# FOOTBALL

# IN FRANCE

# 1894 to 2020

# INTRODUCTION

This book features a statistical history of football in France from 1894 to 2020. Although the French Cup didn't begin until 1917-18 and the French Professional League 1932-33, regional championships had been contested prior to this with various national play-offs also occurring. This book contains information about all of these competitions.

In addition to the results of all League matches and Final League tables, a list of the top goal-scorers and results of the latter stages of the national Cup competition are included.

The full names of clubs are used whenever possible with name-changes, mergers etc. shown as and when they occur. The club names are listed in the following format:   Club Name (Home Town/City/Village).

British Library Cataloguing in Publication Data

A catalogue record for this book is available from the British Library

ISBN  978-1-86223-450-5

Copyright © 2020, SOCCER BOOKS LIMITED. (01472 696226)
72 St. Peter's Avenue, Cleethorpes, N.E. Lincolnshire, DN35 8HU, England

**Manufactured in the UK by Severn**

# 1894

**USFSA Final**  (29/04/1894)

| STANDARD ATHLETIC CLUB (PARIS) | 2-2  (aet) | The White Rovers (Paris) |
|---|---|---|

**USFSA Final Replay**  (05/05/1894)

| STANDARD ATHLETIC CLUB (PARIS) | 2-0 | The White Rovers (Paris) |
|---|---|---|

**Semi-Finals**  (22/04/1894)

| Standard Athletic Club (Paris) | 5-0 | Cercle Pédestre d'Asnières (Paris) |
|---|---|---|
| The White Rovers (Paris) | 1-0 | Club Français (Paris) |

# 1895

**USFSA Final**  (24/03/1895)

| STANDARD ATHLETIC CLUB (PARIS) | 3-1 | The White Rovers (Paris) |
|---|---|---|

**Semi-Finals**  (17/03/1895)

| Standard Athletic Club (Paris) | 18-0 | Stade de Neuilly-sur-Seine (Paris) |
|---|---|---|
| The White Rovers (Paris) | 2-1  (aet) | Club Français (Paris) |

**Qualifying Round**

| Club Français (Paris) | 11-0 | FC Levallois (Paris) |
|---|---|---|
| Stade de Neuilly-sur-Seine (Paris) | 2-1 | Cercle Pédestre d'Asnières (Paris) |
| Standard Athletic Club (Paris) | 13-0 | United Sport Club (Paris) |
| The White Rovers (Paris) | 8-1 | Paris Star (Paris) |

# 1896

| | USFSA League | Pd | Wn | Dw | Ls | GF | GA | Pts |
|---|---|---|---|---|---|---|---|---|
| 1. | CLUB FRANÇAIS (PARIS) | 8 | 8 | - | - | 33 | 2 | 16 |
| 2. | The White Rovers (Paris) | 8 | 7 | - | 1 | 36 | 6 | 14 |
| 3. | Standard Athletic Club (Paris) | 7 | 5 | - | 2 | 24 | 11 | 10 |
| 4. | FC Levallois (Paris) | 8 | 2 | 3 | 3 | 11 | 6 | 7 |
| 5. | Cercle Pédestre d'Asnières (Paris) | 7 | 3 | - | 4 | 10 | 8 | 6 |
| 6. | Paris Star (Paris) | 8 | 2 | 2 | 4 | 4 | 12 | 6 |
| 7. | Stade de Neuilly-sur-Seine (Paris) | 8 | 2 | 1 | 5 | 10 | 11 | 5 |
| 8. | United Sport Club (Paris) | 8 | 2 | - | 6 | 12 | 20 | 4 |
| 9. | Union Athlétique du Premier Arrondisement (Paris) | 8 | - | 2 | 6 | 2 | 66 | 2 |
| | | 70 | 31 | 8 | 31 | 142 | 142 | 70 |

# 1897

## Play-off

STANDARD ATHLETIC CLUB (PARIS)          3-2 – w/o          The White Rovers (Paris)

(the match was declared void and a replay was ordered but White Rovers declined to play)

| | USFSA League | Pd | Wn | Dw | Ls | GF | GA | Pts |
|---|---|---|---|---|---|---|---|---|
| 1. | Standard Athletic Club (Paris) | 8 | 6 | 2 | - | 31 | 4 | 14 |
| 1. | The White Rovers (Paris) | 8 | 7 | - | 1 | 33 | 8 | 14 |
| 3. | Club Français (Paris) | 8 | 5 | 2 | 1 | 19 | 10 | 12 |
| 4. | Racing Club de France (Paris) | 8 | 4 | 1 | 3 | 17 | 13 | 9 |
| 5. | Paris Star (Paris) | 8 | 4 | - | 4 | 15 | 24 | 8 |
| 6. | United Sport Club (Paris) | 8 | 3 | 1 | 4 | 11 | 18 | 7 |
| 7. | FC Levallois (Paris) | 8 | 2 | - | 6 | 15 | 2 | 4 |
| 8. | Union Athlétique du Premier Arrondisement (Paris) | 8 | 1 | - | 7 | 12 | 32 | 2 |
| 9. | Cercle Pédestre d'Asnières (Paris) | 8 | 1 | - | 7 | - | 22 | 2 |
| | | 72 | 33 | 6 | 33 | 153 | 153 | 72 |

# 1898

## Play-off

STANDARD ATHLETIC CLUB (PARIS)          3-2          Club Français (Paris)

| | USFSA League | Pd | Wn | Dw | Ls | GF | GA | Pts |
|---|---|---|---|---|---|---|---|---|
| 1. | Standard Athletic Club (Paris) | 10 | 9 | - | 1 | 50 | 5 | 18 |
| 1. | Club Français (Paris) | 10 | 9 | - | 1 | 27 | 6 | 18 |
| 3. | United Sport Club (Paris) | 10 | 5 | 1 | 4 | 10 | 22 | 11 |
| 4. | Racing Club de France (Paris) | 10 | 3 | 2 | 5 | 11 | 31 | 8 |
| 5. | Paris Star (Paris) | 10 | 2 | 1 | 7 | 3 | 37 | 5 |
| 6. | The White Rovers (Paris) | 10 | - | - | 10 | - | - | - |
| | | 60 | 28 | 4 | 28 | 101 | 101 | 60 |

# 1899

## USFSA Final

HAVRE AC (LE HAVRE)          w/o          Club Français (Paris)

## Semi-Finals

Havre Athletic Club (Le Havre)          1-0          Iris Club Lillois (Lille)
Club Français (Paris) received a bye

## Paris League Play-Off

CLUB FRANÇAIS (PARIS)          3-2          Standard Athletic Club (Paris)

| Paris League | Pd | Wn | Dw | Ls | GF | GA | Pts |
|---|---|---|---|---|---|---|---|
| 1. Club Français (Paris) | 12 | 10 | - | 2 | 51 | 17 | 20 |
| 1. Standard Athletic Club (Paris) | 12 | 10 | - | 2 | 48 | 14 | 20 |
| 3. The White Rovers (Paris) | 12 | 7 | - | 5 | 43 | 22 | 14 |
| 4. United Sport Club (Paris) | 12 | 7 | - | 5 | 19 | 23 | 14 |
| 5. Racing Club de France (Paris) | 12 | 4 | - | 8 | 12 | 48 | 8 |
| 6. Paris Star (Paris) | 12 | 2 | 2 | 8 | 12 | 31 | 6 |
| 7. Cercle Pédestre d'Asnières (Paris) | 12 | - | 2 | 10 | 8 | 38 | 2 |
| | 84 | 40 | 4 | 40 | 193 | 193 | 84 |

# 1900

## USFSA Final (06/05/1900)

| HAVRE AC (LE HAVRE) | 1-0 | Club Français (Paris) |
|---|---|---|

### Semi-Finals

| Havre Athletic Club (Le Havre) | 4-1 | US Tourquennoise (Tourcoing) |
|---|---|---|

Club Français (Paris) received a bye.

| Paris League | Pd | Wn | Dw | Ls | GF | GA | Pts |
|---|---|---|---|---|---|---|---|
| 1. CLUB FRANÇAIS (PARIS) | 14 | 13 | - | 1 | 45 | 10 | 26 |
| 2. Standard Athletic Club (Paris) | 14 | 12 | - | 2 | 42 | 14 | 24 |
| 3. United Sport Club (Paris) | 14 | 8 | 2 | 4 | 31 | 24 | 18 |
| 4. Racing Club de France (Paris) | 14 | 8 | 1 | 5 | 20 | 17 | 17 |
| 5. Paris Star (Paris) | 14 | 7 | 1 | 6 | 30 | 15 | 15 |
| 6. Cercle Pédestre d'Asnières (Paris) | 14 | 4 | - | 10 | 8 | 44 | 8 |
| 7. Union Athlétique du Premier Arrond. (Paris) | 14 | 2 | - | 12 | 4 | 56 | 4 |
| 8. The White Rovers (Paris) | 14 | - | - | 14 | - | - | - |
| | 112 | 54 | 4 | 54 | 180 | 180 | 112 |

# 1901

## USFSA Final

| STANDARD AC (PARIS) | 1-1 (aet) | Havre Athletic Club (Le Havre) |
|---|---|---|

### Replay (26/04/1901)

| STANDARD AC (PARIS) | 6-1 | Havre Athletic Club (Le Havre) |
|---|---|---|

### Semi-Finals

| Iris Club Lillois (Lille) | 1-6 | Havre Athletic Club (Le Havre) |
|---|---|---|

Standard Athletic Club (Paris) received a bye

# 1902

## USFSA Final

| | | |
|---|---|---|
| RACING CLUB DE ROUBAIX (ROUBAIX) | 3-4 (aet) | Racing Club de France (Paris) |

## Semi-Finals

| | | |
|---|---|---|
| Racing Club de France (Paris) | 5-1 | Havre Athletic Club (Le Havre) |
| Racing Club de Roubaix (Roubaix) | 12-1 | Sports Athlétiques Sézannais (Sézanne) |

# 1903

## USFSA Final  (15/04/03)

| | | |
|---|---|---|
| RACING CLUB DE ROUBAIX (ROUBAIX) | 2-2 (aet) | Racing Club de France (Paris) |

## Replay  (17/04/03)

| | | |
|---|---|---|
| RACING CLUB DE ROUBAIX (ROUBAIX) | 3-1 | Racing Club de France (Paris) |

## Semi-Finals

| | | |
|---|---|---|
| Racing Club de Roubaix (Roubaix) | w/o | Havre Athletic Club (Le Havre) |
| Union Athlétique du Licée Malherbe (Caen) | 1-5 | Racing Club de France (Paris) |

## Quarter-Finals

| | | |
|---|---|---|
| Havre Athletic Club (Le Havre) | 3-0 | Sports Athlétiques Sézannais (Sézanne) |
| Racing Club de France (Paris) | 5-0 | Stade Bordelais Université Club (Bordeaux) |
| Racing Club de Roubaix (Roubaix) | w/o | Amiens Athletic Club (Amiens) |
| Union Athlétique du Lycée Malherbe (Caen) | 4-1 | FC Rennais (Rennes) |

# 1904

## USFSA Final

| | | |
|---|---|---|
| RACING CLUB DE ROUBAIX (ROUBAIX) | 4-2 | United Sport Club (Paris) |

## Semi-Finals

| | | |
|---|---|---|
| Racing Club de Roubaix (Roubaix) | 10-1 | Stade Rennais Université Club (Rennes) |
| United Sport Club (Paris) | 4-0 | Olympique de Marseille (Marseille) |

## Quarter-Finals

| | | |
|---|---|---|
| Burdigalia (Bordeaux) | 2-2, Replay 0-2 | Olympique de Marseille (Marseille) |
| Racing Club de Roubaix (Roubaix) | w/o | CS Havrais (Le Havre) |
| United Sport Club (Paris) | 8-0 | Sports Athlétiques Sézannais (Sézanne) |

Stade Rennais Université Club (Rennes) received a bye.

# 1905

## USFSA Final (16/04/05)

| | | |
|---|---|---|
| GALLIA CLUB (PARIS) | 1-0 | Racing Club de Roubaix (Roubaix) |

### Semi-Finals

| | | |
|---|---|---|
| Racing Club de Roubaix (Roubaix) | 5-1 | Amiens Athletic Club (Amiens) |
| Stade Olymp. des Étudiantes Toulousains | 0-5 | Gallia Club (Paris) |

### Quarter-Finals

| | | |
|---|---|---|
| Amiens Athletic Club (Amiens) | w/o | Sports Athlétiques Sézannais (Sézanne) |
| Gallia Club (Paris) | 3-1 | US Servannaise (Saint-Servain) |
| Havre Athletic Club (Le Havre) | 1-2 | Racing Club de Roubaix (Roubaix) |
| Stade Olymp. des Étudiantes Toulousains | 5-0 | Olympique de Marseille (Marseille) |

### FGSPF Final

| | | |
|---|---|---|
| FC ÉTOILE DES DEUX-LACS (PARIS) | 2-1 | Gallia Club (Paris) |

# 1906

## USFSA Final

| | | |
|---|---|---|
| RACING CLUB DE ROUBAIX (ROUBAIX) | 4-1 | Cercle Athlétique de Paris (Paris) |

### Semi-Finals

| | | |
|---|---|---|
| Stade Olymp. des Étudiantes Toulousains | 1-2 | Cercle Athlétique de Paris (Paris) |
| Stade Rémois (Reims) | 0-7 | Racing Club de Roubaix (Roubaix) |

### Quarter-Finals

| | | |
|---|---|---|
| Racing Club de Roubaix (Roubaix) | 6-2 | Havre Athletic Club (Le Havre) |
| Stade Olymp. des Étudiantes Toulousains | 4-1 | Olympique de Marseille (Marseille) |
| Stade Rémois (Reims) | 4-1 | Amiens Athletic Club (Amiens) |
| Stade Universitaire Caennais (Caen) | 0-8 | Cercle Athlétique de Paris (Paris) |

### Round 1

| | | |
|---|---|---|
| Amiens Athletic Club (Amiens) | w/o | Stade Ardennais (Sedan) |
| Lyon Olympique (Lyon) | 2-2, Replay w/o | Olympique de Marseille (Marseille) |
| Stade Bordelais Université (Bordeaux) | 1-5 | Stade Olympique des Étudiantes Toulousains |
| Stade Lorrain (Nancy) | 1-3 | Stade Rémois (Reims) |
| Stade Universitaire Caennais (Caen) | 2-1 | Stade Rennais Université Club (Rennes) |

Cercle Athlétique de Paris (Paris), Havre AC (Le Havre) and Racing Club de Roubaix (Roubaix) all received byes.

### FGSPF Final

| | | |
|---|---|---|
| FC ÉTOILE DES DEUX-LACS (PARIS) | 5-2 | Notre-Dame des Toutes Grâces (Rennes) |

## Semi-Finals

| | | |
|---|---|---|
| Union Sportive Saint-Joseph (Orléans) | 1-6 | FC Étoile des Deux-Lacs (Paris) |

Notre-Dame des Toutes Grâces (Rennes) received a bye.

## Qualifying Round

| | | |
|---|---|---|
| Union Sportive Saint-Jean (Douai) | 0-5 | FC Étoile des Deux-Lacs (Paris) |
| Union Sportive Saint-Joseph (Orléans) | 5-0 | Association de la Jeunesse Auxerroise |

Notre-Dame des Toutes Grâces (Rennes) received a bye.

| | |
|---|---|
| **FCAF** | SOCIÉTÉ MUNICIPALE DE PUTEAUX (PUTEAUX) |

# 1907

## CFI Final (Trophée de France 12/03/07)

| | | |
|---|---|---|
| FC ÉTOILE DES DEUX-LACS (PARIS) | 8-3 | FC Simotain (Bordeaux) |

### Semi-Finals

| | | |
|---|---|---|
| Cercle Athlétique Joinville-Champigny | 1-2 | FC Simotain (Bordeaux) |
| FC Étoile des Deux-Lacs (Paris) | 5-4 | Société Municipale de Puteaux (Puteaux) |

## FGSPF Final

| | | |
|---|---|---|
| FC ÉTOILE DES DEUX-LACS (PARIS) | w/o | Club Sportive Maisons-Laffite (Paris) |

### Semi-Finals

| | | |
|---|---|---|
| Club Sportive Maisons-Laffite (Paris) | 4-1 | Assoc. de la Jeunesse Auxerroise (Auxerre) |
| GS Patronage (Compiègne) | 0-11 | FC Étoile des Deux-Lacs (Paris) |

### Qualifying Round

| | | |
|---|---|---|
| Cadets de Bretagnes (Rennes) | 1-11 | FC Étoile des Deux-Lacs (Paris) |
| Club Sportive Maisons-Laffite (Paris) | 2-0 | Furséens (Lagny) |

## USFSA Final

| | | |
|---|---|---|
| RACING CLUB DE FRANCE (PARIS) | 3-2 | Racing Club de Roubaix (Roubaix) |

### Semi-Finals

| | | |
|---|---|---|
| Havre Athletic Club (Le Havre) | 1-1, Replay 1-7 | Racing Club de Roubaix (Roubaix) |
| Racing Club de France (Paris) | 3-1 | Olympique de Marseille (Marseille) |

### Quarter-Finals

| | | |
|---|---|---|
| Havre Athletic Club (Le Havre) | w/o | US & SC Mans (Le Mans) |
| Olympique de Marseille (Marseille) | 1-0 | Stade Olympique des Étudiants Toulousains |
| Racing Club de France (Paris) | 5-0 | Union Sportive Servannais (Saint-Servain) |
| Racing Club de Roubaix (Roubaix) | 7-0 | CP et Nautique Châlonnais (Châlons/Marne) |

## Qualifying Round

| | | |
|---|---|---|
| CP Nautique Châlonnais (Châlons/M.) | 1-0 | Sporting Club Abbevillois (Abbeville) |
| Olympique de Marseille (Marseille) | 8-1 | Lyon Olympique (Lyon) |
| Stade Olymp. des Étudiantes Toulousains | 7-1 | Burdigalia (Bordeaux) |

Havre Athletic Club (Le Havre), Racing Club de France (Paris), US & SC Mans (Le Mans), Racing Club de Roubaix (Roubaix) and US Servannaise (Saint-Servain) all received byes.

## Preliminary Round

| | | |
|---|---|---|
| CP Nautique Châlonnais (Châlons/M.) | 5-0 | GS Nancéien (Nancy) |
| Olympique Cette (Sète) | 0-5 | Stade Olympique des Étudiantes Toulousains |
| Olympique de Marseille (Marseille) | 9-1 | Sporting Club Dracénois (Draguignan) |

**FAA**     CERCLE ATHLÉTIQUE JOINVILLE-CHAMPIGNY (JOINVILLE)

**FASO**             FC SIMOTAIN (BORDEAUX)

**FCAF**     SOCIÉTÉ MUNICIPALE DE PUTEAUX (PUTEAUX)

# 1908

## CFI Final (Trophée de France)

| | | |
|---|---|---|
| PATRONAGE OLIER (PARIS) | 3-0 | Société Municipale de Puteaux (Puteaux) |

### Semi-Finals

| | | |
|---|---|---|
| Patronage Olier (Paris) | 12-2 | Société Athlétique Montrepos (Bordeaux) |

Société Municipale de Puteaux (Puteaux) received a bye.

## USFSA Final

| | | |
|---|---|---|
| RACING CLUB DE ROUBAIX (ROUBAIX) | 2-1 | Racing Club de France (Paris) |

### Semi-Finals

| | | |
|---|---|---|
| Olympique de Marseille (Marseille) | 1-2 | Racing Club de France (Paris) |
| Racing Club de Roubaix (Roubaix) | 4-0 | Havre Sports (Le Havre) |

### Quarter-Finals

| | | |
|---|---|---|
| Olympique de Marseille (Marseille) | 3-0 | Stade Olympien Vélo Sport (Toulouse) |
| Racing Club de France (Paris) | 3-1 | Club des Sports Stade Lorrain (Nancy) |
| Racing Club de Roubaix (Roubaix) | 4-2 | Union Athlétique du Lycée Malherbe (Caen) |
| Stade Rennais Université (Rennes) | 0-1 | Havre Sports (Le Havre) |

## Qualifying Round

| | | |
|---|---|---|
| Olympique de Marseille (Marseille) | 4-0 | Stade Raphaëlois (Saint-Raphaël) |
| FC de Rouen (Rouen) | w/o | Havre Sports (Le Havre) |
| Club Sports Stade Lorrain (Nancy) | 3-2 | Amiens Athletic Club (Amiens) |
| Stade Olympien Vélo Sport (Toulouse) | 18-0 | JVA Jarnacais (Jarnac) |
| Stade Rennais Université (Rennes) | w/o | Racing Club Angevin (Angers) |

Racing Club de France (Paris), Racing Club de Roubaix (Roubaix) and Union Athlétique du Lycée Malherbe (Caen) all received byes.

## Preliminary Round

| | | |
|---|---|---|
| Sporting Club Nîmois (Nîmes) | 2-5 | Olympique de Marseille (Marseille) |
| Stade Bordelais Université (Bordeaux) | 2-4 | Stade Olympien Vélo Sport (Toulouse) |
| Stade Raphaëlois (Saint-Raphaël) | 2-1 | FC de Lyon (Lyon) |

## FGSPF

| | | |
|---|---|---|
| PATRONAGE OLIER (PARIS) | 8-0 | Cadets de Bretagne (Rennes) |

## FASO            SOCIÉTÉ ATHLÉTIQUE MONTREPOS (BORDEAUX)

## FCAF            SOCIÉTÉ MUNICIPALE DE PUTEAUX (PUTEAUX)

# 1909

## CFI Final (Trophée de France)

| | | |
|---|---|---|
| JEUNESSE ATHÈTIQUE (SAINT-OUEN) | w/o | AS Les Bons Gars de Bordeaux (Bordeaux) |

## FGSPF Final

| | | |
|---|---|---|
| AS LES BONS GARS DE BORDEAUX | 5-1 | Association de la Jeunesse Auxerroise |

### Semi-Finals

| | | |
|---|---|---|
| AS Les Bons Gars de Bordeaux (Bordeaux) | 4-2 | Patronage Olier (Paris) |

Association de la Jeunesse Auxerroise (Auxerre) received a bye.

## Qualifying Round

| | | |
|---|---|---|
| Cadets de Bretagne (Rennes) | 1-4, Replay 1-3 | Patronage Olier (Paris) |
| | (the match was replayed after a protest) | |

## USFSA Final

| | | |
|---|---|---|
| STADE HELVÉTIQUE DE MARSEILLE | 3-2 | Cercle Athlétique de Paris (Paris) |

### Semi-Finals

| | | |
|---|---|---|
| Cercle Athlétique de Paris (Paris) | 1-0 | Union Sportive Tourquennoise (Tourcoing) |
| Stade Helvétique de Marseille (Marseille) | w/o | Sports Athlétiques Bordelais (Bordeaux) |

## Quarter-Finals

| | | |
|---|---|---|
| Cercle Athlétique de Paris (Paris) | 8-3 | Stade Rennais Université Club (Rennes) |
| Sports Athlétiques Bordelais (Bordeaux) | 4-0 | Stade Nantais Université Club (Nantes) |
| Stade Helvétique de Marseille (Marseille) | 12-2 | FC de Lyon (Lyon) |
| US Tourquennoise (Tourcoing) | 3-0 | Racing Club de Reims (Reims) |

## Previous Round

| | | |
|---|---|---|
| Cercle Athlétique de Paris (Paris) | 17-1 | Angers Université Club (Angers) |
| FC de Lyon (Lyon) | 5-2 | Racing Club Franc-Comtois (Besançon) |
| Racing Club de Reims (Reims) | 4-1 | Amiens Athletic Club (Amiens) |
| Sports Athlétiques Bordelais (Bordeaux) | 2-1 | Olympique Cettois (Sète) |
| Stade Helvétique de Marseille (Marseille) | w/o | Stade Raphaëlois (Saint-Raphaël) |
| Stade Nantais Université (Nantes) | 1-0 | Stade Toulousain (Toulouse) |
| Stade Rennais Université (Rennes) | 5-1 | Havre Athletic Club (Le Havre) |
| US Tourquennoise (Tourcoing) | 3-0 | Club des Sports Stade Lorrain (Nancy) |

| | | |
|---|---|---|
| **FCAF** | **JEUNESSE ATHLÉTIQUE (SAINT-OUEN)** | |

## "Display" Final

| | | |
|---|---|---|
| STAR CLUB CAUDRÉSIEN (CAUDRY) | 4-2 | Association Sportive Alfortville (Alfortville) |

# 1910

## CFI Final (Trophée de France)

| | | |
|---|---|---|
| PATRONAGE OLIER (PARIS) | 2-0 | Club Athlétique de Vitry (Vitry-sur-Seine) |

## FGSPF Final

| | | |
|---|---|---|
| PATRONAGE OLIER (PARIS) | 11-0 | AS Les Bons Gars de Bordeaux (Bordeaux) |

## Semi-Finals

| | | |
|---|---|---|
| Association de la Jeunesse Auxerroise | 0-9 | Patronage Olier (Paris) |

AS Les Bons Gars de Bordeaux (Bordeaux) received a bye.

## Qualifying Round

| | | |
|---|---|---|
| Jeunesse Sportive (Crépy-en-Valois) | 1-5 | Patronage Olier (Paris) |
| Alliance (Dreux) | 2-5 | Jeunesse Sportive (Crépy-en-Valois) |
| AS Les Bons Gars de Bordeaux (Bordeaux) | 4-2 | Étoile Sportive de Mont-de-Marson |

## FCAF Final

| | | |
|---|---|---|
| CA DE VITRY (VITRY-SUR-SEINE) | 4-2 | Racing Club de Saint-Quentin (St-Quentin) |

## Semi-Finals

| | | |
|---|---|---|
| Vie au Grand Air du Médoc (Bordeaux) | 1-5 | Club Athlétique de Vitry (Vitry-sur-Seine) |
| Racing Club de Saint-Quentin (Saint-Quentin) | w/o | FC International Croisien (Croissy) |

## USFSA Final

| | | |
|---|---|---|
| US TOURQUENNOISE (TOURCOING) | 7-2 | Stade Helvétique de Marseille (Marseille) |

## Semi-Finals

| | | |
|---|---|---|
| Stade Helvétique de Marseille (Marseille) | 4-1 | Stade Bordelais Université Club (Bordeaux) |
| US Tourquennoise (Tourcoing) | 3-0 | Union Sportive Servannaise (Saint-Servain) |

## Quarter-Finals

| | | |
|---|---|---|
| Amiens Athletic Club (Amiens) | 0-5 | Union Sportive Tourquennoise (Tourcoing) |
| Stade Bordelais Université (Bordeaux) | 3-1 | Olympique Cettois (Sète) |
| Stade Helvétique de Marseille (Marseille) | 5-0 | Lyon Olympique (Lyon) |
| US Servannaise (Saint-Servain) | 2-0 | Stade Français (Paris) |

## First Round

| | | |
|---|---|---|
| Amiens Athletic Club (Amiens) | 2-1 | Cercle des Sports Stade Lorrain (Nancy) |
| Lyon Olympique (Lyon) | 4-1 | Racing Club Franc-Comtois (Besançon) |
| Club Malherbe Caennais (Caen) | 0-3 | Stade Français (Paris) |
| Olympique Cettois (Sète) | 3-1 | Stade Toulousain (Toulouse) |
| Stade Bordelais Université (Bordeaux) | 3-1 | Stade Nantais Université Club (Nantes) |
| Stade Helvétique de Marseille (Marseille) | 11-0 | AS de Cannes (Cannes) |
| US Servannaise (Saint-Servain) | 7-1 | Union Sportive du Mans (Le Mans) |
| US Tourquennoise (Tourcoing) | 5-0 | FC de Braux (Braux) |

## Qualifying Round

| | | |
|---|---|---|
| FC de Rouen (Rouen) | 0-1 | Amiens Athletic Club (Amiens) |
| Cercle des Sports Stade Lorrain | 1-1, 2-1 | Racing Club de Reims (Reims) |
| Union Sportive de Tours (Tours) | 1-4 | Union Sportive du Mans (Le Mans) |

# 1911

## CFI Final (Trophée de France)

| | | |
|---|---|---|
| CERCLE ATHLÉTIQUE DE PARIS (PARIS) | 1-0 | FC Étoile des Deux-Lacs (Paris) |

## Semi-Finals

| | | |
|---|---|---|
| Cercle Athlétique de Paris (Paris) | 5-0 | Jeunesse Athlétique de Saint-Ouen |
| FC Étoile des Deux-Lacs (Paris) received a bye. | | |

## FGSPF Final

| | | |
|---|---|---|
| FC ÉTOILE DES DEUX-LACS (PARIS) | 6-1 | Étoile Sportive de Mont-de-Marsan |

## Semi-Finals

| | | |
|---|---|---|
| Ass. de la Jeunesse Auxerroise (Auxerre) | 1-8 | FC Étoile des Deux-Lacs (Paris) |
| Étoile Sportive de Mont-de-Marsan | w/o | Cadets de Bretagne (Rennes) |

## Quarter-Finals

| | | |
|---|---|---|
| Ass. de la Jeunesse Auxerroise (Auxerre) | 7-1 | Sports Athlétiques Provençaux (Marseille) |
| Cadets de Bretagne (Rennes) | 13-0 | La Vaillante Sports (Angers) |
| FC Étoile des Deux-Lacs (Paris) | 5-0 | GSP Creil (Creil) |
| Union Amicales de Cognac (Cognac) | 3-8 | Étoile Sportive de Mont-de-Marsan |

## FCAF Final

| | | |
|---|---|---|
| JEUNESSE ATHLÉTIQUE DE SAINT-OUEN | w/o | Racing Club de Saint-Quentin |

## Semi-Finals

| | | |
|---|---|---|
| Jeunesse Athlétique de Saint-Ouen | 4-2 | Vie au Grand Air du Médoc (Bordeaux) |

Racing Club de Saint-Quentin (Saint-Quentin) received a bye.

## USFSA Final

| | | |
|---|---|---|
| STADE HELVÉTIQUE DE MARSEILLE | 3-2 | Racing Club de France (Paris) |

## Semi-Finals

| | | |
|---|---|---|
| Olympique Cettois (Sète) | 0-4 | Stade Helvétique de Marseille (Marseille) |
| FC Rouennais (Rouen) | 1-2 | Racing Club de France (Paris) |

## Quarter-Finals

| | | |
|---|---|---|
| FC International (Lyon) | 0-2 | Stade Helvétique de Marseille (Marseille) |
| Olympique Cettois (Sète) | 3-0 | Sports Athlétiques Bordelais (Bordeaux) |
| Racing Club de France (Paris) | 1-0 | Union Sportive Servannaise (Saint-Servain) |
| FC Rouennais (Rouen) | 4-1 | Olympique Lillois (Lille) |

## First Round

| | | |
|---|---|---|
| FC International (Lyon) | 2-1 | Sporting Club Dauphinois (Grenoble) |
| Olympique Cettois (Sète) | 3-1 | Stade Toulousain (Toulouse) |
| Olympique Lillois (Lille) | 8-1 | FC de Braux (Braux) |
| FC Rouennais (Rouen) | 5-1 | Racing Club de Reims (Reims) |
| Sp. Athlétiques Bordelais (Bordeaux) | 6-0 | US Angérienne (Saint-Jean d'Angély) |
| Stade Helvétique de Marseille | 9-0 | Stade Raphaëlois (Saint-Raphaël) |
| AS Trouville-Deauville (Trouville) | 1-3 | Racing Club de France (Paris) |
| US Servannaise (Saint-Servain) | 0-2 | Angers Université Club (Angers) |

(Anger UC were later expelled from the competition and US Servannaise reinstated)

## Qualifying Round

| | | |
|---|---|---|
| Amiens Athletic Club (Amiens) | 1-6 | FC Rouennais (Rouen) |
| Angers Université Club (Angers) | 12-0 | Union Sportive de Tours (Tours) |
| FC International (Lyon) | 3-0 | Racing Club Franc-Comtois (Besançon) |
| Racing Club de Reims (Reims) | 5-0 | Cercle des Sports Stade Lorrain (Nancy) |

**LFA**      CERCLE ATHLÉTIQUE DE PARIS (PARIS)

## CFI Final

| | | |
|---|---|---|
| FC ÉTOILE DES DEUX-LACS (PARIS) | 3-1 | Red Star Amical Club (Saint-Ouen) |

### Semi-Finals

| | | |
|---|---|---|
| FC Étoile des Deux-Lacs (Paris) | 2-1 | Vie au Grand Air du Médoc (Bordeaux) |
| Red Star Amical Club (Saint-Ouen) received a bye. | | |

## FGSPF Final

| | | |
|---|---|---|
| FC ÉTOILE DES DEUX-LACS (PARIS) | 6-2 | AS Les Bons Gars de Bordeaux (Bordeaux) |

### Semi-Finals

| | | |
|---|---|---|
| FC Étoile des Deux-Lacs (Paris) | w/o | Entente Sportive Cherbourg (Cherbourg) |
| AS Les Bons Gars de Bordeaux (Bordeaux) | 4-2 | Étoile Sportive de Mont-de-Marsan |

### Quarter-Finals

| | | |
|---|---|---|
| Bousbotte Association (Besançon) | 1-9 | FC Étoile des Deux-Lacs (Paris) |
| Entente Sportive Cherbourg (Cherbourg) | 6-3 | Association de la Jeunesse Auxerroise |
| AS Les Bons Gars de Bordeaux (Bordeaux) | 6-0 | Union Sportive de Beauregard (Laval) |
| Étoile Sportive de Mont-de-Marsan (Mont-de-Marsan) received a bye. | | |

### First Round

| | | |
|---|---|---|
| Ass. de la Jeunesse Auxerroise (Auxerre) | 1-0 | Jeunesse Sportive Clodoaldiennes (Saint-Cloud) |
| FC Étoile des Deux-Lacs (Paris) | w/o | Légion Saint-Michel (Paris) |
| Étoile Sportive de Mont-deMarsan | 5-0 | Bleuets (Hendaye) |
| Jeanne d'Arc (Epinal) | 0-4 | Bousbotte Association (Besançon) |
| Patronage Saint-Louis (Cognac) | 4-9 | AS Les Bons Gars de Bordeaux (Bordeaux) |
| Union Sportive Beauregard (Laval) | 6-1 | V. (Fontenay-le-Comte) |
| Entente Sportive Cherbourg (Cherbourg) received a bye. | | |

### Qualifying Round

| | | |
|---|---|---|
| Dijon Association (Dijon) | 1-2 | Jeanne d'Arc (Epinal) |
| JS Clodoaldienne (Saint-Cloud) | 2-2, Replay 2-1 | Jeunesse Sportive (Crépy-en-Valois) |
| Légion Saint-Michel (Paris) | 6-2 | Alliance (Dreux) |

## FCAF Final

| | | |
|---|---|---|
| VIE AU GRAND AIR DU MÉDOC | 1-2 | Club Athlétique de Vitry (Vitry-sur-Seine) |
| (CA de Vitry left the field before the end of the game so the match was awarded to VGAM) | | |

### Semi-Finals

| | | |
|---|---|---|
| Vie au Grand Air du Médoc (Bordeaux) | 2-0 | Racing Club de Saint-Quentin (Saint-Quentin) |
| Club Athlétique de Vitry (Vitry-sur-Seine) received a bye. | | |

## USFSA Final

| | | |
|---|---|---|
| STADE RAPHAËLOIS (ST-RAPHAËL) | 2-1 | Association Sportive Française (Paris) |

### Semi-Finals

| | | |
|---|---|---|
| Association Sportive Française (Paris) | 6-1 | Olympique Cettois (Sète) |
| Stade Raphaëlois (Saint-Raphaël) | 2-0 | Union Sportive Tourquennoise (Tourcoing) |

### Quarter-Finals

| | | |
|---|---|---|
| Olympique Cettois (Sète) | 3-2 | Stade Bordelais Université Club (Bordeaux) |
| US Servannaise (Saint-Servain) | 1-3 | Association Sportive Française (Paris) |
| Stade Raphaëlois (Saint-Raphaël) | 2-0 | FC de Lyon (Lyon) |
| US Tourquennoise (Tourcoing) | 3-2 | FC Rouennais (Rouen) |

### First Round

| | | |
|---|---|---|
| FC de Lyon (Lyon) | 9-1 | Racing Club Franc-Comtois (Besançon) |
| US Servannaise (Saint-Servain) | 13-0 | CA de la Société Générale (Orléans) |
| Stade Bordelais Université Club (Bordeaux) | 10-0 | SC Angérien (Saint-Jean d'Angély) |
| US Tourquennoise (Tourcoing) | 5-1 | Cercle des Sports Stade Lorrain (Nancy) |

### Qualifying Round

| | | |
|---|---|---|
| Sporting Club Dauphinois (Grenoble) | 1-3 | FC de Lyon (Lyon) |
| Club Malherbe Caennais (Caen) | 0-5 | Association Sportive Française (Paris) |
| Société Nautique Bayonne | 0-4 | Stade Bordelais Université Club (Bordeaux) |
| Olympique Cettois (Sète) | 4-3 | Stade Toulousain (Toulouse) |
| FC Rouennais (Rouen) | 3-1 | Amiens Athletic Club (Amiens) |
| US Servannaise (Saint-Servain) | 5-0 | Angers Université Club (Angers) |
| CA de la Société Générale (Orléans) | 4-1 | Union Sportive du Mans (Le Mans) |
| Cercle des Sports Stade Lorrain (Nancy) | 4-3 | Racing Club de Reims (Reims) |
| Stade Raphaëlois (Saint-Raphaël) | 2-2, Replay 2-1 | Stade Helvétique de Marseille (Marseille) |
| US Tourquennoise (Tourcoing) | 5-0 | FC de Braux (Braux) |

| | |
|---|---|
| **LFA** | RED STAR AMICAL CLUB (SAINT-OUEN) |

# 1913

## CFI Final (Trophée de France)

| | | |
|---|---|---|
| CERCLE ATHÉTIQUE DE PARIS (PARIS) | 2-1 | Vie au Grand Air du Médoc (Bordeaux) |

### Semi-Finals

| | | |
|---|---|---|
| Cercle Athlétique de Paris (Paris) | 4-2 (aet) | FC Étoile des Deux-Lacs (Paris) |
| Vie au Grand Air du Médoc (Bordeaux) | 2-1 | FC Rouennais (Rouen) |

## FGSPF Final

| | | |
|---|---|---|
| FC ÉTOILE DES DEUX-LACS (PARIS) | 5-1 | AS Les Bons Gars de Bordeaux (Bordeaux) |

## Semi-Finals

| | | |
|---|---|---|
| Bousbotte Association (Besançon) | 0-8 | FC Étoile des Deux-Lacs (Paris) |
| AS Les Bons Gars de Bordeaux (Bordeaux) | 3-0 | Étoile Sportive de Mont-de-Marsan |

## Quarter-Finals

| | | |
|---|---|---|
| Bousbotte Association (Besançon) | 5-0 | Association de la Jeunesse Auxerroise |
| FC Étoile des Deux-Lacs (Paris) | 8-1 | La Vaillante Sports (Angers) |
| AS Les Bons Gars de Bordeaux (Bordeaux) | 9-0 | Jeunesse Sportive (Crépy-en-Valois) |
| Sports Athlétiques Provençaux (Marseille) | 2-4 | Étoile Sportive de Mont-de-Marsan |

## Previous Round

| | | |
|---|---|---|
| AS de la Jeunesse Auxerroise (Auxerre) | 2-1 | Jeunesse Sportive Clodoaldienne (Saint-Cloud) |
| Bousbotte Association (Besançon) | 4-0 | Étoile Sportive Chazelloise (Chazelle) |
| Étoile Sportive de Mont-de-Marsan | 12-5 | Étoile Sportive Montauban (Montauban) |
| Jeunesse Sportive (Crépy-en-Valois) | 5-2 | Arago Sports Orléanais (Orléans) |
| AS Les Bons Gars de Bordeaux (Bordeaux) | 15-0 | Patronage Saint-Louis (Cognac) |
| Sporting Club Montpellier (Montpellier) | 0-3 | Sports Athlétiques Provençaux (Marseille) |
| Union Sportive Beauregard (Laval) | w/o | FC Étoile des Deux-Lacs (Paris) |
| La Vaillante Sports (Angers) | 8-1 | Étoile Alençonnaise (Alençon) |

## FCAF Final

| | | |
|---|---|---|
| VIE AU GRAND AIR DU MÉDOC | 2-0 | Association Sportive Alfortville (Alfortville) |

## Semi-Finals

| | | |
|---|---|---|
| Association Sportive Alfortville (Alfortville) | 2-1 | Racing Club de Saint-Quentin (Saint-Quentin) |

Vie au Grand Air du Médoc (Bordeaux) received a bye.

## USFSA Final

| | | |
|---|---|---|
| STADE HELVÉTIQUE DE MARSEILLE | 1-0 | FC Rouennais (Rouen) |

## Semi-Finals

| | | |
|---|---|---|
| FC Rouennais (Rouen) | 1-0 | CA de la Société Générale (Paris) |
| Stade Helvétique de Marseille (Marseille) | 2-1 | Olympique Cettois (Sète) |

## Quarter-Finals

| | | |
|---|---|---|
| Olympique Cettois (Sète) | 6-1 | Stade Bordelais Université Club (Bordeaux) |
| FC Rouennais (Rouen) | 2-1 | Olympique Lillois (Lille) |
| US Servannaise (Saint-Servain) | 1-3 | CA de la Société Générale (Paris) |
| Stade Helvétique de Marseille (Marseille) | 4-1 | Stade Raphaëlois (Saint-Raphaël) |

## Previous Round

| | | |
|---|---|---|
| Amiens Athletic Club (Amiens) | 0-1 | FC Rouennais (Rouen) |
| FC de Braux (Braux) | 0-2 | Olympique Lillois (Lille) |
| Olympique Cettois (Sète) | w/o | Angers Université Club (Angers) |
| CA de la Société Générale (Paris) | 1-0 | AS Trouville-Deauville (Trouville) |
| US Servannaise (Saint-Servain) | 4-0 | CA de la Société Générale (Orléans) |
| Stade Helvétique de Marseille (Marseille) | 15-0 | Stade Issoirien (Issoire) |
| Stade Raphaëlois (Saint-Raphaël) | 5-1 | Lyon Olympique Universitaire Lyon |
| Stade Toulousain (Toulouse) | 1-4 | Stade Bordelais Université Club (Bordeaux) |

# 1914

## CFI Final (Trophée de France)

| | | |
|---|---|---|
| OLYMPIQUE LILLOIS (LILLE) | 4-1 | Vie au Grand Air du Médoc (Bordeaux) |

### Semi-Finals

| | | |
|---|---|---|
| Olympique Lillois (Lille) | 4-1 | FC Étoile Levallois (Paris) |
| Vie au Grand Air du Médoc (Bordeaux) | 3-2 | Patronage Olier (Paris) |

## FGSPF Final

| | | |
|---|---|---|
| PATRONAGE OLIER (PARIS) | 3-1 | AS Les Bons Gars de Bordeaux (Bordeaux) |

### Semi-Finals

| | | |
|---|---|---|
| Bousbotte Association (Besançon) | 0-8 | Patronage Olier (Paris) |
| AS Les Bons Gars de Bordeaux (Bordeaux) | 3-1 | La Vaillante Sports (Angers) |

### Quarter-Finals

| | | |
|---|---|---|
| Ass. de la Jeunesse Auxerroise (Auxerre) | 1-4 | Patronage Olier (Paris) |
| AS Les Bons Gars de Bordeaux (Bordeaux) | 3-1 | Étoile Sportive Saint-Michel (Saint-Brieuc) |
| Union Sportive Saint-Bruno (Lyon) | 0-4 | Bousbotte Association (Besançon) |
| La Vaillante Sports (Angers) | 4-1 | Étoile Sportive de Mont-de-Marsan |

### Previous Round

| | | |
|---|---|---|
| Ass. de la Jeunesse Auxerroise (Auxerre) | 3-1 | Jeunes de Chaumont (Chaumont) |
| Bousbotte Association (Besançon) | 5-0 | Arago Sports Orléanais (Orléans) |
| Étoile Sportive de Mont-de-Marsan | 6-1 | Sporting Club Montpellier (Montpellier) |
| Étoile Sportive Saint-Michel (Saint-Brieuc) | w/o | Stade Athlétique Amiens (Amiens) |
| Union Amical de Cognac (Cognac) | 1-2 | AS Les Bons Gars de Bordeaux (Bordeaux) |
| Union Sportive Saint-Bruno (Lyon) | w/o | Sports Athlétiques Provençaux (Marseille) |
| La Vaillante Sports (Angers) | 6-0 | Étoile Alençonnaise (Alençon) |

Patronage Olier (Paris) received a bye.

## FCAF Final

| | | |
|---|---|---|
| VIE AU GRAND AIR DU MÉDOC | w/o | Association Sportive Alfortville (Alfortville) |

### Semi-Finals

| | | |
|---|---|---|
| Association Sportive Alfortville (Alfortville) | 1-0 | Club Sportif de Fontainebleau (Fontainebleau) |

Vie au Grand Air du Médoc (Bordeaux) received a bye.

## USFSA Final

| | | |
|---|---|---|
| OLYMPIQUE LILLOIS (LILLE) | 3-0 | Olympique de Cette (Sète) |

## Semi-Finals

| | | |
|---|---|---|
| Olympique de Cette (Sète) | 3-1 | Stade Raphaëlois (Saint-Raphaël) |
| Olympique Lillois (Lille) | 8-1 | Union Sportive Servannaise (Saint-Servain) |

## Quarter-Finals

| | | |
|---|---|---|
| Olympique de Cette (Sète) | 2-1 | Stade Bordelais Université Club (Bordeaux) |
| FC Rouennais (Rouen) | 0-1 | Olympique Lillois (Lille) |
| US Servannaise (Saint-Servain) | 1-0 | Association Sportive Français (Paris) |
| Stade Raphaëlois (Saint-Raphaël) | 2-0 | FC de Lyon (Lyon) |

## First Round

| | | |
|---|---|---|
| FC de Lyon (Lyon) | 3-2 | Stade Helvétique de Marseille (Marseille) |
| Olympique de Cette (Sète) | w/o | SC Angérien (Saint-Jean d'Angély) |
| FC Rouennais (Rouen) | 4-3 | Racing Club de Reims (Reims) |
| Stade Bordelais Université Club (Bordeaux) | 3-1 | Stade Toulousain (Toulouse) |
| Stade Malherbe Caennais (Caen) | 3-3 | Union Sportive Servannaise (Saint-Servain) |

(US Servannaise were awarded a walkover after a dispute over extra-time)

## Qualifying Round

| | | |
|---|---|---|
| FC de Lyon (Lyon) | 5-0 | Association Sportive Montbéliard (Montbéliard) |
| Racing Club de Reims (Reims) | 6-0 | FC de Braux (Braux) |
| FC de Braux (Braux) | 4-2 | Cercle des Sports Stade Lorrain (Nancy) |
| FC de Lyon (Lyon) | 6-2 | Union Sportive d'Annemasse (Annemasse) |
| Assoc. Sportive Montbéliard (Montbéliard) | 5-4 | Red Star Association (Besançon) |
| Racing Club de Reims (Reims) | 7-0 | La Fraternelle (Ailly) |
| Stade Malherbe Caennais (Caen) | 6-1 | Union Sportive du Mans (Le Mans) |

| | |
|---|---|
| **LFA** | FC ÉTOILE LEVALLOIS (PARIS) |

# 1915

| | |
|---|---|
| **FGSPF** | JEANNE DARC LEVALLOIS (PARIS) |
| **LFA** | OLYMPIQUE DE PANTIN (PARIS) |
| **USFSA** | CLUB ATHLÉTIQUE DE LA SOCIÉTÉ GÉNÉRALE (PARIS) |

# 1916

## CFI Final (Trophée de France)

| | | |
|---|---|---|
| OLYMPIQUE DE PANTIN (PARIS) | 2-0 | FC Étoile des Deux-Lacs (Paris) |

## Semi-Finals

| | | |
|---|---|---|
| Olympique de Pantin (Paris) | 2-0 | Vie au Grand Air du Médoc (Bordeaux) |
| FC Étoile des Deux-Lacs (Paris) received a bye | | |

## FGSPF Final

| | | |
|---|---|---|
| FC ÉTOILE DES DEUX-LACS (PARIS) | 2-1 | Bousbotte Association (Besançon) |

### Semi-Finals

| | | |
|---|---|---|
| Bousbotte Association (Besançon) | 3-0 | Union Amicale de Cognac (Cognac) |
| FC Étoile des Deux-Lacs (Paris) | 3-2 | Enghien Sports (Enghien-les-Bains) |

### Quarter-Finals

| | | |
|---|---|---|
| Bousbotte Association (Besançon) | 1-0 | Sports Athlétiques Provençaux (Marseille) |
| Enghien Sports (Enghien-les-Bains) | 8-1 | Alliance (Dreux) |
| FC Étoile des Deux-Lacs (Paris) | 4-0 | Jeunes de Chaumont (Chaumont) |
| Union Amicale de Cognac (Cognac) | 4-1 | Étoile Sportive de Mont-de-Marsan |

## USFSA Final

| | | |
|---|---|---|
| STADE RENNAIS UNIVERSITÉ CLUB | 7-1 | Club Sportif des Terraux (Lyon) |

**LFA**        OLYMPIQUE DE PANTIN (PARIS)

# 1917

## FGSPF Final

| | | |
|---|---|---|
| BOUSBOTTE ASSOCIATION (BESANÇON) | 4-2 | Étoile Sportive de Mont-de-Marsan |

### Semi-Finals

| | | |
|---|---|---|
| Bousbotte Association (Besançon) | 9-0 | Espérance Sportive (Versailles) |
| Étoile Sportive de Mont-de-Marsan | 5-1 | Union Amicale de Cognac (Cognac) |

### Quarter-Finals

| | | |
|---|---|---|
| Bousbotte Association (Besançon) | 1-0 | Eveil de Lyon (Lyon) |
| Espérance Sportive (Versailles) | 8-0 | Arago Sports Orléanais (Orléans) |
| Étoile Sportive de Mont-de-Marsan | 7-3 | AS Les Bons Gars de Bordeaux (Bordeaux) |
| Patronage Olier (Paris) | w/o | Union Amicale de Cognac (Cognac) |

**LFA**        OLYMPIQUE DE PANTIN (PARIS)

## USFSA Final

| | | |
|---|---|---|
| CA DE LA SOCIÉTÉ GÉNÉRALE (PARIS) | 4-1 | FC de Lyon (Lyon) |

The Coupe de France began from season 1917-18 and became the premier tournament in the country until the inauguration of the National League for season 1932-33.

# 1917-18

**Coupe de France Final** (Stade Olivier de Serres, Paris – 05/05/18 – 2,000)

**OLYMPIQUE DE PANTIN (PARIS)**     **3-0**  (HT 2-0)                    FC de Lyon (Lyon)

*Fievet 1-0, 2-0, Darques 3-0*

**Olympique:** Decoux, Van Roey, Lambrechts, Van Steck, Olivan, Lina, Dewaquez, Landauer, Darques, Fievet, Delouys.

**Lyon:** Weber, Orvain, Bellon, Allemand, Ebrard, Meunier, Soulignac, Salmson, Bard, Weber, Ritchie.

## Semi-Finals  (03/03/18)

| | | |
|---|---|---|
| FC de Lyon (Lyon) | 1-0 | Association Sportive Française (Paris) |
| Olympique de Pantin (Paris) | 2-1 | CA de la Société Générale (Paris) |

## Quarter-Finals  (03/02/18)

| | | |
|---|---|---|
| Association Sportive Française (Paris) | 4-2 | Racing Club de France (Paris) |
| FC de Lyon (Lyon) | 2-1 | Stade Rennais Université Club (Rennes) |
| Olympique de Pantin (Paris) | 3-2 | Club Français (Paris) |
| CA de la Société Générale (Paris) | 4-1 | Raincy Sports (Le Raincy) |

# 1918

| | |
|---|---|
| **FGSPF** | ÉTOILE SPORTIVE BIENFAISANCE |
| **LF** | CLUB FRANÇAIS (PARIS) |

# 1918-19

**Coupe de France Final** (Parc des Princes, Paris – 06/04/19 – 10,000)

**CA de la SOCIÉTÉ GÉNÉRALE (PARIS)**   **3-2**  (aet)          Olympique de Paris (Paris)

*Devic 1-0, Hatzfeld 2-2, 3-2*        (HT  1-0,  90 minutes  1-1)        *Darques 1-1, Dewaquez 1-2*

**Société:** Ganneval, Mentha, Frizon, Hadden, Schmer, Devic, E.Devicq, Deydier, Hatzfeld, Boyer, J.Devicq.

**Olympique:** Blochet, Fievet, Vasselin, Jousserand, Ninot, Van Steck, Dewaquez, Landauer, Mainguet, Darques, Dartoux.

## Semi-Finals  (02/02/19)

| | | |
|---|---|---|
| Olympique de Paris (Paris) | 4-3 | Vie au Grand Air du Médoc (Bordeaux) |
| CA de la Société Générale (Paris) | 4-3 | Stade Rennais Université Club (Rennes) |

## Quarter-Finals  (05/01/19)

| | | |
|---|---|---|
| Olympique de Paris (Paris) | 2-1 | Cercle Athlétique de Paris (Paris) |
| CA de la Société Générale (Paris) | 4-2 | Association Sportive Française (Paris) |
| Stade Rennais Université Club (Rennes) | 1-0 | Association Sportive Lyonnaise (Lyon) |
| Vie au Grand Air du Médoc (Bordeaux) | 3-1 | Club Sportif des Terreaux (Lyon) |

# 1919

## USFSA Final

| | | |
|---|---|---|
| HAVRE ATHLETIC CLUB (LE HAVRE) | 4-1 | Olympique de Marseille (Marseille) |

## Semi-Finals

| | | |
|---|---|---|
| Havre Athletic Club (Le Havre) | 4-0 | CS Malouin Servannais (Saint-Servain) |
| Olympique de Marseille (Marseille) | 6-1 | Club Sportif des Terreaux (Lyon) |

## Quarter-Finals

| | | |
|---|---|---|
| Havre Athletic Club (Le Havre) | 1-0 | Racing Club de France (Paris) |
| CS Malouin Servannais (Saint-Servain) | w/o | Club Olympique Choletais (Cholet) |
| Olympique de Marseille (Marseille) | 2-1 | Stade Bordelais Université Club (Bordeaux) |
| Club Sportif des Terreaux (Lyon) | 3-1 | Alliance Vélo Sportive (Auxerre) |

## First Round

| | | |
|---|---|---|
| Club Sportif Alençonnais (Alençon) | 0-4 | CS Malouin Servannais (Saint-Servain) |
| Havre Athletic Club (Le Havre) | 2-0 | Stade Vélo Club Abbevillois (Abbeville) |
| Association Sportive Limousine (Poitiers) | 1-1 | Club Olympique Choletais (Cholet) |

(CO Choletais were awarded a w/o after a dispute over extra-time)

| | | |
|---|---|---|
| Olympique de Marseille (Marseille) | 16-0 | SPMSA Romans |
| Racing Club Bourguignon (Dijon) | 0-5 | Alliance Vélo Sportive (Auxerre) |
| Racing Club de France (Paris) | 2-1 | SS La Courageuse (Romilly-sur-Seine) |
| Stade Bordelais Université Club (Bordeaux) | 6-0 | Stadoceste Tarbais (Tarbes) |
| Club Sportif des Terreaux (Lyon) | w/o | Cercle des Sports Athlétiques de Montluçon |

# 1919-20

## Coupe de France Final    (Stade Bergeyre, Paris – 09/05/20 – 7,000)

| | | |
|---|---|---|
| CERCLE ATHLÉTIQUE DE PARIS | 2-1 | Havre AC (Le Havre) |

*Bard 1-1 (pen), 2-1*                          (HT  0-0)                          *Thorel 0-1*

**Cercle**: Dreyfus, Vanco, Mesnier, McDewitt, Bigué, Allegro, Dupé, Pache, Poullain, Dard, Gravier.

**Havre**: Drancourt, Grivel, Gibbon, Dial, Mérieult, Avenel, Cantais, Accard, Blouin, Thorel, Lenoble.

## Semi-Finals    (11/04/20)

| | | |
|---|---|---|
| Cercle Athlétique de Paris (Paris) | 2-1 | Vie au Grand Air du Médoc (Bordeaux) |
| Havre AC (Le Havre) | 2-0 | AS de Cannes (Cannes) |

## Quarter-Finals    (07/03/20)

| | | |
|---|---|---|
| AS de Cannes (Cannes) | 2-1 | Olympique Lillois (Lille) |
| Cercle Athlétique de Paris (Paris) | 1-1,  2-0 | Red Star Club (Saint-Ouen) |
| Havre AC (Le Havre) | 3-2 | US Athlétiques de Clichy (Clichy) |
| Vie au Grand Air du Médoc (Bordeaux) | 3-0 | CA des Sports Généraux (Paris) |

# 1920-21

**Coupe de France Final**   (Stade Pershing, Paris – 24/04/21 – 18,000)

**RED STAR CLUB (SAINT-OUEN)**      **2-1**      Olympique de Paris (Paris)

*Clavel 53', Naudin 77'*      *Landauer 78'*

**Red Star**: Chayrigues, Meyer, Gamblin, Marion, Hugues, Bonnardel, Bourdin, Brouzes, Nicolas, Naudin, Clavel.

**Olympique**: Cottenet, Langenove, Huysmans, Baron, Parachini, Haas, Dewaquez, Rouches, Landauer, Darques, Rebut.

## Semi-Finals   (03/04/21)

| | | |
|---|---|---|
| Olympique de Paris (Paris) | 3-2  (aet) | US Tourquennoise (Tourcoing) |
| Red Star Club (Saint-Ouen) | 4-3 | Racing Club de France (Paris) |

## Quarter-Finals   (13/03/21)

| | | |
|---|---|---|
| Olympique de Paris (Paris) | 2-1 | Cercle Athlétique de Paris (Paris) |
| Racing Club de France (Paris) | 4-2 | US Suisse (Paris) |
| Red Star Club (Saint-Ouen) | 4-0 | AS de Cannes (Cannes) |
| US Tourquennoise (Tourcoing) | 2-0 | Racing Club de Calais (Calais) |

# 1921-22

**Coupe de France Final**   (Stade Pershing, Paris – 07/05/22 – 25,000)

**RED STAR CLUB (SAINT-OUEN)**      **2-0**      Stade Rennais UC (Rennes)

*Nicolas 14', Sentubéry 87'*

**Red Star**: Chayrigues, Meyer, Gamblin, Marion, Bonnardel, Thédié, Cordon, Nicolas, Joyaut, Naudin, Sentubéry.

**Rennais**: Berthelot, Molles, Lenoble, Scoones, Hugues, P.Gastiger, Bourdin, M.Gastiger, Caballero, Marc, Delalande.

## Semi-Finals   (02/04/22)

| | | |
|---|---|---|
| Red Star Club (Saint-Ouen) | 2-1 | FC Rouennais (Rouen) |
| Stade Rennais UC (Rennes) | 3-0 | Olympique de Paris (Paris) |

## Quarter-Finals   (05/03/22)

| | | |
|---|---|---|
| Olympique de Paris (Paris) | 2-2, 4-1 | Vie au Grand Air du Médoc (Bordeaux) |
| Red Star Club (Saint-Ouen) | 2-1 | US Tourquennoise (Tourcoing) |
| FC Rouennais (Rouen) | 2-1 | CA des Sports Généraux (Paris) |
| Stade Rennais UC (Rennes) | 1-1, 1-0 | Olympique Lillois (Lille) |

# 1922-23

## Coupe de France Final   (Stade Pershing, Paris – 06/05/23 – 20,000)
**RED STAR CLUB (SAINT-OUEN)**                   4-2                    FC de Cette (Sète)
*Naudin 02', 07', Cordon 11', Joyaut 17'*                                      *Cornelius 16', Kramer 27'*
**Red Star**: Chayrigues, Gamblin, Meyer, Joyaut, Hugues, Bonnardel, Cordon, Brouzes, Nicolas, Naudin, Sentubéry.
**Cette**: Encontre, Huot, Gravier, Berntsson, Jourda, Dedieu, Cornelius, Kramer, Parkes, Dangles, Pujol.

## Semi-Finals   (08-29/04/23)

| | | |
|---|---|---|
| FC de Cette (Sète) | 1-0 | FC Rouennais (Rouen) |
| Red Star Club (Saint-Ouen) | 1-0 | Olympique de Paris (Paris) |

## Quarter-Finals   (04/03/23)

| | | |
|---|---|---|
| Olympique de Paris (Paris) | 3-0 | FEC de Levallois (Levallois Perret) |
| Red Star Club (Saint-Ouen) | 4-0 | Racing Club de Roubaix (Roubaix) |
| FC Rouennais (Rouen) | 2-1 | SC de Nîmes (Nîmes) |
| Stade Rennais UC (Rennes) | 1-0, 0-2 | FC de Cette (Sète) |

# 1923-24

## Coupe de France Final   (Stade Yves du Manoir, Colombes – 13/04/24 – 29,000)
**OLYMPIQUE DE MARSEILLE**                   3-2  (aet)                    FC de Cette (Sète)
*Crut 03', --', Boyer 42'*                                      *Cazal 15', Torta 67' (o.g.)*
**Olympique**: R. de Ruymbecke, Jacquier, Seitz, Blanc, Cabassu, Torta, Michel, Boyer, Subrini, Crut, D.de Ruymbecke.
**Cette**: Henric, Gravier, Hewitt, Parachini, Domergue, Jourda, Cornelius, Cazal, Caballero, Dangles, Gibson.

## Semi-Finals   (16/03/24 – 06/04/24)

| | | |
|---|---|---|
| FC de Cette (Sète) | 1-1, 1-1, 2-0 | Havre AC (Le Havre) |
| Olympique de Marseille (Marseille) | 3-1 | FC Rouennais (Rouen) |

## Quarter-Finals   (24/02/24)

| | | |
|---|---|---|
| FC de Cette (Sète) | 0-0 | Stade Rennais UC (Rennes)   *(forfeit)* |
| Havre AC (Le Havre) | 2-1 | Olympique de Paris (Paris) |
| Olympique de Marseille (Marseille) | 2-2, 3-2 | Stade Français (Paris) |
| FC Rouennais (Rouen) | 3-1 | US Servannaise (Saint-Servain) |

# 1924-25

**Coupe de France Final**   (Stade Yves du Manoir, Colombes – 10/05/25 – 18,000)

**CA des SPORTS GÉNÉRAUX (PARIS)**          **1-1**          FC Rouennais (Rouen)

*Auger 70'*                                                    *Boulanger 03'*

**Généaux**: Jou, Liènert, Gollet, Marion, Marquet, Clugnet, Barville, Caillet, Soïka, Tissot, Auger.
**Rouennais**: Barnes, Rault, Canthelou, Witty, Hérubel, Blaizot, Renault, Burel, Boulanger, Halotel, Pozo.

## Final Replay

**CA des SPORTS GÉNÉRAUX (PARIS)**          **3-2**          FC Rouennais (Rouen)

*Soïka 03', Barville 15', Liènert 58' pen*                        *Boulanger 11', 20'*

**Généaux**: Jou, Liènert, Gollet, Marion, Marquet, Clugnet, Barville, Caillet, Soïka, Tissot, Auger.
**Rouennais**: Barnes, Rault, Canthelou, Witty, Hérubel, Blaizot, Renault, Burel, Boulanger, Halotel, Pozo.

## Semi-Finals   (05/04/25)

| | | |
|---|---|---|
| FC Rouennais (Rouen) | 2-1 | Olympique de Paris (Paris) |
| CA des Sports Généraux (Paris) | 1-0 | FC de Cett1 (Sète) |

## Quarter-Finals   (01/03/25)

| | | |
|---|---|---|
| FC de Cette (Sète) | 1-0 | Amiens SC (Amiens) |
| Olympique de Paris (Paris) | 1-0 | Olympique de Marseille (Marseille) |
| FC Rouennais (Rouen) | 2-1 | Stade Français (Paris) |
| CA des Sports Généraux (Paris) | 2-0 | Assoc. Fraternelle de La Garenne Colombes |

# 1925-26

**Coupe de France Final**   (Stade Yves du Manoir, Colombes – 09/05/26 – 30,000)

**OLYMPIQUE DE MARSEILLE**          **4-1**          AS Valentigney (Valentigney)

*Dewaquez 16', 80', D. de Ruymbecke 26', Boyer 33'*                  *Chavey 40'*

**Olympique**: Seitz, Durbec, Jacquier, Subrini, Clere, Blanc, Dewaquez, D. de Ruymbecke, Boyer, Crut, Gallay.
**Valentigney**: Entz, Lovy, Simonin, Rigoulot, Goll, Richard, Grédy, Van Praet, Chavey, Haenni, Schaff.

## Semi-Finals   (28/03/26)

| | | |
|---|---|---|
| Olympique de Marseille (Marseille) | 5-0 | Stade Français (Paris) |
| AS Valentigney (Valentigney) | 2-1 | CA de Vitry (Vitry-sur-Seine) |

## Quarter-Finals   (07/03/26)

| | | |
|---|---|---|
| Olympique de Marseille (Marseille) | 4-2 | US Tourquennoise (Tourcoing) |
| Stade Français (Paris) | 1-2, 4-2 | FC de Cette (Sète) |
| AS Valentigney (Valentigney) | 4-2 | FC Rouennais (Rouen) |
| CA de Vitry (Vitry-sur-Seine) | 2-1 | Club Français (Paris) |

# 1926-27

**Coupe de France Final**   (Stade Yves du Manoir, Colombes – 06/05/27 – 23,800)

**OLYMPIQUE DE MARSEILLE**                          **3-0**                          US Quevillaise (Le Petit Quevilly)

*Durand 34', Gallay 36', Dewaquez 89'*

**Olympique:** Allé, Schnoeck, Jacquier, Clère, Cabassu, Durbec, Dewaquez, Durand, Boyer, Crut, Gallay.

**Quevillaise:** Puddefoot, Demeilliez, Farret, Hecquet, Bonnardel, Groult, Verdin, Willig, Fagris, Guillard, Deans.

## Semi-Finals   (03/04/27)

| | | |
|---|---|---|
| Olympique de Marseille (Marseille) | 1-1 (aet),  6-0 | Cercle Athlétique de Paris (Paris) |
| US Quevillaise (Le Petit Quevilly) | 1-1 (aet),  1-0 | Stade Raphaëlois (Saint-Raphaël) |

## Quarter-Finals   (06/03/27)

| | | |
|---|---|---|
| Cercle Athlétique de Paris (Paris) | 2-2, 2-1 | Club Français (Paris) |
| Olympique de Marseille (Marseille) | 1-0 | Olympique Lillois (Lille) |
| US Quevillaise (Le Petit Quevilly) | 4-1 | US Suisse (Paris) |
| Stade Raphaëlois (Saint-Raphaël) | 2-1 | Stade Havrais (Le Havre) |

# 1927-28

**Coupe de France Final**   (Stade Yves du Manoir, Colombes – 06/05/28 – 30,000)

**RED STAR OLYMPIQUE (SAINT-OUEN)**     **3-1**     Cercle Athlétique de Paris (Paris)

*Wartel 08', Lund 33', Brouzes 61'*                                                                  *Bertrand 45'*

**Red Star:** Espanet, Diaz, Domergue, Chantrel, Baron, Wartel, Lund, Brouzes, Nicolas, Martin, Lebreton.

**Cercle:** Blanc, Fidon, Ottavis, Laurent, Gautheroux, Quentier, Ouvray, Laurent, Bertrand, Langiller, Mahieu.

## Semi-Finals   (01/04/28)

| | | |
|---|---|---|
| Cercle Athlétique de Paris (Paris) | 5-1 | FC de Mulhouse 1893 (Mulhouse) |
| Red Star Olympique (Saint-Ouen) | 8-2 | Stade Français (Paris) |

## Quarter-Finals   (26/02/28)

| | | |
|---|---|---|
| Cercle Athlétique de Paris (Paris) | 0-0, 1-0 | Olympique Lillois (Lille) |
| FC de Mulhouse 1893 (Mulhouse) | 1-0 | Stade Raphaëlois (Saint-Raphaël) |
| Red Star Olympique (Saint-Ouen) | 4-3 | Amiens AC (Amiens) |
| Stade Français (Paris) | 2-1 | FC de Sète (Sète) |

# 1928-29

**Coupe de France Final**  (Stade Yves du Manoir, Colombes – 05/05/29 – 25,000)

**SO MONTPELLIÉRAINS (MONTPELLIER)**    **2-0**                         FC de Sète (Sète)

*A.Kramer 40', E.Kramer 89'*

**Monpelliérains:** Guillard, Olivet, Rolhion, Bousquet, Dedieu, Mistral, E.Kramer, Temple, A.Kramer, G.Kramer, Sekulic.

**Sète:** Henric, Skiller, Chardar, Harrison, Barrett, Féjean, Boutet, Bek, Cazal, Dormoy, Galey.


**Semi-Finals**    (07/04/29)

| | | |
|---|---|---|
| SO Montpelliérains (Montpellier) | 1-0 | Stade Raphaëlois (Saint-Raphaël) |
| FC de Sète (Sète) | 2-1 | Union Racing Dunkerque-Malo (Dunkerque) |


**Quarter-Finals**    (17/03/29)

| | | |
|---|---|---|
| SO Montpelliérains (Montpellier) | 5-0 | Stade Rennais UC (Rennes) |
| FC de Sète (Sète) | 7-1 | AS de Cannes (Cannes) |
| Stade Raphaëlois (Saint-Raphaël) | 1-0 | Cercle Athlétique de Paris (Paris) |
| Union Racing Dunkerque-Malo (Dunkerque) | 1-0 | US Boulonnaise (Boulogne-sur-Mer) |


# 1929-30

**Coupe de France Final**  (Stade Yves du Manoir, Colombes – 27/04/30 – 35,000)

**FC DE SÈTE (SÈTE)**              **3-1  (aet)**              Racing Club de France (Paris)

*Friedman 88', Bek 94', 111'*                                                              *Lhottka 80'*

**Sète:** Frondas, Skiller, Chardar, Cazal, Stevanovic, Féjean, Lucibello, Bek, Dubus, Friedmann, Durand.

**Racing:** Tassin, Anatol, Capelle, Guézou, Gautheroux, Villaplane, Veyssade, Ozenne, Lhottka, Veinante, Galey.


**Semi-Finals**    (05/04/30)

| | | |
|---|---|---|
| Racing Club de France (Paris) | 1-1 (aet), 3-0 | Amiens AC (Amiens) |
| FC de Sète (Sète) | 3-0 | Olympique de Marseille (Marseille) |


**Quarter-Finals**    (09/03/30)

| | | |
|---|---|---|
| Amiens AC (Amiens) | 2-1 | Union Racing Dunkerque-Malo (Dunkerque) |
| Olympique de Marseille (Marseille) | 1-0 | Stade Raphaëlois (Saint-Raphaël) |
| Racing Club de France (Paris) | 3-1 | Cercle Athlétique de Paris (Paris) |
| FC de Sète (Sète) | 4-1 | SO Montpelliérains (Montpellier) |

# 1930-31

**Coupe de France Final**  (Stade Yves du Manoir, Colombes – 03/05/31 – 30,000)

| CLUB FRANÇAIS (PARIS) | **3-0** | SO Montpelliérains (Montpellier) |
|---|---|---|

*Boros 14', Parkes 18' pen., Mercier 32'*

**Français:**  Séchehaye, Huvier, Parkes, Rigolet, Hudry, Logez, Hennequin, Boros, Mercier, Haas, Miramon.

**Montpelliérains:**  Guillard, A.Boutet, D.Boutet, Hornus, Dedieu, Dupont, Matte, Cros, Rolhion, J.Temple, P.Temple.

## Semi-Finals  (12/04/31)

| Club Français (Paris) | 6-1 | Olympique GC de Nice (Nice) |
|---|---|---|
| SO Montpelliérains (Montpellier) | 2-1 | AS de Cannes (Cannes) |

## Quarter-Finals  (08/03/31)

| AS de Cannes (Cannes) | 4-0 | Cercle Athlétique de Paris (Paris) |
|---|---|---|
| Club Français (Paris) | 1-0 | Excelsior AC de Roubaix (Roubaix) |
| SO Montpelliérains (Montpellier) | 2-1 | Amiens AC (Amiens) |
| Olympique GC de Nice (Nice) | 4-1 | CS Jean Bouin (Angers) |

# 1931-32

**Coupe de France Final**  (Stade Yves du Manoir, Colombes – 24/04/32 – 36,143)

| AS DE CANNES (CANNES) | **1-0** | Racing Club de Roubaix (Roubaix) |
|---|---|---|

*Cler 83'*

**Cannes:**  Roux, Tourniaire, Vigouroux, Beraudo, Hillier, Cler, Duthell, Aitken, Bardot, Fechino, Besson.

**Racing:**  Encontre, Cottenier, Mathoré, Lechanteux, Verriest, Kramarik, Hewitt, Depoers, Leveugle, Cossement, Gonce.

## Semi-Finals  (03/04/32)

| AS de Cannes (Cannes) | 1-0 | Racing Club de France (Paris) |
|---|---|---|
| Racing Club de Roubaix (Roubaix) | 3-0 | Olympique GC de Nice (Nice) |

## Quarter-Finals  (06/03/32)

| AS de Cannes (Cannes) | 2-0 | Olympique Lillois (Lille) |
|---|---|---|
| Olympique GC de Nice (Nice) | 3-1 | Iris Club Lillois (Lille) |
| Racing Club de France (Paris) | 0-0, 4-2 | Havre AC (Le Havre) |
| Racing Club de Roubaix (Roubaix) | 3-1 | FC Rouennais (Rouen) |

A National League began in season 1932-33 with two groups of 10 clubs each.

# 1932-33

| 1932-33 Group "A" | Excelsior AC Roubaix | Club Français Paris | Hyères FC | Olympique Lillois | Olympique Marseille | FC de Mulhouse 1893 | Olympique GC Nice | SC de Nîmes | Racing Club de Paris | FC de Sète |
|---|---|---|---|---|---|---|---|---|---|---|
| Excelsior AC | ■ | 4-1 | 2-1 | 2-1 | 2-1 | 2-2 | 2-2 | 4-4 | 1-1 | 0-3 |
| Club Français Paris | 2-2 | ■ | 2-2 | 1-3 | 6-2 | 5-0 | 2-0 | 5-2 | 5-5 | 2-3 |
| Hyères FC | 3-1 | 3-1 | ■ | 0-1 | 1-1 | 1-1 | 1-0 | 2-2 | 1-2 | 1-2 |
| Olymp. Lillois | 2-0 | 5-3 | 2-1 | ■ | 1-2 | 2-0 | 3-0 | 4-0 | 4-1 | 4-2 |
| Olymp. Marseille | 2-2 | 5-1 | 1-2 | 7-0 | ■ | 3-1 | 1-0 | 2-0 | 1-0 | 3-1 |
| FC de Mulhouse | 6-2 | 2-3 | 3-1 | 1-2 | 1-4 | ■ | 5-2 | 3-4 | 3-5 | 3-1 |
| Olymp. GC Nice | 2-2 | 2-0 | 2-1 | 2-3 | 1-0 | 5-2 | ■ | 2-3 | 0-0 | 2-2 |
| SC de Nîmes | 2-0 | 3-1 | 3-0 | 0-3 | 1-3 | 3-1 | 2-0 | ■ | 5-1 | 1-3 |
| RC de Paris | 2-2 | 4-1 | 2-1 | 0-1 | 3-1 | 2-1 | 2-2 | 3-1 | ■ | 5-3 |
| FC de Sète | 0-2 | 3-2 | 1-0 | 1-0 | 1-1 | 1-1 | 1-2 | 1-1 | 3-2 | ■ |

| 1932-33 Group "B" | Olympique Alésien | Antibes Olympique | AS de Cannes | Cercle Athlétique Paris | SC Fivois | FC de Metz | SO Montpelliérains | Red Star Olympique | Stade Rennais UC | FC Sochaux-Montbél. |
|---|---|---|---|---|---|---|---|---|---|---|
| Olymp. Alésien | ■ | 3-3 | 2-4 | 2-1 | 7-4 | 2-3 | 2-2 | 0-0 | 4-4 | 0-1 |
| Antibes Olymp. | 0-0 | ■ | 1-0 | 3-0 | 5-0 | 1-1 | 0-2 | 2-0 | 3-1 | 4-1 |
| AS de Cannes | 2-0 | 3-0 | ■ | 2-2 | 5-5 | 0-1 | 3-0 | 2-1 | 3-0 | 1-1 |
| Cercle Ath. Paris | 2-1 | 2-3 | 1-1 | ■ | 1-2 | 2-1 | 2-2 | 2-2 | 3-1 | 3-5 |
| SC Fivois | 3-0 | 0-5 | 1-1 | 0-2 | ■ | 8-1 | 2-3 | 3-2 | 4-4 | 2-2 |
| FC de Metz | 4-0 | 3-2 | 0-2 | 2-3 | 0-0 | ■ | 2-1 | 1-7 | 1-2 | 0-3 |
| SO Montpelliér. | 2-0 | 2-1 | 1-2 | 3-4 | 4-2 | 7-3 | ■ | 1-1 | 1-0 | 2-0 |
| Red Star Olymp. | 5-0 | 2-3 | 1-1 | 3-4 | 0-1 | 2-2 | 4-0 | ■ | 6-2 | 0-1 |
| Stade Rennais UC | 4-0 | 0-0 | 5-4 | 3-1 | 0-1 | 4-0 | 6-1 | 3-1 | ■ | 1-1 |
| FC Sochaux-Mont. | 5-2 | 1-3 | 2-1 | 1-3 | 6-4 | 5-0 | 2-3 | 1-1 | 2-1 | ■ |

## Play-off

| OLYMPIQUE LILLOIS (LILLE) | 4-3 | AS de Cannes (Cannes) |
|---|---|---|

### Group "A"

| | | Pd | Wn | Dw | Ls | GF | GA | Pts | |
|---|---|---|---|---|---|---|---|---|---|
| 1. | Olympique Lillois (Lille) | 18 | 14 | - | 4 | 41 | 23 | 28 | |
| 2. | Olympique de Marseille (Marseille) | 18 | 10 | 3 | 5 | 40 | 24 | 23 | |
| 3. | Racing Club de Paris (Paris) | 18 | 8 | 5 | 5 | 40 | 36 | 21 | |
| 4. | FC de Sète (Sète) | 18 | 8 | 4 | 6 | 32 | 32 | 20 | |
| 5. | SC de Nîmes (Nîmes) | 18 | 8 | 3 | 7 | 37 | 38 | 19 | |
| 6. | Excelsior AC de Roubaix (Roubaix) | 18 | 5 | 8 | 5 | 32 | 37 | 18 | |
| 7. | Olympique GC de Nice (Nice) | 18 | 5 | 5 | 8 | 26 | 32 | 15 | |
| 8. | Club Français (Paris) | 18 | 5 | 3 | 10 | 43 | 50 | 13 | |
| 9. | Hyères FC (Hyères) | 18 | 4 | 4 | 10 | 22 | 29 | 12 | |
| 10. | FC de Mulhouse 1893 (Mulhouse) | 18 | 4 | 3 | 11 | 36 | 48 | 11 | |
| | | 180 | 71 | 38 | 71 | 349 | 349 | 180 | |

### Group "B"

| | | Pd | Wn | Dw | Ls | GF | GA | Pts | |
|---|---|---|---|---|---|---|---|---|---|
| 1. | Antibes Olympique (Antibes) | 18 | 10 | 4 | 4 | 39 | 21 | 24* | |
| 2. | AS de Cannes (Cannes) | 18 | 8 | 6 | 4 | 37 | 24 | 22* | |
| 3. | FC Sochaux-Montbéliard (Montbéliard) | 18 | 9 | 4 | 5 | 40 | 31 | 22 | |
| 4. | Sports Olympiques Montpelliérains (Montpellier) | 18 | 9 | 3 | 6 | 37 | 36 | 21 | |
| 5. | Cercle Athlétique de Paris (Paris) | 18 | 8 | 4 | 6 | 38 | 37 | 20 | |
| 6. | Stade Rennais Université Club (Rennes) | 18 | 7 | 4 | 7 | 41 | 36 | 18 | |
| 7. | SC Fivois (Fives) | 18 | 6 | 5 | 7 | 42 | 48 | 17 | |
| 8. | Red Star Olympique (Saint-Ouen) | 18 | 4 | 6 | 8 | 38 | 29 | 14 | R |
| 9. | FC de Metz (Metz) | 18 | 5 | 3 | 10 | 25 | 51 | 13 | R |
| 10. | Olympique Alésien (Alès) | 18 | 2 | 5 | 11 | 25 | 49 | 9 | R |
| | | 180 | 68 | 44 | 68 | 362 | 362 | 180 | |

## Top goal-scorers

1) Walter KAISER                   (Stade Rennais UC)    15
    Robert "Mercier" FUROIS      (Club Français Paris)    15
3) José ALCAZAR         (Olympique de Marseille)    14
    Pierre FECCHINO           (AS de Cannes)    14

* Antibes Olympique (Antibes) were banned by the FFF from contesting the championship play-off, being replaced by AS de Cannes (Cannes). The club then changed their name to Antibes-Juan-les-Pins FC (Antibes) prior to the next season.

## Coupe de France Final   (Stade Yves de Manoir, Colombes – 07/05/33 – 38,000)

**EXCELSIOR AC DE ROUBAIX (ROUBAIX)**   **3-1**           Racing Club de Roubaix (Roubaix)

*Langiller 03', Bugé 23', Van Caeneghem 26'*                     *R. Van Vooren 72'*

**Excelsior:** Gianelloni, Payne, Dhulst, Bartlett, Delmer, Barbieux, Burghraeves, Bugé, Van Caeneghem, Liétaer, Langiller.

**Racing:** Encontre, Cottenier, Hewitt, Lechanteux, Verriest, Lerouge, Cossement, A.Van Vooren, Leveugle, Chauvel, R.Van Vooren.

### Semi-Finals   (08-09/04/33)

| | | |
|---|---|---|
| Excelsior AC de Roubaix (Roubaix) | 2-1 | FC de Sète (Sète) |
| Racing Club de Roubaix (Roubaix) | 2-0 | AS de Cannes (Cannes) |

### Quarter-Finals   (26/02/33)

| | | |
|---|---|---|
| AS de Cannes (Cannes) | 3-1 | Antibes Olympique (Antibes) |
| Excelsior AC de Roubaix (Roubaix) | 3-1 | Olympique GC de Nice (Nice) |
| Racing Club de Roubaix (Roubaix) | 3-0 | SO Montpelliérains (Montpellier) |
| FC de Sète (Sète) | 3-2 | FC Sochaux |

Division 2 began next season comprising two groups (Nord = 14 clubs + Sud = 9 clubs).

# 1933-34

| | Division 1 | Pd | Wn | Dw | Ls | GF | GA | Pts |
|---|---|---|---|---|---|---|---|---|
| 1. | FC DE SÈTE (SÈTE) | 26 | 14 | 6 | 6 | 69 | 52 | 34 |
| 2. | SC Fivois (Fives) | 26 | 13 | 7 | 6 | 57 | 31 | 33 |
| 3. | Olympique de Marseille (Marseille) | 26 | 15 | 3 | 8 | 69 | 46 | 33 |
| 4. | Olympique Lillois (Lille) | 26 | 14 | 4 | 8 | 70 | 40 | 32 |
| 5. | Excelsior AC de Roubaix (Roubaix) | 26 | 13 | 4 | 9 | 65 | 59 | 30 |
| 6. | Stade Rennais Université Club (Rennes) | 26 | 11 | 5 | 10 | 67 | 75 | 27 |
| 7. | Antibes-Juan-les-Pins FC (Antibes) | 26 | 11 | 5 | 10 | 52 | 60 | 27* |
| 8. | Sports Olympiques Montpelliérains (Montpellier) | 26 | 10 | 6 | 10 | 53 | 55 | 26 |
| 9. | SC de Nîmes (Nîmes) | 26 | 11 | 3 | 12 | 68 | 72 | 25 |
| 10. | AS de Cannes (Cannes) | 26 | 9 | 7 | 10 | 42 | 52 | 25 |
| 11. | Racing Club de Paris (Paris) | 26 | 9 | 5 | 12 | 51 | 49 | 23 |
| 12. | FC Sochaux-Montbéliard (Montbéliard) | 26 | 9 | 4 | 13 | 60 | 70 | 22 |
| 13. | Olympique GC de Nice (Nice) | 26 | 6 | 5 | 15 | 42 | 69 | 17# |
| 14. | Cercle Athlétique de Paris (Paris) | 26 | 5 | - | 21 | 55 | 90 | 10 |
| | | 364 | 150 | 64 | 150 | 820 | 820 | 364 |

| 1933-34 Division 1 | Antibes-Juan-les-Pins FC | AS de Cannes | Cercle Athlétique de Paris | Excelsior AC de Roubaix | SC Fivois | Olympique Lillois | Olympique de Marseille | SO Montpelliérains | Olympique GC de Nice | SC de Nîmes | Racing Club de Paris | Stade Rennais Université Club | FC de Sète | FC Sochaux-Montbéliard |
|---|---|---|---|---|---|---|---|---|---|---|---|---|---|---|
| Antibes-Juan-les-Pins FC | | 4-1 | 3-1 | 2-1 | 0-7 | 3-1 | 1-3 | 3-3 | 3-2 | 4-2 | 1-0 | 1-1 | 3-0 | 3-1 |
| AS de Cannes | 1-0 | | 3-1 | 1-0 | 0-0 | 2-0 | 1-1 | 3-1 | 2-2 | 1-1 | 6-2 | 0-2 | 4-1 | 4-0 |
| Cercle Athlétique de Paris | 1-3 | 5-1 | | 3-6 | 0-1 | 0-3 | 3-1 | 1-4 | 6-1 | 7-0 | 1-4 | 3-6 | 2-3 | 4-6 |
| Excelsior AC de Roubaix | 2-3 | 3-1 | 3-2 | | 1-1 | 2-0 | 4-3 | 3-2 | 3-1 | 1-0 | 3-6 | 4-2 | 3-3 | 2-1 |
| SC Fivois | 0-0 | 1-2 | 2-0 | 1-0 | | 3-0 | 2-3 | 2-1 | 5-2 | 5-2 | 3-3 | 5-0 | 4-2 | 3-0 |
| Olympique Lillois | 4-0 | 3-1 | 4-1 | 4-2 | 1-1 | | 6-1 | 6-2 | 3-0 | 3-1 | 0-0 | 5-4 | 6-0 | 2-2 |
| Olympique de Marseille | 3-2 | 4-0 | 3-1 | 2-4 | 2-1 | 1-3 | | 3-1 | 4-0 | 7-3 | 4-1 | 7-1 | 3-3 | 4-0 |
| SO Montpelliérains | 3-2 | 0-0 | 3-2 | 2-6 | 4-1 | 2-1 | 3-3 | | 3-1 | 2-4 | 1-0 | 1-2 | 4-1 | 3-2 |
| Olympique GC de Nice | 1-1 | 3-1 | 5-2 | 3-3 | 0-0 | 3-2 | 0-3 | 1-1 | | 1-2 | 2-0 | 4-2 | 1-4 | 2-1 |
| SC de Nîmes | 5-0 | 4-1 | 5-1 | 3-0 | 3-4 | 3-3 | 0-2 | 2-0 | 5-2 | | 3-1 | 5-3 | 0-2 | 7-1 |
| Racing Club de Paris | 5-2 | 5-1 | 4-1 | 3-3 | 1-0 | 1-0 | 0-1 | 3-0 | 4-3 | 1-1 | | 2-3 | 1-1 | 0-2 |
| Stade Rennais Université Club | 2-2 | 2-2 | 8-2 | 5-2 | 1-0 | 1-5 | 1-0 | 2-6 | 2-1 | 6-2 | 2-1 | | 4-4 | 2-2 |
| FC de Sète | 4-2 | 4-0 | 6-2 | 4-2 | 2-2 | 1-0 | 1-0 | 1-1 | 4-0 | 8-2 | 2-1 | 3-1 | | 3-1 |
| FC Sochaux-Montbéliard | 6-4 | 3-3 | 2-3 | 1-2 | 1-3 | 3-5 | 4-1 | 0-0 | 3-1 | 6-3 | 3-2 | 6-2 | 3-2 | |

## Top goal-scorers

1) Istvan LUKACS (FC de Sète) 28
2) WOLWEILER (Stade Rennais UC) 25
3) Roger COURTOIS (FC Sochaux-Montbéliard) 23

\* Antibes-Juan-les-Pins FC (Antibes) changed their name from Antibes Olympique (Antibes).

\# Olympique GC de Nice (Nice) resigned from the league and reverted to amateur status.

| Division 2 (Nord) | | Pd | Wn | Dw | Ls | GF | GA | Pts |
|---|---|---|---|---|---|---|---|---|
| 1. | Red Star Olympique (Saint-Ouen) | 24 | 15 | 5 | 4 | 71 | 37 | 35 |
| 2. | FC de Rouen (Rouen) | 24 | 15 | 5 | 4 | 85 | 46 | 35 |
| 3. | FC de Mulhouse 1893 (Mulhouse) | 24 | 14 | 3 | 7 | 58 | 39 | 31 |
| 4. | Racing Club de Strasbourg (Strasbourg) | 24 | 13 | 4 | 7 | 64 | 42 | 30 |
| 5. | FC de Metz (Metz) | 24 | 11 | 4 | 9 | 51 | 39 | 26 |
| 6. | Racing Club de Roubaix (Roubaix) | 24 | 10 | 3 | 11 | 41 | 47 | 23 |
| 7. | US Valenciennes-Anzin (Valenciennes) | 24 | 7 | 8 | 9 | 47 | 52 | 22 |
| 8. | Amiens AC (Amiens) | 24 | 8 | 3 | 11 | 59 | 65 | 21 |
| 9. | US Tourquennoise (Tourcoing) | 24 | 8 | 4 | 12 | 38 | 51 | 20 |
| 10. | Havre AC (Le Havre) | 24 | 8 | 3 | 13 | 48 | 61 | 19 |
| 11. | US Servannaise et Malouine (St.Malo/St.Servan) | 24 | 7 | 4 | 13 | 39 | 67 | 18 |
| 12. | Club Français (Paris) | 24 | 5 | 7 | 12 | 43 | 73 | 17 |
| 13. | Racing Club de Calais (Calais) | 24 | 5 | 5 | 14 | 31 | 56 | 15 |
| | | 312 | 126 | 58 | 126 | 675 | 675 | 312 |

| Division 2 (Sud) | | Pd | Wn | Dw | Ls | GF | GA | Pts | |
|---|---|---|---|---|---|---|---|---|---|
| 1. | Olympique Alésien (Alès) | 14 | 10 | 1 | 3 | 38 | 19 | 21 | |
| 2. | AS de Saint-Étienne (Saint-Étienne) | 14 | 9 | 1 | 4 | 25 | 16 | 19 | |
| 3. | AS de Monaco (Monaco) | 14 | 7 | 3 | 4 | 40 | 31 | 17 | |
| 4. | Club Deportivo de Bordeaux (Bordeaux) | 14 | 7 | 1 | 6 | 38 | 38 | 15 | * |
| 5. | Hyères FC (Hyères) | 14 | 6 | 1 | 7 | 15 | 21 | 13 | R |
| 6. | Stade Olympique Biterrois (Béziers) | 14 | 4 | 3 | 7 | 31 | 39 | 11 | R |
| 7. | SC de la Bastidienne (Bordeaux) | 14 | 4 | 1 | 9 | 21 | 29 | 9 | * |
| 8. | FC de Lyon (Lyon) | 14 | 2 | 3 | 9 | 21 | 36 | 7 | R |
| | | 112 | 49 | 14 | 49 | 229 | 229 | 112 | |

US Suisse (Paris) and FCA Lyon (Lyon) withdrew from Division 2 Nord and Sud respectively.

Elected: Racing Club Lensois (Lens) and Stade Malherbe Caennais (Caen).

* Club Deportivo de Bordeaux (Bordeaux) and SC de la Bastidienne (Bordeaux) merged and became Football Club Hispano-Bastidien (Bordeaux) for the next season.

## Coupe de France Final   (Stade Yves du Manoir, Colombes – 06/05/34 – 40,600)

**FC DE SÈTE (SÈTE)**        **2-1**        Olympique de Marseille (Marseille)

*Lukacs 22', 75'*        *Zermani 02'*

**Sète**: Llense, Hillier, Gasco, Gabrillargues, Bukovi, Dupont, Monsallier, Bek, Lukacs, Miquel, Benouna.
**Olympique**: Di Lorto, M.Conchy, H.Conchy, Charbit, Drucker, Schillemann, Zermani, Alcazar, Boyer, Eisenhoffer, Kohut.

## Semi-Finals   (08/04/34)

| Olympique de Marseille (Marseille) | 1-0 | Racing Club de Roubaix (Roubaix) |
|---|---|---|
| FC de Sète (Sète) | 1-0 | Olympique Lillois (Lille) |

## Quarter-Finals   (04/03/34)

| Olympique Lillois (Lille) | 3-0 | US Tourquennoise (Tourcoing) |
|---|---|---|
| Olympique de Marseille (Marseille) | 2-2,  4-0 | Stade Rennais UC (Rennes) |
| Racing Club de Roubaix (Roubaix) | 3-2 | FC de Rouen (Rouen) |
| FC de Sète (Sète) | 3-0 | Amiens AC (Amiens) |

# 1934-35

| 1934-35 Division One | Olympique Alésien | Antibes-Juan-les-Pins FC | AS de Cannes | Excelsior AC de Roubaix | SC Fivois | Olympique Lillois | Olympique de Marseille | SO Montpelliérains | FC de Mulhouse 1893 | SC de Nîmes | Racing Club de Paris | Red Star Olympique | Stade Rennais Université Club | FC de Sète | FC Sochaux-Montbéliard | Racing Club de Strasbourg |
|---|---|---|---|---|---|---|---|---|---|---|---|---|---|---|---|---|
| Olympique Alésien | ■ | 2-1 | 5-1 | 0-3 | 2-1 | 3-1 | 1-0 | 1-1 | 2-2 | 2-4 | 7-2 | 3-2 | 3-2 | 3-0 | 0-5 | 1-5 |
| Antibes-Juan-les-Pins FC | 1-0 | ■ | 1-1 | 4-2 | 2-3 | 1-0 | 1-7 | 4-0 | 1-1 | 4-1 | 2-5 | 1-1 | 0-0 | 1-0 | 1-1 | 1-3 |
| AS de Cannes | 6-2 | 3-1 | ■ | 5-2 | 2-0 | 1-2 | 3-0 | 7-2 | 5-0 | 1-0 | 0-2 | 6-2 | 3-0 | 2-0 | 0-2 | 0-1 |
| Excelsior AC de Roubaix | 2-0 | 1-4 | 2-0 | ■ | 0-1 | 2-1 | 0-3 | 6-1 | 1-2 | 4-0 | 5-3 | 2-0 | 0-0 | 0-1 | 0-1 | 1-2 |
| SC Fivois | 1-0 | 2-1 | 1-2 | 0-0 | ■ | 2-1 | 6-3 | 1-0 | 0-2 | 3-1 | 2-1 | 6-0 | 4-1 | 1-2 | 0-3 | 1-3 |
| Olympique Lillois | 2-1 | 10-0 | 0-0 | 4-0 | 3-0 | ■ | 5-0 | 4-1 | 0-1 | 3-1 | 0-0 | 0-4 | 3-1 | 2-0 | 2-1 | 2-1 |
| Olympique de Marseille | 3-2 | 7-2 | 2-2 | 2-4 | 5-1 | 3-1 | ■ | 4-1 | 8-3 | 2-1 | 3-2 | 4-3 | 4-1 | 1-1 | 1-3 | 1-1 |
| SO Montpelliérains | 0-3 | 2-0 | 2-3 | 0-2 | 2-0 | 1-3 | 3-2 | ■ | 5-3 | 0-3 | 3-3 | 0-3 | 4-1 | 0-2 | 0-4 | 0-0 |
| FC de Mulhouse 1893 | 2-0 | 4-1 | 4-0 | 6-1 | 1-0 | 1-0 | 3-4 | 4-1 | ■ | 6-0 | 3-1 | 0-0 | 2-2 | 1-1 | 1-5 | 4-1 |
| SC de Nîmes | 1-1 | 3-1 | 1-2 | 1-1 | 1-4 | 1-2 | 1-1 | 4-5 | 3-2 | ■ | 0-2 | 2-1 | 1-2 | 1-3 | 0-2 | 0-1 |
| Racing Club de Paris | 6-3 | 5-1 | 3-2 | 3-1 | 7-0 | 3-0 | 5-1 | 1-0 | 2-3 | 2-0 | ■ | 2-2 | 2-1 | 6-2 | 1-2 | 2-2 |
| Red Star Olympique | 3-1 | 2-2 | 2-1 | 1-3 | 5-2 | 1-1 | 4-1 | 0-1 | 3-1 | 2-2 | 1-2 | ■ | 2-1 | 3-4 | 2-7 | 1-3 |
| Stade Rennais Université Club | 6-0 | 4-1 | 3-0 | 0-1 | 3-1 | 4-0 | 1-1 | 4-1 | 6-2 | 2-0 | 0-1 | 3-1 | ■ | 4-1 | 3-3 | 0-2 |
| FC de Sète | 1-0 | 1-1 | 1-1 | 2-2 | 4-0 | 3-1 | 6-3 | 3-0 | 2-0 | 2-2 | 2-2 | 2-2 | 2-0 | ■ | 1-1 | 1-0 |
| FC Sochaux-Montbéliard | 6-2 | 3-7 | 4-2 | 0-2 | 2-1 | 5-2 | 4-0 | 9-0 | 8-0 | 1-0 | 3-1 | 4-3 | 2-1 | 0-0 | ■ | 2-3 |
| Racing Club de Strasbourg | 3-2 | 6-1 | 1-1 | 1-1 | 2-1 | 4-1 | 1-0 | 2-1 | 4-2 | 3-0 | 6-0 | 5-2 | 2-1 | 5-2 | 0-1 | ■ |

## Division 1

| | | Pd | Wn | Dw | Ls | GF | GA | Pts | |
|---|---|---|---|---|---|---|---|---|---|
| 1. | FC SOCHAUX-MONTBÉLIARD (MONTBÉLIARD) | 30 | 22 | 4 | 4 | 94 | 36 | 48 | |
| 2. | Racing Club de Strasbourg (Strasbourg) | 30 | 21 | 5 | 4 | 73 | 33 | 47 | |
| 3. | Racing Club de Paris (Paris) | 30 | 16 | 5 | 9 | 77 | 57 | 37 | |
| 4. | FC de Sète (Sète) | 30 | 13 | 10 | 7 | 52 | 45 | 36 | |
| 5. | AS de Cannes (Cannes) | 30 | 14 | 5 | 11 | 62 | 48 | 33 | |
| 6. | FC de Mulhouse 1893 (Mulhouse) | 30 | 14 | 5 | 11 | 66 | 67 | 33 | |
| 7. | Olympique Lillois (Lille) | 30 | 14 | 3 | 13 | 56 | 46 | 31 | |
| 8. | Excelsior AC de Roubaix (Roubaix) | 30 | 13 | 5 | 12 | 51 | 48 | 31 | |
| 9. | Olympique de Marseille (Marseille) | 30 | 13 | 5 | 12 | 76 | 72 | 31 | |
| 10. | Stade Rennais Université Club (Rennes) | 30 | 11 | 5 | 14 | 57 | 49 | 27 | |
| 11. | SC Fivois (Fives) | 30 | 12 | 1 | 17 | 45 | 61 | 25 | |
| 12. | Red Star Olympique (Saint-Ouen) | 30 | 8 | 7 | 15 | 58 | 72 | 23 | |
| 13. | Olympique Alésien (Alès) | 30 | 10 | 3 | 17 | 52 | 73 | 23 | |
| 14. | Antibes-Juan-les-Pins FC (Antibes) | 30 | 8 | 7 | 156 | 49 | 80 | 23 | |
| 15. | Sports Olympiques Montpelliérains (Montpellier) | 30 | 7 | 3 | 20 | 37 | 86 | 17 | R |
| 16. | SC de Nîmes (Nîmes) | 30 | 5 | 5 | 20 | 35 | 67 | 15 | R# |
| | | 480 | 201 | 78 | 201 | 940 | 940 | 480 | |

# SC de Nîmes (Nîmes) resigned from the league and reverted to amateur status for the next season.

## Top goal-scorers

1) André "Trello" ABBEGLEN     (FC Sochaux-Montbéliard)     30
2) Roger COURTOIS     (FC Sochaux-Montbéliard)     29
3) Franz WESSELIK     (FC de Mulhouse 1893)     24

| Division 2 | Pd | Wn | Dw | Ls | GF | GA | Pts | |
|---|---|---|---|---|---|---|---|---|
| 1. Cercle des Sports de Metz (Metz) | 26 | 18 | 5 | 3 | 78 | 22 | 41 | P* |
| 2. US Valenciennes-Anzin (Valenciennes) | 26 | 17 | 3 | 6 | 71 | 44 | 37 | P |
| 3. FC de Rouen (Rouen) | 26 | 16 | 2 | 8 | 80 | 46 | 34 | |
| 4. Racing Club de Roubaix (Roubaix) | 26 | 14 | 5 | 7 | 63 | 45 | 33 | |
| 5. Racing Club de Lens (Lens) | 26 | 12 | 8 | 6 | 70 | 49 | 32 | |
| 6. Racing Club de Calais (Calais) | 26 | 12 | 7 | 7 | 79 | 62 | 31 | |
| 7. Cercle Athlétique de Paris (Paris) | 26 | 9 | 6 | 11 | 52 | 63 | 24 | |
| 8. US Tourquennoise (Tourcoing) | 26 | 10 | 3 | 13 | 46 | 59 | 23 | # |
| 9. AS de Saint-Étienne (Saint-Étienne) | 26 | 10 | 3 | 13 | 46 | 59 | 23 | |
| 10. Havre AC (Le Havre) | 26 | 8 | 6 | 12 | 56 | 72 | 22 | |
| 11. Stade Malherbe Caennais (Caen) | 26 | 9 | 3 | 14 | 61 | 57 | 21 | |
| 12. Amiens AC (Amiens) | 26 | 8 | 3 | 15 | 50 | 76 | 19 | |
| 13. AS Villeurbannaise (Villerbanne) | 26 | 5 | 4 | 17 | 45 | 85 | 14 | |
| 14. FC Hispano-Bastidien (Bordeaux) | 26 | 3 | 4 | 19 | 40 | 98 | 10 | # |
| | 364 | 151 | 62 | 151 | 837 | 837 | 364 | |

* Cercle des Sports de Metz (Metz) changed their name pre-season from FC de Metz (Metz).

# US Tourquennoise (Tourcoing) and FC Hispano-Bastidien (Bordeaux) both resigned from the league and reverted to amateur status for the next season.

Club Français (Paris) & US Servannaise et Malouin (Saint-Malo/Saint-Servain) withdrew from the league.

**Promoted**: US Boulonnaise (Boulogne-sur-Mer), FC de Nancy (Nancy), FC Olympique de Charleville (Charleville), Olympique de Dunkerque (Dunkerque), Olympique GC de Nice (Nice), Stade de Reims (Reims) and AS Troyenne-Savinienne (Troyes).

## Coupe de France Final    (Stade Yves du Manoir, Colombes – 05/05/35 – 40,008)

| **OLYMPIQUE DE MARSEILLE** | **3-0** | Stade Rennais UC (Rennes) |
|---|---|---|

*Roviglione 34', Kohut 38', J.Laurent 43' (o.g.)*

**Olympique:** Di Lorto, M.Conchy, H.Conchy, Charbit, Bruhin, Durand, Zermani, Alcazar, Roviglione, Eisenhoffer, Kohut.

**Rennais:** Collet, Rose, Pleyer, Laurent, Volante, Gardet, Rouxel, Boccon, Bernasconi, Chauvel, Cahours.

## Semi-Finals    (07/04/35)

| Olympique de Marseille (Marseille) | 3-2 | Red Star Olympique (Saint-Ouen) |
|---|---|---|
| Stade Rennais UC (Rennes) | 3-0 | SC Fivois (Fives) |

## Quarter-Finals    (03/03/35)

| SC Fivois (Fives) | 2-1 | Cercle des Sports de Metz (Metz) |
|---|---|---|
| Olympique de Marseille (Marseille) | 3-0 | FC Sochaux-Montbéliard (Montbéliard) |
| Red Star Olympique (Saint-Ouen) | 2-0 | FC de Sète (Sète) |
| Stade Rennais UC (Rennes) | 1-0 | FC de Rouen (Rouen) |

# 1935-36

| 1935-36 Division One | Olympique Alésien | Antibes-Juan-les-Pi. | AS de Cannes | Excelsior de Roubaix | SC Fivois | Olympique Lillois | Olymp. de Marseille | CS de Metz | FC de Mulhouse 1893 | Racing Club de Paris | Red Star Olympique | Stade Rennais UC | FC de Sète | FC Sochaux-Montbél. | RC de Strasbourg | US Valenciennes-Anzin |
|---|---|---|---|---|---|---|---|---|---|---|---|---|---|---|---|---|
| Olympique Alésien | ■ | 1-2 | 3-1 | 3-2 | 0-3 | 1-1 | 3-3 | 1-1 | 3-3 | 0-2 | 0-0 | 2-6 | 1-2 | 0-0 | 0-2 | 3-5 |
| Antibes-Juan-les-Pins FC | 3-2 | ■ | 0-1 | 1-0 | 3-1 | 3-1 | 3-2 | 0-0 | 3-2 | 3-9 | 2-0 | 3-1 | 1-4 | 1-3 | 1-1 | 1-3 |
| AS de Cannes | 3-1 | 2-1 | ■ | 2-3 | 1-0 | 0-0 | 3-1 | 2-1 | 2-2 | 0-2 | 2-1 | 6-0 | 3-2 | 1-0 | 0-2 | 5-1 |
| Excelsior de Roubaix-Tour. | 1-1 | 2-0 | 2-0 | ■ | 4-3 | 1-2 | 1-1 | 2-3 | 4-0 | 0-2 | 6-4 | 1-1 | 2-0 | 2-2 | 2-1 | 3-1 |
| SC Fivois | 1-2 | 1-1 | 5-1 | 1-0 | ■ | 1-1 | 1-2 | 3-0 | 3-0 | 2-0 | 2-1 | 1-3 | 3-0 | 2-1 | 0-1 | 3-2 |
| Olympique Lillois | 3-0 | 6-3 | 1-1 | 3-2 | 1-0 | ■ | 1-0 | 3-0 | 4-0 | 2-1 | 0-0 | 0-2 | 2-3 | 4-0 | 3-0 |  |
| Olympique de Marseille | 2-0 | 4-1 | 3-0 | 2-5 | 3-2 | 1-0 | ■ | 3-0 | 6-2 | 2-5 | 1-4 | 7-1 | 1-0 | 4-1 | 1-0 | 2-2 |
| Cercle des Sports de Metz | 1-1 | 2-1 | 2-1 | 3-5 | 0-2 | 1-2 | 5-2 | ■ | 2-1 | 1-2 | 5-1 | 2-0 | 3-1 | 3-2 | 5-1 | 5-4 |
| FC de Mulhouse 1893 | 3-3 | 2-2 | 2-2 | 0-4 | 3-1 | 2-3 | 3-1 | 3-0 | ■ | 3-0 | 3-2 | 2-2 | 2-1 | 3-6 | 2-4 | 3-2 |
| Racing Club de Paris | 3-1 | 3-2 | 5-0 | 3-2 | 4-0 | 2-3 | 2-2 | 3-5 | 3-1 | ■ | 4-1 | 4-0 | 2-1 | 1-1 | 4-1 | 2-1 |
| Red Star Olympique | 1-2 | 4-1 | 0-3 | 3-2 | 1-4 | 0-2 | 0-2 | 6-2 | 7-1 | 1-4 | ■ | 0-1 | 1-1 | 2-2 | 1-2 | 2-0 |
| Stade Rennais Université Club | 2-0 | 2-1 | 1-3 | 2-2 | 2-3 | 1-1 | 1-1 | 2-0 | 5-1 | 0-3 | 3-0 | ■ | 1-0 | 1-1 | 2-0 | 1-1 |
| FC de Sète | 1-0 | 4-0 | 2-0 | 1-3 | 1-0 | 2-1 | 1-0 | 2-1 | 3-1 | 1-1 | 3-2 | 4-2 | ■ | 1-4 | 3-1 | 1-1 |
| FC Sochaux-Montbéliard | 7-0 | 5-1 | 1-1 | 6-2 | 0-0 | 1-1 | 4-0 | 6-0 | 0-1 | 2-2 | 0-1 | 2-0 | 2-2 | ■ | 1-1 | 12-1 |
| Racing Club de Strasbourg | 6-1 | 2-1 | 0-2 | 1-0 | 2-1 | 3-2 | 4-1 | 4-0 | 3-0 | 0-1 | 6-0 | 8-0 | 4-0 | 2-1 | ■ | 4-0 |
| US Valenciennes-Anzin | 2-4 | 0-0 | 2-5 | 4-0 | 1-2 | 1-5 | 0-1 | 3-1 | 8-2 | 5-3 | 0-2 | 3-1 | 5-3 | 0-5 | 1-1 | ■ |

## Division 1

| | | Pd | Wn | Dw | Ls | GF | GA | Pts | |
|---|---|---|---|---|---|---|---|---|---|
| 1. | RACING CLUB DE PARIS (PARIS) | 30 | 20 | 4 | 6 | 81 | 45 | 44 | |
| 2. | Olympique Lillois (Lille) | 30 | 17 | 7 | 6 | 62 | 32 | 41 | |
| 3. | Racing Club de Strasbourg (Strasbourg) | 30 | 18 | 3 | 9 | 67 | 37 | 39 | |
| 4. | FC Sochaux-Montbéliard (Montbéliard) | 30 | 12 | 11 | 7 | 81 | 38 | 35 | |
| 5. | AS de Cannes (Cannes) | 30 | 15 | 5 | 10 | 53 | 46 | 35 | |
| 6. | Olympique de Marseille (Marseille) | 30 | 14 | 5 | 11 | 61 | 55 | 33 | |
| 7. | FC de Sète (Sète) | 30 | 14 | 4 | 12 | 49 | 48 | 32 | |
| 8. | SC Fivois (Fives) | 30 | 14 | 3 | 13 | 51 | 41 | 31 | |
| 9. | Excelsior de Roubaix-Tourcoing (Roubaix) | 30 | 13 | 5 | 12 | 65 | 56 | 31 | * |
| 10. | Stade Rennais Université Club (Rennes) | 30 | 10 | 8 | 12 | 44 | 62 | 28 | |
| 11. | Cercle des Sports de Metz (Metz) | 30 | 12 | 3 | 15 | 54 | 69 | 27 | |
| 12. | Antibes-Juan-les-Pins FC (Antibes) | 30 | 10 | 5 | 15 | 47 | 68 | 25 | |
| 13. | FC de Mulhouse 1893 (Mulhouse) | 30 | 8 | 6 | 16 | 53 | 89 | 22 | |
| 14. | Red Star Olympique (Saint-Ouen) | 30 | 8 | 3 | 19 | 49 | 68 | 19 | |
| 15. | US Valenciennes-Anzin (Valenciennes) | 30 | 7 | 5 | 18 | 57 | 87 | 19 | R |
| 16. | Olympique Alésien (Alès) | 30 | 5 | 9 | 16 | 39 | 72 | 19 | R |
| | | 480 | 197 | 86 | 197 | 913 | 913 | 480 | |

## Top goal-scorers

| | | | |
|---|---|---|---|
| 1) | Roger COURTOIS | (FC Sochaux-Montbéliard) | 34 |
| 2) | Oskar ROHR | (Racing Club de Strasbourg) | 28 |
| 3) | Roger COUARD | (Racing Club de Paris) | 23 |
| | FRANCESCHETTI | (AS de Cannes) | 23 |

| Division 2 | Pd | Wn | Dw | Ls | GF | GA | Pts | |
|---|---|---|---|---|---|---|---|---|
| 1. FC de Rouen (Rouen) | 34 | 25 | 4 | 5 | 119 | 33 | 54 | P |
| 2. Racing Club de Roubaix (Roubaix) | 34 | 23 | 6 | 5 | 98 | 40 | 52 | P |
| 3. AS de Saint-Étienne (Saint-Étienne) | 34 | 24 | 4 | 6 | 99 | 49 | 52 | |
| 4. Racing Club de Lens (Lens) | 34 | 17 | 10 | 7 | 72 | 43 | 44 | |
| 5. Amiens AC (Amiens) | 34 | 18 | 4 | 12 | 73 | 61 | 40 | |
| 6. Stade Malherbe Caennais (Caen) | 34 | 17 | 5 | 12 | 68 | 57 | 39 | |
| 7. Racing Club de Calais (Calais) | 34 | 14 | 10 | 10 | 75 | 55 | 38 | |
| 8. Sports Olympiques Montpelliérains (Montpellier) | 34 | 15 | 7 | 12 | 54 | 46 | 37 | |
| 9. Olympique GC de Nice (Nice) | 34 | 14 | 6 | 14 | 53 | 39 | 34 | |
| 10. Stade de Reims (Reims) | 34 | 15 | 3 | 16 | 62 | 74 | 33 | |
| 11. Cercle Athlétique de Paris (Paris) | 34 | 12 | 9 | 13 | 43 | 55 | 33 | |
| 12. FC Olympique de Charleville (Charleville) | 34 | 11 | 7 | 16 | 55 | 59 | 29 | |
| 13. AS Troyenne-Savinienne (Troyes) | 34 | 11 | 5 | 18 | 66 | 69 | 27 | |
| 14. US de Boulogne (Boulogne-sur-Mer) | 34 | 12 | 3 | 19 | 57 | 86 | 27 | * |
| 15. Olympique de Dunkerque (Dunkerque) | 34 | 11 | 3 | 20 | 46 | 68 | 25 | |
| 16. Havre AC (Le Havre) | 34 | 8 | 6 | 20 | 47 | 86 | 22 | |
| 17. AS Villeurbannoise (Villeurbanne) | 34 | 5 | 5 | 24 | 40 | 99 | 15 | # |
| 18. FC de Nancy (Nancy) | 34 | 3 | 5 | 26 | 33 | 122 | 11 | |
| --. SC de Nîmes (Nîmes) | --- | --- | --- | --- | --- | ---- | --- | |
| | 612 | 255 | 102 | 255 | 1160 | 1141 | 612 | |

# SC de Nîmes (Nîmes) withdrew from the league.

AS Villeurbannaise (Villeurbanne) resigned from the league at the end of the season.

* US de Boulogne (Boulogne-sur-Mer) changed their name pre-season from US Boulonnaise (Boulogne-sur-Mer).

Note: Girondins Guyenne Sports (Bordeaux) merged with FC de Bordeaux (Bordeaux) to become Girondins de Bordeaux FC (Bordeaux).


## Coupe de France Final   (Stade Yves du Manoir, Colombes – 03/05/36 – 39,725)

**RACING CLUB DE PARIS (PARIS)**          **1-0**          FC Olympique de Charleville (Charleville)
*Couard 67'*

**Racing**: Hiden, Dupuis, Diagne, Banide, Jordan, Delfour, Ozenne, Kennedy, Couard, Veinante, Mathé.
**Olympique**: Darui, Languillat, Herrera, Brembilla, Myrka, Frelin, Woerth, Dujardin, Dufrasne, Bieber, Merveille.


## Semi-Finals   (04-05/04/36)

| FC Olympique de Charleville (Charleville) | 2-1 | Red Star Olympique (Saint-Ouen) |
|---|---|---|
| Racing Club de Paris (Paris) | 3-0 | FC Sochaux-Montbéliard (Montbéliard) |


## Quarter-Finals   (01/03/36)

| FC Olympique de Charleville (Charleville) | 2-0 | Excelsior de Roubaix-Tourcoing (Roubaix) |
|---|---|---|
| Racing Club de Paris (Paris) | 2-2, 3-0 | Olympique Lillois (Lille) |
| Red Star Olympique (Saint-Ouen) | 4-2 | AS Brestoise (Brest) |
| FC Sochaux-Montbéliard (Montbéliard) | 0-0, 2-2, 1-0 | SC Fivois (Fives) |

# 1936-37

| 1936-37 Division 1 | Antibes-Juan-les-Pins FC | AS de Cannes | Excelsior de Roubaix-Tour. | SC Fivois | Olympique Lillois | Olympique de Marseille | FC de Metz | FC de Mulhouse 1893 | Racing Club de Paris | Red Star Olympique | Stade Rennais Université Club | Racing Club de Roubaix | FC de Rouen | FC de Sète | FC Sochaux-Montbéliard | Racing Club de Strasbourg |
|---|---|---|---|---|---|---|---|---|---|---|---|---|---|---|---|---|
| Antibes-Juan-les-Pins FC | | 4-1 | 3-0 | 5-2 | 2-2 | 1-3 | 2-2 | 3-2 | 1-3 | 2-0 | 1-0 | 2-3 | 1-1 | 2-1 | 1-3 | 1-6 |
| AS de Cannes | 2-3 | | 1-4 | 0-0 | 0-2 | 3-0 | 5-1 | 6-4 | 1-2 | 0-2 | 1-2 | 0-0 | 4-1 | 2-2 | 2-1 | 0-0 |
| Excelsior de Roubaix-Tour. | 1-2 | 5-0 | | 4-1 | 0-1 | 0-3 | 2-2 | 5-1 | 4-2 | 2-2 | 3-1 | 3-2 | 0-0 | 3-1 | 1-0 | 3-3 |
| SC Fivois | 1-1 | 1-2 | 6-2 | | 1-0 | 4-3 | 6-0 | 3-0 | 1-3 | 1-2 | 5-1 | 3-2 | 2-1 | 3-2 | 0-1 | 2-0 |
| Olympique Lillois | 3-2 | 4-3 | 5-4 | 1-3 | | 2-1 | 5-0 | 1-1 | 1-0 | 0-0 | 3-1 | 2-3 | 3-3 | 2-0 | 2-1 | 1-2 |
| Olympique de Marseille | 2-0 | 2-0 | 4-4 | 1-0 | 2-1 | | 4-0 | 5-1 | 4-1 | 3-2 | 3-0 | 4-1 | 3-0 | 2-1 | 0-1 | 4-0 |
| FC de Metz | 1-0 | 3-1 | 2-1 | 1-3 | 2-1 | 3-1 | | 8-1 | 3-1 | 4-0 | 2-1 | 4-0 | 4-4 | 4-0 | 2-2 | 0-0 |
| FC de Mulhouse 1893 | 2-3 | 1-1 | 1-4 | 1-0 | 1-3 | 1-3 | 2-4 | | 0-2 | 1-3 | 5-2 | 2-1 | 3-2 | 1-1 | 4-1 | 1-9 |
| Racing Club de Paris | 2-1 | 2-1 | 3-6 | 3-2 | 3-0 | 1-1 | 2-0 | 4-1 | | 4-2 | 3-1 | 2-0 | 2-4 | 4-1 | 1-0 | 2-2 |
| Red Star Olympique | 3-1 | 3-3 | 3-2 | 0-0 | 2-1 | 0-5 | 2-1 | 3-2 | 2-0 | | 0-1 | 2-2 | 0-1 | 1-0 | 2-2 | 1-1 |
| Stade Rennais Université Club | 0-1 | 0-2 | 5-4 | 1-0 | 0-0 | 3-1 | 5-1 | 1-2 | 1-3 | 1-3 | | 1-1 | 0-1 | 3-1 | 1-1 | 2-1 |
| Racing Club de Roubaix | 5-3 | 2-1 | 0-2 | 2-1 | 0-1 | 2-2 | 1-2 | 4-1 | 2-0 | 2-3 | 4-3 | | 3-0 | 1-1 | 3-2 | 2-1 |
| FC de Rouen | 5-1 | 2-2 | 2-1 | 2-1 | 0-2 | 1-0 | 3-2 | 4-2 | 0-1 | 7-1 | 1-0 | 4-0 | | 5-0 | 6-1 | 2-1 |
| FC de Sète | 4-0 | 0-0 | 2-0 | 2-1 | 3-0 | 2-2 | 3-0 | 4-1 | 3-0 | 2-1 | 1-1 | 2-1 | 2-0 | | 1-1 | 1-0 |
| FC Sochaux-Montbéliard | 2-0 | 1-1 | 2-1 | 1-0 | 1-1 | 3-1 | 2-1 | 5-1 | 2-1 | 4-2 | 1-0 | 2-0 | 2-0 | 6-2 | | 3-2 |
| Racing Club de Strasbourg | 2-1 | 1-3 | 0-1 | 1-1 | 2-1 | 1-0 | 1-1 | 7-2 | 0-0 | 3-0 | 3-0 | 5-1 | 4-0 | 1-1 | 3-2 | |

| | Division 1 | Pd | Wn | Dw | Ls | GF | GA | Pts | |
|---|---|---|---|---|---|---|---|---|---|
| 1. | OLYMPIQUE DE MARSEILLE (MARSEILLE) | 30 | 17 | 4 | 9 | 69 | 39 | 38 | |
| 2. | FC Sochaux-Montbéliard (Montbéliard) | 30 | 16 | 6 | 8 | 56 | 42 | 38 | |
| 3. | Racing Club de Paris (Paris) | 30 | 17 | 3 | 10 | 57 | 47 | 37 | |
| 4. | FC de Rouen (Rouen) | 30 | 15 | 5 | 10 | 62 | 48 | 35 | |
| 5. | Olympique Lillois (Lille) | 30 | 14 | 6 | 10 | 51 | 43 | 34 | |
| 6. | Racing Club de Strasbourg (Strasbourg) | 30 | 12 | 9 | 9 | 62 | 39 | 33 | |
| 7. | FC de Metz (Metz) | 30 | 13 | 6 | 11 | 60 | 61 | 32 | * |
| 8. | Excelsior de Roubaix-Tourcoing (Roubaix) | 30 | 13 | 5 | 12 | 72 | 60 | 31 | |
| 9. | Red Star Olympique (Saint-Ouen) | 30 | 12 | 7 | 11 | 47 | 58 | 31 | |
| 10. | FC de Sète (Sète) | 30 | 11 | 8 | 11 | 46 | 48 | 30 | |
| 11. | SC Fivois (Fives) | 30 | 12 | 4 | 14 | 54 | 45 | 28 | |
| 12. | Racing Club de Roubaix (Roubaix) | 30 | 11 | 5 | 14 | 50 | 61 | 27 | |
| 13. | Antibes-Juan-les-Pins FC (Antibes) | 30 | 11 | 4 | 15 | 59 | 64 | 26 | |
| 14. | AS de Cannes (Cannes) | 30 | 8 | 9 | 13 | 48 | 55 | 25 | |
| 15. | Stade Rennais Université Club (Rennes) | 30 | 8 | 4 | 18 | 38 | 58 | 20 | R |
| 16. | FC de Mulhouse 1893 (Mulhouse) | 30 | 6 | 3 | 21 | 48 | 102 | 15 | R |
| | | 480 | 196 | 88 | 196 | 870 | 870 | 480 | |

## Top goal-scorers

1) Oskar ROHR        (Racing Club Strasbourg)    30
2) Mario ZATELLI      (Olympique de Marseille)    28
3) Jean NICOLAS       (FC de Rouen)    27

* FC de Metz (Metz) changed their name pre-season from Cercle des Sports de Metz (Metz).

| | Division 2 | Pd | Wn | Dw | Ls | GF | GA | Pts | |
|---|---|---|---|---|---|---|---|---|---|
| 1. | Racing Club de Lens (Lens) | 32 | 23 | 4 | 5 | 86 | 46 | 50 | P |
| 2. | US Valenciennes-Anzin (Valenciennes) | 32 | 18 | 9 | 5 | 72 | 53 | 45 | P |
| 3. | AS de Saint-Étienne (Saint-Étienne) | 32 | 19 | 2 | 11 | 98 | 50 | 40 | |
| 4. | Havre AC (Le Havre) | 32 | 14 | 8 | 10 | 68 | 50 | 36 | |
| 5. | Olympique GC de Nice (Nice) | 32 | 15 | 5 | 12 | 52 | 41 | 35 | |
| 6. | FC Olympique de Charleville (Charleville) | 32 | 16 | 3 | 13 | 47 | 50 | 35 | |
| 7. | US de Boulogne (Boulogne-sur-Mer) | 32 | 14 | 4 | 14 | 54 | 49 | 32 | |
| 8. | Stade Malherbe Caennais (Caen) | 32 | 12 | 7 | 13 | 44 | 53 | 31 | |
| 9. | Olympique Alésien (Alès) | 32 | 11 | 8 | 13 | 49 | 51 | 30 | |
| 10. | AS Troyenne-Savinienne (Troyes) | 32 | 13 | 4 | 15 | 54 | 63 | 30 | |
| 11. | Amiens AC (Amiens) | 32 | 8 | 14 | 10 | 48 | 56 | 30 | |
| 12. | Olympique de Dunkerque (Dunkerque) | 32 | 11 | 7 | 14 | 59 | 63 | 29 | |
| 13. | Sports Olympiques Montpelliérains (Montpellier) | 32 | 11 | 6 | 15 | 58 | 55 | 28 | |
| 14. | Cercle Athlétique de Paris (Paris) | 32 | 10 | 6 | 16 | 41 | 62 | 26 | |
| 15. | FC de Nancy (Nancy) | 32 | 9 | 6 | 17 | 44 | 64 | 24 | |
| 16. | Stade de Reims (Reims) | 32 | 8 | 7 | 17 | 46 | 66 | 23 | |
| 17. | Racing Club de Calais (Calais) | 32 | 9 | 2 | 21 | 42 | 90 | 20 | |
| | | 544 | 221 | 102 | 221 | 962 | 962 | 544 | |

**Promoted**: Racing Club d'Arras (Arras) and US Tourquennoise (Tourcoing).

Elected: FC Bordeaux-Bouscat (Bordeaux), Sport Réunis de Colmar (Colmar), FC Dieppois (Dieppe), AS Hautmontoise (Hautmont), US du Bassin de Longwy (Longwy) and Toulouse FC (Toulouse).

## Coupe de France Final    (Stade Yves du Manoir, Colombes – 09/05/37 – 39,538)

**FC SOCHAUX-MONTBÉLIARD**      **2-1**      Racing Club de Strasbourg (Strasbourg)

*Lauri 40', Williams 88'*                                                 *Rohr 32'*

**Sochaux**: Di Lorto, Lalloué, Mattler, Hug, Szabo, Lehmann, Lauri, Abegglen, Courtois, Bradac, Williams.
**Racing**: Mayer, Lohr, Schwartz, Halter, Humenberger, Roessler, Keller, Hoffmann, Rohr, Heisserer, Waechter.

## Semi-Finals    (04-05/04/37)

| | | |
|---|---|---|
| Racing Club de Strasbourg (Strasbourg) | 3-1 | FC de Rouen (Rouen) |
| FC Sochaux-Montbéliard (Montbéliard) | 6-0 | US de Boulogne (Boulogne-sur-Mer) |

## Quarter-Finals    (07/03/37)

| | | |
|---|---|---|
| US de Boulogne (Boulogne-sur-Mer) | 1-0 | Racing Club de Paris (Paris) |
| FC de Rouen (Rouen) | 2-0 | Olympique de Dunkerque (Dunkerque) |
| FC Sochaux-Montbéliard (Montbéliard) | 0-0, 3-1 | AS de Cannes (Cannes) |
| Racing Club de Strasbourg (Strasbourg) | 3-1 | Red Star Olympique (Saint-Ouen) |

| 1937-38 Division One | Antibes-Juan-les-Pins | AS de Cannes | Excelsior de Roubaix-T. | SC Fivois | Racing Club de Lens | Olympique Lillois | Olympique de Marseille | FC de Metz | Racing Club de Paris | Red Star Olympique | Racing Club de Roubaix | FC de Rouen | FC de Sète | FC Sochaux-Montbél. | Rac. Club de Strasbourg | US Valenciennes-Anzin |
|---|---|---|---|---|---|---|---|---|---|---|---|---|---|---|---|---|
| Antibes-Juan-les-Pins FC | ■ | 2-0 | 4-2 | 1-1 | 1-1 | 0-0 | 0-3 | 2-0 | 2-2 | 4-1 | 5-0 | 0-1 | 1-1 | 2-1 | 1-2 | 0-0 |
| AS de Cannes | 2-1 | ■ | 2-1 | 1-1 | 5-0 | 3-1 | 1-1 | 4-0 | 2-2 | 5-5 | 2-3 | 6-1 | 3-4 | 0-1 | 2-3 | 5-0 |
| Excelsior de Roubaix-Tour. | 2-1 | 2-2 | ■ | 3-2 | 1-1 | 2-2 | 4-2 | 2-4 | 3-2 | 3-1 | 0-1 | 2-0 | 2-2 | 1-2 | 3-2 | 4-0 |
| SC Fivois | 3-1 | 1-1 | 4-4 | ■ | 2-1 | 0-1 | 2-1 | 3-0 | 1-0 | 3-0 | 3-0 | 0-1 | 1-2 | 1-1 | 1-1 | 2-2 |
| Racing Club de Lens | 2-4 | 2-2 | 2-2 | 3-2 | ■ | 2-1 | 4-3 | 2-3 | 2-1 | 1-3 | 2-1 | 1-1 | 0-2 | 0-2 | 2-3 | 2-1 |
| Olympique Lillois | 4-0 | 0-0 | 1-1 | 2-1 | 3-0 | ■ | 1-1 | 3-1 | 0-1 | 4-1 | 1-1 | 4-0 | 2-1 | 0-0 | 2-0 | 0-1 |
| Olympique de Marseille | 1-0 | 2-2 | 1-1 | 1-1 | 2-2 | 4-0 | ■ | 4-0 | 2-1 | 1-0 | 5-1 | 1-1 | 3-0 | 2-0 | 2-1 | 1-1 |
| FC de Metz | 1-1 | 1-0 | 1-2 | 0-0 | 1-1 | 1-0 | 1-2 | ■ | 4-4 | 3-0 | 1-1 | 1-1 | 2-2 | | 4-0 | 1-0 |
| Racing Club de Paris | 1-2 | 3-1 | 5-1 | 1-1 | 1-3 | 1-0 | 3-3 | 2-2 | ■ | 2-1 | 2-1 | 2-1 | 0-2 | 0-4 | 0-3 | 0-3 |
| Red Star Olympique | 0-1 | 2-1 | 2-2 | 3-2 | 0-1 | 3-2 | 0-1 | 2-2 | 2-2 | ■ | 7-0 | 2-2 | 1-4 | 0-1 | 2-2 | 2-0 |
| Racing Club de Roubaix | 2-1 | 4-1 | 2-1 | 0-0 | 3-1 | 3-0 | 1-3 | 2-3 | 2-1 | 0-0 | ■ | 0-3 | 1-1 | 2-2 | 0-2 | 3-2 |
| FC de Rouen | 2-0 | 1-0 | 1-3 | 2-2 | 3-1 | 0-0 | 2-2 | 2-1 | 3-1 | 4-0 | 2-0 | ■ | 3-1 | 1-3 | 3-0 | 4-1 |
| FC de Sète | 0-0 | 1-1 | 3-0 | 1-0 | 3-1 | 3-1 | 1-1 | 4-1 | 2-2 | 3-1 | 0-1 | 1-0 | ■ | 0-1 | 3-0 | 3-0 |
| FC Sochaux-Montbéliard | 1-0 | 1-1 | 1-1 | 6-2 | 4-0 | 2-0 | 1-2 | 3-2 | 4-0 | 3-1 | 3-0 | 5-0 | 0-1 | ■ | 3-3 | 6-1 |
| Racing Club de Strasbourg | 3-0 | 1-0 | 3-3 | 2-0 | 2-2 | 0-0 | 2-2 | 1-1 | 1-3 | 9-3 | 4-0 | 3-3 | 0-2 | 1-6 | ■ | 10-0 |
| US Valenciennes-Anzin | 1-1 | 0-1 | 1-1 | 1-0 | 1-3 | 0-4 | 1-2 | 5-2 | 1-3 | 3-2 | 2-4 | 1-9 | 0-0 | 0-0 | 1-2 | ■ |

## Division 1

| | | Pd | Wn | Dw | Ls | GF | GA | Pts | |
|---|---|---|---|---|---|---|---|---|---|
| 1. | FC SOCHAUX-MONTBÉLIARD (MONTBÉLIARD) | 30 | 18 | 8 | 4 | 69 | 26 | 44 | |
| 2. | Olympique de Marseille (Marseille) | 30 | 15 | 12 | 3 | 61 | 35 | 42 | |
| 3. | FC de Sète (Sète) | 30 | 16 | 9 | 5 | 52 | 28 | 41 | |
| 4. | FC de Rouen (Rouen) | 30 | 14 | 8 | 8 | 57 | 44 | 36 | |
| 5. | Racing Club de Strasbourg (Strasbourg) | 30 | 12 | 9 | 9 | 66 | 54 | 33 | |
| 6. | Excelsior de Roubaix-Tourcoing (Roubaix) | 30 | 10 | 11 | 9 | 59 | 57 | 31 | |
| 7. | Olympique Lillois (Lille) | 30 | 10 | 9 | 11 | 39 | 33 | 29 | |
| 8. | Racing Club de Roubaix (Roubaix) | 30 | 11 | 6 | 13 | 39 | 60 | 28 | |
| 9. | AS de Cannes (Cannes) | 30 | 8 | 11 | 11 | 56 | 47 | 27 | |
| 10. | Antibes-Juan-les-Pins FC (Antibes) | 30 | 9 | 9 | 12 | 38 | 40 | 27 | |
| 11. | FC de Metz (Metz) | 30 | 8 | 11 | 11 | 45 | 36 | 27 | |
| 12. | SC Fivois (Fives) | 30 | 7 | 12 | 11 | 42 | 43 | 26 | |
| 13. | Racing Club de Paris (Paris) | 30 | 9 | 8 | 13 | 48 | 119 | 26 | |
| 14. | Racing Club de Lens (Lens) | 30 | 9 | 8 | 13 | 45 | 63 | 26 | |
| 15. | Red Star Olympique (Saint-Ouen) | 30 | 6 | 7 | 17 | 47 | 31 | 19 | R |
| 16. | US Valenciennes-Anzin (Valenciennes) | 30 | 6 | 6 | 18 | 30 | 77 | 18 | R |
| | | 480 | 168 | 144 | 168 | 793 | 793 | 480 | |

## Top goal-scorers

1) Jean NICOLAS (FC de Rouen) 26
2) Oskar ROHR (Racing Club de Strasbourg) 25
3) Dezsõ "Koranyi" KRONENBERGER (FC de Sète) 24

## Division 2 (Phase 2 Promotion)

| | | Pd | Wn | Dw | Ls | GF | GA | Pts | |
|---|---|---|---|---|---|---|---|---|---|
| 1. | Havre AC (Le Havre) | 30 | 20 | 4 | 6 | 77 | 40 | 44 | P |
| 2. | AS de Saint-Étienne (Saint-Étienne) | 30 | 17 | 7 | 6 | 72 | 40 | 41 | P |
| 3. | Stade Rennais Université Club (Rennes) | 30 | 17 | 6 | 7 | 49 | 33 | 40 | |
| 4. | Sport Réunis de Colmar (Colmar) | 30 | 17 | 5 | 8 | 54 | 41 | 39 | |
| 5. | Olympique de Dunkerque (Dunkerque) | 30 | 13 | 8 | 9 | 58 | 52 | 34 | |
| 6. | Racing Club d'Arras (Arras) | 30 | 12 | 8 | 10 | 46 | 43 | 32 | |
| 7. | Toulouse FC (Toulouse) | 30 | 13 | 5 | 12 | 40 | 43 | 31 | |
| 8. | Olympique GC de Nice (Nice) | 30 | 11 | 7 | 12 | 53 | 50 | 29 | |
| 9. | Cercle Athlétique de Paris (Paris) | 30 | 12 | 4 | 14 | 60 | 50 | 28 | |
| 10. | Stade de Reims (Reims) | 30 | 12 | 3 | 15 | 48 | 50 | 27 | |
| 11. | FC de Nancy (Nancy) | 30 | 10 | 7 | 13 | 45 | 49 | 27 | |
| 12. | Olympique Alésien (Alès) | 30 | 9 | 6 | 15 | 35 | 44 | 24 | |
| 13. | US Boulogne (Boulogne-sur-Mer) | 30 | 10 | 4 | 16 | 49 | 66 | 24 | |
| 14. | Stade Malherbe Caennais (Caen) | 30 | 9 | 5 | 16 | 47 | 71 | 23 | |
| 15. | FC de Mulhouse 1893 (Mulhouse) | 30 | 9 | 4 | 17 | 41 | 62 | 22 | |
| 16. | US Tourquennoise (Tourcoing) | 30 | 5 | 5 | 20 | 37 | 85 | 15 | |
| | | 480 | 196 | 84 | 196 | 811 | 819 | 480 | |

## Division 2 (Phase 2 Relegation)

| | | Pd | Wn | Dw | Ls | GF | GA | Pts | |
|---|---|---|---|---|---|---|---|---|---|
| 1. | FC Olympique de Charleville (Charleville) | 16 | 8 | 3 | 5 | 29 | 23 | 19 | |
| 2. | AS Hautmontoise (Hautmont) | 16 | 7 | 4 | 5 | 36 | 29 | 18 | |
| 3. | FC Bordeaux-Bouscat (Bordeaux) | 16 | 8 | 1 | 7 | 29 | 26 | 17 | |
| 4. | FC Dieppois (Dieppe) | 16 | 8 | 1 | 7 | 27 | 33 | 17 | |
| 5. | Sports Olympiques Montpelliérains (Montpellier) | 16 | 7 | 2 | 7 | 30 | 25 | 16 | |
| 6. | US du Bassin de Longwy (Longwy) | 16 | 7 | 2 | 7 | 36 | 39 | 16 | |
| 7. | AS Troyenne-Savinienne (Troyes) | 16 | 6 | 3 | 7 | 28 | 29 | 15 | |
| 8. | Nîmes Olympique (Nîmes) | 16 | 5 | 4 | 7 | 24 | 23 | 14 | |
| 9. | Racing Club de Calais (Calais) | 16 | 5 | 2 | 9 | 21 | 33 | 12 | R |
| | | 144 | 61 | 22 | 61 | 260 | 260 | 144 | |

## Division 2 (Phase 1 Nord)

| | | Pd | Wn | Dw | Ls | GF | GA | Pts |
|---|---|---|---|---|---|---|---|---|
| 1. | Racing Club d'Arras (Arras) | 10 | 7 | 1 | 2 | 19 | 9 | 15 |
| 2. | US de Boulogne (Boulogne-sur-Mer) | 10 | 5 | 3 | 2 | 21 | 13 | 13 |
| 3. | Olympique de Dunkerque (Dunkerque) | 10 | 4 | 3 | 3 | 18 | 12 | 11 |
| 4. | US Tourquennoise (Tourcoing) | 10 | 3 | 2 | 5 | 13 | 17 | 8 |
| 5. | AS Hautmontoise (Hautmont) | 10 | 3 | 1 | 6 | 15 | 22 | 7 |
| 6. | Racing Club de Calais (Calais) | 10 | 2 | 2 | 6 | 9 | 22 | 6 |
| | | 60 | 24 | 12 | 24 | 95 | 95 | 60 |

## Division 2 (Phase 1 Ouest)

| | | Pd | Wn | Dw | Ls | GF | GA | Pts |
|---|---|---|---|---|---|---|---|---|
| 1. | Havre AC (Le Havre) | 8 | 6 | 1 | 1 | 21 | 7 | 13 |
| 2. | Stade Rennais Université Club (Rennes) | 8 | 3 | 3 | 2 | 15 | 12 | 9 |
| 3. | Cercle Athlétique de Paris (Paris) | 8 | 4 | - | 4 | 13 | 12 | 8 |
| 4. | Stade Malherbe Caennais (Caen) | 8 | 3 | 2 | 3 | 17 | 19 | 8 |
| 5. | FC Dieppois (Dieppe) | 8 | 1 | - | 7 | 10 | 26 | 2 |
| | | 40 | 17 | 6 | 17 | 76 | 76 | 40 |

| Division 2 (Phase 1 Est) | Pd | Wn | Dw | Ls | GF | GA | Pts |
|---|---|---|---|---|---|---|---|
| 1. FC de Nancy (Nancy) | 12 | 8 | - | 4 | 38 | 17 | 16 |
| 2. Sport Réunis de Colmar (Colmar) | 12 | 7 | 1 | 4 | 28 | 11 | 15 |
| 3. Stade de Reims (Reims) | 12 | 7 | 1 | 4 | 31 | 24 | 15 |
| 4. FC de Mulhouse 1893 (Mulhouse) | 12 | 6 | 1 | 5 | 21 | 23 | 13 |
| 5. FC Olympique de Charleville (Charleville) | 12 | 4 | 3 | 5 | 22 | 20 | 11 |
| 6. AS Troyenne-Savinienne (Troyes) | 12 | 4 | 2 | 6 | 30 | 28 | 10 |
| 7. US du Bassin de Longwy (Longwy) | 12 | 2 | - | 10 | 11 | 58 | 4 |
|  | 84 | 38 | 8 | 38 | 181 | 181 | 84 |

| Division 2 (Phase 1 Sud) | Pd | Wn | Dw | Ls | GF | GA | Pts |
|---|---|---|---|---|---|---|---|
| 1. AS de Saint-Étienne (Saint-Étienne) | 12 | 7 | 3 | 23 | 31 | 13 | 17 |
| 2. Toulouse FC (Toulouse) | 12 | 6 | 4 | 2 | 21 | 22 | 16 |
| 3. Olympique Alésien (Alès) | 12 | 5 | 5 | 2 | 24 | 12 | 15 |
| 4. Olympique GC de Nice (Nice) | 12 | 5 | 5 | 2 | 26 | 19 | 15 |
| 5. Sports Olympiques Montpelliérains (Montpellier) | 12 | 4 | 3 | 5 | 19 | 19 | 11 |
| 6. FC Bordeaux-Bouscat (Bordeaux) | 12 | 1 | 3 | 8 | 23 | 33 | 5 |
| 7. Nîmes Olympique (Nîmes) | 12 | 1 | 3 | 8 | 12 | 38 | 5 |
|  | 84 | 29 | 26 | 29 | 156 | 156 | 84 |

## Coupe de France Final  (Parc des Princes, Paris – 08/05/38 – 33,044)

**OLYMPIQUE DE MARSEILLE**          **2-1  (aet)**          FC de Metz (Metz)

*Kohut 49', Aznar 118'*          *Rohrbracher 84'*

**Olympique**: *Vasconcelos, Ben Bouali, H.Conchy, Bastien, Bruhin, Gonzales, Zermani, Olej, Zatelli, Aznar, Kohut.*

**Metz**: *Kappé, Nock, Zehren, Hibst, Fosset, Marchal, Lauer, Ignace, Müller, Hes, Rohrbracher.*

## Semi-Finals   (03/04/38)

| Olympique de Marseille (Marseille) | 0-0,  1-0 | Havre AC (Le Havre) |
|---|---|---|
| FC de Metz (Metz) | 1-0 | SC Fivois (Fives)*(aet)* |

## Quarter-Finals   (06/03/38)

| SC Fivois (Fives) | 2-2,  0-0,  2-0 | Olympique Lillois (Lille) |
|---|---|---|
| Havre AC (Le Havre) | 1-0 | Red Star Olympique (Saint-Ouen) |
| Olympique de Marseille (Marseille) | 6-2 | Racing Club de Paris (Paris) |
| FC de Metz (Metz) | 3-0 | AS de Cannes (Cannes) |

# 1938-39

| 1938-39 Division One | Antibes-Juan-les-Pins FC | AS de Cannes | Excelsior de Roubaix-Tour. | SC Fivois | Havre AC | Racing Club de Lens | Olympique Lillois | Olympique de Marseille | FC de Metz | Racing Club de Paris | Racing Club de Roubaix | FC de Rouen | AS de Saint-Étienne | FC de Sète | FC Sochaux-Montbéliard | Racing Club de Strasbourg |
|---|---|---|---|---|---|---|---|---|---|---|---|---|---|---|---|---|
| Antibes-Juan-les-Pins FC | | 0-0 | 3-0 | 0-3 | 1-0 | 1-0 | 0-3 | 2-2 | 1-1 | 1-1 | 1-0 | 0-0 | 0-4 | 0-2 | 0-0 | 1-1 |
| AS de Cannes | 3-0 | | 2-1 | 1-5 | 3-2 | 2-1 | 1-2 | 2-4 | 2-1 | 1-2 | 4-1 | 2-0 | 1-2 | 3-2 | 0-0 | 1-1 |
| Excelsior de Roubaix-Tour. | 0-2 | 3-5 | | 3-1 | 3-3 | 0-1 | 1-1 | 1-2 | 3-1 | 6-2 | 4-2 | 1-1 | 1-0 | 2-3 | 3-2 | 6-1 |
| SC Fivois | 4-1 | 3-1 | 4-2 | | 7-3 | 0-4 | 3-1 | 0-0 | 1-1 | 0-1 | 1-3 | 1-0 | 3-2 | 1-3 | 2-4 | 2-0 |
| Havre AC | 2-0 | 3-0 | 1-3 | 0-0 | | 2-2 | 1-0 | 2-0 | 0-3 | 2-1 | 5-2 | 1-1 | 2-4 | 2-1 | 2-1 | 2-1 |
| Racing Club de Lens | 1-1 | 6-2 | 2-2 | 1-0 | 4-2 | | 3-1 | 2-3 | 2-1 | 1-1 | 3-1 | 0-2 | 1-0 | 1-2 | 2-2 | 1-1 |
| Olympique Lillois | 2-0 | 0-0 | 4-2 | 1-2 | 1-0 | 2-0 | | 0-1 | 3-2 | 0-2 | 2-1 | 5-3 | 31 | 1-0 | 2-0 | 0-1 |
| Olympique de Marseille | 5-2 | 0-1 | 4-2 | 2-0 | 0-2 | 2-0 | 2-0 | | 5-1 | 5-2 | 6-0 | 1-0 | 3-1 | 1-1 | 1-0 | 1-0 |
| FC de Metz | 6-0 | 2-1 | 1-1 | 1-3 | 2-1 | 1-1 | 0-1 | 5-1 | | 3-0 | 1-0 | 2-2 | 1-0 | 0-2 | 0-3 | 2-1 |
| Racing Club de Paris | 3-0 | 5-1 | 3-1 | 2-2 | 3-0 | 1-0 | 2-2 | 1-1 | 3-2 | | 1-1 | 3-0 | 1-1 | 3-0 | 6-1 | 3-2 |
| Racing Club de Roubaix | 2-2 | 1-1 | 1-1 | 3-3 | 1-1 | 1-5 | 0-0 | 1-0 | 1-2 | 0-3 | | 1-2 | 2-2 | 1-0 | 1-4 | 2-0 |
| FC de Rouen | 0-1 | 2-1 | 2-2 | 2-3 | 1-4 | 3-0 | 0-0 | 1-2 | 2-2 | 3-1 | 0-0 | | 0-2 | 0-1 | 1-0 | 1-1 |
| AS de Saint-Étienne | 1-0 | 2-0 | 2-2 | 2-0 | 0-0 | 1-1 | 2-0 | 1-0 | 0-1 | 0-1 | 5-0 | 2-1 | | 3-1 | 2-1 | 0-0 |
| FC de Sète | 4-0 | 3-0 | 4-2 | 2-0 | 3-2 | 2-2 | 2-2 | 1-2 | 6-3 | 5-0 | 3-1 | 2-0 | 2-1 | | 2-1 | 2-0 |
| FC Sochaux-Montbéliard | 2-0 | 7-3 | 8-0 | 5-2 | 8-0 | 0-2 | 4-1 | 2-0 | 0-1 | 1-0 | 3-1 | 2-0 | 1-2 | 1-1 | | 2-0 |
| Racing Club de Strasbourg | 2-1 | 1-3 | 3-1 | 3-1 | 3-1 | 3-2 | 1-2 | 1-0 | 0-0 | 1-1 | 2-0 | 5-1 | 1-1 | 1-3 | 2-0 | |

## Division 1

| | | Pd | Wn | Dw | Ls | GF | GA | Pts |
|---|---|---|---|---|---|---|---|---|
| 1. | FC DE SÈTE (SÈTE) | 30 | 19 | 4 | 7 | 65 | 36 | 42 |
| 2. | Olympique de Marseille (Marseille) | 30 | 18 | 4 | 8 | 56 | 34 | 40 |
| 3. | Racing Club de Paris (Paris) | 30 | 15 | 8 | 7 | 58 | 43 | 38 |
| 4. | AS de Saint-Étienne (Saint-Étienne) | 30 | 14 | 7 | 9 | 46 | 30 | 35 |
| 5. | Olympique Lillois (Lille) | 30 | 14 | 6 | 10 | 42 | 38 | 34 |
| 6. | FC Sochaux-Montbéliard (Montbéliard) | 30 | 14 | 4 | 12 | 65 | 39 | 32 |
| 7. | Racing Club de Lens (Lens) | 30 | 11 | 9 | 10 | 51 | 42 | 31 |
| 8. | FC de Metz (Metz) | 30 | 12 | 7 | 11 | 49 | 46 | 31 |
| 9. | SC Fivois (Fives) | 30 | 13 | 5 | 12 | 57 | 54 | 31 |
| 10. | Racing Club de Strasbourg (Strasbourg) | 30 | 10 | 8 | 12 | 39 | 43 | 28 |
| 11. | Havre AC (Le Havre) | 30 | 11 | 6 | 13 | 48 | 59 | 28 |
| 12. | AS de Cannes (Cannes) | 30 | 11 | 5 | 14 | 47 | 62 | 27 |
| 13. | Excelsior de Roubaix-Tourcoing (Roubaix) | 30 | 8 | 8 | 14 | 60 | 71 | 24 |
| 14. | FC de Rouen (Rouen) | 30 | 6 | 9 | 15 | 31 | 48 | 21 |
| 15. | Antibes-Juan-les-Pins FC (Antibes) | 30 | 6 | 9 | 15 | 21 | 54 | 21 |
| 16. | Racing Club de Roubaix (Roubaix) | 30 | 4 | 9 | 17 | 31 | 67 | 17 |
| | | 480 | 186 | 108 | 186 | 766 | 766 | 480 |

## Top goal-scorers

| | | | |
|---|---|---|---|
| 1) | Roger COURTOIS | (FC Sochaux-Montbéliard) | 27 |
| | Dezsõ "Koranyi" KRONENBERGER | (FC de Sète) | 27 |
| 3) | VAN CAENEGHEM | (SC Fivois) | 21 |

| Division 2 | Pd | Wn | Dw | Ls | GF | GA | Pts | |
|---|---|---|---|---|---|---|---|---|
| 1. Red Star Olympique (Saint-Ouen) | 40 | 27 | 10 | 3 | 107 | 51 | 64 | P |
| 2. Stade Rennais Université Club (Rennes) | 40 | 27 | 6 | 7 | 112 | 51 | 60 | P |
| 3. FC de Nancy (Nancy) | 40 | 21 | 7 | 12 | 68 | 50 | 49 | |
| 4. Toulouse FC (Toulouse) | 40 | 20 | 8 | 12 | 79 | 49 | 48 | |
| 5. Sport Réunis de Colmar (Colmar) | 40 | 18 | 12 | 10 | 83 | 60 | 48 | |
| 6. Stade de Reims (Reims) | 40 | 19 | 9 | 12 | 70 | 46 | 47 | |
| 7. FC de Mulhouse 1893 (Mulhouse) | 40 | 19 | 9 | 12 | 92 | 77 | 47 | |
| 8. Olympique GC de Nice (Nice) | 40 | 19 | 6 | 15 | 79 | 54 | 44 | |
| 9. FC Olympique de Charleville (Charleville) | 40 | 18 | 7 | 15 | 72 | 77 | 43 | |
| 10. US de Boulogne (Boulogne-sur-Mer) | 40 | 15 | 6 | 19 | 84 | 85 | 36 | |
| 11. FC Bordeaux-Bouscat (Bordeaux) | 40 | 15 | 6 | 19 | 70 | 78 | 36 | |
| 12. US Valenciennes-Anzin (Valenciennes) | 40 | 15 | 5 | 20 | 59 | 69 | 35 | |
| 13. Cercle Athlétique de Paris (Paris) | 40 | 12 | 10 | 18 | 70 | 69 | 34 | |
| 14. Nîmes Olympique (Nîmes) | 40 | 12 | 10 | 18 | 49 | 81 | 34 | |
| 15. US du Bassin de Longwy (Longwy) | 40 | 14 | 4 | 22 | 80 | 96 | 32 | |
| 16. Racing Club d'Arras (Arras) | 40 | 10 | 12 | 18 | 47 | 64 | 32 | |
| 17. Stade Olympique Montpelliérain (Montpellier) | 40 | 11 | 9 | 20 | 52 | 76 | 31 | * |
| 18. AS Troyenne-Savinienne (Troyes) | 40 | 13 | 5 | 22 | 61 | 96 | 31 | |
| 19. Olympique Alésien (Alès) | 40 | 12 | 6 | 22 | 50 | 76 | 30 | |
| 20. Olympique de Dunkerque (Dunkerque) | 40 | 11 | 8 | 21 | 76 | 119 | 30 | |
| 21. AS Hautmontoise (Hautmont) | 40 | 8 | 13 | 19 | 61 | 97 | 29 | |
| | 840 | 336 | 168 | 336 | 1521 | 1521 | 840 | |

* Stade Olympique Montpelliérain (Montpellier) changed their name pre-season from Sports Olympiques Montpelliérains (Montpellier).


## Coupe de France Final   (Stade Yves du Manoir, Colombes – 14/05/39 – 52,431)

**RACING CLUB DE PARIS (PARIS)**          **3-1**                    Olympique Lillois (Lille)

*Perez 04', Veinante 25', Mathé 40'*                                              *Kalocsai 19'*

**Racing**: Hiden, Dupuis, Diagne, De Zabalo, Jordan, Louys, Perez, Heisserer, Ozenne, Veinante, Mathé.

**Olympique**: Darui, Vandooren, Walczak, Carly, Moré, Cléau, Bigot, Cheuva, Delannoy, Prévost, Kalocsai.


## Semi-Finals   (02/04/39)

| Olympique Lillois (Lille) | 1-0 | FC de Sète (Sète) |
|---|---|---|
| Racing Club de Paris (Paris) | 1-0 | SC Fivois (Fives) |


## Quarter-Finals   (05/03/39)

| SC Fivois (Fives) | 3-0 | SO Montpelliérains (Montpellier) |
|---|---|---|
| Olympique Lillois (Lille) | 1-1, 4-1 | FC de Nancy (Nancy) |
| Racing Club de Paris (Paris) | 3-1 | Racing Club de Roubaix (Roubaix) |
| FC de Sète (Sète) | 5-0 | Stade de Reims (Reims) |


The league was suspended due to the outbreak of World War 2 and did not resume until season 1945-46, however regional competitions were contested during the war years.

# 1939-40

| 1939-1940 Zone Nord | Racing Club d'Arras | US de Boulogne | Cercle Ath. Paris | Excelsior de Roubaix | Havre AC | Racing Club de Lens | Racing Club de Paris | Red Star Olympique | Stade de Reims | FC de Rouen |
|---|---|---|---|---|---|---|---|---|---|---|
| Racing Club d'Arras | ■ | --- | 3-3 | 4-0 | 5-0 | 2-3 | 1-0 | 3-1 | 3-4 | --- |
| US de Boulogne | 0-3 | ■ | --- | 0-1 | 0-2 | --- | --- | 3-0 | 0-5 | 4-5 |
| Cercle Athlétique Paris | 0-2 | --- | ■ | 0-1 | --- | 4-4 | 5-3 | 0-0 | 4-2 | 3-4 |
| Excelsior de Roubaix-Tour. | 4-3 | 1-1 | 1-4 | ■ | 0-1 | --- | --- | 3-4 | --- | --- |
| Havre AC | 2-1 | 2-0 | --- | 3-1 | ■ | 1-0 | 4-2 | 1-0 | 6-2 | --- |
| Racing Club de Lens | 6-1 | 5-1 | 1-2 | 6-2 | 2-1 | ■ | --- | 3-0 | 3-2 | 1-1 |
| Racing Club de Paris | 2-0 | --- | --- | --- | --- | --- | ■ | 2-2 | --- | 2-7 |
| Red Star Olympique | --- | 6-1 | --- | 0-3 | 0-3 | --- | 0-3 | ■ | --- | --- |
| Stade de Reims | 3-2 | --- | 4-0 | 10-1 | 4-1 | 7-2 | 2-2 | 5-3 | ■ | 3-1 |
| FC de Rouen | 3-2 | 9-1 | 3-3 | --- | 2-1 | 5-0 | 3-1 | 3-0 | 2-1 | ■ |

The following results were changed to 3-0 or 0-3: Boulogne 2-1 (0-3) Arras; Boulogne 0-2 (3-0) Red Star; Red Star 4-2 (0-3) Excelsior; Red Star 1-2 (0-3) Havre; Red Star 2-5 (0-3) Racing CP; Rouen 4-4 (3-0) Red Star.

## Zone Nord

|  |  | Pd | Wn | Dw | Ls | GF | GA | Pts |  |
|---|---|---|---|---|---|---|---|---|---|
| 1. | FC DE ROUEN (ROUEN) | 13 | 10 | 2 | 1 | 48 | 22 | 22 | |
| 2. | Havre AC (Le Havre) | 14 | 10 | - | 4 | 28 | 19 | 20 | |
| 3. | Stade de Reims (Reims) | 14 | 9 | 1 | 4 | 54 | 30 | 19 | |
| 4. | Racing Club de Lens (Lens) | 13 | 7 | 2 | 4 | 36 | 29 | 16 | # |
| 5. | Racing Club d'Arras (Arras) | 15 | 6 | 1 | 8 | 35 | 31 | 13 | # |
| 6. | Cercle Athlétique de Paris (Paris) | 12 | 4 | 4 | 4 | 28 | 28 | 12 | |
| 7. | Excelsior de Roubaix-Tourcoing (Roubaix) | 12 | 4 | 1 | 7 | 18 | 36 | 9 | # |
| 8. | Racing Club de Paris (Paris) | 9 | 2 | 2 | 5 | 17 | 24 | 6 | |
| 9. | Red Star Olympique (Saint-Ouen) | 13 | 2 | 2 | 9 | 16 | 33 | 6 | |
| 10. | US Boulogne (Boulogne-sur-Mer) | 11 | 1 | 1 | 9 | 11 | 39 | 3 | # |
|  |  | 126 | 55 | 16 | 55 | 291 | 291 | 126 | |

| 1939-1940 Zone Sud-Est | Antibes-Juan-les-Pins FC | AS de Cannes | Olympique de Marseille | Olympique GC de Nice | AS de Saint-Étienne |
|---|---|---|---|---|---|
| Antibes-Juan-les-Pins FC | ■ | 1-3 | 0-9 | 0-1 | 1-3 |
| AS de Cannes | 9-0 | ■ | 3-1 | 2-2 | 5-2 |
| Olympique de Marseille | 3-0 | 4-1 | ■ | 0-0 | 3-2 |
| Olympique GC de Nice | 4-1 | 2-2 | 6-0 | ■ | 5-0 |
| AS de Saint-Étienne | 10-1 | 4-2 | 0-2 | 0-7 | ■ |

| 1939 1940 Zone Sud-Ouest | Olympique Alésien | Girondins de Bordeaux FC | Stade Olympique Montpelliérain | Nîmes Olympique | FC de Sète | Toulouse FC |
|---|---|---|---|---|---|---|
| Olympique Alésien | ■ | 1-3 | 3-7 | 2-2 | 1-1 | 4-1 |
| Girondins de Bordeaux FC | 8-0 | ■ | 3-2 | 6-2 | 3-0 | 9-1 |
| Stade Olymp. Montpelliérain | 7-3 | 0-2 | ■ | 2-2 | 1-1 | 6-0 |
| Nîmes Olympique | 4-0 | 4-1 | 2-0 | ■ | 2-4 | 4-4 |
| FC de Sète | 3-0 | 6-1 | 2-3 | 6-1 | ■ | 3-1 |
| Toulouse FC | 2-2 | 2-4 | 0-3 | 3-1 | 5-4 | ■ |

## Zone Sud Play-Off

OLYMPIQUE GC DE NICE (NICE)          +:-          Girondins de Bordeaux (Bordeaux)
(The match ended 0-3 but OGC Nice were awarded the title by forfeit)

| Zone Sud-Est | Pd | Wn | Dw | Ls | GF | GA | Pts | |
|---|---|---|---|---|---|---|---|---|
| 1. Olympique GC de Nice (Nice) | 8 | 5 | 3 | - | 27 | 5 | 13 | |
| 2. Olympique de Marseille (Marseille) | 8 | 5 | 1 | 2 | 22 | 12 | 11 | |
| 3. AS de Cannes (Cannes) | 8 | 4 | 2 | 2 | 27 | 16 | 10 | |
| 4. AS de Saint-Étienne (Saint-Étienne) | 8 | 3 | - | 5 | 21 | 26 | 6 | |
| 5. Antibes-Juan-les-Pins FC (Antibes) | 8 | - | - | 8 | 4 | 42 | - | # |
| | 40 | 17 | 6 | 17 | 101 | 101 | 40 | |

| Zone Sud-Ouest | Pd | Wn | Dw | Ls | GF | GA | Pts |
|---|---|---|---|---|---|---|---|
| 1. Girondins de Bordeaux FC (Bordeaux) | 10 | 8 | - | 2 | 40 | 18 | 16 |
| 2. FC de Sète (Sète) | 10 | 5 | 2 | 3 | 30 | 18 | 12 |
| 3. Stade Olympique Montpelliérain (Montpellier) | 10 | 5 | 2 | 3 | 31 | 18 | 12 |
| 4. Nîmes Olympique (Nîmes) | 10 | 3 | 3 | 4 | 24 | 28 | 9 |
| 5. Toulouse FC (Toulouse) | 10 | 2 | 2 | 6 | 19 | 40 | 6 |
| 6. Olympique Alésien (Alès) | 10 | 1 | 3 | 6 | 16 | 38 | 5 |
| | 60 | 24 | 12 | 24 | 160 | 160 | 60 |

The match Toulouse FC 2-2 SO Montpelliérain was later awarded as a 0-3 forfeit to Montpellier.

Clubs marked with a # were not in the league for the next season.


## Coupe de France Final   (Stade Yves du Manoir, Colombes – 05/05/40 – 25,969)

**RACING CLUB DE PARIS (PARIS)**          **2-1**          Olympique de Marseille (Marseille)
*Roulier 25', Mathé 70'*                                                                 *Aznar 16'*

**Racing**: Hiden, Dupuis, Diagne, Zabalo, Jordan, Rouellé, Mathé, Hiltl, Roulier, Heisserer, Weiskopf.
**Olympique**: Delachet, Gonzales, Malvy, Bastien, M.Conchy, Durand, Dard, Heiss, Aznar, Eisenhoffer, Donnenfeld.


## Semi-Finals   (07/04/40)

| Olympique de Marseille (Marseille) | 9-1 | Racing Club de Lens (Lens) |
|---|---|---|
| Racing Club de Paris (Paris) | 8-4 | FC de Rouen (Rouen) |


## Quarter-Finals   (03/03/40)

| Racing Club de Lens (Lens) | 2-1 | Cercle Athlétique de Paris (Paris) |
|---|---|---|
| Olympique de Marseille (Marseille) | 1-0 | FC de Sète (Sète) |
| Racing Club de Paris (Paris) | 3-1 | FC Sochaux-Montbéliard (Montbéliard) |
| FC de Rouen (Rouen) | 2-1 | SC Fivois (Fives) |

# 1940-41

| 1940-1941 Zone Nord | Girondins-AS du Port Bordeaux | Cercle Athlétique de Paris | Havre AC | Racing Club de Paris | Red Star Olympique | Stade de Reims | FC de Rouen |
|---|---|---|---|---|---|---|---|
| Girondins-AS du Bordeaux | ■ | 2-1 | 3-2 | 3-1 | 0-2 | 1-1 | 0-3 |
| Cercle Athlétique de Paris | 1-4 | ■ | 3-1 | 0-2 | 0-0 | 0-4 | 3-1 |
| Havre AC | 0-3 | 2-0 | ■ | 8-3 | 1-3 | 3-2 | 3-0 |
| Racing Club de Paris | 1-3 | 1-3 | 3-2 | ■ | 0-2 | 4-1 | 2-4 |
| Red Star Olympique | 2-0 | 4-0 | 2-1 | 3-0 | ■ | 1-0 | 7-1 |
| Stade de Reims | 2-0 | 3-0 | 1-1 | 2-3 | 1-1 | ■ | 2-1 |
| FC de Rouen | 4-2 | 1-1 | 4-3 | 4-3 | 4-1 | 2-1 | ■ |

| 1940-1941 Zone Sud | Olympique Alésien | AS de Cannes | Olympique de Marseille | Stade Olympique Montpelliérain | Olympique GC de Nice | Nîmes Olympique | AS de Saint-Étienne | FC de Sète | Toulouse FC |
|---|---|---|---|---|---|---|---|---|---|
| Olympique Alésien | ■ | 0-0 | 0-4 | 1-1 | 0-4 | 3-2 | 3-1 | 0-1 | 0-2 |
| AS de Cannes | 2-1 | ■ | 2-2 | 3-1 | 2-1 | 0-2 | 2-1 | 3-1 | 1-3 |
| Olympique de Marseille | 7-0 | 1-1 | ■ | 5-1 | 3-2 | 4-0 | 4-1 | 0-0 | 2-1 |
| Stade Olymp. Montpelliérain | 4-0 | 1-5 | 2-2 | ■ | 1-1 | 7-2 | 1-3 | 0-1 | 2-1 |
| Olympique GC de Nice | 4-1 | 2-2 | 0-2 | 2-2 | ■ | 3-0 | 4-1 | 2-1 | 0-0 |
| Nîmes Olympique | 2-0 | 1-0 | 1-4 | 4-1 | 1-0 | ■ | 5-2 | 1-0 | 2-1 |
| AS de Saint-Étienne | 0-2 | 0-1 | 1-2 | 1-2 | 1-0 | 1-0 | ■ | 1-2 | 1-2 |
| FC de Sète | 0-0 | 3-0 | 1-0 | 1-0 | 0-1 | 3-0 | 0-0 | ■ | 0-2 |
| Toulouse FC | 2-0 | 3-1 | 3-2 | 4-2 | 2-0 | 6-1 | 4-2 | 1-1 | ■ |

### Zone Nord

| | | Pd | Wn | Dw | Ls | GF | GA | Pts | |
|---|---|---|---|---|---|---|---|---|---|
| 1. | RED STAR OLYMPIQUE (SAINT-OUEN) | 12 | 9 | 2 | 1 | 28 | 8 | 20 | |
| 2. | FC de Rouen (Rouen) | 12 | 7 | 1 | 4 | 29 | 28 | 15 | |
| 3. | Girondins-AS du Port (Bordeaux) | 12 | 6 | 1 | 5 | 21 | 20 | 13 | * |
| 4. | Stade de Reims (Reims) | 12 | 4 | 3 | 5 | 20 | 17 | 11 | |
| 5. | Havre AC (Le Havre) | 12 | 4 | 1 | 7 | 27 | 27 | 9 | |
| 6. | Cercle Athlétique de Paris (Paris) | 12 | 3 | 2 | 7 | 12 | 25 | 8 | |
| 7. | Racing Club de Paris (Paris) | 12 | 4 | - | 8 | 23 | 35 | 8 | |
| | | 84 | 37 | 10 | 37 | 160 | 160 | 84 | |

* Girondins-AS du Port (Bordeaux) changed their name pre-season from Girondins de Bordeaux FC (Bordeaux).

### Zone Sud

| | | Pd | Wn | Dw | Ls | GF | GA | Pts |
|---|---|---|---|---|---|---|---|---|
| 1. | OLYMPIQUE DE MARSEILLE (MARSEILLE) | 16 | 10 | 4 | 2 | 44 | 16 | 24 |
| 2. | Toulouse FC (Toulouse) | 16 | 11 | 2 | 3 | 37 | 17 | 24 |
| 3. | FC de Sète (Sète) | 16 | 7 | 4 | 5 | 15 | 11 | 18 |
| 4. | AS de Cannes (Cannes) | 16 | 7 | 4 | 5 | 25 | 23 | 18 |
| 5. | Olympique GC de Nice (Nice) | 16 | 6 | 4 | 6 | 26 | 19 | 16 |
| 6. | Nîmes Olympique (Nîmes) | 16 | 8 | - | 8 | 24 | 35 | 16 |
| 7. | Stade Olympique Montpelliérain (Montpellier) | 16 | 4 | 4 | 8 | 28 | 36 | 12 |
| 8. | Olympique Alésien (Alès) | 16 | 3 | 3 | 10 | 11 | 36 | 9 |
| 9. | AS de Saint-Étienne (Saint-Étienne) | 16 | 3 | 1 | 12 | 17 | 34 | 7 |
| | | 144 | 59 | 26 | 59 | 227 | 227 | 144 |

# Coupe de France Final

(Zone Occupée et Interdite/Zone Non Occupée – Stade Municipal, Saint-Ouen – 25/05/41 – 15,230)

**GIRONDINS-AS DU PORT (BORDEAUX)**     **2-0**                    SC Fivois (Fives)

*Urtizberea 60', 84'*

**Bordeaux**: Gérard, Homar, Mancisidor, Ben Ali, Plesiak, Rummelhardt, Szego, Lopez, Urtizberea, Pruvot, Arnaudeau.

**Fivois**: Juszczyk, Pollet, Gyselinck, Trenelle, Jadrejak, Bourbotte, Sommerlynck, Tancré, Van Caeneghem, Dudziak, Waggi.

## Final   (Zone Occupée/Zone Interdite – Colombes – 18/05/41)

| | | |
|---|---|---|
| Girondins-AS du Port (Bordeaux) | 3-1 | Toulouse FC (Toulouse) |

## Final   (Zone Interdite – Lille – 01/04/41)

| | | |
|---|---|---|
| SC Fivois (Fives) | 3-1  (aet) | Excelsior de Roubaix-Tourcoing (Roubaix) |

## Semi-Finals

| | | |
|---|---|---|
| SC Fivois (Fives) | 2-0 | Racing Club de Lens (Lens) |
| Excelsior de Roubaix-Tourcoing | 1-0 | US Valenciennes-Anzin (Valenciennes) |

## Final   (Zone Occupée – Paris – 13/03/41)

| | | |
|---|---|---|
| Girondins-AS du Port (Bordeaux) | 3-1 | Red Star Olympique (Saint-Ouen) |

## Semi-Finals

| | | |
|---|---|---|
| Girondins-AS du Port (Bordeaux) | 4-1 | FC de Rouen (Rouen) |
| Red Star Olympique (Saint-Ouen) | 2-0 | Stade de Reims (Reims) |

## Final   (Zone Non Occupée – Marseille – 06/04/41)

| | | |
|---|---|---|
| Toulouse FC (Toulouse) | 1-0 | AS de Saint-Étienne (Saint-Étienne) |

## Semi-Finals

| | | |
|---|---|---|
| AS de Saint-Étienne (Saint Étienne) | 0-0,  0-0,  4-1 | Olympique Alésien (Alès) |
| Toulouse FC (Toulouse) | 2-0 | Hyères FC (Hyères) |

# 1941-42

| 1941-1942 Zone Nord | Amiens AC | Girondins-AS du Port Bordeaux | Cercle Athlétique de Paris | Havre AC | Racing Club de Paris | Red Star Olympique | Stade de Reims | Stade Rennais Université Club | FC de Rouen |
|---|---|---|---|---|---|---|---|---|---|
| Amiens AC | | 0-0 | 0-1 | 1-2 | 2-4 | 1-3 | 2-6 | 1-2 | 2-2 |
| Gir.-AS du Bordeaux | 5-0 | | 0-1 | 5-3 | 3-0 | 0-3 | 1-2 | 2-1 | 0-1 |
| Cercle Ath. de Paris | 2-2 | 1-1 | | 1-3 | 2-0 | 0-1 | 0-2 | 1-2 | 1-2 |
| Havre AC | 3-1 | 3-4 | 1-0 | | 2-5 | 4-1 | 0-1 | 2-1 | 2-3 |
| Racing Club de Paris | 3-1 | 3-3 | 1-3 | 3-1 | | 3-2 | 0-3 | 1-0 | 3-1 |
| Red Star Olympique | 9-1 | 2-0 | 4-2 | 4-1 | 1-1 | | 2-1 | 3-1 | 0-0 |
| Stade de Reims | 2-0 | 0-2 | 1-1 | 3-2 | 5-3 | 2-0 | | 5-0 | 0-0 |
| Stade Rennais UC | 4-3 | 1-1 | 1-2 | 2-2 | 2-2 | 0-2 | 0-0 | | 1-1 |
| FC de Rouen | 5-1 | 3-1 | 3-2 | 4-1 | 4-0 | 4-1 | 1-1 | 0-4 | |

| 1941-42 Zone Sud | Olympique Alésien | AS de Cannes | Olympique de Marseille | US Olympique de Montpellier | Olympique GC de Nice | Nîmes Olympique | AS de Saint-Étienne | FC de Sète | Toulouse FC |
|---|---|---|---|---|---|---|---|---|---|
| Olympique Alésien | | 4-2 | 3-2 | 4-1 | 4-1 | 0-0 | 1-2 | 2-1 | 0-0 |
| AS de Cannes | 2-0 | | 2-2 | 1-1 | 3-4 | 1-2 | 1-1 | 0-0 | 3-0 |
| Olympique de Marseille | 4-0 | 2-0 | | 3-0 | 2-2 | 0-0 | 8-3 | 0-1 | 0-0 |
| US Olymp. de Montpell. | 0-1 | 2-1 | 3-0 | | 1-3 | 1-0 | 1-0 | 0-1 | 1-1 |
| Olympique GC de Nice | 0-0 | 0-1 | 1-3 | 1-0 | | 1-0 | 2-0 | 2-3 | 0-0 |
| Nîmes Olympique | 3-0 | 2-2 | 1-0 | 1-0 | 1-1 | | 1-0 | 1-3 | 0-1 |
| AS de Saint-Étienne | 1-1 | 1-0 | 4-3 | 2-1 | 3-0 | 3-0 | | 1-0 | 0-4 |
| FC de Sète | 1-0 | 0-0 | 2-2 | 2-1 | 3-1 | 4-0 | 3-1 | | 1-0 |
| Toulouse FC | 5-1 | 0-3 | 3-0 | 6-1 | 3-0 | 4-0 | 4-0 | 0-1 | |

## Zone Nord

| | | Pd | Wn | Dw | Ls | GF | GA | Pts | |
|---|---|---|---|---|---|---|---|---|---|
| 1. | STADE DE REIMS (REIMS) | 16 | 10 | 4 | 2 | 34 | 14 | 24 | |
| 2. | FC de Rouen (Rouen) | 16 | 9 | 5 | 2 | 34 | 20 | 23 | |
| 3. | Red Star Olympique (Saint-Ouen) | 16 | 10 | 2 | 4 | 38 | 21 | 22 | |
| 4. | Racing Club de Paris (Paris) | 16 | 7 | 3 | 6 | 32 | 35 | 17 | |
| 5. | Girondins-AS du Port (Bordeaux) | 16 | 6 | 4 | 6 | 28 | 24 | 16 | |
| 6. | Cercle Athlétique de Paris (Paris) | 16 | 5 | 3 | 8 | 20 | 24 | 13 | * |
| 7. | Stade Rennais Université Club (Rennes) | 16 | 4 | 5 | 7 | 22 | 28 | 13 | |
| 8. | Havre AC (Le Havre) | 16 | 6 | 1 | 9 | 32 | 39 | 13 | |
| 9. | Amiens AC (Amiens) | 16 | - | 3 | 13 | 18 | 53 | 3 | |
| | | 144 | 57 | 30 | 57 | 258 | 258 | 144 | |

* Cercle Athlétique de Paris (Paris) merged with Stade Français (Paris) to become Stade Français-CA de Paris (Paris) for the next season.

## Zone Sud

| | | Pd | Wn | Dw | Ls | GF | GA | Pts | |
|---|---|---|---|---|---|---|---|---|---|
| 1. | FC DE SÈTE (SÈTE) | 16 | 11 | 3 | 2 | 26 | 11 | 25 | |
| 2. | Toulouse FC (Toulouse) | 16 | 8 | 4 | 4 | 31 | 11 | 20 | |
| 3. | Olympique Alésien (Alès) | 16 | 6 | 4 | 6 | 21 | 25 | 16 | |
| 4. | AS de Saint-Étienne (Saint-Étienne) | 16 | 7 | 2 | 7 | 22 | 30 | 16 | |
| 5. | Olympique de Marseille (Marseille) | 16 | 5 | 5 | 6 | 31 | 25 | 15 | |
| 6. | AS de Cannes (Cannes) | 16 | 4 | 6 | 6 | 22 | 21 | 14 | |
| 7. | Olympique GC de Nice (Nice) | 16 | 5 | 4 | 7 | 19 | 27 | 14 | |
| 8. | Nîmes Olympique (Nîmes) | 16 | 5 | 4 | 7 | 12 | 21 | 14 | |
| 9. | US Olympique de Montpellier (Montpellier) | 16 | 4 | 2 | 10 | 14 | 27 | 10 | * |
| | | 144 | 55 | 34 | 55 | 198 | 198 | 144 | |

* US Olympique de Montpellier (Montpellier) were formed by the merger of Stade Olympique Montpelliérain (Montpellier) and US Montpelliéraine (Montpellier).

**Coupe de France Final**  (Zone Occupée et Interdite/Zone Non Occupée – Stade Yves du Manoir, Colombes – 17/05/41)

**RED STAR OLYMPIQUE (SAINT-OUEN)**  **2-0**  FC de Sète (Sète)

*Vandevelde 46', Aston 72'*

**Red Star**: Darui, Herrera, Roessler, Meuris, Braun, Sergent, Aston, Simonyi, Bersoullé, Joncourt, Vandevelde.
**Sète**: Erevanian, Mathieu, Franques, Robisco, Leduc, Laurent, Laid, Novicki, Koranyi, Danzelle, Miramon.

**Final**  (Zone Occupée/Zone Interdite – Saint-Ouen – 03/05/42  +  Colombes – 10/05/42)

| Red Star Olympique (Saint-Ouen) | 1-1, 5-2 | Racing Club de Lens (Lens) |

**Final**   (Zone Interdite – Fives – 12/04/42)

| Racing Club de Lens (Lens) | 3-1 | Olympique Iris Club Lillois (Lille)*(aet)* |

## Semi-Finals

| Olympique IC Lillois (Lille) | 3-2 | Racing Club Franc-Comtois (Besançon) |
| Racing Club de Lens (Lens) | 5-1 | US Bruaysienne (Bruay-en-Artois) |

## Quarter-Finals

| Racing Club Franc-Comtois (Besançon) | 6-3 | CS d'Homécourt (Homécourt) |
| US Bruaysienne (Bruay-en-Artois) | 3-2 | US Tourquennoise (Tourcoing) |
| Racing Club de Lens (Lens) | 2-0 | US Valenciennes-Anzin (Valenciennes) |
| Olympique IC Lillois (Lille) | 1-0 | ES de Bully (Bully-les-Mines) |

**Final**   (Zone Occupée –Paris – 12/04/42)

| Red Star Olympique (Saint-Ouen) | 1-0 | Stade de Reims (Reims) |

## Semi-Finals

| Red Star Olympique (Saint-Ouen) | 2-1 | Girondins-AS du Port (Bordeaux) |
| Stade de Reims (Reims) | 1-0 | US Quevillaise (Le Petit Quevilly) |

## Quarter-Finals

| Girondins-AS du Port (Bordeaux) | 4-2 | US de Mans (Le Mans) |
| US Quevillaise (Le Petit Quevilly) | 0-1, 1-0 | Racing Club de Paris (Paris) |

(the first match was abandoned due to a snowstorm)

| Red Star Olympique (Saint-Ouen) | 4-1 | FC de Rouen (Rouen) |
| Stade de Reims (Reims) | 5-0 | CA Montreuillois (Montreuil) |

**Final**   (Zone Non Occupée – Marseille – 12/04/42)

| FC de Sète (Sète) | 2-1 | AS de Cannes (Cannes) |

## Semi-Finals

| AS de Cannes (Cannes) | 3-1 | US Olympique de Montpellier (Montpellier) |
| FC de Sète (Sète) | 3-0 | Toulouse FC (Toulouse) |

## Quarter-Finals

| AS de Cannes (Cannes) | 2-1 | Olympique Alésien (Alès) |
| US Olympique de Montpellier | 4-1 | AS de Monaco (Monaco) |
| FC de Sète (Sète) | 1-0 | Nîmes Olympique (Nîmes) |
| Toulouse FC (Toulouse) | 1-0 | FC d'Annecy (Annecy) |

# 1942-43

| 1942-1943 Zone Nord | Amiens AC | GAS du Port Bordeaux | Excelsior Roubaix-Tour. | SC Fivois | Stade Français-CAP | Havre AC | Racing Club de Lens | Olympique Iris Lillois | US du Mans | Racing Club de Paris | Red Star Olympique | Stade de Reims | Stade Rennais Université Club | FC de Rouen | Sochaux-Valentigney | Troyenne-Savinienne |
|---|---|---|---|---|---|---|---|---|---|---|---|---|---|---|---|---|
| Amiens AC | ■ | 1-1 | 4-2 | 2-0 | 2-0 | 2-1 | 0-0 | 0-0 | 0-1 | 0-3 | 2-1 | 0-1 | 3-1 | 1-2 | 5-2 | 0-0 |
| GAS du Port Bordeaux | 3-0 | ■ | 3-0 | 1-1 | 4-1 | 5-0 | 1-2 | 4-0 | 3-1 | 5-2 | 4-2 | 3-2 | 3-1 | 1-1 | 2-4 | 3-1 |
| Excelsior de Roubaix-Tour. | 1-1 | 2-4 | ■ | 2-4 | 0-0 | 1-4 | 3-6 | 1-3 | 2-1 | 5-2 | 1-2 | 2-4 | 6-2 | 0-0 | 3-0 | 3-2 |
| SC Fivois | 4-0 | 2-2 | 1-1 | ■ | 4-1 | 3-1 | 4-5 | 4-1 | 1-1 | 0-2 | 2-5 | 3-2 | 4-4 | 0-1 | 3-2 | 5-0 |
| Stade Français-CAP | 3-0 | 4-1 | 1-3 | 1-4 | ■ | 1-3 | 2-5 | 0-5 | 0-1 | 2-0 | 2-2 | 0-1 | 2-1 | 3-2 | 1-3 | 4-4 |
| Havre AC | 1-0 | 3-2 | 1-1 | 3-0 | 4-2 | ■ | 1-2 | 2-0 | 0-1 | 1-0 | 2-1 | 1-2 | 1-2 | 2-0 | 1-2 | 1-0 |
| Racing Club de Lens | 5-0 | 2-1 | 8-0 | 3-0 | 4-2 | 1-1 | ■ | 3-0 | 3-2 | 6-0 | 3-1 | 5-0 | 4-1 | 0-2 | 4-2 | 4-0 |
| Olympique Iris Lillois | 2-1 | 2-1 | 3-1 | 0-2 | 3-1 | 2-3 | 3-4 | ■ | 1-2 | 3-0 | 0-2 | 1-1 | 5-0 | 2-2 | 1-3 | 1-2 |
| US du Mans | 1-2 | 0-2 | 1-0 | 3-5 | 2-3 | 4-0 | 1-3 | 2-4 | ■ | 2-2 | 1-1 | 3-1 | 3-2 | 0-1 | 1-3 | 3-1 |
| Racing Club de Paris | 1-0 | 2-1 | 1-3 | 3-0 | 1-2 | 1-3 | 3-3 | 3-1 | 1-3 | ■ | 3-0 | 1-1 | 7-1 | 0-0 | 1-0 | 6-1 |
| Red Star Olympique | 4-0 | 1-1 | 5-1 | 1-4 | 0-3 | 0-1 | 1-0 | 0-4 | 3-2 | 2-3 | ■ | 1-3 | 2-1 | 1-5 | 5-2 | 3-3 |
| Stade de Reims | 4-0 | 2-2 | 2-3 | 2-2 | 3-1 | 0-0 | 1-1 | 5-0 | 2-1 | 1-2 | 0-1 | ■ | 7-1 | 1-0 | 4-0 | 4-0 |
| Stade Rennais Université Club | 2-2 | 1-2 | 1-2 | 1-2 | 4-1 | 2-2 | 0-5 | 3-3 | 2-2 | 0-7 | 1-4 | 1-0 | ■ | 2-1 | 2-2 | 5-3 |
| FC de Rouen | 0-0 | 3-1 | 4-1 | 2-2 | 4-2 | 1-1 | 3-4 | 2-2 | 1-1 | 1-2 | 2-0 | 2-2 | 2-2 | ■ | 1-0 | 4-3 |
| Sochaux-Valentigney | 3-1 | 3-0 | 2-2 | 0-3 | 1-5 | 3-1 | 3-1 | 0-2 | 6-3 | 3-3 | 4-3 | 2-1 | 4-1 | 0-1 | ■ | 6-0 |
| Troyenne-Savinienne | 1-1 | 1-3 | 2-1 | 0-5 | 0-1 | 1-2 | 1-2 | 2-4 | 1-2 | 3-2 | 3-4 | 0-3 | 4-1 | 0-5 | 2-1 | ■ |

| | **Zone Nord** | **Pd** | **Wn** | **Dw** | **Ls** | **GF** | **GA** | **Pts** | |
|---|---|---|---|---|---|---|---|---|---|
| 1. | RACING CLUB DE LENS (LENS) | 30 | 23 | 4 | 3 | 98 | 39 | 50 | |
| 2. | FC de Rouen (Rouen) | 30 | 13 | 11 | 6 | 55 | 36 | 37 | |
| 3. | SC Fivois (Fives) | 30 | 15 | 7 | 8 | 74 | 52 | 37 | |
| 4. | Girondins-AS du Port (Bordeaux) | 30 | 15 | 6 | 9 | 69 | 47 | 36 | |
| 5. | Stade de Reims (Reims) | 30 | 14 | 7 | 9 | 62 | 39 | 35 | |
| 6. | Havre AC (Le Havre) | 30 | 15 | 5 | 10 | 47 | 42 | 35 | |
| 7. | Racing Club de Paris (Paris) | 30 | 14 | 5 | 11 | 64 | 53 | 33 | |
| 8. | FC Sochaux-Valentigney (Montbéliard) | 30 | 14 | 3 | 13 | 66 | 63 | 31 | * |
| 9. | Olympique Iris Club Lillois (Lille) | 30 | 12 | 5 | 13 | 58 | 56 | 29 | |
| 10. | Red Star Olympique (Saint-Ouen) | 30 | 12 | 4 | 14 | 58 | 63 | 28 | |
| 11. | US de Mans (Le Mans) | 30 | 11 | 5 | 14 | 51 | 56 | 27 | |
| 12. | Excelsior de Roubaix-Tourcoing (Roubaix) | 30 | 9 | 6 | 15 | 53 | 74 | 24 | |
| 13. | Amiens AC (Amiens) | 30 | 8 | 8 | 14 | 30 | 50 | 24 | |
| 14. | Stade Français-Cercle Athlétique de Paris (Paris) | 30 | 10 | 3 | 17 | 51 | 71 | 23 | |
| 15. | Stade Rennais Université Club (Rennes) | 30 | 5 | 7 | 18 | 48 | 95 | 17 | |
| 16. | AS Troyenne-Savinienne (Troyes) | 30 | 5 | 4 | 21 | 41 | 89 | 14 | |
| | | 480 | 195 | 90 | 195 | 925 | 925 | 480 | |

* FC Sochaux-Montbéliard (Montbéliard) merged with AS de Valentigney (Valentigney) to become FC Sochaux-Valentigney.

| 1942-1943 Zone Sud | Olympique Alésien | FC d'Annecy | AS Avignonnaise | ES Aiglons Brivistes | AS de Cannes | AS Clermont-Ferrand | FC de Grenoble | Lyon Olympique Univers. | Olympique de Marseille | Olympique de Montpellier | Olympique GC de Nice | Nîmes Olympique | USA Perpignannaise | FC de Sète | AS de Saint-Étienne | Toulouse FC |
|---|---|---|---|---|---|---|---|---|---|---|---|---|---|---|---|---|
| Olympique Alésien | | 3-1 | 4-2 | 3-2 | 0-1 | 3-1 | 0-1 | 1-1 | 0-2 | 2-0 | 4-09 | 1-2 | 1-1 | 1-2 | 0-1 | 0-3 |
| FC d'Annecy | 2-0 | | 3-1 | 3-1 | 3-2 | 0-2 | 2-2 | 0-1 | 0-0 | 0-0 | 1-0 | 1-1 | 4-1 | 3-2 | 3-6 | 2-2 |
| AS Avignonnaise | 1-0 | 1-1 | | 3-3 | 2-1 | 2-0 | 0-0 | 3-1 | 0-4 | 1-4 | 1-2 | 1-3 | 2-0 | 2-4 | 1-2 | 2-5 |
| ES Aiglons Brivistes | 4-1 | 2-1 | 4-0 | | 4-2 | 0-0 | 1-4 | 3-2 | 2-1 | 4-2 | 5-4 | 0-1 | 0-1 | 0-2 | 4-0 | 6-2 |
| AS de Cannes | 5-0 | 3-0 | 1-2 | 1-2 | | 1-0 | 0-1 | 2-1 | 3-3 | 2-0 | 3-0 | 3-0 | 1-0 | 2-3 | 2-1 | 1-3 |
| AS Clermont-Ferrand | 4-1 | 2-0 | 4-1 | 2-1 | 3-3 | | 1-3 | 4-2 | 2-5 | 1-2 | 1-1 | 1-0 | 2-1 | 1-1 | 2-4 | 0-2 |
| FC de Grenoble | 2-0 | 0-0 | 3-0 | 9-1 | 0-2 | 3-1 | | 2-1 | 2-1 | 2-0 | 3-1 | 1-0 | 1-0 | 2-0 | 0-1 | 1-1 |
| Lyon Olympique Univers. | 0-0 | 1-1 | 4-2 | 1-2 | 0-2 | 3-2 | 1-3 | | 1-2 | 4-0 | 1-1 | 3-2 | 2-1 | 2-0 | 0-1 | 1-0 |
| Olympique de Marseille | 2-0 | 9-1 | 20-2 | 2-3 | 1-1 | 4-2 | 4-1 | 8-2 | | 4-1 | 7-1 | 6-1 | 1-1 | 1-4 | 3-1 | 3-3 |
| Olympique de Montpellier | 1-1 | 1-3 | 0-0 | 4-3 | 3-1 | 4-1 | 1-0 | 1-3 | 1-1 | | 0-2 | 0-3 | 2-4 | 0-0 | 1-1 | 3-0 |
| Olympique GC de Nice | 2-0 | 3-1 | 1-1 | 1-0 | 5-2 | 2-1 | 1-1 | 0-1 | 0-1 | 3-1 | | 3-0 | 2-0 | 4-2 | 1-0 | 1-4 |
| Nîmes Olympique | 0-0 | 1-2 | 1-1 | 1-1 | 3-1 | 1-1 | 1-2 | 3-3 | 2-0 | 3-0 | 2-1 | | 3-0 | 2-1 | 2-1 | 1-1 |
| USA Perpignannaise | 0-2 | 2-0 | 4-2 | 2-0 | 1-1 | 1-1 | 1-1 | 0-0 | 2-2 | 3-0 | 3-0 | 3-1 | | 0-3 | 8-2 | 0-2 |
| FC de Sète | 6-0 | 2-2 | 2-0 | 1-0 | 1-1 | 3-1 | 6-0 | 3-0 | 1-1 | 1-0 | 5-0 | 1-0 | 3-1 | | 1-1 | 1-0 |
| AS de Saint-Étienne | 1-4 | 0-0 | 0-1 | 2-0 | 3-1 | 0-1 | 1-1 | 3-0 | 0-1 | 6-1 | 1-3 | 2-1 | 3-0 | 3-1 | | 1-1 |
| Toulouse FC | 6-0 | 4-2 | 4-0 | 3-0 | 6-1 | 7-0 | 9-0 | 3-0 | 3-1 | 2-1 | 3-0 | 6-1 | 2-0 | 1-0 | 5-2 | |

| | Zone Sud | Pd | Wn | Dw | Ls | GF | GA | Pts | |
|---|---|---|---|---|---|---|---|---|---|
| 1. | TOULOUSE FC (TOULOUSE) | 30 | 21 | 5 | 4 | 93 | 31 | 47 | |
| 2. | FC de Grenoble (Grenoble) | 30 | 17 | 7 | 6 | 51 | 38 | 41 | |
| 3. | Olympique de Marseille (Marseille) | 30 | 16 | 8 | 6 | 100 | 43 | 40 | |
| 4. | FC de Sète (Sète) | 30 | 17 | 6 | 7 | 62 | 31 | 40 | |
| 5. | AS de Saint-Étienne (Saint-Étienne) | 30 | 13 | 5 | 12 | 50 | 49 | 31 | |
| 6. | Olympique GC de Nice (Nice) | 30 | 13 | 4 | 13 | 45 | 55 | 30 | * |
| 7. | Êtoile Sportive-Aiglons Brivistes (Brive) | 30 | 13 | 3 | 14 | 58 | 61 | 29 | |
| 8. | AS de Cannes (Cannes) | 30 | 12 | 5 | 13 | 52 | 51 | 29 | |
| 9. | Nîmes Olympique (Nîmes) | 30 | 11 | 7 | 12 | 42 | 47 | 29 | |
| 10. | FC d'Annecy (Annecy) | 30 | 9 | 10 | 11 | 42 | 55 | 28 | |
| 11. | Lyon Olympique Universitaire (Lyon) | 30 | 10 | 6 | 14 | 42 | 55 | 26 | |
| 12. | US Athlétiques Perpignanais (Perpignan) | 30 | 9 | 7 | 14 | 41 | 46 | 25 | |
| 13. | AS Clermont-Ferrand (Clermont-Ferrand) | 30 | 9 | 6 | 15 | 44 | 61 | 24 | |
| 14. | Olympique Alésien (Alès) | 30 | 8 | 5 | 17 | 32 | 56 | 21 | |
| 15. | US Olympique de Montpellier (Montpellier) | 30 | 7 | 6 | 17 | 34 | 61 | 20 | |
| 16. | AS Avignonnaise (Avignon) | 30 | 7 | 6 | 17 | 37 | 85 | 20 | |
| | | 480 | 192 | 96 | 192 | 825 | 825 | 480 | |

* Olympique GC de Nice (Nice) changed their name to Olympique GC de Nice-Sportsmen (Nice) for the 1944 season only.

## Coupe de France Final    (Stade Yves du Manoir, Colombes – 09/05/43)

**OLYMPIQUE DE MARSEILLE**                2-2                Girondins-AS du Port (Bordeaux)

*Pironti 04', Robin 55'*                                          *Patrone 56', Persillon 82'*

**Marseille**: Delachet, Patrone, Gonzales, Veneziano, Bastien, "Olej", Dard, Scotti, Aznar, Robin, Pironti.

**Girondins**: Gérard, Homar, Normand, Ben Ali, Mateo, Ben Arab, Rolland, Nemeur, Urtizberea, Persillon, Arnaudeau.


## Final Replay    (Parc des Princes, Paris – 22/05/43 – 32,212)

**OLYMPIQUE DE MARSEILLE**                4-0                Girondins-AS du Port (Bordeaux)

*Aznar 32', 63', Dard 56', Pironti 78'*

**Marseille**: Delachet, Patrone, Gonzales, Veneziano, Bastien, "Olej", Dard, Scotti, Aznar, Robin, Pironti.

**Girondins**: Gérard, Homar, Normand, Ben Ali, Mateo, Ben Arab, Rolland, Pruvot, Urtizberea, Persillon, Arnaudeau.


## Final    (Zone Nord/Zone Interdite – Colombes – 02/05/43)

Girondins-AS du Port (Bordeaux)          2-1                Racing Club de Lens (Lens)


## Final    (Zone Interdite – Fives – 04/04/43)

Racing Club de Lens (Lens)               2-0                Olympique Iris Club Lillois (Lille)


## Semi-Finals

Racing Club de Lens (Lens)               5-0       FC Sochaux-Valentigney (Montbéliard)
Olympique IC Lillois (Lille)             4-1       Excelsior de Roubaix-Tourcoing (Roubaix)


## Final    (Zone Nord – Paris – 03/04/43  +  Bordeaux – 18/04/43)

Girondins-AS du Port (Bordeaux)      0-0,  6-3       Stade Française-Cercle Athlétique de Paris


## Semi-Finals

Girondins-AS du Port (Bordeaux)          3-0                Nîmes Olympique (Nîmes)
Stade Française CA de Paris               4-0                FC de Rouen (Rouen)


## Final    (Zone Sud – Marseille – 04/04/93)

Olympique de Marseille (Marseille)       3-0       US Athlétiques Perpignanais (Perpignan)


## Semi-Finals

Olympique de Marseille (Marseille)       3-0                Nîmes Olympique (Nîmes)
US Athlétiques Perpignanais               4-1       Êtoile Sportive-Aiglons Brivistes (Brive)

# 1943-44

| 1943-1944 Championship Fédérale | EF Bordeaux-Guyenne | EF Clermont-Auvergne | EF Grenoble-Dauphiné | EF Lens-Artois | EF Lilles-Flandres | EF Lyon-Lyonnais | EF Marseille-Provence | EF Montpellier-Languedoc | EF Nancy-Lorraine | EF Nice-Côte d'Azur | EF Paris-Capitale | EF Paris-Ile de France | EF Reims-Champagne | EF Rennes-Bretagne | EF Rouen-Normandie | EF Toulouse-Pyrénées |
|---|---|---|---|---|---|---|---|---|---|---|---|---|---|---|---|---|
| EF Bordeaux-Guyenne | ■ | 7-2 | 3-0 | 1-0 | 1-2 | 3-0 | 2-2 | 5-2 | 3-2 | 3-3 | 3-1 | 1-0 | 4-2 | 3-1 | 1-1 | 0-3 |
| EF Clermont-Auvergne | 1-1 | ■ | 4-0 | 3-4 | 0-4 | 4-1 | 0-3 | 1-5 | 2-2 | 0-0 | 1-8 | 0-1 | 4-0 | 0-1 | 1-1 | 2-1 |
| EF Grenoble-Dauphiné | 1-1 | 7-0 | ■ | 0-8 | 0-1 | 1-4 | 0-3 | 0-2 | 1-5 | 1-2 | 1-4 | 2-3 | 1-0 | 1-1 | 2-2 | 2-1 |
| EF Lens-Artois | 4-0 | 3-1 | 7-3 | ■ | 0-1 | 6-1 | 1-0 | 5-0 | 1-2 | 7-1 | 2-4 | 2-3 | 4-1 | 1-0 | 0-0 | 3-3 |
| EF Lilles-Flandres | 1-0 | 7-1 | 4-1 | 0-4 | ■ | 3-1 | 4-2 | 8-0 | 8-1 | 2-1 | 6-2 | 2-1 | 2-1 | 0-1 | 2-3 | 2-2 |
| EF Lyon-Lyonnais | 1-2 | 2-1 | 2-1 | 1-2 | 0-3 | ■ | 1-4 | 4-1 | 1-3 | 3-0 | 3-1 | 0-2 | 0-3 | 1-2 | 3-1 | 7-3 |
| EF Marseille-Provence | 4-0 | 4-0 | 1-2 | 2-3 | 3-1 | 0-2 | ■ | 2-1 | 7-1 | 0-5 | 0-2 | 0-2 | 2-1 | 1-0 | 3-1 | 1-1 |
| EF Montpellier-Languedoc | 0-2 | 3-3 | 1-0 | 7-0 | 4-3 | 0-0 | 0-2 | ■ | 4-0 | 1-3 | 1-5 | 1-1 | 1-6 | 1-3 | 1-2 | 2-3 |
| EF Nancy-Lorraine | 1-1 | 2-2 | 3-1 | 2-5 | 3-3 | 3-3 | 3-0 | 2-1 | ■ | 1-0 | 5-3 | 0-2 | 5-1 | 6-3 | 2-2 | 4-2 |
| EF Nice-Côte d'Azur | 1-2 | 1-1 | 3-1 | 0-3 | 2-1 | 1-0 | 4-0 | 7-0 | 0-0 | ■ | 1-3 | 2-1 | 1-1 | 3-1 | 3-0 | 1-1 |
| EF Paris-Capitale | 4-0 | 1-3 | 6-0 | 1-2 | 5-1 | 1-2 | 1-0 | 1-0 | 5-1 | 1-1 | ■ | 2-3 | 4-2 | 4-1 | 5-2 | 2-1 |
| EF Paris-Ile de France | 0-1 | 2-2 | 3-1 | 1-1 | 2-0 | 4-1 | 0-1 | 2-1 | 2-2 | 0-1 | 0-0 | ■ | 1-1 | 1-1 | 1-1 | 1-3 |
| EF Reims-Champagne | 2-0 | 3-0 | 8-2 | 1-4 | 0-2 | 1-1 | 1-0 | 3-2 | 5-2 | 2-1 | 0-0 | 0-0 | ■ | 6-1 | 1-2 | 1-1 |
| EF Rennes-Bretagne | 2-0 | 3-2 | 8-1 | 2-1 | 3-3 | 0-3 | 0-0 | 4-2 | 2-2 | 2-1 | 5-1 | 0-2 | 2-2 | ■ | 3-3 | 1-1 |
| EF Rouen-Normandie | 1-1 | 3-2 | 2-0 | 0-6 | 0-0 | 3-0 | 2-1 | 3-0 | 5-0 | 2-0 | 2-3 | 2-3 | 0-4 | 2-3 | ■ | 0-2 |
| EF Toulouse-Pyrénées | 7-0 | 6-2 | 7-0 | 0-6 | 0-2 | 3-1 | 1-2 | 5-1 | 7-3 | 3-1 | 1-3 | 2-3 | 3-5 | 5-2 | 7-2 | ■ |

## Championship Fédérale

| | | Pd | Wn | Dw | Ls | GF | GA | Pts |
|---|---|---|---|---|---|---|---|---|
| 1. | EF LENS-ARTOIS (LENS) | 30 | 20 | 3 | 7 | 95 | 41 | 43 |
| 2. | EF Lille-Flandres (Lille) | 30 | 18 | 4 | 8 | 78 | 44 | 40 |
| 3. | EF Paris-Capitale (Paris) | 30 | 18 | 3 | 9 | 84 | 50 | 39 |
| 4. | EF Paris-Ile de France (Paris) | 30 | 14 | 9 | 7 | 47 | 33 | 37 |
| 5. | EF Bordeaux-Guyenne (Bordeaux) | 30 | 14 | 7 | 9 | 51 | 51 | 35 |
| 6. | EF Toulouse-Pyrénées (Toulouse) | 30 | 13 | 6 | 11 | 85 | 62 | 32 |
| 7. | EF Rennes-Bretagne (Rennes) | 30 | 12 | 8 | 10 | 58 | 60 | 32 |
| 8. | EF Reims-Champagne (Reims) | 30 | 12 | 7 | 11 | 64 | 52 | 31 |
| 9. | EF Nice-Côte d'Azur (Nice) | 30 | 12 | 7 | 11 | 50 | 43 | 31 |
| 10. | EF Marseille-Provence (Marseille) | 30 | 14 | 3 | 13 | 50 | 42 | 31 |
| 11. | EF Nancy-Lorraine (Nancy) | 30 | 11 | 9 | 10 | 68 | 82 | 31 |
| 12. | EF Rouen-Normandie (Rouen) | 30 | 10 | 9 | 11 | 50 | 60 | 29 |
| 13. | EF Lyon-Lyonnais (Lyon) | 30 | 11 | 3 | 16 | 49 | 62 | 25 |
| 14. | EF Clermont-Auvergne (Clermont-Ferrand) | 30 | 5 | 8 | 17 | 45 | 86 | 18 |
| 15. | EF Montpellier-Languedoc (Montpellier) | 30 | 6 | 3 | 21 | 45 | 85 | 15 |
| 16. | EF Grenoble-Dauphiné (Grenoble) | 30 | 4 | 3 | 23 | 33 | 99 | 11 |
| | | 480 | 194 | 92 | 194 | 952 | 952 | 480 |

## Top goal-scorer

1) Stefan "Stanis" DEMBICKI     (EF Lens-Artois)    41

EF Grenoble-Dauphiné 2-2 EF Marseille-Provence was later awarded as a 0-3 forfeit.

EF Bordeaux-Guyenne 3-0 EF Lyon-Lyonnais was later awarded as a 3-0 forfeit.

EF Rouen-Normandie 3-0 EF Lyon-Lyonnais was later as a 0-3 forfeit.


Olympique Iris Club Lillois (Lille) merged in 1944 with SC Fivois (Fives) to become Lille Olympique SC (Lille).

US Olympique de Montpellier (Montpellier) changed their name to Stade Olympique Montpelliérain (Montpellier).

Olympique GC de Nice-Sportsmen (Nice) reverted to Olympique GC de Nice (Nice).

Stade Français-Cercle Athlétique de Paris (Paris) separated and reverted to Stade Français (Paris) and Cercle Athlétique de Paris (Paris).

SC du Temple (Toulon) merged with Jeunesse Sportive Toulonnais (Toulon) to become SC de Toulon (Toulon).


The championship reverted to club competitions for next season, being played in regional groups (Nord and Sud) in preparation for the recommencement of the official championship during the following season 1945-46.


## Coupe de France Final    (Parc des Princes, Paris – 07/05/44 – 31,995)

| **EF NANCY-LORRAINE (NANCY)** | **4-0** | EF Reims-Champagne (Reims) |
|---|---|---|

*Parmeggiani 21', Poblomme 54', 74', Jacques 66'*


**Nancy**: "Coulon", Rué, Mathieu, Givert, Magnin, Grandidier, Sesia, Pessonneaux, Poblomme, Parmeggiani, Jacques.
**Reims**: Dambach, Prince, Carrara, Ignace, Brembilla, Roessler, Pradel, Batteux, Flamion, Petitfils, "Szego".


## Semi-Finals    (01/04/44)

| EF Nancy-Lorraine (Nancy) | 2-1 | EF Bordeaux-Guyenne (Bordeaux) |
|---|---|---|
| EF Reims-Champagne (Reims) | 0-0,  2-1 | EF Lens-Artois (Lens) |

## Quarter-Finals    (05/03/44)

| EF Bordeaux-Guyenne (Bordeaux) | 1-0 | EF Montpellier-Languedoc (Montpellier) |
|---|---|---|
| EF Lens-Artois (Lens) | 3-1 | EF Paris-Capitale (Paris) |
| EF Nancy-Lorraine (Nancy) | 4-3 | Girondins-AS du Port (Bordeaux) |
| EF Reims-Champagne (Reims) | 3-1 | EF Rouen-Normandie (Rouen) |

| 1944-1945 Groupe Nord | Excelsior de Roubaix-Tour. | Stade Français | Havre AC | Racing Club de Lens | Lille Olympique SC | US du Mans | Racing Club de Paris | Red Star Olympique | Stade de Reims | Stade Rennais Université | FC de Rouen | US Valenciennes-Anzin |
|---|---|---|---|---|---|---|---|---|---|---|---|---|
| Excelsior de Roubaix-Tour. | | 1-1 | 0-0 | 3-4 | 4-6 | 1-2 | 0-0 | 0-4 | 1-1 | 2-2 | 1-3 | 2-1 |
| Stade Français | 5-2 | | 2-2 | 0-3 | 1-2 | 1-3 | 1-1 | 1-2 | 0-4 | 0-1 | 0-3 | 1-3 |
| Havre AC | 2-2 | 1-1 | | 2-3 | 2-5 | 3-0 | 0-10 | 3-0 | 3-0 | 0-1 | 0-1 | 1-4 |
| Racing Club de Lens | 7-0 | 4-1 | 5-0 | | 2-1 | 9-0 | 2-0 | 1-0 | 3-2 | 1-1 | 0-1 | 6-2 |
| Lille Olympique SC | 5-3 | 2-0 | 9-2 | 4-0 | | 3-0 | 2-3 | 1-2 | 3-1 | 3-0 | 1-0 | 3-0 |
| US du Mans | 2-2 | 2-2 | 2-0 | 1-2 | 1-4 | | 0-0 | 0-1 | 0-2 | 7-3 | 0-3 | 4-1 |
| Racing Club de Paris | 5-3 | 2-3 | 5-0 | 4-1 | 4-3 | 4-2 | | 0-0 | 1-1 | 2-3 | 2-0 | 1-6 |
| Red Star Olympique | 3-1 | 4-1 | 8-2 | 5-1 | 2-0 | 1-0 | 2-1 | | 0-5 | 5-2 | 2-2 | 8-3 |
| Stade de Reims | 5-1 | 3-1 | 5-0 | 1-0 | 4-2 | 10-1 | 9-2 | 3-3 | | 0-3 | 4-0 | 1-2 |
| Stade Rennais Université | 3-3 | 2-4 | 4-1 | 1-1 | 0-7 | 4-0 | 2-5 | 1-1 | 0-6 | | 0-2 | 2-5 |
| FC de Rouen | 2-0 | 1-1 | 2-1 | 2-1 | 3-1 | 5-1 | 5-1 | 5-1 | 3-3 | 6-1 | | 3-1 |
| US Valenciennes-Anzin | 2-0 | 3-3 | 2-1 | 1-2 | 3-2 | 3-1 | 0-2 | -:- | 1-0 | 4-0 | 1-2 | |

## Play-off

| FC DE ROUEN (ROUEN) | 4-0 | Lyon Olympique Universitaire (Lyon) |
|---|---|---|

| **Groupe Nord** | | **Pd** | **Wn** | **Dw** | **Ls** | **GF** | **GA** | **Pts** | |
|---|---|---|---|---|---|---|---|---|---|
| 1. | FC de Rouen (Rouen) | 22 | 16 | 3 | 3 | 54 | 23 | 35 | |
| 2. | Racing Club de Lens (Lens) | 22 | 14 | 2 | 6 | 58 | 32 | 30 | |
| 3. | Red Star Olympique (Saint-Ouen) | 22 | 13 | 4 | 5 | 54 | 33 | 30 | * |
| 4. | Stade de Reims (Reims) | 22 | 12 | 4 | 6 | 70 | 30 | 28 | |
| 5. | Lille Olympique SC (Lille) | 22 | 14 | - | 8 | 69 | 37 | 28 | |
| 6. | Racing Club de Paris (Paris) | 22 | 10 | 4 | 8 | 55 | 45 | 24 | |
| 7. | US Valenciennes-Anzin (Valenciennes) | 22 | 11 | 1 | 10 | 48 | 45 | 23 | |
| 8. | Stade Rennais Université Club (Rennes) | 22 | 6 | 5 | 11 | 36 | 65 | 17 | |
| 9. | Stade Français (Paris) | 22 | 4 | 6 | 12 | 30 | 51 | 14 | |
| 10. | US du Mans (Le Mans) | 22 | 5 | 3 | 14 | 29 | 64 | 13 | |
| 11. | Excelsior de Roubaix-Tourcoing (Roubaix) | 22 | 2 | 7 | 13 | 32 | 65 | 11 | * |
| 12. | Havre AC (Le Havre) | 22 | 3 | 3 | 16 | 26 | 71 | 9 | |
| | | 264 | 110 | 42 | 112 | 561 | 561 | 262 | |

Excelsior de Roubaix-Tourcoing (Roubaix) 0-0 Havre AC (Le Havre) – the points were later awarded to Excelsior.
Stade Français (Paris) 1-1 Racing Club de Paris (Paris) was later changed to a win for Stade Français (Paris).
US Valenciennes-Anzin (Valenciennes) – Red Star Olympique (Paris) was later given as a defeat to both teams.

## Groupe Nord Top goal-scorers

| 1) | René BIHEL | (Lille Olympique SC) | 30 |
|---|---|---|---|
| | Pierre SINIBALDI | (Stade de Reims) | 30 |

| 1944-1945 Groupe Sud | Olympique Alésien | Girondins-AS du Port | AS de Cannes | Stade Clermontois | Lyon Olympique Univ. | Olympique de Marseille | SO Montpelliérain | Olympique GC de Nice | Nîmes Olympique | AS de Saint-Étienne | FC de Sète | Toulouse FC |
|---|---|---|---|---|---|---|---|---|---|---|---|---|
| Olympique Alésien | | 2-5 | 3-2 | 1-3 | 1-1 | 0-1 | 2-2 | 3-1 | 1-3 | 1-0 | 3-0 | 2-3 |
| Girondins-AS du Port | 3-1 | | 1-1 | 1-1 | 4-0 | 2-3 | 7-2 | 2-2 | 8-3 | 2-2 | 2-1 | 4-0 |
| AS de Cannes | 0-0 | 1-1 | | 2-2 | 1-4 | 1-3 | 0-1 | 2-1 | 3-0 | 2-0 | 2-2 | 3-4 |
| Stade Clermontois | 2-2 | 3-2 | 3-0 | | 1-1 | 6-0 | 1-0 | 3-0 | 4-5 | 2-1 | 3-1 | 3-2 |
| Lyon Olympique Univ. | 6-2 | 5-1 | 6-1 | 7-1 | | 3-0 | 2-0 | 3-0 | 2-0 | 3-0 | 0-0 | 8-2 |
| Olympique de Marseille | 9-0 | 0-3 | 2-0 | 1-1 | 1-3 | | 8-3 | 3-1 | 3-1 | 7-3 | 5-2 | 6-1 |
| SO Montpelliérain | 1-5 | 1-6 | 0-1 | 3-1 | 1-0 | 2-1 | | 4-2 | 2-2 | 5-4 | 0-2 | 2-2 |
| Olympique GC de Nice | 2-4 | 1-4 | 1-0 | 1-0 | 0-1 | 4-1 | 0-1 | | 3-0 | 5-0 | 3-1 | 2-1 |
| Nîmes Olympique | 1-0 | 2-6 | 6-2 | 2-1 | 2-2 | 0-0 | 5-1 | 3-3 | | 2-2 | 0-2 | 1-3 |
| AS de Saint-Étienne | 6-0 | 1-4 | 2-1 | 3-1 | 2-2 | 2-1 | 3-4 | 2-0 | 5-1 | | 2-3 | 0-0 |
| FC de Sète | 4-0 | 2-0 | 0-0 | 2-2 | 1-1 | 3-1 | 0-3 | 2-2 | 7-1 | 5-2 | | 3-1 |
| Toulouse FC | 6-1 | 1-2 | 4-2 | 2-4 | 1-2 | 6-2 | 4-3 | 5-0 | 5-2 | 3-3 | 1-1 | |

| | Groupe Sud | Pd | Wn | Dw | Ls | GF | GA | Pts | |
|---|---|---|---|---|---|---|---|---|---|
| 1. | Lyon Olympique Universitaire (Lyon) | 22 | 14 | 6 | 2 | 62 | 22 | 34 | |
| 2. | Girondins-AS du Port (Bordeaux) | 22 | 16 | 2 | 4 | 74 | 35 | 34 | |
| 3. | FC de Sète (Sète) | 22 | 10 | 6 | 6 | 44 | 34 | 26 | |
| 4. | Stade Clermontois (Clermont-Ferrand) | 22 | 11 | 4 | 7 | 48 | 39 | 26 | |
| 5. | Olympique de Marseille (Marseille) | 22 | 11 | 2 | 9 | 58 | 47 | 24 | |
| 6. | Toulouse FC (Toulouse) | 22 | 9 | 4 | 9 | 57 | 56 | 22 | |
| 7. | Stade Olympique Montpelliérain (Montpellier) | 22 | 9 | 3 | 10 | 41 | 58 | 21 | |
| 8. | AS de Saint-Étienne (Saint-Étienne) | 22 | 6 | 5 | 11 | 45 | 54 | 17 | |
| 9. | Olympique GC de Nice (Nice) | 22 | 7 | 3 | 12 | 34 | 45 | 17 | |
| 10. | Nîmes Olympique (Nîmes) | 22 | 5 | 5 | 12 | 42 | 65 | 15 | |
| 11. | Olympique Alésien (Alès) | 22 | 6 | 3 | 13 | 34 | 61 | 15 | |
| 12. | AS de Cannes (Cannes) | 22 | 5 | 3 | 14 | 27 | 50 | 13 | * |
| | | 264 | 109 | 46 | 109 | 566 | 566 | 264 | |

AS de Cannes (Cannes) changed their name to AS Cannes-Grasse (Cannes) for the next season.

Excelsior de Roubaix-Tourcoing (Roubaix) merged with Racing Club de Roubaix (Roubaix) to become Club Olympique Roubaix-Tourcoing (Roubaix) for the next season.

Red Star Olympique (Saint-Ouen) merged with Sports Olympique Audonien (Paris) to become Red Star Olympique Audonien (Saint-Ouen) for the next season.

## Groupe Sud Top goal-scorer

1) PLANTÉ                    (Girondins de Bordeaux FC)    25

## Coupe de France Final   (Stade Yves du Manoir, Colombes – 06/05/45 – 49,983)

**RACING CLUB DE PARIS (PARIS)**    **3-0**    Lille Olympique SC (Lille)

*Philippot 30', Ponsetti 40', Heisserer 65'*

**Racing**: Molinuevo, Dupuis, Salva, Samuel, Jordan, Jasseron, Philippot, Heisserer, Bongiorni, Ponsetti, Vaast.
**Lille**: Da Rui, "Jadrejak", Cardon, Bourbotte, Stefaniak, Bigot, Vandooren, Baratte, Bihel, Carré, Lechantre.

## Semi-Finals   (15/04/45)

| | | |
|---|---|---|
| Lille Olympique SC (Lille) | 4-0 | Toulouse FC (Toulouse) |
| Racing Club de Paris (Paris) | 2-1 | Olympique GC de Nice (Nice) |

## Quarter-Finals   (17-18/03/45)

| | | |
|---|---|---|
| Lille Olympique SC (Lille) | 3-2 | Lyon Olympique Universitaire (Lyon) |
| Olympique GC de Nice (Nice) | 4-0 | FC de Rouen (Rouen) |
| Racing Club de Paris (Paris) | 1-0 | Arago Sports Orléanais (Orléans) |
| Toulouse FC (Toulouse) | 4-3 | Racing Club de Lens (Lens) |

# 1945-46

| 1945-1946 Division One | Girondins-AS Port | AS Cannes-Grasse | Havre AC | Racing Club de Lens | Lille Olympique SC | Lyon Olympique U. | Olympique Marseille | FC de Metz | Racing Club de Paris | Red Star Olympique | Stade de Reims | Stade Rennais Université Club | CO Roubaix-Tourcoing | FC de Rouen | AS de Saint-Étienne | FC de Sète | Sochaux-Montbéliard | Racing Strasbourg |
|---|---|---|---|---|---|---|---|---|---|---|---|---|---|---|---|---|---|---|
| Girondins-AS Port | ■ | 4-1 | 1-2 | 2-2 | 1-5 | 0-1 | 1-1 | 8-0 | 3-1 | 2-1 | 5-1 | 4-1 | 0-2 | 4-1 | 1-3 | 0-3 | 3-2 | 4-3 |
| AS Cannes-Grasse | 0-0 | ■ | 3-2 | 1-0 | 2-1 | 1-1 | 0-2 | 0-1 | 1-1 | 3-1 | 1-1 | 2-2 | 1-1 | 3-1 | 1-4 | 2-1 | 4-1 | 3-1 |
| Havre AC | 3-2 | 1-2 | ■ | 1-0 | 1-2 | 0-0 | 4-3 | 3-0 | 3-5 | 0-1 | 2-3 | 0-0 | 4-1 | 1-0 | 0-2 | 4-1 | 1-0 | 3-0 |
| Racing Club de Lens | 1-1 | 2-1 | 7-1 | ■ | 3-1 | 9-2 | 3-1 | 5-3 | 2-3 | 1-1 | 2-2 | 2-2 | 2-1 | 1-0 | 6-1 | 5-1 | 3-0 | 0-4 |
| Lille Olympique SC | 5-0 | 5-1 | 1-0 | 3-1 | ■ | 4-0 | 4-4 | 7-0 | 0-1 | 3-1 | 3-0 | 2-5 | 0-2 | 2-2 | 8-0 | 5-2 | 3-1 | 4-1 |
| Lyon Olympique U. | 0-0 | 2-2 | 1-0 | 2-0 | 1-2 | ■ | 1-1 | 2-0 | 1-0 | 2-2 | 1-2 | 3-5 | 0-5 | 2-1 | 3-3 | 2-0 | 3-4 | 3-2 |
| Olympique Marseille | 3-0 | 6-1 | 3-0 | 4-1 | 2-2 | 1-1 | ■ | 2-1 | 0-0 | 2-1 | 3-5 | 2-2 | 0-2 | 2-3 | 1-4 | 1-2 | 3-1 | 5-0 |
| FC de Metz | 2-0 | 1-0 | 2-2 | 2-3 | 0-3 | 1-4 | 3-1 | ■ | 2-1 | 2-4 | 2-2 | 0-1 | 4-2 | 0-0 | 0-3 | 2-1 | 2-0 | 1-3 |
| Racing Club de Paris | 2-2 | 0-3 | 4-1 | 2-0 | 2-1 | 1-3 | 2-6 | 2-0 | ■ | 1-0 | 2-1 | 3-0 | 0-2 | 0-1 | 4-1 | 4-1 | 3-0 | 2-1 |
| Red Star Olympique Audonien | 4-2 | 0-0 | 3-0 | 1-1 | 2-2 | 2-2 | 2-2 | 2-3 | 0-1 | ■ | 0-3 | 0-4 | 3-0 | 3-1 | 3-2 | 6-0 | 4-1 | 4-2 |
| Stade de Reims | 2-2 | 2-4 | 4-0 | 1-2 | 1-1 | 6-0 | 4-1 | 1-1 | 1-0 | 4-0 | ■ | 5-0 | 1-1 | 4-1 | 1-3 | 2-1 | 1-0 | 0-1 |
| Stade Rennais Université Club | 4-2 | 0-2 | 0-1 | 3-0 | 1-4 | 3-1 | 0-0 | 1-0 | 1-0 | 1-0 | 1-1 | ■ | 1-1 | 2-0 | 2-3 | 3-3 | 5-1 | 0-1 |
| CO Roubaix-Tourcoing | 3-1 | 2-0 | 1-1 | 3-0 | 1-1 | 5-0 | 1-1 | 4-0 | 1-0 | 3-5 | 0-1 | 1-1 | ■ | 0-0 | 3-2 | 3-1 | 2-2 | 1-1 |
| FC de Rouen | 1-1 | 1-1 | 6-0 | 2-1 | 2-1 | 2-1 | 6-0 | 4-1 | 2-0 | 1-1 | 1-0 | 1-1 | 2-1 | ■ | 2-1 | 0-3 | 1-1 | 5-0 |
| AS de Saint-Étienne | 3-1 | 2-1 | 5-1 | 2-1 | 3-1 | 4-0 | 2-4 | 3-1 | 3-2 | 3-2 | 2-3 | 4-2 | 1-3 | 3-1 | ■ | 6-2 | 1-0 | 0-0 |
| FC de Sète | 2-4 | 1-0 | 3-0 | 0-0 | 1-2 | 6-2 | 2-3 | 3-1 | 3-2 | 4-0 | 1-1 | 2-0 | 0-0 | 4-1 | 1-1 | ■ | 4-0 | 0-1 |
| Sochaux-Montbéliard | 0-3 | 2-2 | 2-4 | 0-3 | 0-0 | 1-3 | 1-0 | 0-0 | 2-4 | 0-2 | 1-1 | 0-2 | 0-1 | 2-0 | 4-4 | 1-3 | ■ | 4-2 |
| Racing Strasbourg | 1-1 | 3-2 | 0-2 | 3-3 | 0-1 | 3-2 | 3-0 | 0-2 | 4-1 | 1-1 | 3-1 | 1-1 | 2-1 | 0-1 | 3-2 | 1-1 | 2-1 | ■ |

| Division 1 | Pd | Wn | Dw | Ls | GF | GA | Pts | |
|---|---|---|---|---|---|---|---|---|
| 1. LILLE OLYMPIQUE SC (LILLE) | 34 | 19 | 7 | 8 | 89 | 44 | 45 | |
| 2. AS de Saint-Étienne (Saint-Étienne) | 34 | 20 | 4 | 10 | 86 | 68 | 44 | |
| 3. Club Olympique Roubaix-Tourcoing (Roubaix) | 34 | 15 | 11 | 8 | 60 | 38 | 41 | |
| 4. Stade de Reims (Reims) | 34 | 15 | 10 | 9 | 68 | 48 | 40 | |
| 5. Stade Rennais Université Club (Rennes) | 34 | 13 | 11 | 10 | 57 | 52 | 37 | |
| 6. Racing Club de Lens (Lens) | 34 | 14 | 8 | 12 | 72 | 57 | 36 | |
| 7. FC de Rouen (Rouen) | 34 | 14 | 8 | 12 | 53 | 47 | 36 | |
| 8. Racing Club de Paris (Paris) | 34 | 16 | 3 | 15 | 56 | 52 | 35 | |
| 9. Olympique de Marseille (Marseille) | 34 | 12 | 10 | 12 | 70 | 65 | 34 | |
| 10. AS Cannes-Grasse (Cannes) | 34 | 12 | 10 | 12 | 51 | 55 | 34 | |
| 11. Red Star Olympique Audonien (Saint-Ouen) | 34 | 12 | 9 | 13 | 62 | 59 | 33 | |
| 12. Racing Club de Strasbourg (Strasbourg) | 34 | 13 | 7 | 14 | 53 | 62 | 33 | |
| 13. FC de Sète (Sète) | 34 | 13 | 6 | 15 | 63 | 65 | 32 | |
| 14. Girondins-AS du Port (Bordeaux) | 34 | 11 | 9 | 14 | 65 | 66 | 31 | |
| 15. Lyon Olympique Universitaire (Lyon) | 34 | 11 | 9 | 14 | 52 | 78 | 31 | R |
| 16. Havre AC (Le Havre) | 34 | 13 | 4 | 17 | 48 | 68 | 30 | |
| 17. FC de Metz (Metz) | 34 | 10 | 5 | 19 | 40 | 77 | 25 | |
| 18. FC Sochaux-Montbéliard (Montbéliard) | 34 | 4 | 7 | 23 | 35 | 79 | 15 | R |
| | 612 | 237 | 138 | 237 | 1080 | 1080 | 612 | |

## Top goal-scorer

1)  René BIHEL          (Lille Olympique SC)      28

| Division 2 (Nord) | Pd | Wn | Dw | Ls | GF | GA | Pts | |
|---|---|---|---|---|---|---|---|---|
| 1. FC de Nancy (Nancy) | 26 | 22 | 2 | 2 | 84 | 28 | 46 | P |
| 2. Stade Français (Paris) | 26 | 18 | 4 | 4 | 64 | 31 | 40 | P |
| 3. SC de l'Ouest Angers (Angers) | 26 | 15 | 3 | 8 | 47 | 42 | 33 | |
| 4 AS des Charentes (Angoulême) | 26 | 12 | 4 | 10 | 45 | 37 | 28 | |
| 5. FC de Nantes (Nantes) | 26 | 11 | 4 | 11 | 47 | 43 | 26 | |
| 6. Sports Réunis de Colmar (Colmar) | 26 | 10 | 6 | 10 | 51 | 51 | 26 | |
| 7. US Valenciennes-Anzin (Valenciennes) | 26 | 10 | 5 | 11 | 47 | 44 | 25 | |
| 8. Cercle Athlétique de Paris (Paris) | 26 | 11 | 2 | 13 | 48 | 52 | 24 | |
| 9. Racing Club Franc-Comtois (Besançon) | 26 | 10 | 3 | 13 | 47 | 52 | 23 | |
| 10. Amiens AC (Amiens) | 26 | 8 | 4 | 14 | 40 | 49 | 20 | |
| 11. US du Mans (Le Mans) | 26 | 7 | 5 | 14 | 35 | 47 | 19 | |
| 12. Sporting Amical Douaisien (Douai) | 26 | 7 | 5 | 14 | 39 | 64 | 19 | |
| 13. AS Troyenne-Savinienne (Troyes) | 26 | 6 | 7 | 13 | 35 | 61 | 19 | |
| 14. FC de Mulhouse 1893 (Mulhouse) | 26 | 6 | 4 | 16 | 39 | 67 | 16 | R |
| | 364 | 153 | 58 | 153 | 668 | 668 | 364 | |

| Division 2 (Sud) | Pd | Wn | Dw | Ls | GF | GA | Pts | |
|---|---|---|---|---|---|---|---|---|
| 1. Stade Olympique Montpelliérain (Montpellier) | 26 | 20 | 2 | 4 | 64 | 21 | 42 | P |
| 2. Toulouse FC (Toulouse) | 26 | 19 | 4 | 3 | 88 | 32 | 42 | P |
| 3. Olympique Alésien (Alès) | 26 | 14 | 7 | 5 | 60 | 35 | 35 | |
| 4. Nîmes Olympique (Nîmes) | 26 | 17 | - | 9 | 69 | 46 | 34 | |
| 5. Olympique GC de Nice (Nice) | 26 | 12 | 5 | 9 | 46 | 36 | 29 | |
| 6. Stade Clermontois (Clermont-Ferrand) | 26 | 11 | 6 | 9 | 52 | 45 | 28 | |
| 7. AS Avignonnaise (Avignon) | 26 | 11 | 5 | 10 | 62 | 45 | 27 | |
| 8. FC de Grenoble (Grenoble) | 26 | 11 | 5 | 10 | 52 | 53 | 27 | # |
| 9. Olympique d'Antibes-Juan-les-Pins (Antibes) | 26 | 9 | 6 | 11 | 36 | 51 | 24 | |
| 10. SC de Toulon (Toulon) | 26 | 10 | 2 | 14 | 52 | 50 | 22 | |
| 11. US Athlétiques Perpignanais (Perpignan) | 26 | 10 | 2 | 14 | 38 | 61 | 22 | |
| 12. Sporting Club de Vichy (Vichy) | 26 | 8 | 3 | 15 | 56 | 76 | 19 | # |
| 13. AS Biterroise (Beziers) | 26 | 2 | 4 | 20 | 18 | 92 | 8 | |
| 14. Étoile-Sportive-Aiglons Brivistes (Brive) | 26 | - | 5 | 21 | 27 | 77 | 5 | R |
| | 364 | 154 | 56 | 154 | 720 | 720 | 364 | |

# FC de Grenoble (Grenoble) and SC de Vichy (Vichy) both reverted to amateur status for the next season.


## Coupe de France Final   (Stade Yves du Manoir, Colombes – 26/05/46 – 59,692)

**LILLE OLYMPIQUE SC (LILLE)**  **4-2**  Red Star Olympique Audonien (Saint-Ouen)

*Tempowski 13', Bihel 24', Vandooren 51', 85'*                    *Moulet 47', Leduc 69'*

**Lille**: Hatz, "Jadrejak", Sommerlynck, Bourbotte, Prévost, Carré, Vandooren, Baratte, Bihel, Tempowski, Lechantre.

**Red Star**: Germain, Planques, Nuevo, Bersoullé, Mindonnet, Leduc, Aston, Kadmiri, Simonyi, Lozia, Moulet.


## Semi-Finals   (27/04/46)

| | | |
|---|---|---|
| Lille Olympique SC (Lille) | 7-1 | Stade Clermontois (Clermont-Ferrand) |
| Red Star Olympique Audonien (Saint-Ouen) | 3-2 | Stade Français (Paris) |


## Quarter-Finals   (31/03/46)

| | | |
|---|---|---|
| Stade Clermontois (Clermont-Ferrand) | 4-1 | Girondins-AS du Port (Bordeaux) |
| Lille Olympique SC (Lille) | 2-1 | Racing Club de Paris (Paris) |
| Red Star Olympique Audonien (Saint-Ouen) | 2-0 | Lyon Olympique Universitaire (Lyon) |
| Stade Français (Paris) | 3-1 | Olympique de Marseille (Marseille) |

# 1946-47

| 1946-1947 Division One | Gir. Bordeaux | AS de Cannes | Stade Français | Havre AC | Racing Lens | Lille Olymp. | Oly. Marseille | FC de Metz | SO Montpellier | FC de Nancy | Racing Paris | Red Star Oly. | Stade Reims | Stade Rennais | CO Roubaix-T. | FC de Rouen | AS St-Étienne | FC de Sète | RC Strasbourg | Toulouse FC |
|---|---|---|---|---|---|---|---|---|---|---|---|---|---|---|---|---|---|---|---|---|
| Girondins de Bordeaux | ■ | 1-4 | 1-4 | 1-2 | 3-2 | 1-0 | 2-2 | 4-3 | 4-0 | 1-1 | 0-6 | 3-2 | 1-3 | 0-1 | 1-3 | 2-1 | 3-1 | 4-3 | 2-5 | 1-1 |
| AS de Cannes | 2-0 | ■ | 1-0 | 2-1 | 2-0 | 0-2 | 2-1 | 1-0 | 2-2 | 2-1 | 1-0 | 1-0 | 1-0 | 0-2 | 3-1 | 3-1 | 7-0 | 5-2 | 2-2 | 3-2 |
| Stade Français | 0-1 | 2-0 | ■ | 4-4 | 3-1 | 0-2 | 4-1 | 0-0 | 6-2 | 1-0 | 2-2 | 0-1 | 2-2 | 5-3 | 4-3 | 0-1 | 3-0 | 1-1 | 2-4 | 5-1 |
| Havre AC | 1-0 | 1-0 | 2-3 | ■ | 0-2 | 1-4 | 1-1 | 1-2 | 2-0 | 3-2 | 0-1 | 0-0 | 1-0 | 2-2 | 0-3 | 4-1 | 0-0 | 5-1 | 1-2 | 0-2 |
| Racing Lens | 1-0 | 2-1 | 0-1 | 8-1 | ■ | 3-3 | 0-0 | 5-1 | 1-2 | 2-3 | 5-2 | 2-0 | 1-1 | 5-1 | 3-1 | 1-1 | 1-1 | 1-1 | 2-1 | 3-1 |
| Lille Olympique | 4-1 | 8-2 | 5-0 | 5-0 | 1-1 | ■ | 5-1 | 5-3 | 5-3 | 4-1 | 3-1 | 3-0 | 5-0 | 2-0 | 0-1 | 0-0 | 4-3 | 2-3 | 2-2 | 1-1 |
| Olympique Marseille | 1-3 | 4-1 | 0-1 | 5-3 | 5-2 | 1-1 | ■ | 3-3 | 2-1 | 3-1 | 5-3 | 4-0 | 3-2 | 1-0 | 1-1 | 4-0 | 2-0 | 3-1 | 2-1 | 3-0 |
| FC de Metz | 1-1 | 7-1 | 1-1 | 2-3 | 2-1 | 4-1 | 1-1 | ■ | 7-2 | 6-0 | 5-0 | 8-0 | 2-2 | 6-0 | 1-1 | 0-0 | 4-4 | 1-1 | 0-2 | 1-4 |
| SO Montpellier | 0-0 | 0-1 | 2-6 | 2-0 | 2-1 | 0-1 | 3-1 | 3-0 | ■ | 4-1 | 0-1 | 4-4 | 2-0 | 1-0 | 2-2 | 3-0 | 3-1 | 3-2 | 0-1 | 3-1 |
| FC de Nancy | 2-4 | 0-0 | 0-0 | 7-0 | 2-0 | 3-1 | 1-1 | 3-1 | 3-1 | ■ | 0-2 | 1-3 | 7-0 | 2-0 |  | 0-1 | 1-1 | 3-1 | 1-0 | 3-1 |
| Racing Paris | 0-1 | 4-0 | 4-2 | 3-1 | 1-3 | 1-0 | 1-2 | 3-3 | 2-3 | 4-3 | ■ | 1-2 | 0-3 | 2-3 | 2-1 | 0-0 | 3-4 | 0-2 | 2-3 | 8-2 |
| Red Star Olympique Audonien | 2-1 | 2-0 | 2-0 | 1-0 | 6-2 | 5-1 | 2-2 | 3-1 | 1-1 | 1-2 | 1-3 | ■ | 1-0 | 1-1 | 2-0 | 4-1 | 0-0 | 1-1 | 0-2 | 2-1 |
| Stade de Reims | 3-1 | 5-1 | 5-1 | 3-1 | 3-1 | 1-0 | 1-0 | 4-0 | 1-0 | 2-1 | 1-0 |  | ■ | 1-0 | 1-2 | 3-0 | 5-0 | 3-0 | 3-0 | 3-1 |
| Stade Rennais | 3-2 | 2-1 | 0-1 | 3-1 | 3-0 | 0-0 | 2-0 | 4-6 | 2-1 | 3-1 | 2-2 | 2-2 | 2-3 | ■ | 2-3 | 2-0 | 2-1 | 5-2 | 1-6 | 3-0 |
| CO Roubaix-Tourcoing | 1-0 | 1-0 | 1-3 | 1-0 | 4-1 | 1-0 | 2-0 | 2-1 | 5-2 | 1-1 | 2-1 | 2-0 | 1-1 | 2-3 | ■ | 1-0 | 7-3 | 2-1 | 2-0 | 1-0 |
| FC de Rouen | 2-2 | 0-0 | 0-2 | 2-2 | 3-1 | 0-3 | 2-3 | 0-1 | 0-2 | 0-0 | 0-2 | 3-0 | 1-0 | 1-1 | 0-1 | ■ | 3-0 | 6-0 | 1-3 | 1-5 |
| AS Saint-Étienne | 4-2 | 4-3 | 1-1 | 2-0 | 4-1 | 2-1 | 3-1 | 6-2 | 3-0 | 2-2 | 0-3 | 3-1 | 1-1 | 1-5 | 2-0 | 1-0 | ■ | 1-1 | 1-1 | 4-2 |
| FC de Sète | 6-1 | 2-1 | 3-1 | 1-1 | 2-1 | 2-1 | 1-1 | 2-2 | 1-0 | 2-2 | 2-2 | 1-1 | 2-1 | 5-0 | 2-5 | 1-3 | 2-1 | ■ | 1-2 | 1-0 |
| RC Strasbourg | 1-1 | 2-0 | 1-2 | 2-0 | 2-0 | 1-2 | 1-0 | 2-2 | 2-1 | 0-1 | 8-1 | 4-1 | 3-0 | 3-2 | 1-1 | 3-1 | 3-3 | 2-1 | ■ | 1-3 |
| Toulouse FC | 1-4 | 2-1 | 1-2 | 5-0 | 2-0 | 3-4 | 0-0 | 3-3 | 2-1 | 2-1 | 4-2 | 0-4 | 0-2 | 1-0 | 1-2 | 3-2 | 4-3 | 5-1 | 3-1 | ■ |

## Division 1

| | | Pd | Wn | Dw | Ls | GF | GA | Pts | |
|---|---|---|---|---|---|---|---|---|---|
| 1. | CLUB OLYMPIQUE ROUBAIX-TOURCOING | 38 | 24 | 5 | 9 | 71 | 47 | 53 | |
| 2. | Stade de Reims (Reims) | 38 | 22 | 5 | 11 | 72 | 40 | 49 | |
| 3. | Racing Club de Strasbourg (Strasbourg) | 38 | 21 | 7 | 10 | 79 | 50 | 49 | |
| 4. | Lille Olympique SC (Lille) | 38 | 20 | 7 | 11 | 89 | 52 | 47 | |
| 5. | Stade Français (Paris) | 38 | 19 | 8 | 11 | 72 | 58 | 46 | |
| 6. | Olympique de Marseille (Marseille) | 38 | 17 | 11 | 10 | 69 | 55 | 45 | |
| 7. | Red Star Olympique Audonien (Saint-Ouen) | 38 | 15 | 9 | 14 | 56 | 61 | 39 | |
| 8 | AS Cannes-Grasse (Cannes) | 38 | 17 | 4 | 17 | 57 | 66 | 38 | |
| 9. | Stade Rennais Université Club (Rennes) | 38 | 16 | 6 | 16 | 67 | 78 | 38 | |
| 10. | FC de Metz (Metz) | 38 | 12 | 13 | 13 | 93 | 75 | 37 | |
| 11. | AS de Saint-Étienne (Saint-Étienne) | 38 | 13 | 11 | 14 | 71 | 84 | 37 | |
| 12. | FC de Nancy (Nancy) | 38 | 13 | 10 | 15 | 61 | 59 | 36 | |
| 13. | FC de Sète (Sète) | 38 | 12 | 11 | 15 | 65 | 79 | 35 | |
| 14. | Toulouse FC (Toulouse) | 38 | 15 | 4 | 19 | 70 | 80 | 34 | |
| 15. | Racing Club de Paris (Paris) | 38 | 14 | 5 | 19 | 76 | 81 | 33 | |
| 16. | Stade Olympique Montpelliérain (Montpellier) | 38 | 14 | 5 | 19 | 59 | 71 | 33 | |
| 17. | Racing Club de Lens (Lens) | 38 | 12 | 7 | 19 | 67 | 72 | 31 | R |
| 18. | Girondins-AS du Port (Bordeaux) | 38 | 12 | 7 | 19 | 58 | 81 | 31 | R |
| 19. | Havre AC (Le Havre) | 38 | 9 | 7 | 22 | 44 | 83 | 25 | R |
| 20. | FC de Rouen (Rouen) | 38 | 7 | 10 | 21 | 37 | 61 | 24 | R |
| | | 760 | 304 | 152 | 304 | 1333 | 1333 | 760 | |

## Top goal-scorers

1) Pierre SINIBALDI (Stade de Reims) 33
2) KEMP (FC de Metz) 30
3) Jean BARATTE (Lille Olympique SC) 28

| Division 2 | Pd | Wn | Dw | Ls | GF | GA | Pts | |
|---|---|---|---|---|---|---|---|---|
| 1. FC Sochaux-Montbéliard (Montbéliard) | 42 | 25 | 13 | 4 | 141 | 61 | 63 | P |
| 2. Olympique Alésien (Alès) | 42 | 26 | 6 | 10 | 110 | 68 | 58 | P |
| 3. SC de l'Ouest Angers (Angers) | 42 | 24 | 8 | 10 | 98 | 55 | 56 | |
| 4. US Valenciennes-Anzin (Valenciennes) | 42 | 22 | 11 | 9 | 68 | 47 | 55 | |
| 5. Lyon Olympique Universitaire (Lyon) | 42 | 23 | 7 | 12 | 81 | 48 | 53 | |
| 6. AS des Charentes (Angoulême) | 42 | 18 | 15 | 9 | 88 | 61 | 51 | |
| 7. Sports Réunis de Colmar (Colmar) | 42 | 19 | 11 | 12 | 80 | 75 | 49 | |
| 8. FC de Nantes (Nantes) | 42 | 16 | 13 | 13 | 66 | 70 | 45 | |
| 9. Nîmes Olympique (Nîmes) | 42 | 15 | 12 | 15 | 69 | 68 | 42 | |
| 10. AS Avignonnaise (Avignon) | 42 | 18 | 6 | 18 | 75 | 81 | 42 | |
| 11. Sporting Amical Douaisien (Douai) | 42 | 13 | 15 | 14 | 62 | 60 | 41 | |
| 12. Cercle Athlétique de Paris (Paris) | 42 | 15 | 11 | 16 | 76 | 74 | 41 | |
| 13. Amiens AC (Amiens) | 42 | 15 | 8 | 19 | 63 | 77 | 38 | |
| 14. Racing Club Franc-Comtois (Besançon) | 42 | 15 | 7 | 20 | 54 | 58 | 37 | |
| 15. AS Biterroise (Beziers) | 42 | 12 | 13 | 17 | 57 | 62 | 37 | |
| 16. AS Troyenne-Savinienne (Troyes) | 42 | 11 | 15 | 16 | 59 | 68 | 37 | |
| 17. Stade Clermontois (Clermont-Ferrand) | 42 | 12 | 13 | 17 | 69 | 81 | 37 | # |
| 18. Olympique GC de Nice (Nice) | 42 | 14 | 8 | 20 | 56 | 73 | 36 | |
| 19. US du Mans (Le Mans) | 42 | 13 | 7 | 22 | 66 | 95 | 33 | |
| 20. SC de Toulon (Toulon) | 42 | 12 | 8 | 22 | 69 | 64 | 32 | R |
| 21. US Athlétiques Perpignanais (Perpignan) | 42 | 8 | 6 | 28 | 57 | 130 | 22 | R |
| 22. Olympique d'Antibes-Juan-les-Pins (Antibes) | 42 | 7 | 5 | 30 | 42 | 120 | 19 | R |
| | 924 | 353 | 218 | 353 | 1606 | 1596 | 924 | |

# Stade Clermontois (Clermont-Ferrand) reverted to amateur status for the next season.

## Coupe de France Final (Stade Yves du Manoir, Colombes – 11/05/47 – 50,852)

**LILLE OLYMPIQUE SC (LILLE)**  **2-0**  Racing Club de Strasbourg (Strasbourg)

*Vandooren 01', Lang 66' (o.g.)*

**Lille:** Germain, "Jadrejak", Sommerlynck, Dubreucq, Prévost, Bigot, Vandooren, Tempowski, Baratte, Carré, Lechantre.

**Strasbourg:** Lergenmuller, Pascual, Braun, Heine, Mateo, Lang, Heckel, Heisserer, Woehl, Vanags, Rolland.

## Semi-Finals (27/04/47)

| | | |
|---|---|---|
| Lille Olympique SC (Lille) | 3-0 | Girondins-AS du Port (Bordeaux) |
| Racing Club de Strasbourg (Strasbourg) | 6-0 | AS des Charentes (Angoulême) |

## Quarter-Finals (30/03/47)

| | | |
|---|---|---|
| AS des Charentes (Angoulême) | 2-1 | Stade de Reims (Reims) |
| Girondins-AS du Port (Bordeaux) | 3-2 | Havre AC (Le Havre) |
| Lille Olympique SC (Lille) | 3-2 | FC de Metz (Metz) |
| Racing Club de Strasbourg (Strasbourg) | 2-1 | Stade Français (Paris) |

# 1947-48

| 1947-1948 Division One | Olympique Alésien | AS Cannes-Grasse | Stade Français | Lille Olympique SC | Olympique Marseille | FC de Metz | SO Montpelliérain | FC de Nancy | Racing Club Paris | Red Star Olympique | Stade de Reims | Stade Rennais Université Club | CO Roubaix-Tourcoing | AS Saint-Étienne | FC de Sète | FC Sochaux-Montbéliard | Racing Strasbourg | Toulouse FC |
|---|---|---|---|---|---|---|---|---|---|---|---|---|---|---|---|---|---|---|
| Olympique Alésien | | 2-1 | 2-2 | 1-1 | 2-3 | 3-0 | 3-0 | 1-1 | 0-5 | 3-1 | 0-1 | 1-1 | 1-1 | 2-2 | 1-1 | 2-2 | 0-2 | 3-2 |
| AS Cannes-Grasse | 4-1 | | 2-0 | 0-2 | 0-2 | 1-1 | 1-1 | 2-1 | 4-4 | 1-0 | 0-4 | 5-2 | 1-1 | 0-3 | 1-2 | 3-0 | 2-2 | 1-0 |
| Stade Français | 3-1 | 1-4 | | 1-1 | 1-1 | 7-1 | 4-1 | 2-3 | 1-0 | 4-0 | 2-1 | 3-1 | 0-2 | 2-1 | 4-1 | 2-2 | 2-2 | 2-1 |
| Lille Olympique SC | 5-2 | 3-0 | 1-3 | | 3-0 | 3-1 | 4-1 | 4-1 | 2-1 | 2-0 | 0-0 | 1-1 | 4-0 | 0-0 | 5-3 | 6-1 | 1-1 | 3-0 |
| Olympique Marseille | 8-0 | 2-1 | 5-1 | 4-1 | | 6-3 | 2-1 | 5-0 | 4-1 | 3-0 | 1-0 | 1-1 | 6-0 | 4-1 | 4-1 | 3-1 | 1-0 | 3-2 |
| FC de Metz | 4-4 | 1-1 | 0-1 | 6-2 | 0-1 | | 1-0 | 4-3 | 2-1 | 2-0 | 1-3 | 6-1 | 0-1 | 2-2 | 4-2 | 2-0 | 4-1 | 1-0 |
| SO Montpelliérain | 1-3 | 0-2 | 6-2 | 0-1 | 1-0 | 5-2 | | 3-1 | 6-0 | 0-0 | 2-3 | 2-2 | 1-1 | 2-0 | 1-1 | 2-0 | 1-1 | 1-3 |
| FC de Nancy | 1-0 | 1-1 | 0-0 | 2-1 | 4-0 | 4-2 | 2-2 | | 1-3 | 5-1 | 1-2 | 1-0 | 0-4 | 4-0 | 2-0 | 2-1 | 3-0 | 0-0 |
| Racing Club Paris | 0-0 | 2-3 | 5-1 | 1-4 | 1-1 | 4-2 | 6-1 | 3-0 | | 2-1 | 2-1 | 2-4 | 2-1 | 2-2 | 7-1 | 2-1 | 4-2 | 2-0 |
| Red Star Olympique Audonien | 3-1 | 3-2 | 0-7 | 1-2 | 2-2 | 0-1 | 3-4 | 2-0 | 1-3 | | 0-2 | 3-5 | 1-1 | 0-5 | 1-0 | 0-0 | 0-5 | 1-2 |
| Stade de Reims | 1-0 | 3-0 | 0-3 | 2-2 | 3-0 | 4-2 | 1-0 | 5-0 | 2-2 | 1-0 | | 1-0 | 1-1 | 6-0 | 3-0 | 4-0 | 2-2 | 4-0 |
| Stade Rennais Université Club | 4-1 | 0-0 | 0-3 | 4-2 | 1-1 | 0-2 | 4-1 | 0-0 | 2-0 | 1-0 | 1-0 | | 4-4 | 1-3 | 3-0 | 0-3 | 7-1 | 2-0 |
| CO Roubaix-Tourcoing | 1-0 | 3-1 | 1-0 | 1-5 | 1-1 | 1-2 | 7-0 | 3-0 | 5-2 | 1-0 | 2-1 | 1-2 | | 0-3 | 2-4 | 3-1 | 3-2 | 1-3 |
| AS Saint-Étienne | 3-3 | 2-0 | 1-1 | 8-3 | 3-2 | 3-0 | 2-2 | 2-0 | 1-4 | 4-1 | 3-2 | 1-0 | 1-2 | | 3-1 | 2-1 | 1-1 | 4-2 |
| FC de Sète | 2-3 | 4-0 | 3-2 | 1-2 | 1-3 | 2-1 | 0-1 | 4-3 | 3-2 | 1-2 | 4-2 | 2-0 | 1-5 | 4-2 | | 1-5 | 3-2 | 2-2 |
| FC Sochaux-Montbéliard | 2-0 | 5-1 | 4-0 | 1-2 | 2-2 | 4-3 | 1-0 | 2-2 | 3-2 | 0-1 | 0-3 | 2-0 | 5-1 | 2-2 | 2-2 | | 1-0 | 4-0 |
| Racing Strasbourg | 9-3 | 8-2 | 1-1 | 2-0 | 1-1 | 8-4 | 0-1 | 1-1 | 1-2 | 3-1 | 2-2 | 6-1 | 3-0 | 2-0 | 3-1 | 2-2 | | 3-1 |
| Toulouse FC | 2-0 | 0-0 | 4-0 | 1-4 | 3-1 | 4-3 | 4-2 | 4-0 | 1-0 | 2-1 | 1-3 | 0-1 | 2-1 | 0-2 | 2-1 | 2-3 | 0-3 | |

## Division 1

| | | Pd | Wn | Dw | Ls | GF | GA | Pts | |
|---|---|---|---|---|---|---|---|---|---|
| 1. | OLYMPIQUE DE MARSEILLE (MARSEILLE) | 34 | 20 | 8 | 6 | 83 | 43 | 48 | |
| 2. | Lille Olympique SC (Lille) | 34 | 20 | 7 | 7 | 82 | 51 | 47 | |
| 3. | Stade de Reims (Reims) | 34 | 20 | 6 | 8 | 73 | 34 | 46 | |
| 4. | AS de Saint-Étienne (Saint-Étienne) | 34 | 16 | 9 | 9 | 72 | 58 | 41 | |
| 5. | Stade Français (Paris) | 34 | 15 | 8 | 11 | 68 | 58 | 38 | * |
| 6. | Racing Club de Strasbourg (Strasbourg) | 34 | 13 | 11 | 10 | 82 | 58 | 37 | |
| 7. | Racing Club de Paris (Paris) | 34 | 16 | 5 | 13 | 79 | 64 | 37 | |
| 8. | Club Olympique Roubaix-Tourcoing (Roubaix) | 34 | 15 | 7 | 12 | 62 | 60 | 37 | |
| 9. | FC Sochaux-Montbéliard (Montbéliard) | 34 | 13 | 8 | 13 | 63 | 59 | 34 | |
| 10. | Stade Rennais Université Club (Rennes) | 34 | 13 | 8 | 13 | 56 | 59 | 34 | |
| 11. | FC de Metz (Metz) | 34 | 13 | 4 | 17 | 70 | 82 | 30 | |
| 12. | FC de Nancy (Nancy) | 34 | 11 | 8 | 15 | 49 | 64 | 30 | |
| 13. | Toulouse FC (Toulouse) | 34 | 13 | 3 | 18 | 50 | 62 | 29 | |
| 14. | AS Cannes-Grasse (Cannes) | 34 | 10 | 9 | 15 | 47 | 66 | 29 | |
| 15. | Stade Olympique Montpelliérain (Montpellier) | 34 | 10 | 8 | 16 | 52 | 67 | 28 | |
| 16. | FC de Sète (Sète) | 34 | 11 | 4 | 19 | 59 | 85 | 26 | |
| 17. | Olympique Alésien (Alès) | 34 | 7 | 11 | 16 | 49 | 79 | 25 | R |
| 18. | Red Star Olympique Audonien (Saint-Ouen) | 34 | 6 | 4 | 24 | 30 | 77 | 16 | R* |
| | | 612 | 242 | 128 | 242 | 1126 | 1126 | 612 | |

## Top goal-scorers

1) Jean BARATTE          (Lille Olympique SC)     31
2) Pierre SINIBALDI       (Stade de Reims)         25
3) Boleslav TEMPOWSKI   (Lille Olympique SC)     23

\* Red Star Olympique Audonien (Saint-Ouen) merged with Stade Français (Paris) to become Stade Français-Red Star (Paris) for the next season.

| | Division 2 | Pd | Wn | Dw | Ls | GF | GA | Pts | |
|---|---|---|---|---|---|---|---|---|---|
| 1. | Olympique GC de Nice (Nice) | 38 | 26 | 6 | 6 | 109 | 36 | 58 | P |
| 2. | Sports Réunis de Colmar (Colmar) | 38 | 23 | 6 | 9 | 83 | 43 | 52 | P |
| 3. | Havre AC (Le Havre) | 38 | 22 | 6 | 10 | 77 | 40 | 50 | |
| 4. | FC de Rouen (Rouen) | 38 | 19 | 11 | 8 | 69 | 42 | 49 | |
| 5. | Girondins-AS du Port (Bordeaux) | 38 | 18 | 9 | 11 | 77 | 47 | 45 | |
| 6. | Lyon Olympique Universitaire (Lyon) | 38 | 19 | 5 | 14 | 71 | 59 | 43 | |
| 7. | SC de l'Ouest Angers (Angers) | 38 | 19 | 5 | 14 | 70 | 64 | 43 | |
| 8. | Racing Club de Lens (Lens) | 38 | 15 | 11 | 12 | 71 | 52 | 41 | |
| 9. | Amiens AC (Amiens) | 38 | 18 | 5 | 15 | 70 | 72 | 41 | |
| 10. | US Valenciennes-Anzin (Valenciennes) | 38 | 16 | 8 | 14 | 76 | 63 | 40 | |
| 11. | FC de Nantes (Nantes) | 38 | 16 | 6 | 16 | 79 | 81 | 38 | |
| 12. | Racing Club Franc-Comtois (Besançon) | 38 | 15 | 7 | 16 | 69 | 72 | 37 | |
| 13. | Nîmes Olympique (Nîmes) | 38 | 13 | 9 | 16 | 68 | 67 | 35 | |
| 14. | Sporting Amical Douaisien (Douai) | 38 | 13 | 7 | 18 | 56 | 84 | 33 | |
| 15. | AS d'Angoulême (Angoulême) | 38 | 11 | 7 | 20 | 58 | 106 | 29 | * |
| 16. | AS Biterroise (Beziers) | 38 | 9 | 10 | 19 | 52 | 79 | 28 | |
| 17. | AS Troyenne-Savinienne (Troyes) | 38 | 9 | 9 | 20 | 56 | 101 | 27 | |
| 18. | US du Mans (Le Mans) | 38 | 8 | 9 | 21 | 50 | 74 | 25 | |
| 19. | Cercle Athlétique de Paris (Paris) | 38 | 10 | 4 | 24 | 60 | 77 | 24 | |
| 20. | Olympique Avignonnais (Avignon) | 38 | 9 | 4 | 25 | 42 | 101 | 22 | R# |
| | | 760 | 308 | 144 | 308 | 1363 | 1360 | 760 | |

\* Olympique Avignonnais (Avignon) reverted to amateur status for the next season.
**Elected:** AS de Monaco (Monaco) and SC de Toulon (Toulon)

## Coupe de France Final   (Stade Yves du Manoir, Colombes – 10/05/48 – 60,739)

**LILLE OLYMPIQUE SC (LILLE)**          **3-2**          Racing Club de Lens (Lens)

*Vandooren 23', Baratte 52', 86'*                                *Stanis 39', 77'*

**Lille:** Witkowski, "Jadrejak", Sommerlynck, Dubreucq, Prévost, Bigot, Vandooren, Tempowski, Baratte, Carré Lechantre.

**Lens:** Duffuler, Gouillard, Mellul, "Siklo", Golinski, Ourdouillé, Mankowski, "Marresch", "Stanis", Pachurka, Habera.

## Semi-Finals   (18/04/48)

| | | |
|---|---|---|
| Lille Olympique SC (Lille) | 2-1 | FC de Nancy (Nancy) |
| Racing Club de Lens (Lens) | 5-1 | Sports Réunis de Colmar (Colmar) |

## Quarter-Finals   (21/03/48)

| | | |
|---|---|---|
| Sports Réunis de Colmar (Colmar) | 1-0 | Girondins-AS du Port (Bordeaux) |
| Racing Club de Lens (Lens) | 2-1 | Stade Français (Paris) |
| Lille Olympique SC (Lille) | 3-3, 2-1 | Racing Club de Paris (Paris) |
| FC de Nancy (Nancy) | 4-1 | FC Sochaux-Montbéliard (Montbéliard) |

# 1948-49

| 1948-1949 Division One | AS Cannes-Grasse | SR de Colmar | Stade Français-RS | Lille Olympique SC | Olympique Marseille | FC de Metz | SO Montpelliérain | FC de Nancy | Olympique GC Nice | Racing Club Paris | Stade de Reims | Stade Rennais Université Club | CO Roubaix-Tourcoing | AS Saint-Étienne | FC de Sète | FC Sochaux-Montbéliard | Racing Strasbourg | Toulouse FC |
|---|---|---|---|---|---|---|---|---|---|---|---|---|---|---|---|---|---|---|
| AS Cannes-Grasse | ■ | 4-2 | 4-1 | 1-6 | 1-0 | 1-1 | 3-0 | 4-1 | 1-2 | 2-1 | 1-3 | 1-1 | 3-0 | 1-0 | 0-2 | 1-1 | 1-1 | 2-1 |
| SR de Colmar | 1-1 | ■ | 3-0 | 2-2 | 1-1 | 5-1 | 1-3 | 0-2 | 1-2 | 3-0 | 3-3 | 2-2 | 5-0 | 3-1 | 5-1 | 0-3 | 2-1 | 2-0 |
| Stade Français-RS | 6-3 | 5-2 | ■ | 1-0 | 1-0 | 2-6 | 3-0 | 3-3 | 1-1 | 1-0 | 3-5 | 0-0 | 1-1 | 4-1 | 2-2 | 2-2 | 1-1 | 3-1 |
| Lille Olympique SC | 2-0 | 8-0 | 2-1 | ■ | 2-2 | 5-0 | 5-0 | 4-0 | 4-1 | 2-3 | 2-1 | 3-0 | 6-2 | 5-0 | 6-1 | 3-1 | 1-2 | 1-1 |
| Olympique Marseille | 1-0 | 7-2 | 1-1 | 2-1 | ■ | 4-2 | 6-3 | 3-1 | 2-2 | 3-0 | 3-4 | 1-3 | 4-2 | 6-1 | 3-1 | 3-1 | 5-0 | 4-0 |
| FC de Metz | 2-1 | 2-0 | 2-3 | 3-1 | 1-4 | ■ | 2-2 | 2-0 | 2-2 | 1-2 | 2-3 | 1-6 | 3-0 | 2-0 | 0-2 | 4-1 | 3-0 | 2-1 |
| SO Montpelliérain | 1-3 | 0-1 | 6-1 | 2-1 | 1-2 | 4-1 | ■ | 3-4 | 1-1 | 0-4 | 0-1 | 2-1 | 4-1 | 2-2 | 1-0 | 2-1 | 2-0 | 2-1 |
| FC de Nancy | 1-0 | 1-2 | 3-1 | 0-1 | 3-2 | 2-1 | 1-0 | ■ | 1-1 | 3-1 | 0-1 | 1-2 | 1-2 | 4-2 | 3-0 | 2-2 | 3-3 | 2-0 |
| Olympique GC Nice | 2-0 | 2-0 | 2-2 | 1-2 | 0-5 | 5-2 | 0-0 | 0-0 | ■ | 3-0 | 2-2 | 8-0 | 4-2 | 1-0 | 4-1 | 5-4 | 1-0 | 2-1 |
| Racing Club Paris | 3-0 | 3-3 | 4-0 | 4-3 | 5-4 | 2-2 | 1-1 | 5-1 | 1-1 | ■ | 3-1 | 2-3 | 1-1 | 1-2 | 5-1 | 0-1 | 4-2 | 5-0 |
| Stade de Reims | 5-2 | 1-2 | 4-0 | 2-4 | 2-0 | 6-1 | 6-4 | 3-3 | 6-1 | 1-0 | ■ | 4-2 | 1-0 | 2-3 | 2-0 | 2-2 | 3-0 | 2-0 |
| Stade Rennais Université Club | 1-0 | 2-0 | 1-1 | 1-1 | 6-1 | 4-3 | 3-0 | 4-0 | 2-0 | 0-0 | 1-0 | ■ | 3-1 | 1-3 | 3-1 | 1-0 | 1-1 | 2-0 |
| CO Roubaix-Tourcoing | 4-0 | 3-2 | 2-2 | 1-4 | 2-10 | 2-2 | 2-3 | 3-1 | 2-1 | 2-2 | 1-5 | 3-2 | ■ | 2-2 | 2-1 | 5-1 | 1-0 | 3-1 |
| AS Saint-Étienne | 3-1 | 5-2 | 2-2 | 2-2 | 4-1 | 3-1 | 0-4 | 4-1 | 2-0 | 3-3 | 2-3 | 1-1 | 6-0 | ■ | 0-0 | 1-1 | 5-1 | 4-2 |
| FC de Sète | 1-0 | 3-4 | 1-0 | 1-0 | 1-1 | 1-1 | 2-1 | 1-0 | 3-2 | 0-2 | 1-2 | 0-0 | 0-0 | 1-1 | ■ | 3-0 | 0-1 | 0-0 |
| FC Sochaux-Montbéliard | 4-0 | 2-0 | 0-2 | 1-3 | 1-1 | 2-1 | 4-2 | 3-2 | 2-0 | 1-2 | 3-0 | 3-1 | 5-1 | 6-0 | 7-0 | ■ | 3-0 | 3-0 |
| Racing Strasbourg | 1-0 | 0-0 | 3-2 | 0-6 | 1-2 | 2-1 | 3-0 | 4-2 | 3-1 | 3-1 | 1-4 | 3-0 | 1-2 | 1-2 | 0-0 | 0-3 | ■ | 0-1 |
| Toulouse FC | 1-0 | 7-0 | 4-1 | 1-4 | 2-1 | 1-0 | 4-1 | 2-1 | 3-0 | 2-1 | 2-0 | 2-1 | 2-0 | 5-1 | 0-2 | 3-0 | 5-1 | ■ |

## Division 1

| | | Pd | Wn | Dw | Ls | GF | GA | Pts | |
|---|---|---|---|---|---|---|---|---|---|
| 1. | STADE DE REIMS (REIMS) | 34 | 22 | 4 | 8 | 90 | 54 | 48 | |
| 2. | Lille Olympique SC (Lille) | 34 | 21 | 5 | 8 | 102 | 40 | 47 | |
| 3. | Olympique de Marseille (Marseille) | 34 | 18 | 6 | 10 | 95 | 58 | 42 | |
| 4. | Stade Rennais Université Club (Rennes) | 34 | 16 | 9 | 9 | 61 | 49 | 41 | |
| 5. | FC Sochaux-Montbéliard (Montbéliard) | 34 | 16 | 6 | 12 | 74 | 52 | 38 | |
| 6. | Racing Club de Paris (Paris) | 34 | 14 | 8 | 12 | 71 | 56 | 36 | |
| 7. | Olympique GC de Nice (Nice) | 34 | 13 | 10 | 11 | 60 | 58 | 36 | |
| 8. | AS de Saint-Étienne (Saint-Étienne) | 34 | 13 | 9 | 12 | 68 | 72 | 35 | |
| 9. | Toulouse FC (Toulouse) | 34 | 16 | 2 | 16 | 56 | 53 | 34 | |
| 10. | Stade Français-Red Star (Paris) | 34 | 10 | 12 | 12 | 59 | 72 | 32 | |
| 11. | Sports Réunis de Colmar (Colmar) | 34 | 12 | 7 | 15 | 61 | 78 | 31 | # |
| 12. | Stade Olympique Montpelliérain (Montpellier) | 34 | 12 | 5 | 17 | 57 | 71 | 29 | |
| 13. | Club Olympique Roubaix-Tourcoing (Roubaix) | 34 | 11 | 7 | 16 | 55 | 89 | 29 | |
| 14. | FC de Sète (Sète) | 34 | 10 | 9 | 15 | 34 | 58 | 29 | |
| 15. | FC de Nancy (Nancy) | 34 | 11 | 6 | 17 | 53 | 69 | 28 | |
| 16. | FC de Metz (Metz) | 34 | 10 | 6 | 18 | 60 | 79 | 26 | |
| 17. | Racing Club de Strasbourg (Strasbourg) | 34 | 10 | 6 | 18 | 40 | 68 | 26 | R# |
| 18. | AS Cannes-Grasse (Cannes) | 34 | 10 | 5 | 19 | 42 | 62 | 25 | R |
| | | 612 | 245 | 122 | 245 | 1138 | 1138 | 612 | |

## Top goal-scorers

1) Jean BARATTE (Lille Olympique SC) 26
   Jozsef "Pepi" HUMPAL (FC Sochaux-Montbéliard) 26
3) Henri BAILLOT (Lille Olympique SC) 25

# Sports Réunis de Colmar (Colmar) reverted to amateur status for the next season. As a result of this Racing Club de Strasbourg (Strasbourg) retained their Division 1 status.

| | Division 2 | Pd | Wn | Dw | Ls | GF | GA | Pts | |
|---|---|---|---|---|---|---|---|---|---|
| 1. | Racing Club de Lens (Lens) | 36 | 21 | 11 | 4 | 64 | 27 | 53 | P |
| 2. | Girondins-AS du Port (Bordeaux) | 36 | 24 | 5 | 7 | 107 | 49 | 53 | P |
| 3. | FC de Rouen (Rouen) | 36 | 20 | 11 | 5 | 67 | 37 | 51 | |
| 4. | Havre AC (Le Havre) | 36 | 19 | 10 | 7 | 64 | 30 | 48 | |
| 5. | Nîmes Olympique (Nîmes) | 36 | 16 | 10 | 10 | 89 | 51 | 42 | |
| 6. | Olympique Alésien (Alès) | 36 | 16 | 10 | 10 | 76 | 57 | 42 | |
| 7. | Racing Club Franc-Comtois (Besançon) | 36 | 15 | 10 | 11 | 81 | 59 | 40 | |
| 8. | AS de Monaco (Monaco) | 36 | 17 | 4 | 15 | 70 | 62 | 38 | |
| 9. | FC de Nantes (Nantes) | 36 | 13 | 12 | 11 | 58 | 53 | 38 | |
| 10. | Lyon Olympique Universitaire (Lyon) | 36 | 16 | 6 | 14 | 65 | 72 | 38 | |
| 11. | SC de l'Ouest Angers (Angers) | 36 | 11 | 15 | 10 | 61 | 49 | 37 | |
| 12. | AS Biterroise (Beziers) | 36 | 13 | 5 | 18 | 58 | 65 | 31 | |
| 13. | SC de Toulon (Toulon) | 36 | 11 | 8 | 17 | 54 | 70 | 30 | |
| 14. | Amiens AC (Amiens) | 36 | 12 | 5 | 19 | 46 | 70 | 29 | |
| 15. | US du Mans (Le Mans) | 36 | 11 | 6 | 19 | 60 | 92 | 28 | |
| 16. | AS Troyenne-Savinienne (Troyes) | 36 | 9 | 7 | 20 | 52 | 90 | 25 | |
| 17. | US Valenciennes-Anzin (Valenciennes) | 36 | 8 | 8 | 20 | 38 | 76 | 24 | |
| 18. | Cercle Athlétique de Paris (Paris) | 36 | 5 | 10 | 21 | 35 | 82 | 20 | |
| 19. | Sporting Amical Douaisien (Douai) | 36 | 5 | 7 | 24 | 36 | 90 | 17 | R# |
| | | 684 | 262 | 160 | 262 | 1181 | 1181 | 684 | |

# Sporting Amical Douaisien (Douai) reverted to amateur status for the next season.

**Elected:** Group Sporting Club de Marseille "2" (Marseille).

## Coupe de France Final (Stade Yves du Manoir, Colombes – 08/05/49 – 61,473)

**RACING CLUB DE PARIS (PARIS)**  **5-2**  Lille Olympique SC (Lille)

*Gabet 28', 35', Quenolle 30', Vaast 52', "Jadrejak" 59' (o.g.)*  *Lechantre 74', Strappe 83'*

**Racing:** Vignal, Arens, Salva, Grizzetti, Lamy, Leduc, Gabet, Tessier, Quenolle, Vaast, Moreel.
**Lille:** Witkowski, "Jadrejak", Nuevo, Dubreucq, Prévost, Carré, Walter, Vandooren, Baratte, Strappe, Lechantre.

## Semi-Finals (10/04/49)

| Lille Olympique SC (Lille) | 1-0 | Stade Français-Red Star (Paris) |
|---|---|---|
| Racing Club de Paris (Paris) | 2-2, 2-0 | FC de Metz (Metz) |

## Quarter-Finals (20/03/49)

| Stade Français-Red Star (Paris) | 3-1 | FC de Sète (Sète) |
|---|---|---|
| Lille Olympique SC (Lille) | 2-1 | Olympique GC de Nice (Nice) |
| FC de Metz (Metz) | 6-0 | Racing Club d'Arras (Arras) |
| Racing Club de Paris (Paris) | 2-1 | Nîmes Olympique (Nîmes) |

# 1949-50

| 1949-1950 Division One | Girondins Bordeaux | Stade Français-RS | Racing Club de Lens | Lille Olympique SC | Olympique Marseille | FC de Metz | SO Montpelliérain | FC de Nancy | Olympique GC Nice | Racing Club de Paris | Stade de Reims | Stade Rennais Université Club | CO Roubaix-Tourcoing | AS de Saint-Étienne | FC de Sète | Sochaux-Montbéliard | Racing Strasbourg | Toulouse FC |
|---|---|---|---|---|---|---|---|---|---|---|---|---|---|---|---|---|---|---|
| Girondins Bordeaux | ■ | 2-1 | 5-1 | 1-1 | 3-1 | 1-1 | 7-0 | 5-0 | 2-1 | 4-0 | 4-0 | 2-1 | 4-2 | 5-2 | 4-2 | 2-1 | 6-0 | 1-2 |
| Stade Français-RS | 0-4 | ■ | 4-3 | 1-1 | 1-1 | 5-0 | 1-2 | 0-4 | 0-2 | 2-1 | 2-0 | 3-1 | 2-2 | 2-2 | 4-0 | 2-5 | 0-0 | 1-3 |
| Racing Club de Lens | 1-3 | 2-1 | ■ | 1-0 | 1-2 | 5-3 | 3-0 | 2-1 | 2-1 | 0-0 | 0-0 | 3-3 | 3-2 | 2-4 | 2-3 | 1-2 | 1-2 | 0-3 |
| Lille Olympique SC | 4-2 | 5-1 | 4-1 | ■ | 1-2 | 2-1 | 5-0 | 2-1 | 4-1 | 2-2 | 4-0 | 1-0 | 0-0 | 3-1 | 3-2 | 2-0 | 7-1 | 4-1 |
| Olympique Marseille | 3-0 | 2-1 | 1-4 | 2-3 | ■ | 4-0 | 3-2 | 1-2 | 1-0 | 1-1 | 2-2 | 3-1 | 2-0 | 2-0 | 3-4 | 3-0 | 2-2 | 2-2 |
| FC de Metz | 2-3 | 1-1 | 1-1 | 0-0 | 1-3 | ■ | 5-2 | 3-0 | 0-3 | 1-4 | 2-4 | 1-2 | 2-2 | 1-4 | 1-1 | 0-2 | 6-3 | 1-4 |
| SO Montpelliérain | 0-1 | 1-2 | 4-2 | 4-3 | 1-0 | 5-2 | ■ | 2-1 | 2-2 | 3-1 | 0-1 | 5-6 | 0-1 | 1-1 | 3-2 | 1-4 | 3-0 | 1-0 |
| FC de Nancy | 0-0 | 1-1 | 0-0 | 0-1 | 4-0 | 7-2 | 2-1 | ■ | 2-2 | 1-1 | 0-2 | 3-1 | 2-2 | 2-1 | 4-0 | 0-0 | 1-2 | 2-1 |
| Olympique GC Nice | 3-2 | 3-0 | 1-1 | 3-2 | 6-4 | 0-2 | 1-0 | 4-0 | ■ | 1-4 | 1-1 | 2-1 | 3-2 | 1-1 | 5-0 | 5-0 | 5-1 | 0-5 |
| Racing Club de Paris | 3-4 | 2-1 | 1-2 | 3-1 | 5-0 | 2-2 | 6-0 | 4-1 | 1-2 | ■ | 2-4 | 1-2 | 4-3 | 2-1 | 2-1 | 3-0 | 1-1 | |
| Stade de Reims | 0-2 | 0-3 | 5-0 | 2-1 | 2-0 | 6-2 | 2-1 | 1-0 | 1-1 | 3-2 | ■ | 3-1 | 2-1 | 0-0 | 2-1 | 5-3 | 6-1 | 1-0 |
| Stade Rennais Université Club | 0-0 | 5-0 | 1-1 | 0-3 | 1-1 | 3-1 | 5-1 | 2-1 | 5-2 | 1-2 | 1-1 | ■ | 1-1 | 3-1 | 4-2 | 1-2 | 1-1 | 0-0 |
| CO Roubaix-Tourcoing | 0-0 | 2-2 | 1-0 | 1-2 | 1-1 | 3-1 | 4-0 | 0-1 | 1-0 | 1-3 | 1-1 | 2-2 | ■ | 2-0 | 3-1 | 0-2 | 2-0 | 0-1 |
| AS de Saint-Étienne | 1-1 | 2-0 | 2-0 | 3-4 | 2-0 | 1-3 | 5-1 | 3-5 | 2-0 | 1-1 | 1-2 | 2-2 | 0-0 | ■ | 1-0 | 1-0 | 5-0 | 3-0 |
| FC de Sète | 2-2 | 3-2 | 3-1 | 0-2 | 1-2 | 4-1 | 2-0 | 4-0 | 1-0 | 5-0 | 3-1 | 0-1 | 3-3 | 2-0 | ■ | 1-2 | 2-1 | 1-1 |
| Sochaux-Montbéliard | 3-3 | 1-2 | 1-0 | 3-1 | 4-0 | 3-1 | 2-2 | 3-4 | 0-3 | 0-2 | 2-0 | 2-1 | 1-1 | 6-2 | 8-1 | ■ | 0-0 | 1-2 |
| Racing Strasbourg | 1-1 | 3-1 | 3-2 | 2-1 | 1-1 | 2-1 | 2-1 | 3-0 | 0-0 | 2-0 | 2-1 | 2-3 | 2-4 | 1-3 | 1-1 | 0-1 | ■ | 4-1 |
| Toulouse FC | 1-2 | 5-2 | 1-1 | 2-0 | 1-1 | 8-2 | 3-1 | 2-0 | 2-3 | 2-0 | 1-1 | 3-2 | 1-1 | 2-0 | 3-1 | 0-0 | 1-1 | ■ |

## Division 1

| | | Pd | Wn | Dw | Ls | GF | GA | Pts | |
|---|---|---|---|---|---|---|---|---|---|
| 1. | GIRONDINS DE BORDEAUX FC (BORDEAUX) | 34 | 21 | 9 | 4 | 88 | 40 | 51 | * |
| 2. | Lille Olympique SC (Lille) | 34 | 20 | 5 | 9 | 79 | 44 | 45 | |
| 3. | Stade de Reims (Reims) | 34 | 18 | 8 | 8 | 62 | 47 | 44 | |
| 4. | Toulouse FC (Toulouse) | 34 | 16 | 10 | 8 | 65 | 41 | 42 | |
| 5. | Olympique GC de Nice (Nice) | 34 | 16 | 7 | 11 | 67 | 52 | 39 | |
| 6. | FC Sochaux-Montbéliard (Montbéliard) | 34 | 16 | 6 | 12 | 65 | 51 | 38 | |
| 7. | Racing Club de Paris (Paris) | 34 | 14 | 8 | 12 | 67 | 56 | 36 | |
| 8. | Olympique de Marseille (Marseille) | 34 | 13 | 9 | 12 | 56 | 60 | 35 | |
| 9. | Stade Rennais Université Club (Rennes) | 34 | 12 | 10 | 12 | 64 | 58 | 34 | |
| 10. | Club Olympique Roubaix-Tourcoing (Roubaix) | 34 | 9 | 15 | 10 | 49 | 46 | 33 | |
| 11. | AS de Saint-Étienne (Saint-Étienne) | 34 | 12 | 8 | 14 | 60 | 58 | 32 | |
| 12. | FC de Nancy (Nancy) | 34 | 12 | 7 | 15 | 52 | 58 | 31 | |
| 13. | Racing Club de Strasbourg (Strasbourg) | 34 | 11 | 9 | 14 | 46 | 73 | 31 | |
| 14. | FC de Sète (Sète) | 34 | 12 | 5 | 17 | 59 | 72 | 29 | |
| 15. | Racing Club de Lens (Lens) | 34 | 9 | 8 | 17 | 49 | 68 | 26 | |
| 16. | Stade Français-Red Star (Paris) | 34 | 9 | 8 | 17 | 51 | 71 | 26 | * |
| 17. | Stade Olympique Montpelliérain (Montpellier) | 34 | 10 | 3 | 21 | 50 | 87 | 23 | R |
| 18. | FC de Metz (Metz) | 34 | 5 | 7 | 22 | 53 | 100 | 17 | R |
| | | 612 | 235 | 142 | 235 | 1082 | 1082 | 612 | |

## Top goal-scorers

| | | | |
|---|---|---|---|
| 1) | Jean GRUMELLON | (Stade Rennais FC) | 24 |
| 2) | Jean BARATTE | (Lille Olympique SC) | 22 |
| 3) | Bertus DE HARDER | (Girondins de Bordeaux FC) | 21 |

\* Girondins de Bordeaux FC (Bordeaux) changed their name pre-season from Girondins-AS du Port (Bordeaux).

Stade Français-Red Star (Paris) dissolved and re-formed as Stade Français FC (Paris) (playing in Division 1) and Red Star Olympique Audonien (Saint-Ouen) (playing in Division 3) for the next season.

| | Division 2 | Pd | Wn | Dw | Ls | GF | GA | Pts | |
|---|---|---|---|---|---|---|---|---|---|
| 1. | Nîmes Olympique (Nîmes) | 34 | 25 | 7 | 2 | 87 | 28 | 57 | P |
| 2. | Havre AC (Le Havre) | 34 | 24 | 5 | 5 | 85 | 25 | 53 | P |
| 3. | AS Cannes-Grasse (Cannes) | 34 | 17 | 7 | 10 | 65 | 40 | 41 | |
| 4. | AS Biterroise (Béziers) | 34 | 12 | 13 | 9 | 57 | 53 | 37 | |
| 5. | FC de Rouen (Rouen) | 34 | 13 | 10 | 11 | 56 | 45 | 36 | |
| 6. | US Valenciennes-Anzin (Valenciennes) | 34 | 15 | 6 | 13 | 52 | 64 | 36 | |
| 7. | Lyon Olympique Universitaire (Lyon) | 34 | 14 | 7 | 13 | 48 | 51 | 35 | |
| 8. | Olympique Alésien (Alès) | 34 | 13 | 8 | 13 | 52 | 52 | 34 | |
| 9. | Amiens AC (Amiens) | 34 | 13 | 7 | 14 | 55 | 54 | 33 | |
| 10. | SC de Toulon (Toulon) | 34 | 11 | 11 | 12 | 52 | 60 | 33 | |
| 11. | Group Sporting Club de Marseille "2" (Marseille) | 34 | 12 | 7 | 15 | 47 | 61 | 31 | |
| 12. | US du Mans (Le Mans) | 34 | 11 | 8 | 15 | 48 | 53 | 30 | |
| 13. | Racing Club Franc-Comtois (Besançon) | 34 | 13 | 4 | 17 | 46 | 53 | 30 | |
| 14. | AS Troyenne-Savinienne (Troyes) | 34 | 9 | 12 | 13 | 38 | 62 | 30 | |
| 15. | SC de l'Ouest Angers (Angers) | 34 | 11 | 7 | 16 | 46 | 57 | 29 | |
| 16. | AS de Monaco (Monaco) | 34 | 11 | 7 | 16 | 40 | 53 | 29 | |
| 17. | FC de Nantes (Nantes | 34 | 9 | 9 | 16 | 44 | 57 | 27 | |
| 18. | Cercle Athlétique de Paris (Paris) | 34 | 3 | 5 | 26 | 36 | 86 | 11 | |
| | | 612 | 236 | 140 | 236 | 954 | 954 | 612 | |

## Coupe de France Final   (Stade Yves du Manoir, Colombes – 14/05/50 – 61,722)

| STADE DE REIMS (REIMS) | 2-0 | Racing Club de Paris (Paris) |
|---|---|---|

*Meano 81', Petitfils 83'*

**Reims:** Paul Sinibaldi, Jacowski, Marché, Penverne, Jonquet, Bini, Batteux, F lamion, Apell, Petitfils, Meano.
**Racing:** Vignal, Grillon, Salva, Gabet, Lamy, Nikitis, Courteaux, Tessier, Quenolle, Gudmundsson, Vaast.

## Semi-Finals   (16/04/50)

| Racing Club de Paris (Paris) | 3-0 | Nîmes Olympique (Nîmes) |
|---|---|---|
| Stade de Reims (Reims) | 6-2 | AS Troyenne-Savinienne (Troyes) |

## Quarter-Finals   (19/03/50)

| Nîmes Olympique (Nîmes) | 4-3 | FC Sochaux-Montbéliard (Montbéliard) |
|---|---|---|
| Racing Club de Paris (Paris) | 2-0 | Lille Olympique SC (Lille) |
| Stade de Reims (Reims) | 2-0 | Union Athlétique Sedan-Torcy (Sedan) |
| AS Troyenne-Savinienne (Troyes) | 3-2 | Racing Club Franc-Comtois (Besançon) |

# 1950-51

| 1950-1951 Division One | Girondins Bordeaux | Stade Français FC | Havre AC | Racing Club de Lens | Lille Olympique SC | Olympique Marseille | FC de Nancy | Olympique FC Nice | Nîmes Olympique | Racing Club de Paris | Stade de Reims | Stade Rennais Université Club | CO Roubaix-Tourcoing | AS Saint-Étienne | FC de Sète | Sochaux-Montbéliard | Racing Strasbourg | Toulouse FC |
|---|---|---|---|---|---|---|---|---|---|---|---|---|---|---|---|---|---|---|
| Girondins Bordeaux | ■ | 4-1 | 0-1 | 4-0 | 1-3 | 0-0 | 3-1 | 2-0 | 2-1 | 0-3 | 2-4 | 1-1 | 2-2 | 1-0 | 4-0 | 3-1 | 3-0 | 3-1 |
| Stade Français FC | 1-2 | ■ | 1-0 | 2-2 | 0-2 | 2-4 | 1-4 | 0-4 | 2-3 | 0-3 | 1-1 | 6-0 | 1-0 | 4-0 | 3-2 | 0-3 | 0-0 | 1-2 |
| Havre AC | 2-2 | 3-0 | ■ | 4-1 | 0-1 | 1-0 | 1-1 | 4-1 | 2-4 | 2-0 | 3-0 | 3-1 | 1-0 | 4-1 | 1-0 | 3-1 | 0-1 | 2-2 |
| Racing Club de Lens | 1-1 | 5-0 | 2-1 | ■ | 2-1 | 1-1 | 0-2 | 2-0 | 4-2 | 1-1 | 2-1 | 1-2 | 4-4 | 2-3 | 3-0 | 3-1 | 1-1 | 2-2 |
| Lille Olympique SC | 3-0 | 1-1 | 1-0 | 5-0 | ■ | 2-1 | 0-0 | 1-3 | 1-0 | 1-1 | 1-1 | 2-0 | 0-1 | 4-3 | 3-1 | 2-1 | 3-1 | 2-0 |
| Olympique Marseille | 3-3 | 0-0 | 3-1 | 3-0 | 1-1 | ■ | 2-1 | 3-0 | 1-1 | 4-2 | 0-2 | 1-1 | 1-2 | 7-0 | 1-2 | 0-0 | 2-2 | 3-1 |
| FC de Nancy | 2-2 | 2-1 | 6-1 | 4-2 | 1-2 | 5-1 | ■ | 1-2 | 3-0 | 0-1 | 0-2 | 3-2 | 2-1 | 4-2 | 2-2 | 3-4 | 2-1 | 0-3 |
| Olympique FC Nice | 4-1 | 5-1 | 0-0 | 5-0 | 4-1 | 2-2 | 5-0 | ■ | 2-0 | 3-0 | 1-2 | 3-6 | 3-0 | 0-0 | 2-1 | 2-1 | 4-1 | 2-1 |
| Nîmes Olympique | 2-2 | 6-2 | 2-3 | 5-3 | 2-4 | 2-1 | 3-0 | 1-1 | ■ | 4-2 | 3-0 | 3-0 | 2-1 | 1-0 | 1-0 | 3-3 | 1-0 | 3-1 |
| Racing Club de Paris | 1-0 | 1-1 | 2-3 | 1-3 | 2-0 | 1-1 | 2-0 | 0-3 | 0-2 | ■ | 0-0 | 4-2 | 1-2 | 2-2 | 3-2 | 4-1 | 2-4 | 1-1 |
| Stade de Reims | 2-3 | 2-0 | 2-0 | 4-2 | 4-3 | 1-1 | 2-2 | 2-4 | 1-1 | 2-2 | ■ | 0-1 | 3-1 | 0-0 | 3-1 | 3-1 | 3-1 | 4-1 |
| Stade Rennais Université Club | 4-2 | 1-3 | 0-4 | 1-2 | 0-0 | 2-1 | 3-5 | 3-1 | 1-2 | 3-4 | 2-2 | ■ | 4-1 | 6-0 | 2-0 | 2-1 | 2-4 | 6-0 |
| CO Roubaix-Tourcoing | 1-1 | 3-1 | 2-3 | 4-1 | 3-0 | 1-1 | 3-0 | 0-0 | 2-0 | 1-4 | 2-1 | 3-0 | ■ | 2-2 | 6-0 | 1-2 | 0-1 | 3-2 |
| AS Saint-Étienne | 1-0 | 3-0 | 1-0 | 4-1 | 5-1 | 1-2 | 3-1 | 3-2 | 1-1 | 2-1 | 1-1 | 3-0 | 3-0 | ■ | 0-2 | 3-0 | 1-1 | 4-0 |
| FC de Sète | 1-0 | 2-0 | 1-2 | 1-1 | 1-1 | 3-1 | 2-1 | 2-1 | 1-1 | 5-1 | 5-2 | 1-2 | 2-0 | 4-1 | ■ | 1-1 | 2-1 | 0-1 |
| Sochaux-Montbéliard | 1-0 | 0-1 | 1-0 | 3-2 | 0-4 | 1-2 | 3-3 | 3-2 | 4-0 | 0-1 | 2-0 | 2-2 | 1-1 | 0-2 | 1-0 | ■ | 5-0 | 2-1 |
| Racing Strasbourg | 0-2 | 2-1 | 1-4 | 1-1 | 1-0 | 2-2 | 1-5 | 2-1 | 2-1 | 3-0 | 0-1 | 1-0 | 3-1 | 2-6 | 1-0 | 2-0 | ■ | 6-1 |
| Toulouse FC | 1-2 | 0-0 | 2-0 | 3-2 | 2-1 | 0-4 | 3-0 | 0-1 | 1-1 | 1-0 | 1-3 | 0-1 | 1-1 | 3-2 | 0-0 | 0-2 | 1-0 | ■ |

## Division 1

| | | Pd | Wn | Dw | Ls | GF | GA | Pts | |
|---|---|---|---|---|---|---|---|---|---|
| 1. | OLYMPIQUE GC DE NICE (NICE) | 34 | 18 | 5 | 11 | 73 | 46 | 41 | |
| 2. | Lille Olympique SC (Lille) | 34 | 17 | 7 | 10 | 57 | 43 | 41 | |
| 3. | Havre AC (Le Havre) | 34 | 18 | 4 | 12 | 59 | 43 | 40 | |
| 4. | Stade de Reims (Reims) | 34 | 15 | 10 | 9 | 61 | 50 | 40 | |
| 5. | Nîmes Olympique (Nîmes) | 34 | 16 | 8 | 10 | 64 | 53 | 40 | |
| 6. | Girondins de Bordeaux FC (Bordeaux) | 34 | 14 | 9 | 11 | 58 | 49 | 37 | |
| 7. | AS de Saint-Étienne (Saint-Étienne) | 34 | 15 | 7 | 12 | 63 | 59 | 37 | |
| 8. | Olympique de Marseille (Marseille) | 34 | 11 | 14 | 9 | 60 | 46 | 36 | |
| 9. | Racing Club de Strasbourg (Strasbourg) | 34 | 14 | 6 | 14 | 49 | 58 | 34 | |
| 10. | Club Olympique Roubaix-Tourcoing (Roubaix) | 34 | 12 | 8 | 14 | 55 | 53 | 32 | |
| 11. | FC de Nancy (Nancy) | 34 | 13 | 6 | 15 | 66 | 66 | 32 | |
| 12. | FC Sochaux-Montbéliard (Montbéliard) | 34 | 13 | 6 | 15 | 52 | 56 | 32 | |
| 13. | Racing Club de Paris (Paris) | 34 | 12 | 8 | 14 | 53 | 59 | 32 | |
| 14. | Stade Rennais Université Club (Rennes) | 34 | 13 | 5 | 16 | 63 | 69 | 31 | |
| 15. | FC de Sète (Sète) | 34 | 12 | 6 | 16 | 47 | 53 | 30 | PO |
| 16. | Racing Club de Lens (Lens) | 34 | 10 | 9 | 15 | 59 | 77 | 29 | PO |
| 17. | Toulouse FC (Toulouse) | 34 | 10 | 7 | 17 | 39 | 64 | 27 | R |
| 18. | Stade Français FC (Paris) | 34 | 7 | 7 | 20 | 38 | 72 | 21 | R |
| | | 612 | 240 | 132 | 240 | 1016 | 1016 | 612 | |

## Top goal-scorers

1) Roger PIANTONI          (FC de Nancy)    28
2) Jean COURTEAUX       (Olympique GC de Nice)    27
3) Henri BAILLOT         (Girondins de Bordeaux FC)    22

| Promotion/Relegation Play-Offs | Pd | Wn | Dw | Ls | GF | GA | Pts | |
|---|---|---|---|---|---|---|---|---|
| 1. Racing Club de Lens (Lens) | 3 | 2 | - | 1 | 9 | 5 | 4 | |
| 2. FC de Sète (Sète) | 3 | 2 | - | 1 | 7 | 4 | 4 | |
| 3. Racing Club Franc-Comtois (Besançon) | 3 | 1 | - | 2 | 4 | 6 | 2 | |
| 4. FC de Rouen (Rouen) | 3 | 1 | - | 2 | 3 | 8 | 2 | |
| | 12 | 6 | - | 6 | 23 | 23 | 12 | |

| Division 2 | Pd | Wn | Dw | Ls | GF | GA | Pts | |
|---|---|---|---|---|---|---|---|---|
| 1. Olympique Lyonnais (Lyon) | 32 | 23 | 4 | 5 | 75 | 41 | 50 | P* |
| 2. FC de Metz (Metz) | 32 | 20 | 6 | 6 | 74 | 32 | 46 | P |
| 3. FC de Rouen (Rouen) | 32 | 18 | 4 | 10 | 51 | 43 | 40 | PO |
| 4. Racing Club Franc-Comtois (Besançon) | 32 | 17 | 4 | 11 | 66 | 49 | 38 | PO |
| 5. AS de Monaco (Monaco) | 32 | 13 | 11 | 8 | 56 | 43 | 37 | |
| 6. AS Cannes-Grasse (Cannes) | 32 | 13 | 9 | 10 | 76 | 47 | 35 | |
| 7. Amiens AC (Amiens) | 32 | 10 | 12 | 10 | 53 | 42 | 32 | |
| 8. Stade Olympique Montpelliérain (Montpellier) | 32 | 13 | 6 | 13 | 46 | 40 | 32 | |
| 9. AS Troyenne-Savinienne (Troyes) | 32 | 14 | 3 | 15 | 42 | 54 | 31 | |
| 10. FC de Nantes (Nantes) | 32 | 11 | 7 | 14 | 54 | 56 | 29 | |
| 11. SC de Toulon (Toulon) | 32 | 11 | 7 | 14 | 52 | 59 | 29 | |
| 12. US Valenciennes-Anzin (Valenciennes) | 32 | 10 | 8 | 14 | 41 | 55 | 28 | |
| 13. Olympique Alésien (Alès) | 32 | 10 | 8 | 14 | 34 | 56 | 28 | |
| 14. SC de l'Ouest Angers (Angers) | 32 | 7 | 9 | 16 | 47 | 67 | 23 | |
| 15. AS Biterroise (Béziers) | 32 | 7 | 8 | 17 | 39 | 60 | 22 | |
| 16. US du Mans (Le Mans) | 32 | 8 | 6 | 18 | 39 | 72 | 22 | |
| 17. Cercle Athlétique de Paris (Paris) | 32 | 9 | 4 | 19 | 31 | 61 | 22 | |
| 18. Group Sporting Club de Marseille "2" (Marseille) | -- | - | - | - | -- | -- | -- | # |
| | 544 | 214 | 116 | 214 | 876 | 877 | 544 | |

* Olympique Lyonnais (Lyon) changed their name pre-season from Lyon Olympique Universitaire.

# Group Sporting Club de Marseille "2" (Marseille) withdrew from the league and reverted to amateur status.

**Elected**: FC de Grenoble (Grenoble).

## Coupe de France Final   (Stade Yves du Manoir, Colombes – 06/05/51 – 61,492)

**RACING CLUB DE STRASBOURG**          **3-0**          US Valenciennes-Anzin (Valenciennes)

*Bihel 24', Krug 34', Nagy 87'*

**Strasbourg**: Schaeffer, Hauss, Démaret, Krug, Wawrzniak, Vanags, Battistella, Nagy, Bihel, Jacques, Haan.
**Valenciennes**: Witkowski, Pazur, Gaillard, Izidorczyk, Blaszczyk, Wassmer, Vrand, Eozé, Verdeal, Léturgeon, Goffart.


## Semi-Finals   (15/04/51)

| | | |
|---|---|---|
| Racing Club de Strasbourg (Strasbourg) | 3-1 | FC de Nancy (Nancy) |
| US Valenciennes-Anzin (Valenciennes) | 3-1 | AS de Saint-Étienne (Saint-Étienne) |


## Quarter-Finals   (18/03/51)

| | | |
|---|---|---|
| FC de Nancy (Nancy) | 3-1 | Stade Français FC (Paris) |
| AS de Saint-Étienne (Saint-Étienne) | 0-0, 0-0, 5-1 | Havre AC (Le Havre) |
| Racing Club de Strasbourg (Strasbourg) | 5-3 | Olympique GC de Nice (Nice) |
| US Valenciennes-Anzin (Valenciennes) | 2-2, 1-0 | Racing Club de Paris (Paris) |


# 1951-52

| 1951-1952 Division One | Girondins Bordeaux | Havre AC | Racing Club de Lens | Lille Olympique SC | Olympique Lyonnais | Olympique Marseille | FC de Metz | FC de Nancy | Olympique GC Nice | Nîmes Olympique | Racing Club de Paris | Stade de Reims | Stade Rennais Université Club | CO Roubaix-Tourcoing | AS Saint-Étienne | FC de Sète | Sochaux-Montbéliard | Racing Strasbourg |
|---|---|---|---|---|---|---|---|---|---|---|---|---|---|---|---|---|---|---|
| Girondins Bordeaux | | 4-1 | 4-1 | 6-0 | 6-1 | 6-1 | 3-2 | 4-1 | 1-3 | 4-2 | 3-0 | 2-0 | 3-2 | 4-0 | 9-0 | 2-1 | 2-1 | 1-1 |
| Havre AC | 0-0 | | 0-1 | 2-0 | 2-0 | 2-0 | 1-1 | 1-1 | 3-1 | 2-0 | 0-2 | 4-2 | 1-2 | 2-0 | 0-2 | 3-2 | 1-2 | 5-1 |
| Racing Club de Lens | 0-0 | 1-1 | | 0-2 | 4-2 | 2-1 | 0-1 | 4-0 | 1-2 | 0-1 | 3-1 | 3-1 | 3-0 | 0-0 | 2-5 | 4-2 | 3-1 | 5-1 |
| Lille Olympique SC | 2-2 | 1-3 | 5-0 | | 3-0 | 3-3 | 3-2 | 0-3 | 6-0 | 2-1 | 5-1 | 1-0 | 9-1 | 2-1 | 5-1 | 6-1 | 7-3 | 3-1 |
| Olympique Lyonnais | 0-1 | 3-0 | 4-1 | 0-3 | | 2-2 | 2-2 | 0-1 | 0-2 | 4-3 | 1-1 | 2-5 | 3-2 | 0-0 | 4-2 | 2-6 | 0-0 | 2-3 |
| Olympique Marseille | 6-0 | 0-0 | 1-0 | 0-2 | 3-1 | | 4-0 | 3-2 | 2-4 | 3-1 | 0-0 | 1-3 | 1-1 | 1-1 | 3-10 | 2-2 | 1-1 | 2-1 |
| FC de Metz | 2-1 | 0-4 | 1-1 | 2-1 | 2-0 | 2-1 | | 1-2 | 0-2 | 1-2 | 2-2 | 0-0 | 4-0 | 0-0 | 2-2 | 3-1 | 3-1 | 2-0 |
| FC de Nancy | 2-1 | 2-1 | 3-2 | 0-2 | 4-0 | 0-1 | 2-2 | | 1-1 | 0-0 | 6-3 | 1-1 | 9-1 | 0-2 | 2-0 | 2-2 | 2-1 | 2-2 |
| Olympique GC Nice | 3-1 | 0-1 | 3-2 | 3-1 | 6-1 | 2-0 | 2-0 | 1-1 | | 3-0 | 1-0 | 2-1 | 3-0 | 2-1 | 3-0 | 2-1 | 0-1 | 2-1 |
| Nîmes Olympique | 2-3 | 2-0 | 4-1 | 5-0 | 0-0 | 1-0 | 0-0 | 1-2 | 3-1 | | 2-2 | 2-0 | 7-0 | 3-3 | 5-1 | 1-2 | 3-1 | 2-1 |
| Racing Club de Paris | 1-0 | 2-6 | 3-1 | 2-1 | 4-0 | 5-1 | 1-2 | 3-1 | 3-2 | 1-2 | | 5-2 | 1-5 | 2-1 | 1-3 | 0-2 | 0-4 | 5-2 |
| Stade de Reims | 6-1 | 3-1 | 5-2 | 1-0 | 1-0 | 8-1 | 2-0 | 0-0 | 2-1 | 1-0 | 1-1 | | 4-0 | 2-1 | 1-0 | 6-0 | 1-5 | 0-0 |
| Stade Rennais Université Club | 2-2 | 2-2 | 0-0 | 2-2 | 2-0 | 1-2 | 0-1 | 1-1 | 0-3 | 2-0 | 4-1 | 2-0 | | 2-2 | 2-3 | 2-0 | 5-1 | 2-1 |
| CO Roubaix-Tourcoing | 2-1 | 3-1 | 1-2 | 2-2 | 3-0 | 5-2 | 0-0 | 2-1 | 3-0 | 1-2 | 3-2 | 1-0 | 2-0 | | 1-2 | 4-0 | 2-0 | 5-0 |
| AS Saint-Étienne | 1-4 | 1-1 | 1-1 | 1-3 | 1-0 | 4-2 | 3-0 | 1-2 | 1-1 | 0-2 | 0-3 | 1-1 | 5-0 | 1-0 | | 2-1 | 4-1 | 5-0 |
| FC de Sète | 1-0 | 3-1 | 1-1 | 0-0 | 0-2 | 2-0 | 1-0 | 0-0 | 1-1 | 1-3 | 2-0 | 2-0 | 3-3 | 2-1 | 4-2 | | 3-1 | 0-0 |
| Sochaux-Montbéliard | 0-2 | 0-1 | 3-1 | 1-1 | 2-0 | 1-1 | 0-0 | 3-1 | 2-0 | 2-0 | 1-0 | 4-1 | 5-1 | 1-2 | 1-1 | 0-3 | | 0-1 |
| Racing Strasbourg | 2-5 | 0-2 | 1-2 | 0-2 | 1-2 | 1-1 | 1-2 | 3-2 | 1-3 | 3-1 | 2-2 | 2-3 | 1-2 | 2-2 | 1-3 | 0-2 | 1-1 | |

| | Division 1 | Pd | Wn | Dw | Ls | GF | GA | Pts | |
|---|---|---|---|---|---|---|---|---|---|
| 1. | OLYMPIQUE GC DE NICE (NICE) | 34 | 21 | 4 | 9 | 65 | 42 | 46 | |
| 2. | Girondins de Bordeaux FC (Bordeaux) | 34 | 20 | 5 | 9 | 88 | 49 | 45 | |
| 3. | Lille Olympique SC (Lille) | 34 | 19 | 6 | 9 | 85 | 50 | 44 | |
| 4. | Stade de Reims (Reims) | 34 | 16 | 6 | 12 | 64 | 48 | 38 | |
| 5. | FC de Metz (Metz) | 34 | 14 | 10 | 10 | 48 | 45 | 38 | |
| 6. | Nîmes Olympique (Nîmes) | 34 | 16 | 5 | 13 | 63 | 47 | 37 | |
| 7. | Havre AC (Le Havre) | 34 | 15 | 7 | 12 | 55 | 44 | 37 | |
| 8. | Club Olympique Roubaix-Tourcoing (Roubaix) | 34 | 14 | 8 | 12 | 57 | 44 | 36 | |
| 9. | AS de Saint-Étienne (Saint-Étienne) | 34 | 15 | 6 | 13 | 69 | 68 | 36 | |
| 10. | FC de Sète (Sète) | 34 | 14 | 8 | 12 | 54 | 56 | 36 | |
| 11. | FC de Nancy (Nancy) | 34 | 12 | 11 | 11 | 59 | 53 | 35 | |
| 12. | FC Sochaux-Montbéliard (Montbéliard) | 34 | 12 | 7 | 15 | 51 | 54 | 31 | |
| 13. | Racing Club de Lens (Lens) | 34 | 12 | 7 | 15 | 54 | 61 | 31 | |
| 14. | Racing Club de Paris (Paris) | 34 | 13 | 5 | 16 | 60 | 71 | 31 | |
| 15. | Stade Rennais Université Club (Rennes) | 34 | 10 | 8 | 16 | 51 | 85 | 28 | |
| 16. | Olympique de Marseille (Marseille) | 34 | 9 | 9 | 16 | 52 | 76 | 27 | PO |
| 17. | Olympique Lyonnais (Lyon) | 34 | 7 | 6 | 21 | 38 | 78 | 20 | R |
| 18. | Racing Club de Strasbourg (Strasbourg) | 34 | 4 | 8 | 22 | 38 | 80 | 16 | R |
| | | 612 | 243 | 126 | 243 | 1051 | 1051 | 612 | |

## Top goal-scorers

| | | | |
|---|---|---|---|
| 1) | Gunnar ANDERSSON | (Olympique de Marseille) | 31 |
| 2) | Bertus DE HARDER | (Girondins de Bordeaux FC) | 25 |
| | ROUVIÈRE | (Nîmes Olympique) | 25 |

## Promotion/Relegation Play-Off

US Valenciennes-Anzin (Valenciennes)     3-1, 0-4     Olympique de Marseille (Marseille)

| | Division 2 | Pd | Wn | Dw | Ls | GF | GA | Pts | |
|---|---|---|---|---|---|---|---|---|---|
| 1. | Stade Français FC (Paris) | 34 | 27 | 2 | 5 | 100 | 38 | 56 | P |
| 2. | Stade Olympique Montpelliérain (Montpellier) | 34 | 21 | 5 | 8 | 68 | 37 | 47 | P |
| 3. | US Valenciennes-Anzin (Valenciennes) | 34 | 17 | 9 | 8 | 68 | 44 | 43 | PO |
| 4. | FC de Nantes (Nantes) | 34 | 17 | 8 | 9 | 61 | 57 | 42 | |
| 5. | AS de Monaco (Monaco) | 34 | 16 | 8 | 10 | 54 | 40 | 40 | |
| 6. | SC de l'Ouest Angers (Angers) | 34 | 16 | 8 | 10 | 64 | 57 | 40 | |
| 7. | FC de Grenoble (Grenoble) | 34 | 16 | 4 | 14 | 64 | 55 | 36 | |
| 8. | Racing Club Franc-Comtois (Besançon) | 34 | 13 | 9 | 12 | 83 | 65 | 35 | |
| 9. | SC de Toulon (Toulon) | 34 | 14 | 7 | 13 | 56 | 63 | 35 | |
| 10. | FC de Rouen (Rouen) | 34 | 13 | 8 | 13 | 64 | 44 | 34 | |
| 11. | AS Troyenne-Savinienne (Troyes) | 34 | 13 | 8 | 13 | 58 | 56 | 34 | |
| 12. | Toulouse FC (Toulouse) | 34 | 14 | 6 | 14 | 52 | 57 | 34 | |
| 13. | AS de Cannes (Cannes) | 34 | 12 | 3 | 19 | 57 | 77 | 27 | * |
| 14. | Cercle Athlétique de Paris (Paris) | 34 | 12 | 3 | 19 | 38 | 52 | 27 | |
| 15. | AS Biterroise (Béziers) | 34 | 9 | 6 | 19 | 41 | 63 | 24 | |
| 16. | Amiens AC (Amiens) | 34 | 7 | 8 | 19 | 43 | 84 | 22 | # |
| 17. | US du Mans (Le Mans) | 34 | 7 | 5 | 22 | 45 | 87 | 19 | # |
| 18. | Olympique Alésien (Alès) | 34 | 5 | 7 | 22 | 41 | 84 | 17 | |
| | | 612 | 249 | 114 | 249 | 1057 | 1060 | 612 | |

\* AS de Cannes (Cannes) changed their name pre-season from AS Cannes-Grasse (Cannes).
\# Amiens AC (Amiens) and US du Mans (Le Mans) both reverted to amateur status for the next season.

**Elected**: Perpignan FC (Perpignan) and Red Star Olympique Audonien (Saint-Ouen).

## Coupe de France Final  (Stade Yves du Manoir, Colombes – 04/05/52 – 61,485)

**OLYMPIQUE GC DE NICE (NICE)**        **5-3**        Girondins de Bordeaux FC (Bordeaux)

*Nurenberg 10', Carniglia 12', Belver 32', Ben Tifour 61', Césari 65'*        *Baillot 11', 55', Kargulewicz 40'*

**Nice**: Domingo, Firoud, Gonzales, Bonifaci, Poitevin, Belver, Courteaux, Nurenberg, Césari, Carniglia, Ben Tifour.

**Bordeaux**: Villenave, Meynieu, Swiatek, Gallice, Garriga, De Kubber, Baillot, Persillon, Kargulewicz, Doye, De Harder.

## Semi-Finals  (06/04/52)

| | | |
|---|:---:|---|
| Girondins de Bordeaux FC (Bordeaux) | 2-1 | Lille Olympique SC (Lille) |
| Olympique GC de Nice (Nice) | 3-1 | FC de Rouen (Rouen) |

## Quarter-Finals  (16/03/52)

| | | |
|---|:---:|---|
| Girondins de Bordeaux FC (Bordeaux) | 2-2, 4-2 | Stade Rennais Université Club (Rennes) |
| Lille Olympique SC (Lille) | 4-0 | AS de Monaco (Monaco) |
| Olympique GC de Nice (Nice) | 3-0 | US Valenciennes-Anzin (Valenciennes) |
| FC de Rouen (Rouen) | 2-1 | FC Sochaux-Montbéliard (Montbéliard) |

# 1952-53

| 1952-1953 Division One | Girondins Bordeaux | Stade Français FC | Havre AC | Racing Club de Lens | Lille Olympique SC | Olympique Marseille | FC de Metz | SO Montpelliérain | FC de Nancy | Olympique GC Nice | Nîmes Olympique | Racing Club Paris | Stade de Reims | Stade Rennais UC | CO Roubaix-Tourcoing | AS Saint-Étienne | FC de Sète | Sochaux-Montbéliard |
|---|---|---|---|---|---|---|---|---|---|---|---|---|---|---|---|---|---|---|
| Girondins Bordeaux | | 2-1 | 6-0 | 2-0 | 1-5 | 2-0 | 4-0 | 6-0 | 4-1 | 7-3 | 3-2 | 3-1 | 1-0 | 7-0 | 4-2 | 0-0 | 3-0 | 4-1 |
| Stade Français FC | 0-2 | | 2-2 | 1-1 | 2-0 | 2-3 | 2-1 | 2-4 | 4-1 | 0-1 | 4-2 | 5-0 | 1-5 | 2-0 | 1-3 | 2-1 | 2-0 | 1-2 |
| Havre AC | 3-1 | 1-3 | | 1-0 | 0-1 | 2-1 | 3-0 | 1-1 | 0-1 | 2-0 | 1-1 | 4-1 | 3-4 | 1-1 | 2-0 | 3-0 | 2-0 | 2-2 |
| Racing Club de Lens | 1-1 | 1-1 | 2-0 | | 0-3 | 1-1 | 3-1 | 2-1 | 4-1 | 2-0 | 2-1 | 2-1 | 1-3 | 5-0 | 1-3 | 1-2 | 3-0 | 5-1 |
| Lille Olympique SC | 0-0 | 2-1 | 3-1 | 0-0 | | 2-0 | 1-2 | 2-2 | 6-2 | 1-1 | 3-2 | 3-0 | 2-5 | 1-1 | 2-1 | 0-2 | 5-0 | 3-1 |
| Olympique Marseille | 3-0 | 1-0 | 3-1 | 1-1 | 3-0 | | 3-0 | 5-1 | 4-3 | 3-1 | 4-1 | 3-0 | 2-1 | 2-2 | 4-2 | 1-0 | 3-3 | 1-6 |
| FC de Metz | 0-2 | 2-0 | 6-1 | 3-0 | 0-3 | 1-3 | | 1-1 | 2-0 | 2-0 | 2-0 | 0-2 | 0-0 | 0-1 | 1-1 | 5-0 | 0-1 | 1-2 |
| SO Montpelliérain | 4-1 | 0-3 | 2-1 | 2-1 | 1-1 | 2-1 | 1-1 | | 0-1 | 2-1 | 2-5 | 0-1 | 2-6 | 2-2 | 1-1 | 2-0 | 1-1 | 2-3 |
| FC de Nancy | 3-0 | 5-1 | 0-3 | 1-3 | 1-3 | 1-0 | 1-0 | 3-0 | | 2-1 | 2-0 | 1-0 | 1-1 | 1-2 | 1-0 | 3-2 | 0-1 | 1-2 |
| Olympique GC Nice | 1-2 | 2-1 | 0-2 | 3-1 | 0-0 | 3-1 | 1-2 | 0-0 | 2-1 | | 2-0 | 1-2 | 0-4 | 3-1 | 4-1 | 2-0 | 3-2 | 5-3 |
| Nîmes Olympique | 5-1 | 0-0 | 7-1 | 0-0 | 2-0 | 2-0 | 2-1 | 4-2 | 2-1 | 1-0 | | 4-2 | 1-0 | 2-0 | 1-0 | 0-0 | 3-1 | 2-0 |
| Racing Club Paris | 3-3 | 2-2 | 1-1 | 1-1 | 1-0 | 1-1 | 0-2 | 2-1 | 1-2 | 1-3 | 1-2 | | 1-3 | 2-0 | 0-2 | 2-1 | 2-1 | 2-1 |
| Stade de Reims | 2-3 | 1-2 | 5-0 | 5-0 | 1-1 | 3-1 | 2-1 | 3-2 | 0-2 | 3-1 | 2-0 | 5-1 | | 5-1 | 1-0 | 2-0 | 2-0 | 3-0 |
| Stade Rennais Université Club | 1-0 | 0-0 | 2-0 | 3-2 | 1-1 | 3-1 | 4-2 | 0-1 | 0-1 | 0-0 | 2-0 | 1-0 | 0-1 | | 3-2 | 0-1 | 3-0 | 1-1 |
| CO Roubaix-Tourcoing | 3-1 | 0-0 | 0-0 | 0-1 | 1-2 | 0-0 | 1-0 | 1-0 | 0-1 | 2-2 | 2-4 | 0-1 | 1-1 | 3-2 | | 2-0 | 2-0 | 2-2 |
| AS Saint-Étienne | 1-1 | 1-1 | 1-0 | 2-3 | 2-1 | 2-2 | 2-2 | 2-0 | 6-0 | 2-1 | 4-2 | 3-1 | 2-6 | 1-0 | 1-1 | | 2-2 | 1-3 |
| FC de Sète | 2-0 | 2-2 | 3-1 | 2-0 | 3-1 | 2-0 | 0-0 | 1-0 | 1-2 | 1-0 | 1-1 | 0-1 | 2-1 | 2-0 | 1-0 | 5-0 | | 0-0 |
| Sochaux-Montbéliard | 8-2 | 1-3 | 3-2 | 1-0 | 3-3 | 2-1 | 1-1 | 2-1 | 1-0 | 3-2 | 1-1 | 3-3 | 1-0 | 2-0 | 3-1 | 3-0 | 4-2 | |

| | Division 1 | Pd | Wn | Dw | Ls | GF | GA | Pts | |
|---|---|---|---|---|---|---|---|---|---|
| 1. | STADE DE REIMS (REIMS) | 34 | 22 | 4 | 8 | 86 | 36 | 48 | |
| 2. | FC Sochaux-Montbéliard (Montbéliard) | 34 | 18 | 8 | 8 | 72 | 58 | 44 | |
| 3. | Girondins de Bordeaux FC (Bordeaux) | 34 | 19 | 5 | 10 | 79 | 56 | 43 | |
| 4. | Lille Olympique SC (Lille) | 34 | 15 | 10 | 9 | 61 | 43 | 40 | |
| 5. | Nîmes Olympique (Nîmes) | 34 | 17 | 6 | 11 | 62 | 47 | 40 | |
| 6. | Olympique de Marseille (Marseille) | 34 | 15 | 7 | 12 | 62 | 53 | 37 | |
| 7. | Racing Club de Lens (Lens) | 34 | 13 | 8 | 13 | 50 | 48 | 34 | |
| 8. | FC de Nancy (Nancy) | 34 | 16 | 2 | 16 | 48 | 58 | 34 | |
| 9. | Stade Français FC (Paris) | 34 | 12 | 9 | 13 | 54 | 51 | 33 | |
| 10. | FC de Sète (Sète) | 34 | 13 | 7 | 14 | 42 | 49 | 33 | |
| 11. | AS de Saint-Étienne (Saint-Étienne) | 34 | 11 | 8 | 15 | 44 | 59 | 30 | |
| 12. | FC de Metz (Metz) | 34 | 11 | 7 | 16 | 44 | 48 | 29 | |
| 13. | Olympique GC de Nice (Nice) | 34 | 12 | 5 | 17 | 49 | 57 | 29 | |
| 14. | Havre AC (Le Havre) | 34 | 11 | 7 | 16 | 47 | 63 | 29 | |
| 15. | Club Olympique Roubaix-Tourcoing (Roubaix) | 34 | 9 | 10 | 15 | 42 | 49 | 28 | |
| 16. | Stade Rennais Université Club (Rennes) | 34 | 9 | 10 | 15 | 42 | 49 | 28 | PO |
| 17. | Racing Club de Paris (Paris) | 34 | 11 | 6 | 17 | 40 | 64 | 28 | R |
| 18. | Stade Olympique Montpelliérain (Montpellier) | 34 | 8 | 9 | 17 | 43 | 67 | 25 | R |
| | | 612 | 243 | 126 | 243 | 962 | 962 | 612 | |

## Top goal-scorers

| | | | |
|---|---|---|---|
| 1) | Gunnar ANDERSSON | (Olympique de Marseille) | 35 |
| 2) | Abraham APPEL | (Stade de Reims) | 30 |
| 3) | Ben Mohamed ABDESSELEM | (Girondins de Bordeaux FC) | 22 |

## Promotion/Relegation Play-Off

Racing Club de Strasbourg (Strasbourg)    4-0, 3-1    Stade Rennais Université Club (Rennes)

| | Division 2 | Pd | Wn | Dw | Ls | GF | GA | Pts | |
|---|---|---|---|---|---|---|---|---|---|
| 1. | Toulouse FC (Toulouse) | 34 | 26 | 4 | 4 | 92 | 29 | 56 | P |
| 2. | AS de Monaco (Monaco) | 34 | 24 | 7 | 3 | 88 | 23 | 55 | P |
| 3. | Racing Club de Strasbourg (Strasbourg) | 34 | 23 | 7 | 4 | 87 | 32 | 53 | PO |
| 4. | AS Troyenne-Savinienne (Troyes) | 34 | 17 | 8 | 9 | 59 | 33 | 42 | |
| 5. | Racing Club Franc-Comtois (Besançon) | 34 | 18 | 5 | 11 | 69 | 47 | 41 | |
| 6. | FC de Nantes (Nantes) | 34 | 16 | 7 | 11 | 60 | 59 | 39 | |
| 7. | FC de Grenoble (Grenoble) | 34 | 14 | 8 | 12 | 57 | 62 | 36 | |
| 8. | Olympique Lyonnais (Lyon) | 34 | 12 | 9 | 13 | 41 | 54 | 33 | |
| 9. | Perpignan FC (Perpignan) | 34 | 12 | 8 | 14 | 59 | 64 | 32 | |
| 10. | AS de Cannes (Cannes) | 34 | 11 | 10 | 13 | 48 | 54 | 32 | |
| 11. | FC de Rouen (Rouen) | 34 | 11 | 9 | 14 | 48 | 43 | 31 | |
| 12. | SC de l'Ouest Angers (Angers) | 34 | 12 | 6 | 16 | 50 | 61 | 30 | |
| 13. | US Valenciennes-Anzin (Valenciennes) | 34 | 8 | 9 | 17 | 45 | 72 | 25 | |
| 14. | AS Biterroise (Béziers) | 34 | 8 | 9 | 17 | 41 | 69 | 25 | |
| 15. | SC de Toulon (Toulon) | 34 | 9 | 6 | 19 | 37 | 64 | 24 | |
| 16. | Cercle Athlétique de Paris (Paris) | 34 | 8 | 5 | 21 | 32 | 65 | 21 | |
| 17. | Red Star Olympique Audonien (Saint-Ouen) | 34 | 7 | 6 | 21 | 33 | 81 | 20 | |
| 18. | Olympique Alésien (Alès) | 34 | 5 | 7 | 22 | 21 | 55 | 17 | |
| | | 612 | 241 | 130 | 241 | 967 | 967 | 612 | |

### Coupe de France Final  (Stade Yves du Manoir, Colombes – 31/05/53 – 58,993)

**LILLE OLYMPIQUE SC (LILLE)**  2-1  FC de Nancy (Nancy)
*Vincent 17', Lefèvre 81'*  *Belaid 41'*

**Lille**: Ruminski, Pazur, Vuye, Bieganski, Van der Hart, Sommerlynck, Jensen, Strappe, Baratte, Vincent, Lefevre.
**Nancy**: Favre, Cecchini, Collot, Nunge, Mindonnet, Bottollier, Clemens, Lorenzo, Belaid, Piantoni, Deladerriere.

### Semi-Finals  (26/04/53)

| | | |
|---|---|---|
| Lille Olympique SC (Lille) | 1-0 | AS de Saint-Étienne (Saint-Étienne) |
| FC de Nancy (Nancy) | 1-0 | AS Troyenne-Savinienne (Troyes) |

### Quarter-Finals  (29/03/53)

| | | |
|---|---|---|
| Lille Olympique SC (Lille) | 4-2 | Olympique GC de Nice (Nice) |
| FC de Nancy (Nancy) | 2-0 | FC de Grenoble (Grenoble) |
| AS de Saint-Étienne (Saint-Étienne) | 1-0 | FC de Sète (Sète) |
| AS Troyenne-Savinienne (Troyes) | 3-0 | Stade Français FC (Paris) |

# 1953-54

| 1953-1954 Division One | Girondins Bordeaux | Stade Français FC | Havre AC | Racing Club de Lens | Lille Olympique SC | Olympique Marseille | FC de Metz | AS de Monaco | FC de Nancy | Olympique GC Nice | Nîmes Olympique | Stade de Reims | CO Roubaix-Tourcoing | AS Saint-Étienne | FC de Sète | Sochaux-Montbéliard | Racing Strasbourg | Toulouse FC |
|---|---|---|---|---|---|---|---|---|---|---|---|---|---|---|---|---|---|---|
| Girondins Bordeaux | | 3-2 | 1-4 | 1-2 | 1-3 | 3-0 | 3-0 | 4-3 | 1-0 | 4-1 | 2-1 | 0-0 | 5-0 | 1-0 | 1-0 | 7-1 | 5-2 | 0-0 |
| Stade Français FC | 0-1 | | 1-2 | 5-2 | 0-0 | 1-1 | 2-1 | 0-4 | 4-0 | 1-1 | 1-3 | 1-2 | 1-1 | 1-2 | 2-2 | 4-1 | 0-1 | 0-0 |
| Havre AC | 2-3 | 1-3 | | 1-2 | 1-1 | 1-0 | 3-1 | 1-2 | 2-2 | 2-2 | 0-1 | 0-0 | 3-1 | 2-0 | 10-0 | 2-1 | 2-0 | 1-1 |
| Racing Club de Lens | 1-1 | 1-2 | 3-1 | | 0-2 | 4-1 | 4-0 | 0-0 | 3-2 | 2-3 | 4-1 | 0-0 | 4-1 | 2-0 | 2-2 | 2-0 | 3-1 | 1-1 |
| Lille Olympique SC | 1-0 | 1-1 | 2-1 | 1-0 | | 4-0 | 2-2 | 0-0 | 3-0 | 3-1 | 0-0 | 0-1 | 2-0 | 1-0 | 3-1 | 0-0 | 3-0 | 1-0 |
| Olympique Marseille | 3-2 | 3-1 | 5-1 | 2-0 | 1-1 | | 1-1 | 5-1 | 0-1 | 0-0 | 0-4 | 0-2 | 3-2 | 3-1 | 2-0 | 0-0 | 5-1 | 0-1 |
| FC de Metz | 2-2 | 1-0 | 2-1 | 1-1 | 2-2 | 3-2 | | 1-0 | 2-4 | 0-0 | 2-0 | 0-1 | 4-2 | 5-1 | 1-0 | 1-1 | 2-1 | 2-2 |
| AS de Monaco | 1-2 | 1-4 | 4-1 | 0-1 | 0-1 | 1-1 | 2-0 | | 2-0 | 0-3 | 2-0 | 2-1 | 0-2 | 1-1 | 2-1 | 0-0 | 4-2 | 2-3 |
| FC de Nancy | 2-2 | 0-0 | 3-0 | 3-1 | 1-1 | 2-1 | 2-1 | 1-1 | | 1-5 | 4-2 | 1-0 | 2-1 | 0-1 | 3-1 | 2-3 | 0-0 | 4-2 |
| Olympique GC Nice | 3-4 | 1-1 | 4-0 | 6-1 | 3-0 | 2-4 | 0-1 | 1-2 | 2-1 | | 1-1 | 1-1 | 3-1 | 5-2 | 5-0 | 4-1 | 4-3 | 0-2 |
| Nîmes Olympique | 2-0 | 1-0 | 2-0 | 3-1 | 1-1 | 2-1 | 2-1 | 1-3 | 1-0 | 1-1 | | 1-1 | 1-0 | 1-0 | 5-2 | 4-1 | 1-2 | 0-1 |
| Stade de Reims | 1-2 | 1-3 | 4-2 | 0-0 | 0-3 | 6-0 | 3-1 | 2-1 | 4-1 | 4-3 | 2-1 | | 2-2 | 0-1 | 2-0 | 4-1 | 2-2 | 1-1 |
| CO Roubaix-Tourcoing | 0-2 | 1-1 | 3-1 | 0-4 | 0-3 | 1-0 | 3-0 | 2-0 | 4-2 | 3-2 | 4-2 | 2-2 | | 0-1 | 1-0 | 1-1 | 0-0 | 4-1 |
| AS Saint-Étienne | 2-0 | 2-1 | 0-1 | 5-2 | 0-0 | 0-0 | 3-2 | 1-1 | 3-1 | 2-1 | 2-1 | 0-1 | 2-1 | | 6-3 | 2-4 | 1-0 | 1-1 |
| FC de Sète | 0-2 | 0-0 | 4-4 | 3-1 | 0-1 | 2-1 | 4-1 | 1-1 | 1-0 | 1-1 | 2-1 | 0-2 | 4-0 | 1-2 | | 0-0 | 0-0 | 1-1 |
| Sochaux-Montbéliard | 1-1 | 4-0 | 0-1 | 1-1 | 2-2 | 1-1 | 3-0 | 1-0 | 7-1 | 4-1 | 2-1 | 1-3 | 0-1 | 1-2 | 2-2 | | 7-1 | 1-3 |
| Racing Strasbourg | 1-2 | 2-0 | 4-0 | 5-2 | 2-1 | 2-1 | 2-2 | 3-0 | 1-2 | 2-2 | 2-1 | 2-4 | 4-2 | 2-1 | 4-0 | 1-0 | | 2-0 |
| Toulouse FC | 3-1 | 2-1 | 5-1 | 1-1 | 1-0 | 2-2 | 0-0 | 1-1 | 3-2 | 4-1 | 1-0 | 1-3 | 3-1 | 1-1 | 2-0 | 2-2 | 3-1 | |

| | Division 1 | Pd | Wn | Dw | Ls | GF | GA | Pts | |
|---|---|---|---|---|---|---|---|---|---|
| 1. | LILLE OLYMPIQUE SC (LILLE) | 34 | 17 | 13 | 4 | 49 | 22 | 47 | |
| 2. | Stade de Reims (Reims) | 34 | 18 | 10 | 6 | 62 | 36 | 46 | |
| 3. | Girondins de Bordeaux FC (Bordeaux) | 34 | 20 | 6 | 8 | 69 | 44 | 46 | |
| 4. | Toulouse FC (Toulouse) | 34 | 15 | 14 | 5 | 55 | 39 | 44 | |
| 5. | AS de Saint-Étienne (Saint-Étienne) | 34 | 16 | 6 | 12 | 48 | 47 | 38 | |
| 6. | Racing Club de Strasbourg (Strasbourg) | 34 | 15 | 6 | 13 | 60 | 61 | 36 | |
| 7. | Racing Club de Lens (Lens) | 34 | 13 | 9 | 12 | 58 | 56 | 35 | |
| 8. | Olympique GC de Nice (Nice) | 34 | 12 | 10 | 12 | 73 | 59 | 34 | |
| 9. | Nîmes Olympique (Nîmes) | 34 | 14 | 5 | 15 | 49 | 46 | 33 | |
| 10. | AS de Monaco (Monaco) | 34 | 11 | 9 | 14 | 44 | 48 | 31 | |
| 11. | FC Sochaux-Montbéliard (Montbéliard) | 34 | 9 | 12 | 13 | 55 | 57 | 30 | |
| 12. | FC de Nancy (Nancy) | 34 | 12 | 6 | 16 | 50 | 65 | 30 | |
| 13. | FC de Metz (Metz) | 34 | 10 | 10 | 14 | 45 | 59 | 30 | |
| 14. | Olympique de Marseille (Marseille) | 34 | 10 | 9 | 15 | 49 | 56 | 29 | |
| 15. | Club Olympique Roubaix-Tourcoing (Roubaix) | 34 | 11 | 6 | 17 | 47 | 65 | 28 | |
| 16. | Stade Français FC (Paris) | 34 | 8 | 11 | 15 | 44 | 49 | 27 | PO |
| 17. | Havre AC (Le Havre) | 34 | 10 | 6 | 18 | 54 | 69 | 26 | R |
| 18. | FC de Sète (Sète) | 34 | 6 | 10 | 18 | 38 | 71 | 22 | R |
| | | 612 | 227 | 158 | 227 | 949 | 949 | 612 | |

## Top goal-scorers

| | | | |
|---|---|---|---|
| 1) | Edouard KARGULEWICZ | (Girondins de Bordeaux FC) | 27 |
| 2) | Abraham APPEL | (Stade de Reims) | 23 |
| 3) | Gunnar ANDERSSON | (Olympique de Marseille) | 19 |

## Promotion/Relegation Play-Off

Racing Club de Paris (Paris)　　　　3-2, 1-1　　　　Stade Français FC (Paris)

| | Division 2 | Pd | Wn | Dw | Ls | GF | GA | Pts | |
|---|---|---|---|---|---|---|---|---|---|
| 1. | Olympique Lyonnais (Lyon) | 38 | 25 | 8 | 5 | 108 | 44 | 58 | P |
| 2. | AS Troyenne-Savinienne (Troyes) | 38 | 24 | 7 | 7 | 101 | 34 | 55 | P |
| 3. | Racing Club de Paris (Paris) | 38 | 25 | 5 | 8 | 107 | 48 | 55 | PO |
| 4. | FC de Rouen (Rouen) | 38 | 23 | 6 | 9 | 81 | 47 | 52 | |
| 5. | Union Athlétique Sedan-Torcy (Sedan) | 38 | 19 | 11 | 8 | 77 | 41 | 49 | |
| 6. | Stade Rennais Université Club (Rennes) | 38 | 19 | 6 | 13 | 86 | 53 | 44 | |
| 7. | Red Star Olympique Audonien (Saint-Ouen) | 38 | 20 | 4 | 14 | 71 | 59 | 44 | |
| 8. | Perpignan FC (Perpignan) | 38 | 16 | 7 | 15 | 49 | 63 | 39 | |
| 9. | FC de Nantes (Nantes) | 38 | 14 | 8 | 16 | 68 | 62 | 36 | |
| 10. | US Valenciennes-Anzin (Valenciennes) | 38 | 16 | 4 | 18 | 56 | 62 | 36 | |
| 11. | SC de l'Ouest Angers (Angers) | 38 | 12 | 11 | 15 | 53 | 58 | 35 | |
| 12. | AS Aixoise (Aix-en-Provence) | 38 | 14 | 7 | 17 | 53 | 67 | 35 | |
| 13. | AS de Cannes (Cannes) | 38 | 12 | 10 | 16 | 49 | 55 | 34 | |
| 14. | Racing Club Franc-Comtois (Besançon) | 38 | 11 | 11 | 16 | 50 | 65 | 33 | |
| 15. | FC de Grenoble (Grenoble) | 38 | 12 | 9 | 17 | 54 | 80 | 33 | |
| 16. | AS Biterrois (Béziers) | 38 | 10 | 7 | 21 | 41 | 92 | 27 | |
| 17. | Olympique Alésien (Alès) | 38 | 10 | 7 | 21 | 31 | 83 | 27 | |
| 18. | SC de Toulon (Toulon) | 38 | 11 | 4 | 23 | 45 | 82 | 26 | |
| 19. | Cercle Athlétique de Paris (Paris) | 38 | 8 | 7 | 23 | 56 | 91 | 23 | |
| 20. | Stade Olympique Montpelliérain (Montpellier) | 38 | 5 | 9 | 24 | 23 | 73 | 19 | |
| | | 760 | 306 | 148 | 306 | 1259 | 1259 | 760 | |

## Coupe de France Final   (Stade Yves du Manoir, Colombes – 23/05/54 – 56,803)

**OLYMPIQUE GC DE NICE (NICE)**      **2-1**      Olympique de Marseille (Marseille)

*Nurenberg 06', Carniglia 11'*                                              *Andersson 55'*

**Nice:** Hairabedian, Ben Nacef, Gonzales, Cuissard, Poitevin, Mahjoub, Ujlaki, Antonio, Carniglia, Fontaine, Nurenberg.

**Marseille:** Angel, Gransart, Abdesselem, Mesas, Johansson, Rossi, Palluch, Ben Barek, Andersson, Scotti, Mercurio.

## Semi-Finals   (25/04/54)

| | | |
|---|---|---|
| Olympique de Marseille (Marseille) | 2-1 | Union Athlétique Sedan-Torcy (Sedan) |
| Olympique GC de Nice (Nice) | 2-1 | AS Troyenne-Savinienne (Troyes) |

## Quarter-Finals   (28/03/54)

| | | |
|---|---|---|
| Olympique de Marseille (Marseille) | 3-2 | FC de Rouen (Rouen) |
| Olympique GC de Nice (Nice) | 1-1,  3-0 | Girondins de Bordeaux FC (Bordeaux) |
| Union Athlétique Sedan-Torcy (Sedan) | 2-1 | Racing Club Franc-Comtois (Besançon) |
| AS Troyenne-Savinienne (Troyes) | 4-1 | AS de Cannes (Cannes) |

# 1954-55

| 1954-1955 Division One | Girondins Bordeaux | Racing Club de Lens | Lille Olympique SC | Olympique Lyonnais | Olympique Marseille | FC de Metz | AS de Monaco | FC de Nancy | Olympique GC Nice | Nîmes Olympique | Racing Club de Paris | Stade de Reims | CO Roubaix-Tourcoing | AS Saint-Étienne | Sochaux-Montbéliard | Racing Strasbourg | Toulouse FC | Troyenne-Savinienne |
|---|---|---|---|---|---|---|---|---|---|---|---|---|---|---|---|---|---|---|
| Girondins Bordeaux | | 2-1 | 4-2 | 3-1 | 2-1 | 2-0 | 4-1 | 2-3 | 7-2 | 3-1 | 0-0 | 5-0 | 5-1 | 2-1 | 1-2 | 0-1 | 1-1 | 3-1 |
| Racing Club de Lens | 1-3 | | 2-1 | 1-0 | 1-0 | 2-3 | 2-0 | 1-1 | 2-2 | 3-1 | 3-1 | 0-0 | 4-3 | 2-1 | 6-2 | 2-1 | 1-1 | 2-0 |
| Lille Olympique SC | 2-2 | 3-3 | | 3-1 | 2-1 | 4-2 | 3-1 | 2-5 | 1-3 | 6-1 | 6-0 | 3-2 | 4-0 | 0-1 | 0-0 | 0-0 | 1-1 | 1-2 |
| Olympique Lyonnais | 3-1 | 1-1 | 2-1 | | 3-0 | 4-2 | 0-2 | 2-1 | 3-4 | 2-2 | 2-2 | 1-1 | 4-2 | 1-1 | 3-2 | 2-1 | 3-2 | 1-0 |
| Olympique Marseille | 3-1 | 4-0 | 5-1 | 1-0 | | 1-1 | 1-1 | 2-2 | 2-0 | 0-1 | 3-1 | 1-3 | 5-2 | 4-0 | 3-0 | 2-0 | 4-0 | 3-0 |
| FC de Metz | 1-0 | 1-1 | 0-0 | 1-2 | 2-1 | | 2-1 | 0-0 | 4-0 | 1-0 | 1-4 | 1-0 | 0-0 | 0-2 | 1-0 | 3-3 | 1-5 | 4-2 |
| AS de Monaco | 1-0 | 6-0 | 1-1 | 0-0 | 1-2 | 5-0 | | 0-2 | 1-1 | 1-0 | 1-1 | 1-2 | 1-0 | 2-0 | 0-0 | 4-0 | 1-1 | 1-2 |
| FC de Nancy | 1-1 | 1-3 | 1-0 | 0-1 | 3-0 | 7-0 | 0-0 | | 4-1 | 3-1 | 1-0 | 2-4 | 4-0 | 2-1 | 2-2 | 1-5 | 0-1 | 4-1 |
| Olympique GC Nice | 1-1 | 1-2 | 2-1 | 7-3 | 0-0 | 2-3 | 1-1 | 2-2 | | 1-0 | 3-2 | 3-3 | 5-2 | 2-0 | 4-0 | 2-1 | 5-0 | 5-1 |
| Nîmes Olympique | 2-0 | 1-0 | 0-1 | 2-2 | 2-2 | 2-0 | 2-0 | 1-0 | 6-2 | | 2-0 | 0-2 | 3-0 | 1-0 | 2-1 | 2-1 | 0-0 | 1-0 |
| Racing Club de Paris | 2-0 | 1-1 | 1-3 | 5-0 | 3-3 | 4-0 | 1-2 | 0-0 | 3-1 | 1-0 | | 2-5 | 2-2 | 4-0 | 0-3 | 4-2 | 2-0 | 4-1 |
| Stade de Reims | 3-0 | 4-2 | 4-2 | 3-1 | 2-0 | 6-0 | 3-1 | 5-2 | 3-2 | 4-1 | 0-3 | | 0-2 | 2-4 | 3-1 | 1-2 | 2-1 | 3-0 |
| CO Roubaix-Tourcoing | 3-0 | 2-2 | 3-1 | 2-1 | 1-1 | 0-2 | 0-1 | 2-1 | 4-2 | 1-5 | 3-3 | 2-1 | | 1-4 | 2-0 | 1-0 | 2-2 | 1-6 |
| AS Saint-Étienne | 3-1 | 1-1 | 2-2 | 4-2 | 3-0 | 2-0 | 0-0 | 2-0 | 4-2 | 4-2 | 0-1 | 0-2 | 5-1 | | 3-1 | 5-1 | 2-3 | 0-2 |
| Sochaux-Montbéliard | 3-2 | 1-1 | 1-2 | 2-0 | 4-0 | 1-0 | 5-2 | 3-2 | 4-1 | 6-2 | 3-2 | 4-1 | 5-0 | 0-0 | | 1-2 | 1-0 | 0-0 |
| Racing Strasbourg | 1-1 | 2-2 | 2-1 | 1-1 | 4-1 | 3-3 | 5-0 | 4-0 | 7-1 | 3-2 | 3-1 | 1-1 | 3-0 | 5-0 | 2-5 | | 2-0 | 4-0 |
| Toulouse FC | 1-1 | 2-0 | 2-1 | 1-0 | 1-0 | 6-2 | 3-2 | 3-1 | 1-1 | 2-0 | 0-1 | 1-1 | 6-2 | 2-0 | 2-1 | 4-1 | | 1-1 |
| Troyenne-Savinienne | 1-3 | 2-1 | 1-0 | 2-2 | 4-2 | 0-1 | 1-1 | 2-1 | 3-4 | 0-0 | 3-1 | 2-2 | 2-5 | 0-3 | 2-0 | 2-1 | 2-1 | |

| | Division 1 | Pd | Wn | Dw | Ls | GF | GA | Pts | |
|---|---|---|---|---|---|---|---|---|---|
| 1. | STADE DE REIMS (REIMS) | 34 | 19 | 6 | 9 | 78 | 53 | 44 | |
| 2. | Toulouse FC (Toulouse) | 34 | 15 | 10 | 9 | 57 | 45 | 40 | |
| 3. | Racing Club de Lens (Lens) | 34 | 13 | 12 | 9 | 56 | 55 | 38 | |
| 4. | Racing Club de Strasbourg (Strasbourg) | 34 | 15 | 7 | 12 | 74 | 55 | 37 | |
| 5. | FC Sochaux-Montbéliard (Montbéliard) | 34 | 15 | 6 | 13 | 64 | 53 | 36 | |
| 6. | Girondins de Bordeaux FC (Bordeaux) | 34 | 14 | 7 | 13 | 63 | 51 | 35 | |
| 7. | AS de Saint-Étienne (Saint-Étienne) | 34 | 15 | 5 | 14 | 58 | 51 | 35 | |
| 8. | Racing Club de Paris (Paris) | 34 | 13 | 8 | 13 | 62 | 57 | 34 | |
| 9. | Olympique GC de Nice (Nice) | 34 | 13 | 8 | 13 | 75 | 81 | 34 | |
| 10. | Olympique de Marseille (Marseille) | 34 | 13 | 7 | 14 | 58 | 51 | 33 | |
| 11. | Nîmes Olympique (Nîmes) | 34 | 14 | 5 | 15 | 48 | 52 | 33 | |
| 12. | Olympique Lyonnais (Lyon) | 34 | 12 | 9 | 13 | 54 | 63 | 33 | |
| 13. | FC de Nancy (Nancy) | 34 | 12 | 8 | 14 | 59 | 54 | 32 | |
| 14. | AS de Monaco (Monaco) | 34 | 10 | 11 | 13 | 43 | 45 | 31 | |
| 15. | FC de Metz (Metz) | 34 | 12 | 7 | 15 | 42 | 72 | 31 | |
| 16. | Lille Olympique SC (Lille) | 34 | 11 | 8 | 15 | 61 | 58 | 30 | PO |
| 17. | AS Troyenne-Savinienne (Troyes) | 34 | 12 | 6 | 16 | 48 | 66 | 30 | R* |
| 18. | Club Olympique Roubaix-Tourcoing (Roubaix) | 34 | 10 | 6 | 18 | 52 | 90 | 26 | R |
| | | 612 | 238 | 136 | 238 | 1052 | 1052 | 612 | |

## Top goal-scorers

| | | | |
|---|---|---|---|
| 1) | René BLIARD | (Stade de Reims) | 30 |
| 2) | Ernst STOJASMAL | (Racing Club de Strasbourg) | 23 |
| 3) | Gunnar ANDERSSON | (Olympique de Marseille) | 21 |

* Red Star Olympique Audonien were barred from promotion. AS Troyenne-Savinienne retained Division 1 status.

## Promotion/Relegation Play-Off

| Stade Rennais Université Club (Rennes) | 0-1, 1-6 | Lille Olympique SC (Lille) |
|---|---|---|

| | Division 2 | Pd | Wn | Dw | Ls | GF | GA | Pts | |
|---|---|---|---|---|---|---|---|---|---|
| 1. | Union Athlétique Sedan-Torcy (Sedan) | 38 | 26 | 9 | 3 | 102 | 30 | 61 | P |
| 2. | Red Star Olympique Audonien (Saint-Ouen) | 38 | 24 | 7 | 7 | 99 | 43 | 55 | * |
| 3. | Stade Rennais Université Club (Rennes) | 38 | 22 | 8 | 8 | 83 | 48 | 52 | PO |
| 4. | Havre AC (Le Havre) | 38 | 19 | 11 | 8 | 74 | 54 | 49 | |
| 5. | US Valenciennes-Anzin (Valenciennes) | 38 | 20 | 7 | 11 | 90 | 66 | 47 | |
| 6. | SC de l'Ouest Angers (Angers) | 38 | 19 | 8 | 11 | 71 | 52 | 46 | |
| 7. | FC de Sète (Sète) | 38 | 15 | 13 | 10 | 40 | 30 | 43 | |
| 8. | FC de Rouen (Rouen) | 38 | 17 | 8 | 13 | 59 | 47 | 42 | |
| 9. | Olympique Alésien (Alès) | 38 | 12 | 12 | 14 | 54 | 52 | 36 | |
| 10. | FC de Nantes (Nantes) | 38 | 13 | 9 | 16 | 69 | 78 | 35 | |
| 11. | AS Biterroise (Béziers) | 38 | 12 | 11 | 15 | 48 | 65 | 35 | |
| 12. | SC de Toulon (Toulon) | 38 | 12 | 10 | 16 | 53 | 78 | 34 | |
| 13. | Stade Français FC (Paris) | 38 | 12 | 9 | 17 | 59 | 71 | 33 | |
| 14. | AS de Cannes (Cannes) | 38 | 9 | 13 | 16 | 55 | 67 | 31 | |
| 15. | AS Aixoise (Aix-en-Provence) | 38 | 10 | 10 | 18 | 54 | 80 | 30 | |
| 16. | Racing Club Franc-Comtois (Besançon) | 38 | 13 | 3 | 22 | 72 | 96 | 29 | |
| 17. | Stade Olympique Montpelliérain (Montpellier) | 38 | 10 | 9 | 19 | 49 | 88 | 29 | |
| 18. | Perpignan FC (Perpignan) | 38 | 10 | 6 | 22 | 45 | 66 | 26 | |
| 19. | FC de Grenoble (Grenoble) | 38 | 7 | 12 | 19 | 50 | 77 | 26 | |
| 20. | Cercle Athlétique de Paris (Paris) | 38 | 4 | 13 | 21 | 38 | 76 | 21 | |
| | | 760 | 286 | 188 | 286 | 1264 | 1264 | 760 | |

## Coupe de France Final  (Stade Yves du Manoir, Colombes – 29/05/55 – 49,411)

**LILLE OLYMPIQUE SC (LILLE)**  **5-2**  Girondins de Bordeaux FC (Bordeaux)

*Vincent 07', Douis 28', 31', Bourbotte 35', 75'*  *Wozniesko 41', Skander 63'*

**Lille**: Van Gool, Pazur, Lemaitre, Clauws, Bieganski, Sommerlynck, Bourbotte, Douis, Vincent, Strappe, Lefevre.

**Bordeaux**: Astresses, Janczewski, Grimonpon, Debelleix, Garriga, De Kubber, Skander, Wozniesko, Abdesselem, Kargulewicz, Doye.


## Semi-Finals  (08/05/55)

| | | |
|---|---|---|
| Girondins de Bordeaux FC (Bordeaux) | 3-2 | Olympique GC de Nice (Nice) |
| Lille Olympique SC (Lille) | 4-0 | Racing Club de Strasbourg (Strasbourg) |


## Quarter-Finals  (17/04/55)

| | | |
|---|---|---|
| Girondins de Bordeaux FC (Bordeaux) | 1-0 | Havre AC (Le Havre) |
| Lille Olympique SC (Lille) | 1-0 | Toulouse FC (Toulouse) |
| Olympique GC de Nice (Nice) | 1-1,  5-0 | SC Draguignan-Le Muy (Draguignan) |
| Racing Club de Strasbourg (Strasbourg) | 4-3 | FC de Nancy (Nancy) |


# 1955-56

| 1955-1956 Division One | Girondins Bordeaux | Racing Club de Lens | Lille Olympique SC | Olympique Lyonnais | Olympique Marseille | FC de Metz | AS de Monaco | FC de Nancy | Olympique GC Nice | Nîmes Olympique | Racing Club de Paris | Stade de Reims | AS Saint-Étienne | Union Athlétique Sedan-Torcy | Sochaux-Montbéliard | Racing Strasbourg | Toulouse FC | Troyenne-Savinienne |
|---|---|---|---|---|---|---|---|---|---|---|---|---|---|---|---|---|---|---|
| Girondins Bordeaux | | 1-2 | 2-1 | 2-0 | 1-0 | 2-1 | 0-2 | 3-3 | 1-2 | 2-1 | 1-4 | 2-3 | 4-3 | 2-1 | 0-1 | 3-0 | 3-4 | 2-2 |
| Racing Club de Lens | 2-0 | | 1-0 | 1-0 | 4-0 | 4-1 | 1-2 | 3-2 | 4-0 | 3-1 | 7-3 | 4-1 | 2-2 | 4-0 | 2-1 | 1-0 | 1-0 | 3-1 |
| Lille Olympique SC | 2-1 | 1-1 | | 4-1 | 0-3 | 4-1 | 2-0 | 1-2 | 2-1 | 3-2 | 6-1 | 2-2 | 0-2 | 0-1 | 1-2 | 4-0 | 1-2 | 4-0 |
| Olympique Lyonnais | 5-2 | 0-1 | 2-1 | | 1-1 | 2-1 | 1-1 | 2-0 | 2-4 | 0-0 | 3-1 | 2-1 | 2-1 | 0-0 | 3-1 | 2-0 | 2-2 | 3-0 |
| Olympique Marseille | 3-0 | 2-2 | 2-1 | 5-1 | | 4-0 | 1-1 | 1-2 | 0-0 | 2-0 | 1-4 | 1-0 | 2-2 | 2-2 | 1-0 | 3-1 | 3-0 | 3-0 |
| FC de Metz | 1-1 | 2-3 | 2-0 | 1-1 | 2-3 | | 1-2 | 2-0 | 2-0 | 2-2 | 1-3 | 1-1 | 5-2 | 3-1 | 3-1 | 2-2 | 1-0 | 2-1 |
| AS de Monaco | 4-2 | 5-2 | 2-0 | 2-1 | 3-0 | 4-0 | | 2-2 | 4-2 | 1-0 | 0-0 | 2-1 | 2-3 | 0-2 | 1-0 | 0-0 | 1-0 | 1-1 |
| FC de Nancy | 1-0 | 1-0 | 3-1 | 2-0 | 0-0 | 1-2 | 1-3 | | 2-0 | 3-1 | 2-3 | 1-4 | 2-2 | 4-2 | 0-1 | 3-1 | 1-2 | 1-0 |
| Olympique GC Nice | 2-0 | 5-2 | 7-1 | 2-0 | 1-2 | 1-0 | 1-1 | 3-0 | | 2-1 | 2-0 | 1-0 | 2-1 | 3-2 | 1-2 | 2-1 | 1-0 | 2-0 |
| Nîmes Olympique | 3-0 | 3-1 | 2-0 | 2-1 | 1-1 | 0-0 | 6-2 | 6-1 | 1-1 | | 1-5 | 2-2 | 1-1 | 6-2 | 1-0 | 4-0 | 2-1 | 5-2 |
| Racing Club de Paris | 3-0 | 0-1 | 2-1 | 1-2 | 4-0 | 1-2 | 2-1 | 3-4 | 4-2 | 3-2 | | 2-1 | 3-0 | 4-0 | 2-5 | 2-2 | 3-0 | 1-1 |
| Stade de Reims | 3-0 | 3-0 | 1-1 | 3-0 | 1-1 | 5-2 | 0-2 | 1-2 | 1-3 | 1-1 | 2-1 | | 1-2 | 1-1 | 3-0 | 6-2 | 0-1 | 2-1 |
| AS Saint-Étienne | 3-0 | 0-0 | 4-1 | 0-1 | 3-1 | 5-0 | 1-0 | 1-1 | 3-3 | 3-1 | 3-2 | 3-1 | | 3-2 | 0-0 | 3-1 | 0-0 | 4-0 |
| Union Athlétique Sedan-Torcy | 1-1 | 1-0 | 2-1 | 2-2 | 2-1 | 4-2 | 2-1 | 1-0 | 0-1 | 2-1 | 3-0 | 1-1 | 3-0 | | 2-1 | 5-2 | 1-1 | 1-3 |
| Sochaux-Montbéliard | 2-4 | 3-1 | 3-3 | 1-2 | 3-1 | 0-1 | 3-1 | 0-0 | 0-0 | 1-0 | 1-1 | 4-3 | 2-3 | 0-2 | | 2-2 | 0-0 | 5-1 |
| Racing Strasbourg | 1-1 | 1-0 | 3-1 | 1-2 | 5-0 | 3-1 | 2-1 | 4-0 | 1-0 | 2-1 | 1-4 | 0-1 | 5-2 | 3-0 | 1-0 | | 1-2 | 2-1 |
| Toulouse FC | 2-1 | 4-2 | 4-2 | 2-1 | 2-3 | 4-1 | 3-1 | 1-0 | 1-1 | 2-2 | 0-0 | 0-2 | 2-2 | 1-1 | 0-1 | 4-4 | | 2-1 |
| Troyenne-Savinienne | 1-1 | 3-0 | 1-6 | 1-3 | 0-1 | 1-1 | 2-5 | 4-4 | 2-2 | 4-2 | 0-2 | 2-3 | 1-1 | 2-1 | 1-1 | 3-0 | 0-2 | |

| | Division 1 | Pd | Wn | Dw | Ls | GF | GA | Pts | |
|---|---|---|---|---|---|---|---|---|---|
| 1. | OLYMPIQUE GC DE NICE (NICE) | 34 | 18 | 7 | 9 | 60 | 43 | 43 | |
| 2. | Racing Club de Lens (Lens) | 34 | 19 | 4 | 11 | 65 | 49 | 42 | |
| 3. | AS de Monaco (Monaco) | 34 | 17 | 7 | 10 | 63 | 45 | 41 | |
| 4. | AS de Saint-Étienne (Saint-Étienne) | 34 | 15 | 11 | 8 | 68 | 53 | 41 | |
| 5. | Olympique de Marseille (Marseille) | 34 | 16 | 81 | 0 | 54 | 49 | 40 | |
| 6. | Racing Club de Paris (Paris) | 34 | 17 | 5 | 12 | 74 | 58 | 39 | |
| 7. | Toulouse FC (Toulouse) | 34 | 14 | 10 | 10 | 51 | 46 | 38 | |
| 8. | Olympique Lyonnais (Lyon) | 34 | 15 | 7 | 12 | 50 | 49 | 37 | |
| 9. | Union Athlétique Sedan-Torcy (Sedan) | 34 | 14 | 89 | 12 | 53 | 56 | 36 | |
| 10. | Stade de Reims (Reims) | 34 | 13 | 8 | 13 | 61 | 60 | 34 | |
| 11. | FC Sochaux-Montbéliard (Montbéliard) | 34 | 12 | 8 | 14 | 47 | 50 | 32 | |
| 12. | FC de Nancy (Nancy) | 34 | 13 | 6 | 15 | 51 | 60 | 32 | |
| 13. | Nîmes Olympique (Nîmes) | 34 | 11 | 9 | 14 | 64 | 56 | 31 | |
| 14. | Racing Club de Strasbourg (Strasbourg) | 34 | 12 | 6 | 16 | 54 | 66 | 30 | |
| 15. | FC de Metz (Metz) | 34 | 11 | 7 | 16 | 49 | 68 | 29 | |
| 16. | Lille Olympique SC (Lille) | 34 | 10 | 4 | 20 | 58 | 65 | 24 | PO |
| 17. | Girondins de Bordeaux FC (Bordeaux) | 34 | 9 | 6 | 19 | 45 | 69 | 24 | R |
| 18. | AS Troyenne-Savinienne (Troyes) | 34 | 5 | 9 | 20 | 43 | 78 | 19 | R |
| | | 612 | 241 | 130 | 241 | 1010 | 1010 | 612 | |

## Top goal-scorers

| | | | |
|---|---|---|---|
| 1) | Tadeusz CISOWSKI | (Racing Club de Paris) | 31 |
| 2) | Rachid MEKLOUFI | (AS de Saint-Étienne) | 21 |
| 3) | Gunnar ANDERSSON | (Olympique de Marseille) | 20 |
| | Jacques FOIX | (AS de Saint-Étienne) | 20 |

## Promotion/Relegation Play-Off

US Valenciennes-Anzin (Valenciennes)     1-0, 1-2, 4-0          Lille Olympique SC (Lille)

| | Division 2 | Pd | Wn | Dw | Ls | GF | GA | Pts | |
|---|---|---|---|---|---|---|---|---|---|
| 1. | Stade Rennais Université Club (Rennes) | 38 | 23 | 8 | 7 | 69 | 38 | 54 | P |
| 2. | SC de l'Ouest Angers (Angers) | 38 | 25 | 3 | 10 | 90 | 42 | 53 | P |
| 3. | US Valenciennes-Anzin (Valenciennes) | 38 | 22 | 7 | 9 | 80 | 39 | 51 | PO |
| 4. | AS Biterroise (Béziers) | 38 | 20 | 11 | 7 | 69 | 43 | 51 | |
| 5. | Stade Français FC (Paris) | 38 | 17 | 12 | 9 | 75 | 56 | 46 | |
| 6. | Olympique Alésien (Alès) | 38 | 17 | 11 | 10 | 64 | 51 | 45 | |
| 7. | Red Star Olympique Audonien (Saint-Ouen) | 38 | 16 | 10 | 12 | 76 | 69 | 42 | |
| 8. | FC de Grenoble (Grenoble) | 38 | 12 | 15 | 11 | 46 | 41 | 39 | |
| 9. | Racing Club Franc-Comtois (Besançon) | 38 | 14 | 11 | 13 | 54 | 54 | 39 | |
| 10. | Club Olympique Roubaix-Tourcoing (Roubaix) | 38 | 16 | 4 | 18 | 63 | 64 | 36 | |
| 11. | AS de Cannes (Cannes) | 38 | 13 | 9 | 16 | 48 | 69 | 35 | |
| 12. | Havre AC (Le Havre) | 38 | 12 | 10 | 16 | 45 | 37 | 34 | |
| 13. | SC de Toulon (Toulon) | 38 | 10 | 13 | 15 | 54 | 62 | 33 | |
| 14. | AS Aixoise (Aix-en-Provence) | 38 | 11 | 10 | 17 | 56 | 59 | 32 | |
| 15. | Perpignan FC (Perpignan) | 38 | 10 | 12 | 16 | 36 | 57 | 32 | |
| 16. | FC de Rouen (Rouen) | 38 | 12 | 7 | 19 | 47 | 56 | 31 | |
| 17. | FC de Nantes (Nantes) | 38 | 10 | 10 | 18 | 54 | 84 | 30 | |
| 18. | FC de Sète (Sète) | 38 | 10 | 7 | 21 | 42 | 74 | 27 | |
| 19. | Cercle Athlétique de Paris (Paris) | 38 | 8 | 10 | 20 | 45 | 66 | 26 | |
| 20. | Stade Olympique Montpelliérain (Montpellier) | 38 | 7 | 10 | 21 | 48 | 80 | 24 | |
| | | 760 | 285 | 190 | 285 | 1161 | 1141 | 760 | |

## Coupe de France Final   (Stade Yves du Manoir, Colombes – 27/05/56 – 47,258)

**UNION ATHLÉTIQUE SEDAN-TORCY**   **3-1**   AS Troyenne-Savinienne (Troyes)

*Cuenca 13', Thuane 34' (o.g.), Tillon 57'*                    *De Vlaeminck 62'*

**Sedan**: Vincent, Carpentier, Fulgenzi, Pascal, Eloy, Christian Oliver, Brény, Lefevre, Tillon, Célestin Oliver, Cuenca.

**Troyenne**: Landi, Thuane, Czapski, Tkomas, Diebold, Ferrad, Jensen, Hjalmarsson, De Vlaeminck, Delcampe, Flamion.

### Semi-Finals   (06/05/56)

| | | |
|---|---|---|
| Union Athlétique Sedan-Torcy (Sedan) | 1-0 | Olympique Lyonnais (Lyon) |
| AS Troyenne-Savinienne (Troyes) | 3-2 | FC de Nancy (Nancy) |

### Quarter-Finals   (08/04/56)

| | | |
|---|---|---|
| Olympique Lyonnais (Lyon) | 3-0 | Olympique GC de Nice (Nice) |
| FC de Nancy (Nancy) | 3-1 | Racing Club de Lens (Lens) |
| Union Athlétique Sedan-Torcy (Sedan) | 2-0 | AS de Saint-Étienne (Saint-Étienne) |
| AS Troyenne-Savinienne (Troyes) | 3-2 | Stade de Reims (Reims) |

# 1956-57

| 1956-1957 Division One | SC l'Ouest Angers | Racing Club de Lens | Olympique Lyonnais | Olympique Marseille | FC de Metz | AS de Monaco | FC de Nancy | Olympique GC Nice | Nîmes Olympique | Racing Club de Paris | Stade de Reims | Stade Rennais Université Club | AS Saint-Étienne | Union Athlétique Sedan-Torcy | Sochaux-Montbéliard | Racing Strasbourg | Toulouse FC | Valenciennes-Anzin |
|---|---|---|---|---|---|---|---|---|---|---|---|---|---|---|---|---|---|---|
| SC l'Ouest Angers | | 1-0 | 0-2 | 2-2 | 0-3 | 0-2 | 3-0 | 0-1 | 1-1 | 1-1 | 2-2 | 2-0 | 0-1 | 0-0 | 4-0 | 4-1 | 2-5 | 2-0 |
| Racing Club de Lens | 0-3 | | 3-1 | 2-0 | 3-1 | 3-1 | 3-1 | 6-1 | 4-0 | 2-0 | 2-1 | 3-0 | 0-2 | 1-0 | 3-1 | 0-2 | 4-1 | 0-0 |
| Olympique Lyonnais | 2-1 | 3-0 | | 2-0 | 1-0 | 1-0 | 0-1 | 1-0 | 4-1 | 1-2 | 0-3 | 2-0 | 1-3 | 1-1 | 0-1 | 3-1 | 1-3 | 1-0 |
| Olympique Marseille | 0-0 | 1-4 | 3-2 | | 3-3 | 2-0 | 3-1 | 3-1 | 3-1 | 0-3 | 1-2 | 1-0 | 4-3 | 3-0 | 2-3 | 3-1 | 3-0 | 4-1 |
| FC de Metz | 0-1 | 1-5 | 3-1 | 1-0 | | 1-2 | 1-1 | 3-3 | 3-1 | 2-2 | 2-5 | 1-1 | 1-2 | 3-1 | 1-3 | 2-0 | 4-1 | 2-2 |
| AS de Monaco | 1-1 | 1-2 | 2-0 | 1-0 | 2-1 | | 0-2 | 2-1 | 4-1 | 1-1 | 1-1 | 4-0 | 3-1 | 2-1 | 2-1 | 1-2 | 1-1 | 6-0 |
| FC de Nancy | 2-2 | 0-2 | 2-2 | 0-1 | 0-2 | 0-2 | | 4-2 | 1-0 | 2-5 | 0-0 | 4-0 | 1-7 | 3-2 | 1-3 | 3-3 | 1-1 | 1-4 |
| Olympique GC Nice | 1-1 | 3-2 | 1-0 | 1-3 | 1-1 | 0-2 | 3-2 | | 5-2 | 1-1 | 2-1 | 0-2 | 2-2 | 1-0 | 4-2 | 1-0 | 1-0 | 2-2 |
| Nîmes Olympique | 3-1 | 2-3 | 2-0 | 2-0 | 1-1 | 3-1 | 4-0 | 3-2 | | 4-2 | 1-2 | 2-1 | 0-0 | 2-1 | 3-0 | 4-1 | 0-1 | 2-3 |
| Racing Club de Paris | 6-2 | 5-0 | 1-2 | 1-3 | 4-1 | 2-1 | 6-1 | 3-2 | 0-0 | | 4-2 | 3-0 | 1-2 | 1-2 | 3-1 | 2-0 | 6-2 | 3-1 |
| Stade de Reims | 1-2 | 3-2 | 4-1 | 1-1 | 2-1 | 5-1 | 4-1 | 3-1 | 2-0 | 2-4 | | 3-1 | 4-5 | 0-1 | 1-0 | 3-1 | 2-0 | 1-1 |
| Stade Rennais Université Club | 4-1 | 1-4 | 2-1 | 1-1 | 1-0 | 0-1 | 0-3 | 2-3 | 2-1 | 2-2 | 1-1 | | 1-0 | 2-0 | 2-0 | 2-1 | 1-0 | 3-0 |
| AS Saint-Étienne | 3-0 | 3-1 | 3-2 | 6-3 | 2-0 | 0-1 | 6-1 | 4-2 | 4-0 | 3-1 | 0-0 | 2-0 | | 2-2 | 6-0 | 2-2 | 0-0 | 5-4 |
| Union Athlétique Sedan-Torcy | 1-1 | 4-4 | 2-2 | 1-1 | 3-2 | 3-3 | 1-1 | 3-3 | 1-0 | 1-1 | 0-4 | 1-1 | 2-6 | | 1-0 | 3-1 | 1-1 | 3-0 |
| Sochaux-Montbéliard | 0-0 | 2-2 | 3-1 | 3-0 | 1-1 | 1-1 | 3-1 | 4-2 | 3-1 | 3-5 | 2-0 | 3-1 | 1-1 | 5-2 | | 6-0 | 1-3 | 4-0 |
| Racing Strasbourg | 0-2 | 1-4 | 2-0 | 2-3 | 1-0 | 2-4 | 0-0 | 2-2 | 0-4 | 2-1 | 1-3 | 2-0 | 1-1 | 0-0 | 3-2 | | 0-0 | 6-0 |
| Toulouse FC | 5-0 | 1-2 | 2-2 | 0-1 | 1-2 | 3-0 | 1-2 | 4-3 | 0-1 | 3-3 | 4-0 | 6-0 | 3-0 | 2-3 | 2-0 | 1-1 | | 4-0 |
| Valenciennes-Anzin | 1-0 | 2-1 | 1-2 | 2-2 | 1-1 | 2-1 | 0-0 | 2-1 | 0-0 | 3-1 | 1-5 | 5-2 | 1-0 | 0-4 | 3-1 | 0-1 | 1-0 | |

| | Division 1 | Pd | Wn | Dw | Ls | GF | GA | Pts | |
|---|---|---|---|---|---|---|---|---|---|
| 1. | AS DE SAINT-Étienne (SAINT-Étienne) | 34 | 20 | 9 | 5 | 88 | 45 | 49 | |
| 2. | Racing Club de Lens (Lens) | 34 | 21 | 3 | 10 | 77 | 49 | 45 | |
| 3. | Stade de Reims (Reims) | 34 | 18 | 7 | 9 | 73 | 47 | 43 | |
| 4. | Racing Club de Paris (Paris) | 34 | 17 | 8 | 9 | 86 | 55 | 42 | |
| 5. | AS de Monaco (Monaco) | 34 | 17 | 6 | 11 | 57 | 44 | 40 | |
| 6. | Olympique de Marseille (Marseille) | 34 | 16 | 7 | 11 | 60 | 53 | 39 | |
| 7. | FC Sochaux-Montbéliard (Montbéliard) | 34 | 14 | 5 | 15 | 63 | 62 | 33 | |
| 8. | Toulouse FC (Toulouse) | 34 | 12 | 8 | 14 | 61 | 49 | 32 | |
| 9. | Union Athlétique Sedan-Torcy (Sedan) | 34 | 9 | 14 | 11 | 51 | 59 | 32 | |
| 10. | Nîmes Olympique (Nîmes) | 34 | 13 | 5 | 16 | 52 | 56 | 31 | |
| 11. | SC de l'Ouest Angers (Angers) | 34 | 10 | 11 | 13 | 42 | 51 | 31 | |
| 12. | Olympique Lyonnais (Lyon) | 34 | 13 | 4 | 17 | 45 | 53 | 30 | |
| 13. | Olympique GC de Nice (Nice) | 34 | 11 | 8 | 15 | 59 | 72 | 30 | |
| 14. | US Valenciennes-Anzin (Valenciennes) | 34 | 10 | 9 | 15 | 43 | 72 | 29 | |
| 15. | FC de Metz (Metz) | 34 | 9 | 10 | 15 | 51 | 58 | 28 | |
| 16. | Stade Rennais Université Club (Rennes) | 34 | 11 | 5 | 18 | 36 | 63 | 27 | PO |
| 17. | Racing Club de Strasbourg (Strasbourg) | 34 | 9 | 8 | 17 | 43 | 66 | 26 | R |
| 18. | FC de Nancy (Nancy) | 34 | 8 | 9 | 17 | 43 | 76 | 25 | R |
| | | 612 | 238 | 136 | 238 | 1030 | 1030 | 612 | |

## Top goal-scorers

| | | | |
|---|---|---|---|
| 1) | Tadeusz CISOWSKI | (Racing Club de Paris) | 33 |
| 2) | Just FONTAINE | (Stade de Reims) | 30 |
| 3) | Egon JÖNSSON | (Racing Club de Lens) | 29 |
| | Eugène NJO-LEA | (AS de Saint-Étienne) | 29 |

## Promotion/Relegation Play-Off

Stade Rennais Université Club (Rennes)     2-0, 1-3, 1-2       Lille Olympique SC (Lille)

| | Division 2 | Pd | Wn | Dw | Ls | GF | GA | Pts | |
|---|---|---|---|---|---|---|---|---|---|
| 1. | Olympique Alésien (Alès) | 38 | 24 | 8 | 6 | 58 | 36 | 56 | P |
| 2. | AS Biterroise (Béziers) | 38 | 20 | 13 | 5 | 58 | 38 | 53 | P |
| 3. | Lille Olympique SC (Lille) | 38 | 21 | 10 | 7 | 99 | 51 | 52 | PO |
| 4. | AS Troyenne-Savinienne (Troyes) | 38 | 17 | 11 | 10 | 71 | 46 | 45 | |
| 5. | Girondins de Bordeaux FC (Bordeaux) | 38 | 15 | 13 | 10 | 67 | 48 | 43 | |
| 6. | FC de Grenoble (Grenoble) | 38 | 16 | 9 | 13 | 63 | 49 | 41 | |
| 7. | SC de Toulon (Toulon) | 38 | 18 | 5 | 15 | 70 | 56 | 41 | |
| 8. | Havre AC (Le Havre) | 38 | 15 | 11 | 12 | 62 | 55 | 41 | |
| 9. | FC de Rouen (Rouen) | 38 | 16 | 8 | 14 | 64 | 48 | 40 | |
| 10. | Stade Français FC (Paris) | 38 | 14 | 11 | 13 | 53 | 51 | 39 | |
| 11. | Stade Olympique Montpelliérain (Montpellier) | 38 | 16 | 6 | 16 | 56 | 71 | 38 | |
| 12. | FC de Sète (Sète) | 38 | 14 | 9 | 15 | 47 | 53 | 37 | |
| 13. | FC de Nantes (Nantes) | 38 | 13 | 10 | 15 | 56 | 64 | 36 | |
| 14. | Perpignan FC (Perpignan) | 38 | 12 | 12 | 14 | 35 | 44 | 36 | |
| 15. | Club Olympique Roubaix-Tourcoing (Roubaix) | 38 | 14 | 4 | 20 | 49 | 55 | 32 | |
| 16. | Racing Club Franc-Comtois (Besançon) | 38 | 13 | 6 | 19 | 46 | 60 | 32 | |
| 17. | AS Aixoise (Aix-en-Provence) | 38 | 11 | 5 | 22 | 40 | 61 | 27 | |
| 18. | AS de Cannes (Cannes) | 38 | 7 | 13 | 18 | 39 | 60 | 27 | |
| 19. | Cercle Athlétique de Paris (Paris) | 38 | 6 | 11 | 21 | 41 | 82 | 23 | |
| 20. | Red Star Olympique Audonien (Saint-Ouen) | 38 | 7 | 7 | 24 | 42 | 88 | 21 | |
| | | 760 | 289 | 182 | 289 | 1116 | 1116 | 760 | |

**Elected**: US de Forbach (Forbach) and Limoges FC (Limoges).

Division 2 was extended to 22 clubs for the next season.

## Coupe de France Final   (Stade Yves du Manoir, Colombes – 26/05/57 – 43,125)

| **TOULOUSE FC (TOULOUSE)** | **6-3** | SC de l'Ouest Angers (Angers) |

*Dereuddre 11', 24', Bouchouk 28', Bocchi 61',*
*Di Loreto 85', Brahimi 89'*                                   *Biancheri 35', Boucher 83' (o.g.), Bourrigault 88'*

**Toulouse**: Roussel, Boucher, Nungesser, Bocchi, Pleimelding, Cahuzac, Brahimi, Dereuddre, Di Loreto, Rytkonen, Bouchouk.

**Angers**: Fragassi, Kowalski, Pasquini, Hnatow, Sbroglia, Bourrigault, Le Gall, Schindlauer, Tison, Biancheri, Loncle

## Semi-Finals   (05/05/57)

| SC de l'Ouest Angers (Angers) | 1-0 | Girondins de Bordeaux FC (Bordeaux) |
| Toulouse FC (Toulouse) | 3-2 | Olympique GC de Nice (Nice) |

## Quarter-Finals   (07/04/57)

| SC de l'Ouest Angers (Angers) | 0-0, 4-1 | Nîmes Olympique (Nîmes) |
| Girondins de Bordeaux FC (Bordeaux) | 2-1 | AS de Cannes (Cannes) |
| Olympique GC de Nice (Nice) | 2-2, 7-1 | Lille Olympique SC (Lille) |
| Toulouse FC (Toulouse) | 3-2 | Union Athlétique Sedan-Torcy (Sedan) |

# 1957-58

| 1957-1958 Division One | Olympique Alésien | SC de l'Ouest Angers | AS Biterroise Béziers | Racing Club de Lens | Lille Olympique SC | Olympique Lyonnais | Olympique Marseille | FC de Metz | AS de Monaco | Olympique GC Nice | Nîmes Olympique | Racing Club de Paris | Stade de Reims | AS Saint-Étienne | Union Athlétique Sedan | Sochaux-Montbéliard | Toulouse FC | Valenciennes-Anzin |
|---|---|---|---|---|---|---|---|---|---|---|---|---|---|---|---|---|---|---|
| Olympique Alésien | | 0-0 | 2-0 | 0-1 | 2-1 | 2-2 | 1-0 | 4-1 | 1-1 | 1-1 | 1-1 | 1-3 | 2-0 | 0-2 | 2-0 | 2-1 | 2-0 | 0-1 |
| SC de l'Ouest Angers | 1-1 | | 3-1 | 5-0 | 0-0 | 2-1 | 2-2 | 3-1 | 3-2 | 2-1 | 1-2 | 0-0 | 0-1 | 2-2 | 1-1 | 5-1 | 0-1 | 3-4 |
| AS Biterroise Béziers | 3-2 | 4-4 | | 1-1 | 2-0 | 1-1 | 0-0 | 0-1 | 0-3 | 0-1 | 0-1 | 1-0 | 2-0 | 2-2 | 0-2 | 2-1 | 2-0 | 3-1 |
| Racing Club de Lens | 5-0 | 2-1 | 3-1 | | 1-0 | 4-4 | 3-1 | 2-2 | 0-1 | 1-0 | 1-1 | 1-1 | 0-1 | 1-3 | 2-3 | 1-1 | 3-1 | 2-0 |
| Lille Olympique SC | 1-0 | 2-3 | 10-1 | 4-1 | | 3-0 | 3-1 | 2-1 | 1-1 | 1-0 | 3-1 | 1-3 | 2-1 | 1-2 | 3-0 | 3-2 | 1-3 | 2-3 |
| Olympique Lyonnais | 2-0 | 2-3 | 2-1 | 3-1 | 2-0 | | 1-1 | 2-0 | 2-0 | 1-1 | 1-0 | 2-0 | 1-2 | 0-2 | 0-3 | 1-1 | 3-1 | 1-1 |
| Olympique Marseille | 1-0 | 1-2 | 0-1 | 2-2 | 3-1 | 2-3 | | 0-0 | 0-1 | 0-1 | 1-0 | 1-1 | 0-0 | 1-0 | 1-1 | 0-3 | 3-0 | 1-1 |
| FC de Metz | 0-1 | 0-3 | 4-0 | 1-4 | 2-3 | 2-1 | 1-2 | | 0-0 | 1-1 | 0-1 | 1-1 | 3-1 | 0-2 | 3-2 | 1-0 | 2-1 | 1-0 |
| AS de Monaco | 3-1 | 0-2 | 2-0 | 2-1 | 1-0 | 1-2 | 3-2 | 2-1 | | 1-1 | 1-1 | 3-2 | 3-0 | 0-0 | 1-1 | 5-2 | 0-2 | 4-0 |
| Olympique GC Nice | 6-1 | 0-0 | 6-1 | 0-2 | 5-5 | 2-2 | 3-0 | 6-2 | 0-1 | | 2-0 | 2-0 | 1-2 | 6-1 | 8-0 | 4-3 | 2-2 | 1-1 |
| Nîmes Olympique | 3-0 | 5-1 | 2-0 | 2-3 | 2-0 | 2-0 | 5-0 | 1-1 | 0-0 | 3-2 | | 0-1 | 3-0 | 2-2 | 2-2 | 2-0 | 3-2 | 5-0 |
| Racing Club de Paris | 3-2 | 1-2 | 1-0 | 5-0 | 1-3 | 2-4 | 4-3 | 1-2 | 2-3 | 3-1 | 3-1 | | 1-5 | 1-1 | 4-2 | 6-4 | 1-2 | 2-2 |
| Stade de Reims | 4-2 | 2-3 | 5-0 | 5-0 | 3-1 | 4-0 | 4-1 | 5-1 | 1-1 | 3-2 | 2-1 | 4-1 | | 4-0 | 3-0 | 3-1 | 2-2 | 4-2 |
| AS Saint-Étienne | 2-2 | 0-3 | 1-2 | 3-1 | 6-2 | 1-1 | 1-1 | 2-2 | 2-1 | 1-1 | 1-1 | 0-1 | 0-0 | | 3-3 | 2-2 | 1-1 | 5-1 |
| Union Athlétique Sedan-Torcy | 5-2 | 1-0 | 8-4 | 2-3 | 3-2 | 2-3 | 2-1 | 6-3 | 2-1 | 3-2 | 3-1 | 2-0 | 2-5 | 1-1 | | 4-1 | 3-0 | 2-1 |
| Sochaux-Montbéliard | 3-1 | 2-1 | 4-0 | 1-0 | 2-4 | 1-0 | 1-2 | 1-0 | 1-2 | 4-0 | 1-1 | 5-0 | 0-4 | 4-1 | 2-1 | | 4-2 | 1-0 |
| Toulouse FC | 2-3 | 1-3 | 3-2 | 3-2 | 1-2 | 3-1 | 1-1 | 4-1 | 0-0 | 2-1 | 4-0 | 1-1 | 1-0 | 2-3 | 2-1 | 0-0 | | 3-2 |
| Valenciennes-Anzin | 0-0 | 2-1 | 1-1 | 1-1 | 0-1 | 2-0 | 2-1 | 2-2 | 0-0 | 1-1 | 0-3 | 0-5 | 0-6 | 0-0 | 3-1 | 1-1 | 2-0 | |

| | Division 1 | Pd | Wn | Dw | Ls | GF | GA | Pts | |
|---|---|---|---|---|---|---|---|---|---|
| 1. | STADE DE REIMS (REIMS) | 34 | 22 | 4 | 8 | 89 | 42 | 48 | |
| 2. | Nîmes Olympique (Nîmes) | 34 | 16 | 9 | 9 | 61 | 39 | 41 | |
| 3. | AS de Monaco (Monaco) | 34 | 15 | 11 | 8 | 50 | 35 | 41 | |
| 4. | SC de l'Ouest Angers (Angers) | 34 | 16 | 9 | 9 | 65 | 46 | 41 | |
| 5. | Union Athlétique Sedan-Torcy (Sedan) | 34 | 16 | 6 | 12 | 74 | 70 | 38 | |
| 6. | Lille Olympique SC (Lille) | 34 | 17 | 3 | 14 | 71 | 59 | 37 | |
| 7. | AS de Saint-Étienne (Saint-Étienne) | 34 | 10 | 17 | 7 | 55 | 52 | 37 | |
| 8. | Olympique Lyonnais (Lyon) | 34 | 13 | 9 | 12 | 51 | 53 | 35 | |
| 9. | Racing Club de Paris (Paris) | 34 | 13 | 7 | 14 | 61 | 62 | 33 | |
| 10. | Toulouse FC (Toulouse) | 34 | 13 | 7 | 14 | 53 | 57 | 33 | |
| 11. | Racing Club de Lens (Lens) | 34 | 13 | 7 | 14 | 55 | 62 | 33 | |
| 12. | FC Sochaux-Montbéliard (Montbéliard) | 34 | 13 | 6 | 15 | 61 | 61 | 32 | |
| 13. | Olympique GC de Nice (Nice) | 34 | 10 | 11 | 13 | 71 | 53 | 31 | |
| 14. | Olympique Alésien (Alès) | 34 | 10 | 8 | 16 | 41 | 59 | 28 | |
| 15. | US Valenciennes-Anzin (Valenciennes) | 34 | 8 | 12 | 14 | 37 | 64 | 28 | |
| 16. | Olympique de Marseille (Marseille) | 34 | 8 | 10 | 16 | 46 | 65 | 26 | |
| 17. | FC de Metz (Metz) | 34 | 9 | 8 | 17 | 45 | 68 | 26 | R |
| 18. | AS Biterroise (Béziers) | 34 | 9 | 6 | 19 | 38 | 77 | 24 | R |
| | | 612 | 231 | 150 | 231 | 1024 | 1024 | 612 | |

## Top goal-scorers

| | | | |
|---|---|---|---|
| 1) | Just FONTAINE | (Stade de Reims) | 34 |
| 2) | Fernand DE VLAEMINCK | (Lille Olympique SC) | 23 |
| 3) | Alberto MURO | (Olympique GC de Nice) | 21 |
| | Ernie SCHULTZ | (Toulouse FC) | 21 |

Division 1 was extended to 20 clubs for the next season.

| | Division 2 | Pd | Wn | Dw | Ls | GF | GA | Pts | |
|---|---|---|---|---|---|---|---|---|---|
| 1. | FC de Nancy (Nancy) | 42 | 25 | 11 | 6 | 89 | 50 | 61 | P |
| 2. | Stade Rennais Université Club (Rennes) | 42 | 23 | 12 | 7 | 93 | 40 | 58 | P |
| 3. | Limoges FC (Limoges) | 42 | 25 | 5 | 12 | 85 | 41 | 55 | P |
| 4. | Racing Club de Strasbourg (Strasbourg) | 42 | 22 | 10 | 10 | 89 | 52 | 54 | P |
| 5. | Girondins de Bordeaux FC (Bordeaux) | 42 | 25 | 3 | 14 | 82 | 53 | 53 | |
| 6. | US de Forbach (Forbach) | 42 | 22 | 9 | 11 | 60 | 51 | 53 | |
| 7. | Havre AC (Le Havre) | 42 | 19 | 11 | 12 | 65 | 50 | 49 | |
| 8. | AS Troyenne-Savinienne (Troyes) | 42 | 20 | 9 | 13 | 51 | 42 | 49 | |
| 9. | FC de Rouen (Rouen) | 42 | 19 | 10 | 13 | 66 | 51 | 48 | |
| 10. | Club Olympique Roubaix-Tourcoing (Roubaix) | 42 | 19 | 9 | 14 | 75 | 68 | 47 | |
| 11. | SC de Toulon (Toulon) | 42 | 18 | 6 | 18 | 71 | 71 | 42 | |
| 12. | Red Star Olympique Audonien (Saint-Ouen) | 42 | 15 | 12 | 15 | 60 | 60 | 42 | |
| 13. | FC de Nantes (Nantes) | 42 | 13 | 11 | 18 | 53 | 65 | 37 | |
| 14. | Perpignan FC (Perpignan) | 42 | 15 | 7 | 20 | 42 | 57 | 37 | |
| 15. | AS de Cannes (Cannes) | 42 | 13 | 10 | 19 | 60 | 79 | 36 | |
| 16. | Stade Français FC (Paris) | 42 | 13 | 7 | 22 | 48 | 75 | 33 | |
| 17. | Stade Olympique Montpelliérain (Montpellier) | 42 | 12 | 7 | 23 | 48 | 75 | 31 | |
| 18. | Cercle Athlétique de Paris (Paris) | 42 | 10 | 10 | 22 | 49 | 80 | 30 | |
| 19. | FC de Grenoble (Grenoble) | 42 | 7 | 15 | 20 | 53 | 74 | 29 | |
| 20. | AS Aixoise (Aix-en-Provence) | 42 | 7 | 13 | 22 | 53 | 90 | 27 | |
| 21. | FC de Sète (Sète) | 42 | 7 | 13 | 22 | 47 | 81 | 27 | |
| 22. | Racing Club Franc-Comtois (Besançon) | 42 | 9 | 8 | 25 | 49 | 83 | 26 | |
| | | 924 | 358 | 208 | 358 | 1388 | 1388 | 924 | |

Division 2 was reduced to 20 clubs for the next season.

## Coupe de France Final   (Stade du Manoir, Colombes – 18/05/58 – 56,523)

**STADE DE REIMS (REIMS)**  3-1  Nîmes Olympique (Nîmes)

*Bliard 42', 89', Fontaine 56'*                                              *Mazzouz 49'*

**Reims**: Colonna, Zimny, Giraudo, Penverne, Jonquet, Siatka, Lamartine, Bliard, Fontaine, Piantoni, Vincent.
**Nîmes**: Roszak, Bettache, Venturi, Schwager, Lafont, Barlaguet, Salaber, Akesbi, Skiba, Mazzouz, Rahis.

## Semi-Finals   (27/04/58)

| | | |
|---|---|---|
| Nîmes Olympique (Nîmes) | 2-1 | AS de Monaco (Monaco) |
| Stade de Reims (Reims) | 2-1 | Racing Club de Lens (Lens) |

## Quarter-Finals   (06/04/58)

| | | |
|---|---|---|
| Racing Club de Lens (Lens) | 1-0 | Girondins de Bordeaux FC (Bordeaux) |
| AS de Monaco (Monaco) | 2-1 | Racing Club de Strasbourg (Strasbourg) |
| Nîmes Olympique (Nîmes) | 2-0 | FC de Sète (Sète) |
| Stade de Reims (Reims) | 7-4 | Club Olympique Roubaix-Tourcoing |

# 1958-59

### 1958-1959 Division One

| | OAl | SCOA | RLe | LiO | LiF | OLy | OMa | ASM | FCN | OGCN | NîO | RPa | StR | StRe | ASSE | UAST | SoM | RCS | ToF | Val |
|---|---|---|---|---|---|---|---|---|---|---|---|---|---|---|---|---|---|---|---|---|
| Olympique Alésien | ■ | 1-3 | 2-6 | 1-2 | 0-2 | 1-2 | 2-1 | 2-1 | 0-3 | 0-0 | 0-4 | 1-1 | 3-6 | 0-1 | 1-1 | 1-1 | 2-1 | 0-1 | 1-0 | 3-0 |
| SC de l'Ouest Angers | 1-0 | ■ | 2-2 | 2-0 | 4-0 | 3-1 | 3-2 | 0-0 | 4-2 | 1-2 | 1-1 | 1-2 | 3-0 | 0-0 | 0-1 | 3-1 | 1-1 | 2-2 | 3-1 | 4-0 |
| Racing Lens | 2-4 | 1-1 | ■ | 2-2 | 1-1 | 2-1 | 4-1 | 2-1 | 2-4 | 0-0 | 0-1 | 2-1 | 2-1 | 2-0 | 0-2 | 0-2 | 3-2 | 6-0 | 0-1 | 2-0 |
| Lille Olympique | 5-0 | 1-1 | 1-1 | ■ | 2-0 | 2-1 | 2-2 | 2-2 | 2-0 | 0-0 | 0-0 | 1-6 | 0-2 | 4-4 | 2-4 | 0-3 | 3-0 | 2-3 | 3-2 | 6-1 |
| Limoges FC | 2-2 | 2-2 | 2-1 | 5-0 | ■ | 1-0 | 1-0 | 2-1 | 0-0 | 0-2 | 3-2 | 1-1 | 2-2 | 2-4 | 4-0 | 1-1 | 1-2 | 1-2 | 0-0 | 1-0 |
| Olympique Lyonnais | 1-1 | 1-0 | 2-0 | 1-0 | 2-1 | ■ | 1-1 | 4-1 | 1-3 | 1-0 | 2-1 | 3-2 | 1-5 | 5-2 | 2-0 | 4-3 | 2-0 | 2-2 | 1-1 | 2-2 |
| Olympique Marseille | 2-1 | 2-3 | 0-2 | 0-0 | 2-0 | 1-1 | ■ | 0-2 | 4-2 | 2-0 | 0-2 | 1-2 | 2-3 | 1-3 | 4-1 | 1-1 | 0-0 | 3-3 | 1-1 | 3-1 |
| AS de Monaco | 1-1 | 1-0 | 0-0 | 3-0 | 0-0 | 4-1 | 2-0 | ■ | 1-0 | 1-1 | 1-1 | 4-1 | 0-2 | 1-0 | 0-3 | 0-3 | 1-0 | 2-1 | 1-0 | 2-1 |
| FC de Nancy | 3-0 | 3-2 | 2-1 | 1-1 | 0-2 | 4-3 | 2-2 | 2-2 | ■ | 3-6 | 2-1 | 1-2 | 3-5 | 2-1 | 0-1 | 0-1 | 2-2 | 0-1 | 0-1 | 1-1 |
| Olympique GC Nice | 4-2 | 0-3 | 3-1 | 2-1 | 3-1 | 2-0 | 6-1 | 2-0 | 3-0 | ■ | 2-0 | 3-2 | 4-0 | 2-0 | 1-0 | 3-1 | 5-0 | 4-2 | 3-2 | 1-0 |
| Nîmes Olympique | 3-0 | 5-3 | 4-2 | 3-0 | 3-0 | 4-1 | 1-1 | 1-0 | 1-0 | 1-1 | ■ | 0-0 | 2-2 | 3-0 | 2-1 | 2-2 | 2-1 | 1-1 | 3-1 | 2-0 |
| Racing Paris | 5-2 | 5-0 | 5-0 | 7-2 | 4-1 | 2-2 | 2-1 | 2-0 | 4-4 | 1-1 | 2-2 | ■ | 0-1 | 1-0 | 2-2 | 1-1 | 0-2 | 5-2 | 2-0 | 3-0 |
| Stade Reims | 1-1 | 1-1 | 4-1 | 4-3 | 1-0 | 1-2 | 2-1 | 3-2 | 7-1 | 1-2 | 3-1 | 0-0 | ■ | 4-0 | 3-0 | 1-1 | 1-3 | 2-3 | 3-1 | 2-1 |
| Stade Rennais | 4-2 | 3-2 | 1-1 | 3-0 | 0-1 | 2-4 | 2-2 | 2-1 | 3-1 | 0-3 | 1-2 | 0-1 | 2-2 | ■ | 0-2 | 3-1 | 4-0 | 2-2 | 3-0 | 4-0 |
| AS Saint-Étienne | 1-0 | 1-1 | 2-1 | 1-0 | 2-1 | 2-0 | 4-2 | 3-5 | 4-0 | 3-4 | 0-1 | 3-3 | 4-4 | 2-2 | ■ | 2-1 | 4-3 | 1-5 | 4-3 | 1-1 |
| Union Athlétique Sedan-Torcy | 2-0 | 2-2 | 1-2 | 1-1 | 3-1 | 3-1 | 6-1 | 2-2 | 1-2 | 1-0 | 1-2 | 0-3 | 0-0 | 1-1 | 5-0 | ■ | 0-1 | 1-3 | 1-1 | 4-0 |
| Sochaux-Montbéliard | 4-5 | 2-1 | 2-1 | 2-3 | 3-1 | 5-3 | 5-1 | 3-2 | 2-1 | 1-0 | 3-2 | 1-1 | 3-1 | 2-1 | 3-1 | 2-2 | ■ | 3-0 | 2-2 | 1-1 |
| RC Strasbourg | 2-0 | 4-2 | 1-0 | 2-0 | 1-1 | 3-0 | 3-1 | 1-1 | 1-1 | 2-2 | 1-5 | 0-2 | 0-2 | 0-1 | 3-3 | 1-3 | 2-1 | ■ | 1-2 | 3-2 |
| Toulouse FC | 4-2 | 1-1 | 3-1 | 3-1 | 2-1 | 0-1 | 3-0 | 1-2 | 3-2 | 2-2 | 2-4 | 1-1 | 1-1 | 1-1 | 2-0 | 4-1 | 1-1 | 5-1 | ■ | 1-2 |
| Valenciennes | 1-0 | 4-0 | 3-1 | 3-2 | 2-3 | 1-0 | 5-1 | 2-2 | 1-1 | 2-1 | 0-0 | 1-0 | 3-1 | 1-1 | 3-1 | 1-1 | 1-1 | 4-1 | 2-0 | ■ |

| Division 1 | Pd | Wn | Dw | Ls | GF | GA | Pts | |
|---|---|---|---|---|---|---|---|---|
| 1. OLYMPIQUE GC DE NICE (NICE) | 38 | 24 | 8 | 6 | 80 | 38 | 56 | |
| 2. Nîmes Olympique (Nîmes) | 38 | 21 | 11 | 6 | 75 | 40 | 53 | |
| 3. Racing Club de Paris (Paris) | 38 | 18 | 13 | 7 | 84 | 47 | 49 | |
| 4. Stade de Reims (Reims) | 38 | 19 | 10 | 9 | 84 | 59 | 48 | |
| 5. FC Sochaux-Montbéliard (Montbéliard) | 38 | 17 | 9 | 12 | 72 | 66 | 43 | |
| 6. AS de Saint-Étienne (Saint-Étienne) | 38 | 16 | 8 | 14 | 68 | 73 | 40 | |
| 7. SC de l'Ouest Angers (Angers) | 38 | 14 | 11 | 13 | 66 | 58 | 39 | |
| 8. AS de Monaco (Monaco) | 38 | 14 | 11 | 13 | 52 | 51 | 39 | |
| 9. Olympique Lyonnais (Lyon) | 38 | 16 | 7 | 15 | 62 | 68 | 39 | |
| 10. Union Athlétique Sedan-Torcy (Sedan) | 38 | 12 | 14 | 12 | 65 | 53 | 38 | |
| 11. Racing Club de Strasbourg (Strasbourg) | 38 | 14 | 10 | 14 | 65 | 76 | 38 | |
| 12. Stade Rennais Université Club (Rennes) | 38 | 13 | 10 | 15 | 63 | 63 | 36 | |
| 13. US Valenciennes-Anzin (Valenciennes) | 38 | 13 | 10 | 15 | 53 | 63 | 36 | |
| 14. Toulouse FC (Toulouse) | 38 | 12 | 11 | 15 | 59 | 59 | 35 | |
| 15. Limoges FC (Limoges) | 38 | 12 | 10 | 16 | 48 | 57 | 34 | |
| 16. Racing Club de Lens (Lens) | 38 | 12 | 8 | 18 | 56 | 66 | 32 | |
| 17. FC de Nancy (Nancy) | 38 | 10 | 9 | 19 | 58 | 79 | 29 | R |
| 18. Lille Olympique SC (Lille) | 38 | 9 | 11 | 18 | 56 | 78 | 29 | R |
| 19. Olympique Alésien (Alès) | 38 | 8 | 8 | 22 | 45 | 83 | 24 | R |
| 20. Olympique de Marseille (Marseille) | 38 | 6 | 11 | 21 | 50 | 84 | 23 | R |
| | 760 | 280 | 200 | 280 | 1261 | 1261 | 760 | |

## Top goal-scorers

| 1) | Tadeusz CISOWSKI | (Racing Club de Paris) | 30 |
|---|---|---|---|
| 2) | Hassan AKESBI | (Nîmes Olympique) | 24 |
| | Just FONTAINE | (Stade de Reims) | 24 |

| Division 2 | Pd | Wn | Dw | Ls | GF | GA | Pts | |
|---|---|---|---|---|---|---|---|---|
| 1. Havre AC (Le Havre) | 38 | 24 | 7 | 7 | 93 | 40 | 55 | P |
| 2. Stade Français FC (Paris) | 38 | 21 | 10 | 7 | 86 | 46 | 52 | P |
| 3. SC de Toulon (Toulon) | 38 | 17 | 10 | 11 | 82 | 63 | 44 | P |
| 4. Girondins de Bordeaux FC (Bordeaux) | 38 | 17 | 10 | 11 | 69 | 56 | 44 | P |
| 5. FC de Grenoble (Grenoble) | 38 | 18 | 6 | 14 | 65 | 51 | 42 | |
| 6. FC de Metz (Metz) | 38 | 13 | 15 | 10 | 49 | 50 | 41 | |
| 7. Racing Club Franc-Comtois (Besançon) | 38 | 14 | 12 | 12 | 69 | 54 | 40 | |
| 8. FC de Sète (Sète) | 38 | 17 | 6 | 15 | 44 | 57 | 40 | |
| 9. Stade Olympique Montpelliérain (Montpellier) | 38 | 16 | 7 | 15 | 64 | 55 | 39 | |
| 10. AS Biterroise (Béziers) | 38 | 13 | 12 | 13 | 58 | 54 | 38 | |
| 11. US de Forbach (Forbach) | 38 | 16 | 6 | 16 | 60 | 64 | 38 | |
| 12. FC de Rouen (Rouen) | 38 | 14 | 9 | 15 | 74 | 59 | 37 | |
| 13. AS Troyenne-Savinienne (Troyes) | 38 | 13 | 11 | 14 | 49 | 51 | 37 | |
| 14. FC de Nantes (Nantes) | 38 | 13 | 9 | 16 | 49 | 59 | 35 | |
| 15. Perpignan FC (Perpignan) | 38 | 11 | 13 | 14 | 42 | 58 | 35 | # |
| 16. Club Olympique Roubaix-Tourcoing (Roubaix) | 38 | 11 | 12 | 15 | 57 | 63 | 34 | |
| 17. AS de Cannes (Cannes) | 38 | 10 | 12 | 16 | 50 | 64 | 32 | |
| 18. AS Aixoise (Aix-en-Provence) | 38 | 11 | 6 | 21 | 49 | 74 | 28 | |
| 19. Red Star Olympique Audonien (Saint-Ouen) | 38 | 9 | 8 | 21 | 34 | 72 | 26 | |
| 20. Cercle Athlétique de Paris (Paris) | 38 | 7 | 9 | 22 | 34 | 87 | 23 | |
| | 760 | 285 | 190 | 285 | 1177 | 1177 | 760 | |

# Perpignan FC (Perpignan) reverted to amateur status for the next season.

**Elected**: US de Boulogne (Boulogne-sur-Mer).

## Coupe de France Final  (Stade Yves du Manoir, Colombes – 03/05/59 – 50,778)

**HAVRE AC (LE HAVRE)**     **2-2** (aet)     FC Sochaux-Montbéliard (Montbéliard)

*Ferrari 02', Bouchache 113'*            *Eloy 45' (o.g.), Gardien 109'*

**Havre:** Villenave, Hassouna, Lagadec, Salzborn, Eloy, Meyer, Saunier, Ferrari, Strappe, Bouchache, N'Doumbé.
**Soch.:** Barthelmebs, Lubrano, Mille, Bout, Mazimann, J.Tellechea, Edimo, Brodd, Stopyra, Bourdoncle, Gardien.

## Final Replay  (Stade Yves du Manoir, Colombes – 18/05/59 – 36,655)

**HAVRE AC (LE HAVRE)**     **3-0**     FC Sochaux-Montbéliard (Montbéliard)

*Meyer 21', N'Doumbé 31', Navarro 87'*

**Havre:** Villenave, Hassouna, Lagadec, Salzborn, Eloy, Meyer, Navarro, Ferrari, Strappe, Bouchache, N'Doumbé.
**Sochaux:** Wendé, Lubrano, Mille, Bout, Mazimann, J.Tellechea, Edimo, Brodd, Stopyra, R.Tellechea, Gardien.

### Semi-Finals  (12/04/59)

| | | |
|---|---|---|
| Havre AC (Le Havre) | 1-0 | Nîmes Olympique (Nîmes) |
| FC Sochaux-Montbéliard (Montbéliard) | 2-1 | Stade Rennais Université Club (Rennes) |

### Quarter-Finals  (29/03/59)

| | | |
|---|---|---|
| Havre AC (Le Havre) | 2-0 | FC de Metz (Metz) |
| Nîmes Olympique (Nîmes) | 4-0 | Racing Club de Paris (Paris) |
| Stade Rennais Université Club (Rennes) | 3-2 | Olympique Lyonnais (Lyon) |
| FC Sochaux-Montbéliard (Montbéliard) | 2-1 | Toulouse FC (Toulouse) |

# 1959-60

| 1959-1960 Division One | SC de l'O. Angers | Gir. de Bordeaux | Stade Français | Havre AC | Racing Lens | Limoges FC | Olymp. Lyonnais | AS de Monaco | Olymp. GC Nice | Nîmes Olympique | Racing Paris | Stade Reims | Stade Rennais | AS Saint-Étienne | UA Sedan-Torcy | Sochaux-Montbél. | RC Strasbourg | SC de Toulon | Toulouse FC | Valenciennes |
|---|---|---|---|---|---|---|---|---|---|---|---|---|---|---|---|---|---|---|---|---|
| SC de l'Ouest Angers | ▓ | 4-1 | 3-0 | 4-2 | 4-1 | 1-0 | 1-1 | 1-1 | 2-2 | 0-0 | 0-0 | 6-1 | 2-0 | 3-3 | 0-0 | 1-0 | 3-1 | 3-2 | 2-0 | 1-2 |
| Girondins de Bordeaux | 1-1 | ▓ | 3-3 | 0-1 | 2-3 | 2-1 | 2-2 | 4-2 | 0-3 | 1-3 | 1-5 | 2-1 | 0-1 | 0-0 | 1-4 | 6-4 | 0-1 | 2-1 | 3-5 | 3-7 |
| Stade Français | 2-0 | 0-2 | ▓ | 0-1 | 0-1 | 2-3 | 2-1 | 3-2 | 2-3 | 0-0 | 3-3 | 0-3 | 1-2 | 3-2 | 1-5 | 2-1 | 2-1 | 3-1 | 3-1 | 1-2 |
| Havre AC | 5-0 | 2-0 | 1-2 | ▓ | 3-1 | 2-0 | 1-2 | 2-0 | 3-1 | 0-3 | 2-2 | 2-2 | 4-2 | 0-0 | 3-3 | 2-2 | 2-1 | 2-0 | 0-3 | 3-2 |
| Racing Lens | 4-2 | 3-1 | 3-2 | 1-1 | ▓ | 0-0 | 1-0 | 1-2 | 1-0 | 3-1 | 3-2 | 2-5 | 1-0 | 0-0 | 1-1 | 3-1 | 2-1 | 6-2 | 4-0 | 1-0 |
| Limoges FC | 2-0 | 3-0 | 1-0 | 0-0 | 1-2 | ▓ | 0-1 | 0-2 | 2-1 | 2-1 | 1-0 | 2-2 | 1-2 | 2-1 | 2-2 | 1-0 | 8-0 | 2-0 | 2-1 | 1-1 |
| Olympique Lyonnais | 2-0 | 2-2 | 0-0 | 1-1 | 0-1 | 1-0 | ▓ | 0-4 | 0-2 | 1-2 | 0-0 | 0-1 | 0-0 | 0-0 | 0-1 | 3-1 | 3-2 | 1-2 | 1-2 | 3-0 |
| AS de Monaco | 2-1 | 5-0 | 3-0 | 0-1 | 2-1 | 0-0 | 4-1 | ▓ | 2-0 | 3-3 | 2-2 | 5-0 | 1-1 | 2-1 | 1-0 | 4-2 | 1-3 | 3-0 | 1-0 |  |
| Olympique GC Nice | 1-5 | 2-1 | 1-3 | 2-2 | 3-0 | 3-3 | 3-1 | 3-2 | ▓ | 2-1 | 2-6 | 1-1 | 3-1 | 0-0 | 0-0 | 0-0 | 0-0 | 4-2 | 1-0 | 1-1 |
| Nîmes Olympique | 1-1 | 4-0 | 3-1 | 4-1 | 0-0 | 2-0 | 2-2 | 5-1 | 5-1 | ▓ | 0-2 | 0-3 | 3-0 | 2-0 | 2-0 | 2-1 | 2-1 | 4-1 | 2-2 | 3-0 |
| Racing Paris | 4-1 | 6-1 | 1-1 | 9-0 | 3-0 | 4-0 | 4-0 | 1-1 | 1-2 | 1-2 | ▓ | 3-3 | 0-2 | 4-0 | 2-0 | 8-0 | 2-2 | 7-1 | 1-3 | 6-4 |
| Stade Reims | 6-0 | 8-2 | 4-0 | 8-2 | 5-1 | 1-0 | 3-0 | 2-1 | 2-2 | 1-2 | 0-0 | ▓ | 2-1 | 3-0 | 1-0 | 4-1 | 5-0 | 3-0 | 5-2 | 2-1 |
| Stade Rennais | 2-3 | 1-0 | 2-3 | 2-2 | 2-0 | 0-2 | 1-2 | 1-2 | 3-1 | 1-1 | 3-2 | 0-1 | ▓ | 0-0 | 1-2 | 0-1 | 4-0 | 3-3 | 1-0 | 2-1 |
| AS Saint-Étienne | 1-1 | 4-2 | 1-1 | 3-1 | 6-0 | 2-0 | 2-1 | 1-0 | 4-1 | 2-2 | 3-4 | 2-5 | 2-1 | ▓ | 3-3 | 0-3 | 7-3 | 3-1 | 3-3 | 3-1 |
| Union Athlétique Sedan-Torcy | 2-0 | 2-3 | 2-1 | 0-3 | 2-2 | 0-0 | 0-0 | 2-1 | 2-0 | 2-3 | 1-4 | 1-3 | 2-0 | 3-1 | ▓ | 2-1 | 2-2 | 1-2 | 3-4 | 2-2 |
| Sochaux-Montbéliard | 2-0 | 0-0 | 3-2 | 0-0 | 1-0 | 0-0 | 1-3 | 1-0 | 1-2 | 1-1 | 3-6 | 1-2 | 2-2 | 2-0 | 0-0 | ▓ | 1-1 | 1-2 | 0-2 | 0-0 |
| RC Strasbourg | 4-2 | 2-1 | 2-5 | 1-2 | 0-0 | 1-3 | 2-1 | 0-2 | 1-4 | 3-1 | 2-5 | 1-3 | 1-1 | 3-0 | 3-3 | 0-1 | ▓ | 3-2 | 2-0 | 0-0 |
| SC de Toulon | 1-0 | 2-0 | 1-2 | 3-3 | 1-1 | 3-1 | 1-1 | 3-1 | 3-2 | 1-3 | 1-1 | 0-1 | 0-1 | 2-1 | 2-2 | 1-4 |  | ▓ | 0-1 | 1-2 |
| Toulouse FC | 5-1 | 2-1 | 1-3 | 2-1 | 1-0 | 6-0 | 1-0 | 1-1 | 4-1 | 2-3 | 1-1 | 2-2 | 1-2 | 2-1 | 1-1 | 3-0 | 2-1 | 3-0 | ▓ | 2-1 |
| Valenciennes | 3-1 | 2-2 | 1-0 | 2-0 | 0-1 | 0-0 | 1-4 | 0-2 | 4-3 | 3-1 | 1-4 | 3-0 | 3-0 | 2-0 | 2-1 | 1-1 | 2-0 | 3-1 | 5-3 | ▓ |

| | Division 1 | Pd | Wn | Dw | Ls | GF | GA | Pts | |
|---|---|---|---|---|---|---|---|---|---|
| 1. | STADE DE REIMS (REIMS) | 38 | 26 | 8 | 4 | 109 | 46 | 60 | |
| 2. | Nîmes Olympique (Nîmes) | 38 | 22 | 9 | 7 | 78 | 43 | 53 | |
| 3. | Racing Club de Paris (Paris) | 38 | 19 | 11 | 8 | 118 | 56 | 49 | |
| 4. | AS de Monaco (Monaco) | 38 | 19 | 7 | 12 | 70 | 45 | 45 | |
| 5. | Toulouse FC (Toulouse) | 38 | 19 | 6 | 13 | 74 | 61 | 44 | |
| 6. | Racing Club de Lens (Lens) | 38 | 18 | 8 | 12 | 55 | 57 | 44 | |
| 7. | Havre AC (Le Havre) | 38 | 15 | 12 | 11 | 63 | 68 | 42 | |
| 8. | US Valenciennes-Anzin (Valenciennes) | 38 | 16 | 8 | 14 | 65 | 60 | 40 | |
| 9. | Olympique GC de Nice (Nice) | 38 | 17 | 6 | 15 | 71 | 74 | 40 | |
| 10. | Limoges FC (Limoges) | 38 | 14 | 10 | 14 | 46 | 46 | 38 | |
| 11. | Union Athlétique Sedan-Torcy (Sedan) | 38 | 12 | 13 | 13 | 62 | 62 | 37 | |
| 12. | AS de Saint-Étienne (Saint-Étienne) | 38 | 12 | 12 | 14 | 62 | 65 | 36 | |
| 13. | SC de l'Ouest Angers (Angers) | 38 | 13 | 10 | 15 | 60 | 67 | 36 | |
| 14. | Stade Français FC (Paris) | 38 | 14 | 6 | 18 | 59 | 70 | 34 | |
| 15. | Stade Rennais Université Club (Rennes) | 38 | 13 | 7 | 18 | 47 | 59 | 33 | |
| 16. | Olympique Lyonnais (Lyon) | 38 | 10 | 11 | 17 | 41 | 52 | 31 | |
| 17. | FC Sochaux-Montbéliard (Montbéliard) | 38 | 8 | 11 | 19 | 40 | 67 | 27 | R |
| 18. | Racing Club de Strasbourg (Strasbourg) | 38 | 9 | 7 | 22 | 55 | 92 | 25 | R |
| 19. | SC de Toulon (Toulon) | 38 | 9 | 7 | 22 | 50 | 85 | 25 | R |
| 20. | Girondins de Bordeaux FC (Bordeaux) | 38 | 7 | 7 | 24 | 52 | 102 | 21 | R |
| | | 760 | 292 | 176 | 292 | 1277 | 1277 | 760 | |

## Top goal-scorers

| | | | |
|---|---|---|---|
| 1) | Just FONTAINE | (Stade de Reims) | 28 |
| 2) | Tadeusz CISOWSKI | (Racing Club de Paris) | 27 |
| 3) | Gines LIRON | (AS de Saint-Étienne) | 23 |

| | Division 2 | Pd | Wn | Dw | Ls | GF | GA | Pts | |
|---|---|---|---|---|---|---|---|---|---|
| 1. | FC de Grenoble (Grenoble) | 38 | 22 | 7 | 9 | 55 | 33 | 51 | P |
| 2. | FC de Nancy (Nancy) | 38 | 19 | 12 | 7 | 61 | 39 | 50 | P |
| 3. | FC de Rouen (Rouen) | 38 | 21 | 5 | 12 | 77 | 45 | 47 | P |
| 4. | AS Troyenne-Savinienne (Troyes) | 38 | 21 | 5 | 12 | 65 | 54 | 47 | P |
| 5. | Red Star Olympique Audonien (Saint-Ouen) | 38 | 21 | 4 | 13 | 69 | 45 | 46 | # |
| 6. | FC de Metz (Metz) | 38 | 18 | 9 | 11 | 58 | 42 | 45 | |
| 7. | Stade Olympique Montpelliérain (Montpellier) | 38 | 18 | 8 | 12 | 57 | 48 | 44 | |
| 8. | FC de Nantes (Nantes) | 38 | 16 | 9 | 13 | 58 | 48 | 41 | |
| 9. | Olympique Alésien (Alès) | 38 | 13 | 14 | 11 | 48 | 42 | 40 | |
| 10. | Olympique de Marseille (Marseille) | 38 | 16 | 5 | 17 | 57 | 63 | 37 | |
| 11. | Lille Olympique SC (Lille) | 38 | 12 | 12 | 14 | 62 | 62 | 36 | |
| 12. | AS Biterroise (Béziers) | 38 | 12 | 12 | 14 | 51 | 59 | 36 | |
| 13. | Racing Club Franc-Comtois (Besançon) | 38 | 14 | 7 | 17 | 50 | 44 | 35 | |
| 14. | FC de Sète (Sète) | 38 | 13 | 9 | 16 | 43 | 52 | 35 | # |
| 15. | US de Forbach (Forbach) | 38 | 10 | 13 | 15 | 52 | 57 | 33 | |
| 16. | Cercle Athlétique de Paris (Paris) | 38 | 14 | 3 | 21 | 61 | 68 | 31 | |
| 17. | AS de Cannes (Cannes) | 38 | 11 | 9 | 18 | 45 | 74 | 31 | |
| 18. | Club Olympique Roubaix-Tourcoing (Roubaix) | 38 | 7 | 14 | 17 | 48 | 65 | 28 | |
| 19. | US de Boulogne (Boulogne-sur-Mer) | 38 | 8 | 11 | 19 | 42 | 73 | 27 | |
| 20. | AS Aixoise (Aix-en-Provence) | 38 | 6 | 8 | 24 | 33 | 79 | 20 | |
| | | 760 | 292 | 176 | 292 | 1092 | 1092 | 760 | |

# Red Star Olympique Audonien (Saint-Ouen) and FC de Sète (Sète) reverted to amateur status for the next season.

**Elected:** AS Cherbourgeoise-Stella (Cherbourg).

## Coupe de France Final   (Stade Yves du Manoir, Colombes – 15/05/60 – 38,298)

**AS DE MONACO (MONACO)**                    **4-2  (aet)**                    AS de Saint-Étienne (Saint-Étienne)

*Roy 05', 114', Biancheri 88', Ludwikowski 103'*                              *Liron 43', Domingo 86'*

**Monaco:** Alberto, Nowak, Thomas, Ludwikowski, Kaelbel, Biancheri, Hess, Hidalgo, Roy, Cossou, Carlier.

**Saint-Étienne:** Abbes, Tylinski, Wicart, Domingo, Herbin, Derrier, Peyroche, Glovacki, Liron, Oleksiak, Balboa.

## Semi-Finals   (24/04/60)

| AS de Monaco (Monaco) | 2-1 | Stade de Reims (Reims) |
| AS de Saint-Étienne (Saint-Étienne) | 3-2 | Havre AC (Le Havre) |

## Quarter-Finals   (03/04/60)

| Havre AC (Le Havre) | 4-2 | AS de Cannes (Cannes) |
| AS de Monaco (Monaco) | 3-1 | Olympique GC de Nice (Nice) |
| Stade de Reims (Reims) | 1-0 | FC de Sète (Sète) |
| AS de Saint-Étienne (Saint-Étienne) | 3-1 | Lille Olympique SC (Lille) |

# 1960-61

| 1960-1961 Division One | SC de l'Ouest Angers | Stade Français | FC de Grenoble | Havre AC | Racing de Lens | Limoges FC | Olympique Lyonnais | AS de Monaco | FC de Nancy | Olympique GC Nice | Nîmes Olympique | Racing Paris | Stade Reims | Stade Rennais | FC de Rouen | AS Saint-Étienne | Union Athlétique Sedan-Torcy | Toulouse FC | AS Troyenne | Valenciennes |
|---|---|---|---|---|---|---|---|---|---|---|---|---|---|---|---|---|---|---|---|---|
| SC de l'Ouest Angers | | 1-0 | 2-2 | 1-0 | 3-2 | 4-0 | 3-0 | 1-4 | 1-2 | 5-0 | 4-2 | 0-3 | 3-2 | 1-1 | 1-3 | 2-4 | 0-0 | 1-0 | 5-1 | 3-1 |
| Stade Français | 1-0 | | 1-0 | 3-1 | 0-0 | 0-1 | 3-1 | 1-1 | 0-2 | 1-3 | 2-1 | 3-3 | 0-1 | 3-1 | 0-1 | 5-0 | 3-1 | 1-3 | 2-1 | 3-0 |
| FC de Grenoble | 0-0 | 1-0 | | 0-1 | 2-1 | 2-0 | 2-2 | 0-0 | 2-2 | 3-1 | 1-2 | 0-2 | 3-2 | 1-1 | 0-0 | 1-1 | 6-3 | 4-0 | 1-0 | 0-0 |
| Havre AC | 0-0 | 0-0 | 1-1 | | 3-2 | 2-1 | 3-2 | 1-1 | 1-1 | 3-2 | 3-0 | 2-2 | 2-1 | 3-2 | 0-2 | 2-1 | 1-0 | 3-0 | 5-2 | 0-1 |
| Racing de Lens | 2-2 | 2-2 | 1-1 | 2-1 | | 1-1 | 0-1 | 0-1 | 1-0 | 1-0 | 2-1 | 1-3 | 2-0 | 3-1 | 1-0 | 1-3 | 0-0 | 3-1 | 1-0 | 2-0 |
| Limoges FC | 1-3 | 4-3 | 1-0 | 2-1 | 5-2 | | 3-1 | 1-5 | 0-0 | 4-2 | 4-1 | 0-1 | 0-1 | 0-0 | 3-2 | 1-1 | 1-2 | 1-1 | 1-0 | 2-1 |
| Olympique Lyonnais | 1-1 | 2-1 | 1-1 | 1-3 | 1-2 | 2-1 | | 2-0 | 0-1 | 4-3 | 2-2 | 4-2 | 0-2 | 4-0 | 4-1 | 2-2 | 1-1 | 1-0 | 5-2 | 0-0 |
| AS de Monaco | 2-0 | 2-4 | 1-0 | 2-2 | 2-1 | 3-2 | 3-1 | | 2-0 | 5-1 | 3-0 | 3-0 | 2-0 | 3-0 | 1-0 | 3-0 | 2-0 | 3-1 | 5-0 | 1-0 |
| FC de Nancy | 0-2 | 5-1 | 1-1 | 0-0 | 2-2 | 0-0 | 2-1 | 0-4 | | 3-3 | 2-2 | 1-1 | 2-0 | 2-0 | 0-1 | 2-2 | 2-1 | 1-0 | 3-2 | 4-0 |
| Olympique GC Nice | 3-2 | 0-0 | 4-2 | 3-3 | 1-0 | 2-1 | 2-2 | 6-0 | 1-4 | | 0-1 | 0-1 | 1-4 | 3-1 | 3-0 | 1-0 | 3-1 | 1-1 | 1-1 | 2-0 |
| Nîmes Olympique | 3-2 | 4-3 | 2-2 | 2-1 | 1-2 | 3-2 | 3-0 | 1-1 | 3-4 | 4-1 | | 2-2 | 2-0 | 1-0 | 3-1 | 0-2 | 5-0 | 3-0 | 2-0 | 2-0 |
| Racing Paris | 5-3 | 3-1 | 6-3 | 4-4 | 3-2 | 3-1 | 3-2 | 3-0 | 2-0 | 4-2 | 3-2 | | 1-1 | 0-2 | 0-1 | 4-2 | 2-0 | 3-0 | 3-3 | 1-1 |
| Stade Reims | 1-0 | 2-0 | 1-0 | 2-0 | 1-0 | 2-2 | 2-0 | 3-0 | 3-0 | 3-0 | 5-1 | 5-3 | | 1-1 | 3-1 | 0-1 | 4-3 | 4-2 | 3-1 | 4-0 |
| Stade Rennais | 2-0 | 0-2 | 1-0 | 3-2 | 4-2 | 3-2 | 6-1 | 1-3 | 1-0 | 1-2 | 0-0 | 1-1 | 2-2 | | 0-0 | 2-2 | 2-0 | 3-2 | 2-2 | 1-2 |
| FC de Rouen | 1-0 | 0-0 | 2-0 | 3-1 | 6-2 | 3-1 | 0-1 | 2-3 | 3-1 | 1-0 | 2-1 | 0-3 | 2-1 | 1-0 | | 1-0 | 1-0 | 7-0 | 1-0 | 3-0 |
| AS Saint-Étienne | 2-2 | 2-0 | 3-1 | 2-1 | 1-0 | 3-1 | 4-2 | 0-1 | 1-1 | 0-0 | 2-1 | 1-2 | 3-1 | 1-3 | 1-1 | | 0-0 | 1-0 | 7-1 | 1-0 |
| Union Athlétique Sedan-Torcy | 1-2 | 4-0 | 3-0 | 2-1 | 0-0 | 1-1 | 2-1 | 4-1 | 2-1 | 4-3 | 1-3 | 1-3 | 0-4 | 2-1 | 4-0 | 2-2 | | 1-1 | 4-1 | 2-1 |
| Toulouse FC | 3-1 | 1-0 | 2-1 | 4-1 | 0-0 | 2-1 | 2-0 | 3-0 | 2-2 | 0-0 | 0-0 | 1-1 | 3-1 | 2-0 | 2-0 | 0-1 | 0-2 | | 3-3 | 2-2 |
| AS Troyenne | 1-2 | 5-3 | 3-3 | 4-3 | 1-3 | 3-2 | 2-3 | 0-1 | 2-1 | 0-5 | 0-2 | 1-4 | 1-4 | 2-3 | 0-2 | 4-0 | 3-7 | 0-3 | | 0-2 |
| Valenciennes | 0-1 | 0-0 | 1-0 | 1-0 | 0-1 | 3-1 | 1-2 | 1-3 | 2-1 | 3-1 | 2-2 | 1-3 | 0-2 | 1-0 | 2-1 | 3-1 | 1-3 | 1-2 | 1-0 | |

| | Division 1 | Pd | Wn | Dw | Ls | GF | GA | Pts | |
|---|---|---|---|---|---|---|---|---|---|
| 1. | AS DE MONACO (MONACO) | 38 | 26 | 5 | 7 | 77 | 42 | 57 | |
| 2. | Racing Club de Paris (Paris) | 38 | 23 | 10 | 5 | 93 | 57 | 56 | |
| 3. | Stade de Reims (Reims) | 38 | 23 | 4 | 11 | 78 | 44 | 50 | |
| 4. | FC de Rouen (Rouen) | 38 | 21 | 4 | 13 | 56 | 42 | 46 | |
| 5. | AS de Saint-Étienne (Saint-Étienne) | 38 | 16 | 11 | 11 | 60 | 54 | 43 | |
| 6. | Nîmes Olympique (Nîmes) | 38 | 17 | 8 | 13 | 70 | 61 | 42 | |
| 7. | SC de l'Ouest Angers (Angers) | 38 | 16 | 8 | 14 | 64 | 56 | 40 | |
| 8. | FC de Nancy (Nancy) | 38 | 13 | 13 | 12 | 55 | 52 | 39 | |
| 9. | Union Athlétique Sedan-Torcy (Sedan) | 38 | 15 | 8 | 15 | 64 | 63 | 38 | |
| 10. | Racing Club de Lens (Lens) | 38 | 14 | 9 | 15 | 50 | 54 | 37 | |
| 11. | Havre AC (Le Havre) | 38 | 13 | 10 | 15 | 61 | 62 | 36 | |
| 12. | Toulouse FC (Toulouse) | 38 | 13 | 10 | 15 | 49 | 58 | 36 | |
| 13. | Olympique GC de Nice (Nice) | 38 | 13 | 8 | 17 | 66 | 73 | 34 | |
| 14. | Stade Rennais Université Club (Rennes) | 38 | 12 | 10 | 16 | 52 | 59 | 34 | |
| 15. | Olympique Lyonnais (Lyon) | 38 | 13 | 8 | 17 | 60 | 71 | 34 | |
| 16. | Stade Français FC (Paris) | 38 | 12 | 8 | 18 | 52 | 59 | 32 | |
| 17. | FC de Grenoble (Grenoble) | 38 | 8 | 15 | 15 | 47 | 55 | 31 | R |
| 18. | Limoges FC (Limoges) | 38 | 11 | 8 | 19 | 55 | 69 | 30 | R |
| 19. | US Valenciennes-Anzin (Valenciennes) | 38 | 12 | 6 | 20 | 35 | 57 | 30 | R |
| 20. | AS Troyenne-Savinienne (Troyes) | 38 | 5 | 5 | 28 | 52 | 108 | 15 | R |
| | | 760 | 296 | 168 | 296 | 1196 | 1196 | 760 | |

## Top goal-scorers

| | | | |
|---|---|---|---|
| 1) | Roger PIANTONI | (Stade de Reims) | 28 |
| 2) | KELLER | (AS Troyenne-Savinienne) | 23 |
| 3) | Hassan AKESBI | (Nîmes Olympique) | 21 |
| | Jozsef UJLAKI | (Racing Club de Paris) | 21 |

| | Division 2 | Pd | Wn | Dw | Ls | GF | GA | Pts | |
|---|---|---|---|---|---|---|---|---|---|
| 1. | Stade Olympique Montpelliérain (Montpellier) | 36 | 22 | 4 | 10 | 68 | 35 | 48 | P |
| 2. | FC de Metz (Metz) | 36 | 19 | 10 | 7 | 69 | 37 | 48 | P |
| 3. | FC Sochaux-Montbéliard (Montbéliard) | 36 | 18 | 10 | 8 | 58 | 36 | 46 | P |
| 4. | Racing Club de Strasbourg (Strasbourg) | 36 | 19 | 7 | 10 | 70 | 38 | 45 | P |
| 5. | AS Biterroise (Béziers) | 36 | 13 | 16 | 7 | 54 | 52 | 42 | |
| 6. | Olympique de Marseille (Marseille) | 36 | 15 | 11 | 10 | 56 | 42 | 41 | |
| 7. | AS de Cannes (Cannes) | 36 | 17 | 7 | 12 | 71 | 59 | 41 | |
| 8. | Girondins de Bordeaux FC (Bordeaux) | 36 | 14 | 13 | 9 | 59 | 50 | 41 | |
| 9. | Lille Olympique SC (Lille) | 36 | 14 | 12 | 10 | 49 | 43 | 40 | |
| 10. | US de Boulogne (Boulogne-sur-Mer) | 36 | 18 | 3 | 15 | 63 | 62 | 39 | |
| 11. | FC de Nantes (Nantes) | 36 | 15 | 6 | 15 | 61 | 64 | 36 | |
| 12. | Club Olympique Roubaix-Tourcoing (Roubaix) | 36 | 13 | 7 | 16 | 59 | 63 | 33 | |
| 13. | AS de Cherbourg (Cherbourg) | 36 | 10 | 9 | 17 | 45 | 58 | 29 | * |
| 14. | SC de Toulon (Toulon) | 36 | 10 | 9 | 17 | 36 | 59 | 29 | |
| 15. | US de Forbach (Forbach) | 36 | 10 | 7 | 19 | 51 | 68 | 27 | |
| 16. | Olympique Alésien (Alès) | 36 | 10 | 7 | 19 | 39 | 62 | 27 | # |
| 17. | Racing Club Franc-Comtois (Besançon) | 36 | 8 | 9 | 19 | 50 | 79 | 25 | |
| 18. | Cercle Athlétique de Paris (Paris) | 36 | 9 | 7 | 20 | 33 | 56 | 25 | |
| 19. | AS Aixoise (Aix-en-Provence) | 36 | 7 | 8 | 21 | 37 | 65 | 22 | |
| | | 684 | 261 | 162 | 261 | 1028 | 1028 | 684 | |

*   AS de Cherbourg (Cherbourg) changed their name pre-season from AS Cherbourgeoise-Stella (Cherbourg).
#   Olympique Alésien (Alès) reverted to amateur status for the next season.

**Elected:** Red Star Olympique Audonien (Saint-Ouen).

**Coupe de France Final**   (Stade Yves du Manoir, Colombes – 07/05/61 – 39,070)

**UNION ATHLÉTIQUE SEDAN-TORCY**   **3-1**   Nîmes Olympique (Nîmes)

*Fulgenzi 16', Brény 74', Salem 82'*   *Constantino 86'*

**Sedan:** Bernard, Noah, Lemasson, Synakowski, Polak, Hatchi, Salaber, Mouchel, Salem, Fulgenzi, Brény.

**Nîmes:** Roszak, Bettache, Bandera, Barlaguet, Charles-Alfred, Oliver, Garnier, Constantino, Akesbi, Cassar, Rahis.

**Semi-Finals**   (16/04/61)

| | | |
|---|---|---|
| Nîmes Olympique (Nîmes) | 2-1 | Stade Olympique Montpelliérain |
| Union Athlétique Sedan-Torcy (Sedan) | 2-2, 1-0 | Girondins de Bordeaux FC (Bordeaux) |

**Quarter-Finals**   (26/03/61)

| | | |
|---|---|---|
| Girondins de Bordeaux FC (Bordeaux) | 2-2, 1-1, 2-0 | AS de Saint-Étienne (Saint-Étienne) |
| Stade Olympique Montpelliérain | 2-0 | Stade de Reims (Reims) |
| Nîmes Olympique (Nîmes) | 3-2 | Racing Club de Paris (Paris) |
| Union Athlétique Sedan-Torcy (Sedan) | 2-1 | Olympique GC de Nice (Nice) |

# 1961-62

| 1961-1962 Division One | SC de l'Ouest Angers | Stade Français | Havre AC | Racing de Lens | Olympique Lyonnais | FC de Metz | AS de Monaco | SO Montpellier | FC de Nancy | Olympique GC Nice | Nîmes Olympique | Racing Paris | Stade Reims | Stade Rennais | FC de Rouen | AS St. Étienne | UA Sedan-Torcy | Sochaux-Montbéliard | RC Strasbourg | Toulouse FC |
|---|---|---|---|---|---|---|---|---|---|---|---|---|---|---|---|---|---|---|---|---|
| SC de l'Ouest Angers | | 2-2 | 0-0 | 0-2 | 1-1 | 3-1 | 2-0 | 1-0 | 2-2 | 0-0 | 8-3 | 2-3 | 2-0 | 1-1 | 1-0 | 2-1 | 2-2 | 3-1 | 1-1 | 1-2 |
| Stade Français | 1-1 | | 1-1 | 2-2 | 2-1 | 2-2 | 1-1 | 3-0 | 1-0 | 4-0 | 1-0 | 2-0 | 2-4 | 2-2 | 2-4 | 1-1 | 4-2 | 1-1 | 0-1 | 3-4 |
| Havre AC | 0-1 | 1-0 | | 0-0 | 1-2 | 2-1 | 0-1 | 2-2 | 1-1 | 3-0 | 1-2 | 0-4 | 1-2 | 2-0 | 1-1 | 1-0 | 1-1 | 3-1 | 0-2 | 2-0 |
| Racing de Lens | 2-1 | 2-1 | 2-0 | | 1-0 | 5-2 | 5-0 | 5-1 | 4-1 | 4-2 | 3-1 | 2-3 | 3-4 | 1-0 | 1-0 | 2-1 | 1-0 | 3-1 | 0-0 | 4-0 |
| Olympique Lyonnais | 2-0 | 1-2 | 1-1 | 3-0 | | 1-0 | 2-4 | 1-2 | 1-3 | 1-2 | 0-0 | 2-0 | 1-3 | 0-0 | 1-1 | 4-0 | 2-2 | 1-0 | 2-1 | 1-3 |
| FC de Metz | 1-2 | 0-2 | 0-0 | 1-0 | 2-1 | | 1-1 | 1-1 | 0-1 | 2-1 | 3-1 | 2-4 | 2-1 | 0-1 | 0-1 | 6-0 | 2-2 | 1-1 | 2-0 | 1-1 |
| AS de Monaco | 5-0 | 2-0 | 2-2 | 2-1 | 3-1 | 4-0 | | 5-3 | 1-1 | 1-2 | 1-1 | 1-2 | 0-1 | 4-2 | 0-0 | 1-0 | 2-1 | 1-1 | 0-2 | 4-3 |
| SO Montpellier | 0-0 | 4-0 | 1-1 | 2-0 | 4-2 | 2-0 | 0-2 | | 1-0 | 3-2 | 3-5 | 2-1 | 1-3 | 3-1 | 4-1 | 4-3 | 5-0 | 4-1 | 1-1 | 3-3 |
| FC de Nancy | 3-2 | 2-1 | 1-1 | 1-0 | 5-1 | 3-0 | 1-2 | 3-1 | | 2-0 | 0-0 | 0-0 | 1-1 | 2-2 | 2-1 | 2-1 | 0-0 | 1-0 | 0-1 | 2-1 |
| Olympique GC Nice | 0-2 | 1-0 | 4-0 | 2-0 | 0-2 | 2-1 | 1-1 | 1-0 | 3-1 | | 1-3 | 1-0 | 4-1 | 1-0 | 1-1 | 3-1 | 3-2 | 1-1 | 3-2 | 3-1 |
| Nîmes Olympique | 2-0 | 4-0 | 3-2 | 2-1 | 2-1 | 3-1 | 1-1 | 3-1 | 1-1 | 3-0 | | 2-4 | 2-1 | 3-0 | 3-2 | 1-0 | 0-1 | 2-1 | 1-0 | 2-0 |
| Racing Paris | 4-3 | 3-1 | 4-1 | 1-0 | 0-4 | 11-2 | 3-0 | 2-1 | 2-0 | 3-1 | 0-4 | | 2-6 | 3-1 | 0-2 | 1-2 | 2-2 | 2-2 | 3-3 | 2-0 |
| Stade Reims | 2-0 | 0-4 | 3-0 | 4-1 | 0-4 | 5-3 | 1-0 | 2-1 | 2-0 | 5-0 | 2-0 | 1-4 | | 2-3 | 2-2 | 1-1 | 1-3 | 2-1 | 5-1 | 5-1 |
| Stade Rennais | 2-1 | 2-3 | 1-0 | 2-1 | 2-0 | 1-2 | 4-6 | 1-1 | 3-0 | 2-2 | 4-2 | 2-3 | 2-2 | | 3-2 | 1-1 | 1-0 | 2-1 | 1-0 | 1-1 |
| FC de Rouen | 2-1 | 2-1 | 0-0 | 0-3 | 3-4 | 3-2 | 2-1 | 3-2 | 0-2 | 2-1 | 1-2 | 2-1 | 2-2 | 4-1 | | 3-1 | 2-3 | 2-2 | 1-0 | 0-1 |
| AS St. Étienne | 2-3 | 1-1 | 1-1 | 3-4 | 2-0 | 2-2 | 5-1 | 1-1 | 1-1 | 1-2 | 5-0 | 1-1 | 2-0 | 2-1 | 2-0 | | 1-0 | 2-2 | 0-1 | 4-1 |
| Union Athlétique Sedan-Torcy | 0-2 | 1-1 | 2-0 | 1-1 | 3-1 | 2-0 | 2-0 | 1-0 | 1-1 | 2-2 | 5-1 | 0-1 | 0-3 | 0-0 | 2-2 | 1-0 | | 4-1 | 5-0 | 1-0 |
| Sochaux-Montbéliard | 5-2 | 2-3 | 6-1 | 1-2 | 1-2 | 1-1 | 1-4 | 1-1 | 0-1 | 2-0 | 3-1 | 4-3 | 2-1 | 1-2 | 1-1 | 0-2 | 2-0 | | 0-0 | 2-0 |
| RC Strasbourg | 2-1 | 0-0 | 3-1 | 3-1 | 5-2 | 0-1 | 0-1 | 1-2 | 2-2 | 2-0 | 2-1 | 1-3 | 1-1 | 1-1 | 1-0 | 2-1 | 1-2 | 1-1 | | 0-1 |
| Toulouse FC | 2-0 | 0-1 | 1-0 | 2-0 | 1-1 | 6-1 | 2-0 | 1-2 | 2-0 | 3-1 | 0-1 | 1-1 | 1-2 | 3-3 | 1-0 | 1-1 | 1-4 | 6-1 | 4-1 | |

| | Division 1 | Pd | Wn | Dw | Ls | GF | GA | Pts | |
|---|---|---|---|---|---|---|---|---|---|
| 1. | STADE DE REIMS (REIMS) | 38 | 21 | 6 | 11 | 83 | 60 | 48 | |
| 2. | Racing Club de Paris (Paris) | 38 | 21 | 6 | 11 | 86 | 63 | 48 | |
| 3. | Nîmes Olympique (Nîmes) | 38 | 21 | 5 | 12 | 68 | 60 | 47 | |
| 4. | FC de Nancy (Nancy) | 38 | 16 | 12 | 10 | 52 | 46 | 44 | |
| 5. | Union Athlétique Sedan-Torcy (Sedan) | 38 | 16 | 11 | 11 | 63 | 49 | 43 | |
| 6. | AS de Monaco (Monaco) | 38 | 17 | 9 | 12 | 65 | 57 | 43 | |
| 7. | Racing Club de Lens (Lens) | 38 | 19 | 4 | 15 | 67 | 52 | 42 | |
| 8. | Stade Olympique Montpelliérain (Montpellier) | 38 | 15 | 9 | 14 | 69 | 64 | 39 | |
| 9. | FC de Rouen (Rouen) | 38 | 14 | 10 | 14 | 57 | 56 | 38 | |
| 10. | Stade Français FC (Paris) | 38 | 13 | 12 | 13 | 58 | 57 | 38 | |
| 11. | Toulouse FC (Toulouse) | 38 | 16 | 6 | 16 | 62 | 61 | 38 | |
| 12. | Stade Rennais Université Club (Rennes) | 38 | 13 | 12 | 13 | 58 | 63 | 38 | |
| 13. | Olympique GC de Nice (Nice) | 38 | 16 | 6 | 16 | 53 | 64 | 38 | |
| 14. | SC de l'Ouest Angers (Angers) | 38 | 13 | 10 | 15 | 56 | 59 | 36 | |
| 15. | Racing Club de Strasbourg (Strasbourg) | 38 | 12 | 10 | 16 | 45 | 54 | 34 | |
| 16. | Olympique Lyonnais (Lyon) | 38 | 13 | 7 | 18 | 57 | 62 | 33 | |
| 17. | AS de Saint-Étienne (Saint-Étienne) | 38 | 10 | 10 | 18 | 55 | 60 | 30 | R |
| 18. | FC Sochaux-Montbéliard (Montbéliard) | 38 | 8 | 12 | 18 | 55 | 69 | 28 | R |
| 19. | Havre AC (Le Havre) | 38 | 7 | 14 | 17 | 34 | 57 | 28 | R |
| 20. | FC de Metz (Metz) | 38 | 9 | 9 | 20 | 49 | 79 | 27 | R |
| | | 760 | 290 | 180 | 290 | 1192 | 1192 | 760 | |

## Top goal-scorers

| | | | |
|---|---|---|---|
| 1) | TOURÉ Sékou | (Stade Olympique Montpelliérain) | 25 |
| 2) | Hassan AKESBI | (Stade de Reims) | 23 |
| 3) | Michel LAFRANCESCHINA | (Racing Club de Lens) | 20 |

| | Division 2 | Pd | Wn | Dw | Ls | GF | GA | Pts | |
|---|---|---|---|---|---|---|---|---|---|
| 1. | FC de Grenoble (Grenoble) | 36 | 23 | 6 | 7 | 65 | 35 | 52 | P |
| 2. | US Valenciennes-Anzin (Valenciennes) | 36 | 19 | 8 | 9 | 59 | 30 | 46 | P |
| 3. | Girondins de Bordeaux FC (Bordeaux) | 36 | 17 | 12 | 7 | 54 | 31 | 46 | P |
| 4. | Olympique de Marseille (Marseille) | 36 | 17 | 10 | 9 | 50 | 38 | 44 | P |
| 5. | AS Troyenne-Savinienne (Troyes) | 36 | 15 | 11 | 10 | 69 | 59 | 41 | |
| 6. | FC de Nantes (Nantes) | 36 | 16 | 8 | 12 | 43 | 43 | 40 | |
| 7. | Racing Club Franc-Comtois (Besançon) | 36 | 15 | 9 | 12 | 38 | 37 | 39 | |
| 8. | Lille Olympique SC (Lille) | 36 | 14 | 9 | 13 | 64 | 56 | 37 | |
| 9. | SC de Toulon (Toulon) | 36 | 13 | 10 | 13 | 42 | 38 | 36 | |
| 10. | Red Star Olympique Audonien (Saint-Ouen) | 36 | 13 | 10 | 13 | 50 | 51 | 36 | |
| 11. | Limoges FC (Limoges) | 36 | 14 | 71 | 15 | 64 | 60 | 35 | |
| 12. | AS Aixoise (Aix-en-Provence) | 36 | 11 | 13 | 12 | 36 | 40 | 35 | |
| 13. | AS de Cannes (Cannes) | 36 | 14 | 6 | 16 | 53 | 57 | 34 | |
| 14. | US de Boulogne (Boulogne-sur-Mer) | 36 | 12 | 7 | 17 | 47 | 59 | 31 | |
| 15. | AS de Cherbourg (Cherbourg) | 36 | 11 | 7 | 18 | 47 | 64 | 29 | |
| 16. | US de Forbach (Forbach) | 36 | 6 | 14 | 16 | 42 | 58 | 26 | |
| 17. | AS Biterroise (Béziers) | 36 | 8 | 10 | 18 | 46 | 64 | 26 | |
| 18. | Cercle Athlétique de Paris (Paris) | 36 | 7 | 12 | 17 | 34 | 49 | 26 | |
| 19. | Club Olympique Roubaix-Tourcoing (Roubaix) | 36 | 8 | 9 | 19 | 40 | 66 | 25 | |
| | | 684 | 253 | 178 | 253 | 943 | 935 | 684 | |

## Coupe de France Final  (Stade Yves du Manoir, Colombes – 13/05/62 – 30,654)

**AS DE SAINT-Étienne (ST-Étienne)**              **1-0**              FC de Nancy (Nancy)

*Baulu 86'*

**Saint-Étienne**: Abbes, Casado, Sbaiz, Herbin, Tylinski, Domingo, Baulu, Guillas, Liron, Ferrier, Oleksiak.
**Nancy**: Ferrero, Adamczyk, Collot, Amanieu, Gauthier, Brezniak, Viaene, Florindo, Muro, Chevalier, Chrétien.

## Semi-Finals  (01/04/62)

| | | |
|---|---|---|
| FC de Nancy (Nancy) | 1-0 | FC de Metz (Metz) |
| AS de Saint-Étienne (Saint-Étienne) | 1-0 | SC de l'Ouest Angers (Angers) |

## Quarter-Finals  (11/03/62)

| | | |
|---|---|---|
| SC de l'Ouest Angers (Angers) | 1-0 | Olympique de Marseille (Marseille) |
| FC de Metz (Metz) | 1-0 | AS de Monaco (Monaco) |
| FC de Nancy (Nancy) | 1-0 | Stade de Reims (Reims) |
| AS de Saint-Étienne (Saint-Étienne) | 3-0 | AS Biterroise (Béziers) |

# 1962-63

| 1962-1963 Division One | SC de l'Ouest Angers | Girondins de Bordeaux | Stade Français | FC de Grenoble | Racing de Lens | Olympique Lyonnais | Olympique Marseille | AS de Monaco | SO Montpellier | FC de Nancy | Olympique GC Nice | Nîmes Olympique | Racing Paris | Stade Reims | Stade Rennais | FC de Rouen | Union Athlétique Sedan-Torcy | RC Strasbourg | Toulouse FC | Valenciennes |
|---|---|---|---|---|---|---|---|---|---|---|---|---|---|---|---|---|---|---|---|---|
| SC de l'Ouest Angers | | 0-3 | 2-0 | 2-1 | 2-2 | 2-2 | 3-0 | 4-2 | 2-1 | 1-1 | 3-0 | 0-0 | 2-1 | 0-1 | 2-3 | 3-1 | 0-1 | 2-2 | 1-3 | 0-0 |
| Girondins de Bordeaux | 0-0 | | 1-0 | 1-1 | 3-0 | 1-2 | 1-3 | 0-1 | 2-0 | 2-0 | 0-2 | 0-0 | 2-1 | 2-3 | 6-0 | 4-1 | 4-4 | 3-0 | 0-0 | 2-2 |
| Stade Français | 0-3 | 0-0 | | 1-1 | 2-0 | 1-0 | 2-2 | 2-2 | 5-2 | 2-0 | 2-0 | 4-2 | 1-2 | 0-4 | 3-3 | 1-2 | 4-2 | 2-1 | 1-2 | 1-3 |
| FC de Grenoble | 0-2 | 2-1 | 1-1 | | 1-0 | 1-2 | 0-3 | 0-1 | 3-1 | 1-1 | 3-1 | 0-0 | 1-1 | 0-3 | 1-1 | 1-1 | 1-1 | 3-3 | 1-0 | 1-1 |
| Racing de Lens | 3-3 | 3-3 | 2-1 | 2-0 | | 2-1 | 8-1 | 1-0 | 3-0 | 0-1 | 2-2 | 2-1 | 1-2 | 0-0 | 2-2 | 1-4 | 1-2 | 0-0 | 1-1 | 1-2 |
| Olympique Lyonnais | 3-0 | 1-0 | 1-0 | 0-1 | 1-0 | | 1-1 | 1-1 | 1-1 | 3-0 | 3-1 | 0-0 | 1-1 | 0-0 | 1-1 | 0-1 | 0-2 | 3-1 | 3-3 | 1-1 |
| Olympique Marseille | 1-0 | 1-1 | 1-3 | 2-2 | 3-3 | 1-2 | | 2-4 | 3-2 | 2-1 | 1-1 | 0-3 | 1-3 | 1-0 | 4-2 | 0-1 | 0-0 | 1-3 | 0-1 | 1-3 |
| AS de Monaco | 5-1 | 0-2 | 1-1 | 4-0 | 2-0 | 1-0 | 2-1 | | 3-1 | 0-1 | 6-2 | 4-1 | 1-1 | 5-2 | 5-0 | 3-1 | 0-1 | 1-0 | 0-0 | 3-1 |
| SO Montpellier | 1-2 | 0-3 | 4-5 | 2-0 | 2-1 | 1-1 | 2-0 | 0-1 | | 5-3 | 1-0 | 1-1 | 4-1 | 3-0 | 1-1 | 3-1 | 1-0 | 1-1 | 1-1 | 0-4 |
| FC de Nancy | 0-0 | 2-2 | 0-0 | 1-0 | 1-3 | 3-2 | 1-0 | 2-1 | 2-1 | | 1-1 | 0-4 | 2-2 | 0-2 | 2-2 | 1-3 | 2-0 | 1-1 | 1-2 | 2-0 |
| Olympique GC Nice | 1-1 | 1-1 | 0-2 | 3-2 | 3-1 | 3-5 | 1-0 | 2-2 | 3-1 | 2-0 | | 1-0 | 3-3 | 4-0 | 3-3 | 1-0 | 2-1 | 3-1 | 2-1 | 2-0 |
| Nîmes Olympique | 5-0 | 1-2 | 4-0 | 1-0 | 4-2 | 1-0 | 3-0 | 1-2 | 1-1 | 3-0 | 6-3 | | 4-1 | 0-0 | 2-1 | 2-1 | 1-2 | 5-1 | 3-1 | 1-3 |
| Racing Paris | 2-4 | 1-3 | 0-2 | 2-0 | 2-1 | 1-1 | 3-0 | 2-3 | 9-1 | 4-2 | 3-4 | 2-2 | | 3-3 | 2-1 | 3-0 | 4-3 | 1-1 | 2-2 | 3-2 |
| Stade Reims | 4-0 | 1-3 | 6-2 | 1-1 | 3-1 | 5-1 | 1-0 | 1-1 | 1-1 | 5-1 | 4-2 | 4-1 | 3-2 | | 4-0 | 4-0 | 2-3 | 1-1 | 1-0 | 2-2 |
| Stade Rennais | 1-1 | 1-3 | 2-0 | 3-0 | 4-2 | 2-1 | 3-2 | 2-0 | 3-1 | 1-1 | 3-1 | 1-1 | 3-5 | 2-0 | | 0-3 | 3-1 | 4-1 | 3-1 | 3-1 |
| FC de Rouen | 3-1 | 1-1 | 3-1 | 0-2 | 3-2 | 0-1 | 3-0 | 3-3 | 3-1 | 2-1 | 4-2 | 0-1 | 0-2 | 1-2 | 2-0 | | 2-1 | 0-0 | 2-2 | 3-2 |
| Union Athlétique Sedan-Torcy | 0-1 | 1-1 | 3-0 | 3-1 | 2-1 | 1-3 | 4-0 | 3-0 | 2-0 | 2-0 | 0-0 | 3-0 | 0-0 | 1-2 | 3-3 | 0-1 | | 2-1 | 2-1 | 4-2 |
| RC Strasbourg | 3-1 | 0-0 | 1-1 | 4-0 | 1-3 | 0-3 | 0-0 | 2-2 | 1-1 | 1-0 | 7-0 | 2-1 | 2-2 | 3-2 | 1-1 | 3-0 | 1-5 | | 3-1 | 0-2 |
| Toulouse FC | 4-0 | 0-0 | 5-2 | 4-2 | 1-2 | 0-1 | 3-1 | 0-5 | 2-1 | 2-0 | 4-0 | 2-0 | 1-1 | 3-2 | 2-1 | 1-2 | 0-2 | 1-1 | | 5-1 |
| Valenciennes | 4-0 | 2-0 | 0-0 | 1-1 | 1-1 | 0-0 | 0-1 | 0-0 | 2-0 | 2-0 | 2-2 | 1-1 | 4-0 | 2-0 | 0-0 | 1-1 | 1-1 | 4-0 | 1-2 | |

| | Division 1 | Pd | Wn | Dw | Ls | GF | GA | Pts | |
|---|---|---|---|---|---|---|---|---|---|
| 1. | AS DE MONACO (MONACO) | 38 | 20 | 10 | 8 | 77 | 44 | 50 | |
| 2. | Stade de Reims (Reims) | 38 | 19 | 9 | 10 | 79 | 52 | 47 | |
| 3. | Union Athlétique Sedan-Torcy (Sedan) | 38 | 19 | 8 | 11 | 68 | 46 | 46 | |
| 4. | Girondins de Bordeaux FC (Bordeaux) | 38 | 15 | 15 | 8 | 63 | 38 | 45 | |
| 5. | Olympique Lyonnais (Lyon) | 38 | 15 | 13 | 10 | 52 | 41 | 43 | |
| 6. | Nîmes Olympique (Nîmes) | 38 | 16 | 10 | 12 | 67 | 46 | 42 | |
| 7. | Toulouse FC (Toulouse) | 38 | 16 | 10 | 12 | 64 | 52 | 42 | |
| 8. | FC de Rouen (Rouen) | 38 | 18 | 6 | 14 | 59 | 57 | 42 | |
| 9. | US Valenciennes-Anzin (Valenciennes) | 38 | 13 | 15 | 10 | 60 | 45 | 41 | |
| 10. | Racing Club de Paris (Paris) | 38 | 14 | 13 | 11 | 80 | 71 | 41 | |
| 11. | Stade Rennais Université Club (Rennes) | 38 | 14 | 13 | 11 | 69 | 71 | 41 | |
| 12.. | Olympique GC de Nice (Nice) | 38 | 14 | 10 | 14 | 64 | 79 | 38 | |
| 13. | SC de l'Ouest Angers (Angers) | 38 | 13 | 11 | 14 | 51 | 64 | 37 | |
| 14. | Racing Club de Strasbourg (Strasbourg) | 38 | 9 | 16 | 13 | 54 | 63 | 34 | |
| 15. | Stade Français FC (Paris) | 38 | 11 | 10 | 17 | 54 | 70 | 32 | |
| 16. | Racing Club de Lens (Lens) | 38 | 10 | 10 | 18 | 60 | 67 | 30 | |
| 17. | FC de Grenoble (Grenoble) | 38 | 7 | 14 | 17 | 36 | 61 | 28 | R |
| 18. | FC de Nancy (Nancy) | 38 | 9 | 10 | 19 | 37 | 66 | 28 | R |
| 19. | Stade Olympique Montpelliérain (Montpellier) | 38 | 9 | 9 | 20 | 50 | 77 | 27 | R |
| 20. | Olympique de Marseille (Marseille) | 38 | 9 | 8 | 21 | 42 | 75 | 26 | R |
| | | 760 | 270 | 220 | 270 | 1186 | 1186 | 760 | |

## Top goal-scorers

| | | | |
|---|---|---|---|
| 1) | Serge MASNAGHETTI | (US Valenciennes-Anzin) | 35 |
| 2) | Lucien COSSOU | (AS de Monaco) | 28 |
| 3) | Hassan AKESBI | (Stade de Reims) | 24 |

Division 1 was reduced to 18 clubs for the next season.

| | Division 2 | Pd | Wn | Dw | Ls | GF | GA | Pts | |
|---|---|---|---|---|---|---|---|---|---|
| 1. | AS de Saint-Étienne (Saint-Étienne) | 36 | 25 | 8 | 3 | 86 | 46 | 58 | P |
| 2. | FC de Nantes (Nantes) | 36 | 25 | 4 | 7 | 82 | 38 | 54 | P |
| 3. | FC Sochaux-Montbéliard (Montbéliard) | 36 | 21 | 9 | 6 | 68 | 33 | 51 | |
| 4. | Havre AC (Le Havre) | 36 | 18 | 11 | 7 | 63 | 43 | 47 | |
| 5. | Red Star Olympique Audonien (Saint-Ouen) | 36 | 17 | 9 | 10 | 69 | 60 | 43 | |
| 6. | US de Boulogne (Boulogne-sur-Mer) | 36 | 15 | 9 | 12 | 66 | 55 | 39 | |
| 7. | Lille Olympique SC (Lille) | 36 | 15 | 8 | 13 | 63 | 59 | 38 | |
| 8. | Limoges FC (Limoges) | 36 | 14 | 9 | 13 | 57 | 60 | 37 | |
| 9. | FC de Metz (Metz) | 36 | 12 | 12 | 12 | 62 | 46 | 36 | |
| 10. | AS Biterroise (Béziers) | 36 | 15 | 6 | 15 | 64 | 62 | 36 | |
| 11. | AS de Cannes (Cannes) | 36 | 16 | 3 | 17 | 67 | 70 | 35 | |
| 12. | Racing Club Franc-Comtois (Besançon) | 36 | 12 | 8 | 16 | 65 | 72 | 32 | |
| 13. | US de Forbach (Forbach) | 36 | 11 | 7 | 18 | 36 | 53 | 29 | |
| 14. | Club Olympique Roubaix-Tourcoing (Roubaix) | 36 | 9 | 10 | 17 | 46 | 53 | 28 | # |
| 15. | Cercle Athlétique de Paris (Paris) | 36 | 9 | 10 | 17 | 39 | 62 | 28 | # |
| 16. | AS de Cherbourg (Cherbourg) | 36 | 7 | 13 | 16 | 46 | 62 | 27 | |
| 17. | AS Troyenne-Savinienne (Troyes) | 36 | 8 | 10 | 18 | 50 | 76 | 26 | # |
| 18. | SC de Toulon (Toulon) | 36 | 7 | 9 | 20 | 41 | 70 | 23 | |
| 19. | AS Aixoise (Aix-en-Provence) | 36 | 6 | 5 | 25 | 32 | 73 | 17 | |
| | | 684 | 262 | 160 | 262 | 1102 | 1093 | 684 | |

# Cercle Athlétique de Paris (Paris), Club Olympique Roubaix-Tourcoing (Roubaix) and AS Troyenne-Savinienne (Troyes) all reverted to amateur status for the next season.

## Coupe de France Final  (Stade Yves du Manoir, Colombes – 12/05/63 – 32,923)

**AS DE MONACO (MONACO)**          **0-0  (aet)**          Olympique Lyonnais (Lyon)

**Mon.**: Hernandez, Casolari, Thomas, Hidalgo, Artelesa, Biancheri, Djibrill, Douis, Cossou, Szkudlapski, Taberner.
**Lyon**: Aubour, Nowak, Mignot, Degeorges, Polak, Leborgne, Nurenberg, Di Nallo, Combin, Linder, Rambert.

### Final Replay  (Parc des Princes, Paris – 23/05/63 – 24,910)

**AS DE MONACO (MONACO)**          **2-0**          Olympique Lyonnais (Lyon)

*Cossou 56', Casolari 84'*

**Monaco**: Hernandez, Casolari, Thomas, Hidalgo, Artelesa, Biancheri, Djibrill, Douis, Cossou, Szkudlapski, Carlier.
**Lyon**: Aubour, Nowak, Mignot, Degeorges, Polak, Leborgne, Nurenberg, Hatchi, Combin, Linder, Rambert.

## Semi-Finals  (21/04/63)

| | | |
|---|---|---|
| AS de Monaco (Monaco) | 3-2 | Stade de Reims (Reims) |
| Olympique Lyonnais (Lyon) | 3-1 | SC de Toulon (Toulon) |

## Quarter-Finals  (31/03/63)

| | | |
|---|---|---|
| Olympique Lyonnais | 1-0 | Union Athlétique Sedan-Torcy (Sedan) |
| AS de Monaco (Monaco) | 2-0 | Girondins de Bordeaux FC (Bordeaux) |
| Stade de Reims (Reims) | 4-3 | Limoges FC (Limoges) |
| SC de Toulon (Toulon) | 1-0 | AS Brestoise (Brest) |

# 1963-64

| 1963-1964 Division One | SC de l'Ouest Angers | Girondins Bordeaux | Stade Français FC | Racing Club de Lens | Olympique Lyonnais | AS de Monaco | FC de Nantes | Olympique GC Nice | Nîmes Olympique | Racing Club de Paris | Stade de Reims | Stade Rennais UC | FC de Rouen | AS Saint-Étienne | UA Sedan-Torcy | Racing Strasbourg | Toulouse FC | Valenciennes-Anzin |
|---|---|---|---|---|---|---|---|---|---|---|---|---|---|---|---|---|---|---|
| SC de l'Ouest Angers | | 1-1 | 1-3 | 1-2 | 1-1 | 4-4 | 3-3 | 0-3 | 0-1 | 2-1 | 3-1 | 1-1 | 3-0 | 3-1 | 1-0 | 1-1 | 4-3 | 3-2 |
| Girondins Bordeaux | 3-0 | | 4-1 | 1-1 | 4-0 | 0-0 | 2-0 | 6-2 | 2-2 | 2-2 | 4-2 | 3-1 | 2-0 | 2-3 | 3-2 | 2-0 | 2-1 | 0-3 |
| Stade Français FC | 2-2 | 2-0 | | 1-0 | 1-2 | 1-0 | 4-0 | 2-2 | 0-0 | 2-3 | 0-2 | 4-2 | 5-2 | 1-3 | 3-2 | 1-0 | 0-0 | 0-2 |
| Racing Club de Lens | 4-0 | 8-1 | 3-0 | | 1-2 | 0-0 | 2-0 | 2-1 | 4-2 | 10-2 | 2-1 | 5-0 | 0-2 | 4-2 | 3-1 | 2-1 | 2-1 | 2-0 |
| Olympique Lyonnais | 2-2 | 3-1 | 2-0 | 1-1 | | 5-1 | 1-1 | 0-0 | 2-1 | 5-1 | 3-1 | 4-1 | 0-1 | 4-5 | 2-0 | 1-1 | 1-2 | 1-1 |
| AS de Monaco | 0-1 | 2-0 | 0-1 | 5-0 | 0-1 | | 3-1 | 0-0 | 2-0 | 5-3 | 1-0 | 3-2 | 2-1 | 2-1 | 3-1 | 4-2 | 5-0 | 3-0 |
| FC de Nantes | 1-0 | 4-1 | 3-1 | 2-1 | 3-1 | 1-3 | | 3-0 | 2-1 | 1-0 | 0-0 | 2-1 | 7-1 | 1-3 | 0-0 | 0-1 | 0-0 | 0-1 |
| Olympique GC Nice | 3-1 | 2-0 | 3-1 | 3-2 | 1-2 | 0-2 | 1-2 | | 3-2 | 0-2 | 1-1 | 0-2 | 2-0 | 1-1 | 2-4 | 1-1 | 2-4 | 1-3 |
| Nîmes Olympique | 2-0 | 0-0 | 3-0 | 1-1 | 5-0 | 1-0 | 3-0 | 0-0 | | 3-1 | 4-0 | 3-1 | 0-2 | 0-2 | 4-2 | 1-1 | 1-0 | 2-0 |
| Racing Club de Paris | 3-4 | 3-1 | 3-2 | 3-2 | 1-3 | 1-5 | 3-0 | 3-2 | 5-0 | | 2-1 | 0-2 | 2-2 | 1-3 | 2-2 | 3-0 | 1-1 | 1-3 |
| Stade de Reims | 1-1 | 1-0 | 0-3 | 1-0 | 2-2 | 2-3 | 1-1 | 2-0 | 0-0 | 1-4 | | 2-4 | 2-1 | 1-1 | 1-0 | 0-0 | 4-2 | 2-1 |
| Stade Rennais Université Club | 2-4 | 2-2 | 4-3 | 0-0 | 2-3 | 2-1 | 3-1 | 3-1 | 2-2 | 2-0 | | | 2-1 | 1-1 | 1-0 | 0-0 | 4-2 | 2-1 |
| FC de Rouen | 0-0 | 0-0 | 2-0 | 3-0 | 2-2 | 4-0 | 5-2 | 3-0 | 1-0 | 1-2 | 3-4 | 3-1 | | 0-0 | 2-2 | 3-0 | 2-1 | 0-4 |
| AS Saint-Étienne | 2-2 | 4-0 | 0-1 | 1-0 | 2-1 | 4-1 | 6-1 | 2-2 | 3-0 | 2-1 | 1-1 | 3-0 | 4-0 | | 2-1 | 2-2 | 7-1 | 1-1 |
| Union Athlétique Sedan-Torcy | 2-1 | 2-4 | 2-0 | 2-3 | 2-0 | 4-0 | 2-0 | 8-1 | 3-1 | 1-0 | 2-0 | 5-0 | 2-1 | 3-0 | | 2-1 | 1-1 | 0-2 |
| Racing Strasbourg | 2-1 | 3-1 | 1-1 | 1-2 | 5-0 | 1-0 | 0-0 | 2-1 | 3-0 | 2-1 | 1-2 | 2-1 | 1-0 | 2-0 | 2-0 | | 1-1 | 1-0 |
| Toulouse FC | 4-0 | 0-1 | 0-2 | 4-2 | 1-0 | 1-1 | 1-0 | 2-1 | 1-1 | 2-2 | 2-2 | 1-1 | 2-2 | 4-0 | 2-0 | 3-2 | | 2-1 |
| Valenciennes-Anzin | 1-3 | 1-0 | 0-0 | 0-0 | 0-1 | 0-0 | 0-0 | 7-2 | 1-0 | 1-3 | 2-1 | 0-0 | 2-1 | 1-2 | 2-0 | 1-0 | 2-3 | |

| | Division 1 | Pd | Wn | Dw | Ls | GF | GA | Pts | |
|---|---|---|---|---|---|---|---|---|---|
| 1. | AS DE SAINT-Étienne (SAINT-Étienne) | 34 | 18 | 8 | 8 | 71 | 48 | 44 | |
| 2. | AS de Monaco (Monaco) | 34 | 17 | 7 | 10 | 62 | 45 | 41 | |
| 3. | Racing Club de Lens (Lens) | 34 | 17 | 6 | 11 | 71 | 46 | 40 | |
| 4. | Olympique Lyonnais (Lyon) | 34 | 15 | 9 | 10 | 58 | 53 | 39 | |
| 5. | Toulouse FC (Toulouse) | 34 | 13 | 11 | 10 | 56 | 54 | 37 | |
| 6. | US Valenciennes-Anzin (Valenciennes) | 34 | 14 | 7 | 13 | 49 | 39 | 35 | |
| 7. | Girondins de Bordeaux FC (Bordeaux) | 34 | 13 | 8 | 13 | 55 | 58 | 34 | |
| 8. | FC de Nantes (Nantes) | 34 | 13 | 8 | 13 | 51 | 59 | 34 | |
| 9. | Racing Club de Strasbourg (Strasbourg) | 34 | 11 | 11 | 12 | 43 | 41 | 33 | |
| 10. | SC de l'Ouest Angers (Angers) | 34 | 11 | 11 | 12 | 54 | 62 | 33 | |
| 11. | Stade Rennais Université Club (Rennes) | 34 | 12 | 9 | 13 | 54 | 65 | 33 | |
| 12. | Union Athlétique Sedan-Torcy (Sedan) | 34 | 14 | 4 | 16 | 62 | 52 | 32 | |
| 13. | Nîmes Olympique (Nîmes) | 34 | 12 | 8 | 14 | 45 | 45 | 32 | |
| 14. | FC de Rouen (Rouen) | 34 | 12 | 8 | 14 | 50 | 51 | 32 | |
| 15. | Stade Français FC (Paris) | 34 | 13 | 6 | 15 | 48 | 53 | 32 | PO |
| 16. | Racing Club de Paris (Paris) | 34 | 12 | 7 | 15 | 66 | 76 | 31 | PO |
| 17. | Stade de Reims (Reims) | 34 | 8 | 11 | 15 | 37 | 56 | 27 | R |
| 18. | Olympique GC de Nice (Nice) | 34 | 7 | 9 | 18 | 45 | 74 | 23 | R |
| | | 612 | 232 | 148 | 232 | 977 | 977 | 612 | |

## Top goal-scorers

| | | | |
|---|---|---|---|
| 1) | Ahmed OUDJANI | (Racing Club de Lens) | 30 |
| 2) | André GUY | (AS de Saint-Étienne) | 28 |
| 3) | Nestor COMBIN | (Olympique Lyonnais) | 23 |

| | Promotion/Relegation Play-Offs | Pd | Wn | Dw | Ls | GF | GA | Pts | |
|---|---|---|---|---|---|---|---|---|---|
| 1. | Stade Français FC (Paris) | 4 | 2 | 1 | 1 | 10 | 8 | 5 | |
| 2. | SC de Toulon (Toulon) | 4 | 2 | - | 2 | 9 | 9 | 4 | P |
| 3. | Racing Club de Paris (Paris) | 4 | 2 | - | 2 | 8 | 9 | 4 | R |
| 4. | FC de Metz (Metz) | 4 | 1 | 1 | 2 | 8 | 9 | 3 | |
| | | 12 | 7 | 2 | 7 | 35 | 35 | 16 | |

| | Division 2 | Pd | Wn | Dw | Ls | GF | GA | Pts | |
|---|---|---|---|---|---|---|---|---|---|
| 1. | Lille Olympique SC (Lille) | 34 | 22 | 6 | 6 | 62 | 29 | 50 | P |
| 2. | FC Sochaux-Montbéliard (Montbéliard) | 34 | 16 | 12 | 6 | 62 | 39 | 44 | P |
| 3. | FC de Metz (Metz) | 34 | 15 | 11 | 8 | 54 | 40 | 41 | PO |
| 4. | SC de Toulon (Toulon) | 34 | 19 | 3 | 12 | 55 | 43 | 41 | PO |
| 5. | Olympique de Marseille (Marseille) | 34 | 15 | 10 | 9 | 59 | 57 | 40 | |
| 6. | FC de Grenoble (Grenoble) | 34 | 14 | 11 | 9 | 46 | 36 | 39 | |
| 7. | Havre AC (Le Havre) | 34 | 14 | 8 | 12 | 58 | 55 | 36 | # |
| 8. | Stade Olympique Montpelliérain (Montpellier) | 34 | 12 | 11 | 11 | 55 | 57 | 35 | |
| 9. | Limoges FC (Limoges) | 34 | 14 | 7 | 13 | 53 | 58 | 35 | |
| 10. | AS Aixoise (Aix-en-Provence) | 34 | 13 | 8 | 13 | 45 | 40 | 34 | |
| 11. | Red Star Olympique Audonien (Saint-Ouen) | 34 | 11 | 10 | 13 | 53 | 61 | 32 | |
| 12. | Racing Club Franc-Comtois (Besançon) | 34 | 9 | 11 | 14 | 46 | 56 | 29 | |
| 13. | AS de Cherbourg (Cherbourg) | 34 | 8 | 12 | 14 | 55 | 69 | 28 | |
| 14. | AS de Cannes (Cannes) | 34 | 10 | 8 | 16 | 67 | 54 | 28 | |
| 15. | US de Boulogne (Boulogne-sur-Mer) | 34 | 9 | 9 | 16 | 50 | 61 | 27 | |
| 16. | FC de Nancy (Nancy) | 34 | 10 | 7 | 17 | 45 | 61 | 27 | # |
| 17. | US de Forbach (Forbach) | 34 | 6 | 14 | 14 | 28 | 42 | 26 | |
| 18. | AS Biterroise (Béziers) | 34 | 5 | 10 | 19 | 23 | 47 | 20 | |
| | | 612 | 222 | 168 | 222 | 916 | 905 | 612 | |

# Havre AC (Le Havre) and FC de Nancy (Nancy) both reverted to amateur status for the next season.

## Coupe de France Final   (Stade Yves du Manoir, Colombes – 10/05/64 – 32,777)

**OLYMPIQUE LYONNAIS (LYON)**  2-0  Girondins de Bordeaux FC (Bordeaux)

*Combin 11', 26'*

**Lyonnais**: Aubour, Djorkaeff, Mignot, Degeorges, Polak, Leborgne, Dumas, Di Nallo, Combin, Hatchi, Rambert.
**Bordeaux**: Ranouilh, Moevi, Chorda, Navarro, Rey, Calleja, Keita, Abossolo, De Bourgoing, Gori, Robuschi.

## Semi-Finals   (17-19/04/64)

| | | |
|---|---|---|
| Girondins de Bordeaux FC (Bordeaux) | 2-0 | FC de Nantes (Nantes) |
| Olympique Lyonnais (Lyon) | 2-0 | US Valenciennes-Anzin (Valenciennes) |

## Quarter-Finals   (22/03/64)

| | | |
|---|---|---|
| Girondins de Bordeaux FC (Bordeaux) | 2-0 | Red Star Olympique Audonien (Saint-Ouen) |
| Olympique Lyonnais (Lyon) | 2-1 | Racing Club de Lens (Lens) |
| FC de Nantes (Nantes) | 4-1 | Olympique GC de Nice (Nice) |
| US Valenciennes-Anzin (Valenciennes) | 1-0 | FC de Rouen (Rouen) |

# 1964-65

**1964-1965 Division One**

| | Angers | Bordeaux | St Français | Lens | Lille | Lyonnais | Monaco | Nantes | Nîmes | St Rennais | Rouen | St-Étienne | Sedan-Torcy | Sochaux | Strasbourg | Toulon | Toulouse | Valenciennes |
|---|---|---|---|---|---|---|---|---|---|---|---|---|---|---|---|---|---|---|
| SC de l'Ouest Angers | ■ | 2-1 | 1-0 | 3-1 | 1-1 | 2-1 | 0-0 | 2-2 | 5-0 | 1-2 | 3-0 | 0-1 | 3-0 | 1-0 | 0-0 | 0-0 | 2-4 | 2-2 |
| Girondins Bordeaux | 2-1 | ■ | 2-1 | 0-0 | 2-0 | 0-2 | 2-0 | 2-2 | 2-1 | 1-0 | 1-2 | 1-1 | 5-1 | 1-0 | 1-0 | 3-0 | 4-2 | 1-0 |
| Stade Français FC | 2-0 | 0-0 | ■ | 0-0 | 0-0 | 1-1 | 3-2 | 1-1 | 3-1 | 2-1 | 2-0 | 2-3 | 1-0 | 3-3 | 2-2 | 3-2 | 2-0 | 0-3 |
| Racing Club de Lens | 1-0 | 3-2 | 5-2 | ■ | 0-1 | 1-2 | 2-0 | 0-3 | 3-1 | 1-1 | 2-2 | 4-1 | 3-1 | 2-3 | 0-3 | 2-1 | 1-1 | 3-2 |
| Lille Olympique SC | 3-4 | 3-1 | 1-1 | 4-0 | ■ | 2-2 | 3-0 | 2-2 | 2-1 | 3-2 | 1-0 | 3-3 | 3-0 | 3-0 | 1-1 | 5-0 | 0-2 | 1-1 |
| Olympique Lyonnais | 5-2 | 0-0 | 4-0 | 1-1 | 1-0 | ■ | 0-1 | 1-1 | 0-3 | 1-0 | 1-1 | 0-1 | 2-0 | 2-1 | 2-1 | 1-0 | 2-1 | 1-0 |
| AS de Monaco | 3-1 | 0-0 | 1-0 | 2-1 | 1-1 | 3-2 | ■ | 4-1 | 1-1 | 2-1 | 1-0 | 0-2 | 0-4 | 2-0 | 0-1 | 1-0 | 2-1 | 1-1 |
| FC de Nantes | 2-1 | 2-0 | 4-2 | 1-1 | 1-1 | 3-0 | 2-1 | ■ | 0-2 | 2-3 | 3-0 | 4-1 | 2-2 | 3-0 | 3-2 | 5-1 | 4-0 | 1-0 |
| Nîmes Olympique | 2-1 | 0-3 | 3-0 | 2-2 | 2-1 | 1-2 | 1-0 | 0-3 | ■ | 2-3 | 2-0 | 1-0 | 0-3 | 3-0 | 2-1 | 0-1 | 0-4 | 2-1 |
| Stade Rennais Université Club | 6-0 | 1-2 | 2-0 | 3-3 | 3-3 | 3-0 | 1-0 | 4-0 | 4-0 | ■ | 4-0 | 2-1 | 3-2 | 1-1 | 1-2 | 4-1 | 1-1 | 3-1 |
| FC de Rouen | 0-1 | 1-0 | 1-1 | 0-1 | 2-1 | 1-1 | 1-1 | 1-3 | 1-0 | 1-0 | ■ | 0-1 | 2-0 | 0-4 | 1-3 | 1-0 | 3-0 | 1-1 |
| AS Saint-Étienne | 2-1 | 0-1 | 0-0 | 2-2 | 3-3 | 6-0 | 2-0 | 2-0 | 1-2 | 3-1 | 1-3 | ■ | 1-1 | 0-0 | 1-1 | 1-0 | 1-0 | 0-1 |
| Union Athlétique Sedan-Torcy | 1-0 | 0-1 | 0-3 | 3-1 | 0-0 | 4-1 | 2-1 | 2-2 | 4-2 | 2-2 | 0-2 | 1-0 | ■ | 0-0 | 5-2 | 3-2 | 6-0 | 1-3 |
| Sochaux-Montbéliard | 2-0 | 4-1 | 4-1 | 2-3 | 2-1 | 2-1 | 3-0 | 1-1 | 1-1 | 3-0 | 2-3 | 3-2 | 2-2 | ■ | 0-2 | 2-0 | 0-2 | 3-2 |
| Racing Strasbourg | 0-1 | 0-0 | 2-0 | 3-0 | 3-2 | 3-3 | 3-3 | 1-1 | 3-2 | 2-3 | 3-0 | 1-0 | 2-0 | 0-0 | ■ | 0-0 | 5-3 | 3-3 |
| SC de Toulon | 4-0 | 2-0 | 2-1 | 1-3 | 3-1 | 1-1 | 0-6 | 0-1 | 1-2 | 4-1 | 1-0 | 1-3 | 1-0 | 0-1 | 0-0 | ■ | 0-2 | 1-3 |
| Toulouse FC | 1-3 | 1-1 | 1-1 | 2-2 | 1-1 | 3-2 | 0-2 | 3-0 | 1-0 | 0-1 | 0-2 | 2-2 | -0 | 1-0 | 3-1 | 0-1 | ■ | 1-0 |
| Valenciennes-Anzin | 0-0 | 0-0 | 0-0 | 6-1 | 3-0 | 1-1 | 3-0 | 2-1 | 1-0 | 0-0 | 3-0 | 2-0 | 1-1 | 1-0 | 3-0 | 1-0 | 1-1 | ■ |

| Division 1 | Pd | Wn | Dw | Ls | GF | GA | Pts | |
|---|---|---|---|---|---|---|---|---|
| 1. FC DE NANTES (NANTES) | 34 | 16 | 11 | 7 | 66 | 45 | 43 | |
| 2. Girondins de Bordeaux FC (Bordeaux) | 34 | 16 | 9 | 9 | 43 | 32 | 41 | |
| 3. US Valenciennes-Anzin (Valenciennes) | 34 | 14 | 12 | 8 | 52 | 30 | 40 | |
| 4. Stade Rennais Université Club (Rennes) | 34 | 14 | 10 | 10 | 67 | 48 | 38 | |
| 5. Racing Club de Strasbourg (Strasbourg) | 34 | 13 | 12 | 9 | 56 | 46 | 38 | |
| 6. Olympique Lyonnais (Lyon) | 34 | 12 | 12 | 10 | 46 | 50 | 36 | |
| 7. AS de Saint-Étienne (Saint-Étienne) | 34 | 13 | 9 | 12 | 48 | 43 | 35 | |
| 8. Racing Club de Lens (Lens) | 34 | 12 | 11 | 11 | 55 | 61 | 35 | |
| 9. Lille Olympique SC (Lille) | 34 | 10 | 14 | 10 | 57 | 48 | 34 | |
| 10. FC Sochaux-Montbéliard (Montbéliard) | 34 | 13 | 8 | 13 | 49 | 45 | 34 | |
| 11. Toulouse FC (Toulouse) | 34 | 12 | 9 | 13 | 50 | 52 | 33 | |
| 12. AS de Monaco (Monaco) | 34 | 13 | 7 | 14 | 41 | 45 | 33 | |
| 13. SC de l'Ouest Angers (Angers) | 34 | 12 | 7 | 15 | 44 | 51 | 31 | |
| 14. Union Athlétique Sedan-Torcy (Sedan) | 34 | 11 | 8 | 15 | 51 | 58 | 30 | |
| 15. Stade Français FC (Paris) | 34 | 9 | 12 | 13 | 40 | 52 | 30 | |
| 16. FC de Rouen (Rouen) | 34 | 12 | 6 | 16 | 31 | 48 | 30 | PO |
| 17. Nîmes Olympique (Nîmes) | 34 | 13 | 3 | 18 | 42 | 58 | 29 | PO |
| 18. SC de Toulon (Toulon) | 34 | 9 | 4 | 21 | 31 | 57 | 22 | R |
| | 612 | 224 | 164 | 224 | 869 | 869 | 612 | |

## Top goal-scorers

| | | | |
|---|---|---|---|
| 1) | Jacques  SIMON | (FC de Nantes) | 24 |
| 2) | Daniel  RODIGHIERO | (Stade Rennais Université Club) | 20 |
| 3) | André  PERRIN | (Union Athlétique Sedan-Torcy) | 18 |

| Promotion/Relegation Play-Offs | Pd | Wn | Dw | Ls | GF | GA | Pts |
|---|---|---|---|---|---|---|---|
| 1. FC de Rouen (Rouen) | 4 | 2 | 1 | 1 | 12 | 4 | 5 |
| 2. Nîmes Olympique (Nîmes) | 4 | 2 | - | 2 | 5 | 4 | 4 |
| 3. US de Boulogne (Boulogne-sur-Mer) | 4 | 2 | - | 2 | 4 | 10 | 4 |
| 4. Limoges FC (Limoges) | 4 | 1 | 1 | 2 | 4 | 7 | 3 |
| | 16 | 7 | 2 | 7 | 25 | 25 | 16 |

Division 1 was extended to 20 clubs for the next season.

| Division 2 | | Pd | Wn | Dw | Ls | GF | GA | Pts | |
|---|---|---|---|---|---|---|---|---|---|
| 1. | Olympique GC de Nice (Nice) | 30 | 19 | 4 | 7 | 52 | 32 | 42 | P |
| 2. | Red Star Olympique Audonien (Saint-Ouen) | 30 | 15 | 11 | 4 | 54 | 28 | 41 | P |
| 3. | AS de Cannes (Cannes) | 30 | 15 | 10 | 5 | 59 | 35 | 40 | P |
| 4. | Limoges FC (Limoges) | 30 | 16 | 5 | 9 | 47 | 31 | 37 | PO |
| 5. | US de Boulogne (Boulogne-sur-Mer) | 30 | 15 | 6 | 9 | 49 | 37 | 36 | PO |
| 6. | Stade Olympique Montpelliérain (Montpellier) | 30 | 12 | 10 | 8 | 41 | 36 | 34 | |
| 7. | FC de Grenoble (Grenoble) | 30 | 12 | 7 | 11 | 36 | 50 | 31 | |
| 8. | AS Aixoise (Aix-en-Provence) | 30 | 12 | 5 | 13 | 33 | 29 | 30 | |
| 9. | FC de Metz (Metz) | 30 | 11 | 8 | 11 | 42 | 43 | 30 | |
| 10. | Stade de Reims (Reims) | 30 | 12 | 5 | 13 | 54 | 38 | 29 | |
| 11. | AS de Cherbourg (Cherbourg) | 30 | 9 | 11 | 10 | 40 | 45 | 29 | |
| 12. | Racing Club de Paris (Paris) | 30 | 10 | 4 | 16 | 36 | 48 | 24 | |
| 13. | Racing Club Franc-Comtois (Besançon) | 30 | 8 | 6 | 16 | 35 | 54 | 22 | |
| 14. | Olympique de Marseille (Marseille) | 30 | 7 | 7 | 16 | 26 | 38 | 21 | |
| 15. | US de Forbach (Forbach) | 30 | 7 | 6 | 17 | 30 | 56 | 20 | |
| 16. | AS Biterroise (Béziers) | 30 | 4 | 6 | 20 | 18 | 61 | 14 | |
| | | 480 | 184 | 111 | 185 | 652 | 661 | 480 | |

**Elected**: Gazélec FC Ajaccien (Ajaccio), Sporting Étoile Club Bastiais (Bastia) and US de Marignane (Marignane).

Division 2 was extended to 19 clubs for the next season.


## Coupe de France Final   (Parc des Princes, Paris – 23/05/65 – 36,789)

**STADE RENNAIS UC (RENNES)**          **2-2**          Union Athlétique Sedan-Torcy (Sedan)

*Ascensio 44', Rodighiero 61*                                                      *Marie 11', Perrin 15'*

**Rennais**: Lamia, Lavaud, Cardiet, Boutet, Cédolin, Loncle, Prigent, Ascensio, Rodighiero, Dubaele, Pellegrini.
**Sedan**: Tordo, Fulgenzi, Rastoll, Gasparini, Lemerre, Cardoni, Salaber, Herbet, Perrin, Marie, Roy.


## Final Replay   (Parc des Princes, Paris – 26/05/65 – 26,792)

**STADE RENNAIS UC (RENNES)**          **3-1**          Union Athlétique Sedan-Torcy (Sedan)

*Rodighiero 47', 86' pen, Loncle 77'*                                                      *Herbet 20'*

**Rennais**: Lamia, Lavaud, Cardiet, Boutet, Brucato, Loncle, Prigent, Ascensio, Rodighiero, Dubaele, Pellegrini.
**Sedan**: Tordo, Fulgenzi, Rastoll, Gasparini, Lemerre, Cardoni, Salaber, Herbet, Perrin, Marie, Roy.


## Semi-Finals   (30/04/65 – 02/05/65)

| Stade Rennais Université Club (Rennes) | 3-0 | AS de Saint-Étienne (Saint-Étienne) |
|---|---|---|
| Union Athlètique Sedan-Torcy (Sedan) | 4-3 | Stade Français FC (Paris) |


## Quarter-Finals   (04/04/65)

| Stade Français FC (Paris) | 2-1 | Racing Club de Strasbourg (Strasbourg) |
|---|---|---|
| Stade Rennais Université Club (Rennes) | 5-2 | Olympique GC de Nice (Nice) |
| AS de Saint-Étienne (Saint-Étienne) | 3-2 | US Valenciennes-Anzin (Valenciennes) |
| Union Athlétique Sedan-Torcy (Sedan) | 3-1 | SC de Toulon (Toulon) |

# 1965-66

| 1965-1966 Division One | SC de l'O. Angers | Gir. de Bordeaux | AS de Cannes | Stade Français | Racing de Lens | Lille Olympique | Olymp. Lyonnais | AS de Monaco | FC de Nantes | Olymp. GC Nice | Nîmes Olymp. | Red Star Olymp. | Stade Rennais | FC de Rouen | AS Saint-Étienne | UA Sedan-Torcy | Sochaux-Montbél. | RC Strasbourg | Toulouse FC | Valenciennes |
|---|---|---|---|---|---|---|---|---|---|---|---|---|---|---|---|---|---|---|---|---|
| SC de l'Ouest Angers | ■ | 0-0 | 4-1 | 0-0 | 3-2 | 3-1 | 4-1 | 1-1 | 1-1 | 1-0 | 3-0 | 2-2 | 5-3 | 6-0 | 1-1 | 2-0 | 2-2 | 0-3 | 2-0 | 0-1 |
| Girondins de Bordeaux | 2-0 | ■ | 1-0 | 10-0 | 2-1 | 1-0 | 2-2 | 5-0 | 1-2 | 0-2 | 5-2 | 6-0 | 2-1 | 4-1 | 4-0 | 4-2 | 4-2 | 4-0 | 3-0 | 2-0 |
| AS de Cannes | 2-5 | 2-1 | ■ | 0-4 | 1-1 | 2-0 | 0-0 | 0-3 | 1-6 | 1-3 | 1-2 | 1-1 | 1-0 | 1-2 | 2-8 | 2-1 | 1-1 | 2-1 | 5-3 | 0-1 |
| Stade Français | 2-1 | 2-4 | 3-1 | ■ | 3-1 | 1-1 | 0-1 | 1-0 | 0-1 | 2-1 | 2-1 | 1-1 | 2-1 | 0-0 | 1-2 | 1-1 | 1-1 | 0-2 | 2-0 | 1-1 |
| Racing de Lens | 2-2 | 0-1 | 1-0 | 1-0 | ■ | 2-0 | 2-1 | 0-0 | 1-1 | 4-2 | 1-1 | 3-0 | 4-1 | 0-0 | 2-1 | 1-1 | 0-1 | 0-0 | 0-1 | 1-1 |
| Lille Olympique | 1-0 | 0-0 | 2-0 | 3-3 | 1-1 | ■ | 1-0 | 2-1 | 0-1 | 2-1 | 1-2 | 3-0 | 1-3 | 2-1 | 3-0 | 1-1 | 2-1 | 2-1 | 1-0 | 6-1 |
| Olympique Lyonnais | 2-1 | 1-4 | 2-0 | 2-0 | 3-2 | 6-3 | ■ | 1-0 | 0-2 | 2-0 | 3-1 | 0-0 | 1-2 | 0-0 | 1-1 | 2-1 | 1-0 | 2-1 | 0-1 | 0-1 |
| AS de Monaco | 1-3 | 0-2 | 0-0 | 3-1 | 3-0 | 2-0 | 2-0 | ■ | 1-3 | 0-3 | 4-0 | 2-1 | 1-1 | 3-0 | 1-1 | 3-3 | 1-1 | 0-0 | 2-3 | 0-2 |
| FC de Nantes | 5-3 | 2-2 | 1-0 | 2-1 | 4-2 | 3-1 | 2-0 | 2-1 | ■ | 2-1 | 4-1 | 7-2 | 4-0 | 2-1 | 5-0 | 4-2 | 2-1 | 2-0 | 2-0 | 1-1 |
| Olympique GC Nice | 5-2 | 1-2 | 1-1 | 1-1 | 0-3 | 2-0 | 4-2 | 1-2 | 0-0 | ■ | 4-1 | 4-0 | 3-2 | 6-0 | 4-2 | 1-0 | 3-1 | 0-2 | 2-1 | 1-1 |
| Nîmes Olympique | 1-0 | 1-1 | 1-1 | 0-0 | 4-5 | 4-1 | 0-0 | 4-0 | 1-2 | 1-0 | ■ | 3-1 | 2-2 | 2-1 | 1-1 | 1-0 | 1-0 | 4-1 | 2-0 | 2-2 |
| Red Star Olympique Audonien | 0-2 | 2-0 | 3-2 | 1-5 | 1-2 | 6-4 | 2-2 | 2-0 | 0-3 | 2-3 | 3-3 | ■ | 0-2 | 0-1 | 1-5 | 3-3 | 1-1 | 2-2 | 1-1 | 2-0 |
| Stade Rennais | 4-4 | 2-0 | 2-2 | 4-3 | 4-1 | 4-0 | 5-2 | 0-1 | 2-0 | 3-0 | 3-1 | 2-1 | ■ | 4-0 | 2-0 | 4-2 | 4-3 | 2-1 | 2-1 | 1-1 |
| FC de Rouen | 4-0 | 0-0 | 1-0 | 2-1 | 1-3 | 1-1 | 0-0 | 1-2 | 0-0 | 1-0 | 1-0 | 1-0 | 2-2 | ■ | 2-0 | 3-1 | 1-1 | 0-0 | 0-1 | 1-3 |
| AS Saint-Étienne | 4-0 | 2-1 | 1-1 | 0-0 | 2-0 | 7-4 | 2-1 | 1-3 | 5-1 | 2-1 | 7-0 | 4-0 | 2-2 |  | ■ | 2-1 | 3-1 | 5-1 | 3-0 | 5-1 |
| Union Athlétique Sedan-Torcy | 3-1 | 1-1 | 3-1 | 0-0 | 1-3 | 1-0 | 2-0 | 0-2 | 3-0 | 2-0 | 5-2 | 3-1 | 4-4 | 4-1 |  | ■ | 3-0 | 0-0 | 0-1 | 2-2 |
| Sochaux-Montbéliard | 3-2 | 0-1 | 3-1 | 1-0 | 3-2 | 1-0 | 7-2 | 2-1 | 3-1 | 1-0 | 3-1 | 3-0 | 3-2 | 4-0 | 2-3 | 0-1 | ■ | 2-1 | 0-1 | 1-1 |
| RC Strasbourg | 1-1 | 3-0 | 5-0 | 4-0 | 1-0 | 4-1 | 0-0 | 1-1 | 1-0 | 1-3 | 1-0 | 7-1 | 3-1 | 0-0 | 0-1 | 3-3 | 5-1 | ■ | 2-2 | 0-0 |
| Toulouse FC | 1-0 | 0-0 | 6-1 | 1-1 | 4-1 | 2-0 | 1-0 | 5-1 | 0-0 | 2-1 | 0-0 | 4-1 | 6-5 | 2-0 | 2-2 | 1-1 | 2-0 |  | ■ | 1-2 |
| Valenciennes | 4-1 | 2-2 | 3-0 | 1-0 | 2-0 | 2-0 | 1-0 | 1-0 | 2-2 | 4-2 | 3-0 | 1-0 | 2-1 | 1-1 | 3-1 | 0-4 | 0-0 | 3-2 | 1-1 | ■ |

## Division 1

| | Pd | Wn | Dw | Ls | GF | GA | Pts | |
|---|---|---|---|---|---|---|---|---|
| 1. FC DE NANTES (NANTES) | 38 | 26 | 8 | 4 | 84 | 36 | 60 | |
| 2. Girondins de Bordeaux FC (Bordeaux) | 38 | 22 | 9 | 7 | 84 | 36 | 53 | |
| 3. US Valenciennes-Anzin (Valenciennes) | 38 | 19 | 14 | 5 | 58 | 44 | 52 | |
| 4. Toulouse FC (Toulouse) | 38 | 19 | 8 | 11 | 61 | 46 | 46 | |
| 5. AS de Saint-Étienne (Saint-Étienne) | 38 | 19 | 7 | 12 | 85 | 62 | 45 | |
| 6. Stade Rennais Université Club (Rennes) | 38 | 18 | 6 | 14 | 80 | 70 | 42 | |
| 7. FC Sochaux-Montbéliard (Montbéliard) | 38 | 15 | 9 | 14 | 61 | 56 | 39 | |
| 8. Racing Club de Strasbourg (Strasbourg) | 38 | 13 | 12 | 13 | 59 | 47 | 38 | |
| 9. Union Athlétique Sedan-Torcy (Sedan) | 38 | 13 | 12 | 13 | 68 | 58 | 38 | * |
| 10. Olympique GC de Nice (Nice) | 38 | 16 | 4 | 18 | 66 | 59 | 36 | |
| 11. SC de l'Ouest Angers (Angers) | 38 | 13 | 10 | 15 | 68 | 66 | 36 | |
| 12. Racing Club de Lens (Lens) | 38 | 13 | 10 | 15 | 55 | 57 | 36 | |
| 13. AS de Monaco (Monaco) | 38 | 13 | 9 | 16 | 48 | 54 | 35 | |
| 14. FC de Rouen (Rouen) | 38 | 10 | 14 | 14 | 41 | 62 | 34 | |
| 15. Stade Français FC (Paris) | 38 | 10 | 13 | 15 | 45 | 57 | 33 | * |
| 16. Olympique Lyonnais (Lyon) | 38 | 12 | 9 | 17 | 43 | 56 | 33 | |
| 17. Nîmes Olympique (Nîmes) | 38 | 12 | 9 | 17 | 52 | 67 | 33 | PO |
| 18. Lille Olympique SC (Lille) | 38 | 12 | 6 | 20 | 51 | 71 | 30 | PO |
| 19. AS de Cannes (Cannes) | 38 | 6 | 9 | 23 | 37 | 86 | 21 | R |
| 20. Red Star Olympique Audonien (Saint-Ouen) | 38 | 5 | 10 | 23 | 44 | 100 | 20 | R |
| | 760 | 286 | 188 | 286 | 1190 | 1190 | 760 | |

## Top goal-scorers

1) Phillipe GONDET (FC de Nantes) 36
2) Robert HERBIN (AS de Saint-Étienne) 26
3) André GUY (Lille Olympique SC) 22
   Michel LAFRANCESCHINA (FC Sochaux-Montbéliard) 22

| Promotion/Relegation Play-Offs | Pd | Wn | Dw | Ls | GF | GA | Pts | |
|---|---|---|---|---|---|---|---|---|
| 1. Lille Olympique SC (Lille) | 4 | 3 | - | 1 | 5 | 2 | 6 | |
| 2. Nîmes Olympique (Nîmes) | 4 | 2 | 1 | 1 | 10 | 5 | 5 | |
| 3. Sporting Étoile Club Bastiais (Bastia) | 4 | 2 | - | 2 | 7 | 4 | 4 | |
| 4. Limoges FC (Limoges) | 4 | - | 1 | 3 | - | 11 | 1 | |
| | 16 | 7 | 2 | 7 | 22 | 22 | 16 | |

| Division 2 | Pd | Wn | Dw | Ls | GF | GA | Pts | |
|---|---|---|---|---|---|---|---|---|
| 1. Stade de Reims (Reims) | 36 | 22 | 6 | 8 | 76 | 38 | 50 | P |
| 2. Olympique de Marseille (Marseille) | 36 | 20 | 8 | 8 | 58 | 31 | 48 | P |
| 3. Limoges FC (Limoges) | 36 | 18 | 10 | 8 | 50 | 27 | 46 | PO |
| 4. Sporting Étoile Club Bastiais (Bastia) | 36 | 18 | 9 | 9 | 60 | 46 | 45 | PO |
| 5. SC de Toulon (Toulon) | 36 | 17 | 10 | 9 | 56 | 38 | 44 | |
| 6. Olympique Avignonnais (Avignon) | 36 | 17 | 9 | 10 | 68 | 42 | 43 | |
| 7. AS Biterroise (Béziers) | 36 | 19 | 5 | 12 | 59 | 42 | 43 | |
| 8. FC de Metz (Metz) | 36 | 15 | 12 | 9 | 54 | 50 | 42 | |
| 9. US de Boulogne (Boulogne-sur-Mer) | 36 | 15 | 10 | 11 | 60 | 56 | 40 | |
| 10. FC de Grenoble (Grenoble) | 36 | 16 | 7 | 13 | 62 | 58 | 39 | |
| 11. AS de Cherbourg (Cherbourg) | 36 | 12 | 11 | 13 | 39 | 50 | 35 | |
| 12. AS d'Angoulême (Angoulême) | 36 | 11 | 10 | 15 | 48 | 52 | 32 | |
| 13. Stade Olympique Montpelliérain (Montpellier) | 36 | 12 | 6 | 18 | 46 | 60 | 30 | |
| 14. Racing Club Franc-Comtois (Besançon) | 36 | 9 | 11 | 16 | 47 | 72 | 29 | |
| 15. AC Ajaccien (Ajaccio) | 36 | 8 | 11 | 17 | 45 | 65 | 27 | * |
| 16. US de Forbach (Forbach) | 36 | 8 | 9 | 19 | 43 | 67 | 25 | # |
| 17. Racing Club de Paris (Paris) | 36 | 9 | 6 | 21 | 46 | 70 | 24 | * |
| 18. AS Aixoise (Aix-en-Provence) | 36 | 6 | 11 | 19 | 39 | 62 | 23 | |
| 19. US de Marignane (Marignane) | 36 | 7 | 5 | 24 | 32 | 73 | 19 | # |
| | 684 | 259 | 166 | 259 | 988 | 999 | 68 | |

\* AC Ajaccien (Ajaccio) changed their name pre-season from Gazélec AC Ajaccien (Ajaccio)
   Stade Français FC (Paris) changed their name to Stade de Paris FC (Paris) for the next season
   Union Athlétique Sedan-Torcy (Sedan) merged with Racing Club de Paris (Paris) to become Racing Club de
   Paris-Sedan (Sedan) for the next season.

\# US de Forbach (Forbach) and US de Marignane (Marignane) reverted to amateur status for the next season.

**Elected**: Entente Chaumontaise Athletic-Cheminots (Chaumont) and US Dunkerquoise (Dunkerque).

Division 2 was reduced to 18 clubs for the next season.

## Coupe de France Final   (Parc des Princes, Paris – 22/05/66 – 36,285)

**RACING CLUB DE STRASBOURG**   1-0   FC de Nantes (Nantes)

*Sbaïz 51'*

**Strasbourg**: Schuth, Hauss, Sbaïz, Stieber, Devaux, Kaelbel, Gress, Merschel, Farias, Szczepaniak, Hausser.

**Nantes**: Eon, Grabowski, De Michele, Le Chénadec, Budzinski, Suaudeau, Blanchet, Muller, Gondet, Simon, Tourè.

## Semi-Finals   (29/04/66)

| | | |
|---|---|---|
| FC de Nantes (Nantes) | 3-0 | SC de l'Ouest Angers (Angers) |
| Racing Club de Strasbourg (Strasbourg) | 3-1 | Toulouse FC (Toulouse) |

## Quarter-Finals   (03/04/66)

| | | |
|---|---|---|
| SC de l'Ouest Angers (Angers) | 3-1 | Stade de Reims (Reims) |
| FC de Nantes (Nantes) | 2-0 | AC Ajaccien (Ajaccio) |
| Racing Club de Strasbourg (Strasbourg) | 1-0 | AS de Cherbourg (Cherbourg) |
| Toulouse FC (Toulouse) | 2-0 | FC Sochaux-Montbéliard (Montbéliard) |

# 1966-67

| 1966-1967 Division One | SC de l'Ouest Angers | Girondins de Bordeaux | Racing de Lens | Lille Olympique | Olympique Lyonnais | Olympique Marseille | AS de Monaco | FC de Nantes | Olympique GC Nice | Nîmes Olympique | Stade de Paris | Stade de Reims | Stade Rennais | FC de Rouen | AS Saint-Étienne | Racing Club de Paris Sedan | Sochaux-Montbéliard | RC Strasbourg | Toulouse FC | Valenciennes |
|---|---|---|---|---|---|---|---|---|---|---|---|---|---|---|---|---|---|---|---|---|
| SC de l'Ouest Angers | ■ | 2-0 | 2-0 | 2-1 | 0-2 | 5-0 | 0-0 | 1-1 | 1-0 | 1-2 | 1-1 | 2-2 | 0-0 | 5-2 | 0-3 | 2-5 | 1-1 | 3-1 | 1-1 | 3-1 |
| Girondins de Bordeaux | 1-4 | ■ | 1-1 | 1-3 | 4-1 | 2-0 | 1-1 | 0-1 | 1-1 | 2-0 | 0-0 | 1-0 | 2-0 | 3-0 | 1-0 | 2-5 | 1-0 | 4-1 | 2-1 | 0-0 |
| Racing de Lens | 1-1 | 3-2 | ■ | 1-1 | 4-1 | 2-2 | 2-1 | 4-0 | 1-3 | 2-1 | 4-1 | 5-2 | 2-1 | 1-1 | 2-0 | 2-2 | 1-1 | 2-1 | 0-0 | 0-0 |
| Lille Olympique | 0-0 | 1-2 | 2-1 | ■ | 0-1 | 0-0 | 2-1 | 2-4 | 3-0 | 4-0 | 0-0 | 1-1 | 0-0 | 1-0 | 0-1 | 2-2 | 6-0 | 2-1 | 3-1 | 1-0 |
| Olympique Lyonnais | 1-1 | 1-0 | 0-0 | 0-1 | ■ | 2-2 | 1-0 | 1-2 | 1-0 | 3-1 | 0-0 | 3-1 | 2-2 | 1-1 | 3-0 | 0-3 | 0-0 | 2-1 | 1-1 | 0-0 |
| Olympique Marseille | 1-1 | 3-2 | 1-0 | 2-1 | 4-1 | ■ | 1-2 | 1-0 | 1-1 | 4-0 | 1-2 | 0-0 | 1-1 | 0-0 | 2-2 | 1-1 | 1-0 | 0-1 | 2-0 | 2-1 |
| AS de Monaco | 1-5 | 1-1 | 2-1 | 3-0 | 4-0 | 0-1 | ■ | 0-0 | 0-0 | 0-1 | 0-1 | 5-0 | 0-0 | 0-0 | 1-0 | 4-2 | 3-0 | 1-1 | 1-0 | 2-2 |
| FC de Nantes | 2-1 | 1-1 | 3-1 | 4-0 | 5-2 | 3-3 | 2-1 | ■ | 4-1 | 5-3 | 3-0 | 6-2 | 1-0 | 0-0 | 4-1 | 3-1 | 1-1 | 4-0 | 2-2 | 3-1 |
| Olympique GC Nice | 3-1 | 2-1 | 1-0 | 1-2 | 4-3 | 0-0 | 0-0 | 3-1 | ■ | 4-1 | 0-0 | 1-0 | 4-0 | 2-0 | 1-2 | 5-1 | 1-4 | 2-1 | 3-1 | 5-2 |
| Nîmes Olympique | 1-4 | 1-2 | 1-2 | 0-0 | 1-0 | 0-1 | 3-2 | 1-0 | 1-1 | ■ | 0-1 | 2-2 | 1-2 | 1-0 | 1-1 | 2-2 | 3-0 | 1-0 | 2-0 | 1-2 |
| Stade de Paris | 1-1 | 0-0 | 0-1 | 0-2 | 0-1 | 0-2 | 1-1 | 1-0 | 2-0 | 1-2 | ■ | 0-1 | 0-2 | 1-2 | 1-1 | 1-1 | 0-3 | 0-0 | 0-0 | 0-2 |
| Stade de Reims | 0-3 | 4-1 | 4-0 | 0-1 | 2-0 | 1-0 | 2-0 | 1-1 | 2-0 | 1-1 | 1-0 | ■ | 2-4 | 1-0 | 1-2 | 1-4 | 1-1 | 2-1 | 1-3 | 1-0 |
| Stade Rennais | 2-3 | 0-1 | 3-0 | 1-2 | 4-0 | 2-1 | 3-1 | 2-2 | 0-1 | 3-0 | 2-1 | 3-0 | ■ | 2-1 | 1-1 | 5-0 | 1-1 | 4-3 | 1-2 | 1-0 |
| FC de Rouen | 1-0 | 1-1 | 0-2 | 3-0 | 3-2 | 5-1 | 0-0 | 3-3 | 1-0 | 2-0 | 0-1 | 2-0 | 1-0 | ■ | 0-1 | 3-0 | 3-0 | 0-0 | 0-2 | 1-1 |
| AS Saint-Étienne | 4-2 | 1-1 | 4-0 | 4-1 | 2-1 | 2-0 | 1-3 | 3-3 | 7-0 | 3-1 | 7-1 | 3-0 | 4-1 | 3-0 | ■ | 1-0 | 1-0 | 2-1 | 3-0 | 3-1 |
| Racing Club de Paris Sedan | 1-1 | 0-3 | 3-0 | 4-1 | 0-0 | 0-0 | 1-1 | 3-3 | 0-1 | 2-2 | 0-0 | 1-0 | 4-0 | 1-0 | 1-0 | ■ | 1-1 | 3-0 | 1-0 | 0-0 |
| Sochaux-Montbéliard | 2-5 | 1-1 | 2-5 | 1-0 | 1-1 | 0-1 | 0-0 | 1-1 | 4-0 | 2-2 | 3-0 | 1-1 | 3-1 | 3-0 | 0-3 | 1-0 | ■ | 1-0 | 1-0 | 0-1 |
| RC Strasbourg | 0-0 | 0-3 | 1-0 | 3-1 | 0-0 | 2-1 | 4-2 | 1-1 | 3-1 | 1-2 | 1-0 | 5-0 | 5-3 | 1-0 | 2-1 | 0-0 | 3-1 | ■ | 4-0 | 4-1 |
| Toulouse FC | 1-1 | 2-1 | 3-2 | 2-1 | 2-2 | 1-0 | 3-0 | 2-2 | 3-0 | 0-1 | 0-0 | 1-0 | 1-1 | 1-1 | 0-2 | 2-3 | 1-2 | 1-1 | ■ | 0-2 |
| Valenciennes | 0-0 | 0-1 | 1-3 | 3-0 | 0-0 | 2-1 | 2-0 | 0-0 | 0-1 | 2-0 | 2-0 | 2-0 | 3-1 | 3-0 | 0-3 | 0-0 | 2-0 | 1-0 | 2-0 | ■ |

## Division 1

| | Division 1 | Pd | Wn | Dw | Ls | GF | GA | Pts | |
|---|---|---|---|---|---|---|---|---|---|
| 1. | AS DE SAINT-Étienne (SAINT-Étienne) | 38 | 24 | 6 | 8 | 82 | 37 | 54 | |
| 2. | FC de Nantes (Nantes) | 38 | 17 | 16 | 5 | 81 | 51 | 50 | |
| 3. | SC de l'Ouest Angers (Angers) | 38 | 14 | 16 | 8 | 66 | 46 | 44 | |
| 4. | Girondins de Bordeaux FC (Bordeaux) | 38 | 16 | 11 | 11 | 53 | 43 | 43 | |
| 5. | Racing Club de Paris-Sedan (Sedan) | 38 | 13 | 16 | 9 | 58 | 50 | 42 | |
| 6. | Olympique GC de Nice (Nice) | 38 | 17 | 7 | 14 | 53 | 55 | 41 | |
| 7. | US Valenciennes-Anzin (Valenciennes) | 38 | 15 | 10 | 13 | 42 | 37 | 40 | |
| 8. | Racing Club de Lens (Lens) | 38 | 15 | 10 | 13 | 58 | 55 | 40 | |
| 9. | Olympique de Marseille (Marseille) | 38 | 13 | 13 | 12 | 44 | 45 | 39 | |
| 10. | Lille Olympique SC (Lille) | 38 | 15 | 8 | 15 | 48 | 50 | 38 | |
| 11. | Stade Rennais Université Club (Rennes) | 38 | 14 | 9 | 15 | 59 | 56 | 37 | |
| 12. | Racing Club de Strasbourg (Strasbourg) | 38 | 14 | 8 | 16 | 54 | 52 | 36 | |
| 13. | FC Sochaux-Montbéliard (Montbéliard) | 38 | 11 | 13 | 14 | 43 | 53 | 35 | |
| 14. | AS de Monaco (Monaco) | 38 | 10 | 14 | 14 | 44 | 44 | 34 | |
| 15. | Olympique Lyonnais (Lyon) | 38 | 10 | 14 | 14 | 40 | 56 | 34 | |
| 16. | FC de Rouen (Rouen) | 38 | 11 | 11 | 16 | 37 | 44 | 33 | |
| 17. | Toulouse FC (Toulouse) | 38 | 10 | 12 | 16 | 40 | 52 | 32 | PO |
| 18. | Nîmes Olympique (Nîmes) | 38 | 12 | 8 | 18 | 43 | 64 | 32 | PO |
| 19. | Stade de Reims (Reims) | 38 | 11 | 8 | 19 | 40 | 66 | 30 | R |
| 20. | Stade de Paris FC (Paris) | 38 | 6 | 14 | 18 | 18 | 47 | 26 | R |
| | | 760 | 268 | 224 | 268 | 1003 | 1003 | 760 | |

## Top goal-scorers

| | | | |
|---|---|---|---|
| 1) | Hervé REVELLI | (AS de Saint-Étienne) | 31 |
| 2) | Georges LECH | (Racing Club de Lens) | 25 |
| 3) | André GUY | (Lille Olympique SC) | 20 |
| | Daniel RODIGHIERO | (Stade Rennais Université Club) | 20 |

## Promotion/Relegation Play-Offs

| | Promotion/Relegation Play-Offs | Pd | Wn | Dw | Ls | GF | GA | Pts | |
|---|---|---|---|---|---|---|---|---|---|
| 1. | AS Aixoise (Aix-en-Provence) | 4 | 1 | 3 | - | 7 | 5 | 5 | P |
| 2. | Toulouse FC (Toulouse) | 4 | 2 | 1 | 1 | 3 | 3 | 5 | * |
| 3. | Nîmes Olympique (Nîmes) | 4 | 1 | 2 | 1 | 7 | 6 | 4 | R |
| 4. | Sporting Étoile Club Bastiais (Bastia) | 4 | 1 | - | 3 | 2 | 5 | 2 | |
| | | 16 | 5 | 6 | 5 | 19 | 19 | 16 | |

## Division 2

| | | Pd | Wn | Dw | Ls | GF | GA | Pts | |
|---|---|---|---|---|---|---|---|---|---|
| 1. | AC Ajaccien (Ajaccio) | 34 | 18 | 10 | 6 | 52 | 26 | 46 | P |
| 2. | FC de Metz (Metz) | 34 | 17 | 10 | 7 | 46 | 26 | 44 | P |
| 3. | Sporting Étoile Club Bastiais (Bastia) | 34 | 19 | 6 | 9 | 48 | 34 | 44 | PO |
| 4. | AS Aixoise (Aix-en-Provence) | 34 | 15 | 13 | 6 | 59 | 24 | 43 | PO |
| 5. | AS Biterroise (Béziers) | 34 | 16 | 9 | 9 | 46 | 46 | 41 | |
| 6. | Olympique Avignonnais (Avignon) | 34 | 14 | 9 | 11 | 51 | 37 | 37 | |
| 7. | SC de Toulon (Toulon) | 34 | 15 | 7 | 12 | 45 | 44 | 37 | |
| 8. | AS d'Angoulême (Angoulême) | 34 | 15 | 6 | 13 | 48 | 35 | 36 | |
| 9. | AS de Cherbourg (Cherbourg) | 34 | 12 | 11 | 11 | 47 | 52 | 35 | # |
| 10. | FC de Grenoble (Grenoble) | 34 | 11 | 11 | 12 | 44 | 38 | 33 | |
| 11. | Limoges FC (Limoges) | 34 | 10 | 12 | 12 | 48 | 50 | 32 | |
| 12. | Racing Club Franc-Comtois (Besançon) | 34 | 12 | 6 | 16 | 43 | 58 | 30 | |
| 13. | US de Boulogne (Boulogne-sur-Mer) | 34 | 10 | 8 | 16 | 39 | 54 | 28 | |
| 14. | US Dunkerquoise (Dunkerque) | 34 | 11 | 6 | 17 | 38 | 65 | 28 | |
| 15. | AS de Cannes (Cannes) | 34 | 8 | 11 | 15 | 38 | 56 | 27 | |
| 16. | Red Star Olympique Audonien (Saint-Ouen) | 34 | 9 | 8 | 17 | 32 | 49 | 26 | * |
| 17. | Stade Olympique Montpelliérain (Montpellier) | 34 | 8 | 8 | 18 | 32 | 46 | 24 | |
| 18. | Entente Chaumontaise AC (Chaumont) | 34 | 8 | 5 | 21 | 39 | 55 | 21 | |
| | | 612 | 228 | 156 | 228 | 795 | 795 | 612 | |

# AS de Cherbourg (Cherbourg) reverted to amateur status for the next season.

* Toulouse FC (Toulouse) merged with Red Star Olympique Audonien (Saint-Ouen) to become Red Star FC (Saint-Ouen) for the next season.

**Elected**: Bataillon Joinville (Joinville), FC de Lorient (Lorient) and AS Nancy-Lorraine (Nancy).

## Coupe de France Final     (Parc des Princes, Paris – 21/05/67 – 32,523)

**OLYMPIQUE LYONNAIS (LYON)**          **3-1**          FC Sochaux-Montbéliard (Montbéliard)

*Rambert 22', Perrin 81', Di Nallo 89'*                                                      *Leclerc 33'*

**Lyonnais**: Zewulko, Kuffer, Glyczinski, Leborgne, Degeorges, Maison, Rocco, Nouzaret, Perrin, Di Nallo, Rambert.
**Sochaux**: Manolios, Marconnet, Zimmermann, Quittet, Andrieux, Laffon, Dewilder, Leclerc, Wisniewski, Lassalette, Schmitt.

## Semi-Finals     (21/04/67 – 10/05/67)

| | | |
|---|---|---|
| Olympique Lyonnais (Lyon) | 3-3, 1-1, 1-1 | AS d'Angoulême (Angoulême) |

(all games after extra time. Lyon qualified on the drawing of lots)

| | | |
|---|---|---|
| FC Sochaux-Montbéliard (Montbéliard) | 0-0 (aet), 4-3 | Stade Rennais Université Club (Rennes) |

## Quarter-Finals     (02/04/67)

| | | |
|---|---|---|
| AS d'Angoulême (Angoulême) | 2-0 | Racing Club de Lens (Lens) |
| Olympique Lyonnais (Lyon) | 1-0 | SC de l'Ouest Angers (Angers) |
| Stade Rennais Université Club (Rennes) | 2-1 | AS de Monaco (Monaco) |
| FC Sochaux-Montbéliard (Montbéliard) | 1-1, 0-0, 1-0 | Sporting Étoile Club Bastiais (Bastia) |

# 1967-68

| 1967-1968 Division One | AS Aixoise | AC Ajaccien | SC de l'O. Angers | Gir. de Bordeaux | Racing de Lens | Lille Olympique | Olymp. Lyonnais | Olymp. Marseille | FC de Metz | AS de Monaco | FC de Nantes | Olymp. GC Nice | Red Star FC | Stade Rennais | FC de Rouen | AS Saint-Étienne | RC de Paris Sedan | Sochaux-Montbél. | RC Strasbourg | Valenciennes |
|---|---|---|---|---|---|---|---|---|---|---|---|---|---|---|---|---|---|---|---|---|
| AS Aixoise | | 2-4 | 1-3 | 5-1 | 2-2 | 2-1 | 2-0 | 1-2 | 0-1 | 0-0 | 2-6 | 3-1 | 0-0 | 2-3 | 4-1 | 1-1 | 4-2 | 0-0 | 0-3 | 1-1 |
| AC Ajaccien | 8-2 | | 4-0 | 3-0 | 2-0 | 2-1 | 2-2 | 2-2 | 2-1 | 1-2 | 5-3 | 2-1 | 0-0 | 2-0 | 5-3 | 1-1 | 2-0 | 1-1 | 1-0 | 1-4 |
| SC de l'Ouest Angers | 9-1 | 3-0 | | 0-0 | 1-2 | 1-3 | 3-1 | 2-2 | 0-0 | 3-0 | 1-3 | 1-1 | 2-2 | 1-1 | 3-0 | 1-0 | 2-3 | 1-1 | 1-0 | 1-0 |
| Girondins de Bordeaux | 3-0 | 3-0 | 1-2 | | 6-1 | 2-1 | 0-0 | 1-2 | 1-0 | 3-0 | 6-2 | 4-0 | 1-0 | 6-2 | 1-0 | 1-2 | 2-0 | 3-0 | 1-2 | 0-1 |
| Racing de Lens | 4-1 | 1-2 | 4-2 | 2-1 | | 1-1 | 1-0 | 5-1 | 1-1 | 1-3 | 1-3 | 0-0 | 2-4 | 1-1 | 2-1 | 1-3 | 3-0 | 0-2 | 1-0 | 1-0 |
| Lille Olympique | 2-1 | 1-2 | 2-1 | 1-2 | 0-1 | | 1-1 | 2-0 | 0-0 | 0-1 | 2-0 | 0-2 | 1-1 | 2-0 | 1-0 | 2-2 | 2-0 | 0-1 | 0-0 | 0-3 |
| Olympique Lyonnais | 4-3 | 2-1 | 8-0 | 2-0 | 3-0 | 1-1 | | 3-2 | 3-1 | 1-2 | 0-3 | 1-1 | 0-0 | 2-1 | 2-1 | 1-1 | 0-2 | 2-2 | 0-0 | 0-0 |
| Olympique Marseille | 3-2 | 2-0 | 3-1 | 2-0 | 2-0 | 0-0 | 2-1 | | 2-0 | 2-1 | 1-0 | 0-2 | 2-0 | 3-1 | 2-2 | 2-1 | 1-0 | 0-1 | 0-0 | 2-0 |
| FC de Metz | 3-1 | 3-0 | 1-1 | 2-0 | 2-1 | 1-0 | 3-1 | 3-0 | | 2-0 | 1-1 | 1-2 | 1-1 | 6-1 | 1-1 | 1-1 | 1-5 | 2-0 | 1-0 | 2-0 |
| AS de Monaco | 1-1 | 0-1 | 5-0 | 1-2 | 2-3 | 3-1 | 2-1 | 1-0 | 3-1 | | 3-0 | 2-2 | 0-1 | 2-1 | 1-3 | 0-3 | 2-1 | 1-0 | 2-1 | 0-1 |
| FC de Nantes | 5-1 | 1-0 | 1-1 | 1-0 | 2-1 | 1-0 | 1-1 | 1-1 | 0-0 | | 0-0 | 4-2 | 0-0 | 1-1 | 1-1 | 1-1 | 1-1 | 3-0 | 0-2 |
| Olympique GC Nice | 1-0 | 1-0 | 2-1 | 1-1 | 0-0 | 3-1 | 0-3 | 1-1 | 4-1 | 0-2 | 5-1 | | 2-1 | 0-3 | 4-0 | 1-2 | 1-0 | 1-0 | 2-0 | 2-1 |
| Red Star FC | 2-1 | 4-1 | 3-3 | 1-0 | 3-2 | 0-2 | 1-1 | 2-0 | 0-1 | 2-0 | 0-1 | 1-1 | | 3-1 | 0-2 | 1-1 | 3-0 | 1-2 | 0-1 | 1-0 |
| Stade Rennais | 4-0 | 1-0 | 1-1 | 1-0 | 1-0 | 4-1 | 1-0 | 3-1 | 0-0 | 1-1 | 1-1 | 4-0 | 3-0 | | 0-1 | 0-3 | 1-1 | 1-1 | 2-1 | 1-1 |
| FC de Rouen | 5-0 | 3-1 | 0-1 | 3-0 | 0-1 | 1-0 | 3-1 | 1-2 | 0-0 | 2-1 | 1-2 | 1-0 | 0-2 | 2-0 | | 3-0 | 0-0 | 1-0 | 3-2 | 1-2 |
| AS Saint-Étienne | 3-1 | 4-0 | 3-0 | 1-0 | 3-0 | 3-0 | 1-1 | 2-0 | 4-0 | 1-0 | 1-2 | 3-1 | 1-1 | 3-0 | 3-0 | | 2-1 | 2-0 | 4-0 | 3-0 |
| Racing Club de Paris Sedan | 3-0 | 2-0 | 3-1 | 1-2 | 1-1 | 1-1 | 2-3 | 1-1 | 3-0 | 3-0 | 1-0 | 0-1 | 0-0 | 3-0 | 2-0 | 5-2 | | 2-0 | 3-1 | 1-1 |
| Sochaux-Montbéliard | 1-1 | 3-1 | 2-0 | 0-1 | 4-1 | 2-1 | 3-1 | 1-1 | 3-2 | 0-0 | 1-0 | 0-2 | 1-0 | 1-2 | 3-0 | 0-4 | 3-0 | | 1-1 | 3-1 |
| RC Strasbourg | 1-0 | 0-0 | 5-1 | 0-1 | 1-0 | 2-0 | 0-1 | 1-0 | 0-0 | 2-0 | 3-1 | 0-0 | 2-1 | 1-1 | 2-1 | 0-1 | 0-2 | 1-4 | | 0-1 |
| Valenciennes | 1-0 | 0-0 | 2-1 | 2-0 | 1-1 | 3-0 | 2-0 | 1-0 | 1-2 | 1-1 | 2-1 | 0-1 | 1-0 | 2-1 | 0-2 | 1-2 | 3-1 | 0-0 | 0-1 | |

| | Division 1 | Pd | Wn | Dw | Ls | GF | GA | Pts | |
|---|---|---|---|---|---|---|---|---|---|
| 1. | AS DE SAINT-Étienne (SAINT-Étienne) | 38 | 24 | 9 | 5 | 78 | 30 | 57 | |
| 2. | Olympique GC de Nice (Nice) | 38 | 18 | 10 | 10 | 49 | 41 | 46 | |
| 3. | FC Sochaux-Montbéliard (Montbéliard) | 38 | 16 | 11 | 11 | 48 | 39 | 43 | |
| 4. | Olympique de Marseille (Marseille) | 38 | 17 | 9 | 12 | 49 | 46 | 43 | |
| 5. | US Valenciennes-Anzin (Valenciennes) | 38 | 17 | 8 | 13 | 42 | 34 | 42 | |
| 6. | FC de Metz (Metz) | 38 | 18 | 6 | 14 | 49 | 44 | 42 | |
| 7. | FC de Nantes (Nantes) | 38 | 15 | 11 | 12 | 55 | 50 | 41 | |
| 8. | Girondins de Bordeaux FC (Bordeaux) | 38 | 18 | 4 | 16 | 57 | 44 | 40 | |
| 9. | AC Ajaccien (Ajaccio) | 38 | 16 | 7 | 15 | 59 | 59 | 39 | |
| 10. | Racing Club de Paris-Sedan (Sedan) | 38 | 15 | 8 | 15 | 56 | 47 | 38 | |
| 11. | AS de Monaco (Monaco) | 38 | 15 | 7 | 16 | 45 | 48 | 37 | |
| 12. | Olympique Lyonnais (Lyon) | 38 | 12 | 12 | 14 | 53 | 51 | 36 | |
| 13. | Red Star FC (Saint-Ouen) | 38 | 12 | 12 | 14 | 44 | 43 | 36 | |
| 14. | Stade Rennais Université Club (Rennes) | 38 | 13 | 10 | 15 | 49 | 57 | 36 | |
| 15. | FC de Rouen (Rouen) | 38 | 15 | 5 | 18 | 48 | 51 | 35 | |
| 16. | Racing Club de Strasbourg (Strasbourg) | 38 | 13 | 8 | 17 | 34 | 40 | 34 | PO |
| 17. | Racing Club de Lens (Lens) | 38 | 13 | 8 | 17 | 48 | 61 | 34 | PO |
| 18. | SC de l'Ouest Angers (Angers) | 38 | 13 | 8 | 17 | 56 | 70 | 34 | R |
| 19. | Lille Olympique SC (Lille) | 38 | 9 | 9 | 20 | 35 | 52 | 27 | R |
| 20. | AS Aixoise (Aix-en-Provence) | 38 | 6 | 8 | 24 | 48 | 95 | 20 | R |
| | | 760 | 295 | 170 | 295 | 1002 | 1002 | 760 | |

## Top goal-scorers

| | | | |
|---|---|---|---|
| 1) | Étienne SANSONETTI | (AC Ajaccien) | 26 |
| 2) | Hervé REVELLI | (AS de Saint-Étienne) | 23 |
| 3) | Fleury DI NALLO | (Olympique Lyonnais) | 18 |
| | Yegba Maya JOSEPH | (Olympique de Marseille) | 18 |

| Promotion/Relegation Play-Offs | Pd | Wn | Dw | Ls | GF | GA | Pts | |
|---|---|---|---|---|---|---|---|---|
| 1. Racing Club de Strasbourg (Strasbourg) | 4 | 2 | 1 | 1 | 5 | 3 | 5 | |
| 2. Nîmes Olympique (Nîmes) | 4 | 2 | 1 | 1 | 4 | 4 | 5 | P |
| 3. Stade de Reims (Reims) | 4 | 2 | 1 | 1 | 8 | 6 | 5 | |
| 4. Racing Club de Lens (Lens) | 4 | - | 1 | 3 | 5 | 9 | 1 | R |
| | 16 | 6 | 4 | 6 | 22 | 22 | 16 | |

Division 1 was reduced to 18 clubs for the next season.

| Division 2 | Pd | Wn | Dw | Ls | GF | GA | Pts | |
|---|---|---|---|---|---|---|---|---|
| 1. Sporting Étoile Club Bastiais (Bastia) | 34 | 21 | 8 | 5 | 53 | 21 | 50 | P |
| 2. Nîmes Olympique (Nîmes) | 34 | 16 | 12 | 6 | 52 | 24 | 44 | PO |
| 3. Stade de Reims (Reims) | 34 | 18 | 7 | 9 | 69 | 27 | 43 | PO |
| 4. Olympique Avignonnais (Avignon) | 34 | 19 | 5 | 10 | 69 | 48 | 43 | |
| 5. SC de Toulon (Toulon) | 34 | 16 | 9 | 9 | 47 | 40 | 41 | |
| 6. FC de Grenoble (Grenoble) | 34 | 17 | 6 | 11 | 53 | 41 | 40 | |
| 7. Bataillon Joinville (Joinville) | 34 | 15 | 7 | 12 | 50 | 43 | 37 | |
| 8. FC de Lorient (Lorient) | 34 | 12 | 13 | 9 | 38 | 31 | 37 | |
| 9. AS d'Angoulême (Angoulême) | 34 | 15 | 8 | 11 | 44 | 34 | 38 | |
| 10. AS Nancy-Lorraine (Nancy) | 34 | 14 | 8 | 12 | 41 | 38 | 36 | |
| 11. US Dunkerquoise (Dunkerque) | 34 | 9 | 12 | 13 | 39 | 39 | 30 | |
| 12. Entente Chaumontaise AC (Chaumont) | 34 | 11 | 8 | 15 | 55 | 63 | 30 | |
| 13. AS Biterroise (Béziers) | 34 | 10 | 8 | 16 | 35 | 43 | 28 | |
| 14. Limoges FC (Limoges) | 34 | 9 | 8 | 17 | 38 | 45 | 26 | |
| 15. Racing Club Franc-Comtois (Besançon) | 34 | 8 | 10 | 16 | 30 | 57 | 26 | |
| 16. Stade Olympique Montpelliérain (Montpellier) | 34 | 8 | 8 | 18 | 30 | 47 | 24 | |
| 17. AS de Cannes (Cannes) | 34 | 5 | 11 | 18 | 29 | 64 | 21 | |
| 18. US de Boulogne (Boulogne-sur-Mer) | 34 | 6 | 6 | 22 | 32 | 68 | 18 | |
| | 612 | 229 | 154 | 229 | 804 | 773 | 612 | |

Note: Stade de Paris FC (Paris) resigned from the league and reverted to amateur status.

**Elected**: Gazélec FC Ajaccien (Ajaccio).

Division 2 was extended to 21 clubs for the next season.

**Coupe de France Final**  (Stade Yves du Manoir, Colombes – 12/05/68 – 33,959)

**AS DE SAINT-Étienne (ST.Étienne)**　　　　**2-1**　　　　Girondins de Bordeaux FC (Bordeaux)

*Mekhloufi 30', 78' pen*　　　　　　　　　　　　　　　　　　　　　　　　　　*Wojciak 05'*

**Saint-Étienne**: Carnus, Durkovic, Polny, Mitoraj, Bosquier, Jacquet, Fefeu, Herbin, Revelli, Mekhloufi, Bereta.

**Bordeaux**: Montes, Baudet, Chorda, Péri, Desremeaux, Calleja, Couécou, De Bourgoing, Ruiter (Duhayot 75'), Abossolo, Wojciak.

## Semi-Finals  (17-20/04/68)

| | | |
|---|---|---|
| Girondins de Bordeaux FC (Bordeaux) | 2-1 (aet) | US Quevillaise (Le Petit Quevilly) |
| AS de Saint-Étienne (Saint-Étienne) | 1-1 (aet), 2-1 | AS d'Angoulême (Angoulême) |

## Quarter-Finals  (31/03/68)

| | | |
|---|---|---|
| AS d'Angoulême (Angoulême) | 2-1 | FC Sochaux-Montbéliard (Montbéliard) |
| Girondins de Bordeaux FC (Bordeaux) | 1-1, 2-1 | Racing Club de Strasbourg (Strasbourg) |
| US Quevillaise (Le Petit Quevilly) | 4-0 | US Dunkerquoise (Dunkerque) |
| AS de Saint-Étienne (Saint-Étienne) | 1-0 | FC de Metz (Metz) |

# 1968-69

| 1968-1969 Division One | AC Ajaccien | Sporting Étoile Club Bastiais | Girondins Bordeaux | Olympique Lyonnais | Olympique Marseille | FC de Metz | AS de Monaco | FC de Nantes | Olympique GC Nice | Nîmes Olympique | Red Star FC | Stade Rennais Université Club | FC de Rouen | AS de Saint-Étienne | Racing Club de Paris Sedan | Sochaux-Montbéliard | RC de Strasbourg | Valenciennes-Anzin |
|---|---|---|---|---|---|---|---|---|---|---|---|---|---|---|---|---|---|---|
| AC Ajaccien | | 4-0 | 2-2 | 4-1 | 1-1 | 0-1 | 4-3 | 1-0 | 1-0 | 1-0 | 3-1 | 2-2 | 0-1 | 0-2 | 2-0 | 0-2 | 1-1 | 1-1 |
| Sporting Étoile Club Bastiais | 1-0 | | 1-0 | 4-0 | 3-1 | 1-1 | 4-0 | 3-1 | 2-0 | 2-2 | 2-1 | 1-2 | 1-1 | 1-1 | 1-5 | 1-0 | 2-1 | 3-0 |
| Girondins Bordeaux | 5-0 | 8-1 | | 2-1 | 2-2 | 1-0 | 2-1 | 1-1 | 5-0 | 2-1 | 6-1 | 3-2 | 2-1 | 2-0 | 0-2 | 4-0 | 3-0 | 1-0 |
| Olympique Lyonnais | 3-2 | 8-3 | 0-2 | | 2-3 | 0-1 | 2-0 | 3-1 | 3-1 | 1-1 | 0-0 | 1-0 | 0-1 | 1-2 | 1-0 | 6-3 | 2-3 | 1-0 |
| Olympique Marseille | 3-0 | 1-0 | 3-3 | 2-2 | | 0-1 | 0-1 | 3-1 | 3-1 | 4-0 | 0-0 | 3-3 | 1-0 | 0-3 | 4-1 | 4-0 | 0-0 | 1-0 |
| FC de Metz | 0-0 | 2-0 | 1-0 | 1-1 | 3-0 | | 0-0 | 1-0 | 1-0 | 0-0 | 3-1 | 3-0 | 7-3 | 0-1 | 0-1 | 3-0 | 2-0 | 1-0 |
| AS de Monaco | 3-0 | 2-0 | 2-4 | 0-2 | 1-0 | 1-1 | | 2-0 | 0-0 | 0-0 | 1-1 | 2-2 | 1-1 | 1-2 | 0-0 | 2-1 | 2-1 | 0-0 |
| FC de Nantes | 0-0 | 3-0 | 1-2 | 2-1 | 2-1 | 1-2 | 2-0 | | 0-0 | 3-1 | 0-1 | 3-2 | 0-1 | 3-0 | 3-2 | 0-0 | 4-0 | 3-2 |
| Olympique GC Nice | 0-3 | 2-2 | 2-2 | 2-1 | 2-3 | 1-2 | 1-0 | 0-0 | | 3-0 | 1-1 | 1-1 | 2-2 | 2-3 | 2-1 | 0-3 | 1-0 | 1-1 |
| Nîmes Olympique | 3-2 | 2-1 | 1-3 | 1-2 | 0-0 | 0-0 | 1-1 | 1-2 | 2-0 | | 0-0 | 5-1 | 0-0 | 1-0 | 1-0 | 3-1 | 0-0 | 2-2 |
| Red Star FC | 1-0 | 1-1 | 1-2 | 1-2 | 1-1 | 1-0 | 1-0 | 2-3 | 0-2 | 0-2 | | 2-1 | 4-0 | 0-0 | 2-1 | 2-2 | 2-1 | 1-2 |
| Stade Rennais Université Club | 5-0 | 3-1 | 0-1 | 2-1 | 2-1 | 2-0 | 3-1 | 2-1 | 4-2 | 1-0 | 1-1 | | 0-1 | 0-2 | 1-3 | 3-2 | 1-0 | 1-2 |
| FC de Rouen | 1-1 | 1-3 | 2-1 | 2-1 | 2-1 | 1-0 | 3-1 | 3-0 | 4-0 | 1-0 | 1-1 | 1-0 | | 1-5 | 0-1 | 2-1 | 3-0 | 2-2 |
| AS de Saint-Étienne | 2-0 | 7-2 | 3-2 | 0-1 | 1-0 | 4-0 | 1-1 | 3-1 | 2-0 | 1-0 | 4-2 | 3-1 | 2-0 | | 4-2 | 4-1 | 2-0 | 4-0 |
| Racing Club de Paris Sedan | 4-0 | 0-0 | 0-1 | 1-0 | 3-1 | 0-0 | 2-2 | 3-1 | 2-1 | 3-1 | 0-0 | 3-0 | 1-1 | 0-0 | | 2-0 | 1-1 | 1-0 |
| Sochaux-Montbéliard | 0-1 | 2-2 | 0-1 | 2-1 | 3-1 | 5-2 | 0-0 | 2-1 | 3-0 | 1-1 | 3-3 | 1-1 | 2-0 | 1-0 | 3-1 | | 3-0 | 2-0 |
| RC de Strasbourg | 3-0 | 4-0 | 1-1 | 2-2 | 1-2 | 1-1 | 5-0 | 1-0 | 1-0 | 1-0 | 1-0 | 0-0 | 2-0 | 0-2 | 1-2 | 1-0 | | 0-1 |
| Valenciennes-Anzin | 1-0 | 0-1 | 1-1 | 0-0 | 3-1 | 1-1 | 4-2 | 0-0 | 3-0 | 0-0 | 3-0 | 4-1 | 0-1 | 1-1 | 1-1 | 2-1 | 1-1 | |

| | Division 1 | Pd | Wn | Dw | Ls | GF | GA | Pts | |
|---|---|---|---|---|---|---|---|---|---|
| 1. | AS DE SAINT-Étienne (SAINT-Étienne) | 34 | 24 | 5 | 5 | 70 | 26 | 53 | |
| 2. | Girondins de Bordeaux FC (Bordeaux) | 34 | 22 | 7 | 5 | 77 | 34 | 51 | |
| 3. | FC de Metz (Metz) | 34 | 16 | 10 | 8 | 41 | 27 | 42 | |
| 4. | FC de Rouen (Rouen) | 34 | 16 | 8 | 10 | 44 | 43 | 40 | |
| 5. | Racing Club de Paris Sedan (Sedan) | 34 | 15 | 9 | 10 | 49 | 35 | 39 | * |
| 6. | Sporting Étoile Club Bastiais (Bastia) | 34 | 13 | 8 | 13 | 50 | 66 | 34 | |
| 7. | Olympique de Marseille (Marseille) | 34 | 12 | 9 | 13 | 51 | 48 | 33 | |
| 8. | US Valenciennes-Anzin (Valenciennes) | 34 | 10 | 13 | 11 | 38 | 37 | 33 | |
| 9. | Olympique Lyonnais (Lyon) | 34 | 13 | 6 | 15 | 53 | 51 | 32 | |
| 10. | FC de Nantes (Nantes) | 34 | 13 | 6 | 15 | 44 | 45 | 32 | |
| 11. | Stade Rennais Université Club (Rennes) | 34 | 12 | 7 | 15 | 50 | 57 | 31 | |
| 12. | FC Sochaux-Montbéliard (Montbéliard) | 34 | 11 | 7 | 16 | 49 | 55 | 29 | |
| 13. | Nîmes Olympique (Nîmes) | 34 | 8 | 13 | 13 | 32 | 39 | 29 | |
| 14. | Racing Club de Strasbourg (Strasbourg) | 34 | 10 | 9 | 15 | 34 | 41 | 29 | |
| 15. | Red Star FC (Saint-Ouen) | 34 | 8 | 13 | 13 | 35 | 48 | 29 | |
| 16. | AC Ajaccien (Ajaccio) | 34 | 10 | 8 | 16 | 36 | 53 | 28 | |
| 17. | AS de Monaco (Monaco) | 34 | 7 | 13 | 14 | 33 | 50 | 27 | PO |
| 18. | Olympique GC de Nice (Nice) | 34 | 6 | 9 | 19 | 30 | 61 | 21 | R |
| | | 612 | 226 | 160 | 226 | 816 | 816 | 612 | |

## Top goal-scorers

| 1) | André GUY | (Olympique Lyonnais) | 25 |
|---|---|---|---|
| 2) | Hervé REVELLI | (AS de Saint-Étienne) | 22 |
| 3) | Yegba Maya JOSEPH | (Olympique de Marseille) | 21 |
| | Salif KEITA | (AS de Saint-Étienne) | 21 |

## Promotion/Relegation Play-Off

| AS de Monaco (Monaco) | 2-1, 0-1, 0-2 | AS d'Angoulême (Angoulême) |
|---|---|---|

| | Division 2 | Pd | Wn | Dw | Ls | GF | GA | Pts | Bon | Tot | |
|---|---|---|---|---|---|---|---|---|---|---|---|
| 1. | SC de l'Ouest Angers (Angers) | 40 | 29 | 7 | 4 | 128 | 45 | 65 | 21 | 86 | P |
| 2. | AS d'Angoulême (Angoulême) | 40 | 24 | 12 | 4 | 112 | 44 | 60 | 16 | 76 | PO |
| 3. | AS Nancy-Lorraine (Nancy) | 40 | 19 | 9 | 12 | 67 | 47 | 47 | 13 | 60 | |
| 4. | Limoges FC (Limoges) | 40 | 20 | 10 | 10 | 67 | 55 | 50 | 9 | 59 | |
| 5. | SC de Toulon (Toulon) | 40 | 19 | 9 | 12 | 75 | 63 | 47 | 9 | 56 | |
| 6. | AS Aixoise (Aix-en-Provence) | 40 | 17 | 10 | 13 | 63 | 63 | 44 | 10 | 54 | |
| 7. | Racing Club de Lens (Lens) | 40 | 15 | 13 | 12 | 73 | 48 | 43 | 10 | 53 | # |
| 8. | Stade de Reims (Reims) | 40 | 19 | 6 | 15 | 63 | 45 | 44 | 9 | 53 | |
| 9. | FC de Grenoble (Grenoble) | 40 | 15 | 13 | 12 | 64 | 60 | 43 | 8 | 51 | |
| 10. | Gazélec FC Ajaccien (Ajaccio) | 40 | 15 | 8 | 17 | 63 | 62 | 38 | 13 | 51 | |
| 11. | FC de Lorient (Lorient) | 40 | 18 | 6 | 16 | 61 | 61 | 42 | 8 | 50 | |
| 12. | Olympique Avignonnais (Avignon) | 40 | 15 | 12 | 13 | 56 | 53 | 42 | 7 | 49 | |
| 13. | Lille Olympique SC (Lille) | 40 | 14 | 14 | 12 | 56 | 51 | 42 | 6 | 48 | # |
| 14. | AS de Cannes (Cannes) | 40 | 15 | 12 | 13 | 65 | 59 | 42 | 5 | 47 | |
| 15. | Entente Chaumontaise AC (Chaumont) | 40 | 13 | 8 | 19 | 70 | 79 | 34 | 10 | 44 | # |
| 16. | US Dunkerquoise (Dunkerque) | 40 | 14 | 5 | 21 | 49 | 64 | 33 | 6 | 39 | |
| 17. | Stade Olympique Montpelliérain | 40 | 12 | 9 | 19 | 42 | 60 | 33 | 2 | 35 | #* |
| 18. | AS Biterroise (Béziers) | 40 | 11 | 5 | 24 | 48 | 82 | 27 | 7 | 34 | # |
| 19. | Paris-Joinville (Paris) | 40 | 8 | 12 | 20 | 41 | 86 | 28 | 2 | 30 | * |
| 20. | Racing Club Franc-Comtois (Besançon) | 40 | 4 | 11 | 25 | 53 | 126 | 19 | 7 | 26 | |
| 21. | US de Boulogne (Boulogne-sur-Mer) | 40 | 5 | 7 | 28 | 34 | 96 | 17 | 3 | 20 | |
| | | 840 | 321 | 198 | 321 | 1350 | 1349 | 840 | 181 | 1021 | |

\# AS Biterroise (Béziers), Entente Chaumontaise AC (Chaumont), Racing Club de Lens (Lens), Lille Olympique SC (Lille) and Stade Olympique Montpelliérain (Montpellier) all reverted to amateur status for the next season.

\* Racing Club de Paris-Sedan (Sedan) dissolved and re-formed as CS Sedan-Ardennes (Sedan) (professional) and Racing Club de Paris (Paris) (amateur); Stade Olympique Montpelliérain (Montpellier) later reformed as Montpellier-Littoral SC (Montpellier); Paris-Joinville (Paris) changed their name from Bataillon Joinville (Joinville) and later changed their name once again to Racing FC Paris-Neuilly (Neuilly).

## Coupe de France Final   (Stade Yves du Manoir, Colombes – 18/05/69 – 39,460)

**OLYMPIQUE DE MARSEILLE**                **2-0**                Girondins de Bordeaux FC (Bordeaux)

*Papin 82' (o.g.), Joseph 89'*

**Marseille**: Escale, Lopez, Hodoul, Zwunka, Djorkaeff, Novi, Destrumelle, Magnusson, Joseph, Bonnel, Guéniche.

**Bordeaux**: Montes, Papin, Chorda, Baudet, Péri, Calleja, Petyt, Simon, Ruiter, Burdino (Couécou 65'), Wojciak.

## Semi-Finals   (26/04/69 – 03/05/69)

| | | |
|---|---|---|
| SC de l'Ouest Angers (Angers) | 0-0,  1-2 | Olympique de Marseille (Marseille) |
| Racing Club de Paris-Sedan (Sedan) | 0-0,  3-4 | Girondins de Bordeaux FC (Bordeaux) |

## Quarter-Finals   (29/03/69 – 19/04/69)

| | | |
|---|---|---|
| FC de Gueugnon (Gueugnon) | 0-1,  1-2 | SC de l'Ouest Angers (Angers) |
| FC de Mulhouse 1893 (Mulhouse) | 0-2,  0-1 | Girondins de Bordeaux FC (Bordeaux) |
| Stade Saint-Germanois (St-Germain/Laye) | 0-2,  1-5 | Olympique de Marseille (Marseille) |
| Racing Club de Paris-Sedan (Sedan) | 0-1,  1-0,  3-2 | Racing Club de Strasbourg (Strasbourg) |

# 1969-70

| 1969-1970 Division One | AC Ajaccien | SC l'Ouest Angers | AS d'Angoulême | SE Club Bastiais | Girondins Bordeaux | Olympique Lyonnais | Olympique Marseille | FC de Metz | FC de Nantes | Nîmes Olympique | Red Star FC | Stade Rennais UC | FC de Rouen | AS de Saint-Étienne | CS Sedan Ardennes | Sochaux-Montbéliard | RC de Strasbourg | Valenciennes-Anzin |
|---|---|---|---|---|---|---|---|---|---|---|---|---|---|---|---|---|---|---|
| AC Ajaccien | | 0-1 | 0-0 | 2-0 | 1-1 | 2-0 | 2-4 | 0-0 | 2-1 | 1-0 | 2-2 | 4-2 | 1-0 | 1-2 | 0-1 | 1-0 | 1-0 | 3-1 |
| SC l'Ouest Angers | 3-2 | | 2-2 | 5-0 | 3-1 | 3-2 | 2-1 | 0-0 | 0-3 | 1-0 | 5-1 | 1-0 | 1-1 | 0-0 | 1-3 | 2-2 | 4-1 | 0-1 |
| AS d'Angoulême | 2-1 | 1-1 | | 5-1 | 3-2 | 1-1 | 1-3 | 2-1 | 2-2 | 1-0 | 1-1 | 3-0 | 1-1 | 0-1 | 2-1 | 4-0 | 1-1 | 6-1 |
| Sporting Étoile Club Bastiais | 2-0 | 3-1 | 1-1 | | 2-2 | 2-4 | 3-2 | 2-2 | 3-2 | 2-5 | 3-0 | 4-0 | 0-2 | 0-1 | 2-3 | 2-0 | 2-1 | 3-1 |
| Girondins Bordeaux | 2-1 | 1-0 | 5-1 | 1-0 | | 3-0 | 2-2 | 1-0 | 3-0 | 1-0 | 0-1 | 1-1 | 1-1 | 1-4 | 4-1 | 3-0 | 4-2 | 0-2 |
| Olympique Lyonnais | 2-1 | 2-1 | 1-2 | 2-1 | 1-3 | | 1-0 | 2-4 | 2-5 | 3-0 | 2-0 | 4-4 | 3-0 | 1-7 | 4-2 | 2-2 | 0-1 | 1-0 |
| Olympique Marseille | 1-0 | 5-2 | 1-1 | 3-3 | 3-1 | 4-1 | | 3-2 | 4-2 | 4-0 | 4-0 | 1-0 | 2-0 | 2-3 | 2-0 | 0-0 | 2-0 | 3-1 |
| FC de Metz | 1-0 | 2-1 | 3-2 | 3-0 | 4-1 | 4-0 | 2-1 | | 2-2 | 3-1 | 2-1 | 2-0 | 2-0 | 1-2 | 0-2 | 1-2 | 2-2 | 3-0 |
| FC de Nantes | 6-0 | 1-0 | 1-1 | 2-1 | 1-1 | 5-2 | 2-1 | 1-0 | | 1-0 | 1-1 | 6-1 | 0-2 | 2-2 | 2-2 | 1-2 | 0-1 | 1-2 |
| Nîmes Olympique | 2-0 | 1-1 | 2-2 | 4-1 | 3-0 | 5-2 | 1-1 | 2-1 | 4-2 | | 1-3 | 2-3 | 6-1 | 1-3 | 5-1 | 2-0 | 3-2 | 2-1 |
| Red Star FC | 4-1 | 3-4 | 0-0 | 2-1 | 1-1 | 1-5 | 1-6 | 3-1 | 3-0 | 3-0 | | 2-4 | 2-0 | 1-5 | 0-2 | 1-0 | 2-1 | 1-1 |
| Stade Rennais Université Club | 0-1 | 1-0 | 2-0 | 3-1 | 0-0 | 4-3 | 1-1 | 2-0 | 1-2 | 1-1 | 2-2 | | 1-1 | 1-0 | 3-3 | 2-4 | 4-5 | 1-1 |
| FC de Rouen | 2-0 | 5-0 | 0-2 | 3-0 | 0-0 | 1-0 | 1-1 | 1-1 | 1-0 | 1-1 | 2-0 | 4-0 | | 0-2 | 0-0 | 1-3 | 1-1 | 3-3 |
| AS de Saint-Étienne | 3-1 | 1-2 | 1-1 | 4-2 | 2-0 | 6-0 | 2-1 | 2-0 | 2-3 | 2-1 | 0-0 | 8-2 | 5-0 | | 3-1 | 2-0 | 3-0 | 1-0 |
| CS Sedan Ardennes | 2-0 | 2-2 | 2-0 | 0-2 | 1-1 | 1-0 | 0-0 | 0-0 | 4-0 | 1-0 | 3-0 | 3-2 | 1-0 | 1-2 | | 3-0 | 2-1 | 0-0 |
| Sochaux-Montbéliard | 0-2 | 1-1 | 1-0 | 2-1 | 3-2 | 0-2 | 2-2 | 4-1 | 0-3 | 2-2 | 0-3 | 2-2 | 1-1 | 3-3 | 1-0 | | 2-0 | 6-1 |
| RC de Strasbourg | 2-0 | 4-1 | 3-1 | 4-0 | 3-1 | 2-1 | 2-3 | 2-0 | 2-1 | 4-1 | 5-0 | 1-1 | 3-2 | 1-1 | 2-3 | 2-2 | | 4-2 |
| Valenciennes-Anzin | 2-1 | 0-2 | 0-1 | 2-0 | 1-4 | 1-1 | 0-2 | 0-0 | 2-1 | 0-2 | 2-0 | 0-1 | 1-3 | 0-3 | 1-3 | 0-1 | 2-0 | |

| | Division 1 | Pd | Wn | Dw | Ls | GF | GA | Pts | |
|---|---|---|---|---|---|---|---|---|---|
| 1. | AS DE SAINT-Étienne (SAINT-Étienne) | 34 | 25 | 6 | 3 | 88 | 30 | 56 | |
| 2. | Olympique de Marseille (Marseille) | 34 | 18 | 9 | 7 | 75 | 41 | 45 | |
| 3. | CS Sedan Ardennes (Sedan) | 34 | 17 | 8 | 9 | 54 | 42 | 42 | |
| 4. | AS d'Angoulême (Angoulême) | 34 | 12 | 14 | 8 | 53 | 43 | 38 | |
| 5. | Racing Club de Strasbourg (Strasbourg) | 34 | 15 | 6 | 13 | 65 | 55 | 36 | * |
| 6. | Girondins de Bordeaux FC (Bordeaux) | 34 | 13 | 10 | 11 | 54 | 48 | 36 | |
| 7. | SC de l'Ouest Angers (Angers) | 34 | 13 | 9 | 12 | 53 | 53 | 35 | |
| 8. | FC de Metz (Metz) | 34 | 13 | 8 | 13 | 50 | 44 | 34 | |
| 9. | FC Sochaux-Montbéliard (Montbéliard) | 34 | 12 | 10 | 12 | 48 | 55 | 34 | |
| 10. | FC de Nantes (Nantes) | 34 | 13 | 7 | 14 | 62 | 56 | 33 | |
| 11. | Nîmes Olympique (Nîmes) | 34 | 13 | 6 | 15 | 60 | 55 | 32 | |
| 12. | FC de Rouen (Rouen) | 34 | 10 | 12 | 12 | 41 | 45 | 32 | # |
| 13. | Red Star FC (Saint-Ouen) | 34 | 11 | 8 | 15 | 45 | 67 | 30 | * |
| 14. | Stade Rennais Université Club (Rennes) | 34 | 9 | 11 | 14 | 52 | 73 | 29 | |
| 15. | Olympique Lyonnais (Lyon) | 34 | 12 | 4 | 18 | 57 | 78 | 28 | |
| 16. | AC Ajaccien (Ajaccio) | 34 | 11 | 4 | 19 | 34 | 51 | 26 | PO |
| 17. | Sporting Étoile Club Bastiais (Bastia) | 34 | 10 | 4 | 20 | 50 | 74 | 24 | PO |
| 18. | US Valenciennes-Anzin (Valenciennes) | 34 | 8 | 6 | 20 | 32 | 63 | 22 | R** |
| | | 612 | 235 | 142 | 235 | 973 | 973 | 612 | |

## Top goal-scorers

| | | | |
|---|---|---|---|
| 1) | Hervé REVELLI | (AS de Saint-Étienne) | 28 |
| 2) | Yegba Maya JOSEPH | (Olympique de Marseille) | 24 |
| 3) | Salif KEITA | (AS de Saint-Étienne) | 21 |

| | Promotion/Relegation Play-Off | Pd | Wn | Dw | Ls | GF | GA | Pts | |
|---|---|---|---|---|---|---|---|---|---|
| 1. | Sporting Étoile Club Bastiais (Bastia) | 4 | 2 | 1 | 1 | 8 | 5 | 5 | |
| 2. | AS Nancy-Lorraine (Nancy) | 4 | 2 | 1 | 1 | 5 | 4 | 5 | P |
| 3. | AC Ajaccien (Ajaccio) | 4 | 2 | - | 2 | 8 | 5 | 4 | ** |
| 4. | Olympique Avignonnais (Avignon) | 4 | 1 | - | 3 | 5 | 12 | 2 | |
| | | 16 | 7 | 2 | 7 | 26 | 26 | 16 | |

| | Division 2 | Pd | Wn | Dw | Ls | GF | GA | Pts | |
|---|---|---|---|---|---|---|---|---|---|
| 1. | Olympique GC de Nice (Nice) | 30 | 19 | 8 | 3 | 54 | 18 | 46 | P |
| 2. | AS Nancy-Lorraine (Nancy) | 30 | 20 | 5 | 5 | 77 | 31 | 45 | PO |
| 3. | Olympique Avignonnais (Avignon) | 30 | 16 | 8 | 6 | 60 | 26 | 40 | PO |
| 4. | Stade de Reims (Reims) | 30 | 16 | 5 | 9 | 44 | 31 | 37 | P |
| 5. | FC de Grenoble (Grenoble) | 30 | 13 | 10 | 7 | 55 | 36 | 36 | |
| 6. | US de Boulogne (Boulogne-sur-Mer) | 30 | 14 | 6 | 10 | 38 | 35 | 34 | * |
| 7. | Gazélec FC Ajaccien (Ajaccio) | 30 | 12 | 5 | 13 | 42 | 39 | 29 | |
| 8. | AS de Monaco (Monaco) | 30 | 10 | 8 | 12 | 38 | 44 | 28 | |
| 9. | US Dunkerquoise (Dunkerque) | 30 | 10 | 7 | 13 | 30 | 42 | 27 | |
| 10. | AS Aixoise (Aix-en-Provence) | 30 | 9 | 7 | 14 | 36 | 64 | 25 | |
| 11. | FC de Lorient (Lorient) | 30 | 9 | 7 | 14 | 32 | 37 | 25 | |
| 12. | Racing FC Paris-Neuilly (Neuilly) | 30 | 7 | 11 | 12 | 28 | 37 | 25 | |
| 13. | AS de Cannes (Cannes) | 30 | 8 | 8 | 14 | 28 | 49 | 24 | |
| 14. | SC de Toulon (Toulon) | 30 | 8 | 4 | 18 | 32 | 51 | 20 | |
| 15. | Racing Club Franc-Comtois (Besançon) | 30 | 8 | 4 | 18 | 30 | 53 | 20 | |
| 16. | Limoges FC (Limoges) | 30 | 7 | 5 | 18 | 32 | 63 | 19 | |
| | | 480 | 186 | 108 | 186 | 656 | 656 | 480 | |

# FC de Rouen (Rouen) resigned from Division 1 and reverted to amateur status, playing in Division 2 next season.

\* Racing Club de Strasbourg (Strasbourg) merged with CS Pierrots (Strasbourg) to become Racing-Pierrots Strasbourg-Meinau;  Red Star FC (Saint-Ouen) split to become Red Star FC (Saint-Ouen) (Division 1) and US de Toulouse (Toulouse) (Division 2); US de Boulogne (Boulogne-sur-Mer) changed their name to US du Grand Boulogne (Boulogne-sur-Mer) for the next season.

\*\* AC Ajaccien and US Valenciennes-Anzin retained their Division 1 places after the league was extended to 20 clubs for the next season.

Division 2 was split into three groups of 16 teams for the next season.

## Coupe de France Final   (Stade Yves du Manoir, Colombes – 31/05/70 – 32,894)

### AS DE SAINT-Étienne (SAINT-Étienne)   5-0   FC de Nantes (Nantes)

*Parizon 26', Bereta 40', Herbin 51', Revelli 74', 87'*

**Saint-Étienne**: Carnus, Durkovic, Polny, Herbin, Bosquier, Jacquet, Parizon, Larqué, Revelli, Keita, Bereta.

**Nantes**: Fouché, Osman, De Michelle, Lemerre, Esteve, Eo (Arribas 56'), Blanchet, Pech, Gondet, Michel, Levavasseur.

## Semi-Finals   (09/05/70 – 15/05/70)

| | | |
|---|---|---|
| Stade Rennais Université Club (Rennes) | 0-1, 1-1 | AS de Saint-Étienne (Saint-Étienne) |
| US Valenciennes-Anzin (Valenciennes) | 0-2, 0-0 | FC de Nantes (Nantes) |

## Quarter-Finals   (11/04/70 – 18/04/70)

| | | |
|---|---|---|
| SC de l'Ouest Angers (Angers) | 2-2, 0-2 | FC de Nantes (Nantes) |
| Limoges FC (Limoges) | 1-3, 0-4 | Stade Rennais Université Club (Rennes) |
| FC de Metz (Metz) | 1-1, 0-5 | AS de Saint-Étienne (Saint-Étienne) |
| Racing FC Paris-Neuilly (Neuilly) | 2-1, 0-1, 1-2 | US Valenciennes-Anzin (Valenciennes) |

# 1970-71

| | Division 1 | Pd | Wn | Dw | Ls | GF | GA | Pts | |
|---|---|---|---|---|---|---|---|---|---|
| 1. | OLYMPIQUE DE MARSEILLE (MARSEILLE) | 38 | 23 | 9 | 6 | 94 | 48 | 55 | |
| 2. | AS de Saint-Étienne (Saint-Étienne) | 38 | 20 | 11 | 7 | 83 | 45 | 51 | |
| 3. | FC de Nantes (Nantes) | 38 | 17 | 12 | 9 | 61 | 41 | 46 | |
| 4. | Nîmes Olympique (Nîmes) | 38 | 17 | 11 | 10 | 68 | 54 | 45 | |
| 5. | Girondins de Bordeaux FC (Bordeaux) | 38 | 16 | 8 | 14 | 58 | 51 | 40 | |
| 6. | AC Ajaccien (Ajaccio) | 38 | 16 | 8 | 14 | 54 | 52 | 40 | |
| 7. | Olympique Lyonnais (Lyon) | 38 | 14 | 12 | 12 | 51 | 51 | 40 | |
| 8. | FC de Metz (Metz) | 38 | 13 | 14 | 11 | 46 | 56 | 40 | |
| 9. | Stade de Reims (Reims) | 38 | 14 | 11 | 13 | 64 | 54 | 39 | |
| 10. | FC Sochaux-Montbéliard (Montbéliard) | 38 | 14 | 10 | 14 | 58 | 55 | 38 | |
| 11. | Stade Rennais Université Club (Rennes) | 38 | 14 | 9 | 15 | 56 | 53 | 37 | |
| 12. | SC de l'Ouest Angers (Angers) | 38 | 15 | 5 | 18 | 61 | 66 | 35 | |
| 13. | AS Nancy-Lorraine (Nancy) | 38 | 12 | 11 | 15 | 45 | 56 | 35 | |
| 14. | Olympique GC de Nice (Nice) | 38 | 12 | 10 | 16 | 48 | 55 | 34 | |
| 15. | Red Star FC (Saint-Ouen) | 38 | 11 | 11 | 16 | 46 | 65 | 33 | |
| 16. | AS d'Angoulême (Angoulême) | 38 | 10 | 12 | 16 | 30 | 47 | 32 | |
| 17. | Sporting Étoile Club Bastiais (Bastia) | 38 | 12 | 8 | 18 | 52 | 83 | 32 | |
| 18. | Racing-Pierrots Strasbourg-Meinau (Strasbourg) | 38 | 13 | 5 | 20 | 54 | 63 | 31 | R |
| 19. | US Valenciennes-Anzin (Valenciennes) | 38 | 10 | 9 | 19 | 47 | 59 | 29 | R |
| 20. | CS Sedan Ardennes (Sedan) | 38 | 10 | 8 | 20 | 42 | 64 | 28 | R |
| | | 760 | 283 | 194 | 283 | 1118 | 1118 | 760 | |

| 1970-1971 Division One | AC Ajaccien | SC de l'O. Angers | AS Angoulême | SE Club Bastiais | Gir. de Bordeaux | Olymp. Lyonnais | Olymp. Marseille | FC de Metz | Nancy-Lorraine | FC de Nantes | Olymp. GC Nice | Nîmes Olympique | Red Star FC | Stade de Reims | Stade Rennais | AS Saint-Étienne | Sedan Ardennes | Sochaux-Montbél. | RP Strasbourg | Valenciennes |
|---|---|---|---|---|---|---|---|---|---|---|---|---|---|---|---|---|---|---|---|---|
| AC Ajaccien | ■ | 0-0 | 0-0 | 6-1 | 2-0 | 0-0 | 1-2 | 2-0 | 5-0 | 2-1 | 3-1 | 2-2 | 0-1 | 1-0 | 3-0 | 1-1 | 1-0 | 1-0 | 4-0 | 1-0 |
| SC de l'Ouest Angers | 1-1 | ■ | 1-4 | 3-0 | 0-3 | 3-2 | 2-1 | 5-0 | 2-1 | 0-1 | 6-0 | 1-2 | 3-1 | 0-3 | 2-1 | 2-2 | 3-1 | 1-0 | 1-3 | 5-3 |
| AS Angoulême | 2-0 | 1-1 | ■ | 2-2 | 1-1 | 2-2 | 0-0 | 1-0 | 1-0 | 1-0 | 1-1 | 0-2 | 1-0 | 1-3 | 1-0 | 1-1 | 1-0 | 1-0 | 0-1 | 1-0 |
| Sporting Étoile Club Bastiais | 1-4 | 2-0 | 3-1 | ■ | 2-0 | 2-1 | 0-3 | 2-0 | 0-2 | 1-0 | 3-1 | 2-2 | 2-1 | 0-6 | 2-2 | 4-2 | 4-0 | 2-2 | 3-1 | 1-0 |
| Girondins de Bordeaux | 2-2 | 3-0 | 1-0 | 2-0 | ■ | 3-0 | 3-1 | 1-1 | 2-3 | 2-3 | 3-1 | 3-0 | 4-1 | 3-1 | 0-1 | 1-2 | 1-2 | 1-2 | 1-4 | 1-0 |
| Olympique Lyonnais | 3-0 | 1-0 | 3-0 | 1-1 | 2-2 | ■ | 1-4 | 1-2 | 2-1 | 2-0 | 2-1 | 0-1 | 2-1 | 0-0 | 3-2 | 1-2 | 0-0 | 2-0 | 2-2 | 3-1 |
| Olympique Marseille | 1-0 | 5-1 | 5-0 | 5-2 | 3-0 | 2-2 | ■ | 2-1 | 3-0 | 2-2 | 4-0 | 2-2 | 1-1 | 1-0 | 5-0 | 2-2 | 5-0 | 2-2 | 6-3 | 5-2 |
| FC de Metz | 1-3 | 2-1 | 1-0 | 1-0 | 1-0 | 6-1 | 2-1 | ■ | 1-1 | 0-0 | 0-0 | 4-2 | 2-2 | 2-0 | 2-1 | 2-2 | 1-0 | 3-3 | 2-1 | 2-2 |
| Nancy-Lorraine | 3-1 | 0-1 | 2-1 | 3-0 | 0-0 | 0-0 | 2-0 | 1-1 | ■ | 1-2 | 0-0 | 2-0 | 0-0 | 2-2 | 5-0 | 1-1 | 1-0 | 2-1 | 3-2 | 0-2 |
| FC de Nantes | 3-0 | 1-0 | 0-0 | 3-1 | 2-2 | 1-1 | 1-3 | 0-0 | 7-0 | ■ | 3-1 | 5-1 | 1-1 | 3-0 | 1-0 | 2-1 | 2-0 | 1-1 | 1-2 | 2-0 |
| Olympique GC Nice | 2-3 | 2-1 | 3-1 | 2-0 | 0-1 | 2-0 | 1-2 | 0-1 | 0-0 | 3-1 | ■ | 3-0 | 1-1 | 2-0 | 0-1 | 0-0 | 2-2 | 4-5 | 1-0 | 4-2 |
| Nîmes Olympique | 4-0 | 0-1 | 3-1 | 2-0 | 1-1 | 1-1 | 3-0 | 4-0 | 1-0 | 2-2 | 1-1 | ■ | 1-2 | 1-1 | 3-2 | 5-3 | 4-0 | 4-3 | 3-0 | 4-1 |
| Red Star FC | 3-0 | 0-5 | 0-0 | 1-1 | 3-1 | 1-3 | 3-4 | 0-0 | 3-1 | 0-3 | 0-0 | 1-2 | ■ | 2-1 | 1-5 | 1-1 | 4-2 | 0-0 | 2-1 | 3-2 |
| Stade de Reims | 1-0 | 3-1 | 2-0 | 5-2 | 3-0 | 1-0 | 1-2 | 1-1 | 2-1 | 0-0 | 1-1 | 1-1 | 0-1 | ■ | 1-1 | 2-2 | 2-1 | 4-1 | 1-0 | 2-0 |
| Stade Rennais | 0-1 | 1-0 | 0-0 | 3-2 | 3-0 | 2-3 | 2-2 | 0-0 | 5-1 | 4-0 | 1-3 | 2-0 | 3-0 | 0-0 | ■ | 0-3 | 0-0 | 4-0 | 2-0 | 1-1 |
| AS Saint-Étienne | 5-2 | 3-1 | 1-0 | 6-0 | 2-3 | 1-0 | 2-1 | 6-0 | 4-1 | 2-3 | 2-1 | 0-0 | 2-1 | 3-1 | 1-0 | ■ | 8-0 | 1-0 | 2-1 | 4-0 |
| Sedan Ardennes | 3-1 | 6-2 | 1-1 | 5-1 | 0-2 | 3-1 | 1-2 | 1-0 | 2-2 | 0-0 | 0-1 | 1-1 | 5-0 | 1-1 | 0-1 | 3-1 | ■ | 2-1 | 1-0 | 0-1 |
| Sochaux-Montbéliard | 5-1 | 1-0 | 3-0 | 1-1 | 1-3 | 0-0 | 1-1 | 5-1 | 1-0 | 2-0 | 1-0 | 3-0 | 2-1 | 2-1 | 4-2 | 1-1 | 3-1 | ■ | 1-0 | 0-1 |
| RP Strasbourg | 3-0 | 6-2 | 2-1 | 2-2 | 0-1 | 0-1 | 1-2 | 2-1 | 0-2 | 2-2 | 2-2 | 0-2 | 2-1 | 2-0 | 3-4 | 1-0 | 3-0 | 2-1 | ■ | 0-0 |
| Valenciennes | 0-0 | 1-3 | 2-1 | 2-0 | 1-1 | 1-2 | 1-2 | 2-2 | 1-1 | 1-2 | 3-1 | 3-1 | 1-2 | 3-1 | 0-0 | 0-1 | 0-0 | 4-0 | 3-0 | ■ |

## Top goal-scorers

1) Jozsip SKOBLAR     (Olympique de Marseille)    44
2) Salif KEITA     (AS de Saint-Étienne)    42
3) Jacky VERGNES     (Nîmes Olympique)    27

### Division 2 (Nord)

| | | Pd | Wn | Dw | Ls | GF | GA | Pts | |
|---|---|---|---|---|---|---|---|---|---|
| 1. | Lille Olympique SC (Lille) | 30 | 19 | 6 | 5 | 56 | 25 | 44 | P |
| 2. | Entente Chaumontaise Athletic-Cheminots (Chaumont) | 30 | 17 | 8 | 5 | 42 | 19 | 42 | |
| 3. | Racing Club de Lens (Lens) | 30 | 18 | 5 | 7 | 51 | 34 | 41 | |
| 4. | US du Grand Boulogne (Boulogne-sur-Mer) | 30 | 15 | 9 | 6 | 54 | 38 | 39 | |
| 5. | Entente Bagneaux-Fontainebleau-Nemours (Fonbleau) | 30 | 9 | 14 | 7 | 43 | 31 | 32 | |
| 6. | US Dunkerquoise (Dunkerque) | 30 | 11 | 10 | 9 | 42 | 36 | 32 | |
| 7. | Racing-Pierrots Strasbourg-Meinau (Strasbourg) 2nd X1 | 30 | 12 | 7 | 11 | 43 | 45 | 31 | # |
| 8. | FC de Mulhouse 1893 (Mulhouse) | 30 | 9 | 11 | 10 | 32 | 37 | 29 | |
| 9. | Racing Club Franc-Comtois (Besançon) | 30 | 9 | 10 | 11 | 40 | 41 | 28 | |
| 10. | Amiens SC (Amiens) | 30 | 9 | 10 | 11 | 39 | 50 | 28 | |
| 11. | Troyes Aube Football (Troyes) | 30 | 8 | 11 | 11 | 31 | 33 | 27 | |
| 12. | Racing Paris-Joinville (Neuilly) | 30 | 9 | 9 | 12 | 33 | 51 | 27 | |
| 13. | FC Sochaux-Montbéliard (Montbéliard) 2nd X1 | 30 | 8 | 7 | 15 | 33 | 48 | 23 | # |
| 14. | AC Cambrésien (Cambrai) | 30 | 6 | 10 | 14 | 44 | 52 | 22 | |
| 15. | AS de Creil (Creil) | 30 | 8 | 5 | 17 | 32 | 47 | 21 | |
| 16. | US Merlebach | 30 | 2 | 10 | 18 | 27 | 57 | 14 | R |
| | | 480 | 169 | 142 | 169 | 642 | 644 | 480 | |

| Division 2 (Centre) | Pd | Wn | Dw | Ls | GF | GA | Pts | |
|---|---|---|---|---|---|---|---|---|
| 1. Paris Saint-Germain FC (Paris) | 30 | 17 | 11 | 2 | 52 | 23 | 45 | P |
| 2. FC de Rouen (Rouen) | 30 | 16 | 9 | 5 | 53 | 25 | 41 | |
| 3. Limoges FC (Limoges) | 30 | 13 | 10 | 7 | 52 | 35 | 36 | |
| 4. Étoile Montluçonnais des Sports (Montluçon) | 30 | 13 | 9 | 8 | 56 | 39 | 35 | |
| 5. Stade Brestois (Brest) | 30 | 11 | 13 | 6 | 49 | 39 | 35 | |
| 6. FC de Lorient (Lorient) | 30 | 13 | 8 | 9 | 44 | 31 | 34 | |
| 7. US Quevillaise (Le Petit Quevilly) | 30 | 11 | 12 | 7 | 44 | 36 | 34 | |
| 8. Association Amicale de la Jeunesse Blésoise (Blois) | 30 | 13 | 8 | 9 | 33 | 35 | 34 | |
| 9. US du Mans (Le Mans) | 30 | 9 | 11 | 10 | 36 | 40 | 29 | |
| 10. La Berrichonne (Chateauroux) | 30 | 6 | 12 | 12 | 32 | 40 | 24 | |
| 11. Stade Quimperois (Quimper) | 30 | 4 | 16 | 10 | 24 | 45 | 24 | |
| 12. Stade Lavallois (Laval) | 30 | 7 | 9 | 14 | 30 | 49 | 23 | |
| 13. FC de Bourges (Bourges) | 30 | 7 | 9 | 14 | 28 | 48 | 23 | |
| 14. Stade Poitevin-Patronage des École Publiques (Poitiers) | 30 | 4 | 14 | 12 | 25 | 44 | 22 | |
| 15. Stade Malherbe Caennais (Caen) | 30 | 8 | 6 | 16 | 29 | 46 | 22 | |
| 16. Havre AC (Le Havre) | 30 | 6 | 7 | 17 | 37 | 49 | 19 | R |
| | 480 | 158 | 164 | 158 | 624 | 624 | 480 | |

| Division 2 (Sud) | Pd | Wn | Dw | Ls | GF | GA | Pts | |
|---|---|---|---|---|---|---|---|---|
| 1. AS de Monaco (Monaco) | 30 | 22 | 3 | 5 | 71 | 23 | 47 | P |
| 2. Olympique Avignonnais (Avignon) | 30 | 17 | 6 | 7 | 53 | 25 | 40 | |
| 3. AS Aixoise (Aix-en-Provence) | 30 | 17 | 4 | 9 | 50 | 32 | 38 | |
| 4. AS de Cannes (Cannes) | 30 | 14 | 10 | 6 | 43 | 28 | 38 | |
| 5. SC de Toulon (Toulon) | 30 | 13 | 5 | 12 | 37 | 37 | 31 | |
| 6. US de Toulouse (Toulouse) | 30 | 12 | 6 | 12 | 36 | 33 | 30 | |
| 7. FC de Gueugnon (Gueugnon) | 30 | 12 | 6 | 12 | 40 | 45 | 30 | |
| 8. Gazélec FC Ajaccien (Ajaccio) | 30 | 9 | 10 | 11 | 26 | 26 | 28 | |
| 9. FC de Sète (Sète) | 30 | 11 | 6 | 13 | 33 | 43 | 28 | |
| 10. Montpellier-Litoral SC (Montpellier) | 30 | 11 | 6 | 13 | 33 | 43 | 28 | |
| 11. Étoile Sportive et Club Naval Ciotaden (La Ciotat) | 30 | 9 | 9 | 12 | 35 | 45 | 27 | |
| 12. Union Montilienne Sportive (Montélimar) | 30 | 10 | 7 | 13 | 31 | 43 | 27 | |
| 13. AC Arlésien (Arles) | 30 | 9 | 8 | 13 | 33 | 38 | 26 | |
| 14. AS Biterroise (Béziers) | 30 | 10 | 6 | 14 | 33 | 42 | 26 | |
| 15. FC de Grenoble (Grenoble) | 30 | 7 | 6 | 17 | 25 | 45 | 20 | R |
| 16. Olympique d'Alés en Cévennes (Alés) | 30 | 5 | 6 | 19 | 29 | 60 | 16 | R |
| | 480 | 188 | 104 | 188 | 608 | 608 | 480 | |

## Coupe de France Final   (Stade Yves du Manoir, Colombes – 20/06/71 – 46,801)

**STADE RENNAIS UC (RENNES)**                 **1-0**                 Olympique Lyonnais (Lyon)

*Guy 63' (pen)*

**Rennais**: Aubour, Cosnard, Cardiet, Cédolin, Chlosta, Naumovic, Guy, Garcia, Kéruzoré, Betta, Rico.

**Lyonnais**: Chauveau, Domenech, Baeza, Mihajlovic, Valette (L'Homme 79'), Prost, Perrin, Chiesa, Félix, Di Nallo, Ravier.

### Semi-Finals   (27/05/71 – 01/06/71)

| | | |
|---|:---:|---|
| Olympique de Marseille (Marseille) | 1-0, 1-2 (aet) | Stade Rennais UC (Rennes) |

Olympique de Marseille (Marseille) won 3-1 on penalties.

| | | |
|---|:---:|---|
| FC Sochaux-Montbéliard (Montbéliard) | 0-1, 1-1 | Olympique Lyonnais (Lyon) |

### Quarter-Finals   (30/04/71 – 05/05/71)

| | | |
|---|:---:|---|
| Olympique Lyonnais (Lyon) | 3-1, 3-2 | US Dunkerquoise (Dunkerque) |
| Olympique de Marseille (Marseille) | 9-1, 4-2 | Assoc. Amicale de la Jeunesse Blésoise (Blois) |
| AS de Monaco (Monaco) | 2-0, 0-4 | Stade Rennais Université Club (Rennes) |
| FC Sochaux-Montbéliard (Montbéliard) | 2-1, 1-0 | Girondins de Bordeaux FC (Bordeaux) |

# 1971-72

| 1971-1972 Division One | AC Ajaccien | SC de l'Ouest Angers | AS Angoulême | Sporting Étoile Club Bastiais | Girondins de Bordeaux | Lille Olympique SC | Olympique Lyonnais | Olympique Marseille | FC de Metz | AS de Monaco | Nancy-Lorraine | FC de Nantes | Olympique GC Nice | Nîmes Olympique | Paris Saint-Germain FC | Red Star FC | Stade de Reims | Stade Rennais | AS Saint-Étienne | Sochaux-Montbéliard |
|---|---|---|---|---|---|---|---|---|---|---|---|---|---|---|---|---|---|---|---|---|
| AC Ajaccien | | 1-3 | 3-0 | 2-0 | 3-1 | 0-1 | 2-0 | 1-1 | 1-0 | 3-0 | 3-1 | 4-2 | 0-0 | 0-0 | 3-0 | 1-0 | 2-2 | 1-2 | 2-1 | 1-2 |
| SC de l'Ouest Angers | 2-1 | | 8-1 | 2-0 | 3-1 | 3-1 | 2-1 | 1-0 | 1-1 | 4-1 | 1-1 | 2-1 | 2-0 | 0-0 | 2-0 | 1-0 | 3-2 | 1-1 | 1-1 | 2-0 |
| AS Angoulême | 1-3 | 1-0 | | 2-1 | 3-0 | 3-3 | 2-0 | 2-3 | 1-0 | 2-0 | 1-1 | 2-5 | 1-1 | 0-3 | 3-1 | 0-2 | 2-1 | 0-0 | 3-4 | 0-0 |
| Sporting Étoile Club Bastiais | 2-1 | 3-1 | 2-0 | | 1-0 | 1-0 | 1-1 | 2-1 | 1-0 | 1-2 | 2-0 | 2-1 | 3-3 | 1-0 | 1-0 | 2-0 | 3-1 | 4-1 | 3-0 | 6-1 |
| Girondins de Bordeaux | 1-0 | 1-1 | 2-0 | 2-1 | | 3-1 | 0-3 | 0-2 | 0-0 | 3-1 | 1-0 | 2-2 | 2-1 | 1-4 | 2-0 | 2-0 | 1-1 | 2-1 | 0-2 | 0-1 |
| Lille Olympique SC | 3-1 | 0-1 | 4-2 | 1-0 | 0-0 | | 0-1 | 0-2 | 3-0 | 1-1 | 1-1 | 3-0 | 3-3 | 1-1 | 1-3 | 3-1 | 0-0 | 0-0 | 2-0 | 2-3 |
| Olympique Lyonnais | 2-1 | 1-2 | 2-0 | 3-0 | 2-2 | 1-0 | | 3-3 | 2-1 | 2-2 | 3-2 | 1-3 | 2-0 | 3-2 | 3-1 | 5-1 | 5-0 | 0-2 | 2-0 | 1-0 |
| Olympique Marseille | 1-1 | 2-1 | 3-0 | 0-2 | 3-0 | 3-0 | 1-1 | | 3-0 | 4-2 | 1-1 | 2-0 | 1-1 | 3-1 | 4-2 | 6-0 | 0-0 | 1-1 | 2-3 | 3-0 |
| FC de Metz | 3-0 | 0-0 | 1-0 | 2-1 | 1-3 | 4-0 | 1-0 | 1-3 | | 4-0 | 0-1 | 3-0 | 1-0 | 3-1 | 2-0 | 3-0 | 3-0 | 1-2 | 0-4 | 0-1 |
| AS de Monaco | 2-2 | 3-0 | 1-0 | 0-1 | 1-2 | 1-1 | 0-1 | 0-1 | 3-2 | | 4-2 | 2-1 | 0-2 | 1-2 | 2-1 | 0-0 | 1-1 | 0-1 | 1-2 | 1-3 |
| Nancy-Lorraine | 2-0 | 1-0 | 3-2 | 2-0 | 2-1 | 2-1 | 2-2 | 1-2 | 1-1 | 3-0 | | 1-0 | 3-2 | 0-1 | 2-3 | 1-1 | 0-0 | 3-1 | 3-1 | 0-0 |
| FC de Nantes | 2-0 | 1-0 | 5-0 | 4-0 | 0-0 | 2-1 | 2-0 | 1-1 | 5-1 | 1-1 | 2-2 | | 4-0 | 2-0 | 6-0 | 1-1 | 0-2 | 4-0 | 4-3 | 2-0 |
| Olympique GC Nice | 2-0 | 3-1 | 3-0 | 0-1 | 5-1 | 3-0 | 2-1 | 2-0 | 1-1 | 2-0 | 1-0 | 1-1 | | 4-0 | 1-1 | 1-0 | 3-0 | 0-0 | 1-2 | 1-2 |
| Nîmes Olympique | 2-0 | 1-0 | 3-0 | 6-2 | 1-1 | 5-2 | 2-0 | 1-3 | 1-1 | 5-1 | 0-0 | 4-0 | 2-0 | | 4-1 | 2-0 | 2-1 | 3-0 | 4-0 | 2-1 |
| Paris Saint-Germain FC | 1-1 | 0-1 | 3-0 | 4-1 | 0-0 | 4-1 | 1-2 | 1-2 | 3-1 | 0-0 | 1-4 | 2-3 | 1-1 | 1-1 | | 4-1 | 2-4 | 1-1 | 1-3 | 1-0 |
| Red Star FC | 3-1 | 2-1 | 1-1 | 2-1 | 1-0 | 0-0 | 1-1 | 2-4 | 1-1 | 1-0 | 1-1 | 0-1 | 1-1 | 1-5 | 0-0 | | 2-2 | 1-0 | 1-2 | 2-1 |
| Stade de Reims | 3-1 | 2-1 | 3-1 | 0-2 | 2-1 | 2-0 | 0-0 | 1-3 | 0-1 | 1-1 | 3-2 | 0-0 | 1-2 | 1-1 | 3-3 | 0-1 | | 0-2 | 2-1 | 2-3 |
| Stade Rennais | 1-1 | 3-1 | 2-2 | 1-0 | 2-0 | 5-2 | 0-0 | 1-2 | 3-0 | 1-3 | 3-1 | 1-1 | 2-2 | 0-2 | 1-1 | 2-0 | 4-1 | | 2-4 | 0-2 |
| AS Saint-Étienne | 1-1 | 0-1 | 4-0 | 5-3 | 1-1 | 4-0 | 0-1 | 2-1 | 2-0 | 3-2 | 1-3 | 2-1 | 2-2 | 1-3 | 0-1 | 5-1 | 9-1 | 4-2 | | 0-1 |
| Sochaux-Montbéliard | 3-1 | 2-0 | 4-1 | 6-1 | 0-0 | 2-0 | 4-0 | 0-1 | 1-0 | 3-1 | 2-1 | 2-0 | 1-1 | 1-0 | 0-2 | 1-2 | 1-1 | 3-2 | 0-2 | |

| Division 1 | | Pd | Wn | Dw | Ls | GF | GA | Pts | |
|---|---|---|---|---|---|---|---|---|---|
| 1. | OLYMPIQUE DE MARSEILLE (MARSEILLE) | 38 | 24 | 8 | 6 | 78 | 37 | 56 | |
| 2. | Nîmes Olympique (Nîmes) | 38 | 21 | 9 | 8 | 76 | 37 | 51 | |
| 3. | FC Sochaux-Montbéliard (Montbéliard) | 38 | 21 | 5 | 12 | 57 | 42 | 47 | |
| 4. | SC de l'Ouest Angers (Angers) | 38 | 19 | 7 | 12 | 57 | 42 | 45 | |
| 5. | Olympique Lyonnais (Lyon) | 38 | 18 | 9 | 11 | 58 | 45 | 45 | |
| 6. | AS de Saint-Étienne (Saint-Étienne) | 38 | 20 | 4 | 14 | 81 | 59 | 44 | |
| 7. | FC de Nantes (Nantes) | 38 | 17 | 9 | 12 | 70 | 48 | 43 | |
| 8. | Olympique GC de Nice (Nice) | 38 | 15 | 12 | 11 | 58 | 43 | 42 | |
| 9. | Sporting Étoile Club Bastiais (Bastia) | 38 | 20 | 2 | 16 | 58 | 57 | 42 | |
| 10. | AS Nancy-Lorraine (Nancy) | 38 | 14 | 12 | 12 | 56 | 49 | 40 | |
| 11. | Stade Rennais Université Club (Rennes) | 38 | 13 | 12 | 13 | 53 | 54 | 38 | * |
| 12. | Girondins de Bordeaux FC (Bordeaux) | 38 | 12 | 11 | 15 | 39 | 52 | 35 | |
| 13. | AC Ajaccien (Ajaccio) | 38 | 12 | 9 | 17 | 49 | 53 | 33 | |
| 14. | FC de Metz (Metz) | 38 | 13 | 7 | 18 | 44 | 49 | 33 | |
| 15. | Stade de Reims (Reims) | 38 | 9 | 13 | 16 | 46 | 69 | 31 | |
| 16. | Paris Saint-Germain FC (Paris) | 38 | 10 | 10 | 18 | 51 | 67 | 30 | * |
| 17. | Red Star FC (Saint-Ouen) | 38 | 10 | 10 | 18 | 34 | 64 | 30 | |
| 18. | Lille Olympique SC (Lille) | 38 | 8 | 10 | 20 | 43 | 68 | 26 | R |
| 19. | AS de Monaco (Monaco) | 38 | 8 | 10 | 20 | 41 | 68 | 26 | R |
| 20. | AS d'Angoulême (Angoulême) | 38 | 8 | 7 | 23 | 39 | 85 | 23 | R |
| | | 760 | 292 | 176 | 292 | 1088 | 1088 | 760 | |

## Top goal-scorers

| 1) | Jozsip SKOBLAR | (Olympique de Marseille) | 30 |
|---|---|---|---|
| 2) | Salif KEITA | (AS de Saint-Étienne) | 29 |
| 3) | Jacky VERGNES | (Nîmes Olympique) | 26 |

* Paris Saint-Germain FC (Paris) split to become Paris FC (Paris) playing in Division 1 and Paris Saint-Germain FC (Paris) playing in Division 3 due to a league ruling that all Division 1 clubs should have a separate amateur section; Stade Rennais Université Club (Rennes) changed their name to Stade Rennais FC (Rennes) for the next season.

| Division 2 (Group "A") | | Pd | Wn | Dw | Ls | GF | GA | Pts | |
|---|---|---|---|---|---|---|---|---|---|
| 1. | CS Sedan Ardennes (Sedan) | 30 | 22 | 4 | 4 | 85 | 21 | 48 | P |
| 2. | Troyes Aube Football (Troyes) | 30 | 16 | 12 | 2 | 50 | 24 | 44 | |
| 3. | Racing Club de Lens (Lens) | 30 | 18 | 4 | 8 | 48 | 24 | 40 | |
| 4. | FC de Rouen (Rouen) | 30 | 11 | 13 | 6 | 44 | 38 | 35 | |
| 5. | US du Grand Boulogne (Boulogne-sur-Mer) | 30 | 11 | 11 | 8 | 35 | 22 | 33 | |
| 6. | Stade Malherbe Caennais (Caen) | 30 | 12 | 9 | 9 | 32 | 36 | 33 | |
| 7. | Entente Chaumontaise Athletic-Cheminots (Chaumont) | 30 | 13 | 6 | 11 | 37 | 28 | 32 | |
| 8. | FC de Mulhouse 1893 (Mulhouse) | 30 | 9 | 12 | 9 | 36 | 26 | 30 | |
| 9. | US Dunkerquoise (Dunkerque) | 30 | 9 | 9 | 12 | 41 | 35 | 27 | |
| 10. | Racing Club Franc-Comtois (Besançon) | 30 | 11 | 5 | 14 | 37 | 39 | 27 | |
| 11. | Amiens SC (Amiens) | 30 | 10 | 6 | 14 | 34 | 56 | 26 | |
| 12. | US Quevillaise (Le Petit Quevilly) | 30 | 8 | 9 | 13 | 34 | 49 | 25 | R |
| 13. | AC Canbrésien (Cambrai) | 30 | 8 | 9 | 13 | 39 | 59 | 25 | |
| 14. | Amical Club Mouzonnais (Mouzon) | 30 | 6 | 11 | 13 | 45 | 54 | 23 | R |
| 15. | Evreux AC (Evreux) | 30 | 5 | 9 | 16 | 30 | 49 | 19 | R |
| 16. | AS de Creil (Creil) | 30 | 3 | 7 | 20 | 22 | 42 | 13 | R |
| | | 480 | 172 | 136 | 172 | 649 | 602 | 480 | |

| Division 2 (Group "B") | Pd | Wn | Dw | Ls | GF | GA | Pts | |
|---|---|---|---|---|---|---|---|---|
| 1. US Valenciennes-Anzin (Valenciennes) | 30 | 19 | 5 | 6 | 48 | 21 | 43 | P |
| 2. Limoges FC (Limoges) | 30 | 17 | 7 | 6 | 49 | 26 | 41 | |
| 3. Stade Brestois (Brest) | 30 | 15 | 7 | 8 | 50 | 33 | 37 | |
| 4. US du Mans (Le Mans) | 30 | 13 | 7 | 10 | 52 | 35 | 33 | |
| 5. FC de Bourges (Bourges) | 30 | 11 | 11 | 8 | 40 | 44 | 33 | |
| 6. CA Mantais (Mantes-la-Ville) | 30 | 12 | 8 | 10 | 42 | 42 | 32 | R |
| 7. Étoile Montluçonnais des Sports (Montluçon) | 30 | 12 | 8 | 10 | 46 | 49 | 32 | |
| 8. Stade Lavallois (Laval) | 30 | 13 | 6 | 11 | 38 | 46 | 32 | |
| 9. Association Amicale de la Jeunesse Blésoise (Blois) | 30 | 9 | 10 | 11 | 41 | 40 | 28 | |
| 10. La Berrichonne (Chateauroux) | 30 | 10 | 8 | 12 | 31 | 32 | 28 | |
| 11. FC de Lorient (Lorient) | 30 | 9 | 8 | 13 | 54 | 57 | 26 | |
| 12. Stade Poitevin-Patronage des Écoles Publiques (Poitiers) | 30 | 8 | 10 | 12 | 35 | 39 | 26 | |
| 13. Entente Bagneaux-Fontainebleau-Nemours (Fonbleau) | 30 | 9 | 6 | 15 | 31 | 44 | 24 | |
| 14. Entente Sportive Rochelloise (La Rochelle) | 30 | 7 | 9 | 14 | 36 | 48 | 23 | R |
| 15. Racing Paris-Joinville (Neuilly) | 30 | 6 | 10 | 14 | 27 | 42 | 22 | R |
| 16. Stade Quimperois (Quimper) | 30 | 7 | 6 | 17 | 24 | 46 | 20 | R |
| | 480 | 177 | 126 | 177 | 644 | 644 | 480 | |

| Division 2 (Group "C") | Pd | Wn | Dw | Ls | GF | GA | Pts | |
|---|---|---|---|---|---|---|---|---|
| 1. Racing-Pierrots Strasbourg-Meinau (Strasbourg) | 30 | 24 | 4 | 2 | 92 | 19 | 52 | P |
| 2. Olympique Avignonnais (Avignon) | 30 | 13 | 13 | 4 | 51 | 28 | 39 | |
| 3. SC de Toulon (Toulon) | 30 | 15 | 6 | 9 | 48 | 30 | 36 | |
| 4. Étoile Sportive et Club Naval Ciotaden (La Ciotat) | 30 | 12 | 9 | 9 | 30 | 33 | 33 | |
| 5. AS de Cannes (Cannes) | 30 | 12 | 9 | 9 | 46 | 26 | 33 | |
| 6. FC de Gueugnon (Gueugnon) | 30 | 11 | 9 | 10 | 34 | 40 | 31 | |
| 7. AC Arlésien (Arles) | 30 | 13 | 5 | 12 | 28 | 36 | 31 | |
| 8. US de Toulouse (Toulouse) | 30 | 11 | 8 | 11 | 37 | 34 | 30 | |
| 9. Montpellier-Litoral SC (Montpellier) | 30 | 9 | 10 | 11 | 34 | 40 | 28 | |
| 10. Union Montilienne Sportive (Montelimar) | 30 | 11 | 5 | 14 | 36 | 42 | 27 | |
| 11. FC de Sète (Sète) | 30 | 10 | 7 | 13 | 37 | 45 | 27 | |
| 12. CS Cuiseaux-Louhans (Cuiseaux-Louhans) | 30 | 8 | 10 | 12 | 37 | 46 | 26 | |
| 13. AS Biterroise (Béziers) | 30 | 9 | 8 | 13 | 29 | 54 | 26 | R |
| 14. AS Aixoise (Aix-en-Provence) | 30 | 9 | 8 | 13 | 26 | 35 | 26 | R |
| 15. FC de Martigues (Martigues) | 30 | 6 | 8 | 16 | 39 | 53 | 20 | R |
| 16. Gazélec FC Ajaccien (Ajaccio) | 30 | 2 | 11 | 17 | 20 | 59 | 15 | R |
| | 480 | 175 | 130 | 175 | 624 | 620 | 480 | |

## Coupe de France Final  (Parc des Princes, Paris – 04/06/72 – 44,069)

**OLYMPIQUE DE MARSEILLE**  **2-1**  Sporting Étoile Club Bastiais (Bastia)

*Couécou 15', Skoblar 73'*  *Franceschetti 85'*

**Marseille**: Carnus, Lopez, Bosquier, Zwunka, Kula, Novi, Gress, Magnusson, Bonnel (Hodoul 77'), Skoblar, Couécou.

**Bastiais**: Pantelic, Mosa, Tosi, Luccini, Savkovic, Calmettes, "Kanyan", Dogliani, Félix, Franceschetti, Giordani (Papi 77').

### Semi-Finals  (10-14/05/72)

| | | |
|---|---|---|
| Sporting Étoile Club Bastiais (Bastia) | 3-0, 0-2 | Racing Club de Lens (Lens) |
| Stade de Reims (Reims) | 0-0, 2-2 (aet) | Olympique de Marseille (Marseille) |

Olympique de Marseille (Marseille) won 3-1 on penalties.

### Quarter-Finals  (15-19/04/72)

| | | |
|---|---|---|
| Olympique Avignonnais (Avignon) | 0-1, 0-1 | Sporting Étoile Club Bastiais (Bastia) |
| Racing Club de Lens (Lens) | 1-0, 0-0 | Red Star FC (Saint-Ouen) |
| Olympique GC de Nice (Nice) | 1-1, 0-1 | Olympique de Marseille (Marseille) |
| Stade de Reims (Reims) | 2-0, 0-0 | AS Nancy-Lorraine (Nancy) |

# 1972-73

| 1972-1973 Division One | AC Ajaccien | SC de l'Ouest Angers | SEC Bastiais | Girondins de Bordeaux | Olympique Lyonnais | Olympique Marseille | FC de Metz | Nancy-Lorraine | FC de Nantes | Olympique GC Nice | Nîmes Olympique | Paris FC | Red Star FC | Stade de Reims | Stade Rennais | AS Saint-Étienne | Sedan Ardennes | Sochaux-Montbéliard | RP Strasbourg | Valenciennes |
|---|---|---|---|---|---|---|---|---|---|---|---|---|---|---|---|---|---|---|---|---|
| AC Ajaccien | ■ | 1-1 | 0-1 | 2-2 | 4-3 | 1-0 | 0-0 | 2-2 | 1-1 | 0-3 | 1-1 | 2-1 | 2-2 | 2-3 | 2-3 | 2-0 | 2-1 | 2-0 | 0-2 | 3-1 |
| SC de l'Ouest Angers | 4-0 | ■ | 3-0 | 3-1 | 1-0 | 0-2 | 3-2 | 0-0 | 1-0 | 0-0 | 0-1 | 1-1 | 1-0 | 1-1 | 0-2 | 2-0 | 2-2 | 1-0 | 1-0 | 5-1 |
| Sporting Étoile Club Bastiais | 1-0 | 2-0 | ■ | 1-1 | 1-1 | 0-0 | 4-0 | 3-1 | 0-0 | 3-0 | 3-0 | 1-0 | 3-0 | 1-1 | 4-0 | 3-3 | 3-0 | 3-1 | 3-0 | 2-0 |
| Girondins de Bordeaux | 3-0 | 1-2 | 1-1 | ■ | 1-0 | 2-1 | 2-0 | 3-1 | 2-1 | 0-1 | 0-1 | 0-1 | 1-1 | 2-0 | 1-1 | 6-1 | 1-1 | 2-1 | 2-0 | |
| Olympique Lyonnais | 1-0 | 2-1 | 2-0 | 0-1 | ■ | 4-4 | 3-0 | 2-2 | 2-4 | 1-2 | 1-0 | 5-2 | 1-2 | 1-1 | 3-1 | 2-0 | 1-2 | 2-0 | 4-0 | 1-0 |
| Olympique Marseille | 3-0 | 3-2 | 1-0 | 1-1 | 5-2 | ■ | 5-0 | 0-0 | 1-0 | 1-1 | 1-2 | 0-0 | 3-0 | 3-1 | 3-0 | 3-1 | 0-1 | 1-1 | 3-1 | 1-0 |
| FC de Metz | 7-0 | 2-0 | 3-2 | 1-1 | 2-2 | 2-0 | ■ | 1-0 | 0-2 | 1-0 | 0-1 | 0-1 | 3-0 | 1-2 | 2-1 | 1-2 | 4-2 | 2-1 | 1-1 | 1-1 |
| Nancy-Lorraine | 2-1 | 0-0 | 3-2 | 2-1 | 4-1 | 1-0 | 0-2 | ■ | 1-1 | 3-0 | 2-1 | 1-2 | 2-1 | 3-0 | 4-0 | 4-0 | 1-1 | 4-2 | 2-1 | 1-1 |
| FC de Nantes | 6-1 | 2-0 | 1-0 | 3-0 | 3-0 | 1-2 | 0-0 | 2-1 | ■ | 2-2 | 2-1 | 2-0 | 3-1 | 0-0 | 1-0 | 1-0 | 1-0 | 1-3 | 6-2 | 1-0 |
| Olympique GC Nice | 5-3 | 2-4 | 1-0 | 0-1 | 2-2 | 1-1 | 6-0 | 1-0 | 3-0 | ■ | 2-0 | 3-2 | 1-1 | 2-2 | 2-0 | 1-1 | 4-2 | 4-1 | 3-0 | 4-1 |
| Nîmes Olympique | 2-1 | 2-2 | 2-1 | 2-0 | 3-1 | 1-1 | 0-0 | 2-1 | 1-1 | 0-1 | ■ | 2-0 | 1-1 | 2-1 | 1-1 | 4-0 | 2-1 | 3-0 | 3-0 | 1-1 |
| Paris FC | 3-1 | 1-2 | 2-0 | 4-3 | 5-1 | 1-3 | 1-3 | 3-2 | 1-2 | 2-0 | 3-1 | ■ | 3-0 | 0-0 | 2-2 | 1-1 | 2-1 | 0-2 | 1-1 | 1-1 |
| Red Star FC | 3-0 | 1-2 | 2-2 | 3-1 | 0-1 | 1-2 | 1-0 | 0-1 | 1-3 | 1-1 | 1-1 | 2-3 | ■ | 1-2 | 2-0 | 0-3 | 1-1 | 3-3 | 0-0 | 1-0 |
| Stade de Reims | 0-0 | 3-2 | 2-0 | 3-1 | 2-1 | 2-1 | 0-0 | 2-3 | 2-1 | 2-3 | 0-1 | 1-1 | 3-0 | ■ | 1-1 | 0-0 | 5-1 | 1-0 | 1-0 | 1-0 |
| Stade Rennais | 1-1 | 1-2 | 2-1 | 3-0 | 3-2 | 2-3 | 1-0 | 4-1 | 0-0 | 1-0 | 1-0 | 2-1 | 1-1 | 1-0 | ■ | 2-2 | 1-1 | 0-0 | 1-0 | 2-0 |
| AS Saint-Étienne | 3-1 | 5-0 | 2-1 | 6-2 | 1-1 | 2-1 | 1-0 | 1-0 | 1-2 | 0-1 | 3-1 | 3-0 | 1-1 | 2-1 | 2-0 | ■ | 2-0 | 2-2 | 5-1 | 3-2 |
| Sedan Ardennes | 5-0 | 2-2 | 2-1 | 1-0 | 4-1 | 0-2 | 1-1 | 1-0 | 0-3 | 0-5 | 2-1 | 3-1 | 0-1 | 2-0 | 2-3 | 1-3 | ■ | 1-1 | 0-0 | 3-1 |
| Sochaux-Montbéliard | 4-0 | 1-1 | 3-2 | 0-0 | 3-1 | 1-2 | 4-1 | 2-2 | 0-1 | 5-1 | 0-0 | 1-1 | 1-0 | 2-1 | 2-1 | 2-1 | 1-0 | ■ | 1-1 | 3-0 |
| RP Strasbourg | 6-0 | 0-0 | 0-4 | 2-2 | 0-2 | 1-1 | 0-1 | 1-1 | 0-3 | 0-1 | 2-1 | 2-0 | 2-2 | 4-1 | 2-1 | 0-0 | 2-1 | 4-2 | ■ | 1-1 |
| Valenciennes | 3-2 | 3-0 | 1-0 | 3-0 | 1-2 | 1-0 | 1-0 | 0-1 | 1-1 | 1-1 | 1-0 | 1-1 | 0-0 | 1-2 | 2-0 | 0-1 | 5-1 | 0-0 | 1-2 | ■ |

| | Division 1 | Pd | Wn | Dw | Ls | GF | GA | Pts | |
|---|---|---|---|---|---|---|---|---|---|
| 1. | FC DE NANTES (NANTES) | 38 | 23 | 9 | 6 | 67 | 31 | 55 | |
| 2. | Olympique GC de Nice (Nice) | 38 | 20 | 10 | 8 | 70 | 44 | 50 | |
| 3. | Olympique de Marseille (Marseille) | 38 | 19 | 10 | 9 | 64 | 37 | 48 | |
| 4. | AS de Saint-Étienne (Saint-Étienne) | 38 | 18 | 10 | 10 | 64 | 47 | 46 | |
| 5. | SC de l'Ouest Angers (Angers) | 38 | 16 | 11 | 11 | 52 | 47 | 43 | |
| 6. | AS Nancy-Lorraine (Nancy) | 38 | 16 | 10 | 12 | 59 | 47 | 42 | |
| 7. | Nîmes Olympique (Nîmes) | 38 | 16 | 10 | 12 | 48 | 39 | 42 | |
| 8. | Stade de Reims (Reims) | 38 | 15 | 11 | 12 | 50 | 47 | 41 | |
| 9. | Sporting Étoile Club Bastiais (Bastia) | 38 | 15 | 8 | 15 | 59 | 41 | 38 | |
| 10. | Stade Rennais FC (Rennes) | 38 | 14 | 10 | 14 | 46 | 53 | 38 | |
| 11. | FC Sochaux-Montbéliard (Montbéliard) | 38 | 12 | 13 | 13 | 56 | 54 | 37 | |
| 12. | Paris FC (Paris) | 38 | 13 | 10 | 15 | 54 | 58 | 36 | |
| 13. | Olympique Lyonnais (Lyon) | 38 | 14 | 7 | 17 | 62 | 67 | 35 | |
| 14. | Girondins de Bordeaux FC (Bordeaux) | 38 | 12 | 11 | 15 | 49 | 55 | 35 | |
| 15. | FC de Metz (Metz) | 38 | 13 | 9 | 16 | 42 | 52 | 35 | |
| 16. | Racing-Pierrots Strasbourg-Meinau (Strasbourg) | 38 | 9 | 12 | 17 | 44 | 62 | 30 | |
| 17. | CS Sedan Ardennes (Sedan) | 38 | 11 | 8 | 19 | 49 | 71 | 30 | |
| 18. | US Valenciennes-Anzin (Valenciennes) | 38 | 9 | 10 | 19 | 37 | 51 | 28 | R |
| 19. | Red Star FC (Saint-Ouen) | 38 | 7 | 14 | 17 | 38 | 58 | 28 | R |
| 20. | AC Ajaccien (Ajaccio) | 38 | 7 | 9 | 22 | 40 | 89 | 23 | R |
| | | 760 | 279 | 202 | 279 | 1050 | 1050 | 760 | |

## Top goal-scorers

| | | | | |
|---|---|---|---|---|
| 1) | Jozsip SKOBLAR | (Olympique de Marseille) | 26 |
| 2) | Bernard LACOMBE | (Olympique Lyonnais) | 23 |
| 3) | Hervé REVELLI | (Olympique GC de Nice) | 22 |

| | Division 2 (Group "A") | Pd | Wn | Dw | Ls | GF | GA | Pts | |
|---|---|---|---|---|---|---|---|---|---|
| 1. | Racing Club de Lens (Lens) | 34 | 18 | 9 | 7 | 67 | 28 | 45 | P |
| 2. | US du Grand Boulogne (Boulogne-sur-Mer) | 34 | 21 | 3 | 10 | 52 | 34 | 45 | PO |
| 3. | Lille Olympique SC (Lille) | 34 | 19 | 6 | 9 | 60 | 26 | 44 | |
| 4. | US Dunkerquoise (Dunkerque) | 34 | 17 | 8 | 9 | 62 | 41 | 42 | |
| 5. | Stade Poitevin-Patronage des Écoles Publiques (Poitiers) | 34 | 15 | 9 | 10 | 54 | 48 | 39 | |
| 6. | AS d'Angoulême (Angoulême) | 34 | 14 | 11 | 9 | 40 | 34 | 39 | |
| 7. | Stade Brestois (Brest) | 34 | 13 | 11 | 10 | 39 | 36 | 37 | |
| 8. | US du Mans (Le Mans) | 34 | 13 | 11 | 10 | 49 | 54 | 37 | |
| 9. | FC de Rouen (Rouen) | 34 | 16 | 4 | 14 | 62 | 49 | 36 | |
| 10. | Stade Lavallois (Laval) | 34 | 12 | 10 | 12 | 32 | 30 | 34 | |
| 11. | FC de Lorient (Lorient) | 34 | 14 | 5 | 15 | 38 | 36 | 33 | |
| 12. | AC Cambrésien (Cambrai) | 34 | 12 | 6 | 16 | 39 | 57 | 30 | |
| 13. | CA Mantais (Mantes-la-Ville) | 34 | 8 | 12 | 14 | 40 | 51 | 28 | |
| 14. | Association Amicale de la Jeunesse Blésoise (Blois) | 34 | 10 | 8 | 16 | 41 | 57 | 28 | |
| 15. | FC de Bourges (Bourges) | 34 | 9 | 9 | 16 | 39 | 56 | 27 | |
| 16. | La Berrichonne (Châteauroux | 34 | 9 | 6 | 19 | 37 | 66 | 24 | |
| 17. | Stade Malherbe Caennais (Caen) | 34 | 8 | 7 | 19 | 37 | 65 | 23 | R |
| 18. | Amiens SC (Amiens) | 34 | 7 | 7 | 20 | 36 | 56 | 21 | R |
| | | 612 | 235 | 142 | 235 | 824 | 824 | 612 | |

| Division 2 (Group "B") | Pd | Wn | Dw | Ls | GF | GA | Pts | |
|---|---|---|---|---|---|---|---|---|
| 1. Troyes Aube Football (Troyes) | 34 | 23 | 7 | 4 | 71 | 16 | 53 | P |
| 2. AS de Monaco (Monaco) | 34 | 23 | 5 | 6 | 89 | 29 | 51 | PO |
| 3. Olympique Avignonnais (Avignon) | 34 | 17 | 7 | 10 | 53 | 49 | 41 | |
| 4. Entente Chaumontaise Athletic-Cheminots (Chaumont) | 34 | 13 | 13 | 8 | 55 | 39 | 39 | |
| 5. SC de Toulon (Toulon) | 34 | 15 | 9 | 10 | 30 | 41 | 39 | |
| 6. FC de Mulhouse 1893 (Mulhouse) | 34 | 15 | 8 | 11 | 43 | 39 | 38 | |
| 7. AS de Cannes (Cannes) | 34 | 15 | 7 | 12 | 56 | 55 | 37 | |
| 8. Racing Club Franc-Comtois (Besançon) | 34 | 15 | 7 | 12 | 46 | 46 | 37 | |
| 9. Étoile Montluçonnais des Sports (Montluçon) | 34 | 13 | 8 | 13 | 47 | 43 | 34 | |
| 10. US de Toulouse (Toulouse) | 34 | 10 | 13 | 11 | 41 | 42 | 33 | |
| 11. FC de Sète (Sète) | 34 | 12 | 8 | 14 | 33 | 44 | 32 | |
| 12. Limoges FC (Limoges) | 34 | 10 | 10 | 14 | 45 | 56 | 30 | |
| 13. AC Arlésien (Arles) | 34 | 10 | 10 | 14 | 35 | 52 | 30 | |
| 14. Entente Bagneaux-Fontainebleau-Nemours (Fonbleau) | 34 | 8 | 13 | 13 | 43 | 49 | 29 | R |
| 15. FC de Gueugnon (Gueugnon) | 34 | 9 | 9 | 16 | 48 | 39 | 27 | |
| 16. Étoile Sportive et Club Naval Ciotaden (La Ciotat) | 34 | 8 | 9 | 17 | 28 | 56 | 25 | R |
| 17. CS Cuiseaux-Louhans (Cuiseaux-Louhans) | 34 | 6 | 8 | 20 | 27 | 59 | 20 | R |
| 18. Union Montilienne Sportive (Montelimar) | 34 | 3 | 11 | 20 | 20 | 66 | 17 | R |
| | 612 | 225 | 162 | 225 | 810 | 820 | 612 | |

## Promotion Play-Off

US du Grand Boulogne (Boulogne-sur-Mer)  2-2, 1-7    AS de Monaco (Monaco)

\* Paris Saint-Germain FC (Paris) separated from Paris FC (Paris) after winning promotion to Division 2.

## Coupe de France Final    (Parc des Princes, Paris – 17/06/73 – 45,734)

**OLYMPIQUE LYONNAIS (LYON)**    **2-1**    FC de Nantes (Nantes)

*Trivic 29' pen, Lacombe 63'*    *Couécou 86'*

**Lyonnais:**  Chauveau, Domenech, Mihajlovic, Cacchioni, Lhomme, Prost, Trivic, Chiesa, Lacombe, Di Nallo, Ravier.

**Nantes:**  Bertrand-Demanes, Osman, De Michele, Bargas, Gardon, Pech, Blanchet, Michel, Couécou, Rampillon, Maas.

## Semi-Finals    (06-09/06/73)

| Olympique Avignonnais (Avignon) | 1-0,  1-4 | Olympique Lyonnais (Lyon) |
|---|---|---|
| Nîmes Olympique (Nîmes) | 0-0,  0-3 | FC de Nantes (Nantes) |

## Quarter-Finals    (13-18/04/73)

| Olympique de Marseille (Marseille) | 1-0,  0-4 | Olympique Lyonnais (Lyon) |
|---|---|---|
| Nîmes Olympique (Nîmes) | 4-2,  1-2 | Red Star FC (Saint-Ouen) |
| FC de Rouen (Rouen) | 2-0,  0-6 | Olympique Avignonnais (Avignon) |
| AS de Saint-Étienne (Saint-Étienne) | 2-0,  1-5 | FC de Nantes (Nantes) |

# 1973-74

| 1973-1974 Division One | SC Angers | SE Club Bastiais | Gir. de Bordeaux | Racing Lens | Olymp. Lyonnais | Olymp. Marseille | FC de Metz | AS de Monaco | Nancy-Lorraine | FC de Nantes | Olymp. GC Nice | Nîmes Olympique | Paris FC | Stade de Reims | Stade Rennais | AS Saint-Étienne | Sedan Ardennes | Sochaux-Mont. | RC Strasbourg | Troyes Aube |
|---|---|---|---|---|---|---|---|---|---|---|---|---|---|---|---|---|---|---|---|---|
| SC de l'Ouest Angers | ■ | 1-2 | 4-3 | 3-1 | 1-0 | 3-0 | 2-1 | 2-2 | 1-0 | 2-3 | 4-1 | 1-2 | 1-1 | 3-1 | 0-1 | 4-0 | 4-0 | 2-4 | 3-3 | 6-1 |
| Sporting Étoile Club Bastiais | 0-0 | ■ | 2-0 | 0-0 | 5-1 | 4-0 | 0-0 | 4-0 | 3-2 | 0-1 | 1-0 | 2-0 | 1-1 | 1-1 | 1-0 | 1-6 | 2-0 | 2-0 | 0-0 | 1-0 |
| Girondins de Bordeaux | 0-2 | 3-1 | ■ | 1-1 | 3-0 | 0-0 | 3-1 | 1-2 | 1-1 | 2-1 | 4-0 | 1-1 | 6-1 | 3-0 | 0-1 | 0-5 | 2-1 | 1-1 | 2-2 | 4-1 |
| Racing Lens | 1-1 | 3-1 | 0-1 | ■ | 1-1 | 2-3 | 2-1 | 2-1 | 1-0 | 0-1 | 2-0 | 0-1 | 3-2 | 2-1 | 3-0 | 2-3 | 4-2 | 1-1 | 3-1 | 0-0 |
| Olympique Lyonnais | 3-1 | 1-0 | 2-0 | 4-2 | ■ | 2-2 | 2-0 | 0-1 | 4-0 | 3-1 | 5-2 | 2-0 | 5-4 | 4-4 | 2-2 | 0-0 | 2-0 | 2-1 | 3-2 | 2-0 |
| Olympique Marseille | 2-2 | 2-1 | 3-1 | 5-2 | 1-1 | ■ | 3-1 | 0-2 | 2-2 | 3-0 | 2-0 | 1-2 | 3-0 | 1-0 | 2-1 | 0-2 | 4-0 | 1-1 | 6-1 | 2-3 |
| FC de Metz | 0-1 | 3-0 | 1-0 | 1-0 | 0-2 | 1-0 | ■ | 3-2 | 3-3 | 1-1 | 2-0 | 1-1 | 4-0 | 1-0 | 4-0 | 5-1 | 4-1 | 3-2 | 2-0 | 1-1 |
| AS de Monaco | 1-2 | 3-3 | 1-1 | 4-2 | 1-1 | 1-1 | 2-1 | ■ | 3-3 | 1-4 | 1-1 | 0-2 | 3-0 | 3-3 | 2-0 | 2-3 | 3-0 | 2-1 | 1-1 | 1-1 |
| Nancy-Lorraine | 0-3 | 2-0 | 0-2 | 3-2 | 3-1 | 0-0 | 2-1 | 2-1 | ■ | 1-0 | 0-1 | 1-1 | 1-1 | 2-2 | 1-2 | 1-1 | 4-1 | 0-1 | 3-1 | 0-0 |
| FC de Nantes | 1-0 | 3-0 | 3-1 | 4-0 | 1-2 | 4-1 | 2-2 | 2-1 | 0-0 | ■ | 1-1 | 0-2 | 3-0 | 2-1 | 1-1 | 3-1 | 1-0 | 2-1 | 3-0 | 3-0 |
| Olympique GC Nice | 4-0 | 3-0 | 2-1 | 2-4 | 4-1 | 3-0 | 4-0 | 3-2 | 1-1 | 1-1 | ■ | 2-2 | 2-1 | 3-0 | 3-1 | 4-1 | 7-2 | 2-2 | 3-2 | 1-1 |
| Nîmes Olympique | 0-0 | 3-1 | 0-0 | 1-1 | 0-0 | 4-1 | 0-0 | 4-3 | 1-0 | 0-0 | 0-0 | ■ | 1-1 | 2-0 | 0-2 | 1-2 | 2-0 | 1-1 | 1-2 | 1-1 |
| Paris FC | 2-2 | 0-1 | 2-2 | 1-3 | 2-0 | 0-1 | 3-2 | 4-0 | 4-2 | 2-5 | 3-2 | 3-1 | ■ | 3-0 | 0-0 | 0-1 | 3-1 | 2-3 | 3-0 | 0-2 |
| Stade de Reims | 4-2 | 1-0 | 2-0 | 3-1 | 0-0 | 1-0 | 4-0 | 8-4 | 1-2 | 4-2 | 2-2 | 1-0 | 4-0 | ■ | 4-0 | 0-1 | 0-1 | 1-0 | 3-2 | 3-2 |
| Stade Rennais | 1-2 | 1-2 | 4-2 | 0-1 | 1-0 | 3-1 | 1-0 | 1-1 | 3-0 | 0-0 | 1-0 | 1-2 | 1-0 | 2-0 | ■ | 1-0 | 1-1 | 0-2 | 2-1 | 2-1 |
| AS Saint-Étienne | 3-2 | 2-0 | 0-0 | 2-1 | 2-0 | 3-1 | 2-0 | 3-2 | 6-0 | 1-1 | 1-0 | 2-1 | 4-0 | 2-2 | 0-0 | ■ | 4-1 | 2-0 | 3-3 | 2-0 |
| Sedan Ardennes | 0-4 | 1-0 | 2-2 | 1-1 | 1-1 | 3-1 | 1-2 | 0-2 | 2-3 | 0-1 | 2-0 | 2-0 | 2-2 | 4-1 | 1-1 | 0-0 | ■ | 1-1 | 2-1 | 4-3 |
| Sochaux-Montbéliard | 4-2 | 1-0 | 4-1 | 2-3 | 1-1 | 2-0 | 1-0 | 4-1 | 2-0 | 0-1 | 0-1 | 2-1 | 1-2 | 4-1 | 0-2 | 3-0 |  | ■ | 1-0 | 2-0 |
| RC Strasbourg | 2-2 | 3-1 | 0-0 | 3-0 | 1-2 | 2-2 | 2-1 | 3-1 | 2-1 | 3-2 | 0-4 | 2-0 | 1-1 | 4-1 | 2-1 | 1-1 | 2-0 | 2-2 | ■ | 2-0 |
| Troyes Aube | 3-2 | 1-1 | 3-1 | 4-1 | 1-2 | 2-1 | 2-0 | 0-2 | 4-4 | 1-0 | 2-2 | 0-0 | 4-1 | 0-2 | 1-2 | 1-0 | 2-2 | 3-0 | 1-3 | ■ |

## Division 1

| | | Pd | Wn | Dw | Ls | GF | GA | Pts | Bon | Tot | |
|---|---|---|---|---|---|---|---|---|---|---|---|
| 1. | AS SAINT-Étienne (ST-Étienne) | 38 | 23 | 9 | 6 | 73 | 40 | 55 | 11 | 66 | |
| 2. | FC de Nantes (Nantes) | 38 | 19 | 9 | 10 | 63 | 41 | 47 | 11 | 58 | |
| 3. | Olympique Lyonnais (Lyon) | 38 | 18 | 11 | 9 | 64 | 51 | 47 | 8 | 55 | |
| 4. | SC de l'Ouest Angers (Angers) | 38 | 17 | 9 | 12 | 77 | 57 | 43 | 11 | 54 | |
| 5. | Olympique GC de Nice (Nice) | 38 | 16 | 10 | 12 | 69 | 55 | 42 | 12 | 54 | |
| 6. | Stade de Reims (Reims) | 38 | 16 | 7 | 15 | 67 | 62 | 39 | 11 | 50 | |
| 7. | FC Sochaux-Montbéliard (Montbéliard) | 38 | 17 | 8 | 13 | 60 | 45 | 42 | 7 | 49 | |
| 8. | Racing Club de Strasbourg (Strasbourg) | 38 | 13 | 11 | 14 | 60 | 67 | 37 | 8 | 45 | * |
| 9. | Nîmes Olympique (Nîmes) | 38 | 13 | 15 | 10 | 40 | 38 | 41 | 3 | 44 | |
| 10. | Racing Club de Lens (Lens) | 38 | 14 | 8 | 16 | 58 | 65 | 36 | 8 | 44 | |
| 11. | FC de Metz (Metz) | 38 | 14 | 7 | 17 | 53 | 53 | 35 | 8 | 43 | |
| 12. | Olympique de Marseille (Marseille) | 38 | 13 | 9 | 16 | 58 | 62 | 35 | 8 | 43 | |
| 13. | Stade Rennais FC (Rennes) | 38 | 16 | 8 | 14 | 42 | 47 | 40 | 3 | 43 | |
| 14. | Girondins de Bordeaux FC (Bordeaux) | 38 | 11 | 12 | 15 | 55 | 55 | 34 | 8 | 42 | |
| 15. | Sporting Étoile Club Bastiais (Bastia) | 38 | 14 | 8 | 16 | 44 | 49 | 36 | 5 | 41 | |
| 16. | AS de Monaco (Monaco) | 38 | 11 | 11 | 16 | 64 | 72 | 33 | 8 | 41 | |
| 17. | Troyes Aube Football (Troyes) | 38 | 11 | 11 | 16 | 52 | 61 | 33 | 8 | 41 | |
| 18. | AS Nancy-Lorraine (Nancy) | 38 | 10 | 13 | 15 | 51 | 67 | 33 | 8 | 41 | R |
| 19. | Paris FC (Paris) | 38 | 9 | 9 | 20 | 54 | 79 | 27 | 9 | 36 | R |
| 20. | CS Sedan Ardennes (Sedan) | 38 | 8 | 9 | 21 | 42 | 80 | 25 | 3 | 28 | R |
| | | 760 | 283 | 194 | 283 | 1146 | 1146 | 760 | 158 | 918 | |

1 extra bonus point was awarded for scoring 3 or more goals in a match in Division 1 and for winning by 2 goals or more in Division 2.

## Top goal-scorers

1) Carlos BIANCHI      (Stade de Reims)    30
2) Marc BERDOLL      (SC de l'Ouest Angers)    29
3) Nico BRAUN      (FC de Metz)    28

## Division 2 Play-Off

| Lille Olympique SC (Lille) | 5-1, 0-2 | Red Star FC (Saint-Ouen) |
|---|---|---|

| | Division 2 (Group "A") | Pd | Wn | Dw | Ls | GF | GA | Pts | Bon | Tot | |
|---|---|---|---|---|---|---|---|---|---|---|---|
| 1. | Lille Olympique SC (Lille) | 34 | 24 | 8 | 2 | 68 | 21 | 56 | 11 | 67 | P |
| 2. | US Valenciennes-Anzin (Valenciennes) | 34 | 21 | 7 | 6 | 78 | 29 | 49 | 15 | 64 | PO |
| 3. | FC de Rouen (Rouen) | 34 | 18 | 6 | 10 | 59 | 31 | 42 | 14 | 56 | |
| 4. | US du Grand Boulogne (Boulogne/Mer) | 34 | 16 | 10 | 8 | 58 | 39 | 42 | 11 | 53 | |
| 5. | Stade Lavallois (Laval) | 34 | 16 | 10 | 8 | 54 | 40 | 42 | 6 | 48 | |
| 6. | FC de Lorient (Lorient) | 34 | 14 | 10 | 10 | 50 | 34 | 38 | 7 | 45 | |
| 7. | Racing Club Franc-Comtois (Besançon) | 34 | 14 | 8 | 12 | 53 | 50 | 36 | 5 | 41 | |
| 8. | US Dunkerquoise (Dunkerque) | 34 | 13 | 7 | 14 | 49 | 50 | 33 | 7 | 40 | |
| 9. | Stade Brestois (Brest) | 34 | 14 | 8 | 12 | 41 | 42 | 36 | 2 | 38 | |
| 10. | Entente Chaumontaise AC (Chaumont) | 34 | 9 | 12 | 13 | 45 | 58 | 30 | 4 | 34 | |
| 11. | FC de Bourges (Bourges) | 34 | 10 | 10 | 14 | 35 | 54 | 30 | 4 | 34 | |
| 12. | Étoile Montluçonnais des Sports (Mont.) | 34 | 11 | 5 | 18 | 52 | 61 | 27 | 6 | 33 | |
| 13. | AC Cambrésien (Cambrai) | 34 | 11 | 9 | 14 | 42 | 55 | 31 | 2 | 33 | |
| 14. | AA de la Jeunesse Blésoise (Blois) | 34 | 10 | 9 | 15 | 36 | 52 | 29 | 4 | 33 | |
| 15. | SC d'Hazebrouck (Hazebrouck) | 34 | 10 | 8 | 16 | 45 | 54 | 28 | 4 | 32 | |
| 16. | Stade P-P des Écoles Publiques (Poitiers) | 34 | 10 | 7 | 17 | 43 | 61 | 27 | 5 | 32 | R |
| 17. | US du Mans (Le Mans) | 34 | 5 | 8 | 21 | 29 | 63 | 18 | 5 | 23 | R |
| 18. | ES Rochelloise (La Rochelle) | 34 | 5 | 8 | 21 | 29 | 72 | 18 | - | 18 | R |
| | | 612 | 231 | 150 | 231 | 866 | 866 | 612 | 112 | 724 | |

| | Division 2 (Group "B") | Pd | Wn | Dw | Ls | GF | GA | Pts | Bon | Tot | |
|---|---|---|---|---|---|---|---|---|---|---|---|
| 1. | Red Star FC (Saint-Ouen) | 34 | 19 | 12 | 3 | 71 | 29 | 50 | 11 | 61 | P |
| 2. | Paris Saint-Germain FC (Paris) | 34 | 19 | 6 | 9 | 70 | 42 | 44 | 13 | 57 | PO |
| 3. | US de Toulouse (Toulouse) | 34 | 17 | 5 | 12 | 64 | 42 | 39 | 9 | 48 | |
| 4. | Olympique Avignonnais (Avignon) | 34 | 15 | 10 | 9 | 47 | 33 | 40 | 6 | 46 | |
| 5. | SC de Toulon (Toulon) | 34 | 15 | 8 | 11 | 50 | 39 | 38 | 8 | 46 | |
| 6. | CA Mantais (Mantes la Ville) | 34 | 14 | 7 | 13 | 47 | 45 | 35 | 4 | 39 | |
| 7. | AC Ajaccien (Ajaccio) | 34 | 12 | 9 | 13 | 46 | 44 | 33 | 6 | 39 | |
| 8. | AS de Cannes (Cannes) | 34 | 11 | 12 | 11 | 39 | 42 | 34 | 5 | 39 | |
| 9. | AS d'Angoulême (Angoulême) | 34 | 13 | 8 | 13 | 45 | 49 | 34 | 5 | 39 | |
| 10. | FC de Mulhouse 1893 (Mulhouse) | 34 | 12 | 7 | 15 | 49 | 56 | 31 | 7 | 38 | |
| 11. | Ent. Bagneaux-Fontainebleau-Nemours | 34 | 11 | 9 | 14 | 42 | 48 | 31 | 5 | 36 | |
| 12. | FC de Sète (Sète) | 34 | 13 | 8 | 13 | 30 | 49 | 34 | 2 | 36 | |
| 13. | La Berrichonne (Châteauroux) | 34 | 10 | 10 | 14 | 43 | 47 | 30 | 5 | 35 | |
| 14. | FC de Gueugnon (Gueugnon) | 34 | 10 | 9 | 15 | 46 | 56 | 29 | 5 | 34 | |
| 15. | AS Biterroise (Béziers) | 34 | 11 | 8 | 15 | 36 | 46 | 30 | 4 | 34 | |
| 16. | Jeune Garde Athlétique de Nevers | 34 | 10 | 10 | 14 | 37 | 49 | 30 | 4 | 34 | R |
| 17. | AC Arlésien (Arles) | 34 | 9 | 8 | 17 | 44 | 67 | 26 | 4 | 30 | R |
| 18. | CS Vittel (Vittel) | 34 | 8 | 8 | 18 | 27 | 49 | 24 | 2 | 26 | R |
| | | 612 | 229 | 154 | 229 | 833 | 832 | 612 | 105 | 717 | |

## Promotion Play-Off

US Valenciennes-Anzin (Valenciennes)  2-1, 2-4  Paris Saint-Germain FC (Paris)

\* Racing Club de Strasbourg (Strasbourg) changed their name pre-season from Racing-Pierrots Strasbourg-Meinau (Strasbourg).

## Coupe de France Final  (Parc des Princes, Paris – 08/06/74 – 45,813)

**AS DE SAINT-Étienne (ST-Étienne)**  **2-1**  AS de Monaco (Monaco)

*Synaeghel 44', Merchadier 61'*  *Onnis 65'*

**Saint-Étienne**: Curkovic, Repellini, Farison, Piazza, Lopez, Bathenay (Merchadier 58'), Revelli, Larqué, Bereta, Janvion, Synaeghel.

**Monaco**: Montes, Guesdon, Polny, Mosca, Quittet, Chomet, Rosso, Dalger, Onnis, Petit, Tarabini.

## Semi-Finals  (31/05/74)

AS de Monaco (Monaco)  1-0  FC Sochaux-Montbéliard (Montbéliard)
AS de Saint-Étienne (Saint-Étienne)  1-0  Stade de Reims (Reims)

## Quarter-Finals  (04-7/05/74)

Olympique Lyonnais (Lyon)  4-2, 0-2 (aet)  FC Sochaux-Montbéliard (Montbéliard)
FC Sochaux-Montbéliard (Montbéliard) won 4-3 on penalties.
AS de Monaco (Monaco)  2-0, 0-1  Sporting Étoile Club Bastiais (Bastia)
Paris Saint-Germain FC (Paris)  0-5, 2-2  Stade de Reims (Reims)
AS de Saint-Étienne (Saint-Étienne)  2-1, 1-1  FC de Nantes (Nantes)

# 1974-75

| | Division 1 | Pd | Wn | Dw | Ls | GF | GA | Pts | Bon | Tot | |
|---|---|---|---|---|---|---|---|---|---|---|---|
| 1. | AS SAINT-Étienne (ST-Étienne) | 38 | 23 | 6 | 9 | 70 | 30 | 52 | 6 | 58 | |
| 2. | Olympique de Marseille (Marseille) | 38 | 18 | 9 | 11 | 65 | 45 | 45 | 4 | 49 | |
| 3. | Olympique Lyonnais (Lyon) | 38 | 16 | 11 | 11 | 64 | 53 | 43 | 5 | 48 | |
| 4. | Nîmes Olympique (Nîmes) | 38 | 16 | 11 | 11 | 56 | 49 | 43 | 4 | 47 | |
| 5. | FC de Nantes (Nantes) | 38 | 16 | 11 | 11 | 50 | 42 | 43 | 2 | 45 | |
| 6. | Sporting Étoile Club Bastiais (Bastia) | 38 | 15 | 11 | 12 | 54 | 47 | 41 | 4 | 45 | |
| 7. | Racing Club de Lens (Lens) | 38 | 16 | 8 | 14 | 59 | 59 | 40 | 4 | 44 | |
| 8. | FC de Metz (Metz) | 38 | 15 | 10 | 13 | 54 | 56 | 40 | 4 | 44 | |
| 9. | Racing Club de Strasbourg (Strasbourg) | 38 | 16 | 8 | 14 | 49 | 56 | 40 | 3 | 43 | |
| 10. | AS de Monaco (Monaco) | 38 | 18 | 4 | 16 | 64 | 68 | 40 | 2 | 42 | |
| 11. | Stade de Reims (Reims) | 38 | 15 | 8 | 15 | 57 | 57 | 38 | 3 | 41 | |
| 12. | Girondins de Bordeaux FC (Bordeaux) | 38 | 15 | 7 | 16 | 48 | 49 | 37 | 2 | 39 | |
| 13. | Lille Olympique SC (Lille) | 38 | 15 | 5 | 18 | 53 | 56 | 35 | 4 | 39 | |
| 14. | Olympique GC de Nice (Nice) | 38 | 13 | 10 | 15 | 59 | 63 | 36 | 3 | 39 | |
| 15. | Paris Saint-Germain FC (Paris) | 38 | 12 | 12 | 14 | 57 | 65 | 36 | 1 | 37 | |
| 16. | Troyes Aube Football (Troyes) | 38 | 12 | 10 | 16 | 46 | 55 | 34 | 3 | 37 | |
| 17. | FC Sochaux-Montbéliard (Montbéliard) | 38 | 11 | 10 | 17 | 41 | 49 | 32 | 2 | 34 | |
| 18. | SC de l'Ouest Angers (Angers) | 38 | 9 | 10 | 19 | 48 | 69 | 28 | 5 | 33 | R |
| 19. | Stade Rennais FC (Rennes) | 38 | 10 | 11 | 17 | 38 | 52 | 31 | 2 | 33 | R |
| 20. | Red Star FC (Saint-Ouen) | 38 | 7 | 12 | 19 | 43 | 55 | 26 | 3 | 29 | R |
| | | 760 | 288 | 184 | 288 | 1075 | 1075 | 760 | 66 | 826 | |

1 extra bonus point was awarded for scoring 3 or more goals in a match in Division 1 and for winning by 2 goals or more in Division 2.

| 1974-1975 Division One | SC de l'Ouest Angers | Sporting Étoile Club Bastiais | Girondins de Bordeaux | Racing de Lens | Lille Olympique | Olympique Lyonnais | Olympique Marseille | FC de Metz | AS de Monaco | FC de Nantes | Olympique GC Nice | Nîmes Olympique | Paris Saint-Germain FC | Red Star FC | Stade de Reims | Stade Rennais | AS Saint-Étienne | Sochaux-Montbéliard | RC Strasbourg | Troyes Aube |
|---|---|---|---|---|---|---|---|---|---|---|---|---|---|---|---|---|---|---|---|---|
| SC de l'Ouest Angers | | 3-0 | 2-2 | 1-2 | 4-1 | 0-2 | 1-2 | 2-2 | 2-1 | 0-0 | 1-3 | 2-0 | 3-1 | 1-1 | 1-2 | 1-2 | 0-1 | 1-1 | 5-1 | 1-1 |
| Sporting Étoile Club Bastiais | 3-0 | | 1-0 | 0-0 | 2-0 | 2-0 | 2-2 | 0-0 | 1-0 | 1-0 | 2-0 | 4-0 | 0-2 | 2-0 | 0-1 | 3-0 | 1-1 | 3-2 | 2-1 | 5-1 |
| Girondins de Bordeaux | 1-1 | 1-0 | | 2-0 | 4-2 | 1-1 | 1-0 | 3-2 | 0-0 | 2-1 | 2-0 | 0-1 | 1-2 | 2-1 | 2-0 | 1-0 | 1-0 | 2-1 | 4-1 | 6-0 |
| Racing de Lens | 0-0 | 3-3 | 3-0 | | 1-0 | 4-0 | 2-2 | 3-1 | 6-3 | 2-2 | 4-2 | 3-0 | 3-2 | 0-0 | 1-0 | 1-0 | 3-1 | 3-2 | 0-1 | 1-0 |
| Lille Olympique | 1-5 | 0-0 | 2-0 | 1-1 | | 1-2 | 1-0 | 4-0 | 2-0 | 3-0 | 4-2 | 1-1 | 5-0 | 1-0 | 2-1 | 1-0 | 2-0 | 4-0 | 2-1 | 2-0 |
| Olympique Lyonnais | 0-0 | 8-1 | 1-0 | 5-1 | 5-1 | | 0-1 | 2-0 | 1-3 | 1-1 | 0-0 | 2-2 | 4-4 | 2-1 | 3-3 | 4-1 | 1-0 | 1-0 | 4-1 | 2-1 |
| Olympique Marseille | 3-1 | 3-1 | 3-0 | 4-0 | 2-0 | 0-1 | | 1-0 | 4-1 | 2-1 | 4-1 | 1-1 | 4-2 | 3-2 | 1-1 | 3-1 | 1-2 | 2-0 | 1-1 | 0-0 |
| FC de Metz | 2-0 | 0-2 | 3-3 | 2-1 | 2-1 | 3-1 | 1-0 | | 1-0 | 4-0 | 2-2 | 3-0 | 1-3 | 2-1 | 1-1 | 5-2 | 3-0 | 0-1 | 2-1 | 1-1 |
| AS de Monaco | 1-0 | 0-1 | 2-0 | 3-0 | 1-0 | 3-1 | 0-2 | 1-2 | | 1-3 | 3-2 | 3-3 | 3-0 | 4-3 | 2-3 | 2-0 | 3-1 | 3-1 | 1-0 | 3-1 |
| FC de Nantes | 1-0 | 0-0 | 3-0 | 2-1 | 1-0 | 3-1 | 2-0 | 0-2 | 4-2 | | 2-0 | 0-1 | 0-0 | 0-0 | 0-1 | 1-1 | 2-1 | 1-0 | 3-1 | 4-1 |
| Olympique GC Nice | 4-1 | 2-1 | 0-0 | 2-1 | 2-1 | 2-2 | 1-3 | 1-0 | 2-3 | 2-2 | | 2-0 | 4-2 | 2-1 | 0-0 | 4-1 | 1-1 | 5-1 | 2-1 | 2-1 |
| Nîmes Olympique | 4-0 | 3-3 | 2-1 | 3-1 | 2-1 | 1-2 | 3-1 | 2-0 | 3-0 | 0-2 | 2-1 | | 2-1 | 3-0 | 2-0 | 0-0 | 0-0 | 1-0 | 6-0 | 2-2 |
| Paris Saint-Germain FC | 3-2 | 1-1 | 1-0 | 3-1 | 0-0 | 2-2 | 1-1 | 2-2 | 0-1 | 2-3 | 2-1 | 1-1 | | 2-0 | 3-0 | 2-1 | 2-2 | 0-1 | 1-1 | 0-0 |
| Red Star FC | 2-5 | 0-0 | 1-2 | 1-1 | 2-1 | 4-0 | 0-0 | 1-1 | 3-0 | 4-4 | 4-1 | 0-1 | 1-1 | | 2-1 | 0-2 | 1-2 | 0-1 | 0-1 | 2-1 |
| Stade de Reims | 1-1 | 0-1 | 2-1 | 5-1 | 4-3 | 0-2 | 4-3 | 1-2 | 2-3 | 2-1 | 1-1 | 2-1 | 6-1 | 1-1 | | 2-1 | 0-2 | 2-1 | 2-0 | 3-0 |
| Stade Rennais | 2-0 | 1-1 | 1-1 | 1-0 | 3-0 | 0-0 | 1-0 | 0-0 | 1-1 | 0-0 | 0-0 | 2-1 | 2-1 | 0-2 | 2-2 | | 3-1 | 0-1 | 5-1 | 1-1 |
| AS Saint-Étienne | 2-0 | 3-2 | 2-0 | 3-2 | 4-1 | 1-0 | 4-1 | 5-0 | 3-2 | 2-0 | 2-0 | 4-0 | 3-2 | 2-0 | 3-1 | 3-0 | | 1-0 | 2-1 | 5-1 |
| Sochaux-Montbéliard | 0-1 | 3-0 | 5-2 | 0-1 | 1-1 | 3-1 | 1-1 | 1-1 | 4-2 | 0-1 | 1-1 | 2-0 | 0-1 | 0-0 | 1-0 | 2-1 | 1-1 | | 0-0 | 0-1 |
| RC Strasbourg | 1-0 | 3-2 | 1-0 | 2-1 | 3-0 | 2-0 | 3-2 | 3-0 | 2-2 | 2-0 | 2-1 | 1-1 | 2-1 | 1-1 | 3-0 | 2-0 | 0-0 | 1-1 | | 1-0 |
| Troyes Aube | 4-0 | 2-1 | 1-0 | 0-1 | 0-1 | 0-0 | 1-2 | 4-1 | 5-0 | 0-0 | 3-1 | 1-1 | 1-3 | 2-1 | 2-0 | 2-0 | 1-0 | 2-2 | 2-0 | |

## Top goal-scorers

| | | | |
|---|---|---|---|
| 1) | Dellio ONNIS | (AS de Monaco) | 30 |
| 2) | M'PELÉ | (Paris Saint-Germain FC) | 21 |
| 3) | Hugo CURIONI | (FC de Metz) | 19 |

## Division 2 Play-Off

US Valenciennes-Anzin (Valenciennes)     0-0, 0-4     AS Nancy-Lorraine (Nancy)

| Division 2 (Group "A") | Pd | Wn | Dw | Ls | GF | GA | Pts | Bon | Pts | |
|---|---|---|---|---|---|---|---|---|---|---|
| 1. US Valenciennes-Anzin (Valenciennes) | 34 | 19 | 9 | 6 | 59 | 27 | 47 | 6 | 53 | P |
| 2. FC de Rouen (Rouen) | 34 | 19 | 10 | 5 | 59 | 34 | 48 | 4 | 52 | PO |
| 3. FC de Lorient (Lorient) | 34 | 18 | 8 | 8 | 50 | 31 | 44 | 2 | 46 | |
| 4. CS Sedan Ardennes (Sedan) | 34 | 18 | 8 | 8 | 57 | 40 | 44 | 2 | 46 | |
| 5. FC de Gueugnon (Gueugnon) | 34 | 13 | 13 | 8 | 46 | 31 | 39 | 4 | 43 | |
| 6. US Dunkerquoise (Dunkerque) | 34 | 17 | 8 | 9 | 46 | 40 | 42 | - | 42 | |
| 7. AS d'Angoulême (Angoulême) | 34 | 13 | 9 | 12 | 56 | 50 | 35 | 5 | 40 | |
| 8. Amiens SC (Amiens) | 34 | 15 | 6 | 13 | 42 | 41 | 36 | 3 | 39 | |
| 9. US du Grand Boulogne (Boulogne/Mer) | 34 | 13 | 8 | 13 | 40 | 33 | 34 | 3 | 37 | |
| 10. AJ Auxerroise (Auxerre) | 34 | 14 | 8 | 12 | 36 | 31 | 36 | 1 | 37 | |
| 11. Stade Lavallois (Laval) | 34 | 14 | 5 | 15 | 50 | 46 | 33 | 3 | 36 | |
| 12. Ent. Bagneaux-Fontainebleau-Nemours | 34 | 11 | 9 | 14 | 43 | 53 | 31 | 3 | 34 | |
| 13. Stade Brestois (Brest) | 34 | 10 | 10 | 14 | 50 | 52 | 30 | 3 | 33 | |
| 14. SC d'Hazebrouck (Hazebrouck) | 34 | 8 | 12 | 14 | 30 | 49 | 28 | 2 | 30 | |
| 15. Paris FC (Paris) | 34 | 11 | 8 | 15 | 31 | 54 | 30 | - | 30 | |
| 16. AC Cambrésien (Cambrai) | 34 | 6 | 11 | 17 | 35 | 50 | 23 | 2 | 25 | R |
| 17. Stade Quimperois (Quimper) | 34 | 6 | 9 | 19 | 40 | 69 | 21 | 2 | 23 | R |
| 18. CA Mantais (Mantes-la-Ville) | 34 | 4 | 9 | 21 | 31 | 70 | 17 | - | 17 | R |
| | 612 | 229 | 160 | 223 | 801 | 801 | 618 | 45 | 663 | |

| Division 2 (Group "B") | Pd | Wn | Dw | Ls | GF | GA | Pts | Bon | Pts | |
|---|---|---|---|---|---|---|---|---|---|---|
| 1. AS Nancy-Lorraine (Nancy) | 32 | 17 | 8 | 7 | 73 | 34 | 42 | 10 | 52 | P |
| 2. Olympique Avignonnais (Avignon) | 32 | 16 | 9 | 7 | 57 | 31 | 41 | 5 | 46 | PO |
| 3. SC de Toulon (Toulon) | 32 | 18 | 8 | 6 | 44 | 22 | 44 | 2 | 46 | |
| 4. AS de Cannes (Cannes) | 32 | 16 | 7 | 9 | 56 | 37 | 39 | 5 | 44 | |
| 5. Étoile des Sports Montluçonnais (Mont.) | 32 | 14 | 12 | 6 | 40 | 35 | 40 | 1 | 41 | |
| 6. US de Toulouse (Toulouse) | 32 | 13 | 10 | 9 | 49 | 48 | 36 | 3 | 39 | |
| 7. FC de Martigues (Martigues) | 32 | 13 | 9 | 10 | 47 | 44 | 35 | 2 | 37 | |
| 8. FC de Sète (Sète) | 32 | 9 | 11 | 12 | 38 | 27 | 29 | 3 | 32 | |
| 9. Racing Club Franc-Comtois (Besançon) | 32 | 11 | 7 | 14 | 48 | 52 | 29 | 3 | 32 | |
| 10. La Berrichonne (Châteauroux) | 32 | 11 | 8 | 13 | 41 | 44 | 30 | 1 | 31 | |
| 11. FC de Tours (Tours) | 32 | 10 | 9 | 13 | 41 | 50 | 29 | 2 | 31 | |
| 12. Entente Chaumontaise AC (Chaumont) | 32 | 10 | 9 | 13 | 38 | 47 | 29 | 2 | 31 | |
| 13. AS Biterroise (Béziers) | 32 | 10 | 7 | 15 | 49 | 60 | 27 | 3 | 30 | |
| 14. FC de Mulhouse 1893 (Mulhouse) | 32 | 8 | 10 | 14 | 46 | 57 | 26 | 3 | 29 | |
| 15. Stade Athlétique Spinalien (Epinal) | 32 | 8 | 12 | 12 | 32 | 52 | 28 | - | 28 | |
| 16. FC de Bourges (Bourges) | 32 | 7 | 11 | 14 | 26 | 37 | 25 | 2 | 27 | R |
| 17. AA de la Jeunesse Blésoise (Blois) | 32 | 4 | 7 | 12 | 28 | 66 | 15 | 1 | 16 | R |
| | 544 | 195 | 154 | 195 | 753 | 743 | 544 | 48 | 592 | |

## Promotion Play-Off

| Olympique Avignonnais (Avignon) | 3-0, 0-2 | FC de Rouen (Rouen) |
|---|---|---|

\* CS Sedan Ardennes (Sedan) changed their name to CS Sedan-Mouzon Ardennes (Sedan) for the next season; Stade Lavallois (Laval) changed their name to Stade Lavallois FC (Laval) for the next season.

## Coupe de France Final   (Parc des Princes, Paris – 14/06/75 – 44,725)

**AS DE SAINT-Étienne (SAINT-Étienne)**     **2-0**     Racing Club de Lens (Lens)

*Piazza 68', Larqué 79'*

**Saint-Étienne**: Curkovic, Janvion, Farison, Piazza, Lopez, Bathenay, Revelli, Larqué, Revelli, Synaeghel (Santini 77'), Sarramagna.

**Lens**: Lannoy, Hopquin, Notheaux, Marie, Grzegorczyk, Elie, Leclercq, Faber, Kaiser, Bousdira, Zuraszek.

### Semi-Finals   (07/06/75)

| | | |
|---|---|---|
| Racing Club de Lens (Lens) | 3-2  (aet) | Paris Saint-Germain FC (Paris) |
| AS de Saint-Étienne (Saint-Étienne) | 2-0 | Sporting Étoile Club Bastiais (Bastia) |

### Quarter-Finals   (09-13/05/75)

| | | |
|---|---|---|
| Sporting Étoile Club Bastiais (Bastia) | 1-0,  1-0 | SC de l'Ouest Angers (Angers) |
| Olympique de Marseille (Marseille) | 2-2,  0-2 | Paris Saint-Germain FC (Paris) |
| FC de Metz (Metz) | 4-3,  1-3 | Racing Club de Lens (Lens) |
| AS de Saint-Étienne (Saint-Étienne) | 2-0,  1-1 | Racing Club de Strasbourg (Strasbourg) |

# 1975-76

| 1975-1976 Division One | Olymp. Avignonnais | SE Club Bastiais | Gir. de Bordeaux | Racing de Lens | Lille Olympique | Olympique Lyonnais | Olympique Marseille | FC de Metz | AS de Monaco | Nancy-Lorraine | FC de Nantes | Olympique GC Nice | Nîmes Olympique | Paris St-Germain FC | Stade de Reims | AS Saint-Étienne | Sochaux-Montbéliard | RC Strasbourg | Troyes Aube | Valenciennes |
|---|---|---|---|---|---|---|---|---|---|---|---|---|---|---|---|---|---|---|---|---|
| Olympique Avignonnais | | 1-1 | 3-4 | 0-0 | 1-0 | 2-1 | 2-1 | 0-1 | 1-1 | 2-3 | 0-2 | 1-5 | 1-0 | 1-1 | 1-0 | 1-3 | 3-1 | 1-0 | 0-1 | 1-2 |
| Sporting Étoile Club Bastiais | 2-0 | | 2-1 | 0-0 | 1-1 | 4-1 | 2-3 | 3-2 | 3-0 | 3-0 | 0-1 | 1-1 | 1-1 | 3-0 | 2-0 | 2-2 | 1-1 | 2-1 | 3-1 | 1-1 |
| Girondins de Bordeaux | 2-1 | 3-0 | | 2-2 | 2-1 | 3-1 | 3-1 | 3-1 | 3-1 | 0-0 | 2-1 | 1-0 | 1-0 | 2-1 | 2-3 | 1-1 | 1-2 | 1-1 | 2-2 | 0-1 |
| Racing de Lens | 3-1 | 1-1 | 3-2 | | 2-0 | 3-1 | 2-3 | 4-1 | 3-0 | 4-2 | 3-2 | 2-1 | 1-1 | 3-3 | 1-0 | 1-1 | 1-1 | 1-1 | 1-1 | 0-1 |
| Lille Olympique | 4-0 | 2-0 | 3-2 | 4-2 | | 2-1 | 4-3 | 1-1 | 3-3 | 1-2 | 1-0 | 0-3 | 2-1 | 2-1 | 2-2 | 0-0 | 1-1 | 3-0 | 3-0 | 5-1 |
| Olympique Lyonnais | 2-0 | 2-2 | 1-2 | 4-1 | 3-0 | | 2-1 | 2-3 | 4-1 | 1-0 | 3-3 | 1-0 | 1-1 | 2-0 | 1-2 | 0-0 | 1-2 | 2-1 | 2-0 | 1-1 |
| Olympique Marseille | 3-1 | 4-3 | 1-0 | 3-2 | 2-0 | 2-0 | | 2-1 | 1-0 | 1-3 | 1-2 | 2-1 | 0-1 | 2-1 | 1-0 | 4-2 | 0-3 | 1-0 | 3-2 | 3-0 |
| FC de Metz | 1-0 | 4-1 | 2-1 | 2-1 | 5-2 | 3-1 | 1-0 | | 4-1 | 4-1 | 3-0 | 2-2 | 4-3 | 1-2 | 2-4 | 1-1 | 3-1 | 5-0 | 0-1 | 3-0 |
| AS de Monaco | 1-0 | 2-0 | 1-1 | 1-1 | 3-4 | 1-0 | 2-1 | 2-0 | | 1-0 | 4-4 | 4-1 | 3-1 | 3-0 | 1-0 | 0-3 | 0-0 | 1-2 | 1-1 | 3-1 |
| Nancy-Lorraine | 6-0 | 0-1 | 3-2 | 3-0 | 5-0 | 1-4 | 4-2 | 0-0 | 3-0 | | 1-1 | 2-0 | 1-1 | 2-4 | 3-1 | 0-0 | 5-1 | 1-1 | 0-0 | 3-3 |
| FC de Nantes | 4-0 | 1-0 | 5-1 | 1-1 | 4-0 | 2-3 | 0-1 | 2-0 | 3-1 | 3-0 | | 1-1 | 1-0 | 1-2 | 4-1 | 3-0 | 2-2 | 2-1 | 2-2 | 2-0 |
| Olympique GC Nice | 2-0 | 1-1 | 2-0 | 5-0 | 2-2 | 1-0 | 2-1 | 4-2 | 4-1 | 2-1 | 2-2 | | 4-0 | 2-1 | 2-1 | 1-1 | 3-0 | 1-0 | 5-2 | 1-0 |
| Nîmes Olympique | 1-0 | 3-0 | 1-2 | 2-2 | 5-1 | 2-0 | 0-1 | 3-2 | 3-2 | 2-2 | 0-0 | 2-1 | | 2-1 | 0-3 | 2-0 | 0-2 | 2-1 | 1-1 | 1-0 |
| Paris Saint-Germain FC | 6-2 | 1-1 | 2-2 | 4-2 | 2-2 | 2-0 | 2-3 | 3-1 | 1-2 | 1-4 | 2-1 | 0-0 | 2-0 | | 2-3 | 2-1 | 2-3 | 0-0 | 1-0 | 2-0 |
| Stade de Reims | 4-1 | 1-2 | 0-0 | 4-0 | 2-0 | 3-2 | 3-1 | 3-2 | 2-2 | 1-1 | 1-0 | 1-0 | 2-0 | 1-1 | | 3-2 | 1-1 | 6-0 | 1-1 | 5-1 |
| AS Saint-Étienne | 4-0 | 4-2 | 5-2 | 2-0 | 3-1 | 1-1 | 1-0 | 1-0 | 2-2 | 3-0 | 2-2 | 1-1 | 5-2 | 1-1 | 2-1 | | 2-0 | 2-1 | 3-0 | 2-0 |
| Sochaux-Montbéliard | 1-1 | 2-2 | 2-0 | 3-2 | 4-1 | 1-0 | 3-0 | 3-2 | 4-0 | 3-0 | 1-1 | 0-0 | 2-1 | 1-4 | 1-0 | 1-1 | | 1-1 | 2-2 | 3-0 |
| RC Strasbourg | 4-0 | 1-3 | 0-2 | 1-1 | 3-0 | 5-0 | 2-0 | 1-2 | 1-0 | 1-5 | 1-1 | 2-2 | 0-1 | 1-0 | 1-1 | 0-2 | 0-0 | | 2-1 | 1-0 |
| Troyes Aube | 1-1 | 0-2 | 2-0 | 1-1 | 1-0 | 3-4 | 2-2 | 0-1 | 3-1 | 3-0 | 0-0 | 2-2 | 1-1 | 1-1 | 2-1 | 0-1 | 3-0 | 1-1 | | 4-0 |
| Valenciennes | 2-0 | 3-1 | 1-1 | 1-1 | 0-1 | 0-0 | 1-0 | 3-0 | 5-1 | 2-0 | 1-1 | 0-0 | 0-3 | 2-2 | 2-1 | 1-1 | 3-0 | 2-0 | 3-0 | |

1 extra bonus point was awarded for scoring 3 or more goals in a match in Division 1 and for winning by 2 goals or more in Division 2.

| | Division 1 | Pd | Wn | Dw | Ls | GF | GA | Pts | Bon | Tot | |
|---|---|---|---|---|---|---|---|---|---|---|---|
| 1. | AS SAINT-Étienne (ST-Étienne) | 38 | 18 | 15 | 5 | 68 | 39 | 51 | 6 | 57 | |
| 2. | Olympique GC de Nice (Nice) | 38 | 17 | 13 | 8 | 67 | 40 | 47 | 7 | 54 | |
| 3. | FC Sochaux-Montbéliard (Montbéliard) | 38 | 16 | 14 | 8 | 59 | 50 | 46 | 6 | 52 | |
| 4. | FC de Nantes (Nantes) | 38 | 15 | 14 | 9 | 67 | 44 | 44 | 6 | 50 | |
| 5. | Stade de Reims (Reims) | 38 | 17 | 8 | 13 | 68 | 49 | 42 | 5 | 47 | |
| 6. | FC de Metz (Metz) | 38 | 18 | 4 | 16 | 72 | 62 | 40 | 5 | 45 | |
| 7. | AS Nancy-Lorraine (Nancy) | 38 | 14 | 10 | 14 | 67 | 59 | 38 | 7 | 45 | |
| 8. | Sporting Étoile Club Bastiais (Bastia) | 38 | 14 | 13 | 11 | 59 | 53 | 41 | 4 | 45 | |
| 9. | Olympique de Marseille (Marseille) | 38 | 20 | 1 | 17 | 60 | 60 | 41 | 1 | 42 | |
| 10. | Girondins de Bordeaux FC (Bordeaux) | 38 | 15 | 9 | 14 | 59 | 59 | 39 | 1 | 40 | |
| 11. | Nîmes Olympique (Nîmes) | 38 | 14 | 9 | 15 | 50 | 53 | 37 | 3 | 40 | |
| 12. | US Valenciennes-Anzin (Valenciennes) | 38 | 13 | 10 | 15 | 44 | 54 | 36 | 4 | 40 | |
| 13. | Lille Olympique SC (Lille) | 38 | 14 | 8 | 16 | 59 | 73 | 36 | 4 | 40 | |
| 14. | Paris Saint-Germain FC (Paris) | 38 | 13 | 11 | 14 | 63 | 60 | 37 | 2 | 39 | |
| 15. | Racing Club de Lens (Lens) | 38 | 10 | 16 | 12 | 58 | 66 | 36 | 2 | 38 | |
| 16. | Olympique Lyonnais (Lyon) | 38 | 13 | 7 | 18 | 55 | 61 | 33 | 4 | 37 | |
| 17. | Troyes Aube Football (Troyes) | 38 | 9 | 16 | 13 | 48 | 54 | 34 | 3 | 37 | |
| 18. | AS de Monaco (Monaco) | 38 | 12 | 9 | 17 | 53 | 73 | 33 | 2 | 35 | R |
| 19. | Racing Club de Strasbourg (Strasbourg) | 38 | 9 | 11 | 18 | 39 | 56 | 29 | 3 | 32 | R |
| 20. | Olympique Avignonnais (Avignon) | 38 | 7 | 6 | 25 | 30 | 80 | 20 | - | 20 | R |
| | | 760 | 278 | 204 | 278 | 1145 | 1145 | 760 | 75 | 835 | |

## Top goal-scorers

| | | | |
|---|---|---|---|
| 1) | Carlos BIANCHI | (Stade de Reims) | 34 |
| 2) | Dellio ONNIS | (AS de Monaco) | 29 |
| 3) | Hugo CURIONI | (FC de Metz) | 25 |

## Division 2 Play-Off

Stade Rennais FC (Rennes)　　　　　2-3, 4-6　　　　　SC de l'Ouest Angers (Angers)

| | Division 2 (Group "A") | Pd | Wn | Dw | Ls | GF | GA | Pts | Bon | Tot | |
|---|---|---|---|---|---|---|---|---|---|---|---|
| 1. | Stade Rennais FC (Rennes) | 34 | 22 | 6 | 6 | 82 | 22 | 50 | 10 | 60 | P |
| 2. | Stade Lavallois FC (Laval) | 34 | 21 | 8 | 5 | 71 | 28 | 50 | 7 | 57 | PO |
| 3. | FC de Lorient (Lorient) | 34 | 15 | 9 | 10 | 55 | 36 | 39 | 6 | 45 | |
| 4. | FC de Rouen (Rouen) | 34 | 17 | 2 | 15 | 60 | 48 | 36 | 9 | 45 | |
| 5. | Amiens SC (Amiens) | 34 | 15 | 8 | 11 | 47 | 42 | 38 | 6 | 44 | |
| 6. | Stade Malherbe Caennais (Caen) | 34 | 16 | 8 | 10 | 54 | 48 | 40 | 3 | 43 | |
| 7. | SC d'Hazebrouck (Hazebrouck) | 34 | 12 | 12 | 10 | 42 | 34 | 36 | 4 | 40 | |
| 8. | La Berrichonne (Châteauroux) | 34 | 13 | 12 | 9 | 29 | 24 | 38 | - | 38 | |
| 9. | FC de Tours (Tours) | 34 | 14 | 7 | 13 | 47 | 47 | 35 | 3 | 38 | |
| 10. | AS d'Angoulême (Angoulême) | 34 | 13 | 6 | 15 | 51 | 54 | 32 | 3 | 35 | |
| 11. | US Dunkerquoise (Dunkerque) | 34 | 10 | 11 | 13 | 38 | 46 | 31 | 3 | 34 | |
| 12. | Paris FC (Paris) | 34 | 13 | 3 | 18 | 47 | 53 | 29 | 4 | 33 | |
| 13. | Ent. Bagneaux-Fontainebleau-Nemours | 34 | 9 | 11 | 14 | 42 | 51 | 29 | 1 | 30 | |
| 14. | US du Grand Boulogne (Boulogne/Mer) | 34 | 12 | 5 | 17 | 37 | 48 | 29 | 1 | 30 | |
| 15. | Stade Brestois (Brest) | 34 | 9 | 11 | 14 | 34 | 57 | 29 | - | 29 | |
| 16. | CS Sedan-Mouzon Ardennes (Sedan) | 34 | 8 | 9 | 17 | 43 | 75 | 25 | 4 | 29 | R |
| 17. | Stade Olympique Choletais (Cholet) | 34 | 9 | 7 | 18 | 38 | 58 | 25 | 3 | 28 | R |
| 18. | US Municipale de Malakoff (Malakoff) | 34 | 9 | 3 | 22 | 31 | 67 | 21 | 2 | 23 | R |
| | | 612 | 237 | 138 | 237 | 848 | 838 | 612 | 69 | 681 | |

| | Division 2 (Group "B") | Pd | Wn | Dw | Ls | GF | GA | Pts | Bon | Tot | |
|---|---|---|---|---|---|---|---|---|---|---|---|
| 1. | SC de l'Ouest Angers (Angers) | 34 | 18 | 8 | 8 | 68 | 40 | 44 | 9 | 53 | P |
| 2. | Red Star FC (Saint-Ouen) | 34 | 18 | 6 | 10 | 51 | 25 | 42 | 8 | 50 | PO |
| 3. | SC de Toulon (Toulon) | 34 | 17 | 8 | 9 | 50 | 31 | 42 | 3 | 45 | |
| 4. | AS de Cannes (Cannes) | 34 | 16 | 9 | 9 | 47 | 31 | 41 | 2 | 43 | |
| 5. | FC de Gueugnon (Gueugnon) | 34 | 15 | 10 | 9 | 37 | 31 | 40 | 2 | 42 | |
| 6. | US de Toulouse (Toulouse) | 34 | 13 | 11 | 10 | 62 | 53 | 37 | 3 | 40 | |
| 7. | FC de Martigues (Martigues) | 34 | 14 | 9 | 11 | 47 | 41 | 37 | 3 | 40 | |
| 8. | Racing Club Franc-Comtois (Besançon) | 34 | 14 | 9 | 11 | 46 | 40 | 37 | 3 | 40 | |
| 9. | AS Biterroise (Béziers) | 34 | 13 | 9 | 12 | 44 | 36 | 35 | 4 | 39 | |
| 10. | AJ Auxerroise (Auxerre) | 34 | 13 | 11 | 10 | 44 | 36 | 37 | 2 | 39 | |
| 11. | Gazélec FC Ajaccien (Ajaccio) | 34 | 13 | 6 | 15 | 44 | 47 | 32 | 4 | 36 | |
| 12. | Stade Athlétique Spinalien (Epinal) | 34 | 10 | 8 | 16 | 42 | 52 | 28 | 4 | 32 | |
| 13. | Entente Chaumontaise AC (Chaumont) | 34 | 9 | 12 | 13 | 41 | 56 | 30 | 2 | 32 | |
| 14. | Sports Réunis Déodatiens (Saint-Dié) | 34 | 11 | 8 | 15 | 36 | 53 | 30 | 2 | 32 | # |
| 15. | FC de Sète (Sète) | 34 | 8 | 12 | 14 | 44 | 43 | 28 | 3 | 31 | |
| 16. | FC de Mulhouse 1893 (Mulhouse) | 34 | 12 | 5 | 17 | 41 | 63 | 29 | 2 | 31 | R |
| 17. | Étoile des Sports Montluçonnais (Mont.) | 34 | 8 | 9 | 17 | 36 | 57 | 25 | 2 | 27 | R |
| 18. | Jeune Garde Athlétique de Nevers | 34 | 6 | 6 | 22 | 29 | 74 | 18 | 1 | 19 | R |
| | | 612 | 228 | 156 | 228 | 809 | 809 | 612 | 59 | 671 | |

## Promotion Play-Off

| | | |
|---|---|---|
| Red Star FC (Saint-Ouen) | 0-1, 1-2 | Stade Lavallois FC (Laval) |

# Sports Réunis Déodatiens (Saint-Dié) resigned from the league and reverted to amateur status for the next season.

## Coupe de France Final   (Parc des Princes, Paris – 12/06/76 – 45,661)

**OLYMPIQUE DE MARSEILLE**               **2-0**               Olympique Lyonnais (Lyon)

*Nogues 67', Boubacar 84'*

**Marseille**: Migeon, Lemée, Trésor, Zwunka, Bracci, Buigues, Fernandez, Boubacar, Yazalde, Nogues (Martinez 88'), Bereta.

**Lyonnais**: De Rocco, Garrigues, Mihajlovic, Jodar, Domenech, Cacchioni, Maneiro (Valette 74'), Chiesa, Lacombe, Bernad, Ferrigno.

## Semi-Finals   (29/05/76)

| | | |
|---|---|---|
| Olympique Lyonnais (Lyon) | 2-0 | FC de Metz (Metz) |
| Olympique de Marseille (Marseille) | 4-1 | AS Nancy-Lorraine (Nancy) |

## Quarter-Finals   (04-07/05/76)

| | | |
|---|---|---|
| SC de l'Ouest Angers (Angers) | 1-0, 2-0 | Olympique de Marseille (Marseille) |
| Sporting Étoile Club Bastiais (Bastia) | 0-1, 0-0 | FC de Metz (Metz) |
| AS Nancy-Lorraine (Nancy) | 2-0, 1-2 | US Valenciennes-Anzin (Valenciennes) |
| Paris Saint-Germain FC (Paris) | 1-1, 0-2 | Olympique Lyonnais (Lyon) |

# 1976-77

| 1976-1977 Division One | SC de Angers | SE Club Bastiais | Gir. de Bordeaux | Stade Lavallois | Racing de Lens | Lille Olympique | Olymp. Lyonnais | Olymp. Marseille | FC de Metz | Nancy-Lorraine | FC de Nantes | Olymp. GC Nice | Nîmes Olympique | Paris St.Germain | Stade de Reims | Stade Rennais | AS Saint-Étienne | Sochaux-Montbél. | Troyes Aube | Valenciennes |
|---|---|---|---|---|---|---|---|---|---|---|---|---|---|---|---|---|---|---|---|---|
| SC de l'Ouest Angers | | 0-3 | 0-0 | 1-1 | 3-2 | 3-0 | 0-1 | 1-2 | 0-2 | 3-1 | 2-2 | 5-0 | 0-0 | 0-2 | 1-2 | 1-0 | 4-2 | 1-1 | 1-2 | 0-0 |
| Sporting Étoile Club Bastiais | 5-1 | | 4-1 | 3-1 | 3-2 | 1-1 | 3-0 | 4-0 | 2-0 | 3-2 | 3-0 | 2-0 | 5-0 | 5-2 | 3-2 | 3-1 | 1-1 | 2-0 | 3-0 | 4-0 |
| Girondins de Bordeaux | 4-1 | 1-0 | | 0-1 | 5-2 | 2-1 | 1-2 | 5-0 | 3-3 | 2-0 | 1-2 | 3-1 | 0-0 | 5-2 | 3-1 | 2-1 | 2-0 | 2-1 | 3-0 | 0-0 |
| Stade Lavallois | 2-0 | 3-1 | 0-0 | | 1-3 | 1-0 | 3-0 | 2-1 | 1-1 | 1-1 | 1-2 | 1-0 | 0-1 | 2-1 | 0-0 | 0-0 | 3-1 | 0-2 | 1-1 | 1-1 |
| Racing de Lens | 2-0 | 4-3 | 3-3 | 2-1 | | 4-2 | 2-0 | 1-0 | 4-1 | 1-1 | 1-1 | 1-1 | 3-0 | 3-3 | 2-2 | 3-1 | 1-1 | 2-1 | 3-1 | 1-0 |
| Lille Olympique | 0-1 | 0-3 | 2-2 | 3-3 | 0-1 | | 3-0 | 2-0 | 2-0 | 1-1 | 1-3 | 0-2 | 1-2 | 2-0 | 2-1 | 2-2 | 1-0 | 1-1 | 3-1 | 1-1 |
| Olympique Lyonnais | 1-1 | 1-1 | 1-0 | 2-0 | 3-3 | 1-0 | | 2-1 | 1-0 | 2-1 | 2-0 | 4-1 | 4-0 | 1-1 | 2-1 | 1-2 | 0-2 | 3-0 | 0-0 | 2-0 |
| Olympique Marseille | 2-1 | 4-1 | 1-1 | 2-1 | 2-2 | 3-2 | 3-1 | | 3-1 | 2-4 | 1-1 | 0-1 | 1-0 | 2-1 | 0-1 | 3-2 | 1-0 | 1-1 | 2-0 | 1-1 |
| FC de Metz | 4-2 | 1-1 | 4-2 | 5-3 | 0-1 | 3-1 | 2-0 | 3-0 | | 3-0 | 1-2 | 2-2 | 2-0 | 3-1 | 2-0 | 1-0 | 0-0 | 2-0 | 2-1 | 2-2 |
| Nancy-Lorraine | 1-1 | 4-1 | 7-3 | 4-1 | 1-1 | 3-0 | 0-0 | 2-0 | 4-1 | | 3-0 | 1-4 | 3-1 | 1-2 | 4-2 | 3-2 | 2-0 | 3-0 | 2-0 | 3-0 |
| FC de Nantes | 3-0 | 3-1 | 2-0 | 4-0 | 1-1 | 3-1 | 3-0 | 3-0 | 3-2 | 3-1 | | 6-1 | 1-0 | 3-3 | 1-1 | 3-1 | 3-0 | 2-0 | 2-1 | 3-1 |
| Olympique GC Nice | 4-1 | 5-0 | 2-1 | 2-1 | 1-0 | 2-0 | 1-2 | 2-2 | 2-4 | 2-0 | 1-2 | | 1-0 | 1-0 | 2-3 | 4-0 | 2-0 | 1-0 | 2-0 | 2-1 |
| Nîmes Olympique | 3-1 | 3-1 | 3-2 | 4-2 | 0-2 | 1-0 | 1-1 | 2-3 | 1-1 | 2-2 | 0-0 | 3-2 | | 3-0 | 1-1 | 6-2 | 1-1 | 0-1 | 2-0 | 2-2 |
| Paris Saint-Germain FC | 2-0 | 2-2 | 2-1 | 5-0 | 3-1 | 2-1 | 2-4 | 1-1 | 3-1 | 2-0 | 0-1 | 3-0 | 0-0 | | 2-1 | 3-1 | 2-0 | 1-0 | 2-1 | 1-2 |
| Stade de Reims | 2-1 | 1-1 | 2-1 | 1-0 | 2-0 | 3-1 | 1-1 | 1-0 | 0-2 | 3-3 | 0-2 | 0-1 | 2-0 | 2-3 | | 3-0 | 2-2 | 1-1 | 1-3 | 3-0 |
| Stade Rennais | 4-2 | 1-1 | 0-2 | 1-3 | 2-1 | 3-1 | 2-2 | 2-1 | 2-3 | 0-3 | 2-1 | 0-0 | 0-1 | 1-1 | 2-2 | | 0-1 | 2-2 | 2-2 | 0-2 |
| AS Saint-Étienne | 1-1 | 2-1 | 2-0 | 3-1 | 3-0 | 2-0 | 1-1 | 4-0 | 0-0 | 3-2 | 2-0 | 2-0 | 2-0 | 1-0 | 0-0 | 4-0 | | 2-0 | 4-0 | 5-0 |
| Sochaux-Montbéliard | 1-1 | 2-0 | 1-0 | 1-1 | 1-5 | 4-2 | 2-1 | 1-2 | 1-0 | 0-3 | 2-6 | 1-2 | 2-1 | 1-1 | 2-2 | 2-1 | 4-0 | | 2-0 | 2-1 |
| Troyes Aube | 1-1 | 1-0 | 0-1 | 2-1 | 0-2 | 1-0 | 0-3 | 0-0 | 3-2 | 0-1 | 2-3 | 2-2 | 3-1 | 2-1 | 4-1 | 2-1 | 0-0 | 1-0 | | 2-1 |
| Valenciennes | 0-2 | 1-2 | 3-2 | 1-2 | 0-1 | 1-0 | 3-2 | 3-1 | 1-1 | 1-1 | 0-0 | 1-1 | 2-0 | 0-3 | 5-0 | 2-0 | 1-1 | 0-0 | 1-2 | |

## Division 1

| | | Pd | Wn | Dw | Ls | GF | GA | Pts | |
|---|---|---|---|---|---|---|---|---|---|
| 1. | FC DE NANTES (NANTES) | 38 | 25 | 8 | 5 | 80 | 40 | 58 | |
| 2. | Racing Club de Lens (Lens) | 38 | 19 | 11 | 8 | 73 | 53 | 49 | |
| 3. | Sporting Étoile Club Bastiais (Bastia) | 38 | 20 | 7 | 11 | 82 | 53 | 47 | |
| 4. | AS Nancy-Lorraine (Nancy) | 38 | 20 | 5 | 13 | 78 | 53 | 45 | |
| 5. | AS de Saint-Étienne (Saint-Étienne) | 38 | 17 | 11 | 10 | 55 | 36 | 45 | |
| 6. | Olympique Lyonnais (Lyon) | 38 | 17 | 10 | 11 | 54 | 47 | 44 | |
| 7. | Olympique GC de Nice (Nice) | 38 | 19 | 6 | 13 | 60 | 54 | 44 | |
| 8. | FC de Metz (Metz) | 38 | 17 | 9 | 12 | 67 | 54 | 43 | |
| 9. | Paris Saint-Germain FC (Paris) | 38 | 17 | 8 | 13 | 65 | 55 | 42 | |
| 10. | Girondins de Bordeaux FC (Bordeaux) | 38 | 15 | 8 | 15 | 66 | 57 | 38 | |
| 11. | Stade de Reims (Reims) | 38 | 12 | 12 | 14 | 53 | 60 | 36 | |
| 12. | Olympique de Marseille (Marseille) | 38 | 14 | 8 | 16 | 48 | 63 | 36 | |
| 13. | Nîmes Olympique (Nîmes) | 38 | 12 | 10 | 16 | 45 | 56 | 34 | |
| 14. | FC Sochaux-Montbéliard (Montbéliard) | 38 | 12 | 10 | 16 | 44 | 56 | 34 | |
| 15. | Troyes Aube Football (Troyes) | 38 | 13 | 7 | 18 | 41 | 59 | 33 | |
| 16. | Stade Lavallois FC (Laval) | 38 | 11 | 10 | 17 | 46 | 62 | 32 | |
| 17. | US Valenciennes-Anzin (Valenciennes) | 38 | 9 | 13 | 16 | 41 | 56 | 31 | |
| 18. | SC de l'Ouest Angers (Angers) | 38 | 8 | 11 | 19 | 44 | 65 | 27 | R |
| 19. | Lille Olympique SC (Lille) | 38 | 7 | 7 | 24 | 40 | 67 | 21 | R |
| 20. | Stade Rennais FC (Rennes) | 38 | 6 | 9 | 23 | 43 | 79 | 21 | R |
| | | 760 | 290 | 180 | 290 | 1125 | 1125 | 760 | |

## Top goal-scorers

| | | | |
|---|---|---|---|
| 1) | Carlos BIANCHI | (Stade de Reims) | 28 |
| 2) | Michel PLATINI | (AS Nancy-Lorraine) | 25 |
| 3) | Nico BRAUN | (FC de Metz) | 23 |

## Division 2 Play-Off

Racing Club de Strasbourg (Strasbourg)          2-0,  1-1                    AS de Monaco (Monaco)

| | **Division 2 (Group "A")** | **Pd** | **Wn** | **Dw** | **Ls** | **GF** | **GA** | **Pts** | |
|---|---|---|---|---|---|---|---|---|---|
| 1. | AS de Monaco (Monaco) | 34 | 19 | 10 | 5 | 64 | 35 | 48 | P |
| 2. | FC de Gueugnon (Gueugnon) | 34 | 18 | 9 | 7 | 54 | 32 | 45 | PO |
| 3. | SC de Toulon (Toulon) | 34 | 16 | 12 | 6 | 49 | 30 | 44 | |
| 4. | Olympique Avignonnais (Avignon) | 34 | 15 | 10 | 9 | 53 | 31 | 40 | |
| 5. | Association de la Jeunesse Auxerroise (Auxerre) | 34 | 13 | 12 | 9 | 48 | 30 | 38 | |
| 6. | US de Toulouse (Toulouse) | 34 | 15 | 7 | 12 | 72 | 60 | 37 | |
| 7. | AS d'Angoulême (Angoulême) | 34 | 16 | 5 | 13 | 50 | 46 | 37 | |
| 8. | AS Biterroise (Béziers) | 34 | 14 | 9 | 11 | 41 | 50 | 37 | |
| 9. | Red Star FC (Saint-Ouen) | 34 | 14 | 8 | 12 | 51 | 47 | 36 | |
| 10. | FC de Martigues (Martigues) | 34 | 14 | 7 | 13 | 51 | 47 | 35 | |
| 11. | AS de Cannes (Cannes) | 34 | 14 | 7 | 13 | 48 | 33 | 35 | |
| 12. | Paris FC (Paris) | 34 | 12 | 10 | 12 | 49 | 33 | 34 | |
| 13. | Entente Bagneaux-Fontainebleau-Nemours (Font.) | 34 | 13 | 4 | 17 | 40 | 41 | 30 | |
| 14. | AC Arlésien (Arles) | 34 | 9 | 12 | 13 | 37 | 50 | 30 | |
| 15. | Gazélec FC Ajaccien (Ajaccio) | 34 | 9 | 11 | 14 | 33 | 47 | 29 | |
| 16. | FC de Bourges (Bourges) | 34 | 6 | 9 | 19 | 29 | 56 | 21 | R |
| 17. | US Tavaux-Damparis (Tavaux) | 34 | 7 | 7 | 20 | 38 | 69 | 21 | R |
| 18. | FC de Sète (Sète) | 34 | 5 | 5 | 24 | 26 | 89 | 15 | R |
| | | 612 | 229 | 154 | 229 | 833 | 826 | 612 | |

| | **Division 2 (Group "B")** | **Pd** | **Wn** | **Dw** | **Ls** | **GF** | **GA** | **Pts** | |
|---|---|---|---|---|---|---|---|---|---|
| 1. | Racing Club de Strasbourg (Strasbourg) | 34 | 23 | 3 | 8 | 84 | 26 | 49 | P |
| 2. | FC de Rouen (Rouen) | 34 | 17 | 10 | 7 | 62 | 39 | 44 | PO |
| 3. | FC de Tours (Tours) | 34 | 14 | 11 | 9 | 58 | 44 | 39 | |
| 4. | Amicale de Lucé (Lucé) | 34 | 14 | 9 | 11 | 47 | 43 | 37 | |
| 5. | Stade Quimperois (Quimper) | 34 | 15 | 6 | 13 | 48 | 44 | 36 | |
| 6. | Racing Club Franc-Comtois (Besançon) | 34 | 14 | 8 | 12 | 45 | 43 | 36 | |
| 7. | Stade Athlétique Spinalien (Epinal) | 34 | 13 | 9 | 12 | 44 | 50 | 35 | |
| 8. | La Berrichone (Châteauroux) | 34 | 13 | 8 | 13 | 41 | 42 | 34 | |
| 9. | US Noeuxoise (Noeux-les-Mines) | 34 | 11 | 11 | 12 | 31 | 31 | 33 | |
| 10. | Stade Brestois (Brest) | 34 | 12 | 8 | 14 | 39 | 44 | 32 | |
| 11. | Entente Chaumontaise AC (Chaumont) | 34 | 13 | 6 | 15 | 44 | 65 | 32 | |
| 12. | US Dunkerquoise (Dunkerque) | 34 | 9 | 13 | 12 | 42 | 47 | 31 | |
| 13. | Sports Réunis Déodatiens (Saint-Dié) | 34 | 11 | 8 | 15 | 36 | 40 | 30 | |
| 14. | US du Grand Boulogne (Boulogne-sur-Mer) | 34 | 11 | 8 | 15 | 36 | 40 | 30 | |
| 15. | Stade Malherbe Caennais (Caen) | 34 | 11 | 8 | 15 | 43 | 51 | 30 | |
| 16. | FC de Lorient (Lorient) | 34 | 9 | 10 | 15 | 36 | 46 | 28 | R |
| 17. | Amiens SC (Amiens) | 34 | 9 | 10 | 15 | 36 | 56 | 28 | R |
| 18. | SC d'Hazebrouck (Hazebrouck) | 34 | 9 | 9 | 16 | 35 | 48 | 27 | R |
| | | 612 | 228 | 155 | 229 | 807 | 799 | 611 | |

## Promotion Play-Off

FC de Gueugnon (Gueugnon)      2-1, 0-3      FC de Rouen (Rouen)

## Coupe de France Final    (Parc des Princes, Paris – 18/06/77 – 45,454)

### AS DE SAINT-Étienne (ST-Étienne)      **2-1**      Stade de Reims (Reims)

*Bathenay 85' pen, Merchadier 89'*      *Santamaria 63'*

**Saint-Étienne**: Curkovic, Merchadier, Farison, Piazza, Lopez, Bathenay, Rocheteau, Santini, Revelli, Janvion, Revelli.

**Reims**: Laudu, Masclaux, Buisset, Durand, Dubouil, Ravier, Santamaria, Polaniok, Maufroy (Giannetta 74'), Betta, Ducuing.

## Semi-Finals    (11-14/06/77)

| FC de Nantes (Nantes) | 3-0, 1-5 (aet) | AS de Saint-Étienne (Saint-Étienne) |
|---|---|---|
| Olympique GC de Nice (Nice) | 1-2, 0-1 | Stade de Reims (Reims) |

## Quarter-Finals    (12-17/05/77)

| Racing Club de Lens (Lens) | 2-1, 0-1 | FC de Nantes (Nantes) |
|---|---|---|
| FC de Lorient (Lorient) | 2-0, 2-8 | Stade de Reims (Reims) |
| Nîmes Olympique (Nîmes) | 3-3, 0-2 | Olympique GC de Nice (Nice) |
| FC Sochaux-Montbéliard (Montbéliard) | 1-1, 1-3 | AS de Saint-Étienne (Saint-Étienne) |

# 1977-78

| 1977-1978 Division One | SE Club Bastiais | Gir. de Bordeaux | Stade Lavallois | Racing de Lens | Olymp. Lyonnais | Olymp. Marseille | FC de Metz | AS de Monaco | Nancy-Lorraine | FC de Nantes | Olymp. GC Nice | Nîmes Olympique | Paris St Germain | Stade de Reims | FC de Rouen | AS Saint-Étienne | Sochaux-Montbél. | RC Strasbourg | Troyes Aube | Valenciennes |
|---|---|---|---|---|---|---|---|---|---|---|---|---|---|---|---|---|---|---|---|---|
| Sporting Étoile Club Bastiais | ■ | 1-2 | 1-0 | 3-1 | 2-1 | 2-0 | 2-0 | 0-2 | 1-0 | 0-0 | 4-1 | 2-1 | 5-3 | 3-0 | 3-2 | 2-0 | 0-0 | 3-1 | 6-0 | 3-0 |
| Girondins de Bordeaux | 1-0 | ■ | 1-1 | 0-1 | 1-4 | 1-2 | 1-0 | 0-4 | 2-0 | 1-0 | 0-1 | 4-4 | 1-2 | 2-0 | 4-0 | 2-2 | 1-1 | 3-0 | 1-1 | 2-0 |
| Stade Lavallois | 0-1 | 2-1 | ■ | 3-0 | 1-0 | 2-1 | 3-0 | 0-0 | 1-2 | 1-1 | 2-0 | 2-1 | 1-2 | 2-0 | 3-0 | 1-0 | 3-1 | 2-3 | 2-1 | 3-1 |
| Racing de Lens | 3-4 | 2-0 | 1-1 | ■ | 2-3 | 3-2 | 1-2 | 2-3 | 1-0 | 0-1 | 3-1 | 4-1 | 3-1 | 3-1 | 5-1 | 2-0 | 1-3 | 2-2 | 3-2 | 0-2 |
| Olympique Lyonnais | 2-1 | 1-1 | 5-0 | 2-0 | ■ | 4-2 | 4-1 | 1-1 | 1-3 | 1-0 | 1-1 | 3-1 | 3-2 | 0-1 | 4-0 | 2-2 | 0-2 | 1-1 | 0-0 | 0-1 |
| Olympique Marseille | 2-0 | 4-0 | 0-1 | 4-0 | 4-0 | ■ | 2-0 | 2-2 | 1-1 | 2-2 | 2-0 | 1-1 | 2-1 | 2-1 | 2-0 | 3-0 | 4-0 | 1-0 | 0-1 | 3-0 |
| FC de Metz | 0-0 | 5-0 | 1-0 | 2-1 | 1-0 | 0-4 | ■ | 2-1 | 3-0 | 2-2 | 2-0 | 3-0 | 2-1 | 2-1 | 4-1 | 0-2 | 1-1 | 0-0 | 0-0 | 1-1 |
| AS de Monaco | 2-1 | 3-2 | 4-0 | 3-0 | 3-1 | 2-3 | 4-0 | ■ | 2-0 | 1-1 | 2-0 | 2-1 | 0-0 | 2-0 | 6-1 | 3-1 | 2-1 | 3-2 | 1-1 | 3-2 |
| Nancy-Lorraine | 3-0 | 4-1 | 3-0 | 0-0 | 3-1 | 1-1 | 0-0 | 2-2 | ■ | 3-0 | 1-1 | 2-2 | 4-1 | 4-1 | 1-0 | 2-1 | 1-1 | 3-1 | 1-0 | 2-2 |
| FC de Nantes | 2-0 | 4-1 | 3-1 | 2-0 | 2-0 | 1-0 | 2-0 | 1-0 | 2-0 | ■ | 6-1 | 3-1 | 3-1 | 3-1 | 0-0 | 1-0 | 2-0 | 1-1 | 3-0 | 4-1 |
| Olympique GC Nice | 3-1 | 5-3 | 4-2 | 5-4 | 3-1 | 1-1 | 1-1 | 1-1 | 3-7 | 1-0 | ■ | 3-1 | 2-3 | 4-2 | 6-1 | 2-1 | 4-2 | 0-1 | 4-1 | 0-2 |
| Nîmes Olympique | 2-0 | 3-1 | 1-0 | 2-1 | 3-0 | 2-1 | 2-0 | 3-4 | 1-0 | 0-0 | 1-1 | ■ | 2-1 | 1-0 | 3-2 | 0-0 | 1-1 | 0-1 | 1-1 | 1-2 |
| Paris Saint-Germain FC | 3-3 | 1-2 | 2-2 | 2-1 | 3-2 | 5-1 | 3-0 | 1-2 | 1-2 | 0-1 | 0-3 | 5-0 | ■ | 2-2 | 3-1 | 4-1 | 3-1 | 2-2 | 7-2 | 2-0 |
| Stade de Reims | 1-3 | 1-0 | 3-1 | 0-0 | 2-1 | 0-0 | 0-0 | 0-2 | 4-1 | 1-3 | 0-0 | 2-1 | 0-0 | ■ | 3-1 | 0-0 | 1-1 | 0-0 | 5-1 | 3-0 |
| FC de Rouen | 0-0 | 1-2 | 1-1 | 0-0 | 3-2 | 1-4 | 5-2 | 3-4 | 3-2 | 0-0 | 2-0 | 2-0 | 1-3 | 1-2 | ■ | 1-2 | 1-2 | 0-3 | 2-1 | 1-1 |
| AS Saint-Étienne | 0-4 | 5-0 | 1-0 | 0-1 | 1-0 | 2-1 | 2-0 | 1-0 | 2-1 | 2-1 | 1-2 | 2-1 | 1-1 | 2-0 | 2-1 | ■ | 3-1 | 4-3 | 1-0 | 2-1 |
| Sochaux-Montbéliard | 2-0 | 0-0 | 4-1 | 7-2 | 1-0 | 1-2 | 3-0 | 3-2 | 2-0 | 1-1 | 1-2 | 1-1 | 2-1 | 2-3 | 3-0 | 2-3 | ■ | 3-2 | 6-2 | 0-1 |
| RC Strasbourg | 1-1 | 3-0 | 6-2 | 3-0 | 2-2 | 2-1 | 5-1 | 3-0 | 2-0 | 1-0 | 2-1 | 3-0 | 1-1 | 2-1 | 2-0 | 2-0 | 1-1 | ■ | 3-0 | 1-1 |
| Troyes Aube | 1-0 | 1-1 | 0-0 | 0-0 | 0-2 | 0-1 | 0-2 | 3-0 | 2-3 | 1-0 | 3-1 | 2-2 | 3-1 | 3-0 | 3-1 | 1-0 | 1-0 | 0-2 | ■ | 2-1 |
| Valenciennes | 2-0 | 0-1 | 2-3 | 3-3 | 2-1 | 1-2 | 2-1 | 1-1 | 0-1 | 0-2 | 2-4 | 1-1 | 2-1 | 0-0 | 3-0 | 1-1 | 1-2 | 0-0 | 6-1 | ■ |

| Division 1 | | Pd | Wn | Dw | Ls | GF | GA | Pts | |
|---|---|---|---|---|---|---|---|---|---|
| 1. | AS DE MONACO (MONACO) | 38 | 22 | 9 | 7 | 79 | 46 | 53 | |
| 2. | FC de Nantes (Nantes) | 38 | 21 | 10 | 7 | 60 | 26 | 52 | |
| 3. | Racing Club de Strasbourg (Strasbourg) | 38 | 19 | 12 | 7 | 70 | 40 | 50 | |
| 4. | Olympique de Marseille (Marseille) | 38 | 20 | 7 | 11 | 70 | 41 | 47 | |
| 5. | Sporting Étoile Club Bastiais (Bastia) | 38 | 19 | 6 | 13 | 62 | 44 | 44 | |
| 6. | AS Nancy-Lorraine (Nancy) | 38 | 17 | 9 | 12 | 63 | 49 | 43 | |
| 7. | AS de Saint-Étienne (Saint-Étienne) | 38 | 18 | 6 | 14 | 50 | 49 | 42 | |
| 8. | Olympique GC de Nice (Nice) | 38 | 17 | 7 | 14 | 72 | 70 | 41 | |
| 9. | FC Sochaux-Montbéliard (Montbéliard) | 38 | 15 | 10 | 13 | 65 | 54 | 40 | |
| 10. | Stade Lavallois (Laval) | 38 | 15 | 7 | 16 | 50 | 58 | 37 | |
| 11. | Paris Saint-Germain FC (Paris) | 38 | 14 | 8 | 16 | 75 | 66 | 36 | |
| 12. | FC de Metz (Metz) | 38 | 13 | 9 | 16 | 41 | 57 | 35 | |
| 13. | Nîmes Olympique (Nîmes) | 38 | 11 | 11 | 16 | 49 | 63 | 33 | |
| 14. | US Valenciennes-Anzin (Valenciennes) | 38 | 11 | 10 | 17 | 48 | 58 | 32 | |
| 15. | Stade de Reims (Reims) | 38 | 11 | 10 | 17 | 42 | 55 | 32 | |
| 16. | Girondins de Bordeaux FC (Bordeaux) | 38 | 12 | 8 | 18 | 46 | 69 | 32 | |
| 17. | Olympique Lyonnais (Lyon) | 38 | 12 | 7 | 19 | 56 | 59 | 31 | |
| 18. | Racing Club de Lens (Lens) | 38 | 12 | 7 | 19 | 56 | 71 | 31 | R |
| 19. | Troyes Aube Football (Troyes) | 38 | 11 | 9 | 18 | 41 | 69 | 31 | R |
| 20. | FC de Rouen (Rouen) | 38 | 6 | 6 | 26 | 40 | 91 | 18 | R |
| | | 760 | 296 | 168 | 296 | 1135 | 1135 | 760 | |

## Top goal-scorers

| 1) | Carlos BIANCHI | (Paris Saint-Germain FC) | 37 |
|---|---|---|---|
| 2) | Nenad BJEKOVIC | (Olympique GC de Nice) | 29 |
| | Dellio ONNIS | (AS de Monaco) | 29 |

## Division 2 Play-Off

SC de l'Ouest Angers (Angers)          2-1,  3-5                          Lille Olympique SC (Lille)

| Division 2 (Group "A") | | Pd | Wn | Dw | Ls | GF | GA | Pts | |
|---|---|---|---|---|---|---|---|---|---|
| 1. | SC de l'Ouest Angers (Angers) | 34 | 21 | 7 | 6 | 50 | 27 | 49 | P |
| 2. | Racing Club Franc-Comtois (Besançon) | 34 | 19 | 8 | 7 | 52 | 26 | 46 | PO |
| 3. | SC de Toulon (Toulon) | 34 | 18 | 7 | 9 | 61 | 32 | 43 | |
| 4. | Association de la Jeunesse Auxerroise (Auxerre) | 34 | 17 | 7 | 10 | 49 | 36 | 41 | |
| 5. | AS de Cannes (Cannes) | 34 | 15 | 10 | 9 | 50 | 40 | 40 | |
| 6. | Stade Athlétique Spinalien (Epinal) | 34 | 13 | 13 | 8 | 42 | 40 | 39 | |
| 7. | FC de Martigues (Martigues) | 34 | 16 | 5 | 13 | 49 | 37 | 37 | |
| 8. | Olympique Avignonnais (Avignon) | 34 | 12 | 9 | 13 | 43 | 36 | 33 | |
| 9. | Gazélec FC Ajaccien (Ajaccio) | 34 | 12 | 9 | 13 | 42 | 55 | 33 | |
| 10. | Entente Chaumontaise AC (Chaumont) | 34 | 10 | 11 | 13 | 51 | 51 | 31 | |
| 11. | Sports Réunis Déodatiens (Saint-Dié) | 34 | 12 | 7 | 15 | 30 | 44 | 31 | |
| 12. | Olympique d'Alès en Cévennes (Alès) | 34 | 11 | 8 | 15 | 59 | 55 | 30 | |
| 13. | US Melunaise (Melun) | 34 | 10 | 10 | 14 | 33 | 39 | 30 | |
| 14. | AC Arlésien (Arles) | 34 | 8 | 14 | 12 | 33 | 41 | 30 | |
| 15. | AS Biterroise (Béziers) | 34 | 8 | 14 | 12 | 26 | 35 | 30 | |
| 16. | US de Toulouse (Toulouse) | 34 | 9 | 12 | 13 | 36 | 53 | 30 | |
| 17. | Sports Réunis d'Haguenau (Haguenau) | 34 | 7 | 7 | 20 | 23 | 52 | 21 | R |
| 18. | Entente Bagneaux-Fontainebleau-Nemours Font.) | 34 | 5 | 8 | 21 | 25 | 55 | 18 | R |
| | | 612 | 223 | 166 | 223 | 754 | 754 | 612 | |

| Division 2 (Group "B") | Pd | Wn | Dw | Ls | GF | GA | Pts | |
|---|---|---|---|---|---|---|---|---|
| 1. Lille Olympique SC (Lille) | 34 | 21 | 9 | 4 | 75 | 28 | 51 | P |
| 2. Paris FC (Paris) | 34 | 20 | 9 | 5 | 71 | 25 | 49 | PO |
| 3. Red Star FC (Saint-Ouen) | 34 | 20 | 7 | 7 | 58 | 33 | 47 | * |
| 4. US Dunkerquoise (Dunkerque) | 34 | 17 | 9 | 8 | 66 | 34 | 43 | |
| 5. FC de Tours (Tours) | 34 | 17 | 7 | 10 | 58 | 44 | 41 | |
| 6. FC de Gueugnon (Gueugnon) | 34 | 16 | 8 | 10 | 52 | 39 | 40 | |
| 7. AS d'Angoulême (Angoulême) | 34 | 12 | 12 | 10 | 46 | 36 | 36 | * |
| 8. Amicale de Lucé (Lucé) | 34 | 11 | 13 | 10 | 26 | 37 | 35 | |
| 9. La Berrichonne (Châteauroux) | 34 | 10 | 13 | 11 | 37 | 38 | 33 | |
| 10. Stade Brestois (Brest) | 34 | 11 | 11 | 12 | 41 | 48 | 33 | |
| 11. US du Grand Boulogne (Boulogne-sur-Mer) | 34 | 9 | 11 | 14 | 37 | 49 | 29 | |
| 12. Stade Rennais FC (Rennes) | 34 | 9 | 10 | 15 | 43 | 56 | 28 | |
| 13. Stade Quimperois (Quimper) | 34 | 7 | 14 | 13 | 32 | 45 | 28 | |
| 14. En Avant de Guingamp (Guingamp) | 34 | 9 | 10 | 15 | 32 | 57 | 28 | |
| 15. Limoges FC (Limoges) | 34 | 7 | 13 | 14 | 30 | 44 | 27 | |
| 16. Amicale Sportive de Poissy (Poissy) | 34 | 6 | 10 | 18 | 23 | 47 | 22 | R |
| 17. US Noeuxoise (Noeux-les-Mines) | 34 | 6 | 10 | 18 | 26 | 55 | 22 | R |
| 18. Stade Malherbe Caennais (Caen) | 34 | 6 | 8 | 20 | 29 | 66 | 20 | R |
| | 612 | 214 | 184 | 214 | 782 | 781 | 612 | |

## Promotion Play-Off

Paris FC (Paris)                      3-1, 3-2          Racing Club Franc-Comtois (Besançon)

* AS d'Angoulême (Angoulême) changed their name to AS Angoulême-Charentes (Angoulême) for the next season; Red Star FC (Saint-Ouen) dissolved and reformed as amateur club AS Red Star (Saint-Ouen) for the next season.

## Coupe de France Final   (Parc des Princes, Paris – 13/05/78 – 45,998)

### AS NANCY-LORRAINE (NANCY)          1-0          Olympique GC de Nice (Nice)
*Platini 57'*

**Nancy**: Moutier, Perdrieau (Raczynski 79'), Cloet, Neubert, Curbelo, Jeannol, Rouyer, Caron, Platini, Rubio, Chebel.

**Nice**: Baratelli, Zambelli, Morabito, Barraja, Katalinski, Jouve, Sanchez, Huck, Bjekovic, Guillou, Cappadona ("Toko" 75').

## Semi-Finals   (05-08/05/78)

| | | |
|---|---|---|
| Olympique GC de Nice (Nice) | 1-0,  1-1 | AS de Monaco (Monaco) |
| FC Sochaux-Montbéliard (Montbéliard) | 1-0,  0-5 | AS Nancy-Lorraine (Nancy) |

## Quarter-Finals   (15-18/04/78)

| | | |
|---|---|---|
| Sporting Étoile Club Bastiais (Bastia) | 2-1,  0-2 | AS de Monaco (Monaco) |
| Olympique GC de Nice (Nice) | 4-1,  0-1 | FC de Nantes (Nantes) |
| FC Sochaux-Montbéliard (Montbéliard) | 0-0,  1-0 | Olympique de Marseille (Marseille) |
| US Valenciennes-Anzin (Valenciennes) | 0-0,  0-3 | AS Nancy-Lorraine (Nancy) |

# 1978-79

| 1978-1979 Division One | SC de Angers | SE Bastiais | Gir. de Bordeaux | Stade Lavallois | Lille Olympique | Olymp. Lyonnais | Olymp. Marseille | FC de Metz | AS de Monaco | Nancy-Lorraine | FC de Nantes | Olymp. GC Nice | Nîmes Olymp. | Paris FC | Paris St.Germain | Stade de Reims | AS Saint-Étienne | Sochaux-Mont. | RC Strasbourg | Valenciennes |
|---|---|---|---|---|---|---|---|---|---|---|---|---|---|---|---|---|---|---|---|---|
| SC de l'Ouest Angers | | 0-2 | 0-0 | 1-1 | 1-1 | 1-1 | 1-1 | 3-1 | 2-2 | 2-1 | 1-1 | 1-1 | 2-1 | 0-0 | 2-2 | 3-0 | 1-3 | 3-2 | 1-2 | 1-0 |
| Sporting Étoile Club Bastiais | 1-0 | | 1-1 | 2-2 | 0-0 | 1-0 | 1-3 | 1-3 | 4-1 | 5-1 | 1-0 | 5-2 | 1-0 | 5-1 | 1-2 | 3-2 | 0-2 | 3-0 | 1-1 | 2-0 |
| Girondins de Bordeaux | 2-0 | 2-0 | | 1-1 | 1-1 | 4-1 | 2-1 | 1-2 | 0-2 | 0-0 | 1-1 | 2-0 | 0-0 | 1-2 | 2-0 | 0-0 | 2-1 | 1-1 | 1-1 | 1-0 |
| Stade Lavallois | 1-2 | 0-1 | 3-1 | | 3-3 | 3-1 | 2-1 | 0-1 | 0-3 | 1-4 | 0-5 | 1-2 | 2-2 | 5-1 | 2-1 | 1-0 | 2-1 | 1-1 | 2-2 | 1-1 |
| Lille Olympique SC | 0-0 | 2-2 | 1-1 | 5-3 | | 1-1 | 2-0 | 1-1 | 4-2 | 4-3 | 1-3 | 4-0 | 1-1 | 4-2 | 3-1 | 4-0 | 3-0 | 4-2 | 1-2 | 2-1 |
| Olympique Lyonnais | 3-0 | 1-1 | 0-1 | 1-0 | 4-0 | | 1-1 | 3-1 | 1-0 | 2-1 | 0-3 | 4-0 | 3-1 | 2-1 | 4-2 | 1-1 | 2-0 | 1-0 | 0-3 | 3-0 |
| Olympique Marseille | 0-3 | 1-0 | 0-0 | 0-0 | 1-1 | 2-2 | | 2-3 | 1-2 | 3-2 | 1-1 | 0-0 | 2-0 | 1-1 | 4-1 | 1-0 | 2-0 | 2-2 | 1-0 | 1-0 |
| FC de Metz | 1-0 | 3-1 | 1-0 | 5-1 | 4-4 | 1-2 | 2-1 | | 1-1 | 3-1 | 1-3 | 2-0 | 3-0 | 5-1 | 2-1 | 4-1 | 1-0 | 1-0 | 1-2 | 1-0 |
| AS de Monaco | 3-0 | 6-0 | 2-2 | 2-2 | 2-1 | 0-0 | 1-2 | 4-1 | | 1-3 | 2-1 | 6-1 | 1-0 | 2-1 | 2-1 | 3-0 | 0-1 | 1-1 | 0-2 | 2-2 |
| Nancy-Lorraine | 2-2 | 5-1 | 4-1 | 2-3 | 3-1 | 1-1 | 5-0 | 1-1 | 1-2 | | 3-2 | 3-1 | 3-0 | 5-1 | 2-1 | 4-0 | 1-1 | 1-2 | 0-0 | 4-0 |
| FC de Nantes | 5-0 | 1-0 | 1-0 | 2-1 | 0-0 | 5-1 | 2-2 | 1-0 | 3-0 | 3-0 | | 5-0 | 4-0 | 2-0 | 1-0 | 2-0 | 3-1 | 4-0 | 3-0 | 4-0 |
| Olympique GC Nice | 3-1 | 2-2 | 2-1 | 2-1 | 1-1 | 4-0 | 4-2 | 5-0 | 1-2 | 2-2 | 1-1 | | 1-2 | 5-0 | 1-3 | 2-0 | 1-1 | 2-1 | 0-0 | 3-4 |
| Nîmes Olympique | 3-0 | 3-2 | 4-2 | 4-0 | 3-2 | 2-2 | 1-2 | 2-0 | 1-0 | 3-0 | 4-2 | 4-1 | | 2-0 | 1-2 | 4-0 | 2-2 | 2-1 | 0-0 | 5-0 |
| Paris FC | 3-0 | 1-1 | 3-1 | 2-2 | 1-1 | 0-0 | 2-1 | 1-2 | 1-7 | 1-1 | 1-2 | 3-0 | 1-0 | | 1-1 | 2-0 | 0-1 | 3-1 | 0-1 | 0-2 |
| Paris Saint-Germain FC | 1-1 | 4-0 | 2-5 | 3-2 | 0-0 | 2-1 | 4-3 | 0-2 | 3-0 | 2-1 | 1-1 | 1-1 | 3-2 | 2-2 | | 3-2 | 1-1 | 3-1 | 2-1 | 2-0 |
| Stade de Reims | 3-1 | 1-1 | 0-0 | 1-1 | 0-0 | 1-2 | 0-0 | 1-2 | 0-2 | 1-3 | 1-4 | 2-2 | 0-0 | 1-2 | 2-0 | | 0-1 | 0-2 | 1-1 | 2-1 |
| AS Saint-Étienne | 4-0 | 2-1 | 1-3 | 3-0 | 5-1 | 3-0 | 1-0 | 1-0 | 4-1 | 3-2 | 3-1 | 5-1 | 2-0 | 6-0 | 4-1 | 2-0 | | 3-1 | 2-0 | 5-0 |
| Sochaux-Montbéliard | 4-0 | 5-0 | 2-0 | 2-1 | 1-1 | 5-1 | 2-2 | 4-0 | 1-2 | 1-2 | 3-1 | 2-1 | 2-2 | 1-0 | 2-1 | 2-1 | 0-0 | | 1-2 | 3-0 |
| RC Strasbourg | 6-0 | 2-0 | 1-1 | 1-1 | 3-0 | 1-0 | 4-1 | 3-0 | 2-1 | 3-0 | 2-1 | 0-0 | 0-0 | 3-0 | 3-0 | 2-2 | 2-1 | 2-1 | | 5-0 |
| Valenciennes | 1-1 | 3-0 | 0-1 | 1-1 | 4-2 | 3-1 | 0-2 | 2-2 | 0-0 | 1-0 | 1-1 | 0-3 | 2-0 | 1-1 | 1-0 | 3-0 | 0-0 | 0-1 | 2-2 | |

| | Division 1 | Pd | Wn | Dw | Ls | GF | GA | Pts | |
|---|---|---|---|---|---|---|---|---|---|
| 1. | RACING CLUB DE STRASBOURG (STRASBOURG) | 38 | 22 | 12 | 4 | 68 | 28 | 56 | |
| 2. | FC de Nantes (Nantes) | 38 | 23 | 8 | 7 | 85 | 33 | 54 | |
| 3. | AS de Saint-Étienne (Saint-Étienne) | 38 | 24 | 6 | 8 | 77 | 34 | 54 | |
| 4. | AS de Monaco (Monaco) | 38 | 18 | 8 | 12 | 70 | 51 | 44 | |
| 5. | FC de Metz (Metz) | 38 | 19 | 6 | 13 | 61 | 56 | 44 | |
| 6. | Lille Olympique SC (Lille) | 38 | 11 | 18 | 9 | 67 | 62 | 40 | |
| 7. | Olympique Lyonnais (Lyon) | 38 | 15 | 10 | 13 | 53 | 56 | 40 | |
| 8. | Nîmes Olympique (Nîmes) | 38 | 15 | 9 | 14 | 61 | 50 | 39 | |
| 9. | FC Sochaux-Montbéliard (Montbéliard) | 38 | 15 | 9 | 14 | 63 | 53 | 39 | |
| 10. | Girondins de Bordeaux FC (Bordeaux) | 38 | 12 | 15 | 11 | 45 | 42 | 39 | |
| 11. | AS Nancy-Lorraine (Nancy) | 38 | 15 | 8 | 15 | 77 | 61 | 38 | |
| 12. | Olympique de Marseille (Marseille) | 38 | 12 | 13 | 13 | 50 | 55 | 37 | |
| 13. | Paris Saint-Germain FC (Paris) | 38 | 14 | 8 | 16 | 59 | 66 | 36 | |
| 14. | Sporting Étoile Club Bastiais (Bastia) | 38 | 13 | 9 | 16 | 53 | 65 | 35 | |
| 15. | Olympique GC de Nice (Nice) | 38 | 11 | 10 | 17 | 58 | 75 | 32 | |
| 16. | Stade Lavallois (Laval) | 38 | 8 | 14 | 16 | 53 | 73 | 30 | |
| 17. | SC de l'Ouest Angers (Angers) | 38 | 8 | 14 | 16 | 37 | 68 | 30 | |
| 18. | US Valenciennes-Anzin (Valenciennes) | 38 | 9 | 10 | 19 | 36 | 65 | 28 | R* |
| 19. | Paris FC (Paris) | 38 | 9 | 10 | 19 | 42 | 77 | 28 | R* |
| 20. | Stade de Reims (Reims) | 38 | 3 | 11 | 24 | 26 | 71 | 17 | R |
| | | 760 | 276 | 208 | 276 | 1141 | 1141 | 760 | |

## Top goal-scorers

| 1) | Carlos BIANCHI | (Paris Saint-Germain FC) | 27 |
|----|----------------|--------------------------|-----|
| 2) | Dellio ONNIS | (AS de Monaco) | 22 |
| | Eric PÉCOUT | (FC de Nantes) | 22 |

* FC de Gueugnon refused promotion after the FFF turned down their application to stay an amateur club. As a result of this US Valenciennes-Anzin retained their Division 1 status and Paris FC were involved in a promotion/relegation play-off against Racing Club de Lens.

## Promotion/Relegation Play-Off

Paris FC (Paris)  0-0,  0-0 (aet)  Racing Club de Lens (Lens)
Paris FC (Paris) won 3-0 on penalties.

## Division 2 Play-Off

FC de Gueugnon (Gueugnon)  1-0,  2-1  Stade Brestois (Brest)

| | Division 2 (Group "A") | Pd | Wn | Dw | Ls | GF | GA | Pts | |
|-----|---------------------------------------------|-----|-----|-----|-----|-----|-----|-----|-----|
| 1. | FC de Gueugnon (Gueugnon) | 34 | 18 | 10 | 6 | 68 | 40 | 46 | * |
| 2. | Olympique Avignonnais (Avignon) | 34 | 19 | 8 | 7 | 47 | 27 | 46 | PO |
| 3. | AS Biterroise (Béziers) | 34 | 19 | 5 | 10 | 55 | 31 | 43 | |
| 4. | Association de la Jeunesse Auxerroise (Auxerre) | 34 | 19 | 4 | 11 | 56 | 38 | 42 | |
| 5. | Racing Club Franc-Comtois (Besançon) | 34 | 18 | 6 | 10 | 45 | 28 | 42 | |
| 6. | Montpellier Paillade SC (Montpellier) | 34 | 17 | 6 | 11 | 57 | 43 | 40 | |
| 7. | FC de Martigues (Martigues) | 34 | 16 | 5 | 13 | 62 | 49 | 37 | |
| 8. | AS de Cannes (Cannes) | 34 | 13 | 10 | 11 | 38 | 40 | 36 | |
| 9. | Étoile des Sports Montluçonnais (Montluçon) | 34 | 10 | 13 | 11 | 36 | 35 | 33 | |
| 10. | Entente Chaumontaise AC (Chaumont) | 34 | 10 | 13 | 11 | 36 | 49 | 33 | |
| 11. | US de Toulouse (Toulouse) | 34 | 13 | 7 | 14 | 42 | 53 | 33 | |
| 12. | SC de Toulon (Toulon) | 34 | 12 | 6 | 16 | 42 | 43 | 30 | |
| 13. | Sports Réunis Déodatiens (Saint-Dié) | 34 | 10 | 10 | 14 | 33 | 41 | 30 | |
| 14. | Olympique d'Alès en Cévenne (Alès) | 34 | 12 | 4 | 18 | 41 | 51 | 28 | |
| 15. | Gazélec FC Ajaccien (Ajaccio) | 34 | 11 | 6 | 17 | 36 | 53 | 28 | |
| 16. | Stade Athlétique Spinalien (Epinal) | 34 | 9 | 7 | 18 | 40 | 52 | 25 | R |
| 17. | Troyes Aube Football (Troyes) | 34 | 7 | 10 | 17 | 33 | 44 | 24 | R |
| 18. | AC Arlésien (Arles) | 34 | 5 | 6 | 23 | 24 | 72 | 16 | R |
| | | 612 | 238 | 136 | 238 | 791 | 789 | 612 | |

| Division 2 (Group "B") | Pd | Wn | Dw | Ls | GF | GA | Pts | |
|---|---|---|---|---|---|---|---|---|
| 1. Stade Brestois (Brest) | 34 | 25 | 4 | 5 | 69 | 22 | 54 | P |
| 2. Racing Club de Lens (Lens) | 34 | 21 | 9 | 4 | 74 | 26 | 51 | PO |
| 3. US Dunkerquoise (Dunkerque) | 34 | 17 | 12 | 5 | 51 | 29 | 46 | |
| 4. FC de Tours (Tours) | 34 | 15 | 13 | 6 | 53 | 39 | 43 | |
| 5. FC de Rouen (Rouen) | 34 | 13 | 11 | 10 | 52 | 44 | 37 | |
| 6. Limoges FC (Limoges) | 34 | 14 | 9 | 11 | 37 | 32 | 37 | |
| 7. En Avant de Guingamp (Guingamp) | 34 | 12 | 12 | 10 | 35 | 39 | 36 | |
| 8. Stade Rennais FC (Rennes) | 34 | 13 | 10 | 11 | 43 | 33 | 36 | |
| 9. US Orléans Football (Orléans) | 34 | 13 | 8 | 13 | 35 | 42 | 34 | |
| 10. La Berrichonne (Châteauroux) | 34 | 11 | 11 | 12 | 32 | 36 | 33 | |
| 11. Amicale de Lucé (Lucé) | 34 | 13 | 6 | 15 | 41 | 45 | 32 | |
| 12. AS Angoulême-Charentes (Angoulême) | 34 | 9 | 13 | 12 | 33 | 36 | 31 | |
| 13. FC de Mulhouse 1893 (Mulhouse) | 34 | 11 | 7 | 16 | 33 | 43 | 29 | |
| 14. Stade Quimperois (Quimper) | 34 | 11 | 7 | 16 | 46 | 56 | 29 | |
| 15. Association Amicale de la Jeunesse Blésoise (Blois) | 34 | 9 | 10 | 15 | 39 | 57 | 28 | |
| 16. US du Grand Boulogne (Boulogne-sur-Mer) | 34 | 7 | 7 | 20 | 33 | 53 | 21 | R |
| 17. US Melunaise (Melun) | 34 | 6 | 6 | 22 | 28 | 63 | 18 | R |
| 18. Amiens SC (Amiens) | 34 | 3 | 11 | 20 | 28 | 66 | 17 | R |
| | 612 | 223 | 166 | 223 | 762 | 761 | 612 | |

## Promotion Play-Off

| Olympique Avignonnais (Avignon) | 2-0, 1-4 | Racing Club de Lens (Lens)(aet) |
|---|---|---|

## Coupe de France Final  (Parc des Princes, Paris – 16/06/79 – 46,070)

**FC DE NANTES (NANTES)**　　　　**4-1 (aet)**　　Association de la Jeunesse Auxerroise

*Pécout 11', 104', 120', Muller 113'*　　　　　　　　　　　　　　　　　*Mesones 49'*

**Nantes:** Bertrand-Demanes, Bossis, Tusseau, Rio (Denoueix 85'), Michel, Sahnoun, Trossero (Baronchelli 61'), Muller, Pécout, Rampillon, Amisse.

**Auxerroise:** Szeja, Denis, Borel, Roque, Noel, Cuperly, Klose, Brot, Schaer (Truffaut 78'), Mesones, Delancray (Hallet 106').

## Semi-Finals　　(06-09/06/79)

| Association de la Jeunesse Auxerroise | 0-0, 2-2 | Racing Club de Strasbourg (Strasbourg) |
|---|---|---|
| FC de Nantes (Nantes) | 6-2, 1-1 | AS Angoulême-Charentes (Angoulême) |

## Quarter-Finals

| AS Angoulême-Charentes (Angoulême) | 1-0, 1-0 | Olympique Avignonnais (Avignon) |
|---|---|---|
| Association de la Jeunesse Auxerroise | 0-0, 2-1 | Lille Olympique SC (Lille) |
| FC de Gueugnon (Gueugnon) | 0-6, 0-2 | Racing Club de Strasbourg (Strasbourg) |
| FC de Nantes (Nantes) | 3-1, 2-4 | Olympique de Marseille (Marseille) |

# 1979-80

| 1979-1980 Division One | SC de Angers | SE Club Bastiais | Gir. de Bordeaux | Stade Brestois | Stade Lavallois | Racing de Lens | Lille Olympique | Olymp. Lyonnais | Olymp. Marseille | FC de Metz | AS de Monaco | Nancy-Lorraine | FC de Nantes | Olymp. GC Nice | Nîmes Olymp. | Paris St.Germain | AS Saint-Étienne | Sochaux-Mont. | RC Strasbourg | Valenciennes |
|---|---|---|---|---|---|---|---|---|---|---|---|---|---|---|---|---|---|---|---|---|
| SC de l'Ouest Angers | | 3-1 | 3-0 | 2-0 | 3-1 | 2-1 | 2-0 | 1-1 | 3-1 | 2-0 | 1-4 | 1-0 | 0-1 | 2-3 | 0-1 | 1-2 | 0-2 | 1-3 | 1-0 | 2-1 |
| Sporting Étoile Club Bastiais | 1-1 | | 2-1 | 1-0 | 2-1 | 1-2 | 4-0 | 2-0 | 2-0 | 0-1 | 2-0 | 2-2 | 1-0 | 3-0 | 2-0 | 1-0 | 0-1 | 0-1 | 2-1 | 2-1 |
| Girondins de Bordeaux | 2-1 | 2-1 | | 4-1 | 4-1 | 1-1 | 1-1 | 3-0 | 2-0 | 1-3 | 3-1 | 4-1 | 1-3 | 3-1 | 2-1 | 0-1 | 5-1 | 2-3 | 1-3 | 7-0 |
| Stade Brestois | 0-1 | 3-0 | 0-1 | | 2-2 | 0-0 | 1-1 | 5-1 | 7-2 | 1-3 | 1-2 | 3-3 | 0-1 | 1-0 | 2-2 | 0-4 | 0-2 | 1-2 | 2-5 | 1-5 |
| Stade Lavallois | 3-2 | 3-0 | 1-0 | 3-0 | | 0-0 | 2-0 | 1-2 | 3-0 | 3-2 | 0-2 | 0-1 | 0-2 | 3-0 | 3-1 | 3-1 | 2-3 | 3-3 | 0-0 | 3-0 |
| Racing de Lens | 2-0 | 2-0 | 2-1 | 3-0 | 1-0 | | 5-3 | 1-1 | 4-1 | 4-1 | 0-3 | 4-0 | 1-3 | 0-1 | 1-0 | 1-1 | 4-3 | 2-0 | 1-1 | 1-1 |
| Lille Olympique SC | 0-0 | 2-0 | 0-1 | 1-0 | 2-0 | 0-0 | | 1-0 | 1-1 | 3-0 | 3-1 | 2-0 | 1-1 | 4-3 | 4-0 | 4-2 | 0-2 | 1-1 | 2-0 | 0-1 |
| Olympique Lyonnais | 0-1 | 1-1 | 1-1 | 3-0 | 2-0 | 1-1 | 4-2 | | 1-0 | 1-0 | 0-1 | 2-1 | 1-2 | 2-2 | 2-1 | 1-1 | 0-0 | 3-1 | 0-2 | 3-1 |
| Olympique Marseille | 3-1 | 2-1 | 1-1 | 3-0 | 0-2 | 3-1 | 2-0 | 3-1 | | 1-0 | 0-3 | 2-2 | 0-1 | 3-1 | 0-1 | 0-2 | 3-5 | 1-1 | 1-3 | 3-6 |
| FC de Metz | 0-1 | 0-2 | 1-1 | 0-0 | 1-4 | 2-1 | 2-0 | 5-2 | 3-2 | | 0-0 | 2-1 | 0-0 | 2-0 | 0-0 | 5-2 | 1-2 | 0-0 | 0-0 | 1-0 |
| AS de Monaco | 3-0 | 1-0 | 0-0 | 4-0 | 2-1 | 2-0 | 0-1 | 4-0 | 1-0 | 3-0 | | 3-0 | 2-1 | 0-0 | 2-2 | 2-1 | 0-1 | 4-1 | 0-1 | 0-1 |
| Nancy-Lorraine | 1-0 | 3-1 | 3-1 | 5-1 | 2-1 | 1-1 | 1-0 | 5-0 | 0-1 | 2-1 | 2-1 | | 0-2 | 1-2 | 1-0 | 3-2 | 1-1 | 1-2 | 3-4 | 1-0 |
| FC de Nantes | 3-1 | 1-0 | 4-1 | 3-0 | 4-1 | 3-0 | 1-0 | 3-0 | 4-1 | 4-1 | 0-0 | 2-0 | | 5-0 | 4-1 | 4-2 | 2-0 | 3-2 | 2-1 | 0-0 |
| Olympique GC Nice | 0-0 | 2-1 | 0-0 | 3-0 | 0-1 | 1-0 | 0-0 | 3-1 | 0-3 | 4-2 | 1-2 | 1-1 | 1-2 | | 1-2 | 3-0 | 2-4 | 1-2 | 6-1 | 2-0 |
| Nîmes Olympique | 1-1 | 2-0 | 2-0 | 2-0 | 2-0 | 2-1 | 3-2 | 3-2 | 0-0 | 1-1 | 4-2 | 2-1 | 0-1 | 1-2 | | 2-0 | 0-1 | 2-0 | 0-0 | 1-1 |
| Paris Saint-Germain FC | 1-1 | 1-1 | 0-1 | 0-0 | 3-1 | 3-0 | 2-2 | 2-1 | 2-1 | 2-0 | 2-1 | 1-2 | 1-0 | 2-2 | 4-0 | | 2-2 | 3-1 | 1-0 | 3-0 |
| AS Saint-Étienne | 3-3 | 2-0 | 3-3 | 2-1 | 3-1 | 3-1 | 0-0 | 2-0 | 3-1 | 2-1 | 2-1 | 2-2 | 4-2 | 2-1 | 3-1 | 2-0 | | 2-1 | 2-1 | 0-1 |
| Sochaux-Montbéliard | 4-0 | 3-0 | 2-0 | 7-0 | 2-0 | 3-0 | 3-0 | 3-1 | 3-0 | 4-0 | 1-2 | 5-1 | 1-0 | 2-1 | 2-1 | 1-0 | 4-1 | | 1-1 | 0-1 |
| RC Strasbourg | 4-0 | 1-0 | 4-0 | 2-1 | 0-3 | 0-1 | 3-2 | 3-1 | 1-1 | 3-2 | 1-1 | 1-0 | 2-2 | 2-3 | 1-0 | 2-1 | 1-0 | 0-1 | | 2-1 |
| Valenciennes | 2-1 | 5-0 | 0-3 | 2-1 | 1-1 | 3-1 | 0-0 | 1-1 | 1-0 | 2-2 | 0-0 | 0-1 | 1-0 | 1-0 | 4-1 | 1-1 | 0-0 | 1-1 | 1-1 | |

## Division 1

| | | Pd | Wn | Dw | Ls | GF | GA | Pts | |
|---|---|---|---|---|---|---|---|---|---|
| 1. | FC DE NANTES (NANTES) | 38 | 26 | 5 | 7 | 76 | 30 | 57 | |
| 2. | FC Sochaux-Montbéliard (Montbéliard) | 38 | 24 | 6 | 8 | 77 | 36 | 54 | |
| 3. | AS de Saint-Étienne (Saint-Étienne) | 38 | 23 | 8 | 7 | 73 | 50 | 54 | |
| 4. | AS de Monaco (Monaco) | 38 | 21 | 8 | 9 | 61 | 30 | 50 | |
| 5. | Racing Club de Strasbourg (Strasbourg) | 38 | 17 | 9 | 12 | 58 | 50 | 43 | |
| 6. | Girondins de Bordeaux FC (Bordeaux) | 38 | 16 | 8 | 14 | 64 | 53 | 40 | |
| 7. | Paris Saint-Germain FC (Paris) | 38 | 15 | 10 | 13 | 59 | 52 | 40 | |
| 8. | US Valenciennes-Anzin (Valenciennes) | 38 | 14 | 12 | 12 | 47 | 47 | 40 | |
| 9. | Racing Club de Lens (Lens) | 38 | 14 | 10 | 14 | 51 | 52 | 38 | |
| 10. | Nîmes Olympique (Nîmes) | 38 | 15 | 8 | 15 | 45 | 50 | 38 | |
| 11. | AS Nancy-Lorraine (Nancy) | 38 | 15 | 7 | 16 | 55 | 61 | 37 | |
| 12. | Stade Lavallois FC (Laval) | 38 | 15 | 5 | 18 | 57 | 55 | 35 | |
| 13. | Lille Olympique SC (Lille) | 38 | 12 | 11 | 15 | 45 | 49 | 35 | |
| 14. | SC de l'Ouest Angers (Angers) | 38 | 14 | 7 | 17 | 45 | 55 | 35 | |
| 15. | Olympique GC de Nice (Nice) | 38 | 13 | 6 | 19 | 53 | 62 | 32 | |
| 16. | Sporting Étoile Club Bastiais (Bastia) | 38 | 14 | 4 | 20 | 39 | 51 | 32 | |
| 17. | FC de Metz (Metz) | 38 | 12 | 8 | 18 | 45 | 60 | 32 | |
| 18. | Olympique Lyonnais (Lyon) | 38 | 10 | 9 | 19 | 43 | 65 | 29 | PO |
| 19. | Olympique de Marseille (Marseille) | 38 | 9 | 6 | 23 | 45 | 78 | 24 | R |
| 20. | Stade Brestois (Brest) | 38 | 4 | 7 | 27 | 35 | 87 | 15 | R |
| | | 760 | 303 | 154 | 303 | 1073 | 1073 | 760 | |

## Top goal-scorers

| | | | |
|---|---|---|---|
| 1) | Erwin  KOSTEDDE | (Stade Lavallois FC) | 21 |
| | Dellio  ONNIS | (AS de Monaco) | 21 |
| 3) | Pierre  PLEIMELDING | (Lille Olympique SC) | 18 |

## Promotion/Relegation Play-Offs

| | | |
|---|---|---|
| Olympique Lyonnais (Lyon) | 6-0,  2-4 | Olympique Avignonnais (Avignon) |
| Stade Rennais FC (Rennes) | 0-0,  2-3 | Olympique Avignonnais (Avignon) |

## Division 2 Play-Off

| | | |
|---|---|---|
| Association de la Jeunesse Auxerroise | 4-0,  0-1 | FC de Tours (Tours) |

| | Division 2 (Group "A") | Pd | Wn | Dw | Ls | GF | GA | Pts | |
|---|---|---|---|---|---|---|---|---|---|
| 1. | FC de Tours (Tours) | 34 | 22 | 7 | 5 | 59 | 26 | 51 | P |
| 2. | Stade Rennais FC (Rennes) | 34 | 20 | 6 | 8 | 60 | 30 | 46 | PO |
| 3. | En Avant de Guingamp (Guingamp) | 34 | 19 | 8 | 7 | 53 | 36 | 46 | |
| 4. | Racing Club Franc-Comtois (Besançon) | 34 | 14 | 11 | 9 | 53 | 39 | 39 | |
| 5. | US Noeuxoise (Noeux-les-Mines) | 34 | 16 | 7 | 11 | 45 | 35 | 39 | |
| 6. | Stade de Reims (Reims) | 34 | 14 | 11 | 9 | 41 | 35 | 39 | |
| 7. | Havre AC (Le Havre) | 34 | 15 | 8 | 11 | 45 | 32 | 38 | |
| 8. | FC de Rouen (Rouen) | 34 | 16 | 6 | 12 | 44 | 36 | 38 | |
| 9. | AS Angoulême-Charentes (Angoulême) | 34 | 9 | 18 | 7 | 38 | 24 | 36 | |
| 10. | US Dunkerquoise (Dunkerque) | 34 | 11 | 9 | 14 | 39 | 38 | 31 | |
| 11. | US Orléans Football (Orléans) | 34 | 9 | 12 | 13 | 34 | 44 | 30 | |
| 12. | Stade Quimperois (Quimper) | 34 | 11 | 7 | 16 | 38 | 55 | 29 | |
| 13. | Association Amicale de la Jeunesse Blésoise (Blois) | 34 | 9 | 9 | 16 | 28 | 50 | 27 | |
| 14. | La Berrichone (Châteauroux) | 34 | 8 | 10 | 16 | 42 | 55 | 26 | |
| 15. | Limoges FC (Limoges) | 34 | 8 | 10 | 16 | 30 | 44 | 26 | |
| 16. | Union Étoile Sportive Montmorillonnaise (Montmorillon) | 34 | 8 | 10 | 16 | 37 | 58 | 26 | |
| 17. | Amicale de Lucé (Lucé) | 34 | 8 | 7 | 19 | 30 | 62 | 23 | R |
| 18. | Entente Chaumontaise AC (Chaumont) | 34 | 7 | 8 | 19 | 35 | 53 | 22 | R |
| | | 612 | 224 | 164 | 224 | 751 | 752 | 612 | |

| Division 2 (Group "B") | Pd | Wn | Dw | Ls | GF | GA | Pts | |
|---|---|---|---|---|---|---|---|---|
| 1. Association de la Jeunesse Auxerroise (Auxerre) | 34 | 16 | 12 | 6 | 54 | 30 | 44 | P |
| 2. Olympique Avignonnais (Avignon) | 34 | 20 | 4 | 10 | 54 | 41 | 44 | PO |
| 3. AS de Cannes (Cannes) | 34 | 15 | 10 | 9 | 54 | 36 | 40 | |
| 4. CS de Thonon (Thonon) | 34 | 14 | 11 | 9 | 47 | 37 | 39 | |
| 5. FC de Gueugnon (Gueugnon) | 34 | 12 | 13 | 9 | 54 | 37 | 37 | |
| 6. Toulouse FC (Toulouse) | 34 | 14 | 9 | 11 | 47 | 34 | 37 | * |
| 7. Paris FC (Paris) | 34 | 11 | 15 | 8 | 41 | 34 | 37 | |
| 8. Montpellier Paillade SC (Montpellier) | 34 | 14 | 8 | 12 | 55 | 42 | 36 | |
| 9. AS Biterroise (Béziers) | 34 | 14 | 8 | 12 | 42 | 37 | 36 | |
| 10. FC de Martigues (Martigues) | 34 | 11 | 13 | 10 | 43 | 41 | 35 | |
| 11. Thionville FC (Thionville) | 34 | 10 | 11 | 13 | 38 | 49 | 31 | |
| 12. Étoile des Sports Montluçonnais (Montluçon) | 34 | 9 | 12 | 13 | 34 | 49 | 30 | |
| 13. Gazélec FC Ajaccien (Ajaccio) | 34 | 9 | 12 | 13 | 36 | 56 | 30 | |
| 14. US Tavaux-Damparis (Tamparis) | 34 | 11 | 7 | 16 | 38 | 54 | 29 | |
| 15. Sports Réunis Déodatiens (Saint-Dié) | 34 | 9 | 10 | 15 | 40 | 63 | 28 | |
| 16. FC de Mulhouse 1893 (Mulhouse) | 34 | 8 | 11 | 15 | 34 | 45 | 27 | R |
| 17. SC de Toulon (Toulon) | 34 | 8 | 11 | 15 | 36 | 48 | 27 | R |
| 18. Olympique d'Alès en Cévenne (Alès) | 34 | 8 | 9 | 17 | 37 | 60 | 25 | R |
| | 612 | 213 | 186 | 213 | 784 | 784 | 612 | |

## Coupe de France Final   (Parc des Princes, Paris – 07/06/80 – 46,136)

### AS DE MONACO (MONACO)                    3-1                    US Orléans Football (Orléans)

*Marette 06' (o.g.), Emon 47', Onnis 66'*

**Monaco**: Ettori, Zorzetto, Vitalis, Gardon, Moizan, Christophe, Dalger, Petit, Onnis, Ricort (Miller 55'), Emon (Ninot 78').

**Orléans**: Viot, Drouet, Plissonneau, Bodji, Lemée, Germain, Marlette (Froissart 81'), Albaladéjo, Hamerschmitt (Helbert 81'), Loukaka, Berthouloux.

## Semi-Finals   (30/05/80 – 03/06/80)

| AS de Monaco (Monaco) | 2-1, 4-2 | Montpellier Paillade SC (Montpellier) |
|---|---|---|
| US Orléans Football (Orléans) | 3-1, 1-2 | Paris FC (Paris) |

## Quarter-Finals   (09-13/05/80)

| AS Angoulême-Charentes (Angoulême) | 2-0, 1-5 | US Orléans Football (Orléans) |
|---|---|---|
| Montpellier Paillade SC (Montpellier) | 0-0, 1-1 | AS de Saint-Étienne (Saint-Étienne) |
| Paris FC (Paris) | 1-1, 2-0 | Association de la Jeunesse Auxerroise |
| FC Sochaux-Montbéliard (Montbéliard) | 1-0, 0-1 | AS de Monaco (Monaco) |

# 1980-81

| 1980-1981 Division One | SC de Angers | AJ Auxerroise | SEC Bastiais | Gir. de Bordeaux | Stade Lavallois | Racing de Lens | Lille Olympique | Olymp. Lyonnais | FC de Metz | AS de Monaco | Nancy-Lorraine | FC de Nantes | Olymp. GC Nice | Nîmes Olymp. | Paris St.Germain | AS Saint-Étienne | Sochaux-Mont. | RC Strasbourg | FC de Tours | Valenciennes |
|---|---|---|---|---|---|---|---|---|---|---|---|---|---|---|---|---|---|---|---|---|
| SC de l'Ouest Angers | | 4-1 | 1-0 | 0-3 | 2-0 | 1-2 | 3-2 | 1-3 | 0-0 | 1-1 | 2-0 | 0-3 | 1-1 | 1-2 | 1-1 | 1-1 | 1-2 | 0-0 | 2-2 | 1-1 |
| AJ Auxerroise | 2-2 | | 0-0 | 1-2 | 1-0 | 1-1 | 2-2 | 2-2 | 4-2 | 0-0 | 0-2 | 0-0 | 3-1 | 4-2 | 0-1 | 0-2 | 1-1 | 1-1 | 3-2 | 1-1 |
| Sporting Étoile Club Bastiais | 3-0 | 2-0 | | 3-2 | 2-2 | 3-1 | 5-1 | 2-0 | 1-0 | 1-1 | 2-1 | 1-2 | 3-0 | 3-2 | 2-0 | 2-1 | 1-1 | 2-0 | 0-1 | 1-1 |
| Girondins de Bordeaux | 1-0 | 2-0 | 0-0 | | 2-1 | 5-1 | 2-0 | 3-2 | 1-1 | 1-0 | 2-0 | 0-0 | 3-0 | 1-1 | 1-3 | 3-0 | 0-0 | 2-1 | 1-1 | 4-0 |
| Stade Lavallois | 2-0 | 0-0 | 3-0 | 2-4 | | 3-0 | 4-2 | 0-0 | 1-1 | 3-3 | 1-0 | 2-0 | 0-1 | 4-0 | 0-0 | 0-0 | 0-0 | 3-1 | 2-0 | 2-1 |
| Racing de Lens | 1-0 | 1-1 | 5-0 | 0-1 | 3-0 | | 0-0 | 2-2 | 2-2 | 0-0 | 0-0 | 0-0 | 2-0 | 1-1 | 2-3 | 1-1 | 5-1 | 1-2 | 3-0 | 1-2 |
| Lille Olympique SC | 4-0 | 2-3 | 3-1 | 2-2 | 1-1 | 2-1 | | 1-1 | 0-1 | 2-1 | 0-0 | 0-3 | 3-1 | 0-0 | 2-2 | 1-3 | 2-1 | 3-0 | 1-1 | 1-2 |
| Olympique Lyonnais | 5-1 | 1-3 | 2-1 | 1-0 | 1-0 | 4-1 | 2-2 | | 0-0 | 3-2 | 4-2 | 0-0 | 5-1 | 4-2 | 2-0 | 1-1 | 5-1 | 0-0 | 2-3 | 1-1 |
| FC de Metz | 1-0 | 2-2 | 1-0 | 1-1 | 3-2 | 0-2 | 3-0 | 0-1 | | 1-1 | 2-0 | 2-2 | 0-1 | 2-1 | 0-0 | 0-0 | 4-2 | 4-1 | 2-3 | 4-2 |
| AS de Monaco | 2-0 | 2-1 | 3-0 | 0-0 | 3-0 | 1-0 | 1-2 | 2-1 | 2-1 | | 1-0 | 2-1 | 1-0 | 2-1 | 4-0 | 1-2 | 2-1 | 3-1 | 1-1 | 5-1 |
| Nancy-Lorraine | 2-0 | 3-0 | 3-0 | 2-0 | 3-0 | 1-2 | 2-0 | 3-1 | 2-0 | 2-3 | | 1-0 | 3-2 | 2-0 | 2-2 | 0-0 | 2-2 | 2-0 | 1-3 | 7-1 |
| FC de Nantes | 3-1 | 0-1 | 2-1 | 1-0 | 4-1 | 2-0 | 4-1 | 2-0 | 1-0 | 5-0 | 3-0 | | 4-1 | 1-1 | 1-1 | 2-1 | 2-1 | 1-1 | 4-3 | 3-0 |
| Olympique GC Nice | 2-2 | 0-0 | 2-1 | 1-1 | 2-1 | 1-1 | 1-2 | 3-2 | 0-0 | 2-1 | 2-2 | 3-2 | | 0-0 | 1-1 | 0-1 | 4-2 | 0-0 | 2-2 | 4-0 |
| Nîmes Olympique | 0-0 | 0-0 | 3-2 | 0-2 | 2-2 | 1-1 | 2-1 | 1-2 | 3-3 | 1-3 | 1-2 | 2-3 | 1-3 | | 2-1 | 0-1 | 0-0 | 4-2 | 2-1 | 1-1 |
| Paris Saint-Germain FC | 2-2 | 2-3 | 3-1 | 4-0 | 3-2 | 3-0 | 4-1 | 1-1 | 1-1 | 0-0 | 2-1 | 0-2 | 3-1 | 3-2 | | 1-1 | 3-2 | 1-0 | 4-1 | 3-2 |
| AS Saint-Étienne | 5-0 | 2-0 | 3-0 | 2-1 | 1-0 | 0-0 | 3-1 | 3-2 | 3-0 | 5-1 | 4-1 | 0-0 | 3-2 | 0-0 | 0-2 | | 3-0 | 3-0 | 1-2 | 4-0 |
| Sochaux-Montbéliard | 2-0 | 1-1 | 1-0 | 0-0 | 2-1 | 1-2 | 3-0 | 2-2 | 3-0 | 1-1 | 1-1 | 2-4 | 1-1 | 2-1 | 4-0 | 1-2 | | 1-1 | 1-0 | 3-3 |
| RC Strasbourg | 2-0 | 1-0 | 1-1 | 1-1 | 0-0 | 0-1 | 3-2 | 2-1 | 3-3 | 0-0 | 2-0 | 1-2 | 2-1 | 1-0 | 0-2 | 2-0 | 1-0 | | 4-1 | 3-0 |
| FC de Tours | 2-2 | 1-4 | 2-2 | 0-1 | 3-2 | 1-1 | 3-3 | 1-1 | 1-1 | 0-1 | 1-0 | 2-3 | 1-0 | 4-3 | 0-2 | 1-3 | 0-1 | 1-1 | | 2-3 |
| Valenciennes | 0-0 | 2-0 | 1-1 | 2-2 | 4-2 | 1-0 | 0-3 | 2-1 | 3-0 | 0-1 | 3-0 | 3-3 | 1-0 | 1-1 | 2-0 | 0-1 | 2-1 | 1-2 | 1-1 | |

## Division 1

| | | Pd | Wn | Dw | Ls | GF | GA | Pts | |
|---|---|---|---|---|---|---|---|---|---|
| 1. | AS DE SAINT-Étienne (SAINT-Étienne) | 38 | 23 | 11 | 4 | 68 | 26 | 57 | |
| 2. | FC de Nantes (Nantes) | 38 | 22 | 11 | 5 | 74 | 36 | 55 | |
| 3. | Girondins de Bordeaux FC (Bordeaux) | 38 | 18 | 13 | 7 | 57 | 34 | 49 | |
| 4. | AS de Monaco (Monaco) | 38 | 19 | 11 | 8 | 58 | 41 | 49 | |
| 5. | Paris Saint-Germain FC (Paris) | 38 | 17 | 12 | 9 | 62 | 50 | 46 | |
| 6. | Olympique Lyonnais (Lyon) | 38 | 14 | 13 | 11 | 70 | 54 | 41 | |
| 7. | Racing Club de Strasbourg (Strasbourg) | 38 | 14 | 12 | 12 | 44 | 47 | 40 | |
| 8. | AS Nancy Lorraine (Nancy) | 38 | 15 | 7 | 16 | 55 | 49 | 37 | |
| 9. | FC de Metz (Metz) | 38 | 10 | 16 | 12 | 48 | 53 | 36 | |
| 10. | Association de la Jeunesse Auxerroise (Auxerre) | 38 | 10 | 16 | 12 | 46 | 52 | 36 | |
| 11. | US Valenciennes-Anzin (Valenciennes) | 38 | 12 | 12 | 14 | 51 | 70 | 36 | |
| 12. | Sporting Étoile Club Bastiais (Bastia) | 38 | 13 | 9 | 16 | 50 | 55 | 35 | |
| 13. | Racing Club de Lens (Lens) | 38 | 10 | 14 | 14 | 46 | 48 | 34 | |
| 14. | FC Sochaux-Montbéliard (Montbéliard) | 38 | 10 | 14 | 14 | 51 | 59 | 34 | |
| 15. | Olympique GC de Nice (Nice) | 38 | 10 | 12 | 16 | 47 | 61 | 32 | |
| 16. | Stade Lavallois FC (Laval) | 38 | 10 | 11 | 17 | 49 | 55 | 31 | |
| 17. | Lille Olympique SC (Lille) | 38 | 10 | 11 | 17 | 55 | 71 | 31 | |
| 18. | FC de Tours (Tours) | 38 | 9 | 13 | 16 | 54 | 71 | 31 | PO |
| 19. | Nîmes Olympique (Nîmes) | 38 | 6 | 14 | 18 | 46 | 66 | 26 | R |
| 20. | SC de l'Ouest Angers (Angers) | 38 | 5 | 14 | 19 | 33 | 66 | 24 | R |
| | | 760 | 257 | 246 | 257 | 1064 | 1064 | 760 | |

## Top goal-scorers

| | | | |
|---|---|---|---|
| 1) | Dellio ONNIS | (FC de Tours) | 24 |
| 2) | KRAUSE | (Stade Lavallois FC) | 23 |
| 3) | Sime NIKOLIC | (Olympique Lyonnais) | 21 |

## Promotion/Relegation Play-Offs

| | | |
|---|---|---|
| FC de Tours (Tours) | 1-0, 2-2 | Toulouse FC (Toulouse) |
| US Noeuxoise (Noeux-les-Mines) | 2-0, 0-5 | Toulouse FC (Toulouse) |

## Division 2 Play-Off

| | | |
|---|---|---|
| Montpellier Paillade SC (Montpellier) | 2-3, 0-2 | Stade Brestois (Brest) |

| | Division 2 (Group "A") | Pd | Wn | Dw | Ls | GF | GA | Pts | |
|---|---|---|---|---|---|---|---|---|---|
| 1. | Montpellier Paillade SC (Montpellier) | 34 | 21 | 8 | 5 | 54 | 17 | 50 | P |
| 2. | Toulouse FC (Toulouse) | 34 | 20 | 7 | 7 | 66 | 30 | 47 | PO |
| 3. | Racing Club Franc-Comtois (Besançon) | 34 | 20 | 7 | 7 | 57 | 24 | 47 | |
| 4. | AS Biterroise (Béziers) | 34 | 18 | 7 | 9 | 50 | 34 | 43 | |
| 5. | AS Angoulême-Charentes (Angoulême) | 34 | 16 | 10 | 8 | 46 | 24 | 42 | |
| 6. | Olympique de Marseille (Marseille) | 34 | 16 | 7 | 11 | 40 | 33 | 39 | |
| 7. | CS de Thonon (Thonon) | 34 | 14 | 9 | 11 | 40 | 39 | 37 | |
| 8. | FC de Gueugnon (Gueugnon) | 34 | 14 | 8 | 12 | 43 | 32 | 36 | |
| 9. | AS de Cannes (Cannes) | 34 | 13 | 9 | 12 | 42 | 36 | 35 | |
| 10. | FC de Martigues (Martigues) | 34 | 13 | 7 | 14 | 42 | 44 | 33 | |
| 11. | Sports Réunis Déodatiens (Saint-Dié) | 34 | 10 | 9 | 15 | 31 | 42 | 29 | |
| 12. | FC-AS de Grenoble (Grenoble) | 34 | 11 | 6 | 17 | 33 | 52 | 28 | |
| 13. | Gazélec FC Ajaccien (Ajaccio) | 34 | 6 | 16 | 12 | 23 | 41 | 28 | |
| 14. | AS Libournaise (Libourne) | 34 | 8 | 11 | 15 | 32 | 49 | 27 | |
| 15. | Étoile des Sports Montluçonnais (Montluçon) | 34 | 10 | 5 | 19 | 29 | 53 | 25 | |
| 16. | US Tavaux-Damparis (Tavaux) | 34 | 6 | 12 | 16 | 31 | 49 | 24 | R |
| 17. | Olympique Avignonnais (Avignon) | 34 | 7 | 7 | 20 | 37 | 66 | 21 | R |
| 18. | AS Corbeil-Essones (Corbeil-Essones) | 34 | 6 | 9 | 19 | 31 | 62 | 21 | R |
| | | 612 | 229 | 154 | 229 | 727 | 727 | 612 | |

| Division 2 (Group "B") | Pd | Wn | Dw | Ls | GF | GA | Pts | |
|---|---|---|---|---|---|---|---|---|
| 1. Stade Brestois (Brest) | 34 | 20 | 9 | 5 | 59 | 25 | 49 | P |
| 2. US Noeuxoise (Noeux-les-Mines) | 34 | 18 | 8 | 8 | 48 | 28 | 44 | PO |
| 3. FC de Rouen (Rouen) | 34 | 16 | 10 | 8 | 43 | 31 | 42 | |
| 4. Stade Rennais FC (Rennes) | 34 | 16 | 8 | 10 | 41 | 30 | 40 | |
| 5. La Berrichone (Châteauroux) | 34 | 15 | 10 | 9 | 50 | 44 | 40 | |
| 6. Thionville FC (Thionville) | 34 | 13 | 11 | 10 | 44 | 37 | 37 | R |
| 7. En Avant de Guingamp (Guingamp) | 34 | 12 | 11 | 11 | 38 | 35 | 35 | |
| 8. Havre AC (Le Havre) | 34 | 13 | 9 | 12 | 32 | 33 | 35 | |
| 9. US Orléans Football (Orléans) | 34 | 13 | 7 | 14 | 45 | 43 | 33 | |
| 10. Stade de Reims (Reims) | 34 | 13 | 6 | 15 | 55 | 56 | 32 | |
| 11. Sporting Club d'Abbeville (Abbeville) | 34 | 9 | 13 | 12 | 44 | 48 | 31 | |
| 12. Association Amicale de la Jeunesse Blésoise (Blois) | 34 | 9 | 12 | 13 | 34 | 45 | 30 | |
| 13. Stade Quimperois (Quimper) | 34 | 10 | 10 | 14 | 27 | 39 | 30 | |
| 14. Limoges FC (Limoges) | 34 | 11 | 7 | 16 | 32 | 48 | 29 | |
| 15. Paris FC (Paris) | 34 | 9 | 10 | 15 | 36 | 34 | 28 | |
| 16. US Dunkerquoise (Dunkerque) | 34 | 10 | 8 | 16 | 34 | 42 | 28 | |
| 17. Union Étoile Sportive Montmorillonnaise (Montmorillon) | 34 | 9 | 9 | 16 | 38 | 49 | 27 | R |
| 18. Stade Malherbe Caennais (Caen) | 34 | 6 | 10 | 18 | 25 | 58 | 22 | R |
| | 612 | 222 | 168 | 222 | 725 | 725 | 612 | |

## Coupe de France Final    (Parc des Princes, Paris – 13/06/81 – 46,155)

**SPORTING ÉTOILE CLUB BASTIAIS**　　　　**2-1**　　　　AS de Saint-Étienne (Saint-Étienne)

*Marcialis 50', Miller 58'*　　　　　　　　　　　　　　　　　　　　*Santini 72' pen*

**Bastiais:** Hiard, Cazes, Marchioni, Orlanducci, Lacuesta, Desvignes, Marcialis, Fiard, Miller, Henry, Ihily.

**Saint-Étienne:** Castaneda, Battiston, Janvion, Gardon (Primard 18'), Lopez, Santini, Zimako, Elie, Roussey (Paganelli 86'), Platini, Rep.


## Semi-Finals    (05-09/06/81)

| | | |
|---|---|---|
| Sporting Étoile Club Bastiais (Bastia) | 2-0, 1-0 | Racing Club de Lens (Lens) |
| AS de Saint-Étienne (Saint-Étienne) | 2-1, 1-1 | Racing Club de Strasbourg (Strasbourg) |


## Quarter-Finals    (08-19/05/81)

| | | |
|---|---|---|
| Girondins de Bordeaux FC (Bordeaux) | 1-5, 0-4 | Racing Club de Strasbourg (Strasbourg) |
| Racing Club de Lens (Lens) | 3-1, 0-1 | Lille Olympique SC (Lille) |
| FC de Martigues (Martigues) | 3-0, 0-5 | Sporting Étoile Club Bastiais (Bastia) |
| AS de Saint-Étienne (Saint-Étienne) | 2-1, 1-1 | Montpellier Paillade SC (Montpellier) |

# 1981-82

| 1981-1982 Division One | AJ Auxerroise | SEC Bastiais | Gir. de Bordeaux | Stade Brestois | Stade Lavallois | Racing de Lens | Lille Olympique | Olymp. Lyonnais | FC de Metz | AS de Monaco | Montpellier Pail. | Nancy-Lorraine | FC de Nantes | Olymp. FC Nice | Paris St-Germain | AS Saint-Étienne | Sochaux-Mont. | RC Strasbourg | FC de Tours | Valenciennes |
|---|---|---|---|---|---|---|---|---|---|---|---|---|---|---|---|---|---|---|---|---|
| AJ Auxerroise | | 2-2 | 3-2 | 1-1 | 0-1 | 1-1 | 1-2 | 2-2 | 0-0 | 2-0 | 1-1 | 1-0 | 0-1 | 0-0 | 1-0 | 3-1 | 3-0 | 3-0 | 1-2 | 3-0 |
| Sporting Étoile Club Bastiais | 0-1 | | 4-4 | 3-1 | 2-2 | 1-0 | 3-2 | 1-0 | 1-1 | 1-0 | 1-0 | 3-3 | 1-0 | 1-1 | 3-1 | 1-1 | 1-1 | 1-0 | 2-1 | 1-0 |
| Girondins de Bordeaux | 0-2 | 4-0 | | 1-1 | 0-0 | 0-1 | 1-1 | 3-0 | 2-1 | 1-0 | 4-1 | 1-1 | 3-2 | 1-0 | 2-0 | 1-1 | 3-1 | 1-1 | 2-1 | 2-0 |
| Stade Brestois | 2-2 | 2-0 | 3-1 | | 2-2 | 2-0 | 1-0 | 1-0 | 2-0 | 2-2 | 0-1 | 0-1 | 1-2 | 1-0 | 0-3 | 1-1 | 2-1 | 1-2 | 2-1 | 3-0 |
| Stade Lavallois | 2-0 | 2-0 | 1-0 | 1-0 | | 1-0 | 2-0 | 3-1 | 1-0 | 2-3 | 2-1 | 2-1 | 1-1 | 5-0 | 0-3 | 0-0 | 1-1 | 4-2 | 0-0 | 0-0 |
| Racing de Lens | 5-2 | 1-1 | 1-2 | 4-0 | 0-1 | | 1-0 | 2-1 | 2-0 | 0-0 | 1-0 | 2-2 | 1-0 | 1-1 | 1-1 | 2-5 | 3-2 | 0-1 | 4-2 | 1-1 |
| Lille Olympique SC | 1-1 | 4-0 | 0-1 | 1-1 | 1-0 | 0-3 | | 1-0 | 1-0 | 0-2 | 6-1 | 1-2 | 1-0 | 5-0 | 2-1 | 3-4 | 0-0 | 1-1 | 2-0 | 2-0 |
| Olympique Lyonnais | 0-1 | 4-1 | 0-1 | 1-0 | 0-0 | 3-0 | 4-1 | | 3-1 | 0-2 | 2-0 | 2-0 | 1-0 | 1-0 | 2-3 | 0-1 | 1-0 | 1-1 | 2-1 | 3-0 |
| FC de Metz | 1-0 | 2-0 | 1-1 | 1-1 | 1-1 | 0-0 | 1-0 | 1-0 | | 0-0 | 4-0 | 1-2 | 0-0 | 1-1 | 0-0 | 1-1 | 0-0 | 1-1 | 4-2 | 1-1 |
| AS de Monaco | 7-1 | 4-1 | 0-1 | 0-0 | 3-0 | 4-1 | 4-0 | 3-1 | 2-1 | | 1-0 | 5-1 | 1-0 | 1-0 | 0-0 | 1-0 | 2-3 | 1-0 | 3-1 | 3-1 |
| Montpellier Paillade SC | 0-0 | 3-2 | 1-2 | 1-3 | 2-1 | 1-1 | 2-1 | 0-0 | 1-1 | 1-2 | | 3-0 | 2-0 | 2-1 | 2-5 | 0-1 | 1-3 | 0-0 | 1-3 | 0-0 |
| Nancy-Lorraine | 1-1 | 2-1 | 0-0 | 5-0 | 2-2 | 0-0 | 1-1 | 2-1 | 2-2 | 0-3 | 3-2 | | 1-0 | 4-0 | 0-0 | 0-0 | 3-0 | 2-0 | 2-0 | 1-3 |
| FC de Nantes | 2-0 | 1-0 | 6-0 | 3-1 | 1-0 | 4-0 | 1-2 | 0-0 | 2-0 | 3-1 | 7-0 | 5-1 | | 2-0 | 4-0 | 3-0 | 1-1 | 2-0 | 3-1 | 4-1 |
| Olympique FC Nice | 4-0 | 1-1 | 2-2 | 2-4 | 1-2 | 3-1 | 2-0 | 0-0 | 3-1 | 0-2 | 1-0 | 1-2 | 3-0 | | 2-2 | 1-3 | 1-0 | 0-1 | 0-1 | 1-2 |
| Paris Saint-Germain FC | 2-1 | 3-1 | 0-2 | 1-2 | 2-1 | 2-1 | 0-1 | 2-0 | 2-0 | 1-1 | 1-2 | 4-0 | 1-1 | 0-0 | | 0-0 | 1-0 | 2-1 | 4-3 | 4-0 |
| AS Saint-Étienne | 3-0 | 3-0 | 5-0 | 1-0 | 1-1 | 3-1 | 1-1 | 4-0 | 9-2 | 2-0 | 4-0 | 2-1 | 1-0 | 2-0 | 0-0 | | 0-1 | 2-0 | 1-0 | 5-1 |
| Sochaux-Montbéliard | 5-0 | 3-0 | 2-1 | 0-0 | 3-1 | 1-0 | 1-1 | 3-1 | 2-1 | 1-4 | 1-0 | 1-0 | 2-1 | 2-1 | 2-1 | 2-1 | | 2-2 | 4-1 | 2-0 |
| RC Strasbourg | 2-2 | 0-0 | 1-0 | 2-3 | 1-2 | 1-2 | 3-0 | 2-0 | 0-1 | 0-1 | 2-0 | 1-0 | 1-1 | 2-0 | 2-0 | 2-3 | 2-3 | | 1-1 | 4-0 |
| FC de Tours | 2-0 | 4-0 | 1-2 | 5-0 | 2-1 | 1-0 | 4-1 | 3-0 | 2-2 | 1-1 | 1-0 | 1-1 | 2-1 | 3-4 | 1-2 | 2-1 | 3-4 | 1-2 | | 2-1 |
| Valenciennes | 3-1 | 1-2 | 0-1 | 5-2 | 3-1 | 1-1 | 4-0 | 0-1 | 2-0 | 0-0 | 1-0 | 2-1 | 1-2 | 0-0 | 2-2 | 0-2 | 3-0 | 0-0 | 1-1 | |

## Division 1

| | | Pd | Wn | Dw | Ls | GF | GA | Pts | |
|---|---|---|---|---|---|---|---|---|---|
| 1. | AS DE MONACO (MONACO) | 38 | 24 | 7 | 7 | 70 | 29 | 55 | |
| 2. | AS de Saint-Étienne (Saint-Étienne) | 38 | 22 | 10 | 6 | 74 | 31 | 54 | |
| 3. | FC Sochaux-Montbéliard (Montbéliard) | 38 | 20 | 9 | 9 | 59 | 43 | 49 | |
| 4. | Girondins de Bordeaux FC (Bordeaux) | 38 | 19 | 10 | 9 | 55 | 45 | 48 | |
| 5. | Stade Lavallois FC (Laval) | 38 | 16 | 12 | 10 | 49 | 40 | 44 | |
| 6. | FC de Nantes (Nantes) | 38 | 19 | 5 | 14 | 64 | 34 | 43 | |
| 7. | Paris Saint-Germain FC (Paris) | 38 | 17 | 9 | 12 | 58 | 45 | 43 | |
| 8. | AS Nancy-Lorraine (Nancy) | 38 | 13 | 13 | 12 | 50 | 52 | 39 | |
| 9. | Stade Brestois (Brest) | 38 | 14 | 10 | 14 | 48 | 57 | 38 | * |
| 10. | Racing Club de Strasbourg (Strasbourg) | 38 | 12 | 12 | 14 | 41 | 41 | 36 | |
| 11. | FC de Tours (Tours) | 38 | 14 | 7 | 17 | 61 | 59 | 35 | |
| 12. | Sporting Étoile Club Bastiais (Bastia) | 38 | 12 | 11 | 15 | 43 | 65 | 35 | |
| 13. | Racing Club de Lens (Lens) | 38 | 12 | 10 | 16 | 44 | 51 | 34 | |
| 14. | Lille Olympique SC (Lille) | 38 | 13 | 8 | 17 | 46 | 54 | 34 | |
| 15. | Association de la Jeunesse Auxerroise (Auxerre) | 38 | 11 | 12 | 15 | 43 | 58 | 34 | |
| 16. | Olympique Lyonnais (Lyon) | 38 | 13 | 6 | 19 | 38 | 46 | 32 | |
| 17. | FC de Metz (Metz) | 38 | 8 | 16 | 14 | 35 | 49 | 32 | |
| 18. | US Valenciennes-Anzin (Valenciennes) | 38 | 10 | 10 | 18 | 40 | 59 | 30 | PO |
| 19. | Olympique GC de Nice (Nice) | 38 | 7 | 9 | 22 | 34 | 57 | 23 | R |
| 20. | Montpellier Paillade SC (Montpellier) | 38 | 7 | 8 | 23 | 30 | 67 | 22 | R |
| | | 760 | 283 | 194 | 283 | 982 | 982 | 760 | |

## Top goal-scorers

1) Dellio ONNIS                  (FC de Tours)     29
2) Andrzej SZARMACH    (Association Jeunesse Auxerroise)   24
3) Michel PLATINI         (AS de Saint-Étienne)   22

## Promotion/Relegation Play-Offs

| | | |
|---|---|---|
| FC de Mulhouse 1893 (Mulhouse) | 5-2, 1-1 | US Valenciennes-Anzin (Valenciennes) |
| FC de Mulhouse 1893 (Mulhouse) | 3-0, 2-1 | CS de Thonon (Thonon) |

* Stade Brestois (Brest) changed their name to Brest Armorique FC (Brest) for the next season.

## Division 2 Play-Off

| | | |
|---|---|---|
| FC de Rouen (Rouen) | 3-2, 1-2 | Toulouse FC (Toulouse) |

Toulouse FC (Toulouse) won on the away goals rule.

| | Division 2 (Group "A") | Pd | Wn | Dw | Ls | GF | GA | Pts | |
|---|---|---|---|---|---|---|---|---|---|
| 1. | Toulouse FC (Toulouse) | 34 | 18 | 10 | 6 | 50 | 25 | 46 | P |
| 2. | CS de Thonon (Thonon) | 34 | 18 | 10 | 6 | 38 | 23 | 46 | PO |
| 3. | Olympique de Marseille (Marseille) | 34 | 14 | 15 | 5 | 48 | 33 | 43 | |
| 4. | SC de Toulon (Toulon) | 34 | 15 | 10 | 9 | 62 | 50 | 40 | |
| 5. | Club Sportif Cuiseaux-Louhans (Cuiseaux-Louhans) | 34 | 16 | 5 | 13 | 49 | 54 | 37 | |
| 6. | Nîmes Olympique (Nîmes) | 34 | 14 | 7 | 13 | 57 | 49 | 35 | |
| 7. | AS Biterroise (Béziers) | 34 | 12 | 11 | 11 | 39 | 35 | 35 | |
| 8. | AS de Cannes (Cannes) | 34 | 11 | 13 | 10 | 40 | 37 | 35 | |
| 9 | US Orléans Football (Orléans) | 34 | 12 | 11 | 11 | 33 | 37 | 35 | |
| 10. | Paris FC (Paris) | 34 | 11 | 12 | 11 | 46 | 45 | 34 | # |
| 11. | FC de Gueugnon (Gueugnon) | 34 | 10 | 13 | 11 | 33 | 34 | 33 | |
| 12. | FC-AS de Grenoble (Grenoble) | 34 | 7 | 18 | 9 | 31 | 29 | 32 | |
| 13. | FC de Martigues (Martigues) | 34 | 12 | 8 | 14 | 41 | 44 | 32 | |
| 14. | AS Libournaise (Libourne) | 34 | 10 | 11 | 13 | 37 | 38 | 31 | |
| 15. | Fontainebleau-Bagneaux FC (Fontainebleau) | 34 | 10 | 10 | 14 | 45 | 47 | 30 | |
| 16. | Sports Réunis Déodatiens (Saint-Dié) | 34 | 8 | 8 | 18 | 31 | 49 | 24 | R |
| 17. | Gazélec FC Ajaccien (Ajaccio) | 34 | 7 | 9 | 18 | 29 | 52 | 23 | R |
| 18. | Association Amicale de la Jeunesse Blésoise (Blois) | 34 | 6 | 9 | 19 | 26 | 54 | 21 | R |
| | | 612 | 211 | 190 | 211 | 735 | 735 | 612 | |

| Division 2 (Group "B") | Pd | Wn | Dw | Ls | GF | GA | Pts | |
|---|---|---|---|---|---|---|---|---|
| 1. FC de Rouen (Rouen) | 34 | 21 | 9 | 4 | 54 | 19 | 51 | P |
| 2. FC de Mulhouse 1893 (Mulhouse) | 34 | 22 | 6 | 6 | 73 | 40 | 50 | PO |
| 3. US Noeuxoise (Noeux-les-Mines) | 34 | 19 | 11 | 4 | 46 | 22 | 49 | |
| 4. Havre AC (Le Havre) | 34 | 20 | 6 | 8 | 73 | 38 | 46 | |
| 5. Stade Rennais FC (Rennes) | 34 | 17 | 10 | 7 | 45 | 26 | 44 | |
| 6. Stade de Reims (Reims) | 34 | 16 | 9 | 9 | 54 | 26 | 41 | |
| 7. AS Angoulême-Charentes (Angoulême) | 34 | 17 | 7 | 10 | 50 | 33 | 41 | |
| 8. SC de l'Ouest Angers (Angers) | 34 | 12 | 10 | 12 | 42 | 39 | 34 | |
| 9. En Avant de Guingamp (Guingamp) | 34 | 12 | 5 | 17 | 43 | 42 | 29 | |
| 10. Racing Club Franc-Comtois (Besançon) | 34 | 9 | 11 | 14 | 45 | 53 | 29 | |
| 11. Stade Français 92 (Paris) | 34 | 8 | 13 | 13 | 37 | 50 | 29 | |
| 12. US Dunkerquoise (Dunkerque) | 34 | 8 | 12 | 14 | 30 | 39 | 28 | |
| 13. Limoges FC (Limoges) | 34 | 10 | 8 | 16 | 38 | 60 | 28 | |
| 14. La Berrichonne (Châteauroux) | 34 | 8 | 9 | 17 | 38 | 51 | 25 | |
| 15. Sporting Club d'Abbeville (Abbeville) | 34 | 5 | 13 | 16 | 34 | 65 | 23 | |
| 16. Calais Racing Union FC (Calais) | 34 | 8 | 7 | 19 | 28 | 69 | 23 | R |
| 17. Étoile des Sports Montluçonnais (Montluçon) | 34 | 7 | 8 | 19 | 22 | 54 | 22 | R |
| 18. Stade Quimperois (Quimper) | 34 | 6 | 8 | 20 | 33 | 59 | 20 | R |
| | 612 | 225 | 162 | 225 | 785 | 785 | 612 | |

\# Paris FC (Paris) dissolved and later reformed as Paris FC 83 (Paris) for the next season.

## Coupe de France Final   (Parc des Princes, Paris – 15/05/82 – 46,160)

**PARIS SAINT-GERMAIN FC**   **2-2  (aet – 6-5 penalties)**   AS de Saint-Étienne

*Tokomon 58', Rocheteau 120'*   *Platini 76', 99'*

**PSG**: Baratelli, Fermandez, Col (Renaut 118'), Pilorget, Bathenay, Lemoult, Tokomon, Boubacar, Rocheteau, Surjak, Dahleb (N'Gom 84').

**Saint-Étienne**: Castaneda, Battiston, Lestage, Gardon (Nogues 67'), Lopez, Zanon, Paganelli (Roussey 67'), Janvion, Platini, Larios, Rep.

## Semi-Finals   (11/05/82)

| | | |
|---|---|---|
| Paris Saint-Germain FC (Paris) | 0-0  (aet) | FC de Tours (Tours) |
| FC de Tours (Tours) won 2-1 on penalties. | | |
| AS de Saint-Étienne (Saint-Étienne) | 2-0 | Sporting Étoile Club Bastiais (Bastia) |

## Quarter-Finals   (16-20/04/82)

| | | |
|---|---|---|
| Paris Saint-Germain FC (Paris) | 2-0, 1-2 | Girondins de Bordeaux FC (Bordeaux) |
| AS de Saint-Étienne (Saint-Étienne) | 1-0, 0-0 | Stade Lavallois FC (Laval) |
| SC de Toulon (Toulon) | 1-1, 1-2 | FC de Tours (Tours) |
| US Valenciennes-Anzin (Valenciennes) | 1-0, 0-3 | Sporting Étoile Club Bastiais (Bastia) |

# 1982-83

| 1982-1983 Division One | AJ Auxerroise | SEC Bastiais | Gir. de Bordeaux | Brest Armorique | Stade Lavallois | Racing de Lens | Lille Olympique | Olymp. Lyonnais | FC de Metz | AS de Monaco | FC de Mulhouse | Nancy-Lorraine | FC de Nantes | Paris St.Germain | FC de Rouen | AS Saint-Étienne | Sochaux-Mont. | RC Strasbourg | Toulouse FC | FC de Tours |
|---|---|---|---|---|---|---|---|---|---|---|---|---|---|---|---|---|---|---|---|---|
| AJ Auxerroise | ■ | 1-1 | 2-2 | 4-2 | 0-1 | 0-0 | 3-0 | 3-1 | 2-2 | 1-0 | 2-1 | 2-3 | 1-1 | 3-2 | 2-0 | 4-1 | 2-2 | 0-0 | 5-1 | 3-1 |
| Sporting Étoile Club Bastiais | 1-0 | ■ | 1-2 | 1-1 | 1-1 | 4-0 | 0-0 | 2-1 | 0-3 | 2-0 | 2-0 | 3-2 | 1-1 | 1-1 | 0-0 | 2-1 | 0-0 | 1-1 | 1-1 | 4-1 |
| Girondins de Bordeaux | 3-0 | 0-0 | ■ | 0-0 | 4-1 | 3-0 | 2-0 | 5-1 | 2-0 | 3-1 | 2-0 | 3-2 | 1-2 | 2-1 | 3-2 | 1-1 | 3-1 | 1-1 | 1-0 | 1-0 |
| Brest Armorique | 2-2 | 4-2 | 0-1 | ■ | 3-0 | 2-1 | 0-1 | 2-1 | 1-1 | 1-1 | 4-0 | 0-3 | 1-1 | 3-1 | 4-2 | 4-2 | 2-2 | 1-0 | 2-2 | 4-2 |
| Stade Lavallois | 1-0 | 1-0 | 2-0 | 1-1 | ■ | 0-0 | 2-0 | 1-1 | 2-1 | 1-0 | 0-0 | 0-0 | 1-3 | 1-0 | 3-1 | 0-0 | 3-1 | 2-1 | 2-1 | 3-0 |
| Racing de Lens | 0-0 | 2-1 | 2-2 | 2-3 | 2-0 | ■ | 2-0 | 1-0 | 4-2 | 2-0 | 4-2 | 2-1 | 2-2 | 4-0 | 2-0 | 4-2 | 3-0 | 2-1 | 3-1 | 2-1 |
| Lille Olympique SC | 1-2 | 2-0 | 2-1 | 4-0 | 0-0 | 1-1 | ■ | 1-0 | 1-1 | 1-1 | 4-0 | 2-0 | 0-2 | 1-0 | 5-0 | 1-1 | 1-0 | 1-0 | 3-0 | 2-0 |
| Olympique Lyonnais | 1-1 | 3-1 | 3-5 | 2-0 | 2-0 | 2-1 | 3-1 | ■ | 3-3 | 1-1 | 7-3 | 1-2 | 1-2 | 1-3 | 0-4 | 2-1 | 3-1 | 4-2 | 4-1 | 2-0 |
| FC de Metz | 1-1 | 0-0 | 2-1 | 1-0 | 3-2 | 2-1 | 2-0 | 4-1 | ■ | 1-1 | 3-0 | 2-3 | 0-4 | 1-2 | 3-2 | 1-1 | 1-1 | 1-1 | 3-2 | 5-1 |
| AS de Monaco | 1-1 | 3-0 | 3-1 | 5-0 | 4-1 | 2-1 | 0-0 | 3-0 | 2-1 | ■ | 1-0 | 1-0 | 2-2 | 1-1 | 2-0 | 2-2 | 0-0 | 3-0 | 0-0 | 3-0 |
| FC de Mulhouse | 3-2 | 4-1 | 4-4 | 1-1 | 2-1 | 1-3 | 1-0 | 1-1 | 3-4 | 2-1 | ■ | 3-1 | 1-1 | 1-1 | 0-0 | 1-0 | 1-0 | 2-0 | 1-2 | 1-0 |
| Nancy-Lorraine | 3-1 | 2-2 | 2-1 | 1-1 | 1-1 | 1-2 | 2-2 | 5-2 | 4-0 | 2-1 | 6-0 | ■ | 2-2 | 2-3 | 2-0 | 3-1 | 1-2 | 2-1 | 1-2 | 3-3 |
| FC de Nantes | 1-0 | 3-0 | 4-0 | 5-1 | 0-0 | 5-1 | 1-0 | 1-0 | 2-3 | 0-0 | 2-1 | 3-1 | ■ | 2-0 | 1-0 | 4-2 | 4-0 | 3-0 | 3-0 | 2-1 |
| Paris Saint-Germain FC | 0-0 | 1-0 | 2-0 | 2-0 | 0-0 | 4-3 | 4-1 | 3-0 | 3-1 | 0-1 | 5-1 | 2-3 | 2-1 | ■ | 1-0 | 4-1 | 1-0 | 4-3 | 2-1 | 4-2 |
| FC de Rouen | 1-1 | 2-1 | 2-1 | 1-1 | 2-2 | 1-1 | 2-0 | 2-1 | 0-0 | 1-1 | 4-2 | 1-0 | 1-0 | 0-1 | ■ | 0-1 | 1-1 | 2-1 | 3-0 | 4-2 |
| AS Saint-Étienne | 1-0 | 1-1 | 3-1 | 0-0 | 1-1 | 0-1 | 10- | 1-0 | 3-1 | 2-0 | 1-0 | 3-4 | 0-1 | 1-1 | 1-0 | ■ | 0-1 | 0-0 | 2-1 | 0-0 |
| Sochaux-Montbéliard | 2-0 | 2-1 | 0-2 | 4-0 | 1-1 | 1-1 | 2-0 | 1-1 | 4-3 | 1-1 | 1-1 | 0-1 | 1-1 | 1-2 | 2-2 | 3-0 | ■ | 2-2 | 2-3 | 1-1 |
| RC Strasbourg | 0-2 | 2-1 | 0-0 | 0-0 | 1-2 | 2-1 | 1-0 | 2-0 | 2-1 | 0-4 | 2-1 | 2-0 | 2-0 | 1-1 | 1-0 | 2-0 | 1-1 | ■ | 3-0 | 1-1 |
| Toulouse FC | 2-1 | 3-1 | 0-1 | 2-2 | 0-1 | 1-0 | 3-0 | 4-1 | 2-1 | 2-1 | 2-1 | 2-1 | 0-1 | 2-1 | 2-1 | 1-1 | 2-6 | 3-1 | ■ | 1-1 |
| FC de Tours | 3-2 | 0-1 | 1-2 | 2-0 | 4-1 | 5-1 | 5-0 | 3-0 | 3-2 | 2-2 | 1-0 | 1-2 | 0-4 | 3-1 | 3-1 | 0-2 | 1-1 | 2-0 | 2-0 | ■ |

## Division 1

| | | Pd | Wn | Dw | Ls | GF | GA | Pts | |
|---|---|---|---|---|---|---|---|---|---|
| 1. | FC DE NANTES (NANTES) | 38 | 24 | 10 | 4 | 77 | 29 | 58 | |
| 2. | Girondins de Bordeaux FC (Bordeaux) | 38 | 20 | 8 | 10 | 67 | 48 | 48 | |
| 3. | Paris Saint-Germain FC (Paris) | 38 | 20 | 7 | 11 | 66 | 49 | 47 | |
| 4. | Racing Club de Lens (Lens) | 38 | 18 | 8 | 12 | 64 | 55 | 44 | |
| 5. | Stade Lavallois FC (Laval) | 38 | 15 | 14 | 9 | 42 | 41 | 44 | |
| 6. | AS de Monaco (Monaco) | 38 | 14 | 15 | 9 | 55 | 35 | 43 | |
| 7. | AS Nancy-Lorraine (Nancy) | 38 | 17 | 7 | 14 | 74 | 61 | 41 | |
| 8. | Association de la Jeunesse Auxerroise (Auxerre) | 38 | 12 | 14 | 12 | 56 | 48 | 38 | |
| 9. | FC de Metz (Metz) | 38 | 13 | 11 | 14 | 66 | 67 | 37 | |
| 10. | Brest Armorique FC (Brest) | 38 | 11 | 15 | 12 | 53 | 63 | 37 | |
| 11. | Toulouse FC (Toulouse) | 38 | 15 | 6 | 17 | 52 | 66 | 36 | |
| 12. | FC Sochaux-Montbéliard (Montbéliard) | 38 | 9 | 17 | 12 | 52 | 53 | 35 | |
| 13. | Lille Olympique SC (Lille) | 38 | 13 | 8 | 17 | 38 | 45 | 34 | |
| 14. | AS de Saint-Étienne (Saint-Étienne) | 38 | 11 | 12 | 15 | 41 | 52 | 34 | |
| 15. | Racing Club de Strasbourg (Strasbourg) | 38 | 11 | 11 | 16 | 40 | 51 | 33 | |
| 16. | FC de Rouen (Rouen) | 38 | 11 | 10 | 17 | 45 | 54 | 32 | |
| 17. | Sporting Étoile Club Bastiais (Bastia) | 38 | 9 | 14 | 15 | 41 | 52 | 32 | |
| 18. | FC de Tours (Tours) | 38 | 12 | 7 | 19 | 58 | 68 | 31 | PO |
| 19. | Olympique Lyonnais (Lyon) | 38 | 11 | 6 | 21 | 57 | 77 | 28 | R |
| 20. | FC de Mulhouse 1893 (Mulhouse) | 38 | 10 | 8 | 20 | 46 | 76 | 28 | R |
| | | 760 | 276 | 208 | 276 | 1090 | 1090 | 760 | |

143

## Top goal-scorers

| | | | |
|---|---|---:|---:|
| 1) | Vahid HALILHODZIC | (FC de Nantes) | 27 |
| 2) | Andrzej SZARMACH | (Association Jeunesse Auxerroise) | 24 |
| 3) | Merry KRIMAU | (FC de Metz) | 23 |
| 4) | Bérnard LACOMBE | (Girondins de Bordeaux FC) | 20 |
| 5) | BELTRAMINI | (FC de Rouen) | 19 |

## Promotion/Relegation Play-Offs

| | | |
|---|---|---|
| FC de Tours (Tours) | 1-1, 1-3 | Nîmes Olympique (Nîmes) |
| Nîmes Olympique (Nîmes) | 3-1, 0-1 | Stade de Reims (Reims) |

## Division 2 Play-Off

| | | |
|---|---|---|
| SC de Toulon (Toulon) | 0-1, 2-2 | Stade Rennais FC (Rennes) |

| | Division 2 (Group "A") | Pd | Wn | Dw | Ls | GF | GA | Pts | |
|---|---|---:|---:|---:|---:|---:|---:|---:|---|
| 1. | Stade Rennais FC (Rennes) | 34 | 23 | 8 | 3 | 68 | 25 | 54 | P |
| 2. | Nîmes Olympique (Nîmes) | 34 | 19 | 11 | 4 | 65 | 34 | 49 | PO |
| 3. | US Valenciennes-Anzin (Valenciennes) | 34 | 18 | 11 | 5 | 74 | 39 | 47 | |
| 4. | Racing Club de Paris (Paris) | 34 | 17 | 9 | 8 | 60 | 28 | 43 | |
| 5. | Havre AC (Le Havre) | 34 | 15 | 11 | 8 | 54 | 39 | 41 | |
| 6. | AS d'Angoulême (Angoulême) | 34 | 13 | 12 | 9 | 39 | 30 | 38 | |
| 7. | Montpellier Paillade SC (Montpellier) | 34 | 14 | 9 | 11 | 43 | 34 | 37 | |
| 8. | En Avant de Guingamp (Guingamp) | 34 | 11 | 13 | 10 | 47 | 42 | 35 | |
| 9. | SC d'Abbeville (Abbeville) | 34 | 15 | 5 | 14 | 35 | 39 | 35 | |
| 10. | US Noeuxoise (Noeux-les-Mines) | 34 | 9 | 13 | 12 | 29 | 39 | 31 | R |
| 11. | AS Biterroise (Béziers) | 34 | 9 | 11 | 14 | 33 | 43 | 29 | |
| 12. | SC de l'Ouest Angers (Angers) | 34 | 10 | 9 | 15 | 50 | 65 | 29 | |
| 13. | La Berrichonne (Châteauroux) | 34 | 9 | 11 | 14 | 38 | 55 | 29 | |
| 14. | AS Libournaise (Libourne) | 34 | 5 | 18 | 11 | 28 | 39 | 28 | |
| 15. | Limoges FC (Limoges) | 34 | 10 | 8 | 16 | 30 | 51 | 28 | |
| 16. | Olympique d'Alès en Cévenne (Alès) | 34 | 8 | 10 | 16 | 34 | 44 | 26 | |
| 17. | Entente Sportive de Viry-Châtillon (Viry-Châtillon) | 34 | 5 | 9 | 20 | 21 | 58 | 19 | R |
| 18. | AS Corbeil-Essones (Corbeil-Essones) | 34 | 3 | 8 | 23 | 25 | 69 | 14 | R |
| | | 612 | 213 | 186 | 213 | 773 | 773 | 612 | |

| Division 2 (Group "B") | Pd | Wn | Dw | Ls | GF | GA | Pts | |
|---|---|---|---|---|---|---|---|---|
| 1. SC de Toulon (Toulon) | 34 | 21 | 10 | 3 | 68 | 17 | 52 | P |
| 2. Stade de Reims (Reims) | 34 | 24 | 4 | 6 | 70 | 33 | 52 | PO |
| 3. Olympique GC de Nice (Nice) | 34 | 18 | 12 | 4 | 55 | 26 | 48 | |
| 4. Olympique de Marseille (Marseille) | 34 | 16 | 9 | 9 | 38 | 24 | 41 | |
| 5. US Dunkerquoise (Dunkerque) | 34 | 15 | 10 | 9 | 49 | 39 | 40 | |
| 6. FC de Martigues (Martigues) | 34 | 17 | 5 | 12 | 53 | 44 | 39 | |
| 7. AS de Cannes (Cannes) | 34 | 13 | 12 | 9 | 43 | 37 | 38 | |
| 8. US Orléans Football (Orléans) | 34 | 10 | 14 | 10 | 32 | 35 | 34 | |
| 9. FC-AS de Grenoble (Grenoble) | 34 | 11 | 12 | 11 | 42 | 46 | 34 | |
| 10. AS Red Star (Saint-Ouen) | 34 | 11 | 11 | 12 | 38 | 48 | 33 | |
| 11. Racing Club Franc-Comtois (Besançon) | 34 | 11 | 10 | 13 | 39 | 44 | 32 | |
| 12. FC de Gueugnon (Gueugnon) | 34 | 8 | 15 | 11 | 35 | 35 | 31 | |
| 13. CS de Thonon (Thonon) | 34 | 8 | 12 | 14 | 35 | 45 | 28 | |
| 14. Club Sportif Cuiseaux-Louhans (Cuiseaux-Louhans) | 34 | 8 | 10 | 16 | 31 | 47 | 26 | |
| 15. Stade Français 92 (Paris) | 34 | 8 | 9 | 17 | 32 | 50 | 25 | |
| 16. Entente Montceau-les-Mines (Montceau-les-Mines) | 34 | 5 | 12 | 17 | 31 | 55 | 22 | |
| 17. Fontainebleau-Bagneaux FC (Fontainebleau) | 34 | 4 | 13 | 17 | 21 | 55 | 21 | R |
| 18. CS de Blénod (Blénod-les Pont-à-Mousson) | 34 | 4 | 8 | 22 | 18 | 50 | 16 | R |
| | 612 | 212 | 188 | 212 | 730 | 730 | 612 | |

## Coupe de France Final   (Parc des Princes, Paris – 11/06/83 – 46,203)

**PARIS SAINT-GERMAIN FC (PARIS)**          **3-2**                                              FC de Nantes (Nantes)

*Zaremba 03', Susic 65', Tokomon 82'*                                                        *Baronchelli 17', Touré 40'*

**PSG:** Baratelli, Tanasi, Lemoult, Pilorget, Bathenay (Dahleb 50'), Zaremba, Tokomon, Fernandez, Rocheteau, Susic, N'Gom.

**Nantes:** Bertrand-Demanes, Bibard (Picot 82'), Ayache, Rio, Bossis, Adonor, Baronchelli, Tusseau (Muller 73'), Halilhodzic, Touré, Amisse.

## Semi-Finals   (27/05/83 – 07/06/83)

| Lille Olympique SC (Lille) | 0-1, 1-1 | FC de Nantes (Nantes) |
|---|---|---|
| Paris Saint-Germain FC (Paris) | 4-0, 3-3 | FC de Tours (Tours) |

## Quarter-Finals   (03-10/05/83)

| Brest Armorique FC (Brest) | 2-1, 0-2 | Paris Saint-Germain FC (Paris) |
|---|---|---|
| En Avant de Guingamp (Guingamp) | 1-1, 1-3 | FC de Tours (Tours) |
| Lille Olympique SC (Lille) | 2-0, 0-1 | FC de Rouen (Rouen) |
| Racing Paris 1 (Paris) | 2-2, 0-1 | FC de Nantes (Nantes) |

# 1983-84

| 1983-1984 Division One | AJ Auxerroise | SEC Bastiais | Gir. de Bordeaux | Brest Armorique | Stade Lavallois | Racing de Lens | Lille Olympique | FC de Metz | AS de Monaco | Nancy-Lorraine | FC de Nantes | Nîmes Olymp. | Paris St.Germain | Stade Rennais | FC de Rouen | AS Saint-Étienne | Sochaux-Mont. | RC Strasbourg | SC de Toulon | Toulouse FC |
|---|---|---|---|---|---|---|---|---|---|---|---|---|---|---|---|---|---|---|---|---|
| AJ Auxerroise | ■ | 1-1 | 1-4 | 5-0 | 3-0 | 4-0 | 2-0 | 6-1 | 0-0 | 4-0 | 1-0 | 0-0 | 1-2 | 1-0 | 1-0 | 1-0 | 2-0 | 3-0 | 1-1 | 1-1 |
| Sporting Étoile Club Bastiais | 1-0 | ■ | 1-3 | 2-1 | 3-0 | 2-2 | 1-0 | 1-0 | 0-1 | 0-1 | 1-0 | 1-1 | 1-1 | 2-1 | 0-0 | 2-1 | 0-2 | 4-2 | 1-0 | 3-2 |
| Girondins de Bordeaux | 4-1 | 2-1 | ■ | 1-1 | 0-0 | 3-2 | 5-2 | 1-1 | 0-2 | 2-1 | 1-0 | 4-0 | 2-1 | 4-1 | 3-1 | 7-0 | 3-0 | 2-0 | 1-0 | 0-0 |
| Brest Armorique | 2-0 | 3-0 | 0-0 | ■ | 1-0 | 2-1 | 1-1 | 0-2 | 1-1 | 0-1 | 2-0 | 2-2 | 1-1 | 1-0 | 3-2 | 0-0 | 0-0 | 5-2 |  | 0-1 |
| Stade Lavallois | 1-0 | 1-0 | 0-1 | 2-1 | ■ | 3-0 | 3-1 | 1-0 | 2-0 | 1-1 | 0-1 | 1-0 | 2-0 | 2-0 | 0-0 | 1-1 | 1-1 | 1-1 | 0-2 | 1-0 |
| Racing de Lens | 1-3 | 1-0 | 3-1 | 3-2 | 2-1 | ■ | 4-2 | 3-2 | 3-1 | 3-1 | 2-2 | 0-0 | 0-3 | 0-1 | 4-2 | 2-1 | 1-0 | 2-2 | 5-1 | 0-1 |
| Lille Olympique | 1-2 | 0-0 | 1-1 | 2-1 | 1-0 | 3-1 | ■ | 2-0 | 1-1 | 2-0 | 2-0 | 1-0 | 1-0 | 2-0 | 0-1 | 1-1 | 1-2 | 1-1 | 4-2 | 0-0 |
| FC de Metz | 1-2 | 1-0 | 0-0 | 1-0 | 0-0 | 3-0 | 1-0 | ■ | 0-4 | 1-2 | 2-1 | 2-1 | 1-1 | 6-0 | 1-1 | 1-0 | 3-1 | 0-1 | 2-0 | 1-3 |
| AS de Monaco | 0-1 | 1-0 | 2-1 | 2-0 | 3-0 | 3-1 | 1-1 | 2-2 | ■ | 1-1 | 3-0 | 5-1 | 0-1 | 3-2 | 1-0 | 3-1 | 1-1 | 1-0 | 1-0 | 2-3 |
| Nancy-Lorraine | 0-1 | 1-3 | 0-2 | 1-1 | 0-0 | 2-0 | 1-2 | 2-1 | 1-1 | ■ | 0-1 | 2-1 | 1-2 | 1-3 | 2-0 | 2-0 | 0-0 | 3-2 | 2-2 | 2-0 |
| FC de Nantes | 1-2 | 1-0 | 0-1 | 4-0 | 3-1 | 0-0 | 2-1 | 2-1 | 0-0 | 2-1 | ■ | 4-0 | 3-1 | 3-1 | 3-0 | 1-0 | 1-1 | 1-1 | 1-0 | 3-1 |
| Nîmes Olympique | 1-1 | 0-0 | 1-2 | 2-2 | 3-0 | 2-1 | 2-2 | 3-7 | 1-2 | 1-1 | 1-0 | ■ | 1-1 | 1-1 | 2-1 | 1-1 | 2-2 | 0-3 | 1-0 | 3-0 |
| Paris Saint-Germain FC | 1-2 | 1-0 | 2-1 | 1-1 | 0-0 | 3-0 | 4-5 | 2-0 | 0-1 | 1-1 | 0-0 | 0-0 | ■ | 3-2 | 2-0 | 3-1 | 3-1 | 2-0 | 5-1 | 1-0 |
| Stade Rennais | 1-3 | 4-1 | 0-2 | 1-1 | 1-1 | 1-1 | 0-0 | 1-2 | 1-2 | 2-1 | 1-2 | 2-1 | 0-1 | ■ | 2-1 | 1-2 | 0-1 | 3-0 | 1-2 | 1-5 |
| FC de Rouen | 2-0 | 1-2 | 1-0 | 0-1 | 2-0 | 0-2 | 3-1 | 3-0 | 1-0 | 7-1 | 2-0 | 3-0 | 0-1 | 1-0 | ■ | 1-1 | 1-0 | 2-2 | 1-1 | 3-1 |
| AS Saint-Étienne | 0-0 | 0-2 | 0-2 | 1-0 | 1-0 | 0-4 | 2-0 | 2-2 | 0-1 | 1-0 | 0-0 | 3-1 | 2-3 | 1-0 | 1-0 | ■ | 1-0 | 0-1 | 1-0 | 0-1 |
| Sochaux-Montbéliard | 3-0 | 2-0 | 3-1 | 2-0 | 0-1 | 2-2 | 1-0 | 2-0 | 1-1 | 0-1 | 0-1 | 4-1 | 2-1 | 1-0 | 1-1 | 1-1 | ■ | 0-0 | 8-2 | 1-0 |
| RC Strasbourg | 2-1 | 0-0 | 2-2 | 1-0 | 1-0 | 2-1 | 1-1 | 0-0 | 0-1 | 1-1 | 0-0 | 1-0 | 0-0 | 1-1 | 0-0 | 2-0 | 0-0 | ■ | 2-0 | 1-3 |
| SC de Toulon | 1-0 | 1-0 | 1-0 | 1-0 | 2-2 | 3-0 | 0-3 | 0-0 | 1-3 | 0-0 | 1-1 | 3-1 | 1-0 | 0-1 | 1-0 | 0-1 | 1-0 | 1-3 | ■ | 3-2 |
| Toulouse FC | 0-2 | 4-0 | 1-3 | 1-0 | 0-0 | 2-0 | 2-1 | 3-1 | 1-1 | 1-0 | 3-1 | 5-0 | 1-1 | 3-1 | 2-0 | 2-1 | 0-0 | 1-0 | 1-3 | ■ |

## Division 1

| | | Pd | Wn | Dw | Ls | GF | GA | Pts | |
|---|---|---|---|---|---|---|---|---|---|
| 1. | GIRONDINS DE BORDEAUX FC (BORDEAUX) | 38 | 23 | 8 | 7 | 72 | 33 | 54 | |
| 2. | AS de Monaco (Monaco) | 38 | 22 | 10 | 6 | 58 | 29 | 54 | |
| 3. | Association de la Jeunesse Auxerroise (Auxerre) | 38 | 21 | 7 | 10 | 59 | 33 | 49 | |
| 4. | Paris Saint-Germain FC (Paris) | 38 | 18 | 11 | 9 | 56 | 37 | 47 | |
| 5. | Toulouse FC (Toulouse) | 38 | 18 | 9 | 11 | 57 | 41 | 45 | |
| 6. | FC de Nantes (Nantes) | 38 | 18 | 9 | 11 | 46 | 32 | 45 | |
| 7. | FC Sochaux-Montbéliard (Montbéliard) | 38 | 14 | 13 | 11 | 46 | 34 | 41 | |
| 8. | Racing Club de Strasbourg (Strasbourg) | 38 | 11 | 17 | 10 | 36 | 38 | 39 | |
| 9. | Lille Olympique SC (Lille) | 38 | 13 | 11 | 14 | 49 | 49 | 37 | |
| 10. | Sporting Étoile Club Bastiais (Bastia) | 38 | 14 | 8 | 16 | 36 | 43 | 36 | |
| 11. | Stade Lavallois FC (Laval) | 38 | 12 | 12 | 14 | 29 | 36 | 36 | |
| 12. | FC de Metz (Metz) | 38 | 13 | 9 | 16 | 48 | 53 | 35 | |
| 13. | Racing Club de Lens (Lens) | 38 | 14 | 7 | 17 | 57 | 65 | 35 | |
| 14. | FC de Rouen (Rouen) | 38 | 13 | 8 | 17 | 42 | 40 | 34 | |
| 15. | AS Nancy-Lorraine (Nancy) | 38 | 10 | 12 | 16 | 38 | 53 | 32 | |
| 16. | SC de Toulon (Toulon) | 38 | 12 | 8 | 18 | 39 | 60 | 32 | |
| 17. | Brest Armorique FC (Brest) | 38 | 9 | 13 | 16 | 36 | 47 | 31 | |
| 18. | AS de Saint-Étienne (Saint-Étienne) | 38 | 11 | 8 | 19 | 31 | 52 | 30 | PO |
| 19. | Nîmes Olympique (Nîmes) | 38 | 6 | 13 | 19 | 36 | 70 | 25 | R |
| 20. | Stade Rennais FC (Rennes) | 38 | 8 | 7 | 23 | 39 | 65 | 23 | R |
| | | 760 | 280 | 200 | 280 | 910 | 910 | 760 | |

## Top goal-scorers

| | | | |
|---|---|---|---|
| 1) | Patrice GARANDE | (Association Jeunesse Auxerroise) | 21 |
| | Dellio ONNIS | (SC de Toulon) | 21 |
| 3) | Andrzej SZARMACH | (Association Jeunesse Auxerroise) | 20 |

## Promotion/Relegation Play-Offs

| | | |
|---|---|---|
| Racing Club de Paris (Paris) | 0-0, 2-0 | AS de Saint-Étienne (Saint-Étienne) |
| Olympique GC de Nice (Nice) | 2-0, 1-5 | Racing Club de Paris (Paris) |
| Olympique GC de Nice (Nice) | 4-3 (aet) | Havre AC (Le Havre) |
| Racing Club de Paris (Paris) | 3-1 (aet) | Olympique Lyonnais (Lyon) |

## Division 2 Play-Off

| | | |
|---|---|---|
| Olympique de Marseille (Marseille) | 1-1, 2-3 | FC de Tours (Tours) |

| | Division 2 (Group "A") | Pd | Wn | Dw | Ls | GF | GA | Pts | |
|---|---|---|---|---|---|---|---|---|---|
| 1. | Olympique de Marseille (Marseille) | 36 | 22 | 12 | 2 | 92 | 32 | 56 | P |
| 2. | Olympique GC de Nice (Nice) | 36 | 23 | 7 | 6 | 72 | 28 | 53 | PO |
| 3. | Olympique Lyonnais (Lyon) | 36 | 17 | 13 | 6 | 55 | 26 | 47 | PO |
| 4. | Limoges FC (Limoges) | 36 | 17 | 11 | 8 | 55 | 37 | 45 | |
| 5. | Montpellier Paillade SC (Montpellier) | 36 | 16 | 11 | 9 | 57 | 43 | 43 | |
| 6. | AS de Cannes (Cannes) | 36 | 14 | 12 | 10 | 53 | 48 | 40 | |
| 7. | FC-AS de Grenoble (Grenoble) | 36 | 14 | 9 | 13 | 45 | 52 | 37 | |
| 8. | Olympique d'Alès en Cévenne (Alès) | 36 | 10 | 16 | 10 | 37 | 40 | 36 | |
| 9. | CS de Thonon (Thonon) | 36 | 11 | 11 | 14 | 39 | 51 | 33 | |
| 10. | FC de Martigues (Martigues) | 36 | 11 | 10 | 15 | 49 | 59 | 32 | |
| 11. | FC de Sète (Sète) | 36 | 11 | 10 | 15 | 41 | 56 | 32 | |
| 12. | Club Sportif Cuiseaux-Louhans (Cuiseaux-Louhans) | 36 | 9 | 13 | 14 | 37 | 50 | 31 | |
| 13. | FC de Gueugnon (Gueugnon) | 36 | 9 | 12 | 15 | 33 | 38 | 30 | |
| 14. | Racing Club Franc-Comtois (Besançon) | 36 | 8 | 14 | 14 | 48 | 57 | 30 | |
| 15. | AS Biterroise (Béziers) | 36 | 10 | 10 | 16 | 35 | 53 | 30 | |
| 16. | AS Libournaise (Libourne) | 36 | 9 | 11 | 16 | 32 | 48 | 29 | R |
| 17. | FC Yonnais (La Roche-sur-Yon) | 36 | 11 | 6 | 19 | 37 | 60 | 28 | R |
| 18. | AS d'Angoulême (Angoulême) | 36 | 9 | 9 | 18 | 33 | 47 | 27 | R |
| 19. | FC Villefranche-Beaujolais (Villefranche) | 36 | 8 | 9 | 19 | 44 | 69 | 25 | R |
| | | 684 | 239 | 206 | 239 | 894 | 894 | 684 | |

| Division 2 (Group "B") | Pd | Wn | Dw | Ls | GF | GA | Pts | |
|---|---|---|---|---|---|---|---|---|
| 1. FC de Tours (Tours) | 34 | 24 | 5 | 5 | 80 | 30 | 53 | P |
| 2. Racing Club de Paris (Paris) | 34 | 24 | 4 | 6 | 91 | 26 | 52 | PO |
| 3. Havre AC (Le Havre) | 34 | 18 | 11 | 5 | 57 | 29 | 47 | PO |
| 4. Stade de Reims (Reims) | 34 | 20 | 5 | 9 | 68 | 40 | 45 | |
| 5. US Valenciennes-Anzin (Valenciennes) | 34 | 17 | 7 | 10 | 45 | 39 | 41 | |
| 6. US Orléans Football (Orléans) | 34 | 14 | 11 | 9 | 39 | 32 | 39 | |
| 7. FC de Mulhouse 1893 (Mulhouse) | 34 | 15 | 8 | 11 | 60 | 42 | 38 | |
| 8. En Avant de Guingamp (Guingamp) | 34 | 14 | 10 | 10 | 52 | 45 | 38 | |
| 9. Stade Français 92 (Paris) | 34 | 10 | 13 | 11 | 36 | 37 | 33 | |
| 10. La Berrichonne (Châteauroux) | 34 | 12 | 7 | 15 | 41 | 64 | 31 | |
| 11. CS Sedan-Mouzon Ardennes (Sedan) | 34 | 11 | 8 | 15 | 29 | 42 | 30 | |
| 12. SC d'Abbeville (Abbeville) | 34 | 8 | 12 | 14 | 33 | 46 | 28 | |
| 13. US Dunkerquoise (Dunkerque) | 34 | 9 | 9 | 16 | 22 | 51 | 27 | |
| 14. SC de l'Ouest Angers (Angers) | 34 | 9 | 8 | 17 | 33 | 49 | 26 | |
| 15. Stade Quimperois (Quimper) | 34 | 7 | 12 | 15 | 28 | 48 | 26 | |
| 16. AS Red Star (Paris) | 34 | 9 | 8 | 17 | 30 | 52 | 26 | |
| 17. Entente Montceau-les-Mines (Montceau-les-Mines) | 34 | 3 | 11 | 20 | 22 | 51 | 17 | R |
| 18. FC Roubaix (Roubaix) | 34 | 3 | 9 | 22 | 20 | 63 | 15 | R |
| | 612 | 227 | 158 | 227 | 786 | 786 | 612 | |

## Coupe de France Final   (Parc des Princes, Paris – 11/05/84 – 45,384)

**FC DE METZ (METZ)**                    **2-0  (aet)**                    AS de Monaco (Monaco)

*Hinschberger 102', Kurbos 108'*

**Metz**: Ettore, Thys (Sonor 36'), Barraja, Colombo, Zappia, Bracigliano, Rohr (Cangini 66'), Kurbos, Hinschberger, Bernad, Pecout.

**Monaco**: Ettori, Puel, Amoros, Le Roux, Simon, Bijotat, Delamontagne, Bravo, Krause, Genghini, Bellone.

## Semi-Finals   (25/04/84 – 05/05/84)

| AS de Monaco (Monaco) | 4-1, 1-2 | SC de Toulon (Toulon) |
|---|---|---|
| FC de Nantes (Nantes) | 2-1, 0-1 | FC de Metz (Metz) |

## Quarter-Finals

| Racing Club de Lens (Lens) | 0-1, 2-2 | SC de Toulon (Toulon) |
|---|---|---|
| FC de Metz (Metz) | 1-0, 2-1 | Stade Lavallois FC (Laval) |
| AS de Monaco (Monaco) | 4-2, 4-2 | AS de Cannes (Cannes) |
| FC de Nantes (Nantes) | 2-0, 2-3 | FC de Mulhouse 1893 (Mulhouse) |

| 1984-1985 Division One | AJ Auxerroise | SEC Bastiais | Gir. de Bordeaux | Brest Armorique | Stade Lavallois | Racing de Lens | Lille Olympique | FC de Metz | Olymp. Marseille | AS de Monaco | Nancy-Lorraine | FC de Nantes | Paris St.Germain | Racing de Paris | FC de Rouen | Sochaux-Mont. | RC Strasbourg | Toulon et du Var | FC de Tours | Toulouse FC |
|---|---|---|---|---|---|---|---|---|---|---|---|---|---|---|---|---|---|---|---|---|
| AJ Auxerroise | ■ | 3-1 | 1-1 | 3-1 | 2-1 | 0-0 | 3-0 | 2-0 | 4-2 | 2-0 | 1-0 | 1-0 | 2-1 | 1-0 | 2-0 | 0-0 | 2-0 | 1-1 | 1-0 | 2-0 |
| Sporting Étoile Club Bastiais | 2-2 | ■ | 0-0 | 2-0 | 1-0 | 2-1 | 2-1 | 1-3 | 1-0 | 1-0 | 1-1 | 1-1 | 1-2 | 0-0 | 3-0 | 1-1 | 2-1 | 3-2 | 2-2 | 4-0 |
| Girondins de Bordeaux | 6-1 | 4-0 | ■ | 3-0 | 5-2 | 2-1 | 2-0 | 6-0 | 4-1 | 0-0 | 3-1 | 2-1 | 3-1 | 1-0 | 2-0 | 1-0 | 3-2 | 2-0 | 2-1 | 2-1 |
| Brest Armorique | 2-0 | 4-2 | 0-0 | ■ | 3-0 | 3-2 | 0-0 | 0-1 | 3-0 | 0-2 | 2-2 | 4-2 | 3-1 | 3-0 | 0-2 | 1-0 | 1-1 | 0-1 | 3-3 | 2-2 |
| Stade Lavallois | 2-1 | 2-1 | 0-2 | 0-0 | ■ | 1-3 | 1-1 | 1-4 | 4-2 | 0-0 | 2-2 | 0-1 | 0-0 | 1-0 | 2-0 | 2-1 | 2-1 | 1-0 | 3-1 | 3-3 |
| Racing de Lens | 1-0 | 3-0 | 2-1 | 1-1 | 3-0 | ■ | 2-0 | 0-0 | 3-0 | 2-2 | 3-0 | 0-1 | 4-2 | 1-0 | 1-0 | 3-1 | 0-0 | 3-0 | 6-1 | 0-0 |
| Lille Olympique | 1-1 | 1-2 | 0-1 | 2-0 | 0-0 | 2-0 | ■ | 1-0 | 1-1 | 1-1 | 4-0 | 1-1` | 3-1 | 2-1 | 0-0 | 1-1 | 3-0 | 1-1 | 3-0 | 0-0 |
| FC de Metz | 2-1 | 1-0 | 1-1 | 2-0 | 0-2 | 4-1 | 2-0 | ■ | 3-0 | 1-1 | 2-2 | 1-1 | 2-1 | 2-0 | 1-0 | 1-1 | 1-0 | 1-0 | 1-1 | 2-1 |
| Olympique Marseille | 1-1 | 5-0 | 0-1 | 3-2 | 0-0 | 1-2 | 2-0 | 2-1 | ■ | 3-0 | 0-1 | 0-2 | 3-1 | 0-2 | 3-2 | 3-1 | 2-1 | 4-2 | 3-2 | 2-1 |
| AS de Monaco | 0-0 | 4-0 | 3-0 | 0-0 | 0-0 | 3-0 | 6-1 | 7-0 | 3-0 | ■ | 1-0 | 1-1 | 4-1 | 3-0 | 2-0 | 2-0 | 3-0 | 0-2 | 4-0 | 0-0 |
| Nancy-Lorraine | 1-1 | 2-0 | 0-1 | 0-2 | 2-3 | 2-1 | 1-0 | 2-1 | 3-1 | 1-1 | ■ | 1-2 | 6-1 | 4-0 | 2-2 | 2-2 | 1-1 | 0-2 | 1-0 | 1-1 |
| FC de Nantes | 2-1 | 3-0 | 0-1 | 0-2 | 2-0 | 2-0 | 1-0 | 1-0 | 3-0 | 1-0 | 2-1 | ■ | 2-0 | 1-1 | 2-1 | 1-1 | 2-2 | 3-1 | 4-0 | 2-2 |
| Paris Saint-Germain FC | 0-0 | 7-1 | 1-2 | 1-1 | 0-1 | 4-3 | 2-3 | 1-2 | 2-1 | 2-1 | 2-4 | 2-3 | ■ | 2-2 | 3-2 | 1-1 | 2-0 | 0-0 | 2-0 | 3-1 |
| Racing de Paris | 1-3 | 0-0 | 0-0 | 3-0 | 2-0 | 2-1 | 2-2 | 0-2 | 0-2 | 0-1 | 1-0 | 1-2 | 0-1 | ■ | 1-0 | 0-2 | 2-2 | 0-1 | 3-1 | 3-1 |
| FC de Rouen | 1-2 | 1-1 | 0-0 | 2-2 | 2-0 | 1-0 | 0-0 | 1-1 | 1-1 | 2-1 | 0-1 | 1-0 | 0-1 | 1-1 | ■ | 1-1 | 1-0 | 1-0 | 0-0 | 0-2 |
| Sochaux-Montbéliard | 2-1 | 4-0 | 1-1 | 4-2 | 2-0 | 1-2 | 1-0 | 1-1 | 2-0 | 1-2 | 1-0 | 0-1 | 4-1 | 6-1 | 4-0 | ■ | 3-1 | 0-0 | 2-2 | 0-1 |
| RC Strasbourg | 1-1 | 1-1 | 2-2 | 1-1 | 2-0 | 1-1 | 2-1 | 4-1 | 2-1 | 3-3 | 2-1 | 1-3 | 1-1 | 3-0 | 1-1 | 4-2 | ■ | 0-1 | 1-0 | 1-0 |
| Toulon et du Var | 2-0 | 1-0 | 1-2 | 2-1 | 1-1 | 1-0 | 0-1 | 0-2 | 2-0 | 0-1 | 3-1 | 1-2 | 5-1 | 1-1 | 1-0 | 1-0 | 3-1 | ■ | 2-0 | 2-1 |
| FC de Tours | 3-1 | 2-0 | 1-0 | 1-1 | 1-1 | 1-1 | 2-0 | 2-1 | 2-2 | 2-1 | 1-3 | 0-1 | 2-3 | 2-0 | 2-0 | 2-2 | 1-0 | 0-1 | ■ | 2-2 |
| Toulouse FC | 1-3 | 3-0 | 2-1 | 0-0 | 1-1 | 1-0 | 1-0 | 1-1 | 2-0 | 1-2 | 1-0 | 1-3 | 0-1 | 1-3 | 1-1 | 0-0 | 2-1 | 2-0 | 3-1 | ■ |

## Division 1

| | | Pd | Wn | Dw | Ls | GF | GA | Pts | |
|---|---|---|---|---|---|---|---|---|---|
| 1. | GIRONDINS DE BORDEAUX FC (BORDEAUX) | 38 | 25 | 9 | 4 | 70 | 27 | 59 | |
| 2. | FC de Nantes (Nantes) | 38 | 24 | 8 | 6 | 62 | 32 | 56 | |
| 3. | AS de Monaco (Monaco) | 38 | 18 | 12 | 8 | 65 | 28 | 48 | |
| 4. | Association de la Jeunesse Auxerroise (Auxerre) | 38 | 18 | 11 | 9 | 53 | 39 | 47 | |
| 5. | FC de Metz (Metz) | 38 | 18 | 9 | 11 | 50 | 46 | 45 | |
| 6. | SC de Toulon et du Var (Toulon) | 38 | 19 | 6 | 13 | 46 | 37 | 44 | * |
| 7. | Racing Club de Lens (Lens) | 38 | 16 | 8 | 14 | 57 | 43 | 40 | |
| 8. | FC Sochaux-Montbéliard (Montbéliard) | 38 | 12 | 14 | 12 | 56 | 43 | 38 | |
| 9. | Brest Armorique FC (Brest) | 38 | 11 | 14 | 13 | 50 | 51 | 36 | |
| 10. | Stade Lavallois FC (Laval) | 38 | 12 | 12 | 14 | 39 | 52 | 36 | |
| 11. | Toulouse FC (Toulouse) | 38 | 11 | 13 | 14 | 43 | 49 | 35 | |
| 12. | AS Nancy-Lorraine (Nancy) | 38 | 12 | 10 | 16 | 52 | 54 | 34 | |
| 13. | Paris Saint-Germain FC (Paris) | 38 | 13 | 7 | 18 | 58 | 73 | 33 | |
| 14. | Sporting Étoile Club Bastiais (Bastia) | 38 | 11 | 10 | 17 | 39 | 68 | 32 | |
| 15. | Lille Olympique SC (Lille) | 38 | 9 | 13 | 16 | 37 | 45 | 31 | |
| 16. | Racing Club de Strasbourg (Strasbourg) | 38 | 9 | 13 | 16 | 47 | 57 | 31 | |
| 17. | Olympique de Marseille (Marseille) | 38 | 13 | 5 | 20 | 51 | 67 | 31 | |
| 18. | FC de Rouen (Rouen) | 38 | 8 | 13 | 17 | 28 | 46 | 29 | PO |
| 19. | FC de Tours (Tours) | 38 | 9 | 11 | 18 | 44 | 66 | 29 | R |
| 20. | Racing Club de Paris (Paris) | 38 | 9 | 8 | 21 | 32 | 56 | 26 | R |
| | | 760 | 277 | 206 | 277 | 979 | 979 | 760 | |

## Top goal-scorers

1) Vahid HALILHODZIC           (FC de Nantes)   28
2) Bérnard LACOMBE     (Girondins de Bordeaux FC)   22
3) Gérard BUSCHER       (Brest Armorique FC)   19

\* SC de Toulon et du Var (Toulon) changed their name pre-season from SC de Toulon (Toulon).

## Promotion/Relegation Play-Offs

| | | |
|---|---|---|
| Stade Rennais FC (Rennes) | 0-1, 1-0 | FC de Rouen (Rouen) (aet 7-6 pen) |
| Stade Rennais FC (Rennes) | 1-0, 4-2 | FC de Mulhouse 1893 (Mulhouse) |
| AS de Saint-Étienne (Saint-Étienne) | 0-2 | Stade Rennais FC (Rennes) |
| FC de Mulhouse 1893 (Mulhouse) | 2-0 | Nîmes Olympique (Nîmes) |

## Division 2 Play-Off

| | | |
|---|---|---|
| Olympique GC de Nice (Nice) | 2-2, 0-3 | Havre AC (Le Havre) |

| | Division 2 (Group "A") | Pd | Wn | Dw | Ls | GF | GA | Pts | |
|---|---|---|---|---|---|---|---|---|---|
| 1. | Havre AC (Le Havre) | 34 | 24 | 4 | 6 | 69 | 20 | 52 | P |
| 2. | FC de Mulhouse 1893 (Mulhouse) | 34 | 22 | 6 | 6 | 62 | 25 | 50 | PO |
| 3. | Stade Rennais FC (Rennes) | 34 | 20 | 6 | 8 | 51 | 21 | 46 | PO |
| 4. | US Orléans Football (Orléans) | 34 | 15 | 13 | 6 | 34 | 19 | 43 | |
| 5. | En Avant de Guingamp (Guingamp) | 34 | 17 | 8 | 9 | 47 | 33 | 42 | |
| 6. | US Valenciennes-Anzin (Valenciennes) | 34 | 15 | 10 | 9 | 46 | 36 | 40 | |
| 7. | Racing Club Franc-Comtois (Besançon) | 34 | 12 | 12 | 10 | 47 | 36 | 36 | |
| 8. | CS Sedan-Mouzon Ardennes (Sedan) | 34 | 12 | 12 | 10 | 36 | 36 | 36 | |
| 9. | Stade Quimperois (Quimper) | 34 | 11 | 11 | 12 | 40 | 43 | 33 | |
| 10. | AS Red Star (Saint-Ouen) | 34 | 12 | 9 | 13 | 32 | 37 | 33 | |
| 11. | Stade Malherbe Caennais (Caen) | 34 | 11 | 11 | 12 | 33 | 40 | 33 | |
| 12. | Stade de Reims (Reims) | 34 | 10 | 12 | 12 | 31 | 44 | 32 | |
| 13. | Stade Français 92 (Paris) | 34 | 9 | 11 | 14 | 37 | 43 | 29 | |
| 14. | US Dunkerquoise (Dunkerque) | 34 | 9 | 7 | 18 | 33 | 46 | 25 | |
| 15. | SC d'Abbeville (Abbeville) | 34 | 6 | 13 | 15 | 35 | 56 | 25 | |
| 16. | SC de l'Ouest Angers (Angers) | 34 | 8 | 6 | 20 | 37 | 60 | 22 | |
| 17. | Amiens SC (Amiens) | 34 | 6 | 8 | 20 | 23 | 51 | 20 | R |
| 18. | La Berrichonne (Châteauroux) | 34 | 3 | 9 | 22 | 25 | 72 | 15 | R |
| | | 612 | 222 | 168 | 222 | 718 | 718 | 612 | |

| Division 2 (Group "B") | Pd | Wn | Dw | Ls | GF | GA | Pts | |
|---|---|---|---|---|---|---|---|---|
| 1. Olympique GC de Nice (Nice) | 34 | 20 | 10 | 4 | 73 | 29 | 50 | P |
| 2. AS de Saint-Étienne (Saint-Étienne) | 34 | 20 | 8 | 6 | 66 | 22 | 48 | PO |
| 3. Nîmes Olympique (Nîmes) | 34 | 15 | 12 | 7 | 64 | 37 | 42 | PO |
| 4. Montpellier Paillade SC (Montpellier) | 34 | 15 | 11 | 8 | 59 | 37 | 41 | |
| 5. CS de Thonon (Thonon) | 34 | 15 | 8 | 11 | 48 | 39 | 38 | |
| 6. Olympique d'Alès en Cévenne (Alès) | 34 | 12 | 11 | 11 | 33 | 28 | 35 | |
| 7. Olympique Lyonnais (Lyon) | 34 | 13 | 9 | 12 | 41 | 39 | 35 | |
| 8. AS de Cannes (Cannes) | 34 | 12 | 10 | 12 | 41 | 41 | 34 | |
| 9. FC de Gueugnon (Gueugnon) | 34 | 11 | 11 | 12 | 39 | 50 | 33 | |
| 10. FC de Sète (Sète) | 34 | 12 | 8 | 14 | 48 | 59 | 32 | |
| 11. FC-AS de Grenoble (Grenoble) | 34 | 14 | 4 | 16 | 35 | 52 | 32 | |
| 12. FC de Martigues (Martigues) | 34 | 10 | 11 | 13 | 42 | 43 | 31 | |
| 13. Limoges FC (Limoges) | 34 | 9 | 13 | 12 | 37 | 48 | 31 | |
| 14. Club Omnisport du Puy (Le Puy) | 34 | 12 | 7 | 15 | 34 | 45 | 31 | |
| 15. AS Biterroise (Béziers) | 34 | 11 | 8 | 15 | 45 | 56 | 30 | |
| 16. Club Sportif Cuiseaux-Louhans (Cuiseaux-Louhans) | 34 | 10 | 9 | 15 | 39 | 45 | 29 | R |
| 17. Amicale des Écoles Publiques du Bourg (La Roche/Yon) | 34 | 9 | 11 | 14 | 39 | 60 | 29 | R |
| 18. FC de Valence (Valence) | 34 | 3 | 5 | 26 | 28 | 81 | 11 | R |
| | 612 | 223 | 166 | 223 | 811 | 811 | 612 | |

## Coupe de France Final   (Parc des Princes, Paris – 08/06/85 – 45,711)

**AS DE MONACO (MONACO)**　　　　**1-0**　　　　　　Paris Saint-Germain FC (Paris)

*Genghini 14'*

**Monaco**: Ettori, Liégeon, Amoros, Stojkovic, Simon, Bijotat, Tibeuf, Bravo, Anziani, Genghgini, Bellone.

**PSG**: Moutier, Lemoult, Bacconnier, Morin, Jeannol, Charbonnier, Tokomon, Fernandez, Rocheteau, Susic, Lanthier, (Segura 70').

## Semi-Finals   (31/05/85 – 04/06/85)

AS de Monaco (Monaco)　　　　　　2-0,  0-1　　　　　　Lille Olympique SC (Lille)
Toulouse FC (Toulouse)　　　　　2-0,  0-2  (aet)　　　Paris Saint-Germain FC (Paris)
Paris Saint-Germain FC (Paris) won 5-3 on penalties.

## Quarter-Finals   (10-17/05/85)

AS de Monaco (Monaco)　　　　　　3-0,  3-0　　　　　　Racing Club de Paris (Paris)
Paris Saint-Germain FC (Paris)　　1-0,  1-0　　　　　　FC de Nantes (Nantes)
AS de Saint-Étienne (Saint-Étienne)　0-1,  2-0　　　　Lille Olympique SC (Lille)
Toulouse FC (Toulouse)　　　　　　2-0,  3-3　　　FC Sochaux-Montbéliard (Montbéliard)

151

# 1985-86

| 1985-1986 Division One | AJ Auxerroise | SEC Bastiais | Gir. de Bordeaux | Brest Armorique | Havre AC | Stade Lavallois | Racing de Lens | Lille Olympique | Olymp. Marseille | FC de Metz | AS de Monaco | Nancy-Lorraine | FC de Nantes | Olymp. GC Nice | Paris St.Germain | Stade Rennais | Sochaux-Mont. | RC Strasbourg | Toulon et du Var | Toulouse FC |
|---|---|---|---|---|---|---|---|---|---|---|---|---|---|---|---|---|---|---|---|---|
| AJ Auxerroise | ■ | 2-0 | 2-2 | 1-2 | 3-0 | 2-0 | 0-0 | 2-0 | 2-0 | 2-1 | 1-0 | 3-0 | 0-0 | 1-2 | 0-1 | 1-0 | 3-2 | 2-0 | 0-0 | 2-1 |
| Sporting Étoile Club Bastiais | 0-0 | ■ | 0-2 | 3-2 | 2-1 | 0-0 | 0-1 | 2-0 | 0-3 | 0-0 | 0-0 | 2-2 | 2-3 | 0-1 | 2-4 | 0-2 | 0-0 | 2-0 | 2-1 | 0-2 |
| Girondins de Bordeaux | 0-0 | 2-2 | ■ | 4-0 | 5-3 | 2-1 | 2-1 | 1-1 | 2-1 | 3-1 | 5-1 | 1-0 | 2-1 | 1-0 | 0-0 | 3-2 | 1-1 | 1-0 | 2-1 | 1-1 |
| Brest Armorique | 1-3 | 7-0 | 0-1 | ■ | 1-1 | 2-1 | 2-0 | 1-1 | 2-1 | 1-1 | 2-1 | 0-2 | 1-3 | 1-1 | 1-1 | 2-1 | 3-1 | 2-1 | 2-1 | 2-2 |
| Havre AC | 3-3 | 5-2 | 0-1 | 2-0 | ■ | 1-1 | 3-0 | 0-0 | 1-0 | 0-0 | 1-1 | 2-0 | 0-1 | 1-2 | 1-2 | 1-0 | 1-0 | 4-1 | 4-3 | 1-0 |
| Stade Lavallois | 0-0 | 1-0 | 0-0 | 0-0 | 2-2 | ■ | 2-1 | 2-2 | 1-0 | 1-1 | 0-0 | 2-0 | 0-0 | 2-1 | 2-2 | 1-0 | 3-1 | 4-1 | 2-0 | 3-2 |
| Racing de Lens | 2-1 | 6-0 | 1-0 | 1-0 | 4-1 | 3-1 | ■ | 1-4 | 2-1 | 0-0 | 1-1 | 1-0 | 0-0 | 2-0 | 2-3 | 0-0 | 3-1 | 0-0 | 1-1 | 2-0 |
| Lille Olympique | 0-1 | 2-2 | 1-0 | 3-1 | 0-0 | 1-3 | 1-0 | ■ | 0-0 | 1-0 | 2-2 | 3-1 | 0-1 | 1-0 | 2-0 | 2-0 | 2-1 | 2-0 | 1-0 | 2-0 |
| Olympique Marseille | 2-1 | 0-0 | 4-0 | 3-0 | 1-1 | 4-0 | 3-3 | 1-0 | ■ | 0-0 | 2-2 | 2-3 | 1-0 | 2-1 | 0-0 | 1-2 | 1-2 | 0-1 | 2-3 | 1-1 |
| FC de Metz | 2-0 | 3-0 | 2-3 | 3-1 | 3-0 | 2-1 | 2-3 | 4-0 | 3-0 | ■ | 3-2 | 3-1 | 0-0 | 3-0 | 3-1 | 4-1 | 2-0 | 0-0 | 0-2 | 1-1 |
| AS de Monaco | 1-0 | 2-1 | 9-0 | 3-1 | 2-2 | 1-1 | 1-2 | 3-2 | 0-0 | 0-0 | ■ | 1-1 | 1-1 | 0-1 | 1-1 | 1-0 | 1-1 | 2-0 | 0-2 | 3-0 |
| Nancy-Lorraine | 1-0 | 4-1 | 1-1 | 2-0 | 3-0 | 1-0 | 2-1 | 3-0 | 0-2 | 0-2 | 1-1 | ■ | 1-3 | 3-0 | 1-0 | 0-0 | 3-0 | 1-1 | 5-3 | 0-1 |
| FC de Nantes | 2-1 | 2-0 | 0-0 | 3-1 | 2-1 | 1-0 | 4-0 | 5-1 | 0-2 | 1-0 | 1-1 | 2-0 | ■ | 1-1 | 2-0 | 1-0 | 3-2 | 2-0 | 1-1 | 1-0 |
| Olympique GC Nice | 1-1 | 1-0 | 1-1 | 2-2 | 0-3 | 0-0 | 1-1 | 0-0 | 1-0 | 2-0 | 1-0 | 3-1 | 0-0 | ■ | 0-0 | 2-1 | 2-0 | 5-1 | 2-1 | 3-1 |
| Paris Saint-Germain FC | 4-0 | 3-1 | 1-0 | 2-0 | 1-0 | 5-1 | 2-2 | 3-0 | 2-0 | 2-1 | 1-0 | 2-0 | 2-1 | 3-2 | ■ | 1-0 | 4-1 | 1-1 | 1-0 | 3-0 |
| Stade Rennais | 4-1 | 3-1 | 0-0 | 0-4 | 2-1 | 1-0 | 2-0 | 2-0 | 1-2 | 0-0 | 0-1 | 1-0 | 0-0 | 2-0 | 2-3 | ■ | 0-0 | 1-1 | 1-0 | 2-1 |
| Sochaux-Montbéliard | 2-0 | 2-0 | 2-1 | 4-2 | 1-1 | 1-0 | 1-3 | 3-1 | 1-1 | 1-2 | 1-1 | 1-1 | 1-1 | 2-0 | 1-1 | 0-0 | ■ | 3-1 | 1-0 | 4-1 |
| RC Strasbourg | 1-3 | 6-1 | 3-2 | 0-1 | 2-1 | 2-1 | 0-1 | 2-1 | 0-0 | 1-0 | 1-0 | 1-2 | 0-0 | 1-0 | 1-1 | 3-0 |  | ■ | 1-1 | 0-3 |
| Toulon et du Var | 0-1 | 1-1 | 1-1 | 2-3 | 1-0 | 3-0 | 0-0 | 1-1 | 0-0 | 1-1 | 0-0 | 1-1 | 0-0 | 4-0 | 1-1 | 1-1 | 2-2 | 1-0 | ■ | 1-1 |
| Toulouse FC | 2-0 | 3-1 | 1-2 | 2-0 | 1-0 | 2-0 | 1-1 | 1-0 | 1-0 | 2-0 | 2-1 | 4-1 | 4-2 | 0-0 | 1-3 | 4-1 | 3-0 | 3-0 | 4-0 | ■ |

## Division 1

| | | Pd | Wn | Dw | Ls | GF | GA | Pts | |
|---|---|---|---|---|---|---|---|---|---|
| 1. | PARIS SAINT-GERMAIN FC (PARIS) | 38 | 23 | 10 | 5 | 66 | 33 | 56 | |
| 2. | FC de Nantes (Nantes) | 38 | 20 | 13 | 5 | 53 | 27 | 53 | |
| 3. | Girondins de Bordeaux FC (Bordeaux) | 38 | 18 | 13 | 7 | 55 | 46 | 49 | |
| 4. | Toulouse FC (Toulouse) | 38 | 18 | 7 | 13 | 59 | 44 | 43 | |
| 5. | Racing Club de Lens (Lens) | 38 | 15 | 13 | 10 | 51 | 43 | 43 | |
| 6. | FC de Metz (Metz) | 38 | 15 | 12 | 11 | 53 | 34 | 42 | |
| 7. | Association de la Jeunesse Auxerroise (Auxerre) | 38 | 16 | 9 | 13 | 45 | 39 | 41 | |
| 8. | Olympique GC de Nice (Nice) | 38 | 14 | 11 | 13 | 39 | 44 | 39 | |
| 9. | AS de Monaco (Monaco) | 38 | 9 | 19 | 10 | 49 | 42 | 37 | |
| 10. | Lille Olympique SC (Lille) | 38 | 13 | 10 | 15 | 40 | 49 | 36 | |
| 11. | Stade Lavallois FC (Laval) | 38 | 11 | 13 | 14 | 39 | 47 | 35 | |
| 12. | Olympique de Marseille (Marseille) | 38 | 11 | 12 | 15 | 43 | 39 | 34 | |
| 13. | Stade Rennais FC (Rennes) | 38 | 12 | 10 | 16 | 36 | 41 | 34 | |
| 14. | Brest Armorique FC (Brest) | 38 | 13 | 8 | 17 | 53 | 63 | 34 | |
| 15. | FC Sochaux-Montbéliard (Montbéliard) | 38 | 11 | 12 | 15 | 47 | 57 | 34 | |
| 16. | SC de Toulon et du Var (Toulon) | 38 | 9 | 15 | 14 | 43 | 46 | 33 | |
| 17. | Havre AC (Le Havre) | 38 | 11 | 11 | 16 | 49 | 53 | 33 | |
| 18. | AS Nancy-Lorraine (Nancy) | 38 | 13 | 7 | 18 | 45 | 51 | 33 | PO |
| 19. | Racing Club de Strasbourg (Strasbourg) | 38 | 10 | 11 | 17 | 36 | 54 | 31 | R |
| 20. | Sporting Étoile Club Bastiais (Bastia) | 38 | 5 | 10 | 23 | 30 | 79 | 20 | R |
| | | 760 | 267 | 226 | 267 | 931 | 931 | 760 | |

## Top goal-scorers

| | | | |
|---|---|---|---|
| 1) | Jules BOCANDÉ | (FC de Metz) | 23 |
| 2) | RAMOS | (SC de Toulon et du Var) | 19 |
| | Dominique ROCHETEAU | (Paris Saint-Germain FC) | 19 |

## Promotion/Relegation Play-Offs

| | | |
|---|---|---|
| AS Nancy-Lorraine (Nancy) | 3-0, 0-2 | FC de Mulhouse 1893 (Mulhouse) |
| Olympique d'Alès en Cévennes (Alès) | 0-2, 1-1 | FC de Mulhouse 1893 (Mulhouse) |
| Olympique d'Alès en Cévennes (Alès) | 3-0 | En Avant de Guingamp (Guingamp) |
| FC de Mulhouse 1893 (Mulhouse) | 2-1 | Olympique Lyonnais (Lyon) |

## Division 2 Play-Off

| | | |
|---|---|---|
| AS de Saint-Étienne (Saint-Étienne) | 1-1, 2-3 | Racing Club de Paris (Paris) |

| | Division 2 (Group "A") | Pd | Wn | Dw | Ls | GF | GA | Pts | |
|---|---|---|---|---|---|---|---|---|---|
| 1. | AS de Saint-Étienne (Saint-Étienne) | 34 | 18 | 10 | 6 | 50 | 29 | 46 | P |
| 2. | Olympique d'Alès en Cévennes (Alès) | 34 | 16 | 9 | 9 | 33 | 22 | 41 | PO |
| 3. | Olympique Lyonnais (Lyon) | 34 | 14 | 12 | 8 | 47 | 31 | 40 | PO |
| 4. | FC de Sète (Sète) | 34 | 15 | 10 | 9 | 33 | 28 | 40 | |
| 5. | Montpellier Paillade SC (Montpellier) | 34 | 15 | 9 | 10 | 61 | 49 | 39 | |
| 6. | Nîmes Olympique (Nîmes) | 34 | 14 | 10 | 10 | 61 | 35 | 38 | |
| 7. | Club Omnisport du Puy (Le Puy) | 34 | 14 | 7 | 13 | 52 | 41 | 35 | |
| 8. | AS Biterroise (Béziers) | 34 | 13 | 9 | 12 | 43 | 38 | 35 | |
| 9. | FC de Tours (Tours) | 33 | 11 | 12 | 10 | 39 | 37 | 34 | |
| 10. | FC de Gueugnon (Gueugnon) | 34 | 12 | 9 | 13 | 32 | 39 | 33 | |
| 11. | FC de Martigues (Martigues) | 34 | 11 | 10 | 13 | 35 | 45 | 32 | |
| 12. | AS de Cannes (Cannes) | 34 | 8 | 15 | 11 | 35 | 41 | 31 | |
| 13. | CS de Thonon (Thonon) | 34 | 9 | 13 | 12 | 26 | 35 | 31 | |
| 14. | FC Montceau-Bourgogne 71 (Montceau-les-Mines) | 34 | 13 | 4 | 17 | 39 | 44 | 30 | |
| 15. | Istres Sports Football (Istres) | 34 | 8 | 14 | 12 | 39 | 47 | 30 | |
| 16. | AS Red Star (Saint-Ouen) | 34 | 8 | 14 | 12 | 30 | 42 | 30 | |
| 17. | Entente Chaumontaise AC (Chaumont) | 34 | 9 | 8 | 17 | 35 | 58 | 26 | R |
| 18. | FC-AS de Grenoble (Grenoble) | 33 | 5 | 9 | 19 | 31 | 62 | 19 | R |
| | | 610 | 213 | 184 | 213 | 721 | 723 | 610 | |

| Division 2 (Group "B") | Pd | Wn | Dw | Ls | GF | GA | Pts | |
|---|---|---|---|---|---|---|---|---|
| 1. Racing Club de Paris (Paris) | 34 | 24 | 8 | 2 | 78 | 24 | 56 | P |
| 2. FC de Mulhouse 1893 (Mulhouse) | 34 | 20 | 10 | 4 | 64 | 32 | 50 | PO |
| 3. En Avant de Guingamp (Guingamp) | 34 | 17 | 13 | 4 | 68 | 35 | 47 | PO |
| 4. Stade de Reims (Reims) | 34 | 17 | 9 | 8 | 49 | 37 | 43 | |
| 5. Chamois Niortais (Niort) | 34 | 14 | 9 | 11 | 40 | 36 | 37 | |
| 6. Stade Malherbe Caennais (Caen) | 34 | 14 | 9 | 11 | 33 | 31 | 37 | |
| 7. US Orléans Football (Orléans) | 34 | 12 | 9 | 13 | 39 | 42 | 33 | |
| 8. Stade Quimperois (Quimper) | 34 | 11 | 10 | 13 | 38 | 43 | 32 | |
| 9. SC d'Abbeville (Abbeville) | 34 | 12 | 6 | 16 | 41 | 60 | 30 | |
| 10. Limoges FC (Limoges) | 34 | 11 | 7 | 16 | 40 | 43 | 29 | |
| 11. AS Beauvais-Marissel (Beauvais) | 34 | 11 | 7 | 16 | 35 | 52 | 29 | |
| 12. US Valenciennes-Anzin (Valenciennes) | 34 | 9 | 10 | 15 | 45 | 50 | 28 | |
| 13. US Dunkerquoise (Dunkerque) | 34 | 9 | 10 | 15 | 31 | 37 | 28 | |
| 14. Racing Club Franc-Comtois (Besançon) | 34 | 10 | 8 | 16 | 39 | 46 | 28 | |
| 15. SC de l'Ouest Angers (Angers) | 34 | 11 | 6 | 17 | 32 | 47 | 28 | |
| 16. FC de Lorient (Lorient) | 34 | 11 | 6 | 17 | 28 | 53 | 28 | R |
| 17. FC de Rouen (Rouen) | 34 | 11 | 5 | 18 | 32 | 43 | 27 | R |
| 18. CS Sedan-Mouzon Ardennes (Sedan) | 34 | 7 | 8 | 19 | 26 | 47 | 22 | R |
| | 612 | 231 | 150 | 231 | 758 | 758 | 612 | |

## Coupe de France Final   (Parc des Princes, Paris – 30/04/86 – 45,429)

**GIRONDINS DE BORDEAUX FC**          **2-1  (aet)**          Olympique de Marseille (Marseille)

*Tigana 52', Giresse 116'*                                                    *Diallo 45' pen*

**Bordeaux**:  Dropsy, Thouvenel, Rohr, Roche, Battiston, Girard, Tigana, Tusseau, Lacombe (Lassagne 64'), Giresse, Reinders.

**Marseille**:  Bell, Anigo, Galtier, Bade, Bonnevay, Zanon (Lorant 103'), Diallo, Martinez, Audrain (Di Meco 56'), Francini, Brylle.

## Semi-Finals   (15-22/04/86)

| | | |
|---|---|---|
| Olympique de Marseille (Marseille) | 1-0, 1-1 | Stade Rennais FC (Rennes) |
| Paris Saint-Germain FC (Paris) | 1-1, 1-2 | Girondins de Bordeaux FC (Bordeaux) |

## Quarter-Finals   (29/03/86 – 01/04/86)

| | | |
|---|---|---|
| Association de la Jeunesse Auxerroise | 1-1, 1-2 | Stade Rennais FC (Rennes) |
| Racing Club de Lens (Lens) | 2-1, 0-2 | Paris Saint-Germain FC (Paris) |
| Racing Club de Paris (Paris) | 2-1, 1-1 | Olympique de Marseille (Marseille) |
| FC de Tours (Tours) | 0-1, 0-1 | Girondins de Bordeaux FC (Bordeaux) |

# 1986-87

| 1986-1987 Division One | AJ Auxerroise | Gir. de Bordeaux | Brest Armorique | Havre AC | Stade Lavallois | Racing de Lens | Lille Olympique | Olymp. Marseille | FC de Metz | AS de Monaco | Nancy-Lorraine | FC de Nantes | Olymp. GC Nice | Paris St.Germain | Racing de Paris | Stade Rennais | AS Saint-Étienne | Sochaux-Mont. | Toulon et du Var | Toulouse FC |
|---|---|---|---|---|---|---|---|---|---|---|---|---|---|---|---|---|---|---|---|---|
| AJ Auxerroise | ■ | 0-1 | 1-0 | 1-0 | 1-1 | 3-1 | 1-0 | 0-0 | 0-0 | 1-1 | 4-2 | 1-0 | 2-1 | 1-2 | 2-0 | 1-0 | 3-0 | 0-0 | 2-0 | 2-1 |
| Girondins de Bordeaux | 2-0 | ■ | 1-2 | 3-0 | 1-1 | 0-0 | 3-0 | 3-0 | 1-0 | 1-1 | 4-2 | 2-0 | 4-1 | 2-0 | 2-0 | 4-1 | 1-0 | 3-0 | 2-1 | 2-3 |
| Brest Armorique | 0-0 | 1-1 | ■ | 2-0 | 1-2 | 1-3 | 0-0 | 0-0 | 0-0 | 1-0 | 2-0 | 2-1 | 1-3 | 0-0 | 2-0 | 2-1 | 1-0 | 0-0 | 1-1 | 1-2 |
| Havre AC | 1-4 | 1-1 | 1-2 | ■ | 2-1 | 0-0 | 1-1 | 1-3 | 2-2 | 1-1 | 3-0 | 1-0 | 3-0 | 2-0 | 2-2 | 1-1 | 1-0 | 3-1 | 1-1 | 1-1 |
| Stade Lavallois | 0-2 | 1-2 | 1-0 | 2-1 | ■ | 1-1 | 2-1 | 0-0 | 1-1 | 2-0 | 0-0 | 1-1 | 0-0 | 4-3 | 3-1 | 3-0 | 2-1 | 1-1 | 3-2 | 0-0 |
| Racing de Lens | 1-1 | 0-0 | 2-1 | 0-0 | 0-2 | ■ | 1-3 | 3-0 | 0-0 | 1-1 | 0-0 | 2-2 | 4-0 | 1-0 | 0-1 | 2-1 | 2-0 | 0-0 | 2-1 | 1-1 |
| Lille Olympique | 1-1 | 0-0 | 2-1 | 3-2 | 2-1 | 0-1 | ■ | 2-2 | 3-0 | 1-1 | 4-3 | 0-1 | 1-1 | 1-0 | 0-1 | 3-0 | 1-0 | 6-0 | 1-1 | 1-0 |
| Olympique Marseille | 1-1 | 1-1 | 2-2 | 1-1 | 3-0 | 1-3 | 2-0 | ■ | 3-2 | 3-1 | 3-2 | 1-0 | 3-1 | 4-0 | 2-0 | 1-0 | 1-0 | 4-0 | 3-0 | 2-1 |
| FC de Metz | 0-1 | 2-1 | 3-0 | 3-0 | 1-0 | 2-0 | 3-0 | 1-1 | ■ | 4-1 | 2-0 | 3-1 | 1-1 | 0-0 | 0-2 | 6-1 | 1-1 | 5-1 | 4-0 | 2-0 |
| AS de Monaco | 2-0 | 2-2 | 0-1 | 2-1 | 0-0 | 2-1 | 1-0 | 2-0 | 2-1 | ■ | 1-0 | 3-1 | 1-0 | 1-1 | 0-0 | 1-0 | 0-0 | 2-0 | 2-2 | 1-0 |
| Nancy-Lorraine | 1-1 | 0-1 | 0-4 | 0-0 | 3-0 | 1-1 | 0-1 | 0-0 | 0-0 | 1-1 | ■ | 0-0 | 1-0 | 0-1 | 2-1 | 2-0 | 1-0 | 0-1 | 3-0 | 2-0 |
| FC de Nantes | 0-1 | 3-0 | 0-0 | 0-0 | 1-1 | 1-0 | 1-0 | 0-2 | 1-0 | 0-0 | 1-0 | ■ | 1-0 | 0-1 | 2-3 | 3-1 | 1-1 | 2-1 | 1-0 | 2-0 |
| Olympique GC Nice | 2-0 | 0-0 | 0-4 | 3-1 | 2-1 | 3-1 | 1-0 | 2-1 | 3-1 | 1-0 | 1-0 | 1-1 | ■ | 0-2 | 1-0 | 1-0 | 1-0 | 1-0 | 2-2 | 1-4 |
| Paris Saint-Germain FC | 1-0 | 0-0 | 1-0 | 1-1 | 1-0 | 3-1 | 1-1 | 2-0 | 0-0 | 0-1 | 0-0 | 2-1 | 0-3 | ■ | 1-2 | 1-0 | 3-0 | 2-0 | 1-1 | 2-3 |
| Racing de Paris | 3-0 | 1-2 | 2-2 | 2-1 | 1-1 | 5-0 | 1-1 | 0-0 | 1-1 | 1-1 | 1-1 | 3-1 | 0-1 |  | ■ | 2-1 | 1-2 | 0-2 | 2-0 | 0-0 |
| Stade Rennais | 1-3 | 0-1 | 0-2 | 0-1 | 1-2 | 1-2 | 1-0 | 0-0 | 0-1 | 0-1 | 0-0 | 1-3 | 1-0 | 0-0 | 1-0 | ■ | 0-0 | 1-0 | 2-0 | 0-0 |
| AS Saint-Étienne | 1-1 | 2-0 | 1-1 | 1-1 | 0-0 | 1-0 | 1-0 | 0-1 | 0-0 | 0-0 | 0-0 | 0-0 | 1-0 | 1-0 | 4-0 | 2-0 | ■ | 1-1 | 1-0 | 0-0 |
| Sochaux-Montbéliard | 2-2 | 0-2 | 3-0 | 2-1 | 4-0 | 0-0 | 1-0 | 2-2 | 2-2 | 2-1 | 0-1 | 3-1 | 0-0 | 0-1 | 0-1 | 1-1 | 3-3 | ■ | 0-1 | 1-1 |
| Toulon et du Var | 1-1 | 0-0 | 2-3 | 0-0 | 3-0 | 0-0 | 1-0 | 0-1 | 1-3 | 1-0 | 1-1 | 2-0 | 1-1 | 1-0 | 2-0 | 2-1 | 0-0 |  | ■ | 3-2 |
| Toulouse FC | 2-0 | 1-1 | 5-0 | 3-0 | 2-0 | 1-0 | 0-0 | 0-0 | 0-0 | 2-1 | 2-1 | 1-0 | 2-0 | 1-1 | 3-0 | 4-2 | 2-1 | 2-1 | 1-0 | ■ |

## Division 1

| | | Pd | Wn | Dw | Ls | GF | GA | Pts | |
|---|---|---|---|---|---|---|---|---|---|
| 1. | GIRONDINS DE BORDEAUX FC (BORDEAUX) | 38 | 20 | 13 | 5 | 57 | 27 | 53 | |
| 2. | Olympique de Marseille (Marseille) | 38 | 18 | 13 | 7 | 52 | 33 | 49 | |
| 3. | Toulouse FC (Toulouse) | 38 | 18 | 12 | 8 | 54 | 32 | 48 | |
| 4. | Association de la Jeunesse Auxerroise (Auxerre) | 38 | 17 | 13 | 8 | 45 | 32 | 47 | |
| 5. | AS de Monaco (Monaco) | 38 | 15 | 15 | 8 | 41 | 33 | 45 | |
| 6. | FC de Metz (Metz) | 38 | 14 | 15 | 9 | 54 | 32 | 43 | |
| 7. | Paris Saint-Germain FC (Paris) | 38 | 14 | 13 | 11 | 35 | 33 | 41 | |
| 8. | Brest Armorique FC (Brest) | 38 | 14 | 12 | 12 | 43 | 41 | 40 | |
| 9. | Stade Lavallois FC (Laval) | 38 | 12 | 14 | 12 | 40 | 46 | 38 | |
| 10. | Racing Club de Lens (Lens) | 38 | 11 | 15 | 12 | 37 | 40 | 37 | |
| 11. | Olympique GC de Nice (Nice) | 38 | 15 | 7 | 16 | 38 | 49 | 37 | |
| 12. | FC de Nantes (Nantes) | 38 | 12 | 12 | 14 | 35 | 38 | 36 | |
| 13. | Racing Club de Paris (Paris) | 38 | 14 | 8 | 16 | 41 | 45 | 36 | * |
| 14. | Lille Olympique SC (Lille) | 38 | 12 | 10 | 16 | 39 | 38 | 34 | |
| 15. | SC de Toulon et du Var (Toulon) | 38 | 10 | 14 | 14 | 36 | 46 | 34 | |
| 16. | AS de Saint-Étienne (Saint-Étienne) | 38 | 9 | 15 | 14 | 27 | 32 | 33 | |
| 17. | Havre AC (Le Havre) | 38 | 8 | 16 | 14 | 39 | 50 | 32 | |
| 18. | FC Sochaux-Montbéliard (Montbéliard) | 38 | 9 | 13 | 16 | 35 | 51 | 31 | PO |
| 19. | AS Nancy-Lorraine (Nancy) | 38 | 8 | 13 | 17 | 28 | 40 | 29 | R |
| 20. | Stade Rennais FC (Rennes) | 38 | 5 | 7 | 26 | 20 | 58 | 17 | R |
| | | 760 | 255 | 250 | 255 | 796 | 796 | 760 | |

## Top goal-scorers

| | | | |
|---|---|---|---|
| 1) | Bernard ZÉNIER | (FC de Metz) | 18 |
| 2) | Gérard BUSCHER | (Brest Armorique FC) | 15 |
| | Phillipe FARGEON | (Girondins de Bordeaux FC) | 15 |

* Racing Club de Paris (Paris) changed their name to Matra Racing de Paris (Paris) for the next season;  Limoges FC (Limoges) changed their name to Limoges Foot 87 (Limoges) for the next season;  La Roche Amicale des Écoles Publiques du Bourg changed their name pre-season from AEPB (La Roche-sur-Yon).

## Promotion/Relegation Play-Offs

| | | |
|---|---|---|
| FC Sochaux-Montbéliard (Montbéliard) | 1-0, 0-2 | AS de Cannes (Cannes) |
| AS de Cannes (Cannes) | 1-0, 1-1 | Olympique Lyonnais (Lyon) |
| Stade Malherbe Caennais (Caen) | 1-2 | AS de Cannes (Cannes) |
| Olympique Lyonnais (Lyon) | 4-3 | FC de Mulhouse 1893 (Mulhouse) |

## Division 2 Play-Off

| | | |
|---|---|---|
| Chamois Niortais (Niort) | 0-1, 1-3 | Montpellier Paillade SC (Montpellier) |

| | Division 2 (Group "A") | Pd | Wn | Dw | Ls | GF | GA | Pts | |
|---|---|---|---|---|---|---|---|---|---|
| 1. | Chamois Niortais (Niort) | 34 | 24 | 7 | 3 | 48 | 15 | 55 | P |
| 2. | Stade Malherbe Caennais (Caen) | 34 | 21 | 6 | 7 | 62 | 30 | 48 | PO |
| 3. | FC de Mulhouse 1893 (Mulhouse) | 34 | 16 | 14 | 4 | 54 | 29 | 46 | PO |
| 4. | Stade de Reims (Reims) | 34 | 18 | 7 | 9 | 53 | 34 | 43 | |
| 5. | Stade Quimperois (Quimper) | 34 | 14 | 13 | 7 | 48 | 36 | 41 | |
| 6. | AS Beauvais-Marissel (Beauvais) | 34 | 15 | 8 | 11 | 47 | 39 | 38 | |
| 7. | FC de Tours (Tours) | 34 | 11 | 13 | 10 | 37 | 36 | 35 | |
| 8. | US Dunkerquoise (Dunkerque) | 34 | 12 | 9 | 13 | 33 | 41 | 33 | |
| 9. | Racing Club de Strasbourg (Strasbourg) | 34 | 12 | 8 | 14 | 42 | 40 | 32 | |
| 10. | En Avant de Guingamp (Guingamp) | 34 | 10 | 12 | 12 | 48 | 47 | 32 | |
| 11. | US Orléans Football (Orléans) | 34 | 11 | 10 | 13 | 33 | 35 | 32 | |
| 12. | SC de l'Ouest Angers (Angers) | 34 | 9 | 14 | 11 | 34 | 41 | 32 | |
| 13. | US Valenciennes-Anzin (Valenciennes) | 34 | 10 | 11 | 13 | 37 | 39 | 31 | |
| 14. | La Roche Amicales des Écoles Publiques du Bourg | 34 | 9 | 11 | 14 | 34 | 40 | 29 | n/c |
| 15. | SC d'Abbeville (Abbeville) | 34 | 8 | 10 | 16 | 28 | 44 | 26 | |
| 16. | Club Omnisports de Saint-Dizier (Saint-Dizier) | 34 | 6 | 12 | 16 | 34 | 52 | 24 | |
| 17. | Amiens SC (Amiens) | 34 | 5 | 13 | 16 | 25 | 56 | 23 | R |
| 18. | AS Red Star (Saint-Ouen) | 34 | 4 | 4 | 26 | 25 | 68 | 12 | R |
| | | 612 | 215 | 182 | 215 | 722 | 722 | 612 | |

| Division 2 (Group "B") | Pd | Wn | Dw | Ls | GF | GA | Pts | |
|---|---|---|---|---|---|---|---|---|
| 1. Montpellier Paillade SC (Montpellier) | 34 | 22 | 8 | 4 | 73 | 25 | 52 | P |
| 2. Olympique Lyonnais (Lyon) | 34 | 19 | 10 | 5 | 71 | 28 | 48 | PO |
| 3. AS de Cannes (Cannes) | 34 | 20 | 5 | 9 | 57 | 24 | 45 | PO |
| 4. Olympique d'Alès en Cévennes (Alès) | 34 | 16 | 11 | 7 | 47 | 24 | 43 | |
| 5. Sporting Étoile Club Bastiais (Bastia) | 34 | 17 | 7 | 10 | 62 | 49 | 41 | |
| 6. Nîmes Olympique (Nîmes) | 34 | 13 | 12 | 9 | 62 | 45 | 38 | |
| 7. Limoges FC (Limoges) | 34 | 13 | 10 | 11 | 35 | 34 | 36 | R4 |
| 8. FC de Sète (Sète) | 34 | 13 | 9 | 12 | 40 | 41 | 35 | |
| 9. FC Montceau-Bourgogne 71 (Montceau-les-Mines) | 34 | 12 | 10 | 12 | 41 | 38 | 34 | |
| 10. CS Cuiseaux-Louhans (Cuiseaux-Louhans) | 34 | 11 | 12 | 11 | 41 | 44 | 34 | |
| 11. FC de Gueugnon (Gueugnon) | 34 | 10 | 13 | 11 | 31 | 42 | 33 | |
| 12. Club Omnisport du Puy (Le Puy) | 34 | 10 | 10 | 14 | 36 | 40 | 30 | |
| 13. Gazélec FC Ajaccien (Ajaccio) | 34 | 10 | 9 | 15 | 38 | 51 | 29 | |
| 14. Istres Sports Football (Istres) | 34 | 9 | 11 | 14 | 33 | 47 | 29 | |
| 15. FC de Martigues (Martigues) | 34 | 9 | 9 | 16 | 29 | 41 | 27 | |
| 16. CS de Thonon (Thonon) | 34 | 7 | 10 | 17 | 27 | 45 | 24 | R4 |
| 17. FC de Bourges (Bourges) | 34 | 7 | 8 | 19 | 32 | 60 | 22 | R |
| 18. AS Biterroise (Béziers) | 34 | 2 | 8 | 24 | 18 | 95 | 12 | R |
| | 612 | 220 | 172 | 220 | 773 | 773 | 612 | |

## Coupe de France Final  (Parc des Princes, Paris – 10/06/87 – 45,145)

**GIRONDINS DE BORDEAUX FC**           **2-0**           Olympique de Marseille (Marseille)

*Fargeon 14', Zlatko Vujovic 88'*

**Bordeaux:** Dropsy, Thouvenel, Zoran Vujovic, Specht, Roche, Girard, Zlatko Vujovic, Touré, Fargeon, Ferreri, Tigana.

**Marseille:** Bell, Galtier (Cubaynes 53'), Bade, Fòrster, Domergue, Passi, Laurey (Genghini 46'), Giresse, Papin, Sliskovic, Diallo.

## Semi-Finals   (26/05/87 – 02/06/87)

| | | |
|---|---|---|
| Olympique d'Alès en Cévennes (Alès) | 2-2, 0-0 | Girondins de Bordeaux FC (Bordeaux) |
| Olympique de Marseille (Marseille) | 2-0, 5-1 | Stade de Reims (Reims) |

## Quarter-Finals   (12-19/05/87)

| | | |
|---|---|---|
| Olympique d'Alès en Cévennes (Alès) | 2-0, 0-1 | Racing Club de Strasbourg (Strasbourg) |
| Girondins de Bordeaux FC (Bordeaux) | 3-1, 1-2 | Lille Olympique SC (Lille) |
| Stade Lavallois FC (Laval) | 1-0, 0-1 (aet) | Stade de Reims (Reims) |
| Stade de Reims (Reims) won 4-3 on penalties. | | |
| Racing Club de Lens (Lens) | 0-1, 0-0 | Olympique de Marseille (Marseille) |

# 1987-88

| 1987-1988 Division One | AJ Auxerroise | Gir. de Bordeaux | Brest Armorique | AS de Cannes | Havre AC | Stade Lavallois | Racing de Lens | Lille Olympique | Olymp. Marseille | FC de Metz | AS de Monaco | Montpellier Pail. | FC de Nantes | Olymp. GC Nice | Chamois Niort. | Paris St.-Germain | Racing de Paris | AS Saint-Étienne | Toulon et du Var | Toulouse FC |
|---|---|---|---|---|---|---|---|---|---|---|---|---|---|---|---|---|---|---|---|---|
| AJ Auxerroise | ■ | 1-3 | 4-0 | 1-0 | 1-1 | 1-1 | 2-0 | 2-1 | 2-0 | 0-1 | 0-0 | 1-1 | 1-0 | 2-0 | 1-3 | 3-0 | 3-0 | 0-1 | 0-0 | 0-2 |
| Girondins de Bordeaux | 0-0 | ■ | 2-0 | 3-3 | 2-2 | 1-0 | 5-2 | 1-0 | 2-0 | 3-2 | 3-1 | 1-0 | 2-1 | 4-2 | 1-0 | 0-0 | 1-0 | 1-0 | 3-0 | 2-2 |
| Brest Armorique | 1-1 | 1-1 | ■ | 1-0 | 3-1 | 2-1 | 4-1 | 2-2 | 2-1 | 1-0 | 0-2 | 4-0 | 0-0 | 0-1 | 1-0 | 0-0 | 0-0 | 1-0 | 1-0 | 1-0 |
| AS de Cannes | 0-0 | 1-0 | 2-1 | ■ | 3-0 | 1-0 | 2-1 | 1-5 | 1-0 | 3-3 | 1-1 | 0-0 | 1-4 | 0-1 | 2-1 | 1-3 | 3-1 | 1-0 | 1-0 | 1-1 |
| Havre AC | 1-2 | 0-1 | 3-2 | 2-2 | ■ | 2-1 | 0-1 | 0-0 | 1-0 | 1-1 | 0-0 | 1-3 | 1-0 | 2-1 | 3-0 | 0-1 | 1-1 | 1-1 | 1-1 | 0-1 |
| Stade Lavallois | 0-0 | 0-0 | 0-0 | 2-1 | 4-3 | ■ | 4-0 | 0-1 | 0-2 | 3-0 | 0-0 | 1-0 | 1-1 | 1-2 | 2-0 | 2-0 | 1-1 | 4-0 | 0-3 | 1-0 |
| Racing de Lens | 2-1 | 1-0 | 2-1 | 0-0 | 0-0 | 1-2 | ■ | 1-1 | 2-4 | 2-0 | 1-3 | 2-1 | 1-2 | 0-1 | 3-1 | 0-0 | 2-1 | 1-0 | 3-1 | 2-0 |
| Lille Olympique | 0-1 | 1-0 | 2-0 | 0-0 | 0-0 | 0-0 | 1-1 | ■ | 1-1 | 1-0 | 0-1 | 3-1 | 3-0 | 1-0 | 0-1 | 1-0 | 5-0 | 1-2 | 1-0 | 2-0 |
| Olympique Marseille | 0-1 | 1-0 | 1-0 | 3-0 | 3-1 | 2-1 | 4-1 | 0-1 | ■ | 1-0 | 2-0 | 1-1 | 3-0 | 2-0 | 1-0 | 1-2 | 2-0 | 5-1 | 1-1 | 1-0 |
| FC de Metz | 1-0 | 2-0 | 1-1 | 2-3 | 1-0 | 2-1 | 2-2 | 3-1 | 3-1 | ■ | 2-2 | 0-1 | 1-0 | 2-0 | 2-0 | 1-0 | 0-0 | 2-1 | 2-0 | 4-1 |
| AS de Monaco | 3-2 | 1-0 | 2-0 | 4-1 | 2-0 | 2-0 | 3-0 | 1-0 | 3-1 | 2-1 | ■ | 0-0 | 2-1 | 1-0 | 1-3 | 2-1 | 3-0 | 2-1 | 0-0 | 5-1 |
| Montpellier Paillade SC | 2-2 | 0-0 | 6-0 | 4-2 | 3-1 | 2-1 | 4-0 | 3-1 | 4-0 | 1-0 | 2-1 | ■ | 0-0 | 4-1 | 1-0 | 4-1 | 6-1 | 5-0 | 0-1 | 4-2 |
| FC de Nantes | 0-0 | 1-0 | 1-0 | 2-1 | 2-0 | 1-2 | 2-0 | 1-1 | 5-0 | 0-0 | 1-1 | 0-0 | ■ | 0-1 | 2-1 | 0-0 | 1-1 | 2-3 | 1-1 | 3-1 |
| Olympique GC Nice | 1-0 | 0-1 | 2-0 | 1-2 | 1-2 | 0-1 | 0-1 | 2-1 | 3-1 | 0-0 | 0-0 | 2-0 | 3-1 | ■ | 1-0 | 2-0 | 1-2 | 2-3 | 0-2 | 3-0 |
| Chamois Niort. | 0-0 | 0-0 | 3-0 | 0-2 | 1-2 | 0-0 | 1-1 | 1-0 | 1-0 | 1-3 | 0-0 | 1-3 | 0-0 |  | ■ | 1-2 | 2-2 | 2-1 | 2-1 | 0-0 |
| Paris Saint-Germain FC | 1-1 | 1-0 | 0-0 | 1-1 | 2-0 | 0-0 | 4-1 | 1-3 | 1-1 | 0-2 | 0-1 | 2-1 | 0-2 | 0-4 | 1-3 | ■ | 1-1 | 3-0 | 1-0 | 2-0 |
| Racing de Paris | 1-0 | 1-0 | 1-1 | 0-0 | 2-0 | 1-0 | 1-0 | 3-0 | 0-0 | 2-0 | 1-0 | 0-2 | 2-2 | 2-1 | 1-1 | 2-1 | ■ | 2-2 | 0-0 | 0-0 |
| AS Saint-Étienne | 2-1 | 1-1 | 4-0 | 1-0 | 2-1 | 2-1 | 2-1 | 4-3 | 0-1 | 2-0 | 3-0 | 2-1 | 1-1 | 3-2 | 2-0 | 1-3 | 0-2 | ■ | 0-0 | 2-0 |
| Toulon et du Var | 0-0 | 0-1 | 3-0 | 1-0 | 3-0 | 3-0 | 2-0 | 3-0 | 1-2 | 0-0 | 0-0 | 5-2 | 4-1 | 1-1 | 1-0 | 0-0 | 1-1 |  | ■ | 1-0 |
| Toulouse FC | 0-0 | 2-1 | 2-1 | 0-1 | 2-1 | 1-0 | 0-1 | 2-1 | 1-0 | 2-0 | 1-1 | 3-1 | 0-1 | 2-0 | 1-0 | 2-1 | 0-0 | 2-3 | 1-0 | ■ |

## Division 1

| | | Pd | Wn | Dw | Ls | GF | GA | Pts | |
|---|---|---|---|---|---|---|---|---|---|
| 1. | AS DE MONACO (MONACO) | 38 | 20 | 12 | 6 | 53 | 29 | 52 | |
| 2. | Girondins de Bordeaux FC (Bordeaux) | 38 | 18 | 10 | 10 | 46 | 30 | 46 | |
| 3. | Montpellier Paillade SC (Montpellier) | 38 | 18 | 9 | 11 | 68 | 38 | 45 | |
| 4. | AS de Saint-Étienne (Saint-Étienne) | 38 | 18 | 6 | 14 | 54 | 56 | 42 | |
| 5. | SC de Toulon et du Var (Toulon) | 38 | 14 | 13 | 11 | 41 | 26 | 41 | |
| 6. | Olympique de Marseille (Marseille) | 38 | 18 | 5 | 15 | 49 | 43 | 41 | |
| 7. | Matra Racing de Paris (Paris) | 38 | 12 | 17 | 9 | 35 | 42 | 41 | |
| 8. | FC de Metz (Metz) | 38 | 16 | 8 | 14 | 46 | 40 | 40 | |
| 9. | Association de la Jeunesse Auxerroise (Auxerre) | 38 | 12 | 15 | 11 | 37 | 29 | 39 | |
| 10. | FC de Nantes (Nantes) | 38 | 13 | 13 | 12 | 46 | 41 | 39 | |
| 11. | Lille Olympique SC (Lille) | 38 | 14 | 9 | 15 | 45 | 39 | 37 | |
| 12. | AS de Cannes (Cannes) | 38 | 13 | 11 | 14 | 42 | 52 | 37 | |
| 13. | Toulouse FC (Toulouse) | 38 | 14 | 7 | 17 | 35 | 47 | 35 | |
| 14. | Stade Lavallois FC (Laval) | 38 | 12 | 10 | 16 | 38 | 38 | 34 | |
| 15. | Paris Saint-Germain FC (Saint-Germain) | 38 | 12 | 10 | 16 | 36 | 45 | 34 | |
| 16. | Olympique GC de Nice (Nice) | 38 | 15 | 3 | 20 | 42 | 47 | 33 | |
| 17. | Racing Club de Lens (Lens) | 38 | 13 | 7 | 18 | 40 | 62 | 33 | |
| 18. | Chamois Niortais (Niort) | 38 | 11 | 10 | 17 | 34 | 42 | 32 | PO |
| 19. | Brest Armorique FC (Brest) | 38 | 11 | 10 | 17 | 32 | 52 | 32 | R |
| 20. | Havre AC (Le Havre) | 38 | 8 | 11 | 19 | 35 | 56 | 27 | R |
| | | 760 | 282 | 196 | 282 | 854 | 854 | 760 | |

## Top goal-scorers

| | | | |
|---|---|---|---|
| 1) | Jean-Pierre PAPIN | (Olympique de Marseille) | 19 |
| 2) | Patrice GARANDE | (AS de Saint-Étienne) | 17 |
| 3) | Mark HATELEY | (AS de Monaco) | 14 |
| 4) | Klaus ALLOFS | (Olympique de Marseille) | 13 |
| | Phillipe FARGEON | (Girondins de Bordeaux FC) | 13 |
| | Maurice JOHNSTON | (FC de Nantes) | 13 |
| | OUDJANI | (Racing Club de Lens) | 13 |

## Promotion/Relegation Play-Offs

| | | |
|---|---|---|
| Chamois Niortais (Niort) | 1-1,  0-3 | Stade Malherbe Caennais (Caen) |
| Olympique Lyonnais (Lyon) | 2-1,  0-2 | Stade Malherbe Caennais (Caen) |
| Olympique Lyonnais (Lyon) | 4-0 | FC de Mulhouse 1893 (Mulhouse) |
| Stade Malherbe Caennais (Caen) | 1-1  (aet – 4-2 pen) | Olympique d'Alès en Cévennes (Alès) |

## Division 2 Play-Off

| | | |
|---|---|---|
| FC Sochaux-Montbéliard (Montbéliard) | 1-2,  0-1 | Racing Club de Strasbourg (Strasbourg) |

| | Division 2 (Group "A") | Pd | Wn | Dw | Ls | GF | GA | Pts | |
|---|---|---|---|---|---|---|---|---|---|
| 1. | FC Sochaux-Montbéliard (Montbéliard) | 34 | 29 | 3 | 2 | 97 | 17 | 61 | P |
| 2. | Olympique Lyonnais (Lyon) | 34 | 18 | 8 | 8 | 65 | 44 | 44 | PO |
| 3. | Olympique d'Alès en Cévennes (Alès) | 34 | 15 | 11 | 8 | 39 | 30 | 41 | PO |
| 4. | FC Montceau-Bourgogne 71 (Montceau-les-Mines) | 34 | 16 | 8 | 10 | 44 | 42 | 40 | |
| 5. | US Orléans Football (Orléans) | 34 | 13 | 10 | 11 | 42 | 39 | 36 | |
| 6. | Nîmes Olympique (Nîmes) | 34 | 15 | 6 | 13 | 40 | 40 | 36 | |
| 7. | CS Cuiseaux Louhans (Cuiseaux Louhans) | 34 | 12 | 9 | 13 | 35 | 34 | 33 | |
| 8. | Sporting Étoile Club Bastiais (Bastia) | 34 | 15 | 3 | 16 | 41 | 52 | 33 | |
| 9. | FC Grenoble-Dauphiné (Grenoble) | 34 | 11 | 10 | 13 | 48 | 61 | 32 | |
| 10. | FC de Gueugnon (Gueugnon) | 34 | 11 | 9 | 14 | 32 | 28 | 31 | |
| 11. | FC de Martigues (Martigues) | 34 | 9 | 13 | 12 | 41 | 42 | 31 | |
| 12. | FC de Sète (Sète) | 34 | 8 | 13 | 13 | 34 | 46 | 29 | |
| 13. | Club Omnisport du Puy (Le Puy) | 34 | 10 | 8 | 16 | 39 | 46 | 28 | |
| 14. | Istres Sports Football (Istres) | 34 | 10 | 8 | 16 | 39 | 48 | 28 | |
| 15. | Cercle Dijon Football (Dijon) | 34 | 9 | 10 | 15 | 26 | 40 | 28 | |
| 16. | Gazélec FC Ajaccien (Ajaccio) | 34 | 9 | 9 | 16 | 29 | 44 | 27 | R |
| 17. | FC de Tours (Tours) | 34 | 10 | 7 | 17 | 25 | 40 | 27 | R |
| 18. | Stade Olympique Châtelleraudais (Châtellerault) | 34 | 10 | 7 | 17 | 26 | 49 | 27 | R |
| | | 612 | 230 | 152 | 230 | 742 | 742 | 612 | |

| Division 2 (Group "B") | Pd | Wn | Dw | Ls | GF | GA | Pts | |
|---|---|---|---|---|---|---|---|---|
| 1. Racing Club de Strasbourg (Strasbourg) | 34 | 20 | 9 | 5 | 56 | 22 | 49 | P |
| 2. Stade Malherbe Caennais (Caen) | 34 | 20 | 9 | 5 | 54 | 22 | 49 | PO |
| 3. FC de Mulhouse 1893 (Mulhouse) | 34 | 19 | 7 | 8 | 49 | 31 | 45 | PO |
| 4. FC de Rouen (Rouen) | 34 | 16 | 8 | 10 | 65 | 46 | 40 | |
| 5. AS Nancy-Lorraine (Nancy) | 34 | 13 | 12 | 9 | 44 | 31 | 38 | |
| 6. SC de l'Ouest Angers (Angers) | 34 | 14 | 10 | 10 | 39 | 38 | 38 | |
| 7. Stade de Reims (Reims) | 34 | 12 | 11 | 11 | 42 | 40 | 35 | |
| 8. US du Littoral Dunkerquois (Dunkerque) | 34 | 11 | 12 | 11 | 34 | 34 | 34 | n/c |
| 9. US Valenciennes-Anzin (Valenciennes) | 34 | 10 | 13 | 11 | 35 | 43 | 33 | |
| 10. Stade Rennais FC (Rennes) | 34 | 11 | 10 | 13 | 33 | 33 | 32 | |
| 11. SC d'Abbeville (Abbeville) | 34 | 11 | 9 | 14 | 31 | 36 | 31 | |
| 12. En Avant de Guingamp (Guingamp) | 34 | 9 | 13 | 12 | 42 | 55 | 31 | |
| 13. AS Beauvais-Marissel (Beauvais) | 34 | 9 | 13 | 12 | 23 | 37 | 31 | |
| 14. Quimper Cornouailles FC (Quimper) | 34 | 10 | 9 | 15 | 42 | 43 | 29 | n/c |
| 15. La Roche Amicale des Écoles Publiques du Bourg | 34 | 9 | 8 | 17 | 33 | 40 | 26 | |
| 16. Club Omnisports de Saint-Dizier (Saint-Dizier) | 34 | 9 | 7 | 18 | 25 | 40 | 25 | R |
| 17. Entente Melun-Fontainebleau 77 (Melun) | 34 | 7 | 9 | 18 | 23 | 46 | 23 | R |
| 18. FC de Lorient (Lorient) | 34 | 6 | 11 | 17 | 34 | 67 | 23 | R |
| | 612 | 216 | 180 | 216 | 704 | 704 | 612 | |

## Coupe de France Final   (Parc des Princes, Paris – 11/06/88 – 44,531)

**FC DE METZ (METZ)**          **1-1  (aet – 5-4 penalties)**          FC Sochaux-Montbéliard

*Black 45'*                                                                          *Paille 36'*

**Metz:** Ettore, Gaillot, Pons, Cartier (Lopez 77'), Kastendeuch, Pauk (Bracconi 106'), Micciche, Zanon, Black, Hinschberger, Zénier.

**Sochaux:** Rousset, Croci, Peltier, Silvestre, Hadzibegic, Thomas (Colin 97'), Henry, Sauzée, Paille, Bazdarevic, Morin (Madar 65').

## Semi-Finals   (31/05/88 – 08/06/88)

| FC de Metz (Metz) | 4-0, 1-3 | Stade de Reims (Reims) |
|---|---|---|
| Olympique GC de Nice (Nice) | 2-1, 0-2 | FC Sochaux-Montbéliard (Montbéliard) |

## Quarter-Finals   (10-18/05/88)

| Racing Club de Lens (Lens) | 2-2, 0-1 | FC Sochaux-Montbéliard (Montbéliard) |
|---|---|---|
| Olympique GC de Nice (Nice) | 3-0, 1-0 | Lille Olympique SC (Lille) |
| Quimper Cornouailles FC (Quimper) | 1-0, 0-5 | FC de Metz (Metz) |
| Stade de Reims (Reims) | 3-0, 3-1 | Stade Olymp. Châtelleraudais (Châtellerault) |

| 1988-1989 Division One | AJ Auxerroise | Gir. de Bordeaux | Stade Caennais | AS de Cannes | Stade Lavallois | Racing de Lens | Lille Olympique | Olymp. Marseille | FC de Metz | AS de Monaco | Montpellier Pail. | FC de Nantes | Olymp. GC Nice | Paris St.Germain | Racing de Paris | AS Saint-Étienne | Sochaux-Mont. | RC Strasbourg | Toulon et du Var | Toulouse FC |
|---|---|---|---|---|---|---|---|---|---|---|---|---|---|---|---|---|---|---|---|---|
| AJ Auxerroise | ■ | 1-1 | 3-0 | 0-0 | 2-1 | 1-0 | 1-0 | 1-0 | 2-1 | 0-0 | 1-0 | 1-0 | 1-0 | 0-0 | 1-1 | 2-0 | 2-1 | 2-1 | 3-0 | 0-0 |
| Girondins de Bordeaux | 2-0 | ■ | 2-3 | 0-0 | 2-1 | 4-1 | 0-0 | 0-0 | 4-1 | 1-1 | 2-1 | 5-0 | 2-0 | 0-1 | 3-2 | 5-0 | 1-2 | 2-0 | 1-1 | 1-1 |
| Stade Malherbe Caennais | 1-0 | 3-0 | ■ | 3-0 | 1-1 | 1-0 | 2-1 | 0-0 | 0-0 | 0-3 | 0-1 | 2-3 | 2-1 | 0-1 | 1-1 | 2-3 | 0-0 | 3-3 | 2-1 | 3-0 |
| AS de Cannes | 3-0 | 1-1 | 2-0 | ■ | 3-2 | 3-0 | 1-0 | 3-1 | 1-1 | 3-2 | 0-1 | 1-2 | 2-0 | 0-3 | 2-1 | 1-0 | 2-0 | 4-1 | 1-0 | 5-1 |
| Stade Lavallois | 0-1 | 1-0 | 1-1 | 2-0 | ■ | 2-1 | 1-2 | 0-1 | 3-0 | 0-0 | 0-1 | 0-2 | 1-2 | 1-2 | 4-2 | 1-1 | 1-1 | 1-0 | 0-0 | 2-0 |
| Racing de Lens | 0-1 | 0-2 | 5-0 | 2-2 | 0-2 | ■ | 1-2 | 0-1 | 0-2 | 1-1 | 0-0 | 0-0 | 2-0 | 0-0 | 1-1 | 1-3 | 2-2 | 1-3 | 0-1 | 1-1 |
| Lille Olympique | 1-0 | 0-1 | 1-1 | 1-0 | 8-0 | 1-0 | ■ | 2-1 | 1-1 | 2-4 | 3-1 | 0-1 | 2-0 | 2-1 | 3-0 | 2-2 | 2-0 | 1-1 | 0-0 | 0-0 |
| Olympique Marseille | 2-1 | 2-2 | 4-2 | 2-1 | 1-0 | 5-2 | 1-1 | ■ | 3-2 | 2-2 | 1-1 | 1-0 | 3-2 | 1-0 | 2-0 | 0-0 | 3-1 | 1-0 | 3-1 | |
| FC de Metz | 2-1 | 3-0 | 1-0 | 2-1 | 0-0 | 4-0 | 3-1 | 1-3 | ■ | 0-3 | 1-2 | 0-0 | 1-0 | 0-1 | 1-1 | 1-2 | 1-0 | 1-1 | 1-2 | 1-1 |
| AS de Monaco | 1-2 | 4-2 | 3-1 | 2-0 | 1-0 | 1-0 | 1-1 | 3-0 | 1-1 | ■ | 4-2 | 4-1 | 1-1 | 1-0 | 1-0 | 2-2 | 0-0 | 4-1 | 2-2 | 1-0 |
| Montpellier Paillade SC | 1-0 | 2-2 | 1-0 | 0-0 | 6-2 | 2-0 | 2-3 | 1-0 | 5-3 | 4-2 | ■ | 1-4 | 1-1 | 0-0 | 0-0 | 2-0 | 1-2 | 1-0 | 0-1 | 1-0 |
| FC de Nantes | 3-2 | 1-0 | 3-1 | 1-1 | 1-1 | 3-1 | 1-0 | 1-1 | 1-0 | 1-1 | 2-1 | ■ | 0-1 | 1-1 | 1-0 | 1-1 | 0-0 | 2-2 | 0-0 | 1-2 |
| Olympique GC Nice | 1-0 | 1-0 | 5-0 | 2-1 | 1-0 | 3-0 | 0-1 | 2-2 | 1-1 | 1-1 | 3-3 | 1-0 | ■ | 3-1 | 3-2 | 1-0 | 3-2 | 1-0 | 1-0 | 2-0 |
| Paris Saint-Germain FC | 2-2 | 1-1 | 3-0 | 1-0 | 3-0 | 3-2 | 1-1 | 0-0 | 2-2 | 0-2 | 3-2 | 1-0 | 1-0 | ■ | 2-1 | 3-1 | 1-0 | 1-0 | 0-0 | 2-1 |
| Racing de Paris | 1-2 | 4-1 | 3-1 | 1-0 | 2-2 | 3-0 | 1-0 | 1-4 | 3-0 | 4-0 | 2-0 | 1-1 | 0-2 | | ■ | 3-1 | 0-2 | 2-1 | 1-1 | 0-1 |
| AS Saint-Étienne | 1-1 | 1-0 | 1-1 | 1-0 | 1-0 | 2-4 | 2-0 | 0-0 | 0-1 | 0-1 | 1-0 | 1-1 | 0-0 | 0-0 | 4-3 | ■ | 1-2 | 0-0 | 2-1 | 3-2 |
| Sochaux-Montbéliard | 3-2 | 1-1 | 1-0 | 4-0 | 3-0 | 2-1 | 2-0 | 0-0 | 1-0 | 0-0 | 2-0 | 0-1 | 1-0 | 2-1 | 2-0 | 1-0 | ■ | 3-0 | 2-1 | 2-2 |
| RC Strasbourg | 1-0 | 3-2 | 1-2 | 0-0 | 3-0 | 4-1 | 1-3 | 2-3 | 1-2 | 1-2 | 3-1 | 2-0 | 3-0 | 0-0 | 1-1 | 0-1 | 0-3 | ■ | 2-1 | 4-1 |
| Toulon et du Var | 1-2 | 1-0 | 1-0 | 3-0 | 0-0 | 3-1 | 2-1 | 1-2 | 1-0 | 1-0 | 1-1 | 1-0 | 0-0 | 0-1 | 1-0 | 0-0 | 0-0 | | ■ | 1-1 |
| Toulouse FC | 0-0 | 1-1 | 0-0 | 4-1 | 0-0 | 2-1 | 1-1 | 0-0 | 2-1 | 2-0 | 2-2 | 1-2 | 2-1 | 0-0 | 2-1 | 3-1 | 2-1 | 4-0 | 1-0 | ■ |

## Division 1

| | Division 1 | Pd | Wn | Dw | Ls | GF | GA | Pts | |
|---|---|---|---|---|---|---|---|---|---|
| 1. | OLYMPIQUE DE MARSEILLE (MARSEILLE) | 38 | 20 | 13 | 5 | 56 | 35 | 73 | |
| 2. | Paris Saint-Germain FC (Paris) | 38 | 19 | 13 | 6 | 45 | 26 | 70 | |
| 3. | AS de Monaco (Monaco) | 38 | 18 | 14 | 6 | 62 | 38 | 68 | |
| 4. | FC Sochaux-Montbéliard (Montbéliard) | 38 | 19 | 11 | 8 | 50 | 28 | 68 | |
| 5. | Association de la Jeunesse Auxerroise (Auxerre) | 38 | 18 | 9 | 11 | 41 | 32 | 63 | |
| 6. | Olympique GC de Nice (Nice) | 38 | 16 | 9 | 13 | 45 | 40 | 57 | |
| 7. | FC de Nantes (Nantes) | 38 | 15 | 12 | 11 | 41 | 40 | 57 | |
| 8. | Lille Olympique SC (Lille) | 38 | 15 | 11 | 12 | 50 | 38 | 56 | |
| 9. | Montpellier Paillade SC (Montpellier) | 38 | 14 | 10 | 14 | 51 | 53 | 52 | * |
| 10. | Toulouse FC (Toulouse) | 38 | 12 | 15 | 11 | 44 | 46 | 51 | |
| 11. | SC de Toulon et du Var (Toulon) | 38 | 12 | 14 | 12 | 30 | 29 | 50 | |
| 12. | AS de Cannes (Cannes) | 38 | 14 | 8 | 16 | 45 | 47 | 50 | |
| 13. | Girondins de Bordeaux FC (Bordeaux) | 38 | 12 | 13 | 13 | 54 | 46 | 49 | |
| 14. | AS de Saint-Étienne (Saint-Étienne) | 38 | 12 | 12 | 14 | 39 | 50 | 48 | |
| 15. | FC de Metz (Metz) | 38 | 12 | 11 | 15 | 47 | 49 | 47 | |
| 16. | Stade Malherbe Caennais (Caen) | 38 | 10 | 10 | 18 | 39 | 60 | 40 | * |
| 17. | Matra Racing de Paris (Paris) | 38 | 10 | 9 | 19 | 49 | 56 | 39 | * |
| 18. | Racing Club de Strasbourg (Strasbourg) | 38 | 10 | 9 | 19 | 47 | 59 | 39 | PO |
| 19. | Stade Lavallois FC (Laval) | 38 | 8 | 11 | 19 | 33 | 55 | 35 | R |
| 20. | Racing Club de Lens (Lens) | 38 | 3 | 8 | 27 | 32 | 73 | 17 | R |
| | | 760 | 269 | 222 | 269 | 900 | 900 | 1029 | |

## Top goal-scorers

1) Jean-Pierre PAPIN       (Olympique de Marseille)   22
2) Glenn HODDLE            (AS de Monaco)             18
   Zlatko VUJOVIC          (AS de Cannes)             18

* Matra Racing de Paris (Paris) changed their name to Racing Paris 1 (Paris) for the next season.
  Montpellier Paillade SC (Montpellier) changed their name to Montpellier Hérault SC (Montpellier) for the next season.
  Stade Malherbe Caennais (Caen) changed their name to Stade Malherbe Caen-Calvados-Basse Normandie (Caen) for the next season.

## Promotion/Relegation Play-Offs

| | | |
|---|---|---|
| Racing Club de Strasbourg (Strasbourg) | 2-2, 0-1 | Brest Armorique FC (Brest) |
| Brest Armorique FC (Brest) | 3-0, 0-1 | Nîmes Olympique (Nîmes) |
| Brest Armorique FC (Brest) | 4-1 | Havre AC (Le Havre) |
| Nîmes Olympique (Nîmes) | 1-0 | Stade Rennais FC (Rennes) |

## Division 2 Play-Off

| | | |
|---|---|---|
| Olympique Lyonnais (Lyon) | 2-1, 2-1 | FC de Mulhouse 1893 (Mulhouse) |

| | Division 2 (Group "A") | Pd | Wn | Dw | Ls | GF | GA | Pts | |
|---|---|---|---|---|---|---|---|---|---|
| 1. | FC de Mulhouse 1893 (Mulhouse) | 34 | 24 | 4 | 6 | 66 | 28 | 76 | P |
| 2. | Brest Armorique FC (Brest) | 34 | 22 | 9 | 3 | 62 | 24 | 75 | PO |
| 3. | Stade Rennais FC (Rennes) | 34 | 19 | 8 | 7 | 61 | 28 | 65 | PO |
| 4. | Quimper Cornouailles FC (Quimper) | 34 | 19 | 8 | 7 | 55 | 29 | 65 | |
| 5. | AS Nancy-Lorraine (Nancy) | 34 | 18 | 5 | 11 | 52 | 36 | 59 | |
| 6. | En Avant de Guingamp (Guingamp) | 34 | 11 | 12 | 11 | 51 | 52 | 45 | |
| 7. | US Valenciennes-Anzin (Valenciennes) | 34 | 12 | 8 | 14 | 38 | 39 | 44 | |
| 8. | US du Littoral Dunkerquois (Dunkerque) | 34 | 11 | 11 | 12 | 28 | 40 | 44 | |
| 9. | Stade de Reims (Reims) | 34 | 11 | 10 | 13 | 39 | 37 | 43 | |
| 10. | US de Créteil (Créteil) | 34 | 10 | 11 | 13 | 29 | 39 | 41 | |
| 11. | FC de Rouen (Rouen) | 34 | 9 | 13 | 12 | 31 | 35 | 40 | |
| 12. | Angers SC de l'Ouest (Angers) | 34 | 8 | 15 | 11 | 44 | 43 | 39 | n/c |
| 13. | SC d'Abbeville (Abbeville) | 34 | 10 | 9 | 15 | 39 | 54 | 39 | |
| 14. | FC de Gueugnon (Gueugnon) | 34 | 10 | 8 | 16 | 30 | 43 | 38 | |
| 15. | AS Beauvais-Marissel (Beauvais) | 34 | 10 | 8 | 16 | 29 | 42 | 38 | |
| 16. | La Roche Amicale des Écoles Publiques du Bourg | 34 | 9 | 9 | 16 | 26 | 32 | 36 | |
| 17. | Touquet Athletic Club (Le Touquet) | 34 | 5 | 9 | 20 | 20 | 57 | 24 | R |
| 18. | Mans UC 72 (Le Mans) | 34 | 5 | 9 | 20 | 27 | 69 | 24 | R |
| | | 612 | 223 | 166 | 223 | 727 | 727 | 612 | |

| Division 2 (Group "B") | Pd | Wn | Dw | Ls | GF | GA | Pts | |
|---|---|---|---|---|---|---|---|---|
| 1. Olympique Lyonnais (Lyon) | 34 | 19 | 11 | 4 | 66 | 22 | 68 | P |
| 2. Nîmes Olympique (Nîmes) | 34 | 20 | 6 | 8 | 53 | 30 | 66 | PO |
| 3. Havre AC (Le Havre) | 34 | 18 | 11 | 5 | 48 | 21 | 65 | PO |
| 4. FC de Martigues (Martigues) | 34 | 17 | 7 | 10 | 40 | 30 | 58 | |
| 5. Sporting Étoile Club Bastiais (Bastia) | 34 | 14 | 9 | 11 | 46 | 44 | 51 | |
| 6. Cercle Dijon Football (Dijon) | 34 | 14 | 7 | 13 | 38 | 40 | 49 | |
| 7. CS Cuiseaux-Louhans (Cuiseaux-Louhans) | 34 | 12 | 11 | 11 | 34 | 40 | 47 | |
| 8. Olympique d'Alès en Cévenne (Alès) | 34 | 10 | 16 | 8 | 33 | 31 | 46 | |
| 9. FC Montceau-Bourgogne 71 (Montceau-les-Mines) | 34 | 10 | 13 | 11 | 41 | 40 | 43 | |
| 10. US Orléans Football (Orléans) | 34 | 11 | 10 | 13 | 53 | 60 | 43 | |
| 11. FC Grenoble-Dauphiné (Grenoble) | 34 | 11 | 9 | 14 | 33 | 39 | 42 | |
| 12. FC d'Annecy (Annecy) | 34 | 12 | 6 | 16 | 36 | 47 | 42 | |
| 13. Istres Sports Football (Istres) | 34 | 8 | 15 | 11 | 30 | 35 | 39 | |
| 14. Chamois Niortais (Niort) | 34 | 7 | 17 | 10 | 28 | 31 | 38 | |
| 15. FC de Sète (Sète) | 34 | 10 | 8 | 16 | 35 | 41 | 38 | R |
| 16. Stade Rodez Football (Rodez) | 34 | 7 | 12 | 15 | 34 | 48 | 33 | R |
| 17. Clermont-Ferrand FC (Clermont-Ferrand) | 34 | 7 | 10 | 17 | 27 | 51 | 31 | R |
| 18. Club Omnisport du Puy (Le Puy) | 34 | 5 | 10 | 19 | 29 | 54 | 25 | R |
| | 612 | 212 | 188 | 212 | 704 | 704 | 612 | |

## Coupe de France Final   (Parc des Princes, Paris – 10/06/89 – 44,448)

**OLYMPIQUE DE MARSEILLE**                         **4-3**                         AS de Monaco (Monaco)

*Papin 12', 22', 47', Allofs 65'*                                             *Dib 31', 72', Amoros 88' pen*

**Marseille**: Huard, Thys, Di Méco, Förster, Le Roux, Germain, Meyrieu (Eyraud 46'), Sauzée, Papin, Vercruysse (Gastien 69'), Allofs.

**Monaco**: Ettori, Amoros, Valéry, Sonor, Battiston, Poullain (Kurbos 68'), Puel (Fofana 46'), Dib, Weah, Hoddle, Petit.


## Semi-Finals   (25/05/89 – 03/06/89)

| | | |
|---|---|---|
| AS de Monaco (Monaco) | 0-0, 0-0 (aet) | FC Sochaux-Montbéliard (Montbéliard) |
| AS de Monaco (Monaco) won 5-3 on penalties. | | |
| Olympique de Marseille (Marseille) | 2-0, 1-0 | Association de la Jeunesse Auxerroise (Auxerre) |


## Quarter-Finals   (03-09/05/89)

| | | |
|---|---|---|
| AS Beauvais-Marissel (Beauvais) | 1-2, 0-0 | Association de la Jeunesse Auxerroise (Auxerre) |
| Olympique de Marseille (Marseille) | 5-1, 2-2 | Stade Rennais FC (Rennes) |
| US Orléans Football (Orléans) | 1-2, 3-3 | AS de Monaco (Monaco) |
| FC Sochaux-Montbéliard (Montbéliard) | 3-1, 0-1 | FC de Mulhouse 1893 (Mulhouse) |

# 1989-90

| 1989-1990 Division One | AJ Auxerroise | Gir. de Bordeaux | Brest Armorique | SM Caen CBN | AS de Cannes | Lille Olympique | Olymp. Lyonnais | Olymp. Marseille | FC de Metz | AS de Monaco | Montpellier Hér. | Mulhouse-Sud | FC de Nantes | Olymp. GC Nice | Paris St.Germain | Racing Paris 1 | AS Saint-Étienne | Sochaux-Mont. | Toulon et du Var | Toulouse FC |
|---|---|---|---|---|---|---|---|---|---|---|---|---|---|---|---|---|---|---|---|---|
| AJ Auxerroise | ■ | 1-1 | 3-1 | 3-0 | 1-0 | 3-0 | 0-1 | 0-2 | 1-1 | 0-0 | 2-1 | 3-1 | 0-0 | 1-0 | 2-0 | 2-0 | 2-1 | 1-1 | 2-0 | 2-2 |
| Girondins de Bordeaux | 0-1 | ■ | 3-0 | 2-1 | 2-0 | 3-1 | 2-0 | 3-0 | 1-0 | 0-0 | 2-0 | 1-0 | 3-0 | 3-0 | 3-0 | 4-0 | 1-0 | 1-0 | 2-1 | 2-1 |
| Brest Armorique | 2-1 | 2-0 | ■ | 2-1 | 2-0 | 1-0 | 0-2 | 2-1 | 2-0 | 1-1 | 1-1 | 2-0 | 3-2 | 3-0 | 0-1 | 2-0 | 0-0 | 1-0 | 2-1 | 0-0 |
| SM Caen CBN | 1-0 | 1-0 | 2-1 | ■ | 1-0 | 2-0 | 1-1 | 0-2 | 1-0 | 1-1 | 3-2 | 1-0 | 2-0 | 1-1 | 2-0 | 1-0 | 3-2 | 1-1 | 2-2 | 0-1 |
| AS de Cannes | 2-2 | 3-0 | 1-1 | 3-1 | ■ | 3-0 | 2-1 | 2-2 | 1-0 | 0-0 | 1-1 | 4-1 | 2-1 | 1-0 | 3-1 | 3-1 | 0-0 | 1-1 | 0-0 | 2-2 |
| Lille Olympique | 2-1 | 0-1 | 1-2 | 1-0 | 2-1 | ■ | 0-0 | 2-0 | 2-1 | 1-1 | 1-0 | 1-1 | 1-0 | 1-1 | 2-0 | 2-1 | 2-2 | 5-0 | 3-0 | 3-0 |
| Olympique Lyonnais | 1-1 | 0-0 | 4-0 | 2-1 | 0-1 | 2-1 | ■ | 1-4 | 0-0 | 0-2 | 3-1 | 3-1 | 0-0 | 2-0 | 1-2 | 1-1 | 0-0 | 0-4 | 3-2 | 3-0 |
| Olympique Marseille | 1-1 | 2-0 | 1-0 | 1-0 | 1-1 | 4-1 | 0-1 | ■ | 2-1 | 2-2 | 2-0 | 3-1 | 1-0 | 3-0 | 2-1 | 4-1 | 2-0 | 6-1 | 3-0 | 6-1 |
| FC de Metz | 2-1 | 0-0 | 1-1 | 0-0 | 2-2 | 1-1 | 2-3 | 3-2 | ■ | 1-0 | 1-0 | 1-1 | 1-1 | 0-0 | 0-1 | 0-0 | 1-0 | 2-0 | 0-0 | 3-0 |
| AS de Monaco | 2-4 | 2-0 | 2-0 | 2-1 | 0-0 | 1-1 | 1-0 | 1-3 | 1-0 | ■ | 1-0 | 0-0 | 0-0 | 1-0 | 2-0 | 4-0 | 0-0 | 2-1 | 2-1 | 2-0 |
| Montpellier Hérault SC | 1-0 | 1-2 | 1-1 | 5-1 | 4-1 | 5-0 | 2-0 | 1-1 | 1-2 | 0-0 | ■ | 3-3 | 2-1 | 1-0 | 2-0 | 2-1 | 3-3 | 2-0 | 3-0 | 1-0 |
| Mulhouse-Sud | 1-2 | 0-0 | 2-0 | 0-0 | 1-0 | 2-1 | 4-4 | 1-2 | 2-2 | 1-1 | 2-0 | ■ | 0-2 | 1-0 | 1-0 | 4-2 | 1-2 | 1-2 | 4-0 | 1-0 |
| FC de Nantes | 2-1 | 2-1 | 1-0 | 0-0 | 1-0 | 1-0 | 2-1 | 0-0 | 0-0 | 0-0 | 1-1 | 3-2 | ■ | 2-2 | 0-1 | 5-1 | 2-0 | 0-1 | 4-0 | 0-1 |
| Olympique GC Nice | 1-1 | 1-0 | 0-1 | 1-0 | 2-0 | 1-1 | 1-0 | 1-1 | 0-0 | 1-0 | 3-0 | 2-0 | 1-2 | ■ | 3-3 | 2-0 | 1-3 | 2-4 | 1-2 | 1-1 |
| Paris Saint-Germain FC | 1-1 | 1-1 | 3-1 | 3-1 | 5-1 | 2-1 | 0-1 | 2-1 | 1-0 | 2-1 | 2-1 | 1-0 | 2-2 | 2-1 | ■ | 1-2 | 2-0 | 1-0 | 1-1 | 0-1 |
| Racing Paris 1 | 3-1 | 1-3 | 1-1 | 0-0 | 3-2 | 2-0 | 0-1 | 1-1 | 1-1 | 0-0 | 0-0 | 2-1 | 2-1 | 5-1 | 2-2 | ■ | 3-0 | 1-1 | 0-2 | 1-0 |
| AS Saint-Étienne | 4-1 | 1-1 | 2-0 | 0-0 | 1-0 | 2-1 | 1-0 | 0-0 | 4-3 | 0-2 | 1-0 | 3-0 | 0-0 | 0-0 | 1-2 | 0-1 | ■ | 0-2 | 1-2 | 0-3 |
| Sochaux-Montbéliard | 0-0 | 2-0 | 1-0 | 5-0 | 3-0 | 1-0 | 0-2 | .0-0 | 1-0 | 3-1 | 0-0 | 1-3 | 0-0 | 1-1 | 1-0 | 2-0 | 2-3 | ■ | 1-0 | 1-0 |
| Toulon et du Var | 1-0 | 0-2 | 2-0 | 2-0 | 1-1 | 1-1 | 1-0 | 0-4 | 1-1 | 2-0 | 3-0 | 2-1 | 0-0 | 1-0 | 0-3 | 1-0 | 2-1 | | ■ | 0-0 |
| Toulouse FC | 1-1 | 0-1 | 2-1 | 2-1 | 4-0 | 3-1 | 0-0 | 2-1 | 2-0 | 0-1 | 0-0 | 3-0 | 1-1 | 0-1 | 4-1 | 1-0 | 1-1 | 0-0 | 0-0 | ■ |

## Division 1

| | | Pd | Wn | Dw | Ls | GF | GA | Pts | |
|---|---|---|---|---|---|---|---|---|---|
| 1. | OLYMPIQUE DE MARSEILLE (MARSEILLE) | 38 | 22 | 9 | 7 | 75 | 34 | 53 | |
| 2. | Girondins de Bordeaux FC (Bordeaux) | 38 | 22 | 7 | 9 | 51 | 25 | 51 | |
| 3. | AS de Monaco (Monaco) | 38 | 15 | 16 | 7 | 38 | 24 | 46 | |
| 4. | FC Sochaux-Montbéliard (Montbéliard) | 38 | 17 | 9 | 12 | 46 | 39 | 43 | |
| 5. | Paris Saint-Germain FC (Paris) | 38 | 18 | 6 | 14 | 50 | 48 | 42 | |
| 6. | Association de la Jeunesse Auxerroise (Auxerre) | 38 | 14 | 13 | 11 | 49 | 40 | 41 | |
| 7. | FC de Nantes (Nantes) | 38 | 13 | 14 | 11 | 42 | 34 | 40 | |
| 8. | Olympique Lyonnais (Lyon) | 38 | 14 | 11 | 13 | 43 | 41 | 39 | |
| 9. | Toulouse FC (Toulouse) | 38 | 13 | 12 | 13 | 39 | 39 | 38 | |
| 10. | Brest Armorique FC (Brest) | 38 | 15 | 8 | 15 | 39 | 44 | 38 | |
| 11. | AS de Cannes (Cannes) | 38 | 12 | 12 | 14 | 44 | 50 | 36 | |
| 12. | SC de Toulon et du Var (Toulon) | 38 | 12 | 11 | 15 | 35 | 50 | 35 | |
| 13. | Montpellier Hérault SC (Montpellier) | 38 | 12 | 10 | 16 | 49 | 48 | 34 | |
| 14. | FC de Metz (Metz) | 38 | 8 | 18 | 12 | 33 | 36 | 34 | |
| 15. | AS de Saint-Étienne (Saint-Étienne) | 38 | 11 | 12 | 15 | 38 | 46 | 34 | |
| 16. | Stade Malherbe Caen-Calvados-Basse Normandie (Caen) | 38 | 12 | 10 | 16 | 34 | 48 | 34 | |
| 17. | Lille Olympique SC (Lille) | 38 | 12 | 9 | 17 | 43 | 52 | 33 | |
| 18. | Olympique GC de Nice (Nice) | 38 | 9 | 13 | 16 | 34 | 48 | 31 | PO |
| 19. | Racing Paris 1 (Paris) | 38 | 10 | 10 | 18 | 39 | 59 | 30 | R* |
| 20. | FC Mulhouse-Sud Alsace (Mulhouse) | 38 | 9 | 10 | 19 | 42 | 58 | 28 | R* |
| | | 760 | 270 | 220 | 270 | 863 | 863 | 760 | |

## Top goal-scorers

| | | | |
|---|---|---|---|
| 1) | Jean-Pierre PAPIN | (Olympique de Marseille) | 30 |
| 2) | Kalman KOVACS | (Association Jeunesse Auxerroise) | 18 |
| 3) | Bobby LANGERS | (Olympique GC de Nice) | 17 |
| 4) | Milos BURSAC | (SC de Toulon et du Var) | 16 |
| 5) | Ramon DIAZ | (AS de Monaco) | 15 |
| | Fabrice DIVERT | (Stade Malherbe Caen-CBN) | 15 |

\* FC Mulhouse-Sud Alsace (Mulhouse) changed their name pre-season from FC de Mulhouse 1893 (Mulhouse); Racing Paris 1 (Paris) were relegated to Division 3 for the next season at their own request.

## Promotion/Relegation Play-Offs

| | | |
|---|---|---|
| Racing Club de Strasbourg (Strasbourg) | 3-1, 0-6 | Olympique GC de Nice (Nice) |
| Racing Club de Strasbourg (Strasbourg) | 0-0, 3-2 (aet) | US Valenciennes-Anzin (Valenciennes) |
| Racing Club de Strasbourg (Strasbourg) | 2-0 | FC de Rouen (Rouen) |
| US Valenciennes-Anzin & Arr (Valenciennes) | 3-1 | Nîmes Olympique (Nîmes) |

## Division 2 Play-Off

| | | |
|---|---|---|
| Stade Rennais FC (Rennes) | 0-1, 0-1 | AS Nancy-Lorraine (Nancy) |

| | Division 2 (Group "A") | Pd | Wn | Dw | Ls | GF | GA | Pts | |
|---|---|---|---|---|---|---|---|---|---|
| 1. | AS Nancy-Lorraine (Nancy) | 34 | 21 | 8 | 5 | 62 | 24 | 50 | P |
| 2. | Racing Club de Strasbourg (Strasbourg) | 34 | 16 | 11 | 7 | 70 | 39 | 43 | PO |
| 3. | Nîmes Olympique (Nîmes) | 34 | 17 | 9 | 8 | 56 | 34 | 43 | PO |
| 4. | Olympique d'Alès en Cévenne (Alès) | 34 | 15 | 13 | 6 | 46 | 29 | 43 | |
| 5. | FC de Martigues (Martigues) | 34 | 13 | 14 | 7 | 38 | 33 | 40 | |
| 6. | Sporting Club Bastiais (Bastia) | 34 | 14 | 11 | 9 | 46 | 30 | 39 | n/c |
| 7. | Stade de Reims (Reims) | 34 | 13 | 9 | 12 | 37 | 32 | 35 | |
| 8. | Olympique Avignon-Vaucluse (Avignon) | 34 | 13 | 8 | 13 | 43 | 54 | 34 | |
| 9. | Istres Sports Football (Istres) | 34 | 10 | 11 | 13 | 39 | 44 | 31 | |
| 10. | Cercle Dijon Football (Dijon) | 34 | 11 | 9 | 14 | 34 | 45 | 31 | |
| 11. | FC de Gueugnon (Gueugnon) | 34 | 10 | 10 | 14 | 49 | 49 | 30 | |
| 12. | US Orléans Football (Orléans) | 34 | 10 | 10 | 14 | 44 | 49 | 30 | |
| 13. | CS Louhans-Cuiseaux 71 (Cuiseaux-Louhans) | 34 | 8 | 14 | 12 | 38 | 44 | 30 | n/c |
| 14. | FC d'Annecy (Annecy) | 34 | 9 | 12 | 13 | 31 | 43 | 30 | |
| 15. | Entente Chaumontaise Athletic-Cheminots (Chaumont) | 34 | 10 | 9 | 15 | 36 | 52 | 29 | |
| 16. | FC Grenoble-Dauphiné (Grenoble) | 34 | 8 | 12 | 14 | 35 | 46 | 28 | R |
| 17. | AS Red Star 93 (Saint-Ouen) | 34 | 9 | 10 | 15 | 27 | 47 | 28 | |
| 18. | FC Montceau-Bourgogne 71 (Montceau-les-Mines) | 34 | 5 | 8 | 21 | 33 | 62 | 18 | R |
| | | 612 | 212 | 188 | 212 | 764 | 764 | 612 | |

## Division 2 (Group "B")

| | | Pd | Wn | Dw | Ls | GF | GA | Pts | |
|---|---|---|---|---|---|---|---|---|---|
| 1. | Stade Rennais FC (Rennes) | 34 | 18 | 8 | 8 | 39 | 27 | 44 | P |
| 2. | US Valenciennes-Anzin & Arrondissement (Valenciennes) | 34 | 18 | 8 | 8 | 45 | 34 | 44 | PO |
| 3. | FC de Rouen (Rouen) | 34 | 16 | 9 | 9 | 46 | 29 | 41 | PO |
| 4. | Stade Lavallois FC (Laval) | 34 | 15 | 11 | 8 | 49 | 35 | 41 | |
| 5. | Havre AC (Le Havre) | 34 | 16 | 8 | 10 | 46 | 28 | 40 | |
| 6. | AS Beauvais-Oise (Beauvais) | 34 | 12 | 14 | 8 | 33 | 29 | 38 | n/c |
| 7. | Chamois Niortais (Niort) | 34 | 8 | 19 | 7 | 30 | 29 | 35 | |
| 8. | Racing Club de Lens (Lens) | 34 | 13 | 8 | 13 | 42 | 37 | 34 | |
| 9. | US de Créteil (Créteil) | 34 | 10 | 13 | 11 | 33 | 31 | 33 | |
| 10. | SC de l'Ouest Angers (Angers) | 34 | 10 | 13 | 11 | 45 | 44 | 33 | n/c |
| 11. | US du Littoral Dunkerquois (Dunkerque) | 34 | 9 | 15 | 10 | 28 | 36 | 33 | |
| 12. | AS Saint-Seurin-sur-LIsle (Saint-Seurin-sur-LIsle) | 34 | 12 | 7 | 15 | 44 | 43 | 31 | |
| 13. | En Avant de Guingamp (Guingamp) | 34 | 9 | 13 | 12 | 32 | 38 | 31 | |
| 14. | FC de Tours (Tours) | 34 | 11 | 8 | 15 | 46 | 46 | 30 | |
| 15. | La Roche Vendée Football (La Roche-sur-Yon) | 34 | 7 | 14 | 13 | 28 | 38 | 28 | n/c |
| 16. | FC de Lorient (Lorient) | 34 | 9 | 9 | 16 | 32 | 52 | 27 | R |
| 17. | SC d'Abbeville (Abbeville) | 34 | 9 | 9 | 16 | 27 | 47 | 27 | R |
| 18. | Quimper Cornouailles FC (Quimper) | 34 | 4 | 14 | 16 | 21 | 43 | 22 | R |
| | | 612 | 206 | 200 | 206 | 666 | 666 | 612 | |

## Coupe de France Final   (Parc des Princes, Paris – 02/06/90 – 44,067)

**MONTPELLIER HÉRAULT SC**          **2-1  (aet)**          Racing Paris 1 (Paris)

*Blanc 103', Ferhaoui 108'*                                                    *Ginola 109'*

**Montpellier**: Rust, Baills, Lucchesi, Julio Cesar, Blanc, Lemoult, Ferhaoui, Ayache, Xuereb, Guérin, Cantona.

**Racing**: Olmeta, Dangbeto, Bade, Thétis, Milojevic, Ben Mabrouk, Blondeau, Bouderbala (Sobrinko 57'), Ginola, Avenet.

## Semi-Finals   (24-25/05/90)

| Olympique de Marseille (Marseille) | 2-3 | Racing Paris 1 (Paris) |
|---|---|---|
| AS de Saint-Étienne (Saint-Étienne) | 0-1 | Montpellier Hérault SC (Montpellier) |

## Quarter-Finals   (02/05/90)

| Olympique Avignon-Vaucluse (Avignon) | 0-1 | Montpellier Hérault SC (Montpellier) |
|---|---|---|
| AS de Cannes (Cannes) | 0-3 | Olympique de Marseille (Marseille) |
| FC Mulhouse-Sud Alsace (Mulhouse) | 2-2  (aet) | AS de Saint-Étienne (Saint-Étienne) |

AS de Saint-Étienne (Saint-Étienne) won 7-6 on penalties.

| Racing Paris 1 (Paris) | 1-1  (aet) | Girondins de Bordeaux FC |
|---|---|---|

Racing Paris 1 (Paris) won 5-4 on penalties.

# 1990-91

| 1990-1991 Division One | AJ Auxerroise | Gir. de Bordeaux | Brest Armorique | SM Caen CBN | AS de Cannes | Lille Olympique | Olymp. Lyonnais | Olymp. Marseille | FC de Metz | AS de Monaco | Montpellier Hér. | Nancy-Lorraine | FC de Nantes | Olymp. GC Nice | Paris St.Germain | Stade Rennais | AS Saint-Étienne | Sochaux-Mont. | Toulon et du Var | Toulouse FC |
|---|---|---|---|---|---|---|---|---|---|---|---|---|---|---|---|---|---|---|---|---|
| AJ Auxerroise | | 0-0 | 2-2 | 3-0 | 0-3 | 3-2 | 1-0 | 4-0 | 3-1 | 0-1 | 3-2 | 1-1 | 0-2 | 5-1 | 0-1 | 4-0 | 2-0 | 4-1 | 3-0 | 2-1 |
| Girondins de Bordeaux | 1-1 | | 1-4 | 1-1 | 1-1 | 1-1 | 0-0 | 1-1 | 1-1 | 0-0 | 1-0 | 5-0 | 2-0 | 3-0 | 3-0 | 1-0 | 2-1 | 1-0 | 0-1 | 2-1 |
| Brest Armorique | 1-3 | 4-0 | | 5-0 | 3-2 | 1-0 | 3-0 | 1-1 | 1-0 | 1-2 | 1-1 | 3-3 | 1-0 | 4-0 | 0-0 | 0-0 | 0-1 | 0-0 | 2-2 | 0-0 |
| SM Caen CBN | 0-1 | 2-0 | 1-2 | | 0-1 | 0-0 | 1-0 | 0-0 | 4-1 | 0-2 | 1-0 | 4-1 | 1-0 | 2-1 | 2-0 | 1-0 | 2-0 | 2-0 | 2-0 | |
| AS de Cannes | 0-3 | 1-1 | 0-0 | 1-1 | | 2-1 | 3-2 | 0-0 | 0-1 | 1-2 | 2-1 | 1-0 | 2-1 | 2-1 | 2-0 | 1-0 | 0-1 | 1-1 | 0-0 | 0-0 |
| Lille Olympique | 1-0 | 0-0 | 1-0 | 1-0 | 0-2 | | 1-1 | 1-0 | 4-1 | 0-0 | 1-0 | 0-2 | 1-1 | 0-0 | 0-0 | 1-1 | 3-2 | 0-1 | 4-1 | 3-0 |
| Olympique Lyonnais | 1-0 | 1-0 | 2-0 | 3-2 | 1-0 | 2-1 | | 2-2 | 3-1 | 1-0 | 3-3 | 0-1 | 2-0 | 1-0 | 0-0 | 1-1 | 1-0 | 1-1 | 1-1 | 4-1 |
| Olympique Marseille | 1-0 | 2-0 | 3-1 | 2-1 | 2-0 | 7-0 | | | 3-0 | 1-0 | 6-2 | 6-0 | 1-0 | 2-1 | 4-1 | 3-1 | 0-0 | 3-3 | 1-0 | |
| FC de Metz | 1-0 | 1-0 | 0-0 | 1-1 | 0-0 | 2-2 | 1-2 | 0-2 | | 1-1 | 0-0 | 4-0 | 2-0 | 1-0 | 2-2 | 2-0 | 3-1 | 2-2 | 0-0 | 2-1 |
| AS de Monaco | 0-0 | 2-0 | 5-0 | 2-0 | 0-0 | 1-1 | 0-0 | 1-3 | 2-0 | | 3-1 | 2-2 | 2-1 | 2-1 | 2-1 | 2-0 | 1-0 | 2-1 | 2-1 | |
| Montpellier Hérault SC | 1-2 | 2-1 | 1-0 | 0-0 | 0-0 | 1-2 | 1-0 | 0-0 | 5-2 | 2-1 | | 5-0 | 1-1 | 3-0 | 4-0 | 1-0 | 0-0 | 1-0 | 2-0 | |
| Nancy-Lorraine | 1-1 | 0-2 | 0-0 | 0-0 | 2-0 | 1-1 | 2-0 | 2-0 | 0-0 | 4-0 | 1-1 | | 3-2 | 2-1 | 0-2 | 0-0 | 1-0 | 2-0 | 2-1 | 1-1 |
| FC de Nantes | 2-3 | 0-0 | 1-0 | 0-0 | 1-0 | 0-0 | 0-0 | 1-1 | 1-1 | 3-1 | 1-1 | 1-0 | | 2-2 | 2-0 | 2-0 | 2-1 | 0-0 | 0-0 | 0-0 |
| Olympique GC Nice | 1-1 | 0-0 | 2-0 | 0-0 | 0-0 | 4-1 | 1-1 | 0-1 | 1-2 | 0-0 | 2-0 | 3-0 | 1-1 | | 1-1 | 2-2 | 2-0 | 3-0 | 0-0 | 1-1 |
| Paris Saint-Germain FC | 1-1 | 1-0 | 1-1 | 3-2 | 0-0 | 2-0 | 3-0 | 0-1 | 2-1 | 0-2 | 2-0 | 2-1 | 1-1 | 0-2 | | 1-1 | 4-2 | 0-2 | 4-0 | 3-0 |
| Stade Rennais | 2-2 | 2-1 | 3-0 | 1-1 | 1-1 | 1-3 | 2-0 | 1-1 | 0-2 | 1-1 | 1-2 | 1-0 | 2-0 | 0-3 | 2-1 | | 0-2 | 1-1 | 0-0 | 2-0 |
| AS Saint-Étienne | 2-1 | 0-0 | 6-1 | 0-0 | 1-0 | 0-0 | 0-1 | 1-1 | 2-1 | 1-0 | 1-0 | 4-1 | 1-3 | 1-0 | 1-1 | 0-0 | | 2-1 | 3-0 | 1-4 |
| Sochaux-Montbéliard | 0-1 | 1-0 | 1-1 | 1-0 | 0-0 | 0-0 | 1-2 | 2-1 | 1-1 | 0-2 | 0-1 | 1-1 | 0-0 | 0-0 | 4-0 | 2-0 | | | 0-0 | 0-1 |
| Toulon et du Var | 2-3 | 0-2 | 1-2 | 0-0 | 0-0 | 0-0 | 1-0 | 0-1 | 2-1 | 1-1 | 1-1 | 2-0 | 3-1 | 1-2 | 0-0 | 1-0 | 3-0 | 1-0 | | 1-0 |
| Toulouse FC | 0-0 | 0-0 | 0-0 | 3-2 | 2-2 | 2-2 | 3-1 | 0-2 | 2-1 | 1-2 | 0-0 | 0-0 | 2-0 | 1-2 | 2-1 | 2-0 | 0-0 | 0-0 | 1-1 | |

## Division 1

| | | Pd | Wn | Dw | Ls | GF | GA | Pts | |
|---|---|---|---|---|---|---|---|---|---|
| 1. | OLYMPIQUE DE MARSEILLE (MARSEILLE) | 38 | 22 | 11 | 5 | 67 | 28 | 55 | |
| 2. | AS de Monaco (Monaco) | 38 | 20 | 11 | 7 | 51 | 30 | 51 | |
| 3. | Association de la Jeunesse Auxerroise (Auxerre) | 38 | 19 | 10 | 9 | 63 | 36 | 48 | |
| 4. | AS de Cannes (Cannes) | 38 | 12 | 17 | 9 | 32 | 28 | 41 | |
| 5. | Olympique Lyonnais (Lyon) | 38 | 15 | 11 | 12 | 39 | 44 | 41 | |
| 6. | Lille Olympique SC (Lille) | 38 | 11 | 17 | 10 | 39 | 37 | 39 | |
| 7. | Montpelier Hérault SC (Montpellier) | 38 | 12 | 14 | 12 | 44 | 35 | 38 | |
| 8. | Stade Malherbe Caen-Calvados-Basse Normandie (Caen) | 38 | 13 | 12 | 13 | 38 | 36 | 38 | |
| 9. | Paris Saint-Germain FC (Paris) | 38 | 13 | 12 | 13 | 40 | 42 | 38 | |
| 10. | Girondins de Bordeaux FC (Bordeaux) | 38 | 11 | 15 | 12 | 34 | 32 | 37 | # |
| 11. | Brest Armorique FC (Brest) | 38 | 11 | 15 | 12 | 45 | 46 | 37 | # |
| 12. | FC de Metz (Metz) | 38 | 12 | 12 | 14 | 44 | 51 | 36 | |
| 13. | AS de Saint-Étienne (Saint-Étienne) | 38 | 13 | 9 | 16 | 40 | 46 | 35 | |
| 14. | Olympique GC de Nice (Nice) | 38 | 10 | 14 | 14 | 40 | 42 | 34 | # |
| 15. | FC de Nantes (Nantes) | 38 | 9 | 16 | 13 | 34 | 44 | 34 | |
| 16. | SC de Toulon et du Var (Toulon) | 38 | 9 | 16 | 13 | 31 | 41 | 34 | |
| 17. | AS Nancy-Lorraine (Nancy) | 38 | 11 | 11 | 16 | 38 | 58 | 33 | |
| 18. | FC Sochaux-Montbéliard (Montbéliard) | 38 | 8 | 16 | 14 | 24 | 33 | 32 | |
| 19. | Toulouse FC (Toulouse) | 38 | 8 | 15 | 15 | 33 | 45 | 31 | R# |
| 20. | Stade Rennais FC (Rennes) | 38 | 7 | 14 | 17 | 29 | 51 | 28 | R# |
| | | 760 | 246 | 268 | 246 | 805 | 805 | 760 | |

## Top goal-scorers

1) Jean-Pierre PAPIN — (Olympique de Marseille) — 23
2) Kálmán KOVÁCS — (Association Jeunesse Auxerroise) — 16
3) Laurent BLANC — (Montpellier Hérault SC) — 14
   François OMAM-BIYIK — (Stade Rennais FC) — 14
   Enzo SCIFO — (Association Jeunesse Auxerroise) — 14

# Brest Armorique, Girondins de Bordeaux and Olympique GC de Nice were later relegated by the FFF for financial reasons. As a result of this action Toulouse FC and Stade Rennais FC retained their Division 1 status.

## Promotion/Relegation Play-Offs

| | | |
|---|---|---|
| Toulouse FC (Toulouse) | 4-0, 0-1 | Racing Club de Lens (Lens) |
| Racing Club de Strasbourg (Strasbourg) | 1-1, 1-3 | Racing Club de Lens (Lens) |
| Racing Club de Strasbourg (Strasbourg) | 3-1 | Stade Lavallois FC (Laval) |
| Racing Club de Lens (Lens) | 1-0 | US Valenciennes-Anzin & Arrondissement |

## Division 2 Play-Off

| | | |
|---|---|---|
| Havre AC (Le Havre) | 3-0, 0-0 | Nîmes Olympique (Nîmes) |

| | Division 2 (Group "A") | Pd | Wn | Dw | Ls | GF | GA | Pts | |
|---|---|---|---|---|---|---|---|---|---|
| 1. | Nîmes Olympique (Nîmes) | 34 | 17 | 10 | 7 | 40 | 27 | 44 | P |
| 2. | Racing Club de Strasbourg (Strasbourg) | 34 | 19 | 5 | 10 | 70 | 37 | 43 | PO |
| 3. | US Valenciennes-Anzin & Arrondissement (Valenciennes) | 34 | 13 | 17 | 4 | 30 | 17 | 43 | PO |
| 4. | Olympique d'Alès en Cévenne (Alès) | 34 | 17 | 9 | 8 | 37 | 32 | 43 | |
| 5. | FC Istres-Ville Nouvelle (Istres) | 34 | 14 | 9 | 11 | 41 | 41 | 37 | n/c |
| 6. | Sporting Club Bastiais (Bastia) | 34 | 12 | 11 | 11 | 46 | 35 | 35 | |
| 7. | Olympique Avignon-Vaucluse (Avignon) | 34 | 10 | 15 | 9 | 41 | 37 | 35 | R |
| 8. | Stade Rodez Football (Rodez) | 34 | 10 | 14 | 10 | 32 | 38 | 34 | |
| 9. | FC d'Annecy (Annecy) | 34 | 10 | 13 | 11 | 26 | 25 | 33 | |
| 10. | FC Mulhouse-Sud Alsace (Mulhouse) | 34 | 11 | 10 | 13 | 41 | 35 | 32 | |
| 11. | FC de Martigues (Martigues) | 34 | 11 | 10 | 13 | 41 | 38 | 32 | |
| 12. | FC de Gueugnon (Gueugnon) | 34 | 9 | 14 | 11 | 30 | 29 | 32 | |
| 13. | Stade Athlétique Spinalien FC (Epinal) | 34 | 11 | 8 | 15 | 33 | 40 | 30 | |
| 14. | Gazélec FC Ajaccien (Ajaccio) | 34 | 11 | 8 | 15 | 30 | 39 | 30 | |
| 15. | Entente Chaumontaise Athletic-Cheminots (Chaumont) | 34 | 10 | 10 | 14 | 32 | 50 | 30 | R5 |
| 16. | CS Louhans-Cuiseaux 71 (Cuiseaux-Louhans) | 34 | 7 | 14 | 13 | 28 | 36 | 28 | |
| 17. | US du Littoral Dunkerquois (Dunkerque) | 34 | 6 | 14 | 14 | 17 | 36 | 26 | |
| 18. | Cercle Dijon Football (Dijon) | 34 | 7 | 11 | 16 | 29 | 52 | 25 | R4 |
| | | 612 | 205 | 202 | 205 | 644 | 644 | 612 | |

| Division 2 (Group "B") | Pd | Wn | Dw | Ls | GF | GA | Pts | |
|---|---|---|---|---|---|---|---|---|
| 1. Havre AC (Le Havre) | 34 | 18 | 11 | 5 | 52 | 17 | 47 | P |
| 2. Racing Club de Lens (Lens) | 34 | 14 | 14 | 6 | 49 | 26 | 42 | PO |
| 3. Stade Lavallois FC (Laval) | 34 | 16 | 9 | 9 | 49 | 29 | 41 | PO |
| 4. SC de l'Ouest Angers (Angers) | 34 | 16 | 8 | 10 | 52 | 32 | 40 | |
| 5. FC de Rouen (Rouen) | 34 | 15 | 10 | 9 | 46 | 26 | 40 | |
| 6. Stade de Reims (Reims) | 34 | 13 | 11 | 10 | 38 | 29 | 37 | R |
| 7. En Avant de Guingamp (Guingamp) | 34 | 12 | 11 | 11 | 35 | 37 | 35 | |
| 8. AS Saint-Seurin-sur-LIsle (Saint-Seurin-sur-LIsle) | 34 | 10 | 14 | 10 | 33 | 37 | 34 | |
| 9. FC de Tours (Tours) | 34 | 9 | 15 | 10 | 26 | 32 | 33 | |
| 10. AS Red Star 93 (Saint-Ouen) | 34 | 9 | 14 | 11 | 36 | 43 | 32 | |
| 11. AS Beauvais-Oise (Beauvais) | 34 | 9 | 13 | 12 | 21 | 25 | 31 | |
| 12. La Roche Vendée Football (La Roche-sur-Yon) | 34 | 10 | 11 | 13 | 35 | 46 | 31 | |
| 13. FC de Bourges (Bourges) | 34 | 10 | 11 | 13 | 35 | 51 | 31 | |
| 14. Mans Union Club 72 (Le Mans) | 34 | 8 | 14 | 12 | 28 | 33 | 30 | |
| 15. Chamois Niortais (Niort) | 34 | 9 | 11 | 14 | 26 | 33 | 29 | R |
| 16. US Orléans Football (Orléans) | 34 | 7 | 14 | 13 | 29 | 41 | 28 | |
| 17. US de Créteil (Créteil) | 34 | 7 | 12 | 15 | 28 | 52 | 26 | R |
| 18. Olympique Saint-Quentinois (Saint-Quentin) | 34 | 7 | 11 | 16 | 24 | 53 | 25 | |
| | 612 | 199 | 214 | 199 | 642 | 642 | 612 | |

## Coupe de France Final   (Parc des Princes, Paris – 08/06/91 – 44,123)

**AS DE MONACO (MONACO)**                **1-0**                Olympique de Marseille (Marseille)

*Passi 90'*

**Monaco**: Ettori, Puel, Sonor, Petit, Mendy, Dib, Barros, Sauzée, Weah, Djorkaeff (Passi 59'), Fofana (Diaz 75').

**Marseille**: Olmeta, Amoros, Fournier (Stojkovic 46'), Boli, Mozer, Germain, Casoni, Waddle, Papin, Abedi "Pelé", Vercruysse.


## Semi-Finals   (31/05/91 – 02/06/91)

| | | |
|---|---|---|
| Olympique de Marseille (Marseille) | 4-1 | Stade Rodez Football (Rodez) |
| AS de Monaco (Monaco) | 5-0 | FC de Gueugnon (Gueugnon) |


## Quarter-Finals   (14/05/91)

| | | |
|---|---|---|
| AS de Cannes (Cannes) | 1-2 | AS de Monaco (Monaco) |
| FC de Gueugnon (Gueugnon) | 1-0 | Chamois Niortais (Niort) |
| FC de Nantes (Nantes) | 1-2 | Olympique de Marseille (Marseille) |
| Stade Rodez Football (Rodez) | 2-1 | FC Sochaux-Montbéliard (Montbéliard) |

# 1991-92

| 1991-1992 Division One | AJ Auxerroise | SM Caen CBN | AS de Cannes | Havre AC | Racing de Lens | Lille Olympique | Olymp. Lyonnais | Olymp. Marseille | FC de Metz | AS de Monaco | Montpellier Hér. | Nancy-Lorraine | FC de Nantes | Nîmes Olymp. | Paris St.Germain | Stade Rennais | AS Saint-Étienne | Sochaux-Mont. | Toulon et du Var | Toulouse FC |
|---|---|---|---|---|---|---|---|---|---|---|---|---|---|---|---|---|---|---|---|---|
| AJ Auxerroise | | 5-1 | 3-1 | 3-0 | 1-0 | 1-0 | 3-0 | 1-1 | 3-0 | 1-1 | 1-0 | 3-1 | 2-2 | 0-0 | 2-2 | 3-1 | 2-0 | 4-0 | 1-0 | 3-0 |
| SM Caen CBN | 1-0 | | 3-1 | 2-1 | 2-0 | 3-3 | 1-0 | 1-3 | 1-0 | 1-0 | 0-0 | 5-1 | 1-1 | 2-0 | 2-0 | 0-0 | 1-0 | 1-1 | 4-1 | 1-0 |
| AS de Cannes | 1-1 | 2-0 | | 0-0 | 2-1 | 1-1 | 0-0 | 1-2 | 1-1 | 1-2 | 2-0 | 1-1 | 2-0 | 0-0 | 1-1 | 3-1 | 0-2 | 2-1 | 0-1 | 2-0 |
| Havre AC | 1-0 | 0-1 | 1-0 | | 1-0 | 0-0 | 1-0 | 0-2 | 0-0 | 3-0 | 3-1 | 1-2 | 1-1 | 1-1 | 1-1 | 0-0 | 2-1 | 1-0 | 3-0 | 1-1 |
| Racing de Lens | 0-0 | 0-0 | 1-1 | 0-0 | | 0-0 | 4-2 | 2-1 | 0-2 | 0-1 | 1-1 | 1-0 | 0-0 | 0-0 | 1-0 | 0-0 | 1-1 | 1-1 | 2-1 | 4-0 |
| Lille Olympique | 1-0 | 1-2 | 0-0 | 0-0 | 1-2 | | 1-0 | 0-1 | 0-2 | 1-2 | 1-0 | 2-1 | 0-0 | 1-1 | 0-0 | 1-1 | 2-0 | 0-0 | 1-1 | 3-1 |
| Olympique Lyonnais | 1-0 | 2-2 | 0-0 | 0-2 | 1-1 | 1-0 | | 1-1 | 0-0 | 2-0 | 1-0 | 2-1 | 0-1 | 1-0 | 0-1 | 3-1 | 0-0 | 0-1 | 1-1 | 1-0 |
| Olympique Marseille | 2-0 | 5-0 | 2-0 | 2-0 | 1-1 | 1-0 | 0-0 | | 2-0 | 1-1 | 0-0 | 4-0 | 4-0 | 4-2 | 0-0 | 5-1 | 2-0 | 2-2 | 0-1 | 2-0 |
| FC de Metz | 2-1 | 1-2 | 1-2 | 1-1 | 3-2 | 1-0 | 1-1 | 0-0 | | 2-0 | 1-3 | 0-1 | 1-1 | 4-0 | 0-0 | 0-0 | 1-0 | 3-1 | 4-1 | 4-0 |
| AS de Monaco | 2-0 | 2-1 | 3-1 | 0-2 | 0-0 | 1-0 | 1-0 | 0-3 | 3-1 | | 1-1 | 4-1 | 1-0 | 1-1 | 1-0 | 3-1 | 2-0 | 2-0 | 3-0 | 0-2 |
| Montpellier Hérault SC | 1-1 | 3-1 | 3-0 | 2-2 | 0-0 | 0-0 | 3-0 | 0-0 | 1-0 | 1-4 | | 2-0 | 2-1 | 0-0 | 1-1 | 0-0 | 2-0 | 3-2 | 1-0 | 0-0 |
| Nancy-Lorraine | 2-1 | 3-0 | 1-0 | 1-3 | 3-1 | 1-2 | 0-1 | 1-3 | 1-3 | 1-4 | 3-1 | | 3-1 | 2-3 | 0-1 | 1-1 | 0-2 | 3-1 | 0-0 | 1-1 |
| FC de Nantes | 2-0 | 2-1 | 1-0 | 0-0 | 1-0 | 1-2 | 3-0 | 0-1 | 4-1 | 1-4 | 0-0 | 0-0 | | 3-2 | 0-0 | 1-0 | 1-0 | 0-0 | 1-2 | 1-1 |
| Nîmes Olympique | 0-0 | 0-1 | 2-1 | 1-0 | 0-2 | 1-0 | 2-1 | 1-2 | 1-0 | 0-1 | 2-1 | 1-2 | 0-0 | | 0-1 | 1-2 | 1-1 | 2-2 | 1-0 | 2-2 |
| Paris Saint-Germain FC | 1-1 | 3-1 | 3-2 | 1-1 | 1-0 | 2-0 | 3-0 | 0-0 | 3-0 | 2-0 | 1-1 | 1-0 | 1-1 | 2-0 | | 1-0 | 0-0 | 2-0 | 2-3 | 0-0 |
| Stade Rennais | 1-1 | 1-0 | 0-0 | 0-2 | 0-0 | 2-3 | 0-2 | 1-2 | 3-1 | 0-0 | 0-2 | 3-1 | 0-1 | 1-1 | 0-0 | | 0-0 | 2-0 | 0-0 | 1-1 |
| AS Saint-Étienne | 1-1 | 1-1 | 2-0 | 4-0 | 0-4 | 1-1 | 1-2 | 1-1 | 2-0 | 0-1 | 1-1 | 3-0 | 2-1 | 3-0 | 3-0 | 0-1 | | 2-1 | 3-1 | 2-1 |
| Sochaux-Montbéliard | 1-0 | 2-0 | 1-0 | 0-0 | 1-2 | 2-1 | 1-0 | 2-3 | 0-0 | 1-3 | 1-1 | 2-2 | 3-1 | 1-1 | 0-2 | 0-0 | 1-0 | | 2-0 | 0-0 |
| Toulon et du Var | 0-3 | 0-0 | 4-3 | 4-0 | 0-1 | 1-2 | 1-0 | 1-0 | 1-1 | 1-1 | 0-0 | 4-2 | 0-2 | 5-0 | 2-5 | 1-0 | 1-2 | 2-0 | | 1-0 |
| Toulouse FC | 2-3 | 0-0 | 2-0 | 0-0 | 1-1 | 1-0 | 1-0 | 0-2 | 1-0 | 0-0 | 1-1 | 1-0 | 2-1 | 0-1 | 3-0 | 2-0 | 1-1 | 2-1 | 3-0 | |

## Division 1

| | | Pd | Wn | Dw | Ls | GF | GA | Pts | |
|---|---|---|---|---|---|---|---|---|---|
| 1. | OLYMPIQUE DE MARSEILLE (MARSEILLE) | 38 | 23 | 12 | 3 | 67 | 21 | 58 | |
| 2. | AS de Monaco (Monaco) | 38 | 22 | 8 | 8 | 55 | 33 | 52 | |
| 3. | Paris Saint-Germain FC (Paris) | 38 | 15 | 17 | 6 | 43 | 27 | 47 | |
| 4. | Association de la Jeunesse Auxerroise (Auxerre) | 38 | 16 | 12 | 10 | 55 | 32 | 44 | |
| 5. | Stade Malherbe Caen-Calvados-Basse Normandie (Caen) | 38 | 17 | 10 | 11 | 46 | 45 | 44 | |
| 6. | Montpellier Hérault SC (Montpellier) | 38 | 12 | 18 | 8 | 40 | 32 | 42 | |
| 7. | Havre AC (Le Havre) | 38 | 13 | 16 | 9 | 35 | 32 | 42 | |
| 8. | Racing Club de Lens (Lens) | 38 | 11 | 17 | 10 | 36 | 30 | 39 | |
| 9. | FC de Nantes (Nantes) | 38 | 12 | 14 | 12 | 37 | 39 | 38 | |
| 10. | AS de Saint-Étienne (Saint-Étienne) | 38 | 13 | 11 | 14 | 42 | 37 | 37 | |
| 11. | Toulouse FC (Toulouse) | 38 | 11 | 14 | 13 | 33 | 40 | 36 | |
| 12. | FC de Metz (Metz) | 38 | 12 | 11 | 15 | 42 | 43 | 35 | |
| 13. | Lille Olympique SC (Lille) | 38 | 11 | 13 | 14 | 31 | 34 | 35 | |
| 14. | SC de Toulon et du Var (Toulon) | 38 | 13 | 6 | 19 | 41 | 55 | 32 | |
| 15. | Nîmes Olympique (Nîmes) | 38 | 9 | 14 | 15 | 31 | 50 | 32 | |
| 16. | Olympique Lyonnais (Lyon) | 38 | 10 | 11 | 17 | 25 | 39 | 31 | |
| 17. | FC Sochaux-Montbéliard (Montbéliard) | 38 | 9 | 13 | 16 | 35 | 50 | 31 | |
| 18. | Stade Rennais FC (Rennes) | 38 | 6 | 17 | 15 | 25 | 42 | 29 | PO |
| 19. | AS de Cannes (Cannes) | 38 | 8 | 12 | 18 | 34 | 48 | 28 | R |
| 20. | AS Nancy-Lorraine (Nancy) | 38 | 10 | 8 | 20 | 43 | 67 | 28 | R |
| | | 760 | 253 | 254 | 253 | 796 | 796 | 760 | |

## Top goal-scorers

| | | | |
|---|---|---|---|
| 1) | Jean-Pierre PAPIN | (Olympique de Marseille) | 27 |
| 2) | François CALDERARO | (FC de Metz) | 19 |
| 3) | George WEAH | (AS de Monaco) | 18 |
| 4) | Fabrice DIVERT | (Montpellier Hérault SC) | 14 |
| | Stéphane PAILLE | (Stade Malherbe Caen-CBN) | 14 |

\* FC de Nantes (Nantes) changed their name to FC Nantes-Atlantique (Nantes) for next season; Girondins de Bordeaux FC (Bordeaux) dissolved and re-formed as AN des Girondins de Bordeaux FC (Bordeaux); Olympique GC de Nice-Côte d'Azur (Nice) changed their name pre-season from Olympique GC de Nice (Nice).

## Promotion/Relegation Play-Offs

| | | |
|---|---|---|
| Stade Rennais FC (Rennes) | 0-0, 1-4 | Racing Club de Strasbourg (Strasbourg) |
| Angers SC de l'Ouest (Angers) | 1-1, 0-0 | Racing Club de Strasbourg (Strasbourg) |
| Angers SC de l'Ouest (Angers) | 1-0 (aet) | FC Istres-Ville Nouvelle (Istres) |
| Acing Club de Strasbourg (Strasbourg) | 3-1 | Mans Union Club 72 (Le Mans) |

## Division 2 Play-Off

| | | |
|---|---|---|
| AN des Girondins de Bordeaux FC | 4-0, 3-2 | US Valenciennes-Anzin & Arrondissement |

| | Division 2 (Group "A") | Pd | Wn | Dw | Ls | GF | GA | Pts | |
|---|---|---|---|---|---|---|---|---|---|
| 1. | US Valenciennes-Anzin & Arrondissement (Valenciennes) | 32 | 16 | 12 | 4 | 41 | 20 | 44 | P |
| 2. | Angers SC de l'Ouest (Angers) | 32 | 17 | 7 | 8 | 50 | 25 | 41 | PO |
| 3. | Mans Union Club 72 (Le Mans) | 32 | 11 | 15 | 6 | 32 | 24 | 37 | PO |
| 4. | SC Louhans-Cuiseaux 71 (Cuiseaux-Louhans) | 32 | 13 | 10 | 9 | 39 | 31 | 36 | |
| 5. | Stade Lavallois FC (Laval) | 32 | 14 | 8 | 10 | 36 | 29 | 36 | |
| 6. | En Avant de Guingamp (Guingamp) | 32 | 13 | 9 | 10 | 36 | 39 | 35 | |
| 7. | FC de Rouen (Rouen) | 32 | 13 | 8 | 11 | 52 | 38 | 34 | |
| 8. | FC de Bourges (Bourges) | 32 | 12 | 9 | 11 | 36 | 35 | 33 | |
| 9. | FC de Tours (Tours) | 32 | 12 | 9 | 11 | 36 | 47 | 33 | |
| 10. | US du Littoral Dunkerquois (Dunkerque) | 32 | 9 | 13 | 10 | 32 | 34 | 31 | |
| 11. | Racing Club Ancenis (Ancenis) | 32 | 10 | 11 | 11 | 21 | 25 | 31 | |
| 12. | AS Beauvais-Oise (Beauvais) | 32 | 8 | 13 | 11 | 36 | 29 | 29 | |
| 13. | AS Red Star 93 (Saint-Ouen) | 32 | 6 | 15 | 11 | 25 | 30 | 27 | |
| 14. | La Roche Vendée Football (La Roche-sur-Yon) | 32 | 7 | 12 | 13 | 25 | 42 | 26 | |
| 15. | CS Sedan-Ardennes (Sedan) | 32 | 7 | 11 | 14 | 22 | 38 | 25 | |
| 16. | Amiens SC (Amiens) | 32 | 6 | 12 | 14 | 26 | 43 | 24 | |
| 17. | US Orléans Football (Orléans) | 32 | 5 | 12 | 15 | 26 | 42 | 22 | R |
| --. | Brest Armorique FC (Brest) | -- | - | -- | -- | -- | -- | -- | w/d |
| | | 544 | 179 | 186 | 179 | 571 | 571 | 544 | |

| Division 2 (Group "B") | Pd | Wn | Dw | Ls | GF | GA | Pts | |
|---|---|---|---|---|---|---|---|---|
| 1. AN des Girondins de Bordeaux FC (Bordeaux) | 34 | 22 | 8 | 4 | 55 | 24 | 52 | P |
| 2. Racing Club de Strasbourg (Strasbourg) | 34 | 20 | 9 | 5 | 75 | 26 | 49 | PO |
| 3. FC Istres-Ville Nouvelle (Istres) | 34 | 18 | 12 | 4 | 53 | 30 | 48 | PO |
| 4. Sporting Club de Bastia (Bastia) | 34 | 16 | 7 | 11 | 56 | 46 | 39 | |
| 5. Gazélec FC Ajaccien (Ajaccio) | 34 | 14 | 9 | 11 | 40 | 43 | 37 | |
| 6. Stade Rodez Football (Rodez) | 34 | 12 | 12 | 10 | 43 | 35 | 36 | |
| 7. Perpignan FC (Perpignan) | 34 | 11 | 13 | 10 | 31 | 34 | 35 | |
| 8. La Berrichonne (Châteauroux) | 34 | 10 | 15 | 9 | 27 | 32 | 35 | |
| 9. Olympique GC de Nice-Côte d'Azur (Nice) | 34 | 11 | 12 | 11 | 40 | 40 | 34 | |
| 10. Olympique d'Alès en Cévenne (Alès) | 34 | 9 | 14 | 11 | 31 | 31 | 32 | |
| 11. FC Mulhouse-Sud Alsace (Mulhouse) | 34 | 11 | 9 | 14 | 42 | 45 | 31 | |
| 12. FC de Gueugnon (Gueugnon) | 34 | 11 | 9 | 14 | 34 | 43 | 31 | |
| 13. Stade Athlétique Spinalien FC (Epinal) | 34 | 10 | 10 | 14 | 39 | 52 | 30 | |
| 14. FC de Martigues (Martigues) | 34 | 6 | 16 | 12 | 38 | 48 | 28 | |
| 15. FC d'Annecy (Annecy) | 34 | 6 | 14 | 14 | 31 | 39 | 26 | |
| 16. AS Saint-Seurin-sur-LIsle (Saint-Seurin-sur-LIsle) | 34 | 5 | 15 | 14 | 26 | 43 | 25 | R |
| 17. FC Grenoble-Dauphine (Grenoble) | 34 | 8 | 9 | 17 | 25 | 46 | 25 | R |
| 18. Olympique Saint-Quentinois (Saint-Quentin) | 34 | 4 | 11 | 19 | 29 | 58 | 19 | R |
| | 612 | 204 | 204 | 204 | 715 | 715 | 612 | |

## Coupe de France Final

The final was not played due to the fatal accident at the Stade Armand Cesari de Furiani in Bastia prior to the Semi-final match on 05/05/1992.

## Semi-Finals  (28/04/92 – 05/05/92)

| | | |
|---|---|---|
| Sporting Club de Bastia (Bastia) | Not played | Olympique de Marseille (Marseille) |

(The match was not played due to the collapse of a temporary grandstand prior to kick-off which resulted in the deaths of 4 fans and injuries to over 1,000 others)

| | | |
|---|---|---|
| AS de Cannes (Cannes) | 0-0  (aet) | AS de Monaco (Monaco) |

AS de Monaco (Monaco) won 5-3 on penalties.

## Quarter-Finals  (22/04/92)

| | | |
|---|---|---|
| Gazélec FC Ajaccien (Ajaccio) | 0-3 | AS de Monaco (Monaco) |
| Sporting Club de Bastia (Bastia) | 0-0  (aet) | AS Nancy-Lorraine (Nancy) |

Sporting Club de Bastia (Bastia) won 3-0 on penalties.

| | | |
|---|---|---|
| Stade Malherbe Caen-CBN (Caen) | 3-1 | Olympique de Marseille (Marseille) |
| AS de Cannes (Cannes) | 1-0 | AS Red Star 93 (Saint-Ouen) |

# 1992-93

| 1992-1993 Division One | AJ Auxerroise | Gir. de Bordeaux | SM Caen CBN | Havre AC | Racing de Lens | Lille Olympique | Olymp. Lyonnais | Olymp. Marseille | FC de Metz | AS de Monaco | Montpellier Hér. | FC de Nantes | Nîmes Olymp. | Paris St.Germain | AS Saint-Étienne | Sochaux-Mont. | RC Strasbourg | Toulon et du Var | Toulouse FC | Valenciennes |
|---|---|---|---|---|---|---|---|---|---|---|---|---|---|---|---|---|---|---|---|---|
| AJ Auxerroise | | 1-0 | 3-2 | 4-1 | 1-1 | 2-0 | 2-1 | 0-2 | 4-0 | 4-1 | 2-0 | 1-1 | 5-2 | 1-2 | 1-0 | 0-3 | 2-0 | 2-1 | 0-0 | 3-2 |
| Girondins de Bordeaux | 1-0 | | 2-0 | 3-0 | 0-0 | 3-0 | 0-0 | 1-0 | 2-1 | 1-0 | 2-1 | 3-0 | 1-1 | 1-1 | 0-0 | 3-0 | 1-1 | 1-1 | 2-0 | 3-0 |
| SM Caen CBN | 2-1 | 1-0 | | 3-3 | 0-1 | 4-3 | 3-2 | 2-3 | 0-1 | 1-0 | 2-3 | 1-1 | 2-2 | 0-2 | 0-0 | 2-0 | 3-0 | 2-1 | 4-1 | 3-0 |
| Havre AC | 0-0 | 0-1 | 2-3 | | 0-1 | 1-0 | 1-3 | 2-1 | 0-0 | 1-1 | 2-0 | 2-0 | 1-1 | 0-1 | 0-0 | 3-0 | 2-1 | 3-2 | 0-0 | 0-0 |
| Racing de Lens | 0-3 | 1-2 | 0-3 | 0-0 | | 0-0 | 0-3 | 2-2 | 2-0 | 0-0 | 2-0 | 1-0 | 0-0 | 2-1 | 1-1 | 0-0 | 2-0 | 2-1 | 0-2 | 2-1 |
| Lille Olympique | 1-0 | 0-2 | 1-0 | 2-1 | 0-0 | | 1-1 | 2-0 | 1-1 | 1-1 | 0-0 | 1-1 | 2-2 | 0-0 | 0-0 | 0-0 | 2-3 | 1-0 | 2-2 | 1-2 |
| Olympique Lyonnais | 1-1 | 2-3 | 1-0 | 1-1 | 3-1 | 1-3 | | 2-2 | 1-1 | 0-0 | 2-1 | 0-2 | 0-1 | 1-1 | 0-2 | 3-1 | 2-2 | 1-1 | 1-0 | 2-1 |
| Olympique Marseille | 2-0 | 0-0 | 2-1 | 1-1 | 2-0 | 4-1 | 2-1 | | 3-2 | 1-0 | 1-1 | 0-1 | 6-1 | 3-1 | 1-0 | 2-0 | 5-0 | 5-2 | 2-1 | 2-1 |
| FC de Metz | 0-1 | 1-1 | 1-0 | 2-3 | 1-2 | 0-0 | 2-0 | 2-1 | | 1-0 | 1-1 | 4-0 | 3-0 | 2-1 | 2-2 | 5-1 | 3-0 | 0-0 | 1-1 | 0-0 |
| AS de Monaco | 4-0 | 0-0 | 4-2 | 2-0 | 2-1 | 3-0 | 2-1 | 1-0 | 2-0 | | 0-0 | 3-1 | 3-1 | 3-1 | 1-0 | 1-0 | 2-1 | 4-0 | 4-0 | 2-1 |
| Montpellier Hérault SC | 1-0 | 2-0 | 2-0 | 2-0 | 1-2 | 3-0 | 0-2 | 1-1 | 1-0 | 0-0 | | 1-0 | 1-0 | 0-0 | 1-2 | 1-0 | 1-1 | 1-1 | 0-1 | 1-3 |
| FC de Nantes | 2-1 | 1-0 | 1-1 | 5-2 | 3-2 | 4-0 | 1-0 | 0-2 | 0-0 | 1-0 | 6-0 | | 2-0 | 1-0 | 0-0 | 1-1 | 2-2 | 0-0 | 4-1 | 3-1 |
| Nîmes Olympique | 1-2 | 0-0 | 1-2 | 0-2 | 1-1 | 0-0 | 2-3 | 1-3 | 2-2 | 0-1 | 0-0 | 1-1 | | 0-1 | 1-1 | 1-1 | 2-6 | 0-1 | 1-1 | 2-1 |
| Paris Saint-Germain FC | 2-0 | 5-0 | 2-0 | 1-0 | 1-1 | 3-0 | 1-1 | 0-1 | 5-1 | 1-0 | 1-0 | 1-0 | 2-3 | | 3-1 | 2-0 | 1-1 | 2-0 | 0-0 | 2-0 |
| AS Saint-Étienne | 1-0 | 2-1 | 1-1 | 0-0 | 0-0 | 0-0 | 0-2 | 1-0 | 0-0 | 1-0 | 1-0 | 1-0 | 1-2 | | 2-0 | 1-2 | 2-0 | 3-2 | 4-2 | |
| Sochaux-Montbéliard | 0-3 | 0-1 | 1-0 | 3-2 | 1-1 | 1-0 | 1-0 | 2-2 | 2-0 | 1-2 | 1-1 | 0-1 | 1-1 | 1-3 | 1-0 | | 0-0 | 2-1 | 1-0 | 2-1 |
| RC Strasbourg | 1-1 | 0-1 | 1-1 | 3-1 | 4-1 | 2-0 | 2-1 | 2-2 | 1-1 | 3-0 | 3-1 | 2-4 | 1-1 | 0-4 | 2-2 | 6-1 | | 1-1 | 0-0 | 0-0 |
| Toulon et du Var | 1-2 | 0-0 | 1-1 | 1-2 | 2-2 | 1-0 | 0-0 | 0-0 | 1-0 | 4-5 | 1-0 | 1-3 | 1-0 | 0-2 | 0-0 | 0-4 | 0-2 | | 2-0 | 1-2 |
| Toulouse FC | 2-1 | 2-0 | 1-1 | 1-0 | 0-0 | 0-0 | 0-0 | 3-1 | 0-0 | 0-2 | 1-3 | 2-0 | 3-0 | 2-2 | 0-0 | 1-0 | 1-1 | 1-1 | | 1-2 |
| Valenciennes | 3-3 | 1-0 | 3-2 | 4-1 | 0-2 | 0-1 | 0-0 | 0-1 | 0-2 | 1-1 | 1-3 | 1-1 | 1-1 | 1-1 | 0-0 | 1-0 | 1-2 | 3-1 | 1-1 | |

## Division 1

| | | Pd | Wn | Dw | Ls | GF | GA | Pts | |
|---|---|---|---|---|---|---|---|---|---|
| 1. | Olympique de Marseille (Marseille) | 38 | 23 | 9 | 6 | 72 | 36 | 55 | * |
| 2. | Paris Saint-Germain FC (Paris) | 38 | 20 | 11 | 7 | 61 | 29 | 51 | |
| 3. | AS de Monaco (Monaco) | 38 | 21 | 9 | 8 | 56 | 29 | 51 | |
| 4. | FC Girondins de Bordeaux (Bordeaux) | 38 | 18 | 12 | 8 | 42 | 25 | 48 | * |
| 5. | FC Nantes-Atlantique (Nantes) | 38 | 17 | 11 | 10 | 54 | 39 | 45 | |
| 6. | Association de la Jeunesse Auxerroise (Auxerre) | 38 | 18 | 7 | 13 | 57 | 44 | 43 | |
| 7. | AS de Saint-Étienne (Saint-Étienne) | 38 | 13 | 17 | 8 | 34 | 26 | 43 | |
| 8. | Racing Club de Strasbourg (Strasbourg) | 38 | 12 | 16 | 10 | 50 | 57 | 40 | |
| 9. | Racing Club de Lens (Lens) | 38 | 12 | 16 | 10 | 36 | 41 | 40 | |
| 10. | Montpellier Hérault SC (Montpellier) | 38 | 12 | 12 | 14 | 36 | 41 | 36 | |
| 11. | Stade Malherbe Caen-Calvados-Basse Normandie (Caen) | 38 | 13 | 9 | 16 | 55 | 54 | 35 | |
| 12. | FC de Metz (Metz) | 38 | 11 | 13 | 14 | 44 | 45 | 35 | |
| 13. | Toulouse FC (Toulouse) | 38 | 9 | 16 | 13 | 36 | 45 | 34 | |
| 14. | Olympique Lyonnais (Lyon) | 38 | 9 | 15 | 14 | 40 | 45 | 33 | |
| 15. | Havre AC (Le Havre) | 38 | 11 | 11 | 16 | 42 | 53 | 33 | |
| 16. | FC Sochaux-Montbéliard (Montbéliard) | 38 | 11 | 10 | 17 | 33 | 50 | 32 | |
| 17. | Lille Olympique SC (Lille) | 38 | 7 | 16 | 15 | 26 | 48 | 30 | |
| 18. | US Valenciennes-Anzin & Arrondissement (Valenciennes) | 38 | 9 | 11 | 18 | 42 | 57 | 29 | PO |
| 19. | SC de Toulon et du Var (Toulon) | 38 | 6 | 13 | 19 | 31 | 57 | 25 | R3 |
| 20. | Nîmes Olympique (Nîmes) | 38 | 3 | 16 | 19 | 32 | 66 | 22 | R |
| | | 760 | 255 | 250 | 255 | 887 | 887 | 760 | |

## Top goal-scorers

* Olympique de Marseille were stripped of the title after an FFF inquiry found them guilty of trying to bribe players of US Valenciennes-Anzin to lose a match between the clubs. No champions were declared for this season.
FC Girondins de Bordeaux (Bordeaux) changed their name pre-season from AN des Girondins de Bordeaux FC (Bordeaux).

## Promotion/Relegation Play-Offs

| | | |
|---|---|---|
| US Valenciennes-Anzin & Arrondissement | 0-2, 1-1 | AS de Cannes (Cannes) |
| Stade Rennais FC (Rennes) | 0-1, 0-3 | AS de Cannes (Cannes) |
| AS de Cannes (Cannes) | 2-1 | FC de Rouen (Rouen) |
| Stade Rennais FC (Rennes) | 1-0 | Olympique GC de Nice-Côte d'Azur (Nice) |

## Division 2 Play-Off

| | | |
|---|---|---|
| FC de Martigues (Martigues) | 1-1, 4-3 | Angers SC de l'Ouest (Angers) |

| | Division 2 (Group "A") | Pd | Wn | Dw | Ls | GF | GA | Pts | |
|---|---|---|---|---|---|---|---|---|---|
| 1. | FC de Martigues (Martigues) | 34 | 19 | 9 | 6 | 53 | 24 | 47 | P |
| 2. | AS de Cannes (Cannes) | 34 | 19 | 8 | 7 | 63 | 33 | 46 | PO |
| 3. | Olympique GC de Nice-Côte d'Azur (Nice) | 34 | 14 | 13 | 7 | 49 | 32 | 41 | PO |
| 4. | AS Nancy-Lorraine (Nancy) | 34 | 15 | 9 | 10 | 48 | 37 | 39 | |
| 5. | AS d'Origine Arménienne de Valence (Valence) | 34 | 15 | 9 | 10 | 42 | 40 | 39 | |
| 6. | CS Sedan-Ardennes (Sedan) | 34 | 13 | 12 | 9 | 46 | 31 | 38 | |
| 7. | Sporting Club de Bastia (Bastia) | 34 | 11 | 15 | 8 | 52 | 39 | 37 | |
| 8. | FC Istres-Ville Nouvelle (Istres) | 34 | 14 | 9 | 11 | 42 | 44 | 37 | |
| 9. | FC Olympique de Charleville (Charleville) | 34 | 14 | 9 | 11 | 36 | 38 | 37 | |
| 10. | Olympique d'Alès en Cévenne (Alès) | 34 | 14 | 8 | 12 | 42 | 44 | 36 | |
| 11. | FC Mulhouse-Sud Alsace (Mulhouse) | 34 | 12 | 10 | 12 | 49 | 45 | 34 | |
| 12. | CS Louhans-Cuiseaux 71 (Cuiseaux-Louhans) | 34 | 10 | 9 | 15 | 35 | 42 | 29 | R |
| 13. | Gazélec FC Ajaccien (Ajaccio) | 34 | 11 | 6 | 17 | 43 | 55 | 28 | R |
| 14. | Stade Rodez Football (Rodez) | 34 | 9 | 9 | 16 | 30 | 57 | 27 | R |
| 15. | Perpignan FC (Perpignan) | 34 | 7 | 12 | 15 | 31 | 44 | 26 | R |
| 16. | Stade Athlétique Spinalien FC (Epinal) | 34 | 8 | 8 | 18 | 35 | 55 | 24 | R |
| 17. | FC d'Annecy (Annecy) | 34 | 8 | 8 | 18 | 28 | 55 | 24 | R |
| 18. | US de Créteil (Créteil) | 34 | 7 | 9 | 18 | 42 | 51 | 23 | R |
| | | 612 | 220 | 172 | 220 | 766 | 766 | 612 | |

| Division 2 (Group "B") | | Pd | Wn | Dw | Ls | GF | GA | Pts | |
|---|---|---|---|---|---|---|---|---|---|
| 1. | Angers SC de l'Ouest (Angers) | 34 | 20 | 8 | 6 | 47 | 22 | 48 | P |
| 2. | Stade Rennais FC (Rennes) | 34 | 16 | 13 | 5 | 48 | 26 | 45 | PO |
| 3. | FC de Rouen (Rouen) | 34 | 18 | 9 | 7 | 50 | 31 | 45 | PO |
| 4. | AS Red Star 93 (Saint-Ouen) | 34 | 17 | 8 | 9 | 46 | 29 | 42 | |
| 5. | Mans Union Club 72 (Le Mans) | 34 | 15 | 11 | 8 | 44 | 33 | 41 | |
| 6. | US du Littoral Dunkerquois (Dunkerque) | 34 | 12 | 16 | 6 | 39 | 31 | 40 | |
| 7. | FC de Bourges (Bourges) | 34 | 11 | 17 | 6 | 49 | 37 | 39 | |
| 8. | AS Beauvais-Oise (Beauvais) | 34 | 12 | 15 | 7 | 31 | 21 | 39 | |
| 9. | Stade Lavallois FC (Laval) | 34 | 11 | 15 | 8 | 43 | 33 | 37 | |
| 10. | Chamois Niortais (Niort) | 34 | 13 | 11 | 10 | 30 | 24 | 37 | |
| 11. | FC de Gueugnon (Gueugnon) | 34 | 12 | 9 | 13 | 37 | 34 | 33 | |
| 12. | Amiens SC (Amiens) | 34 | 11 | 10 | 13 | 32 | 41 | 32 | R |
| 13. | En Avant de Guingamp (Guingamp) | 34 | 10 | 9 | 15 | 40 | 49 | 29 | R |
| 14. | La Berrichonne (Châteauroux) | 34 | 9 | 9 | 16 | 39 | 49 | 27 | R |
| 15. | FC de Tours (Tours) | 34 | 8 | 9 | 17 | 33 | 60 | 25 | R |
| 16. | La Roche Vendée Football (La Roche-sur-Yon) | 34 | 3 | 14 | 17 | 28 | 49 | 20 | R |
| 17. | Racing Club Ancenis (Ancenis) | 34 | 4 | 10 | 20 | 26 | 59 | 18 | R |
| 18. | FC de Lorient (Lorient) | 34 | 3 | 9 | 22 | 29 | 63 | 15 | R |
| | | 612 | 205 | 202 | 205 | 691 | 691 | 612 | |

## Coupe de France Final   (Parc des Princes, Paris – 12/06/93 – 38,789)

**PARIS SAINT-GERMAIN FC (PARIS)**   **3-0**   FC Nantes-Atlantique (Nantes)

*Kombouaré 49' pen, Ginola 55', Roche 59'*

**PSG**: Lama, Kombouaré, Colleter, Roche, Ricardo, Le Guen, Bravo (Valdo 66'), Guerin (Calderaro 81'), Weah, Fournier, Ginola

**Nantes**: Marraud, Karembeu, Le Dizet, Vulic, Guyot, Ferri, Makelele, Pedros, Ouedec, Ziani (Moreau 63'), Loko (Lima 71').

## Semi-Finals   (06/06/93)

| Paris Saint-Germain FC (Paris) | 1-0 | Stade Lavallois FC (Laval) |
|---|---|---|
| AS de Saint-Étienne (Saint-Étienne) | 0-1 | FC Nantes-Atlantique (Nantes) |

## Quarter-Finals   (18-19/05/93)

| Montpellier Hérault SC (Montpellier) | 1-1 (aet) | FC Nantes-Atlantique (Nantes) |
|---|---|---|
| FC Nantes-Atlantique (Nantes) won 5-4 on penalties. | | |
| Paris Saint-Germain FC (Paris) | 2-0 | FC Girondins de Bordeaux (Bordeaux) |
| AS de Saint-Étienne (Saint-Étienne) | 2-1 | Olympique de Marseille (Marseille) |
| Toulouse FC (Toulouse) | 0-1 | Stade Lavallois FC (Laval) |

# 1993-94

| 1993-1994 Division One | SC de Angers | AJ Auxerroise | Gir. de Bordeaux | SM Caen CBN | AS de Cannes | Havre AC | Racing de Lens | Lille Olympique | Olymp. Lyonnais | Olymp. Marseille | FC Martigues | FC de Metz | AS de Monaco | Montpellier Hér. | FC de Nantes | Paris St.Germain | AS Saint-Étienne | Sochaux-Mont. | RC Strasbourg | Toulouse FC |
|---|---|---|---|---|---|---|---|---|---|---|---|---|---|---|---|---|---|---|---|---|
| Angers SC de l'Ouest | ■ | 2-2 | 1-3 | 2-0 | 1-1 | 0-0 | 1-2 | 1-2 | 3-1 | 0-1 | 1-3 | 1-2 | 1-1 | 2-3 | 0-0 | 1-1 | 1-1 | 1-2 | 1-3 | 0-0 |
| AJ Auxerroise | 0-0 | ■ | 0-1 | 1-0 | 0-0 | 3-0 | 1-0 | 5-0 | 3-2 | 2-2 | 3-0 | 2-0 | 4-0 | 3-1 | 3-1 | 0-0 | 3-0 | 1-0 | 2-1 | 5-1 |
| Girondins de Bordeaux | 1-0 | 2-0 | ■ | 3-0 | 0-0 | 2-1 | 4-2 | 2-1 | 2-0 | 1-0 | 1-1 | 2-0 | 1-0 | 1-1 | 2-0 | 1-0 | 1-2 | 4-1 | 2-0 | 2-0 |
| SM Caen CBN | 2-3 | 1-0 | 1-0 | ■ | 1-1 | 1-1 | 1-0 | 2-3 | 1-0 | 1-0 | 4-1 | 1-1 | 0-1 | 0-0 | 0-0 | 0-2 | 1-0 | 2-1 | 3-1 | 1-0 |
| AS de Cannes | 4-3 | 2-1 | 2-1 | 3-0 | ■ | 1-0 | 3-1 | 2-1 | 1-0 | 2-1 | 2-1 | 2-0 | 0-2 | 2-0 | 4-0 | 0-1 | 0-0 | 1-1 | 1-1 | 2-1 |
| Havre AC | 2-1 | 1-0 | 0-3 | 1-2 | 3-1 | ■ | 1-1 | 1-0 | 0-1 | 1-3 | 2-0 | 0-1 | 1-0 | 0-0 | 0-0 | 0-2 | 0-0 | 0-0 | 0-1 | 1-1 |
| Racing de Lens | 0-1 | 1-1 | 1-0 | 2-0 | 2-1 | 5-1 | ■ | 1-1 | 2-0 | 2-3 | 1-1 | 2-0 | 3-3 | 2-1 | 1-1 | 1-2 | 3-1 | 2-0 | 0-0 | 4-0 |
| Lille Olympique | 1-1 | 1-1 | 1-1 | 3-1 | 1-0 | 2-2 | 0-0 | ■ | 2-1 | 1-2 | 1-1 | 0-4 | 1-1 | 0-0 | 0-0 | 0-2 | 0-2 | 3-1 | 1-1 | 3-0 |
| Olympique Lyonnais | 1-1 | 1-0 | 4-2 | 2-0 | 2-2 | 1-1 | 1-2 | 0-0 | ■ | 1-0 | 0-0 | 2-0 | 1-0 | 3-2 | 2-1 | 1-3 | 1-0 | 1-0 | 2-1 | 1-0 |
| Olympique Marseille | 2-1 | 0-3 | 3-1 | 2-0 | 3-1 | 1-1 | 1-0 | 3-2 | 3-0 | ■ | 0-0 | 0-3 | 2-1 | 1-1 | 3-1 | 1-0 | 3-1 | 1-1 | 2-1 | 5-1 |
| FC Martigues | 0-0 | 0-1 | 0-0 | 4-1 | 4-0 | 3-0 | 1-2 | 2-2 | 0-1 | 0-3 | ■ | 1-1 | 1-3 | 1-1 | 1-2 | 1-1 | 2-1 | 1-1 | 0-3 | 1-1 |
| FC de Metz | 2-0 | 0-0 | 1-0 | 2-0 | 0-0 | 2-1 | 1-1 | 0-1 | 0-0 | 0-0 | 0-0 | ■ | 1-1 | 1-2 | 0-1 | 0-1 | 1-1 | 1-0 | 2-1 | 1-0 |
| AS de Monaco | 3-0 | 0-1 | 3-2 | 3-0 | 2-0 | 1-1 | 0-0 | 1-0 | 1-1 | 0-0 | 7-0 | 1-1 | ■ | 1-2 | 1-0 | 1-1 | 1-1 | 2-0 | 2-1 | 3-0 |
| Montpellier Hérault SC | 2-1 | 1-0 | 1-0 | 0-0 | 2-1 | 2-1 | 0-0 | 1-3 | 1-1 | 0-2 | 1-0 | 3-2 | 0-3 | ■ | 1-0 | 0-0 | 3-0 | 1-0 | 4-0 | 3-1 |
| FC de Nantes | 2-1 | 1-2 | 4-1 | 1-0 | 0-0 | 3-1 | 2-1 | 2-0 | 1-0 | 0-0 | 2-1 | 2-0 | 1-0 | 0-0 | ■ | 3-0 | 1-0 | 2-0 | 2-2 | 4-0 |
| Paris Saint-Germain FC | 3-0 | 4-0 | 4-1 | 2-0 | 2-1 | 0-0 | 1-0 | 2-1 | 0-0 | 1-1 | 2-2 | 1-0 | 1-1 | 1-0 | 1-0 | ■ | 1-0 | 1-0 | 2-0 | 1-0 |
| AS Saint-Étienne | 2-0 | 1-0 | 0-0 | 5-0 | 1-2 | 0-0 | 0-0 | 2-1 | 3-0 | 0-0 | 1-1 | 1-0 | 2-0 | 2-0 | 1-1 | 1-2 | ■ | 0-0 | 0-0 | 2-2 |
| Sochaux-Montbéliard | 4-1 | 1-0 | 2-2 | 0-0 | 1-1 | 4-2 | 1-1 | 1-0 | 0-1 | 1-1 | 1-0 | 2-1 | 2-0 | 1-1 | 1-2 | 3-2 | | ■ | 1-3 | 0-0 |
| RC Strasbourg | 2-2 | 1-1 | 0-2 | 3-0 | 2-2 | 0-3 | 2-0 | 1-1 | 0-1 | 1-1 | 3-0 | 0-1 | 0-1 | 0-3 | 2-2 | 2-0 | 2-0 | | ■ | 1-0 |
| Toulouse FC | 2-1 | 0-0 | 0-0 | 0-1 | 1-2 | 0-0 | 1-1 | 1-1 | 2-0 | 0-0 | 2-2 | 2-2 | 2-1 | 0-0 | 0-3 | 1-2 | 1-2 | 3-2 | 0-0 | ■ |

## Division 1

| | | Pd | Wn | Dw | Ls | GF | GA | Pts | |
|---|---|---|---|---|---|---|---|---|---|
| 1. | PARIS SAINT-GERMAIN FC (PARIS) | 38 | 24 | 11 | 3 | 54 | 22 | 59 | |
| 2. | Olympique de Marseille (Marseille) | 38 | 19 | 13 | 6 | 56 | 33 | 51 | R* |
| 3. | Association de la Jeunesse Auxerroise (Auxerre) | 38 | 18 | 10 | 10 | 54 | 29 | 46 | |
| 4. | FC Girondins de Bordeaux (Bordeaux) | 38 | 19 | 8 | 11 | 54 | 37 | 46 | |
| 5. | FC Nantes-Atlantique (Nantes) | 38 | 17 | 11 | 10 | 47 | 32 | 45 | |
| 6. | AS de Cannes (Cannes) | 38 | 16 | 12 | 10 | 50 | 43 | 44 | |
| 7. | Montpellier Hérault SC (Montpellier) | 38 | 15 | 13 | 10 | 41 | 37 | 43 | |
| 8. | Olympique Lyonnais (Lyon) | 38 | 17 | 8 | 13 | 38 | 40 | 42 | |
| 9. | AS de Monaco (Monaco) | 38 | 14 | 13 | 11 | 52 | 36 | 41 | |
| 10. | Racing Club de Lens (Lens) | 38 | 13 | 13 | 12 | 49 | 40 | 39 | |
| 11. | AS de Saint-Étienne (Saint-Étienne) | 38 | 12 | 13 | 13 | 38 | 36 | 37 | |
| 12. | FC de Metz (Metz) | 38 | 12 | 13 | 13 | 36 | 35 | 37 | |
| 13. | Racing Club de Strasbourg (Strasbourg) | 38 | 10 | 14 | 14 | 43 | 47 | 34 | |
| 14. | FC Sochaux-Montbéliard (Montbéliard) | 38 | 10 | 13 | 15 | 39 | 48 | 33 | |
| 15. | Lille Olympique SC (Lille) | 38 | 8 | 16 | 14 | 41 | 52 | 32 | |
| 16. | Stade Malherbe Caen-Calvados-Basse Normandie (Caen) | 38 | 12 | 7 | 19 | 29 | 54 | 31 | |
| 17. | Havre AC (Le Havre) | 38 | 7 | 15 | 16 | 29 | 48 | 29 | |
| 18. | FC de Martigues (Martigues) | 38 | 5 | 17 | 16 | 37 | 58 | 27 | * |
| 19. | Toulouse FC (Toulouse) | 38 | 4 | 15 | 19 | 26 | 60 | 23 | R |
| 20. | Angers SC de l'Ouest (Angers) | 38 | 4 | 13 | 21 | 37 | 63 | 21 | R |
| | | 760 | 256 | 248 | 256 | 850 | 850 | 760 | |

## Top goal-scorers

| | | | |
|---|---|---|---|
| 1) | Roger BOLI | (Racing Club de Lens) | 20 |
| | Youri DJORKAEFF | (AS de Monaco) | 20 |
| | Nicolas OUÉDEC | (FC Nantes-Atlantique) | 20 |
| 4) | Franck PRIOU | (AS de Cannes) | 18 |
| 5) | "Sonny" ANDERSON da Silva | (Olympique de Marseille) | 16 |

\* Olympique de Marseille were relegated as a result of the 1993 inquiry into bribery allegations. Due to this, FC de Martigues retained their Division 1 status and Sporting Club de Bastia were promoted without a play-off.

| | Division 2 | Pd | Wn | Dw | Ls | GF | GA | Pts | |
|---|---|---|---|---|---|---|---|---|---|
| 1. | Olympique FC de Nice-Côte d'Azur (Nice) | 42 | 18 | 18 | 6 | 47 | 25 | 54 | P |
| 2. | Stade Rennais FC (Rennes) | 42 | 20 | 13 | 9 | 57 | 38 | 53 | P |
| 3. | Sporting Club de Bastia (Bastia) | 42 | 21 | 11 | 10 | 44 | 29 | 53 | P* |
| 4. | Nîmes Olympique (Nîmes) | 42 | 21 | 9 | 12 | 59 | 38 | 51 | |
| 5. | AS Red Star 93 (Saint-Ouen) | 42 | 20 | 9 | 13 | 61 | 45 | 49 | |
| 6. | Stade Briochin (Saint-Brieuc) | 42 | 18 | 11 | 13 | 53 | 52 | 47 | |
| 7. | Stade Lavallois FC (Laval) | 42 | 16 | 14 | 12 | 56 | 47 | 46 | |
| 8. | US du Littoral Dunkerquois (Dunkerque) | 42 | 13 | 16 | 13 | 44 | 51 | 42 | |
| 9. | FC Olympique de Charleville (Charleville) | 42 | 14 | 14 | 14 | 41 | 48 | 42 | |
| 10. | Olympique d'Alès en Cévenne (Alès) | 42 | 13 | 15 | 14 | 47 | 50 | 41 | |
| 11. | CS Sedan-Ardennes (Sedan) | 42 | 14 | 12 | 16 | 44 | 42 | 40 | |
| 12. | AS Nancy-Lorraine (Nancy) | 42 | 15 | 10 | 17 | 49 | 48 | 40 | |
| 13. | FC de Gueugnon (Gueugnon) | 42 | 11 | 18 | 13 | 43 | 43 | 40 | |
| 14. | FC Mulhouse-Sud Alsace (Mulhouse) | 42 | 13 | 14 | 15 | 49 | 52 | 40 | |
| 15. | US Jeunesse d'Origine Arménienne de Valence | 42 | 14 | 11 | 17 | 47 | 47 | 39 | |
| 16. | AS Beauvais-Oise (Beauvais) | 42 | 10 | 19 | 13 | 45 | 51 | 39 | |
| 17. | Mans Union Club 72 (Le Mans) | 42 | 14 | 11 | 17 | 43 | 50 | 39 | |
| 18. | Chamois Niortais FC (Niort) | 42 | 13 | 13 | 16 | 34 | 41 | 39 | |
| 19. | FC de Rouen (Rouen) | 42 | 15 | 7 | 20 | 45 | 53 | 37 | R |
| 20. | US Valenciennes-Anzin & Arrondissement (Val.) | 42 | 12 | 13 | 17 | 45 | 59 | 37 | R |
| 21. | FC de Bourges (Bourges) | 42 | 9 | 12 | 21 | 43 | 60 | 30 | R |
| 22. | FC Istres-Ville Nouvelle (Istres) | 42 | 7 | 12 | 23 | 35 | 62 | 26 | R |
| | | 924 | 321 | 282 | 321 | 1031 | 1031 | 924 | |

**Promoted:** En Avant de Guingamp (Guingamp), FC La Berrichone (Châteauroux) and Perpignan FC (Perpignan).

**Coupe de France Final**   (Parc des Princes, Paris – 14/05/94 – 45,189)

**AJ AUXERROISE (AUXERRE)**          **3-0**          Montpellier Hérault SC (Montpellier)

*Saib 17', Baticle 48', Martins 86'*

**Auxerroise:** Charbonnier, Goma, Silvestre, Verlaat, Mahé, Guerreiro, Saib, Martins, Cocard (Laslandes 87'), Baticle, Vahirua (Rabarivony 86').

**Montpellier:** Barrabé, Reuzeau (Alicarte 57'), Der Zakarian, Laurey, Blanc, Périlleux (Divert 57'), Bonnissel, Carotti, Rizzetto, Sanchez, Lefévre.

## Semi-Finals

| | | |
|---|---|---|
| Association de la Jeunesse Auxerroise (Auxerre) | 1-0 | FC Nantes-Atlantique (Nantes) |
| Racing Club de Lens (Lens) | 0-2 | Montpellier Hérault SC (Montpellier) |

## Quarter-Finals

| | | |
|---|---|---|
| Olympique de Marseille (Marseille) | 0-0  (aet) | Montpellier Hérault SC (Montpellier) |

Montpellier Hérault SC (Montpellier) won 4-3 on penalties.

| | | |
|---|---|---|
| FC de Nantes (Nantes) | 3-1 | US Valenciennes-Anzin & Arrondissement |
| Paris Saint-Germain FC (Paris) | 1-2 | Racing Club de Lens (Lens) |
| Racing Club 92 (Paris) | 1-2 | Assoc. de la Jeunesse Auxerroise (Auxerre) |

# 1994-95

| | Division 1 | Pd | Wn | Dw | Ls | GF | GA | Pts | |
|---|---|---|---|---|---|---|---|---|---|
| 1. | FC NANTES-ATLANTIQUE (NANTES) | 38 | 21 | 16 | 1 | 71 | 34 | 79 | |
| 2. | Olympique Lyonnais (Lyon) | 38 | 19 | 12 | 7 | 56 | 38 | 69 | |
| 3. | Paris Saint-Germain FC (Paris) | 38 | 20 | 7 | 11 | 58 | 41 | 67 | |
| 4. | Association de la Jeunesse Auxerroise (Auxerre) | 38 | 15 | 17 | 6 | 59 | 34 | 62 | |
| 5. | Racing Club de Lens (Lens) | 38 | 15 | 14 | 9 | 48 | 44 | 59 | |
| 6. | AS de Monaco (Monaco) | 38 | 15 | 12 | 11 | 60 | 39 | 57 | |
| 7. | FC Girondins de Bordeaux (Bordeaux) | 38 | 16 | 9 | 13 | 52 | 47 | 57 | |
| 8. | FC de Metz (Metz) | 38 | 16 | 8 | 14 | 50 | 44 | 56 | |
| 9. | AS de Cannes (Cannes) | 38 | 15 | 8 | 15 | 56 | 48 | 53 | |
| 10. | Racing Club de Strasbourg (Strasbourg) | 38 | 13 | 12 | 13 | 43 | 43 | 51 | * |
| 11. | FC de Martigues (Martigues) | 38 | 13 | 12 | 13 | 37 | 49 | 51 | |
| 12. | Havre AC (Le Havre) | 38 | 12 | 13 | 13 | 46 | 49 | 49 | * |
| 13. | Stade Rennais FC (Rennes) | 38 | 12 | 12 | 14 | 53 | 55 | 48 | |
| 14. | Lille Olympique SC Metropole (Lille) | 38 | 13 | 9 | 16 | 29 | 44 | 48 | * |
| 15. | Sporting Club de Bastia (Bastia) | 38 | 11 | 11 | 16 | 44 | 56 | 44 | |
| 16. | Olympique GC de Nice-Côte d'Azur (Nice) | 38 | 11 | 10 | 17 | 39 | 52 | 43 | |
| 17. | Montpellier Hérault SC (Montpellier) | 38 | 9 | 14 | 15 | 38 | 53 | 41 | |
| 18. | AS de Saint-Étienne (Saint-Étienne) | 38 | 9 | 11 | 18 | 45 | 55 | 38 | # |
| 19. | Stade Malherbe Caen-CB Normandie (Caen) | 38 | 10 | 6 | 22 | 38 | 58 | 36 | R |
| 20. | FC Sochaux-Montbéliard (Montbéliard) | 38 | 6 | 5 | 27 | 29 | 68 | 23 | R |
| | | 760 | 271 | 218 | 271 | 951 | 951 | 1031 | |

## Top goal-scorers

1) Patrice LOKO      (FC Nantes-Atlantique)   22
2) Alain CAVEGLIA      (Havre AC)   20
3) Nicolas OUÉDEC      (FC Nantes-Atlantique)   18
4) Youri DJORKAEFF      (AS de Monaco)   14
    Marco GRASSI      (Stade Rennais FC)   14
    Florian MAURICE      (Olympique Lyonnais)   14
    Joël TIEHI      (Racing Club de Lens)   14

| 1994-1995 Division One | AJ Auxerroise | SC de Bastia | Girondins de Bordeaux | SM Caen CBN | AS de Cannes | Havre AC | Racing de Lens | Lille Olympique | Olympique Lyonnais | FC Martigues | FC de Metz | AS de Monaco | Montpellier Hérault SC | Nantes-Atlantique | Olympique GC Nice | Paris Saint-Germain FC | Stade Rennais | AS Saint-Étienne | Sochaux-Montbéliard | RC Strasbourg |
|---|---|---|---|---|---|---|---|---|---|---|---|---|---|---|---|---|---|---|---|---|
| AJ Auxerroise | | 2-1 | 1-0 | 1-1 | 3-0 | 1-1 | 3-0 | 2-0 | 0-0 | 3-0 | 1-1 | 2-2 | 0-1 | 1-2 | 3-0 | 1-1 | 2-2 | 3-0 | 4-0 | 1-0 |
| SC de Bastia | 0-1 | | 0-0 | 1-0 | 6-3 | 3-2 | 1-3 | 3-1 | 0-1 | 2-0 | 0-3 | 0-2 | 1-1 | 2-2 | 1-1 | 1-2 | 1-2 | 2-1 | 1-0 | 0-1 |
| Girondins de Bordeaux | 3-1 | 1-0 | | 2-0 | 0-2 | 0-1 | 1-2 | 1-0 | 1-1 | 1-1 | 4-2 | 0-3 | 2-0 | 1-1 | 1-0 | 3-0 | 2-1 | 2-1 | 2-1 | 2-0 |
| SM Caen CBN | 1-5 | 2-1 | 4-2 | | 0-1 | 2-2 | 0-0 | 2-0 | 0-1 | 0-1 | 2-0 | 0-1 | 1-0 | 0-2 | 0-0 | 1-2 | 5-1 | 3-0 | 3-1 | 4-0 |
| AS de Cannes | 3-1 | 0-0 | 2-0 | 1-0 | | 2-2 | 2-0 | 0-0 | 5-1 | 0-1 | 1-0 | 2-2 | 3-0 | 0-1 | 2-0 | 3-2 | 0-1 | 4-1 | 0-0 | 2-2 |
| Havre AC | 1-4 | 2-2 | 1-1 | 1-1 | 1-0 | | 2-3 | 0-1 | 2-0 | 1-0 | 0-3 | 1-0 | 1-2 | 0-0 | 1-1 | 0-0 | 4-0 | 2-0 | 2-0 | 1-0 |
| Racing de Lens | 1-1 | 3-0 | 2-1 | 2-0 | 0-2 | 1-1 | | 1-1 | 4-0 | 2-1 | 2-2 | 0-0 | 1-1 | 1-1 | 2-1 | 1-2 | 5-0 | 0-0 | 1-0 | 1-0 |
| Lille Olympique | 0-0 | 3-0 | 1-0 | 1-1 | 0-3 | 1-1 | 3-1 | | 1-4 | 1-0 | 1-0 | 1-0 | 0-0 | 1-2 | 1-0 | 1-0 | 1-0 | 1-0 | 1-0 | 1-0 |
| Olympique Lyonnais | 3-0 | 0-0 | 1-1 | 1-0 | 3-1 | 2-0 | 1-1 | 3-1 | | 3-0 | 1-0 | 3-1 | 2-1 | 1-1 | 1-1 | 2-0 | 3-0 | 1-0 | 4-0 | 1-0 |
| FC Martigues | 2-1 | 5-2 | 1-0 | 4-1 | 0-0 | 2-1 | 0-0 | 1-0 | 2-0 | | 1-1 | 1-1 | 2-1 | 3-3 | 0-1 | 1-1 | 1-0 | 1-1 | 2-0 | 0-0 |
| FC de Metz | 1-1 | 1-2 | 2-3 | 4-0 | 3-2 | 2-1 | 3-1 | 1-1 | 2-1 | 0-0 | | 2-0 | 0-0 | 0-2 | 0-0 | 2-0 | 1-0 | 1-0 | 3-0 | 3-2 |
| AS de Monaco | 0-0 | 2-1 | 6-3 | 3-0 | 0-0 | 1-2 | 6-0 | 2-0 | 1-1 | 1-0 | 0-1 | | 2-0 | 2-2 | 0-2 | 2-1 | 0-0 | 0-0 | 3-1 | 3-1 |
| Montpellier Hérault SC | 1-1 | 0-0 | 0-1 | 3-2 | 5-3 | 2-1 | 1-2 | 1-0 | 2-2 | 0-1 | 2-0 | 2-2 | | 2-2 | 0-0 | 0-3 | 0-1 | 3-2 | 1-0 | 1-1 |
| Nantes-Atlantique | 0-0 | 0-0 | 3-3 | 2-1 | 2-1 | 3-2 | 3-0 | 3-0 | 1-1 | 3-0 | 3-1 | 3-3 | 2-2 | | 2-1 | 1-0 | 2-0 | 3-0 | 2-0 | 3-0 |
| Olympique GC Nice | 1-3 | 1-2 | 0-2 | 0-1 | 2-1 | 0-2 | 1-1 | 1-0 | 1-2 | 1-1 | 1-0 | 3-1 | 0-0 | 1-3 | | 0-4 | 1-0 | 3-0 | 1-0 | 3-4 |
| Paris Saint-Germain FC | 1-1 | 3-0 | 0-0 | 2-0 | 2-1 | 2-2 | 1-0 | 3-0 | 4-1 | 3-0 | 3-0 | 1-0 | 3-1 | 0-3 | 2-3 | | 2-1 | 1-0 | 1-1 | 1-0 |
| Stade Rennais | 2-2 | 2-2 | 2-0 | 5-0 | 3-1 | 0-0 | 0-1 | 1-0 | 1-1 | 5-1 | 1-2 | 1-3 | 2-2 | 1-1 | 3-1 | 4-0 | | 2-2 | 2-1 | 1-1 |
| AS Saint-Étienne | 1-1 | 1-2 | 2-1 | 2-0 | 1-0 | 4-1 | 1-2 | 3-3 | 1-1 | 3-0 | 0-1 | 1-0 | 4-0 | 1-1 | 3-3 | 1-3 | 1-1 | | 4-0 | 2-0 |
| Sochaux-Montbéliard | 0-1 | 1-3 | 1-4 | 2-0 | 2-1 | 0-1 | 1-1 | 3-0 | 1-2 | 1-1 | 4-2 | 0-5 | 2-0 | 0-0 | 0-1 | 1-2 | 1-3 | 2-0 | | 0-1 |
| RC Strasbourg | 1-1 | 1-1 | 1-1 | 1-0 | 1-2 | 3-0 | 0-0 | 1-1 | 1-0 | 5-0 | 1-0 | 1-0 | 0-0 | 2-0 | 3-2 | 2-0 | 2-2 | 1-1 | 3-2 | |

\*  Havre AC (Le Havre) changed their name to Havre AC Football Association (Le Havre) for the next season;  Lille Olympique SC Metropole (Lille) changed their name pre-season from Lille Olympique SC (Lille);  Racing Club de Strasbourg (Strasbourg) changed their name to Racing Club de Strasbourg Football (Strasbourg).

| Division 2 | Pd | Wn | Dw | Ls | GF | GA | Pts | |
|---|---|---|---|---|---|---|---|---|
| 1. Olympique de Marseille (Marseille) | 42 | 25 | 9 | 8 | 72 | 34 | 84 | # |
| 2. En Avant de Guingamp (Guingamp) | 42 | 23 | 12 | 7 | 51 | 32 | 81 | P |
| 3. FC de Gueugnon (Gueugnon) | 42 | 24 | 8 | 10 | 63 | 40 | 80 | P |
| 4. Toulouse FC (Toulouse) | 42 | 22 | 11 | 9 | 69 | 43 | 77 | |
| 5. FC La Berrichonne (Châteauroux) | 42 | 19 | 14 | 9 | 56 | 34 | 71 | |
| 6. AS Red Star 93 (Saint-Ouen) | 42 | 19 | 13 | 10 | 55 | 44 | 70 | |
| 7. AS Nancy-Lorraine (Nancy) | 42 | 15 | 18 | 9 | 46 | 39 | 63 | |
| 8. US du Littoral Dunkerquois (Dunkerque) | 42 | 14 | 18 | 10 | 42 | 38 | 60 | |
| 9. Amiens SC (Amiens) | 42 | 15 | 13 | 14 | 59 | 61 | 58 | |
| 10. Olympique d'Alès en Cévenne (Alès) | 42 | 12 | 17 | 13 | 44 | 44 | 53 | |
| 11. FC Olympique de Charleville (Charleville) | 42 | 11 | 19 | 12 | 45 | 49 | 52 | |
| 12. Mans Union Club 72 (Le Mans) | 42 | 11 | 16 | 15 | 46 | 49 | 49 | |
| 13. US Jeunesse d'Origine Arménienne de Valence | 42 | 11 | 16 | 15 | 47 | 52 | 49 | |
| 14. FC Mulhouse-Sud Alsace (Mulhouse) | 42 | 12 | 13 | 17 | 49 | 58 | 49 | |
| 15. Stade Lavallois FC (Laval) | 42 | 9 | 17 | 16 | 42 | 56 | 44 | |
| 16. Perpignan FC (Perpignan) | 42 | 9 | 17 | 16 | 35 | 51 | 44 | |
| 17. Chamois Niortais FC (Niort) | 42 | 8 | 19 | 15 | 34 | 49 | 43 | |
| 18. Angers SC de l'Ouest (Angers) | 42 | 10 | 12 | 20 | 38 | 51 | 42 | |
| 19. Stade Briochin (Saint-Brieuc) | 42 | 11 | 9 | 22 | 38 | 53 | 42 | R |
| 20. AS Beauvais-Oise (Beauvais) | 42 | 9 | 15 | 18 | 50 | 66 | 42 | R |
| 21. CS Sedan-Ardennes (Sedan) | 42 | 10 | 11 | 21 | 34 | 60 | 41 | R |
| 22. Nîmes Olympique (Nîmes) | 42 | 9 | 11 | 22 | 48 | 60 | 38 | R |
| | 924 | 308 | 308 | 308 | 1063 | 1063 | 924 | |

**Promoted**: Stade Athlétique Spinalien FC (Epinal), CS Louhans-Cuiseaux 71 (Cuiseaux-Louhans), FC 56 Lorient (Lorient) and Stade Poitevin Pepp Football (Poitiers).

# Olympique de Marseille were refused promotion due to financial irregularities and the club's debts. As a result of this AS de Saint-Étienne retained their Division 1 status.


## Coupe de France Final   (Parc des Princes, Paris – 13/05/95 – 24,633)

**PARIS SAINT-GERMAIN FC (PARIS)**          **1-0**          Racing Club de Strasbourg (Strasbourg)

*Le Guen 48'*

**PSG**: Lama, Cobos (Llacer 10'), Kombouaré, Roche, Colleter, Guérin, Bravo, Le Guen, Raí (Nouma 90'), Weah, Ginola.

**Strasbourg**: Vencel, Baills, Régis, Leboeuf, Pouliquen, Djetou, Sauzée, Garde (Gohel 83'), Mostovoi, Keller (Bouafia 72'), Gravelaine.


## Semi-Finals

| | | |
|---|---|---|
| Paris Saint-Germain FC (Paris) | 2-0 | Olympique de Marseille (Marseille) |
| Racing Club de Strasbourg (Strasbourg) | 1-0 | FC de Metz (Metz) |


## Quarter-Finals

| | | |
|---|---|---|
| Olympique de Marseille (Marseille) | 2-0 | FC La Berrichonne (Châteauroux) |
| FC de Metz (Metz) | 2-0 | FC Mulhouse-Sud Alsace (Mulhouse) |
| AS Nancy-Lorraine (Nancy) | 0-2 | Paris Saint-Germain FC (Paris) |
| Racing Club de Strasbourg (Strasbourg) | 2-0  (aet) | FC Girondins de Bordeaux (Bordeaux) |

# 1995-96

| 1995-1996 Division One | AJ Auxerroise | SC de Bastia | Gir. de Bordeaux | AS de Cannes | FC Gueugnon | EA Guingamp | Havre AC | Racing de Lens | Lille Olympique | Olymp. Lyonnais | FC Martigues | FC de Metz | AS de Monaco | Montpellier Hér. | Nantes-Atlant. | Olymp. GC Nice | Paris St-Germain | Stade Rennais | AS Saint-Étienne | RC Strasbourg |
|---|---|---|---|---|---|---|---|---|---|---|---|---|---|---|---|---|---|---|---|---|
| AJ Auxerroise | ■ | 3-0 | 2-0 | 5-1 | 4-0 | 1-2 | 1-0 | 0-1 | 1-2 | 2-0 | 4-0 | 0-0 | 1-2 | 1-0 | 2-1 | 2-1 | 3-0 | 2-1 | 2-0 | 1-0 |
| SC de Bastia | 1-1 | ■ | 2-0 | 2-1 | 1-2 | 0-1 | 1-0 | 3-2 | 4-0 | 0-0 | 2-0 | 1-0 | 2-1 | 1-0 | 4-1 | 1-2 | 2-2 | 0-0 | 0-0 | 1-1 |
| Girondins de Bordeaux | 0-1 | 1-3 | ■ | 2-1 | 3-1 | 2-0 | 3-1 | 0-0 | 1-0 | 1-1 | 1-1 | 4-0 | 2-4 | 3-0 | 3-0 | 4-1 | 2-2 | 0-0 | 2-0 | 1-1 |
| AS de Cannes | 0-1 | 1-0 | 1-1 | ■ | 2-0 | 3-0 | 0-0 | 5-2 | 2-1 | 3-0 | 2-1 | 1-2 | 1-1 | 2-1 | 0-2 | 1-3 | 0-2 | 3-0 | 2-0 | 0-3 |
| FC Gueugnon | 0-0 | 1-0 | 2-2 | 1-1 | ■ | 2-2 | 0-1 | 0-1 | 3-1 | 0-0 | 0-0 | 0-0 | 2-2 | 0-2 | 0-1 | 1-0 | 1-3 | 1-0 | 1-0 | 0-1 |
| EA Guingamp | 1-1 | 1-0 | 1-0 | 2-0 | 0-0 | ■ | 2-2 | 1-0 | 0-1 | 1-0 | 2-0 | 0-0 | 0-0 | 0-0 | 3-1 | 0-0 | 0-0 |  | 3-0 | 3-0 |
| Havre AC | 0-4 | 1-0 | 1-0 | 0-0 | 0-2 | 1-0 | ■ | 1-1 | 4-1 | 2-1 | 1-0 | 0-0 | 2-1 | 2-2 | 0-1 | 0-0 | 1-1 | 0-0 | 2-2 | 2-0 |
| Racing de Lens | 0-0 | 3-1 | 0-0 | 1-1 | 2-0 | 0-1 | 2-0 | ■ | 1-1 | 2-2 | 1-0 | 2-0 | 2-1 | 2-1 | 2-1 | 1-0 | 3-1 | 1-0 | 3-0 | 0-0 |
| Lille Olympique | 0-4 | 0-2 | 0-2 | 0-2 | 2-0 | 0-3 | 2-0 | 1-3 | ■ | 2-1 | 0-0 | 0-0 | 0-0 | 1-1 | 0-0 | 1-0 | 0-0 | 0-0 | 1-1 | 2-0 |
| Olympique Lyonnais | 0-1 | 1-1 | 1-0 | 1-0 | 0-0 | 1-1 | 3-2 | 0-0 | 1-1 | ■ | 5-1 | 1-1 | 3-3 | 3-2 | 1-1 | 1-0 | 0-0 | 2-2 | 2-1 | 1-1 |
| FC Martigues | 1-2 | 3-1 | 3-1 | 2-1 | 3-0 | 2-1 | 0-1 | 0-1 | 1-0 | 1-2 | ■ | 0-1 | 0-4 | 0-1 | 0-0 | 0-0 | 2-4 | 1-2 | 1-1 | 2-0 |
| FC de Metz | 3-1 | 2-0 | 2-0 | 0-0 | 1-2 | 3-0 | 2-1 | 2-0 | 2-0 | 0-1 | 2-0 | ■ | 0-3 | 1-0 | 0-0 | 4-0 | 0-3 | 0-0 | 1-2 | 3-2 |
| AS de Monaco | 2-2 | 0-0 | 2-0 | 1-0 | 0-0 | 1-0 | 2-1 | 1-1 | 2-1 | 0-2 | 0-1 | 0-1 | ■ | 3-1 | 4-1 | 1-0 | 1-0 | 3-1 | 2-0 | 5-1 |
| Montpellier Hérault SC | 3-1 | 4-3 | 3-0 | 3-1 | 2-2 | 2-1 | 2-0 | 0-0 | 0-0 | 2-1 | 2-0 | 1-2 | 0-0 | ■ | 1-0 | 0-1 | 3-1 | 1-0 |  | 2-2 |
| Nantes-Atlantique | 1-0 | 3-1 | 2-0 | 2-0 | 1-0 | 0-0 | 1-1 | 1-2 | 0-0 | 3-0 | 1-0 | 2-2 | 1-0 |  | ■ | 1-2 | 2-2 | 2-2 | 2-2 |  |
| Olympique GC Nice | 1-3 | 3-1 | 1-0 | 1-2 | 3-1 | 2-1 | 1-2 | 1-1 | 2-1 | 1-0 | 1-0 | 0-1 | 1-2 | 1-2 | 1-0 | ■ | 1-2 | 0-0 | 2-0 | 2-2 |
| Paris Saint-Germain FC | 3-1 | 5-1 | 3-0 | 2-1 | 1-1 | 1-1 | 2-0 | 1-0 | 0-1 | 2-0 | 0-0 | 2-3 | 2-1 | 2-3 | 5-0 | 3-2 | ■ | 1-1 | 4-0 | 2-0 |
| Stade Rennais | 2-1 | 2-0 | 4-3 | 3-2 | 2-1 | 3-0 | 1-0 | 2-1 | 3-1 | 1-0 | 1-3 | 0-0 | 2-3 | 1-1 | 2-2 | 0-0 | 0-1 | ■ | 3-0 | 0-0 |
| AS Saint-Étienne | 0-5 | 3-0 | 2-0 | 2-2 | 2-0 | 4-0 | 1-1 | 1-1 | 1-1 | 1-1 | 2-2 | 1-1 | 2-4 | 0-2 | 0-0 | 1-1 | 1-1 | 0-0 | ■ | 2-0 |
| RC Strasbourg | 1-0 | 4-3 | 3-0 | 1-0 | 0-0 | 0-0 | 3-0 | 1-2 | 2-0 | 2-2 | 2-0 | 1-2 | 2-0 | 1-0 | 1-1 | 1-1 | 1-0 | 3-1 | 3-1 | ■ |

## Division 1

| | | Pd | Wn | Dw | Ls | GF | GA | Pts | |
|---|---|---|---|---|---|---|---|---|---|
| 1. | ASSOCIATION DE LA JEUNESSE AUXERROISE | 38 | 22 | 6 | 10 | 66 | 30 | 72 | |
| 2. | Paris Saint-Germain FC (Paris) | 38 | 19 | 11 | 8 | 65 | 36 | 68 | |
| 3. | AS de Monaco (Monaco) | 38 | 19 | 11 | 8 | 64 | 39 | 68 | |
| 4. | FC de Metz (Metz) | 38 | 18 | 11 | 9 | 42 | 30 | 65 | |
| 5. | Racing Club de Lens (Lens) | 38 | 16 | 15 | 7 | 45 | 31 | 63 | |
| 6. | Montpellier Hérault SC (Montpellier) | 38 | 17 | 9 | 12 | 51 | 40 | 60 | |
| 7. | FC Nantes-Atlantique (Nantes) | 38 | 14 | 13 | 11 | 44 | 42 | 55 | |
| 8. | Stade Rennais FC (Rennes) | 38 | 13 | 15 | 10 | 44 | 41 | 54 | |
| 9. | Racing Club de Strasbourg Football (Strasbourg) | 38 | 14 | 12 | 12 | 46 | 44 | 54 | |
| 10. | En Avant de Guingamp (Guingamp) | 38 | 13 | 14 | 11 | 34 | 33 | 53 | |
| 11. | Olympique Lyonnais (Lyon) | 38 | 10 | 18 | 10 | 41 | 41 | 48 | |
| 12. | Olympique GC de Nice-Côte d'Azur (Nice) | 38 | 12 | 9 | 17 | 37 | 44 | 45 | |
| 13. | Havre AC Football Association (Le Havre) | 38 | 11 | 12 | 15 | 33 | 45 | 45 | |
| 14. | AS de Cannes (Cannes) | 38 | 12 | 8 | 18 | 45 | 51 | 44 | |
| 15. | Sporting Club de Bastia (Bastia) | 38 | 12 | 8 | 18 | 45 | 55 | 44 | |
| 16. | FC Girondins de Bordeaux (Bordeaux) | 38 | 11 | 9 | 18 | 44 | 52 | 42 | |
| 17. | Lille Olympique SC Metropole (Lille) | 38 | 9 | 12 | 17 | 27 | 50 | 39 | |
| 18. | FC de Gueugnon (Gueugnon) | 38 | 8 | 14 | 16 | 27 | 46 | 38 | R |
| 19. | AS de Saint-Étienne (Saint-Étienne) | 38 | 6 | 16 | 16 | 36 | 59 | 34 | R |
| 20. | FC de Martigues (Martigues) | 38 | 9 | 7 | 22 | 31 | 58 | 34 | R |
| | | 760 | 265 | 230 | 265 | 867 | 867 | 1025 | |

## Top goal-scorers

1) ANDERSON da Silva      (AS de Monaco)    21
2) Anto DROBNJAK      (Sporting Club de Bastia)    20
3) Florian MAURICE      (Olympique Lyonnais)    18

| | Division 2 | Pd | Wn | Dw | Ls | GF | GA | Pts | |
|---|---|---|---|---|---|---|---|---|---|
| 1. | Stade Malherbe Caen-Calvados-Basse Normandie | 42 | 24 | 9 | 9 | 59 | 34 | 81 | P |
| 2. | Olympique de Marseille (Marseille) | 42 | 23 | 11 | 8 | 69 | 35 | 80 | P |
| 3. | AS Nancy-Lorraine (Nancy) | 42 | 20 | 16 | 6 | 56 | 23 | 76 | P |
| 4. | Stade Lavallois FC (Laval) | 42 | 21 | 9 | 12 | 53 | 46 | 72 | |
| 5. | Toulouse FC (Toulouse) | 42 | 18 | 9 | 15 | 40 | 34 | 63 | |
| 6. | Mans Union Club 72 (Le Mans) | 42 | 15 | 17 | 10 | 37 | 36 | 62 | |
| 7. | AS Red Star 93 (Saint-Ouen) | 42 | 16 | 13 | 13 | 56 | 38 | 61 | |
| 8. | Perpignan FC (Perpignan) | 42 | 17 | 10 | 15 | 44 | 53 | 61 | |
| 9. | FC La Berrichonne (Châteauroux) | 42 | 16 | 12 | 14 | 40 | 35 | 60 | |
| 10. | FC Sochaux-Montbéliard (Montbéliard) | 42 | 15 | 14 | 13 | 49 | 40 | 59 | |
| 11. | CS Louhans-Cuiseaux 71 (Cuiseaux-Louhans) | 42 | 16 | 10 | 16 | 57 | 49 | 58 | |
| 12. | FC 56 Lorient (Lorient) | 42 | 16 | 10 | 16 | 44 | 46 | 58 | |
| 13. | Amiens SC (Amiens) | 42 | 13 | 15 | 14 | 43 | 49 | 54 | |
| 14. | FC Mulhouse-Sud Alsace (Mulhouse) | 42 | 13 | 12 | 17 | 44 | 45 | 51 | |
| 15. | US Jeunesse d'Origine Arménienne de Valence | 42 | 11 | 18 | 13 | 34 | 42 | 51 | |
| 16. | Chamois Niortais FC (Niort) | 42 | 13 | 11 | 18 | 48 | 50 | 50 | |
| 17. | FC Olympique de Charleville (Charleville) | 42 | 11 | 15 | 16 | 34 | 54 | 48 | |
| 18. | Stade Olympique Spinalien FC (Epinal) | 42 | 9 | 18 | 15 | 41 | 47 | 45 | |
| 19. | Stade Poitevin Pepp Football (Poitiers) | 42 | 9 | 18 | 15 | 36 | 50 | 45 | R |
| 20. | US du Littoral Dunkerquois (Dunkerque) | 42 | 9 | 16 | 17 | 30 | 43 | 43 | R |
| 21. | Angers SC de l'Ouest (Angers) | 42 | 7 | 16 | 19 | 31 | 53 | 37 | R |
| 22. | Olympique d'Alès en Cévenne (Alès) | 42 | 4 | 13 | 25 | 29 | 72 | 25 | R |
| | | 924 | 316 | 292 | 316 | 974 | 974 | 1240 | |

**Promoted**: AS Beauvais-Oise (Beauvais), Stade Briochin (Saint-Brieuc), SC de Toulon et du Var (Toulon) and Association Troyes Aube Champagne FC (Troyes).

## Coupe de France Final    (Parc des Princes, Paris – 04/05/96 – 44,921)

**ASS. DE LA JEUNESSE AUXERROISE**     **2-1**            Nîmes Olympique (Nîmes)

*Blanc 53', Laslandes 88'*                                                 *Belbey 26'*

**Auxerroise**: Charbonnier, Goma, West, Blanc, Rabarivony, Violeau, Saib (Cocard 87'), Martins, Lamouchi, Laslandes, Diomède.

**Nîmes**: Sence, Touron, Preget, Bochu, Ecker, Jeunechamp (Gros 90'), Zugna (Vosalho 35'), Belbey, Perez, Ramdane (Sabin 69'), Marx.

## Semi-Finals

| | | |
|---|---|---|
| Nîmes Olympique (Nîmes) | 1-0 | Montpellier Hérault SC (Montpellier) |
| Olympique de Marseille (Marseille) | 1-1 | Assoc. de la Jeunesse Auxerroise (Auxerre) |

## Quarter-Finals

| | | |
|---|---|---|
| Olympique de Marseille (Marseille) | 1-0 | Lille Olympique SC Metropole (Lille) |
| Montpellier Hérault SC (Montpellier) | 1-0 | Stade Malherbe Caen-CBN (Caen) |
| Nîmes Olympique (Nîmes) | 3-2 (aet) | Racing Club de Strasbourg Football |
| US Jeunesse d'Origine Armén. de Valence | 0-2 | Assoc. de la Jeunesse Auxerroise (Auxerre) |

# 1996-97

| 1996-1997 Division One | AJ Auxerroise | SC de Bastia | Gir. de Bordeaux | SM Caen CBN | AS de Cannes | EA Guingamp | Havre AC | Racing de Lens | Lille Olympique | Olymp. Lyonnais | Olymp. Marseille | FC de Metz | AS de Monaco | Montpellier Hér. | Nancy-Lorraine | Nantes-Atlant. | Olymp. GC Nice | Paris St.Germain | Stade Rennais | RC Strasbourg |
|---|---|---|---|---|---|---|---|---|---|---|---|---|---|---|---|---|---|---|---|---|
| AJ Auxerroise | ■ | 1-2 | 2-1 | 2-0 | 3-1 | 1-0 | 2-0 | 1-0 | 2-0 | 7-0 | 0-0 | 2-3 | 2-0 | 0-2 | 1-0 | 2-2 | 3-1 | 2-1 | 4-1 | 0-1 |
| SC de Bastia | 2-1 | ■ | 3-1 | 4-2 | 1-0 | 1-0 | 1-2 | 0-1 | 0-0 | 3-1 | 2-0 | 2-1 | 0-0 | 2-2 | 2-0 | 0-0 | 1-0 | 1-1 | 2-0 | 3-1 |
| Girondins de Bordeaux | 0-0 | 3-1 | ■ | 3-1 | 1-0 | 0-0 | 1-0 | 2-1 | 3-0 | 2-2 | 4-0 | 1-0 | 2-1 | 3-1 | 0-1 | 0-0 | 4-1 | 5-3 | 2-0 | 1-2 |
| SM Caen CBN | 2-3 | 2-2 | 0-0 | ■ | 3-0 | 0-1 | 4-0 | 0-2 | 1-0 | 1-1 | 1-0 | 0-0 | 0-1 | 0-1 | 1-1 | 0-0 | 1-2 | 1-3 | 0-0 | 3-0 |
| AS de Cannes | 1-1 | 1-1 | 1-1 | 2-0 | ■ | 1-0 | 2-0 | 0-0 | 0-1 | 0-1 | 0-0 | 0-0 | 0-2 | 1-0 | 0-1 | 1-1 | 1-1 | 0-1 | 1-0 | 2-2 |
| EA Guingamp | 0-0 | 2-1 | 2-2 | 1-1 | 0-1 | ■ | 2-2 | 1-0 | 1-0 | 1-0 | 3-1 | 0-1 | 2-1 | 0-0 | 0-1 | 0-0 | 0-1 | 2-2 | 1-0 | 2-1 |
| Havre AC | 0-2 | 0-1 | 1-2 | 1-1 | 0-0 | 0-1 | ■ | 0-0 | 0-0 | 4-1 | 1-1 | 0-0 | 1-2 | 0-0 | 1-3 | 3-1 | 1-0 | 1-0 | 1-1 | 2-0 |
| Racing de Lens | 2-1 | 1-1 | 3-4 | 0-0 | 0-0 | 2-1 | 0-1 | ■ | 1-0 | 0-1 | 0-0 | 2-2 | 1-3 | 3-2 | 3-1 | 0-4 | 3-2 | 1-2 | 2-0 | 1-2 |
| Lille Olympique | 0-1 | 1-2 | 0-0 | 1-0 | 1-2 | 1-1 | 2-2 | 2-1 | ■ | 1-1 | 1-1 | 1-0 | 1-4 | 0-4 | 2-0 | 3-3 | 3-2 | 0-1 | 3-1 | 2-4 |
| Olympique Lyonnais | 2-0 | 4-2 | 2-2 | 3-0 | 3-1 | 2-1 | 2-1 | 0-0 | 0-0 | ■ | 8-0 | 0-0 | 3-3 | 1-1 | 2-0 | 0-1 | 3-1 | 1-1 | 2-0 | 2-0 |
| Olympique Marseille | 3-0 | 1-0 | 0-0 | 0-1 | 3-1 | 2-1 | 0-0 | 2-1 | 5-1 | 3-1 | ■ | 1-2 | 3-1 | 2-2 | 4-1 | 0-1 | 1-0 | 1-0 | 0-1 | 0-1 |
| FC de Metz | 1-0 | 1-0 | 1-1 | 2-2 | 2-0 | 2-0 | 1-2 | 2-0 | 1-0 | 0-1 | 1-1 | ■ | 2-0 | 1-1 | 1-0 | 0-1 | 0-0 | 0-1 | 2-0 | 3-1 |
| AS de Monaco | 0-0 | 3-1 | 3-1 | 2-2 | 1-0 | 0-0 | 3-0 | 5-1 | 2-0 | 0-0 | 1-1 | 1-1 | ■ | 1-1 | 2-0 | 2-1 | 4-1 | 2-0 | 3-1 | 2-0 |
| Montpellier Hérault SC | 0-0 | 3-1 | 2-0 | 0-0 | 0-1 | 1-0 | 2-1 | 1-0 | 0-1 | 2-1 | 2-0 | 1-0 | 0-1 | ■ | 1-1 | 2-2 | 2-1 | 0-3 | 0-0 | 1-4 |
| Nancy-Lorraine | 0-0 | 2-2 | 1-1 | 1-2 | 1-2 | 2-0 | 0-1 | 1-1 | 2-2 | 2-3 | 0-0 | 2-3 | 1-3 | 0-0 | ■ | 1-3 | 1-0 | 0-0 | 1-0 | 2-0 |
| Nantes-Atlantique | 0-0 | 3-0 | 3-1 | 1-1 | 5-1 | 1-1 | 1-1 | 0-1 | 1-0 | 2-2 | 1-1 | 0-1 | 1-3 | 3-0 | 2-0 | ■ | 7-0 | 0-0 | 3-3 | 3-0 |
| Olympique GC Nice | 0-1 | 1-1 | 0-1 | 1-1 | 0-0 | 1-2 | 0-3 | 1-2 | 1-1 | 0-1 | 0-0 | 3-0 | 0-2 | 1-1 | 1-0 | 1-2 | ■ | 0-1 | 3-1 | 1-1 |
| Paris Saint-Germain FC | 1-1 | 3-0 | 2-2 | 2-0 | 1-1 | 1-1 | 2-0 | 4-0 | 3-1 | 3-0 | 0-0 | 2-0 | 0-0 | 1-1 | 1-2 | 1-0 | 5-0 | ■ | 1-1 | 2-1 |
| Stade Rennais | 1-0 | 1-3 | 1-1 | 1-1 | 3-0 | 1-1 | 1-1 | 2-2 | 2-0 | 2-1 | 4-2 | 1-3 | 0-3 | 2-0 | 1-0 | 0-1 | 3-1 | 2-1 | ■ | 2-0 |
| RC Strasbourg | 2-1 | 1-3 | 1-1 | 2-0 | 2-0 | 2-1 | 1-0 | 1-0 | 3-0 | 3-0 | 2-1 | 0-1 | 0-2 | 2-1 | 3-1 | 0-1 | 3-1 | 0-1 | 3-0 | ■ |

## Division 1

| | | Pd | Wn | Dw | Ls | GF | GA | Pts | |
|---|---|---|---|---|---|---|---|---|---|
| 1. | AS DE MONACO (MONACO) | 38 | 23 | 10 | 5 | 69 | 30 | 79 | |
| 2. | Paris Saint-Germain FC (Paris) | 38 | 18 | 13 | 7 | 57 | 31 | 67 | |
| 3. | FC Nantes-Atlantique (Nantes) | 38 | 16 | 16 | 6 | 61 | 32 | 64 | |
| 4. | FC Girondins de Bordeaux (Bordeaux) | 38 | 16 | 15 | 7 | 59 | 42 | 63 | |
| 5. | FC de Metz (Metz) | 38 | 17 | 11 | 10 | 40 | 30 | 62 | |
| 6. | Association de la Jeunesse Auxerroise (Auxerre) | 38 | 17 | 10 | 11 | 49 | 32 | 61 | |
| 7. | Sporting Club de Bastia (Bastia) | 38 | 17 | 10 | 11 | 54 | 47 | 61 | |
| 8. | Olympique Lyonnais (Lyon) | 38 | 16 | 12 | 10 | 59 | 50 | 60 | |
| 9. | Racing Club de Strasbourg Football (Strasbourg) | 38 | 19 | 3 | 16 | 52 | 49 | 60 | |
| 10. | Montpellier Hérault SC (Montpellier) | 38 | 12 | 15 | 11 | 40 | 40 | 51 | |
| 11. | Olympique de Marseille (Marseille) | 38 | 12 | 13 | 13 | 43 | 48 | 49 | |
| 12. | En Avant de Guingamp (Guingamp) | 38 | 11 | 13 | 14 | 32 | 36 | 46 | |
| 13. | Racing Club de Lens (Lens) | 38 | 12 | 9 | 17 | 40 | 52 | 45 | |
| 14. | Havre AC Football Association (Le Havre) | 38 | 10 | 13 | 15 | 34 | 43 | 43 | |
| 15. | AS de Cannes (Cannes) | 38 | 9 | 14 | 15 | 25 | 41 | 41 | |
| 16. | Stade Rennais FC (Rennes) | 38 | 10 | 10 | 18 | 40 | 58 | 40 | |
| 17. | Stade Malherbe Caen-CBN (Caen) | 38 | 7 | 16 | 15 | 35 | 46 | 37 | R |
| 18. | AS Nancy-Lorraine (Nancy) | 38 | 9 | 10 | 19 | 33 | 51 | 37 | R |
| 19. | Lille Olympique SC Metropole (Lille) | 38 | 8 | 11 | 19 | 32 | 58 | 35 | R |
| 20. | Olympique GC de Nice-Côte d'Azur (Nice) | 38 | 5 | 8 | 25 | 30 | 68 | 23 | R |
| | | 760 | 264 | 232 | 264 | 884 | 884 | 1024 | |

## Top goal-scorers

1) Stéphane GUIVARC'H          (Stade Rennais FC)     22
2) Japhet N'DORAM             (FC Nantes-Atlantique)  21
3) "Sonny" ANDERSON da Silva      (AS de Monaco)      19
   Alain CAVEGLIA            (Olympique Lyonnais)     19
   David ZITELLI        (Racing Club de Strasbourg F.)  19

| Division 2 | Pd | Wn | Dw | Ls | GF | GA | Pts | |
|---|---|---|---|---|---|---|---|---|
| 1. FC La Berrichonne (Châteauroux) | 42 | 20 | 16 | 6 | 54 | 27 | 76 | P |
| 2. Toulouse FC (Toulouse) | 42 | 22 | 9 | 11 | 61 | 32 | 75 | P |
| 3. FC de Martigues (Martigues) | 42 | 17 | 16 | 9 | 54 | 33 | 67 | |
| 4. FC de Gueugnon (Gueugnon) | 42 | 19 | 10 | 13 | 54 | 47 | 67 | |
| 5. Chamois Niortais FC (Niort) | 42 | 16 | 17 | 9 | 44 | 36 | 65 | |
| 6. Mans Union Club 72 (Le Mans) | 42 | 15 | 17 | 10 | 49 | 41 | 62 | |
| 7. AS Beauvais-Oise (Beauvais) | 42 | 15 | 16 | 11 | 43 | 43 | 61 | |
| 8. Stade Lavallois Mayenne FC (Laval) | 42 | 14 | 16 | 12 | 48 | 39 | 58 | |
| 9. FC 56 Lorient (Lorient) | 42 | 15 | 13 | 14 | 50 | 50 | 58 | |
| 10. US Jeunesse d'Origine Arménienne de Valence | 42 | 17 | 7 | 18 | 48 | 53 | 58 | |
| 11. FC Sochaux-Montbéliard (Montbéliard) | 42 | 14 | 15 | 13 | 54 | 47 | 57 | |
| 12. FC Mulhouse-Sud Alsace (Mulhouse) | 42 | 14 | 12 | 16 | 51 | 49 | 54 | |
| 13. AS Red Star 93 (Saint-Ouen) | 42 | 12 | 18 | 12 | 50 | 48 | 54 | |
| 14. SC de Toulon et du Var (Toulon) | 42 | 14 | 12 | 16 | 50 | 57 | 54 | |
| 15. Amiens SC (Amiens) | 42 | 13 | 13 | 16 | 44 | 47 | 52 | |
| 16. Perpignan FC (Perpignan) | 42 | 11 | 18 | 13 | 38 | 42 | 51 | R |
| 17. AS de Saint-Étienne (Saint-Étienne) | 42 | 12 | 15 | 15 | 48 | 56 | 51 | |
| 18. CS Louhans-Cuiseaux 71 (Cuiseaux-Louhans) | 42 | 13 | 12 | 17 | 39 | 52 | 51 | |
| 19. FC Olympique de Charleville (Charleville) | 42 | 10 | 19 | 13 | 37 | 48 | 49 | R |
| 20. Association Troyes Aube Champagne FC (Troyes) | 42 | 10 | 18 | 14 | 36 | 42 | 48 | |
| 21. Stade Athlétique Spinalien FC (Epinal) | 42 | 6 | 8 | 28 | 26 | 75 | 26 | R |
| 22. Stade Briochin (Saint-Brieuc) | 42 | 9 | 11 | 22 | 32 | 46 | 38 | R* |
| | 924 | 308 | 308 | 308 | 1010 | 1010 | 1232 | |

*  Stade Briochin (Saint-Brieuc) dissolved after 31 matches. All the remaining fixtures were awarded 1-0 to their opponents.

**Promoted:** Nîmes Olympique (Nîmes) and Entente Sportive de Wasquehal (Wasquehal).

Division 1 was reduced to 18 clubs for the next season.

**Coupe de France Final**   (Parc des Princes, Paris – 10/05/97 – 44,131)

**OGC DE NICE-CÔTE D'AZUR (NICE)**        1-1        En Avant de Guingamp (Guingamp)

*Salimi 21'*                                                                                *Laspalles 77'*

**Nice:** Valencony, Savini (Crétier 76'), Gomis, Salimi, Tatarian, Fugen (Vermeulen 91'), De Neef, Gioria, Onorati, Chaouch (Debbah 82'), Kubica.

**Guingamp:** Hugues, Foulon (Vannuchi 101'), Jozwiak, Mihali, Laspalles, Michel, Lecomte (Carnot 50'), Baret, Coridon, Moreira (Horlaville 63'), Wreh.

## Semi-Finals

| En Avant de Guingamp (Guingamp) | 2-0 (aet) | Montpellier Hérault SC (Montpellier) |
|---|---|---|
| Stade Lavallois Mayenne FC (Laval) | 0-1 | Olympique FC de Nice-Côte d'Azur (Nice) |

## Quarter-Finals

| FC Girondins de Bordeaux (Bordeaux) | 1-2 | Montpellier Hérault SC (Montpellier) |
|---|---|---|
| Clermont-Ferrand FC (Clermont-Ferrand) | 1-2 (aet) | Olympique GC de Nice-Côte d'Azur (Nice) |
| US de Créteil (Créteil) | 1-3 (aet) | En Avant de Guingamp (Guingamp) |
| Stade Lavallois Mayenne FC (Laval) | 1-0 | Association Troyes Aube Champagne FC |

# 1997-98

| 1997-1998 Division One | AJ Auxerroise | SC de Bastia | Girondins Bordeaux | AS de Cannes | FCLB Châteauroux | EA de Guingamp | Havre AC FA | Racing Club de Lens | Olympique Lyonnais | Olympique Marseille | FC de Metz | AS de Monaco | Montpellier Hérault SC | Nantes-Atlantique | Paris Saint-Germain | Stade Rennais FC | Racing Strasbourg | Toulouse FC |
|---|---|---|---|---|---|---|---|---|---|---|---|---|---|---|---|---|---|---|
| AJ Auxerroise | | 2-0 | 4-2 | 1-1 | 5-0 | 1-0 | 0-0 | 1-1 | 1-2 | 2-1 | 0-0 | 3-1 | 3-1 | 3-1 | 2-3 | 4-0 | 1-2 | 3-1 |
| SC de Bastia | 1-2 | | 4-1 | 5-1 | 1-1 | 1-0 | 2-0 | 1-0 | 0-1 | 1-1 | 0-0 | 1-0 | 2-1 | 2-1 | 2-0 | 0-0 | 2-0 | 0-0 |
| Girondins Bordeaux | 3-2 | 2-0 | | 0-1 | 1-0 | 4-2 | 2-1 | 3-0 | 0-0 | 2-0 | 2-2 | 1-0 | 3-1 | 1-1 | 0-0 | 2-2 | 4-4 | 3-1 |
| AS de Cannes | 2-3 | 1-1 | 0-2 | | 2-2 | 1-3 | 1-1 | 0-2 | 1-0 | 3-3 | 1-1 | 1-2 | 1-0 | 2-3 | 0-1 | 1-1 | 1-0 | 0-1 |
| FCLB Châteauroux | 3-2 | 1-1 | 1-0 | 1-2 | | 2-2 | 2-1 | 2-1 | 2-3 | 0-3 | 1-2 | 0-2 | 0-1 | 1-2 | 2-1 | 1-0 | 2-0 | 2-1 |
| EA de Guingamp | 1-1 | 0-0 | 0-1 | 3-1 | 0-0 | | 1-2 | 2-1 | 0-1 | 1-1 | 0-1 | 1-2 | 1-2 | 1-0 | 0-0 | 1-0 | 0-0 | 2-0 |
| Havre AC FA | 2-2 | 2-1 | 0-0 | 2-0 | 5-0 | 0-0 | | 0-1 | 1-3 | 1-1 | 2-1 | 1-1 | 4-0 | 1-0 | 1-1 | 1-1 | 1-1 | 1-1 |
| Racing Club de Lens | 3-0 | 5-1 | 1-0 | 5-4 | 1-0 | 1-0 | 0-0 | | 3-0 | 0-1 | 1-1 | 1-0 | 0-0 | 0-0 | 3-0 | 3-0 | 3-2 | 2-0 |
| Olympique Lyonnais | 1-0 | 0-2 | 1-1 | 2-0 | 2-1 | 1-0 | 0-1 | 1-3 | | 2-1 | 0-1 | 0-3 | 1-2 | 0-0 | 1-0 | 3-1 | 3-1 | 0-0 |
| Olympique Marseille | 4-0 | 1-0 | 1-0 | 2-0 | 3-0 | 3-1 | 2-3 | 1-0 | 2-0 | | 1-0 | 0-0 | 1-0 | 0-0 | 0-1 | 0-0 | 0-0 | 2-0 |
| FC de Metz | 3-0 | 0-1 | 4-1 | 2-0 | 2-0 | 2-1 | 2-0 | 0-2 | 1-0 | 3-2 | | 3-0 | 0-1 | 3-2 | 2-1 | 1-0 | 1-0 | 2-1 |
| AS de Monaco | 0-1 | 1-0 | 5-2 | 0-1 | 2-2 | 1-0 | 2-0 | 0-1 | 2-1 | 2-0 | 1-2 | | 4-0 | 3-2 | 3-0 | 1-0 | 3-2 | 0-1 |
| Montpellier Hérault SC | 1-1 | 1-1 | 0-1 | 1-0 | 1-0 | 2-3 | 1-1 | 1-2 | 1-1 | 0-0 | 0-1 | 0-2 | | 2-0 | 2-1 | 2-0 | 1-1 | 4-0 |
| Nantes-Atlantique | 0-2 | 0-1 | 1-2 | 1-2 | 3-1 | 2-0 | 2-0 | 1-0 | 3-2 | 1-0 | 1-1 | 1-1 | 1-1 | | 0-0 | 1-1 | 2-1 | 0-1 |
| Paris Saint-Germain | 1-0 | 2-0 | 0-1 | 3-1 | 2-0 | 4-2 | 0-2 | 2-0 | 3-0 | 1-2 | 1-1 | 1-2 | 1-1 | 0-1 | | 4-1 | 2-1 | 1-1 |
| Stade Rennais FC | 1-1 | 2-0 | 0-0 | 2-0 | 3-0 | 1-2 | 2-2 | 2-3 | 0-3 | 0-2 | 2-2 | 2-1 | 2-0 | 3-0 | 1-2 | | 3-1 | 1-0 |
| Racing Strasbourg | 1-1 | 1-1 | 0-0 | 2-0 | 2-0 | 0-1 | 0-1 | 2-1 | 1-2 | 2-0 | 2-0 | 0-0 | 3-0 | 1-2 | 0-3 | 3-1 | | 2-0 |
| Toulouse FC | 2-1 | 1-1 | 2-2 | 1-0 | 1-1 | 3-0 | 1-0 | 1-2 | 0-2 | 0-4 | 0-1 | 1-3 | 1-1 | 1-0 | 0-2 | 1-0 | 1-1 | |

| Division 1 | Pd | Wn | Dw | Ls | GF | GA | Pts | |
|---|---|---|---|---|---|---|---|---|
| 1. RACING CLUB DE LENS (LENS) | 34 | 21 | 5 | 8 | 55 | 30 | 68 | |
| 2. FC de Metz (Metz) | 34 | 20 | 8 | 6 | 48 | 28 | 68 | |
| 3. AS de Monaco (Monaco) | 34 | 18 | 5 | 11 | 51 | 33 | 59 | |
| 4. Olympique de Marseille (Marseille) | 34 | 16 | 9 | 9 | 47 | 27 | 57 | |
| 5. FC Girondins de Bordeaux (Bordeaux) | 34 | 15 | 11 | 8 | 49 | 41 | 56 | |
| 6. Olympique Lyonnais (Lyon) | 34 | 16 | 5 | 13 | 39 | 37 | 53 | |
| 7. Association de la Jeunesse Auxerroise (Auxerre) | 34 | 14 | 9 | 11 | 55 | 45 | 51 | |
| 8. Paris Saint-Germain FC (Paris) | 34 | 14 | 8 | 12 | 43 | 35 | 50 | |
| 9. Sporting Club de Bastia (Bastia) | 34 | 13 | 11 | 10 | 36 | 31 | 50 | |
| 10. Havre AC Football Association (Le Havre) | 34 | 10 | 14 | 10 | 38 | 35 | 44 | |
| 11. FC Nantes-Atlantique (Nantes) | 34 | 11 | 8 | 15 | 35 | 41 | 41 | |
| 12. Montpellier Hérault SC (Montpellier) | 34 | 10 | 11 | 13 | 32 | 42 | 41 | |
| 13. Racing Club de Strasbourg Football (Strasbourg) | 34 | 9 | 10 | 15 | 39 | 43 | 37 | |
| 14. Stade Rennais FC (Rennes) | 34 | 9 | 9 | 16 | 36 | 48 | 36 | |
| 15. Toulouse FC (Toulouse) | 34 | 9 | 9 | 16 | 26 | 46 | 36 | |
| 16. En Avant de Guingamp (Guingamp) | 34 | 9 | 8 | 17 | 30 | 42 | 35 | R |
| 17. FC La Berrichonne (Châteauroux) | 34 | 8 | 7 | 19 | 31 | 59 | 31 | R |
| 18. AS de Cannes (Cannes) | 34 | 7 | 7 | 20 | 32 | 59 | 28 | R |
| | 612 | 229 | 154 | 229 | 722 | 722 | 841 | |

## Top goal-scorers

| 1) | Stéphane GUIVARC'H | (Association Jeunesse Auxerroise) | 21 |
|---|---|---|---|
| 2) | David TREZEGUET | (AS de Monaco) | 18 |
| 3) | Victor IKPEBA NOSA | (AS de Monaco) | 16 |
| 4) | Anto DROBNJAK | (Racing Club de Lens) | 14 |
| | Lilian LASLANDES | (FC Girondins de Bordeaux) | 14 |

| Division 2 | Pd | Wn | Dw | Ls | GF | GA | Pts | |
|---|---|---|---|---|---|---|---|---|
| 1. AS Nancy-Lorraine (Nancy) | 42 | 20 | 16 | 6 | 64 | 37 | 76 | P |
| 2. FC 56 Lorient (Lorient) | 42 | 21 | 12 | 9 | 68 | 38 | 75 | P |
| 3. FC Sochaux-Montbéliard (Montbéliard) | 42 | 18 | 12 | 12 | 56 | 37 | 66 | P |
| 4. Lille Olympique SC Metropole (Lille) | 42 | 17 | 14 | 11 | 62 | 44 | 65 | |
| 5. Association Troyes Aube Champagne FC (Troyes) | 42 | 16 | 15 | 11 | 48 | 38 | 63 | |
| 6. Mans Union Club 72 (Le Mans) | 42 | 16 | 14 | 12 | 54 | 46 | 62 | |
| 7. US Jeunesse d'Origine Arménienne de Valence | 42 | 12 | 22 | 8 | 51 | 45 | 58 | |
| 8. AS Red Star 93 (Saint-Ouen) | 42 | 15 | 12 | 15 | 51 | 61 | 57 | |
| 9. Stade Malherbe Caen-CBN (Caen) | 42 | 15 | 11 | 16 | 61 | 55 | 56 | |
| 10. Chamois Niortais FC (Niort) | 42 | 12 | 19 | 11 | 42 | 38 | 55 | |
| 11. FC de Gueugnon (Gueugnon) | 42 | 16 | 7 | 19 | 47 | 54 | 55 | |
| 12. Amiens SC (Amiens) | 42 | 14 | 13 | 15 | 40 | 49 | 55 | |
| 13. Stade Lavallois Mayenne FC (Laval) | 42 | 14 | 12 | 16 | 50 | 48 | 54 | |
| 14. Olympique GC de Nice-Côte d'Azur (Nice) | 42 | 11 | 19 | 12 | 40 | 40 | 52 | |
| 15. Nîmes Olympique (Nîmes) | 42 | 13 | 13 | 16 | 41 | 51 | 52 | |
| 16. AS Beauvais-Oise (Beauvais) | 42 | 11 | 18 | 13 | 40 | 47 | 51 | |
| 17. AS de Saint-Étienne (Saint-Étienne) | 42 | 12 | 15 | 15 | 47 | 60 | 51 | |
| 18. Entente Sportive de Wasquehal (Wasquehal) | 42 | 14 | 9 | 19 | 49 | 63 | 51 | |
| 19. CS Louhans-Cuiseaux 71 (Cuiseaux-Louhans) | 42 | 13 | 10 | 19 | 41 | 51 | 49 | R |
| 20. SC de Toulon et du Var (Toulon) | 42 | 12 | 10 | 20 | 43 | 62 | 46 | R |
| 21. FC de Martigues (Martigues) | 42 | 10 | 15 | 17 | 37 | 63 | 45 | R |
| 22. FC Mulhouse-Sud Alsace (Mulhouse) | 42 | 9 | 14 | 19 | 51 | 56 | 41 | R |
| | 924 | 311 | 302 | 311 | 1083 | 1083 | 1235 | |

**Promoted**: AC Ajaccio (Ajaccio) and CS Sedan-Ardennes (Sedan).

Division 2 was reduced to 20 clubs for the next season.

## Coupe de France Final   (Stade de France, Saint-Denis – 02/05/98 – 80,000)

**PARIS SAINT-GERMAIN FC (PARIS)**         **2-1**                Racing Club de Lens (Lens)

*Raí 25', Simone 53'*                                                                 *Smièer 83'*

**PSG**: Fernandez, Roche, Rabesandratana, Le Guen, Domi, Algérino, Ducrocq, Gava, Raí, Simone, Maurice (Fournier 87').

**Lens**: Warmuz, Déhu, Wallemme, Magnier, Sikora, Foé, Debève (Brunel 68'), Ziani, Smièer, Drobnjak (Eloi 60'), Vairelles.

## Semi-Finals

| | | |
|---|---|---|
| Racing Club de Lens (Lens) | 2-0 | Olympique Lyonnais (Lyon) |
| Paris Saint-Germain FC (Paris) | 1-0 | En Avant de Guingamp (Guingamp) |

## Quarter-Finals

| | | |
|---|---|---|
| FC Bourg-Péronnas (Bourg-en-Bresse) | 0-1 | Olympique Lyonnais (Lyon) |
| Stade Malherbe Caen-CBN (Caen) | 1-2 | Racing Club de Lens (Lens) |
| En Avant de Guingamp (Guingamp) | 1-0 | FC Mulhouse-Sud Alsace (Mulhouse) |
| Paris Saint-Germain FC (Paris) | 1-0 | AS de Monaco (Monaco) |

# 1998-99

| 1998-1999 Division One | AJ Auxerroise | SC de Bastia | Girondins Bordeaux | Havre AC FA | Racing Club de Lens | FC 56 Lorient | Olympique Lyonnais | Olympique Marseille | FC de Metz | AS de Monaco | Montpellier Hérault SC | AS Nancy-Lorraine | Nantes-Atlantique | Paris Saint-Germain | Stade Rennais FC | Sochaux-Montbéliard | Racing Strasbourg | Toulouse FC |
|---|---|---|---|---|---|---|---|---|---|---|---|---|---|---|---|---|---|---|
| AJ Auxerroise | | 1-0 | 3-1 | 0-0 | 1-2 | 5-0 | 1-0 | 1-1 | 1-0 | 0-3 | 2-2 | 3-2 | 1-1 | 0-1 | 2-0 | 3-1 | 3-1 | 1-2 |
| SC de Bastia | 2-0 | | 2-0 | 2-0 | 1-1 | 2-1 | 4-1 | 0-2 | 3-0 | 3-1 | 2-2 | 1-2 | 1-0 | 2-0 | 0-1 | 1-1 | 0-0 | 1-1 |
| Girondins Bordeaux | 1-0 | 2-0 | | 3-0 | 1-0 | 0-0 | 1-0 | 4-1 | 6-0 | 0-1 | 3-1 | 2-0 | 2-0 | 3-1 | 4-0 | 0-0 | 1-0 | 3-1 |
| Havre AC FA | 2-1 | 1-1 | 2-3 | | 3-1 | 0-1 | 1-0 | 0-0 | 0-0 | 1-2 | 1-1 | 1-1 | 2-1 | 0-4 | 2-0 | 3-0 | 0-1 | 0-0 |
| Racing Club de Lens | 2-2 | 1-0 | 2-4 | 0-1 | | 1-1 | 0-3 | 4-0 | 2-0 | 1-1 | 1-0 | 2-1 | 2-4 | 2-1 | 3-1 | 1-1 | 3-0 | 3-1 |
| FC 56 Lorient | 1-1 | 3-1 | 0-2 | 0-0 | 1-1 | | 0-1 | 1-3 | 1-1 | 1-2 | 1-1 | 0-1 | 1-1 | 2-0 | 1-1 | 4-1 | 0-1 | 1-0 |
| Olympique Lyonnais | 2-1 | 2-1 | 2-1 | 0-0 | 3-1 | 2-2 | | 2-1 | 2-0 | 1-1 | 2-0 | 2-1 | 2-1 | 1-1 | 1-2 | 4-1 | 3-2 | 6-1 |
| Olympique Marseille | 1-0 | 3-1 | 2-2 | 2-0 | 1-0 | 4-1 | 0-0 | | 3-0 | 1-0 | 5-4 | 4-0 | 2-0 | 0-0 | 1-1 | 4-0 | 1-0 | 2-0 |
| FC de Metz | 2-0 | 4-0 | 0-2 | 1-0 | 0-1 | 3-0 | 3-2 | 0-1 | | 1-0 | 3-1 | 2-3 | 1-0 | 1-1 | 0-0 | 1-1 | 1-0 | 0-0 |
| AS de Monaco | 3-2 | 1-1 | 0-2 | 3-0 | 2-0 | 1-0 | 0-1 | 1-2 | 0-0 | | 2-0 | 3-0 | 3-1 | 2-1 | 4-2 | 4-1 | 2-1 | 1-1 |
| Montpellier Hérault SC | 3-0 | 3-0 | 1-1 | 2-0 | 1-0 | 5-1 | 1-3 | 0-1 | 1-1 | 2-3 | | 1-1 | 1-2 | 2-1 | 3-1 | 0-0 | 1-1 | 3-0 |
| AS Nancy-Lorraine | 1-1 | 1-2 | 2-3 | 1-0 | 0-1 | 2-0 | 0-0 | 2-3 | 1-0 | 1-2 | 0-1 | | 1-0 | 0-0 | 0-1 | 1-1 | 1-1 | 2-0 |
| Nantes-Atlantique | 2-2 | 2-0 | 0-0 | 1-1 | 2-0 | 1-1 | 2-0 | 0-0 | 0-0 | 0-1 | 1-1 | 2-0 | | 0-0 | 2-1 | 2-0 | 1-0 | 2-0 |
| Paris Saint-Germain | 2-0 | 2-0 | 2-3 | 3-0 | 0-1 | 1-2 | 0-1 | 2-1 | 2-2 | 1-0 | 0-1 | 1-2 | 0-0 | | 2-1 | 2-1 | 0-0 | 0-0 |
| Stade Rennais FC | 1-0 | 2-0 | 1-1 | 2-1 | 2-0 | 1-0 | 0-0 | 1-1 | 1-0 | 2-1 | 3-2 | 2-1 | 2-3 | 2-1 | | 4-0 | 1-1 | 1-0 |
| Sochaux-Montbéliard | 1-1 | 2-1 | 2-0 | 1-0 | 0-4 | 0-1 | 1-2 | 0-0 | 1-1 | 1-1 | 4-0 | 1-1 | 1-1 | 1-0 | 0-3 | | 1-1 | 2-1 |
| Racing Strasbourg | 2-1 | 1-1 | 3-2 | 0-1 | 1-1 | 2-0 | 0-0 | 0-2 | 0-0 | 1-1 | 2-1 | 1-2 | 2-2 | 0-1 | 1-1 | 1-1 | | 2-0 |
| Toulouse FC | 0-0 | 2-1 | 0-3 | 0-0 | 3-2 | 1-4 | 0-0 | 1-0 | 1-0 | 0-0 | 2-5 | 1-1 | 2-3 | 2-1 | 0-1 | 1-1 | 0-1 | |

| | Division 1 | Pd | Wn | Dw | Ls | GF | GA | Pts | |
|---|---|---|---|---|---|---|---|---|---|
| 1. | FC GIRONDINS DE BORDEAUX (BORDX) | 34 | 22 | 6 | 6 | 66 | 29 | 72 | |
| 2. | Olympique de Marseille (Marseille) | 34 | 21 | 8 | 5 | 56 | 28 | 71 | |
| 3. | Olympique Lyonnais (Lyon) | 34 | 18 | 9 | 7 | 51 | 31 | 63 | |
| 4. | AS de Monaco (Monaco) | 34 | 18 | 8 | 8 | 52 | 32 | 62 | |
| 5. | Stade Rennais FC (Rennes) | 34 | 17 | 8 | 9 | 45 | 38 | 59 | |
| 6. | Racing Club de Lens (Lens) | 34 | 14 | 7 | 13 | 46 | 43 | 49 | |
| 7. | FC Nantes-Atlantique (Nantes) | 34 | 12 | 12 | 10 | 40 | 34 | 48 | |
| 8. | Montpellier Hérault SC (Montpellier) | 34 | 11 | 10 | 13 | 53 | 50 | 43 | |
| 9. | Paris Saint-Germain FC (Paris) | 34 | 10 | 9 | 15 | 34 | 35 | 39 | |
| 10. | FC de Metz (Metz) | 34 | 9 | 12 | 13 | 28 | 37 | 39 | |
| 11. | AS Nancy-Lorraine (Nancy) | 34 | 10 | 9 | 15 | 35 | 45 | 39 | |
| 12. | Racing Club de Strasbourg Football (Strasbourg) | 34 | 8 | 14 | 12 | 30 | 36 | 38 | |
| 13. | Sporting Club de Bastia (Bastia) | 34 | 10 | 8 | 16 | 37 | 46 | 38 | |
| 14. | Association de la Jeunesse Auxerroise (Auxerre) | 34 | 9 | 10 | 15 | 40 | 45 | 37 | |
| 15. | Havre AC Football Association (Le Havre) | 34 | 8 | 11 | 15 | 23 | 38 | 35 | |
| 16. | FC 56 Lorient (Lorient) | 34 | 8 | 11 | 15 | 33 | 49 | 35 | R |
| 17. | FC Sochaux-Montbéliard (Montbéliard) | 34 | 6 | 15 | 13 | 30 | 54 | 33 | R |
| 18. | Toulouse FC (Toulouse) | 34 | 6 | 11 | 17 | 24 | 53 | 29 | R |
| | | 612 | 217 | 178 | 217 | 723 | 723 | 829 | |

## Top goal-scorers

| | | | | |
|---|---|---|---|---|
| 1) | Sylvain WILTORD | (FC Girondins de Bordeaux) | 22 | |
| 2) | Alain CAVEGLIA | (Olympique Lyonnais) | 17 | |
| 3) | Lilian LASLANDES | (FC Girondins de Bordeaux) | 15 | |
| | Shabani NONDA | (Stade Rennais FC) | 15 | |
| 5) | Florian MAURICE | (Olympique de Marseille) | 14 | |

| | Division 2 | Pd | Wn | Dw | Ls | GF | GA | Pts | |
|---|---|---|---|---|---|---|---|---|---|
| 1. | AS de Saint-Étienne (Saint-Étienne) | 38 | 18 | 14 | 6 | 56 | 38 | 68 | P |
| 2. | CS Sedan-Ardennes (Sedan) | 38 | 18 | 12 | 8 | 59 | 31 | 66 | P |
| 3. | Assoc. Troyes Aube Champagne FC (Troyes) | 38 | 17 | 13 | 8 | 48 | 31 | 64 | P |
| 4. | Lille Olympique SC Metropole (Lille) | 38 | 19 | 7 | 12 | 45 | 35 | 64 | |
| 5. | Stade Malherbe Caen-CBN (Caen) | 38 | 16 | 11 | 11 | 47 | 39 | 59 | |
| 6. | FC de Gueugnon (Gueugnon) | 38 | 14 | 15 | 9 | 44 | 39 | 57 | |
| 7. | En Avant de Guingamp (Guingamp) | 38 | 14 | 11 | 13 | 36 | 38 | 53 | |
| 8. | FC La Berrichonne (Châteauroux) | 38 | 12 | 15 | 11 | 38 | 38 | 51 | |
| 9. | AC Ajaccio (Ajaccio) | 38 | 13 | 12 | 13 | 49 | 56 | 51 | |
| 10. | Stade Lavallois Mayenne FC (Laval) | 38 | 12 | 14 | 12 | 37 | 35 | 50 | |
| 11. | Chamois Niortais FC (Niort) | 38 | 11 | 15 | 12 | 41 | 40 | 48 | |
| 12. | AS de Cannes (Cannes) | 38 | 12 | 11 | 15 | 34 | 45 | 47 | |
| 13. | Nîmes Olympique (Nîmes) | 38 | 11 | 13 | 14 | 49 | 46 | 46 | |
| 14. | Olympique GC de Nice-Côte d'Azur (Nice) | 38 | 11 | 13 | 14 | 31 | 34 | 46 | |
| 15. | Entente Sportive de Wasquehal (Wasquehal) | 38 | 11 | 12 | 15 | 35 | 41 | 45 | |
| 16. | Amiens SC Football (Amiens) | 38 | 11 | 11 | 16 | 39 | 43 | 44 | |
| 17. | Mans Union Club 72 (Le Mans) | 38 | 9 | 15 | 14 | 41 | 41 | 42 | |
| 18. | AS d'Origine Arménienne de Valence (Valence) | 38 | 10 | 10 | 18 | 41 | 56 | 40 | R |
| 19. | AS Red Star 93 (Saint-Ouen) | 38 | 9 | 12 | 17 | 52 | 72 | 39 | R |
| 20. | AS Beauvais-Oise (Beauvais) | 38 | 10 | 8 | 20 | 43 | 67 | 38 | R |
| | | 760 | 258 | 246 | 258 | 865 | 865 | 1018 | |

**Promoted**: US de Créteil (Créteil), CS Louhans-Cuiseaux 71 (Cuiseaux-Louhans) and AS d'Origine Arménienne de Valence (Valence).

## Coupe de France Final   (Stade de France, Saint-Denis – 15/05/99 – 78,586)

**FC NANTES-ATLANTIQUE (NANTES)**        1-0                    CS Sedan-Ardennes (Sedan)

*Monterrubio 57' pen*

**Nantes:** Landreau, Chanelet, Decroix, Fabbri (Gillet 67'), Deroff, Carrière, Devineau (Savinaud 87'), Piocelle, Olembé, Monterrubio, Da Rocha (Suffo 90').

**Sedan:** Sachy, Borbiconi (Crosnier 70'), Oliveira (Dangbeto 70'), Satorra, Elzéard, Deblock, Pabois (N'Diefi 61'), Faure, Quint, Di Rocco, Mionnet.

### Semi-Finals

| | | |
|---|---|---|
| FC Nantes-Atlantique (Nantes) | 1-0 | Nîmes Olympique (Nîmes) |
| SC Sedan-Ardennes (Sedan) | 4-3 (aet) | Mans Union Club 72 (Le Mans) |

### Quarter-Finals

| | | |
|---|---|---|
| AS Angoulême-Charentes (Angoulême) | 0-2 | Nîmes Olympique (Nîmes) |
| Grand Rouen | 0-2 | CS Sedan-Ardennes (Sedan) |
| Mans Union Club 72 (Le Mans) | 3-1 | Stade Lavallois Mayenne FC (Laval) |
| FC Nantes-Atlantique (Nantes) | 2-0 | En Avant de Guingamp (Guingamp) |

# 1999-2000

| 1999-2000 Division One | AJ Auxerroise | SC de Bastia | Girondins Bordeaux | Havre AC FA | Racing Club de Lens | Olympique Lyonnais | Olympique Marseille | FC de Metz | AS de Monaco | Montpellier Hérault SC | AS Nancy-Lorraine | Nantes-Atlantique | Paris Saint-Germain | Stade Rennais FC | AS Saint-Étienne | CS Sedan-Ardennes | Racing Strasbourg | Troyes Aube Champagne |
|---|---|---|---|---|---|---|---|---|---|---|---|---|---|---|---|---|---|---|
| AJ Auxerroise | ■ | 3-1 | 1-0 | 2-1 | 3-2 | 2-0 | 2-2 | 1-1 | 0-2 | 2-1 | 2-1 | 1-1 | 1-0 | 4-0 | 2-1 | 3-1 | 0-1 | 0-1 |
| SC de Bastia | 2-0 | ■ | 1-1 | 1-1 | 2-0 | 3-0 | 0-0 | 0-0 | 1-0 | 1-0 | 1-1 | 2-1 | 1-2 | 4-2 | 4-0 | 1-0 | 3-0 | 5-0 |
| Girondins Bordeaux | 1-0 | 3-2 | ■ | 3-0 | 1-2 | 1-3 | 2-1 | 0-0 | 3-2 | 2-0 | 2-1 | 3-0 | 1-1 | 1-0 | 1-2 | 1-1 | 3-0 | 4-0 |
| Havre AC FA | 0-0 | 2-2 | 3-0 | ■ | 1-1 | 0-1 | 0-0 | 1-0 | 1-4 | 2-1 | 0-1 | 0-1 | 3-1 | 0-1 | 1-0 | 2-1 | 0-1 | 2-0 |
| Racing Club de Lens | 2-1 | 4-0 | 3-3 | 4-0 | ■ | 4-3 | 0-0 | 1-0 | 1-0 | 0-1 | 1-2 | 3-2 | 1-1 | 0-2 | 0-3 | 3-0 |  | 0-1 |
| Olympique Lyonnais | 0-0 | 2-1 | 1-1 | 3-0 | 1-0 | ■ | 2-0 | 2-0 | 2-1 | 1-2 | 2-1 | 2-0 | 1-0 | 2-2 | 0-0 | 2-0 | 0-0 | 1-3 |
| Olympique Marseille | 0-1 | 1-1 | 0-2 | 2-0 | 1-2 | 0-1 | ■ | 1-1 | 4-2 | 0-0 | 2-2 | 1-1 | 4-1 | 1-1 | 3-3 | 3-0 | 4-1 | 1-0 |
| FC de Metz | 3-0 | 1-1 | 2-1 | 3-0 | 0-0 | 0-1 | 2-0 | ■ | 1-1 | 2-2 | 2-2 | 2-1 | 1-3 | 0-0 | 1-1 | 1-1 | 0-0 | 3-1 |
| AS de Monaco | 2-0 | 4-0 | 1-0 | 5-2 | 2-0 | 1-0 | 1-1 | 2-2 | ■ | 1-0 | 2-2 | 2-0 | 1-0 | 3-1 | 2-2 | 2-1 | 3-0 | 3-0 |
| Montpellier Hérault SC | 2-0 | 1-1 | 2-2 | 0-0 | 1-1 | 2-2 | 3-1 | 0-1 | 2-3 | ■ | 1-0 | 3-0 | 0-1 | 1-2 | 0-1 | 1-1 | 1-1 | 2-2 |
| AS Nancy-Lorraine | 2-0 | 1-0 | 2-2 | 3-0 | 2-1 | 1-0 | 2-2 | 0-0 | 1-2 | 1-2 | ■ | 2-1 | 1-1 | 3-0 | 1-0 | 0-2 | 2-3 | 1-2 |
| Nantes-Atlantique | 3-1 | 1-1 | 0-1 | 1-0 | 0-1 | 6-1 | 0-0 | 1-3 | 0-3 | 3-0 | 2-0 | ■ | 0-4 | 3-0 | 0-1 | 1-0 | 3-1 | 3-0 |
| Paris Saint-Germain | 1-1 | 2-0 | 2-1 | 2-1 | 4-1 | 2-2 | 0-2 | 2-1 | 0-3 | 3-0 | 1-1 | 0-0 | ■ | 1-0 | 2-0 | 3-2 | 4-2 | 1-0 |
| Stade Rennais FC | 1-0 | 0-0 | 2-1 | 2-1 | 3-0 | 1-2 | 1-2 | 2-0 | 2-1 | 1-3 | 3-1 | 0-0 | 1-3 | ■ | 4-1 | 5-0 | 2-1 | 2-2 |
| AS Saint-Étienne | 0-0 | 1-1 | 1-2 | 3-3 | 0-2 | 1-1 | 5-1 | 2-0 | 3-1 | 5-4 | 2-1 | 0-2 | 1-1 | 1-0 | ■ | 2-3 | 0-1 | 1-0 |
| CS Sedan-Ardennes | 1-1 | 2-0 | 0-1 | 0-1 | 0-0 | 2-0 | 2-2 | 0-2 | 2-1 | 2-1 | 3-1 | 0-0 | 1-1 | 2-1 | 3-2 | ■ | 2-1 | 2-1 |
| Racing Strasbourg | 1-3 | 2-0 | 2-2 | 0-1 | 1-0 | 4-2 | 3-1 | 1-1 | 3-2 | 2-0 | 0-2 | 3-2 | 1-1 | 2-1 | 0-1 | 1-1 | ■ | 2-0 |
| Troyes Aube Champagne | 2-0 | 1-0 | 2-0 | 3-1 | 0-1 | 1-2 | 1-2 | 2-2 | 1-4 | 2-1 | 2-0 | 1-0 | 2-2 | 1-0 | 0-1 | 0-2 | 2-1 | ■ |

| | Division 1 | Pd | Wn | Dw | Ls | GF | GA | Pts | |
|---|---|---|---|---|---|---|---|---|---|
| 1. | AS DE MONACO (MONACO) | 34 | 20 | 5 | 9 | 69 | 38 | 65 | |
| 2. | Paris Saint-Germain FC (Paris) | 34 | 16 | 10 | 8 | 54 | 40 | 58 | |
| 3. | Olympique Lyonnais (Lyon) | 34 | 16 | 8 | 10 | 45 | 42 | 56 | |
| 4. | FC Girondins de Bordeaux (Bordeaux) | 34 | 15 | 9 | 10 | 52 | 40 | 54 | |
| 5. | Racing Club de Lens (Lens) | 34 | 14 | 7 | 13 | 42 | 41 | 49 | |
| 6. | AS Saint-Étienne (Saint-Étienne) | 34 | 13 | 9 | 12 | 46 | 47 | 48 | |
| 7. | CS Sedan-Ardennes (Sedan) | 34 | 13 | 9 | 12 | 43 | 44 | 48 | |
| 8. | Association de la Jeunesse Auxerroise (Auxerre) | 34 | 13 | 8 | 13 | 37 | 39 | 47 | |
| 9. | Racing Club de Strasbourg Football (Strasbourg) | 34 | 13 | 7 | 14 | 42 | 52 | 46 | |
| 10. | Sporting Club de Bastia (Bastia) | 34 | 11 | 12 | 11 | 43 | 39 | 45 | |
| 11. | FC de Metz (Metz) | 34 | 9 | 17 | 8 | 38 | 33 | 44 | |
| 12. | FC Nantes-Atlantique (Nantes) | 34 | 12 | 7 | 15 | 39 | 40 | 43 | |
| 13. | Stade Rennais FC (Rennes) | 34 | 12 | 7 | 15 | 44 | 48 | 43 | |
| 14. | Association Troyes Aube Champagne FC (Troyes) | 34 | 13 | 4 | 17 | 36 | 52 | 43 | |
| 15. | Olympique de Marseille (Marseille) | 34 | 9 | 15 | 10 | 45 | 45 | 42 | |
| 16. | AS Nancy-Lorraine (Nancy) | 34 | 11 | 9 | 14 | 43 | 45 | 42 | R |
| 17. | Havre AC Football Association (Le Havre) | 34 | 9 | 7 | 18 | 30 | 52 | 34 | R |
| 18. | Montpellier Hérault SC (Montpellier) | 34 | 7 | 10 | 17 | 39 | 50 | 31 | R |
| | | 612 | 226 | 160 | 226 | 787 | 787 | 838 | |

## Top goal-scorers

| | | | |
|---|---|---|---|
| 1) | Sonny ANDERSON | (Olympique Lyonnais) | 23 |
| 2) | David TREZEGUET | (AS de Monaco) | 22 |
| 3) | Marco SIMONE | (AS de Monaco) | 21 |
| 4) | CHRISTIAN Correa Dionísio | (Paris Saint-Germain FC) | 16 |
| | Shabani NONDA | (Stade Rennais FC) | 16 |

| | Division 2 | Pd | Wn | Dw | Ls | GF | GA | Pts | |
|---|---|---|---|---|---|---|---|---|---|
| 1. | Lille Olympique SC Metropole (Lille) | 38 | 25 | 8 | 5 | 58 | 25 | 83 | P |
| 2. | En Avant de Guingamp (Guingamp) | 38 | 18 | 13 | 7 | 62 | 41 | 67 | P |
| 3. | Toulouse FC (Toulouse) | 38 | 18 | 9 | 11 | 52 | 31 | 63 | P |
| 4. | FC Sochaux-Montbéliard (Montbéliard) | 38 | 18 | 8 | 12 | 53 | 41 | 62 | |
| 5. | FC de Gueugnon (Gueugnon) | 38 | 13 | 17 | 8 | 47 | 34 | 56 | |
| 6. | Stade Malherbe Caen-Calvados-Basse-Normandie (Caen) | 38 | 12 | 17 | 9 | 50 | 37 | 53 | |
| 7. | AC Ajaccio (Ajaccio) | 38 | 15 | 8 | 15 | 37 | 40 | 53 | |
| 8. | FC La Berrichonne (Châteauroux) | 38 | 13 | 13 | 12 | 44 | 44 | 52 | |
| 8. | Mans Union Club 72 (Le Mans) | 38 | 12 | 16 | 10 | 44 | 44 | 52 | |
| 10. | Stade Lavallois Mayenne FC (Laval) | 38 | 12 | 15 | 11 | 41 | 40 | 51 | |
| 11. | Olympique GC de Nice-Côte d'Azur (Nice) | 38 | 10 | 20 | 8 | 34 | 33 | 50 | |
| 12. | AS de Cannes (Cannes) | 38 | 12 | 12 | 14 | 33 | 38 | 48 | |
| 13. | FC 56 Lorient (Lorient) | 38 | 12 | 11 | 15 | 32 | 39 | 47 | |
| 14. | Nîmes Olympique (Nîmes) | 38 | 11 | 12 | 15 | 39 | 44 | 45 | |
| 15. | Chamois Niortais FC (Niort) | 38 | 10 | 15 | 13 | 42 | 49 | 45 | |
| 16. | Entente Sportive de Wasquehal (Wasquehal) | 38 | 9 | 17 | 12 | 33 | 39 | 44 | |
| 17. | US de Créteil (Créteil) | 38 | 11 | 11 | 16 | 36 | 52 | 44 | |
| 18. | Amiens SC Football (Amiens) | 38 | 7 | 16 | 15 | 30 | 43 | 37 | |
| 19. | AS d'Origine Arménienne de Valence (Valence) | 38 | 6 | 15 | 17 | 36 | 54 | 33 | R |
| 20. | CS Louhans-Cuiseaux 71 (Cuiseaux-Louhans) | 38 | 5 | 9 | 24 | 32 | 67 | 24 | R |
| | | 760 | 249 | 262 | 249 | 835 | 835 | 1009 | |

Promoted: Angers SC de l'Ouest (Angers), AS Beauvais-Oise (Beauvais) and FC de Martigues (Martigues).

## Coupe de France Final   (Stade de France, Saint-Denis – 07/05/00 – 78,717)

**FC NANTES-ATLANTIQUE (NANTES)**          2-1          Calais Racing Union FC (Calais)

*Sibierski 50', 90' pen*                                                              *Dutitre 34'*

**Nantes**: Landreau, Chanelet, Gillet, Fabbri, Olembé, Corrière, Berson, Devineau (Monterrubio 68'), Touré (Caveglia 72'), Sibierski, Da Rocha.

**Calais**: Schille, Merlen, Becque, Baron, Deswarte, Jandau, Hogard, Lefebvre (Canu 53'), Vasseur, Gerard, Dutitre (Millien 53, Lestavel 90').

## Semi-Finals

| | | |
|---|---|---|
| Calais Racing Union FC (Calais) | 3-1  (aet) | FC Girondins de Bordeaux (Bordeaux) |
| AS de Monaco (Monaco) | 0-1 | FC Nantes-Atlantique (Nantes) |

## Quarter-Finals

| | | |
|---|---|---|
| FC Girondins de Bordeaux (Bordeaux) | 1-0 | Nîmes Olympique (Nîmes) |
| Calais Racing Union FC (Calais) | 2-1 | Racing Club de Strasbourg Football (Strasbourg) |
| Olympique Lyonnais (Lyon) | 1-3 | AS de Monaco (Monaco) |
| FC Nantes-Atlantique (Nantes) | 2-1  (aet) | Stade Rennais FC (Rennes) |

# 2000-01

| 2000-2001 Division One | AJ Auxerroise | SC de Bastia | Girondins Bordeaux | En Avant Guingamp | Racing Club de Lens | Lille Olympique SC | Olympique Lyonnais | Olympique Marseille | FC de Metz | AS de Monaco | Nantes-Atlantique | Paris Saint-Germain | Stade Rennais FC | AS Saint-Étienne | CS Sedan-Ardennes | Racing Strasbourg | Toulouse FC | Troyes Aube Champagne |
|---|---|---|---|---|---|---|---|---|---|---|---|---|---|---|---|---|---|---|
| AJ Auxerroise | | 1-0 | 0-2 | 1-1 | 3-2 | 1-1 | 0-3 | 0-1 | 1-0 | 1-0 | 2-2 | 1-0 | 0-1 | 4-3 | 0-1 | 1-2 | 2-0 | 2-2 |
| SC de Bastia | 3-1 | | 2-0 | 2-0 | 1-3 | 1-0 | 2-0 | 3-0 | 1-0 | 0-2 | 3-1 | 1-1 | 0-2 | 0-0 | 0-1 | 3-1 | 5-1 | 2-2 |
| Girondins Bordeaux | 1-0 | 0-0 | | 0-2 | 1-1 | 1-0 | 1-1 | 3-0 | 1-1 | 2-1 | 0-2 | 2-0 | 3-0 | 2-1 | 2-2 | 2-1 | 2-1 | 2-2 |
| En Avant Guingamp | 1-0 | 1-0 | 1-1 | | 0-1 | 0-1 | 2-3 | 1-0 | 1-3 | 2-2 | 0-1 | 1-1 | 1-6 | 2-2 | 0-3 | 2-1 | 2-1 | 1-1 |
| Racing Club de Lens | 1-0 | 4-0 | 2-2 | 3-2 | | 0-1 | 0-0 | 1-0 | 1-1 | 4-3 | 1-4 | 1-1 | 1-2 | 0-0 | 1-1 | 0-0 | 2-1 | 1-0 |
| Lille Olympique SC | 1-1 | 1-0 | 2-2 | 1-1 | 2-1 | | 1-2 | 1-0 | 2-1 | 1-1 | 1-1 | 2-0 | 1-0 | 4-1 | 1-0 | 1-1 | 1-0 | 1-2 |
| Olympique Lyonnais | 2-2 | 1-0 | 2-1 | 0-1 | 3-0 | 0-1 | | 1-1 | 0-0 | 2-1 | 3-1 | 2-0 | 2-2 | 2-1 | 2-2 | 5-0 | 4-1 | 1-0 |
| Olympique Marseille | 0-1 | 2-1 | 0-1 | 3-1 | 0-0 | 0-1 | 1-1 | | 4-1 | 2-1 | 2-1 | 1-0 | 0-1 | 2-1 | 2-1 | 0-0 | 1-1 | 3-1 |
| FC de Metz | 1-2 | 3-2 | 2-0 | 1-1 | 2-1 | 1-1 | 0-0 | 1-0 | | 1-3 | 1-2 | 1-0 | 0-2 | 3-0 | 1-0 | 1-0 | 1-1 | 2-2 |
| AS de Monaco | 1-1 | 2-1 | 2-2 | 1-0 | 0-0 | 1-2 | 0-2 | 0-2 | 6-1 | | 2-5 | 2-0 | 1-2 | 5-3 | 1-0 | 3-0 | 3-0 | 4-3 |
| Nantes-Atlantique | 1-1 | 1-0 | 0-5 | 2-1 | 0-2 | 0-0 | 0-1 | 3-2 | 2-0 | 3-1 | | 1-0 | 1-0 | 1-0 | 4-1 | 1-0 | 3-2 | 4-0 |
| Paris Saint-Germain | 3-0 | 3-1 | 1-2 | 1-3 | 1-0 | 2-2 | 1-1 | 2-0 | 1-0 | 1-1 | 2-1 | | 0-1 | 5-1 | 2-1 | 3-1 | 3-0 | 0-0 |
| Stade Rennais FC | 0-1 | 1-2 | 1-2 | 1-2 | 1-0 | 2-0 | 3-4 | 2-0 | 0-1 | 1-1 | 0-2 | 1-1 | | 3-0 | 2-0 | 3-0 | 1-1 | 0-2 |
| AS Saint-Étienne | 2-0 | 2-1 | 1-0 | 2-2 | 1-1 | 1-1 | 2-2 | 3-0 | 2-0 | 1-0 | 0-2 | 1-0 | 0-2 | | 0-2 | 3-3 | *0-0* | 4-1 |
| CS Sedan-Ardennes | 1-0 | 3-3 | 0-0 | 2-2 | 2-2 | 1-0 | 1-1 | 2-0 | 0-0 | 1-0 | 2-0 | 5-1 | 2-1 | 2-1 | | 1-0 | 2-3 | 2-1 |
| Racing Strasbourg | 1-0 | 1-4 | 0-2 | 0-1 | 1-0 | 0-4 | 0-3 | 1-1 | 0-1 | 1-3 | 0-5 | 1-2 | 1-1 | 3-2 | 3-2 | | 1-0 | 3-3 |
| Toulouse FC | 0-1 | 0-1 | 1-1 | 1-1 | 1-0 | 0-2 | 1-1 | 2-0 | 2-1 | 2-1 | 1-1 | 2-3 | 2-0 | 1-1 | 2-0 | 0-0 | | 2-1 |
| Troyes Aube Champagne | 1-0 | 0-0 | 1-0 | 0-1 | 1-0 | 2-1 | 1-0 | 1-1 | 3-2 | 1-0 | 0-1 | 5-3 | 3-1 | 0-0 | 1-1 | 0-1 | 1-1 | |

| | Division 1 | Pd | Wn | Dw | Ls | GF | GA | Pts | |
|---|---|---|---|---|---|---|---|---|---|
| 1. | FC NANTES-ATLANTIQUE (NANTES) | 34 | 21 | 5 | 8 | 58 | 36 | 68 | |
| 2. | Olympique Lyonnais (Lyon) | 34 | 17 | 13 | 4 | 57 | 30 | 64 | |
| 3. | Lille Olympique SC Metropole (Lille) | 34 | 16 | 11 | 7 | 43 | 27 | 59 | |
| 4. | FC Girondins de Bordeaux (Bordeaux) | 34 | 15 | 12 | 7 | 48 | 33 | 57 | |
| 5. | CS Sedan-Ardennes (Sedan) | 34 | 14 | 10 | 10 | 47 | 40 | 52 | |
| 6. | Stade Rennais FC (Rennes) | 34 | 14 | 6 | 14 | 46 | 39 | 48 | |
| 7. | ES Troyes Aube Champagne (Troyes) | 34 | 11 | 13 | 10 | 45 | 47 | 46 | * |
| 8. | Sporting Club de Bastia (Bastia) | 34 | 13 | 6 | 15 | 45 | 41 | 45 | |
| 9. | Paris Saint-Germain FC (Paris) | 34 | 12 | 8 | 14 | 44 | 45 | 44 | |
| 10. | En Avant de Guingamp (Guingamp) | 34 | 11 | 11 | 12 | 40 | 48 | 44 | |
| 11. | AS de Monaco (Monaco) | 34 | 12 | 7 | 15 | 53 | 50 | 43 | |
| 12. | FC de Metz (Metz) | 34 | 11 | 10 | 13 | 37 | 44 | 43 | |
| 13. | Association de la Jeunesse Auxerroise (Auxerre) | 34 | 11 | 8 | 15 | 31 | 41 | 41 | |
| 14. | Racing Club de Lens (Lens) | 34 | 9 | 13 | 12 | 37 | 39 | 40 | |
| 15. | Olympique de Marseille (Marseille) | 34 | 11 | 7 | 16 | 31 | 40 | 40 | |
| 16. | Toulouse FC (Toulouse) | 34 | 9 | 10 | 15 | 34 | 49 | 37 | R3 |
| 17. | AS de Saint-Étienne (Saint-Étienne) | 34 | 8 | 10 | 16 | 42 | 56 | 34 | R |
| 18. | Racing Club de Strasbourg Football (Strasbourg) | 34 | 7 | 8 | 19 | 28 | 61 | 29 | R |
| | | 612 | 222 | 168 | 222 | 766 | 766 | 834 | |

## Top goal-scorers

| 1) | "Sonny" ANDERSON da Silva | (Olympique Lyonnais) | 22 |
|---|---|---|---|
| 2) | "PAULETA" (Pedro Miguel Carreiro Resendes) | (FC Girondins de Bordeaux) | 20 |
| 3) | Frédéric NEE | (Sporting Club de Bastia) | 16 |
| 4) | Gerald BATICLE | (FC de Metz) | 15 |
| | Victor BONILLA | (Toulouse FC) | 15 |

| | Division 2 | Pd | Wn | Dw | Ls | GF | GA | Pts | |
|---|---|---|---|---|---|---|---|---|---|
| 1. | FC Sochaux-Montbéliard (Montbéliard) | 38 | 21 | 12 | 5 | 67 | 27 | 75 | P |
| 2. | FC 56 Lorient (Lorient) | 38 | 21 | 11 | 6 | 58 | 34 | 74 | P |
| 3. | Montpellier Hérault SC (Montpellier) | 38 | 18 | 14 | 6 | 52 | 26 | 68 | P |
| 4. | Chamois Niortais FC (Niort) | 38 | 15 | 14 | 9 | 58 | 44 | 59 | |
| 5. | AS Nancy-Lorraine (Nancy) | 38 | 15 | 11 | 12 | 46 | 32 | 56 | |
| 6. | FC La Berrichonne (Châteauroux) | 38 | 14 | 14 | 10 | 50 | 38 | 56 | |
| 7. | Havre AC Football Association (Le Havre) | 38 | 14 | 14 | 10 | 48 | 42 | 56 | |
| 8. | Nîmes Olympique (Nîmes) | 38 | 14 | 11 | 13 | 53 | 56 | 53 | |
| 9. | Stade Lavallois Mayenne FC (Laval) | 38 | 15 | 8 | 15 | 39 | 43 | 53 | |
| 10. | FC de Gueugnon (Gueugnon) | 38 | 13 | 11 | 14 | 44 | 50 | 50 | |
| 11. | AS Beauvais-Oise (Beauvais) | 38 | 11 | 14 | 13 | 38 | 42 | 47 | |
| 12. | AC Ajaccio (Ajaccio) | 38 | 12 | 10 | 16 | 32 | 40 | 46 | |
| 13. | Entente Sportive de Wasquehal (Wasquehal) | 38 | 11 | 12 | 15 | 37 | 40 | 45 | |
| 14. | Mans Union Club 72 (Le Mans) | 38 | 9 | 18 | 11 | 37 | 45 | 45 | |
| 15. | Olympique GC de Nice-Côte d'Azur (Nice) | 38 | 13 | 6 | 19 | 39 | 56 | 45 | |
| 16. | US de Créteil (Créteil) | 38 | 10 | 13 | 15 | 37 | 43 | 43 | |
| 17. | Stade Malherbe Caen-CBN (Caen) | 38 | 11 | 10 | 17 | 38 | 53 | 43 | |
| 18. | FC de Martigues (Martigues) | 38 | 8 | 15 | 15 | 30 | 46 | 39 | R |
| 19. | AS de Cannes (Cannes) | 38 | 8 | 10 | 20 | 45 | 66 | 34 | R |
| 20. | Angers SC de l'Ouest (Angers) | 38 | 7 | 12 | 19 | 35 | 60 | 33 | R |
| | | 760 | 260 | 240 | 260 | 883 | 883 | 1020 | |

**Promoted**: Amiens SC Football (Amiens), Grenoble Foot 83 (Grenoble), FC Istres-Ville-Nouvelle (Istres) and FC de Martigues (Martigues).

Note: Saint-Étienne 1-0 Toulouse was later awarded to Toulouse with a 0-0 score as Saint-Étienne had fielded 2 players, Alex Dias (Brazil) and Maxim Levitsky (Ukraine) under false EU passports. Saint-Étienne were also deducted 7 points which was reduced to 3 points and later to 0 points as a result of several appeals and court decisions; AS Monaco also had 2 points deducted for fielding Pablo Conteras (Chile) under a false passport. This deduction was also revoked; FC de Metz 2-2 Stade Rennais was awarded 0-2 as Metz fielded Colombian goalkeeper Farid Mondragón under a false Greek passport; RC Strasbourg 1-0 Metz on 21/12/2001 was abandoned after a linesman was struck by a missile. The game was ordered to be replayed behind closed doors but referees refused to officiate and it was awarded as 0-0 loss to both teams. After an appeal it was to be replayed but referees once again refused to officiate. The match was finally played on 30/05/2002 (1-0 to Metz) but was awarded as a 0-0 win to Strasbourg as Metz fielded goalkeeper Mondragón who was eligible for the replay but was not eligible for the original fixture. On appeal this decision was also revoked and the 1-0 result to Metz was allowed to stand.

## Coupe de France Final   (Stade de France, Saint-Denis – 26/05/01 – 78,641)

**RACING CLUB DE STRASBOURG      0-0  (aet – 5-4 pens)**             Amiens SC Football (Amiens)

**Strasbourg**: Chilavert, Ismaël, Bertin, Njanka, Beye, Camadini (Ljuboja 108'), Fischer, Johansen, Amzine (Rémy 57'), Martins, Luyindula.

**Amiens**: Lachuer, Lebrun, Strzelczak, Abalo, Leroy, Coquelet (Chalier 80'), Duchemin, Ewolo, Rivenet (Adjali 104'), Darbelet, Sampil.

## Semi-Finals

| | | |
|---|---|---|
| Amiens SC Football (Amiens) | 0-0  (aet) | ES Troyes Aube Champagne (Troyes) |
| Amiens SC Football (Amiens) won 4-2 on penalties. | | |
| Racing Club de Strasbourg Football (Strasbourg) | 4-1 | FC Nantes-Atlantique (Nantes) |

## Quarter-Finals

| | | |
|---|---|---|
| Amiens SC Football (Amiens) | 1-0 | Stade de Reims (Reims) |
| Grenoble Foot 38 (Grenoble) | 2-4 | ES Troyes Aube Champagne (Troyes) |
| FC Nantes-Atlantique (Nantes) | 4-1 | Association de la Jeunesse Auxerroise (Auxerre) |
| Racing Club de Strasbourg Football (Strasbourg) | 3-0 | Olympique Lyonnais (Lyon) |

| 2001-2002 Division One | AJ Auxerroise | SC de Bastia | Girondins Bordeaux | En Avant Guingamp | Racing Club de Lens | Lille Olympique SC | FC Lorient Bretagne | Olympique Lyonnais | Olympique Marseille | FC de Metz | AS de Monaco | Montpellier Hérault SC | Nantes-Atlantique | Paris Saint-Germain | Stade Rennais FC | CS Sedan-Ardennes | Sochaux-Montbéliard | Troyes Aube Champagne |
|---|---|---|---|---|---|---|---|---|---|---|---|---|---|---|---|---|---|---|
| AJ Auxerroise | ■ | 1-0 | 0-1 | 2-2 | 1-0 | 2-1 | 2-2 | 0-1 | 2-0 | 3-2 | 2-0 | 1-0 | 2-1 | 1-1 | 2-3 | 2-1 | 2-0 | 1-3 |
| SC de Bastia | 0-1 | ■ | 1-2 | 3-0 | 3-1 | 1-0 | 3-1 | 1-2 | 0-1 | 1-2 | 1-0 | 3-0 | 0-2 | 0-1 | 1-2 | 1-1 | 3-0 | 2-0 |
| Girondins Bordeaux | 1-1 | 2-1 | ■ | 2-0 | 2-1 | 0-0 | 2-1 | 0-1 | 0-0 | 1-0 | 0-0 | 3-1 | 2-0 | 1-0 | 2-1 | 2-1 | 0-1 | 2-3 |
| En Avant Guingamp | 0-0 | 1-0 | 2-1 | ■ | 1-0 | 0-0 | 4-3 | 2-4 | 1-0 | 0-2 | 2-1 | 2-2 | 1-0 | 0-1 | 1-1 | 1-2 | 0-0 | 1-0 |
| Racing Club de Lens | 1-1 | 7-0 | 0-0 | 4-1 | ■ | 1-1 | 1-1 | 2-0 | 2-0 | 2-2 | 1-0 | 2-0 | 3-0 | 1-1 | 2-0 | 1-0 | 3-0 | 0-0 |
| Lille Olympique SC | 2-3 | 2-1 | 2-2 | 1-0 | 0-1 | ■ | 3-1 | 2-0 | 2-0 | 2-0 | 1-1 | 2-1 | 1-0 | 1-0 | 1-0 | 1-1 | 1-2 | 1-0 |
| FC Lorient Bretagne | 0-1 | 0-0 | 0-2 | 6-2 | 2-3 | 2-4 | ■ | 0-3 | 2-2 | 1-0 | 2-0 | 1-0 | 1-2 | 1-2 | 2-0 | 1-1 | 1-1 | 1-0 |
| Olympique Lyonnais | 3-0 | 0-0 | 1-0 | 3-0 | 3-1 | 4-2 | 2-0 | ■ | 4-0 | 4-1 | 1-0 | 0-0 | 4-1 | 3-0 | 4-0 | 2-0 | 1-1 | 3-1 |
| Olympique Marseille | 3-0 | 2-2 | 0-0 | 2-1 | 1-2 | 0-0 | 3-2 | 0-0 | ■ | 1-0 | 1-1 | 1-0 | 2-0 | 1-0 | 2-1 | 2-1 | 4-2 | 0-1 |
| FC de Metz | 2-0 | 0-1 | 1-2 | 2-4 | 0-1 | 0-1 | 1-1 | 2-0 | 0-2 | ■ | 1-0 | 0-0 | 2-0 | 0-2 | 3-1 | 2-3 | 2-0 | 2-1 |
| AS de Monaco | 1-1 | 1-1 | 3-1 | 3-1 | 3-0 | 2-2 | 1-0 | 2-1 | 1-1 | 2-2 | ■ | 0-0 | 1-2 | 2-2 | 3-1 | 2-0 | 0-1 | 2-0 |
| Montpellier Hérault SC | 0-0 | 2-1 | 0-0 | 2-1 | 1-2 | 2-0 | 1-3 | 3-0 | 1-1 | 3-0 | 1-1 | ■ | 3-0 | 0-0 | 0-0 | 0-0 | 0-0 | 2-0 |
| Nantes-Atlantique | 2-2 | 0-2 | 2-1 | 2-0 | 1-2 | 0-1 | 2-0 | 3-0 | 3-1 | 0-0 | 2-1 | 1-2 | ■ | 1-2 | 3-1 | 1-1 | 0-0 | 1-0 |
| Paris Saint-Germain | 0-0 | 1-0 | 1-0 | 1-1 | 2-2 | 1-0 | 5-0 | 2-2 | 0-0 | 2-0 | 1-2 | 0-0 | 1-1 | ■ | 3-0 | 3-0 | 1-0 | 3-1 |
| Stade Rennais FC | 0-5 | 2-1 | 1-0 | 2-1 | 1-2 | 4-0 | 1-1 | 2-2 | 2-0 | 0-0 | 3-0 | 2-0 | 2-0 | 1-2 | ■ | 1-0 | 1-1 | 0-1 |
| CS Sedan-Ardennes | 3-3 | 0-2 | 1-0 | 1-1 | 1-0 | 1-0 | 5-0 | 2-1 | 1-1 | 2-0 | 0-0 | 2-0 | 0-0 | 1-2 | 0-0 | ■ | 2-1 | 0-0 |
| Sochaux-Montbéliard | 1-2 | 4-1 | 2-0 | 1-0 | 0-2 | 0-0 | 2-2 | 2-1 | 3-0 | 2-0 | 3-0 | 0-1 | 0-1 | 0-2 | 4-3 | 3-0 | ■ | 2-2 |
| Troyes Aube Champagne | 1-2 | 3-0 | 2-0 | 3-0 | 1-1 | 0-1 | 4-2 | 0-2 | 1-0 | 2-0 | 3-0 | 2-0 | 0-0 | 1-0 | 1-1 | 1-1 | 2-2 | ■ |

## Division 1

| | | Pd | Wn | Dw | Ls | GF | GA | Pts | |
|---|---|---|---|---|---|---|---|---|---|
| 1. | OLYMPIQUE LYONNAIS (LYON) | 34 | 20 | 6 | 8 | 62 | 32 | 66 | |
| 2. | Racing Club de Lens (Lens) | 34 | 18 | 10 | 6 | 55 | 30 | 64 | |
| 3. | Association de la Jeunesse Auxerroise (Auxerre) | 34 | 16 | 11 | 7 | 48 | 38 | 59 | |
| 4. | Paris Saint-Germain FC (Paris) | 34 | 15 | 13 | 6 | 43 | 24 | 58 | |
| 5. | Lille Olympique SC Metropole (Lille) | 34 | 15 | 11 | 8 | 39 | 32 | 56 | |
| 6. | FC Girondins de Bordeaux (Bordeaux) | 34 | 14 | 8 | 12 | 34 | 31 | 50 | |
| 7. | ES Troyes Aube Champagne (Troyes) | 34 | 13 | 8 | 13 | 40 | 35 | 47 | |
| 8. | FC Sochaux-Montbéliard (Montbéliard) | 34 | 12 | 10 | 12 | 41 | 40 | 46 | |
| 9. | Olympique de Marseille (Marseille) | 34 | 11 | 11 | 12 | 34 | 39 | 44 | |
| 10. | FC Nantes-Atlantique (Nantes) | 34 | 12 | 7 | 15 | 35 | 41 | 43 | |
| 11. | Sporting Club de Bastia (Bastia) | 34 | 12 | 5 | 17 | 38 | 44 | 41 | |
| 12. | Stade Rennais FC (Rennes) | 34 | 11 | 8 | 15 | 40 | 51 | 41 | |
| 13. | Montpellier Hérault SC (Montpellier) | 34 | 9 | 13 | 12 | 28 | 31 | 40 | |
| 14. | CS Sedan-Ardennes (Sedan) | 34 | 8 | 15 | 11 | 35 | 39 | 39 | |
| 15. | AS de Monaco (Monaco) | 34 | 9 | 12 | 13 | 36 | 41 | 39 | |
| 16. | En Avant de Guingamp (Guingamp) | 34 | 9 | 8 | 17 | 34 | 57 | 35 | |
| 17. | FC de Metz (Metz) | 34 | 9 | 6 | 19 | 31 | 47 | 33 | R |
| 18. | FC Lorient Bretagne-Sud (Lorient) | 34 | 7 | 10 | 17 | 43 | 64 | 31 | R |
| | | 612 | 220 | 172 | 220 | 716 | 716 | 832 | |

## Top goal-scorers

| | | | |
|---|---|---|---|
| 1) | Djibril CISSÉ | (Association Jeunesse Auxerroise) | 22 |
| | "PAULETA" (Pedro Miguel Carreiro Resendes) | (FC Girondins de Bordeaux) | 22 |
| 3) | Jean-Claude DARCHEVILLE | (FC Lorient Bretagne-Sud) | 19 |
| 4) | Nicolas GOUSSE | (ES Troyes Aube Champagne) | 15 |

| | Division 2 | Pd | Wn | Dw | Ls | GF | GA | Pts | |
|---|---|---|---|---|---|---|---|---|---|
| 1. | AC Ajaccio (Ajaccio) | 38 | 20 | 12 | 6 | 47 | 25 | 72 | P |
| 2. | Racing Club de Strasbourg Football (Strasbourg) | 38 | 19 | 11 | 8 | 47 | 27 | 68 | P |
| 3. | Olympique GC de Nice-Côte d'Azur (Nice) | 38 | 20 | 6 | 12 | 56 | 40 | 66 | P |
| 4. | Havre AC Football Association (Le Havre) | 38 | 17 | 14 | 7 | 56 | 32 | 65 | P |
| 5. | Mans Union Club 72 (Le Mans) | 38 | 16 | 10 | 12 | 48 | 41 | 58 | |
| 6. | Stade Malherbe Caen-CBN (Caen) | 38 | 16 | 10 | 12 | 59 | 55 | 58 | |
| 7. | AS Beauvais-Oise (Beauvais) | 38 | 13 | 18 | 7 | 37 | 25 | 57 | |
| 8. | FC La Berrichonne (Châteauroux) | 38 | 15 | 8 | 15 | 41 | 42 | 53 | |
| 9. | AS Nancy-Lorraine (Nancy) | 38 | 12 | 15 | 11 | 42 | 38 | 51 | |
| 10. | Stade Lavallois Mayenne FC (Laval) | 38 | 14 | 8 | 16 | 50 | 56 | 50 | |
| 11. | Chamois Niortais FC (Niort) | 38 | 11 | 15 | 12 | 40 | 39 | 48 | |
| 12. | Amiens SC Football (Amiens) | 38 | 11 | 14 | 13 | 46 | 50 | 47 | |
| 13. | AS de Saint-Étienne (Saint-Étienne) | 38 | 11 | 13 | 14 | 35 | 42 | 46 | |
| 14. | FC de Gueugnon (Gueugnon) | 38 | 9 | 17 | 12 | 42 | 49 | 44 | |
| 15. | Entente Sportive de Wasquehal (Wasquehal) | 38 | 11 | 10 | 17 | 43 | 55 | 43 | |
| 16. | Grenoble Foot 38 (Grenoble) | 38 | 10 | 12 | 16 | 38 | 55 | 42 | |
| 17. | FC Istres-Ville Nouvelle (Istres) | 38 | 8 | 17 | 13 | 34 | 43 | 41 | |
| 18. | US de Créteil (Créteil) | 38 | 9 | 14 | 15 | 35 | 46 | 41 | |
| 19. | Nîmes Olympique (Nîmes) | 38 | 5 | 17 | 16 | 33 | 48 | 32 | R |
| 20. | FC de Martigues (Martigues) | 38 | 7 | 11 | 20 | 32 | 53 | 32 | R |
| | | 760 | 254 | 252 | 254 | 861 | 861 | 1014 | |

**Promoted**: Clermont Foot Auvergne (Clermont-Ferrand), Stade de Reims (Reims), Toulouse FC (Toulouse) and AS d'Origine Arménienne de Valence (Valence).

Division 1 was extended to 20 clubs for the next season.

## Coupe de France Final   (Stade de France, Saint-Denis – 21/05/02 – 60,000)

**FC LORIENT BRETAGNE-SUD**   **1-0**   Sporting Club de Bastia (Bastia)

*Darcheville 41'*

**Lorient**: Harnel, Gauvin, Druon (Delhommeau 64'), Martini, Diop, Le Lan, Kroupi-Zahi (Cavalli 58'), Keita, Bedrossian (Esceth-N'i 84'), Feindoune, Darcheville.

**Bastia**: Boumnijal, Uras, Soumah, Mendy, Deguerville (Dieuze 53'), Jau, Nalis, Essien, Jeunechamp (Beneforti 75'), Vairelle, Daye (Leite 87').

## Semi-Finals

| | | |
|---|---|---|
| Sporting Club de Bastia (Bastia) | 1-0 (aet) | CS Sedan-Ardennes (Sedan) |
| FC Lorient Bretagne-Sud (Lorient) | 1-0 | Nîmes Olympique (Nîmes) |

## Quarter-Finals

| | | |
|---|---|---|
| FC Libourne/Saint-Seurin | 0-1 (aet) | Sporting Club de Bastia (Bastia) |
| Nîmes Olympique (Nîmes) | 1-1 (aet) | AS de Monaco (Monaco) |

Nîmes Olympique (Nîmes) won 3-1 on penalties.

| | | |
|---|---|---|
| Paris Saint-Germain FC (Paris) | 0-1 | FC Lorient Bretagne-Sud (Lorient) |
| CS Sedan-Ardennes (Sedan) | 1-0 | Racing Club de Strasbourg Football |

# 2002-03

| 2002-2003 Division One | AC Ajaccio | AJ Auxerroise | SC de Bastia | Gir. de Bordeaux | EA Guingamp | Havre AC FA | Racing de Lens | Lille Olympique | Olymp. Lyonnais | Olymp. Marseille | AS de Monaco | Montpellier Hér. | Nantes-Atlant. | OGC de Nice | Paris St-Germain | Stade Rennais | Sedan-Ardennes | Sochaux-Mont. | RC Strasbourg | ES Troyes Aube |
|---|---|---|---|---|---|---|---|---|---|---|---|---|---|---|---|---|---|---|---|---|
| AC Ajaccio | ■ | 1-0 | 1-1 | 1-6 | 0-2 | 1-2 | 0-0 | 2-2 | 0-1 | 0-2 | 2-4 | 0-0 | 1-0 | 2-0 | 0-0 | 1-0 | 1-0 | 0-1 | 0-0 | 1-0 |
| AJ Auxerroise | 1-0 | ■ | 1-0 | 1-0 | 2-1 | 1-0 | 0-0 | 0-0 | 1-2 | 0-0 | 1-1 | 2-0 | 0-1 | 0-2 | 2-0 | 1-0 | 3-1 | 2-0 | 0-0 | 1-0 |
| SC de Bastia | 1-2 | 2-0 | ■ | 2-1 | 0-2 | 3-1 | 1-1 | 1-0 | 2-0 | 2-0 | 1-0 | 1-2 | 3-1 | 1-1 | 1-0 | 3-1 | 0-1 | 2-2 | 1-1 | 1-1 |
| Girondins de Bordeaux | 1-0 | 0-1 | 0-2 | ■ | 4-2 | 2-0 | 1-0 | 2-0 | 0-1 | 3-1 | 2-2 | 3-1 | 0-0 | 4-0 | 0-0 | 2-0 | 2-2 | 2-0 | 1-2 | 1-0 |
| EA Guingamp | 3-1 | 0-2 | 3-0 | 0-0 | ■ | 1-2 | 1-0 | 1-0 | 3-3 | 0-0 | 3-1 | 3-1 | 2-0 | 0-0 | 3-2 | 3-0 | 0-1 | 2-0 | 2-3 | 2-0 |
| Havre AC FA | 0-1 | 0-1 | 2-0 | 1-0 | 1-2 | ■ | 1-3 | 0-0 | 1-2 | 1-3 | 0-3 | 1-0 | 1-1 | 2-1 | 0-1 | 0-1 | 2-1 | 1-0 | 1-1 | 1-0 |
| Racing de Lens | 1-1 | 3-1 | 2-0 | 3-3 | 1-3 | 1-0 | ■ | 0-0 | 2-2 | 0-1 | 1-0 | 4-0 | 0-1 | 0-0 | 3-2 | 1-0 | 4-0 | 1-1 | 1-1 | 1-0 |
| Lille Olympique SC | 2-0 | 2-2 | 1-1 | 0-3 | 2-1 | 1-0 | 0-2 | ■ | 2-1 | 3-0 | 1-3 | 2-0 | 0-1 | 0-3 | 2-1 | 1-0 | 0-0 | 1-0 | 0-1 | 0-0 |
| Olympique Lyonnais | 3-1 | 3-0 | 4-1 | 4-2 | 1-4 | 2-1 | 1-0 | 0-0 | ■ | 1-0 | 1-3 | 1-1 | 0-0 | 2-2 | 1-0 | 4-1 | 6-1 | 4-1 | 2-1 | 0-0 |
| Olympique Marseille | 3-1 | 0-0 | 2-1 | 2-1 | 0-2 | 2-0 | 1-0 | 2-0 | 1-1 | ■ | 1-1 | 2-0 | 0-2 | 2-0 | 0-3 | 2-0 | 4-2 | 1-0 | 1-0 | 0-0 |
| AS de Monaco | 3-2 | 3-1 | 0-0 | 0-1 | 4-0 | 1-1 | 1-1 | 1-1 | 2-0 | 0-1 | ■ | 3-1 | 2-1 | 0-1 | 3-1 | 2-1 | 3-0 | 1-0 | 2-0 | 6-0 |
| Montpellier Hérault SC | 0-1 | 0-0 | 2-2 | 0-1 | 2-0 | 0-0 | 0-2 | 1-0 | 1-1 | 1-2 | 1-2 | ■ | 1-0 | 2-2 | 1-1 | 1-0 | 2-0 | 0-2 | 2-1 | 2-2 |
| Nantes-Atlantique | 1-0 | 1-4 | 1-0 | 0-0 | 0-4 | 2-0 | 2-2 | 1-0 | 1-0 | 1-0 | 0-2 | 3-1 | ■ | 0-0 | 1-1 | 1-0 | 4-1 | 0-1 | 4-1 | 2-1 |
| OGC de Nice | 3-0 | 1-0 | 2-0 | 1-1 | 1-0 | 1-2 | 0-0 | 2-0 | 0-1 | 2-0 | 1-0 | 2-1 | 1-1 | ■ | 0-0 | 0-0 | 0-0 | 2-2 | 4-0 | 1-0 |
| Paris St-Germain | 2-2 | 1-0 | 1-1 | 1-1 | 5-0 | 1-0 | 0-1 | 1-0 | 2-0 | 3-0 | 2-1 | 1-3 | 0-1 | 1-1 | ■ | 0-0 | 2-0 | 1-1 | 3-0 | 4-2 |
| Stade Rennais | 0-0 | 0-0 | 0-1 | 3-4 | 2-1 | 0-0 | 1-1 | 5-1 | 0-1 | 1-3 | 0-0 | 3-1 | 1-0 | 2-2 | 1-0 | ■ | 1-0 | 2-2 | 2-3 | 0-0 |
| Sedan-Ardennes | 1-1 | 1-2 | 2-2 | 0-1 | 2-0 | 4-0 | 0-1 | 0-1 | 1-1 | 1-2 | 2-2 | 1-2 | 1-0 | 3-0 | 3-1 | 1-3 | ■ | 0-0 | 2-1 | 4-0 |
| Sochaux-Montbéliard | 1-1 | 1-1 | 2-0 | 2-0 | 0-0 | 0-0 | 3-0 | 2-2 | 2-1 | 3-0 | 0-0 | 4-1 | 1-0 | 0-0 | 1-0 | 2-1 | | ■ | 2-0 | 1-0 |
| RC Strasbourg | 1-1 | 1-2 | 2-0 | 1-1 | 3-1 | 1-1 | 2-0 | 2-2 | 0-4 | 0-1 | 1-0 | 3-2 | 2-0 | 0-0 | 0-1 | 1-3 | 1-1 | 1-3 | ■ | 2-1 |
| ES Troyes Aube | 1-0 | 1-2 | 3-0 | 0-1 | 0-2 | 1-1 | 0-0 | 2-0 | 1-1 | 0-0 | 0-4 | 0-2 | 2-0 | 1-0 | 1-2 | 0-1 | 2-0 | 0-2 | 1-0 | ■ |

| | Division 1 | Pd | Wn | Dw | Ls | GF | GA | Pts | |
|---|---|---|---|---|---|---|---|---|---|
| 1. | OLYMPIQUE LYONNAIS (LYON) | 38 | 19 | 11 | 8 | 63 | 41 | 68 | |
| 2. | AS de Monaco (Monaco) | 38 | 19 | 10 | 9 | 66 | 33 | 67 | |
| 3. | Olympique de Marseille (Marseille) | 38 | 19 | 8 | 11 | 41 | 36 | 65 | |
| 4. | FC Girondins de Bordeaux (Bordeaux) | 38 | 18 | 10 | 10 | 57 | 36 | 64 | |
| 5. | FC Sochaux-Montbéliard (Montbéliard) | 38 | 17 | 13 | 8 | 46 | 31 | 64 | |
| 6. | Association de la Jeunesse Auxerroise (Auxerre) | 38 | 18 | 10 | 10 | 38 | 29 | 64 | |
| 7. | En Avant de Guingamp (Guingamp) | 38 | 19 | 5 | 14 | 59 | 46 | 62 | |
| 8. | Racing Club de Lens (Lens) | 38 | 14 | 15 | 9 | 43 | 31 | 57 | |
| 9. | FC Nantes-Atlantique (Nantes) | 38 | 16 | 18 | 14 | 37 | 39 | 56 | |
| 10. | Olympique GC de Nice-Côte d'Azur (Nice) | 38 | 13 | 16 | 9 | 39 | 31 | 55 | |
| 11. | Paris Saint-Germain FC (Paris) | 38 | 14 | 12 | 12 | 47 | 36 | 54 | |
| 12. | Sporting Club de Bastia (Bastia) | 38 | 12 | 11 | 15 | 40 | 48 | 47 | |
| 13. | Racing Club de Strasbourg Football (Strasbourg) | 38 | 11 | 12 | 15 | 40 | 54 | 45 | |
| 14. | Lille Olympique SC Metropole (Lille) | 38 | 10 | 12 | 16 | 29 | 44 | 42 | |
| 15. | Stade Rennais FC (Rennes) | 38 | 10 | 10 | 18 | 35 | 45 | 40 | |
| 16. | Montpellier Hérault SC (Montpellier) | 38 | 10 | 10 | 18 | 37 | 54 | 40 | |
| 17. | AC Ajaccio (Ajaccio) | 38 | 9 | 12 | 17 | 29 | 49 | 39 | |
| 18. | Havre AC Football Association (Le Havre) | 38 | 10 | 8 | 20 | 27 | 47 | 38 | R |
| 19. | CS Sedan-Ardennes (Sedan) | 38 | 9 | 9 | 20 | 41 | 59 | 36 | R |
| 20. | ES Troyes Aube Champagne (Troyes) | 38 | 7 | 10 | 21 | 23 | 48 | 31 | R |
| | | 760 | 274 | 222 | 274 | 837 | 837 | 1034 | |

Auxerre 3-1 Sedan on 21/09/2002 was annulled after Auxerre kicked-off at 1-1 while two Sedan players were still in their half of the field. The match was replayed on 08/04/2003 with a 3-1 result; Sedan 0-1 Lens on 17/08/2002 – the referee booked Sedan player Tarik Oulida twice but forgot to send him off, Johann Charpenet (Sedan) was red-carded on 10 minutes.

## Top goal-scorers

| | | | |
|---|---|---|---|
| 1) | Shabani NONDA | (AS de Monaco) | 26 |
| 2) | "PAULETA" (Pedro Miguel Carreiro Resendes) | (FC Girondins de Bordeaux) | 23 |
| 3) | Didier-Yves DROGBA Tébily | (En Avant de Guingamp) | 17 |

| | **Division 2** | **Pd** | **Wn** | **Dw** | **Ls** | **GF** | **GA** | **Pts** | |
|---|---|---|---|---|---|---|---|---|---|
| 1. | Toulouse FC (Toulouse) | 38 | 21 | 9 | 8 | 50 | 24 | 72 | P |
| 2. | Mans Union Club 72 (Le Mans) | 38 | 18 | 14 | 6 | 49 | 33 | 68 | P |
| 3. | FC de Metz (Metz) | 38 | 19 | 10 | 9 | 52 | 29 | 67 | P |
| 4. | FC Lorient Bretagne-Sud (Lorient) | 38 | 18 | 11 | 9 | 43 | 29 | 65 | |
| 5. | FC La Berrichonne (Châteauroux) | 38 | 16 | 12 | 10 | 40 | 35 | 60 | |
| 6. | Chamois Niortais FC (Niort) | 38 | 14 | 11 | 13 | 44 | 40 | 53 | |
| 7. | Stade Malherbe Caen-CBN (Caen) | 38 | 12 | 16 | 10 | 45 | 40 | 52 | |
| 8. | Stade Lavallois Mayenne FC (Laval) | 38 | 15 | 7 | 16 | 41 | 42 | 52 | |
| 9. | AS de Saint-Étienne (Saint-Étienne) | 38 | 12 | 15 | 11 | 34 | 30 | 51 | |
| 10. | Amiens SC Football (Amiens) | 38 | 12 | 13 | 13 | 30 | 33 | 49 | |
| 11. | FC de Gueugnon (Gueugnon) | 38 | 12 | 13 | 13 | 35 | 42 | 49 | |
| 12. | Grenoble Foot 38 (Grenoble) | 38 | 11 | 14 | 13 | 39 | 29 | 47 | |
| 13. | AS d'Origine Armènienne de Valence (Valence) | 38 | 11 | 13 | 14 | 38 | 42 | 46 | |
| 14. | Clermont Foot Auvergne (Clermont Ferrand) | 38 | 13 | 7 | 18 | 39 | 51 | 46 | |
| 15. | AS Nancy-Lorraine (Nancy) | 38 | 10 | 13 | 15 | 30 | 47 | 43 | |
| 16. | FC Istres-Ville Nouvelle (Istres) | 38 | 10 | 13 | 15 | 32 | 53 | 43 | |
| 17. | US de Crèteil (Crèteil) | 38 | 8 | 18 | 12 | 39 | 42 | 42 | |
| 18. | AS Beauvais-Oise (Beauvais) | 38 | 9 | 10 | 19 | 20 | 32 | 37 | R |
| 19. | Entente Sportive de Wasquehal (Wasquehal) | 38 | 6 | 18 | 14 | 26 | 39 | 36 | R |
| 20. | Stade de Reims (Reims) | 38 | 6 | 17 | 15 | 31 | 45 | 35 | R |
| | | 760 | 253 | 254 | 253 | 757 | 757 | 1013 | |

**Promoted:** Angers SC de l'Ouest (Angers), Besançon Racing Club (Besançon) and FC de Rouen (Rouen).

## Coupe de France Final   (Stade de France, Saint-Denis – 31/05/03 – 78,316)

**AJ AUXERROISE (AUXERRE)**               **2-1**               Paris Saint-Germain FC (Paris)

*Cissé 77', Boumsong 90'*                                                   *Leal 21'*

**Auxerroise:** Cool, Radet, Mexes, Boumsong, Perrier-Doumbe, Lachuer, Mathis, Faye (Benjani 72'), Fadiga (Akale 46'), Cissé, Kapo.

**PSG:** Alonzo, Cristobal, Pochetting, Heinze, Potillon (Aloisio 90'), Leroy, Dehu, Leal, Pedron (Llacer 84'), Fiorese (Paulo Cesar 75'), Ronaldinho.

## Semi-Finals

| | | |
|---|---|---|
| Association de la Jeunesse Auxerroise (Auxerre) | 2-1 | Stade Rennais FC (Rennes) |
| Paris Saint-Germain FC (Paris) | 2-0 | FC Girondins de Bordeaux (Bordeaux) |

## Quarter-Finals   (15-16/03/03)

AS Angoulême-Charentes (Angoulême)   0-0  (aet)   Association de la Jeunesse Auxerroise (Auxerre)
Association de la Jeunesse Auxerroise (Auxerre) won 4-2 on penalties.

| | | |
|---|---|---|
| FC Girondins de Bordeaux (Bordeaux) | 2-0 | FC Lorient Bretagne-Sud (Lorient) |
| FC de Martigues (Martigues) | 0-1 | Paris Saint-Germain FC (Paris) |
| SC Schiltigheim | 1-2 | Stade Rennais FC (Rennes) |

# 2003-2004

| 2003-2004 Division One | AC Ajaccio | AJ Auxerroise | SC de Bastia | Gir. de Bordeaux | EA Guingamp | Racing de Lens | Lille Olympique | Olymp. Lyonnais | Mans Union Club | FC de Metz | Olymp. Marseille | AS Monaco | Montpellier Hér. | FC Nantes | OGC de Nice | Paris St. Germain | Stade Rennais | Sochaux-Mont. | RC Strasbourg | Toulouse FC |
|---|---|---|---|---|---|---|---|---|---|---|---|---|---|---|---|---|---|---|---|---|
| AC Ajaccio | ■ | 1-2 | 1-0 | 1-0 | 0-0 | 2-0 | 0-3 | 2-4 | 2-0 | 3-1 | 0-1 | 0-1 | 0-0 | 1-3 | 1-1 | 0-0 | 1-0 | 1-0 | 0-0 | 2-1 |
| AJ Auxerroise | 1-1 | ■ | 4-1 | 5-0 | 3-0 | 2-0 | 3-0 | 1-2 | 1-0 | 2-1 | 2-0 | 0-0 | 0-1 | 2-0 | 1-2 | 1-1 | 2-1 | 2-1 | 3-2 | 3-2 |
| SC de Bastia | 1-1 | 0-0 | ■ | 0-2 | 4-2 | 3-1 | 0-2 | 0-0 | 0-0 | 0-2 | 4-1 | 0-0 | 1-0 | 1-3 | 2-1 | 0-1 | 3-2 | 2-0 | 0-0 | 1-0 |
| FC Girondins de Bordeaux | 1-0 | 2-0 | 1-1 | ■ | 2-0 | 0-0 | 2-1 | 1-1 | 2-0 | 2-0 | 1-0 | 1-3 | 0-1 | 2-0 | 1-1 | 3-0 | 2-1 | 1-3 | 1-1 | 1-2 |
| En Avant de Guingamp | 2-0 | 2-2 | 1-0 | 1-3 | ■ | 1-0 | 2-1 | 2-0 | 2-4 | 1-1 | 0-1 | 1-2 | 4-3 | 1-1 | 1-2 | 0-2 | 0-2 | 1-2 | 3-2 | 1-0 |
| Racing Club de Lens | 2-0 | 1-3 | 0-0 | 1-0 | 2-1 | ■ | 2-1 | 1-1 | 0-0 | 0-2 | 2-1 | 0-0 | 3-2 | 0-0 | 1-0 | 1-0 | 2-1 | 0-3 | 2-1 | 1-1 |
| Lille Olympique SC | 0-0 | 1-0 | 2-0 | 2-1 | 1-3 | 1-1 | ■ | 1-0 | 1-1 | 1-1 | 0-1 | 1-1 | 1-1 | 2-0 | 1-2 | 1-0 | 1-0 | 2-0 | 0-1 | 0-1 |
| Olympique Lyonnais | 4-0 | 1-1 | 1-0 | 3-0 | 0-1 | 4-0 | 3-0 | ■ | 2-0 | 2-1 | 1-2 | 3-1 | 3-0 | 1-0 | 5-0 | 1-1 | 3-0 | 1-1 | 1-0 | 0-0 |
| Mans Union Club 72 | 0-1 | 2-1 | 1-1 | 0-0 | 2-0 | 3-0 | 1-1 | 0-2 | ■ | 2-0 | 0-0 | 0-1 | 4-0 | 0-1 | 1-1 | 0-1 | 2-2 | 2-2 | 0-3 | 2-1 |
| FC de Metz | 0-1 | 0-2 | 1-0 | 3-1 | 1-1 | 0-2 | 0-1 | 1-2 | 5-0 | ■ | 1-1 | 0-2 | 2-1 | 1-3 | 1-0 | 0-1 | 1-1 | 0-1 | 1-0 | 0-2 |
| Olympique de Marseille | 2-1 | 1-0 | 3-1 | 1-1 | 2-1 | 3-2 | 1-1 | 1-4 | 5-0 | 0-1 | ■ | 1-2 | 1-1 | 1-1 | 0-1 | 2-0 | 2-0 | 4-0 | 1-0 |  |
| AS de Monaco FC | 3-3 | 1-1 | 2-0 | 2-0 | 3-1 | 2-0 | 0-1 | 3-0 | 4-2 | 1-0 | 1-0 | ■ | 4-0 | 0-1 | 1-1 | 1-1 | 1-4 | 1-1 | 2-0 | 3-0 |
| Montpellier Hérault SC | 3-1 | 1-0 | 1-1 | 1-2 | 2-0 | 1-0 | 0-2 | 0-2 | 0-3 | 0-1 | 0-1 | 1-2 | ■ | 4-1 | 2-2 | 3-2 | 1-1 | 1-3 | 1-2 | 0-1 |
| FC Nantes Atlantique | 4-0 | 1-0 | 1-1 | 0-0 | 0-0 | 2-0 | 2-0 | 0-1 | 1-0 | 2-2 | 1-0 | 0-1 | 3-2 | ■ | 3-1 | 0-1 | 1-0 | 3-1 | 1-1 | 1-1 |
| OGC de Nice | 2-2 | 1-1 | 2-0 | 0-0 | 2-0 | 4-0 | 2-0 | 0-1 | 0-1 | 1-1 | 0-0 | 1-2 | 2-1 | 1-0 | ■ | 1-2 | 3-1 | 1-0 | 0-0 | 1-1 |
| Paris Saint-Germain FC | 1-0 | 1-0 | 0-0 | 2-1 | 2-0 | 0-1 | 1-0 | 1-0 | 5-1 | 0-0 | 2-1 | 2-4 | 6-1 | 3-2 | 0-0 | ■ | 1-0 | 1-1 | 3-2 | 2-1 |
| Stade Rennais FC | 4-1 | 0-2 | 4-0 | 3-1 | 0-0 | 1-1 | 2-2 | 3-1 | 2-0 | 0-0 | 4-3 | 1-0 | 4-0 | 0-3 | 0-0 | 1-1 | ■ | 4-0 | 1-1 | 1-0 |
| FC Sochaux-Montbéliard | 2-0 | 3-2 | 2-1 | 1-1 | 2-0 | 0-3 | 2-1 | 1-2 | 3-0 | 2-0 | 2-1 | 1-1 | 3-1 | 2-1 | 0-0 | 0-1 | 1-1 | ■ | 3-0 | 3-1 |
| Racing Club de Strasbourg | 3-2 | 0-2 | 4-2 | 1-1 | 2-0 | 0-1 | 2-2 | 0-1 | 3-0 | 0-2 | 4-1 | 0-0 | 4-2 | 1-0 | 2-2 | 0-0 | 0-3 | 0-2 | ■ | 0-0 |
| Toulouse FC | 3-1 | 0-3 | 0-2 | 1-0 | 0-0 | 1-2 | 0-3 | 0-1 | 1-1 | 1-0 | 2-1 | 1-1 | 2-2 | 0-1 | 1-1 | 0-1 | 2-0 | 0-0 | 1-1 | ■ |

## Division 1

| | | Pd | Wn | Dw | Ls | GF | GA | Pts | |
|---|---|---|---|---|---|---|---|---|---|
| 1. | OLYMPIQUE LYONNAIS (LYON) | 38 | 24 | 7 | 7 | 64 | 26 | 79 | |
| 2. | Paris Saint-Germain FC (Paris) | 38 | 22 | 10 | 6 | 50 | 28 | 76 | |
| 3. | AS de Monaco FC (Monaco) | 38 | 21 | 12 | 5 | 59 | 30 | 75 | |
| 4. | Association de la Jeunesse Auxerroise (Auxerre) | 38 | 19 | 8 | 11 | 60 | 34 | 65 | |
| 5. | FC Sochaux-Montbéliard (Montbéliard) | 38 | 18 | 9 | 11 | 54 | 42 | 63 | |
| 6. | FC Nantes-Atlantique (Nantes) | 38 | 17 | 9 | 12 | 47 | 35 | 60 | |
| 7. | Olympique de Marseille (Marseille) | 38 | 17 | 6 | 15 | 51 | 45 | 57 | |
| 8. | Racing Club de Lens (Lens) | 38 | 15 | 8 | 15 | 34 | 48 | 53 | |
| 9. | Stade Rennais FC (Rennes) | 38 | 14 | 10 | 14 | 56 | 44 | 52 | |
| 10. | Lille Olympique SC Metropole (Lille) | 38 | 14 | 9 | 15 | 41 | 41 | 51 | |
| 11. | Olympique GC de Nice-Côte d'Azur (Nice) | 38 | 11 | 17 | 10 | 42 | 39 | 50 | |
| 12. | FC Girondins de Bordeaux (Bordeaux) | 38 | 13 | 11 | 14 | 40 | 43 | 50 | |
| 13. | Racing Club de Strasbourg Football (Strasbourg) | 38 | 10 | 13 | 15 | 43 | 50 | 43 | |
| 14. | FC de Metz (Metz) | 38 | 11 | 9 | 18 | 34 | 42 | 42 | |
| 15. | AC Ajaccio (Ajaccio) | 38 | 10 | 10 | 18 | 33 | 55 | 40 | |
| 16. | Toulouse FC (Toulouse) | 38 | 9 | 12 | 17 | 31 | 44 | 39 | |
| 17. | Sporting Club de Bastia (Bastia) | 38 | 9 | 12 | 17 | 33 | 49 | 39 | |
| 18. | En Avant de Guingamp (Guingamp) | 38 | 10 | 8 | 20 | 36 | 58 | 38 | R |
| 19. | Mans Union Club 72 (Le Mans) | 38 | 9 | 11 | 18 | 35 | 57 | 38 | R |
| 20. | Montpellier Hérault SC (Montpellier) | 38 | 8 | 7 | 23 | 41 | 74 | 31 | R |
| | | 760 | 281 | 198 | 281 | 884 | 884 | 1041 | |

## Top goal-scorers

| | | | |
|---|---|---|---|
| 1) | Djibril CISSE | (AJ Auxerroise) | 26 |
| 2) | Alexander FREI | (Stade Rennais FC) | 20 |
| 3) | Didier-Yves DROGBA Tébily | (Olympique de Marseille) | 18 |
| | "PAULETA" (Pedro Miguel Carreiro Resendes) | (Paris Saint-Germain FC) | 18 |
| 5) | Pierre-Alain FRAU | (FC Sochaux-Montbéliard) | 17 |

| Division 2 | Pd | Wn | Dw | Ls | GF | GA | Pts | |
|---|---|---|---|---|---|---|---|---|
| 1. AS de Saint-Étienne (Saint-Étienne) | 38 | 22 | 7 | 9 | 44 | 29 | 73 | P |
| 2. Stade Malherbe Caen-CBN (Caen) | 38 | 20 | 11 | 7 | 56 | 31 | 71 | P |
| 3. FC Istres-Ville Nouvelle (Istres) | 38 | 19 | 9 | 10 | 44 | 26 | 66 | P |
| 4. FC Lorient Bretagne-Sud (Lorient) | 38 | 17 | 10 | 11 | 57 | 45 | 61 | |
| 5. CS Sedan-Ardennes (Sedan) | 38 | 15 | 15 | 8 | 42 | 31 | 60 | |
| 6. AS Nancy-Lorraine (Nancy) | 38 | 14 | 13 | 11 | 45 | 36 | 55 | |
| 7. Havre AC Football Association (Le Havre) | 38 | 15 | 10 | 13 | 44 | 46 | 55 | |
| 8. Chamois Niortais FC (Niort) | 38 | 13 | 14 | 11 | 47 | 44 | 53 | |
| 9. Amiens SC Football (Amiens) | 38 | 15 | 8 | 15 | 43 | 45 | 53 | |
| 10. ES Troyes Aube Champagne (Troyes) | 38 | 13 | 13 | 12 | 43 | 48 | 52 | |
| 11. FC La Berrichonne (Châteauroux) | 38 | 13 | 10 | 15 | 44 | 49 | 49 | |
| 12. US de Créteil (Créteil) | 38 | 10 | 15 | 13 | 41 | 47 | 45 | |
| 13. Angers SC de l'Ouest (Angers) | 38 | 11 | 12 | 15 | 36 | 43 | 45 | |
| 14. Clermont Football Auvergne (Clermont Ferrand) | 38 | 9 | 17 | 12 | 36 | 48 | 44 | |
| 15. Grenoble Foot 38 (Grenoble) | 38 | 9 | 16 | 13 | 38 | 43 | 43 | |
| 16. FC de Gueugnon (Gueugnon) | 38 | 9 | 15 | 14 | 40 | 43 | 42 | |
| 17. Stade Lavallois Mayenne FC (Laval) | 38 | 10 | 12 | 16 | 51 | 55 | 42 | |
| 18. AS d'Origine Arménienne de Valance (Valence) | 38 | 9 | 13 | 16 | 45 | 56 | 40 | R |
| 19. Besançon Racing Club (Besançon) | 38 | 8 | 14 | 16 | 37 | 45 | 38 | R |
| 20. FC de Rouen (Rouen) | 38 | 5 | 14 | 19 | 27 | 50 | 29 | R |
| | 760 | 256 | 248 | 256 | 860 | 860 | 1016 | |

**Promoted:** Dijon Football Côte-d'Or (Dijon), Stade Brestois 92 (Brest) and Stade de Reims (Reims)

## Coupe de France Final  (Stade de France, Saint-Denis – 29/05/04 – 77,857)

### PARIS SAINT-GERMAIN FC (PARIS)        1-0        FC La Berrichonne (Châteauroux)

*Pauleta 66'*

**PSG:** Letizi, Mendy, Dehu, Pierre-Fanfan, El-Karkouri, Fiorese, M'Bami, Cana, Boskovic (Benachour 74'), Ljuboja (Rocchi 85'), Pauleta (Touré 90').

**La Berrichonne:** Roche, Algerino, Viator, Bertin, El-Bekri (Paul 77'), Fradin, Ferreira, Sidibe, Roudet, Gueï, Vandenbossche.

## Semi-finals

| | | |
|---|---|---|
| FC La Berrichonne (Châteauroux) | 2-0 | Dijon Foot Côte d'Or (Dijon) |
| FC Nantes-Atlantique (Nantes) | 1-1 (aet) | Paris Saint-Germain FC (Paris) |

Paris Saint-Germain FC won 4-3 on penalties

## Quarter-finals

| | | |
|---|---|---|
| Amiens SC Football (Amiens) | 0-1 | Dijon Foot Côte d'Or (Dijon) |
| Étoile Sportive Briviste (Brive) | 1-2 | Paris Saint-Germain FC (Paris) |
| AS de Monaco (Monaco) | 0-1 | FC la Berrichonne (Châteauroux) |
| FC Nantes-Atlantique (Nantes) | 3-2 | Stade Rennais FC (Rennes) |

199

| 2004-2005 Division One | AC Ajaccio | AJ Auxerroise | SC de Bastia | Giron. Bordeaux | SM Caen | FC Istres | RC de Lens | Lille Olympique | Olym. Lyonnais | Olym. Marseille | FC de Metz | AS Monaco | FC Nantes | OGC de Nice | Paris St.Germain | Stade Rennais | St-Étienne | Sochaux-Mont. | RC Strasbourg | Toulouse FC |
|---|---|---|---|---|---|---|---|---|---|---|---|---|---|---|---|---|---|---|---|---|
| AC Ajaccio | ■ | 4-3 | 1-0 | 0-0 | 2-2 | 0-0 | 0-0 | 0-0 | 1-1 | 2-0 | 1-2 | 3-0 | 1-1 | 0-1 | 1-0 | 1-1 | 1-1 | 3-1 | 2-2 | 1-0 |
| AJ Auxerroise | 1-0 | ■ | 4-1 | 0-0 | 1-0 | 0-0 | 3-0 | 1-3 | 0-3 | 0-0 | 4-0 | 2-2 | 2-1 | 4-3 | 1-1 | 3-1 | 2-2 | 2-0 | 0-0 | 3-2 |
| SC de Bastia | 1-0 | 1-0 | ■ | 1-4 | 2-0 | 2-0 | 3-1 | 3-1 | 1-1 | 0-1 | 1-0 | 0-2 | 0-0 | 2-0 | 1-2 | 1-1 | 0-3 | 1-1 | 2-1 | 2-1 |
| FC Girondins de Bordeaux | 0-0 | 0-0 | 0-0 | ■ | 2-2 | 2-2 | 1-1 | 1-3 | 0-0 | 3-3 | 1-0 | 1-1 | 0-2 | 5-1 | 3-0 | 0-0 | 2-0 | 2-0 | 0-2 | 1-1 |
| Stade Malherbe Caen | 2-2 | 0-2 | 0-1 | 1-1 | ■ | 1-1 | 1-0 | 0-0 | 1-0 | 2-3 | 0-1 | 1-0 | 2-1 | 0-0 | 0-0 | 2-2 | 2-0 | 0-2 | 0-0 | 0-2 |
| FC Istres | 0-1 | 1-0 | 1-0 | 0-1 | 3-2 | ■ | 0-2 | 0-2 | 0-0 | 0-2 | 0-0 | 0-1 | 0-1 | 1-1 | 1-1 | 0-2 | 0-2 | 2-0 | 1-1 | 1-0 |
| Racing Club de Lens | 1-1 | 3-1 | 2-1 | 2-0 | 0-1 | 0-1 | ■ | 1-1 | 0-1 | 0-0 | 2-0 | 1-1 | 2-0 | 0-0 | 2-2 | 5-2 | 3-0 | 3-2 | 2-1 | 1-0 |
| Lille Olympique SC | 0-2 | 2-0 | 2-1 | 0-0 | 2-0 | 8-0 | 2-1 | ■ | 2-1 | 1-2 | 4-0 | 1-1 | 1-1 | 1-0 | 1-0 | 0-0 | 1-0 | 0-0 | 1-1 | 1-1 |
| Olympique Lyonnais | 2-1 | 2-1 | 0-0 | 5-1 | 4-0 | 2-1 | 1-0 | 1-0 | ■ | 1-1 | 2-0 | 0-0 | 2-0 | 0-0 | 0-1 | 2-1 | 3-2 | 1-1 | 1-0 | 4-0 |
| Olympique de Marseille | 1-2 | 0-1 | 1-0 | 1-0 | 2-3 | 1-1 | 2-1 | 3-0 | 0-1 | ■ | 1-3 | 1-1 | 3-1 | 2-0 | 1-1 | 3-1 | 1-1 | 0-2 | 2-0 | 1-0 |
| FC de Metz | 1-0 | 3-0 | 2-0 | 0-0 | 1-2 | 2-1 | 1-1 | 1-1 | 1-1 | 0-1 | ■ | 1-1 | 1-0 | 1-1 | 3-2 | 1-1 | 2-2 | 0-0 | 1-0 | 0-1 |
| AS de Monaco FC | 2-2 | 0-0 | 5-2 | 1-1 | 5-2 | 2-1 | 2-0 | 2-0 | 1-1 | 2-1 | 0-0 | ■ | 2-1 | 3-4 | 2-0 | 2-0 | 1-1 | 1-3 | 3-1 | 2-1 |
| FC Nantes Atlantique | 0-0 | 1-1 | 1-1 | 0-1 | 2-0 | 1-0 | 1-0 | 1-3 | 2-2 | 2-2 | 1-0 | 0-0 | ■ | 0-1 | 1-0 | 2-0 | 0-0 | 2-2 | 2-1 | 2-2 |
| OGC de Nice | 3-0 | 1-0 | 1-1 | 3-3 | 0-1 | 0-0 | 1-1 | 1-1 | 0-1 | 1-1 | 1-1 | 2-1 | 0-0 | ■ | 1-1 | 2-0 | 2-0 | 2-1 | 0-0 | 1-0 |
| Paris Saint-Germain FC | 1-0 | 1-0 | 1-0 | 1-1 | 2-2 | 2-2 | 0-1 | 1-1 | 0-0 | 3-0 | 0-1 | 1-0 | 3-1 | ■ | 1-0 | 2-2 | 2-2 | 1-0 | 0-0 | |
| Stade Rennais FC | 2-0 | 1-0 | 1-0 | 2-0 | 2-2 | 3-1 | 3-1 | 0-1 | 1-2 | 1-0 | 3-1 | 0-0 | 1-0 | 4-1 | 2-1 | ■ | 2-2 | 3-0 | 4-0 | 1-1 |
| AS de Saint-Étienne | 3-0 | 3-1 | 3-0 | 0-0 | 5-0 | 2-0 | 0-0 | 0-0 | 2-3 | 2-0 | 0-0 | 0-1 | 0-0 | 2-1 | 0-0 | 1-0 | ■ | 1-0 | 1-1 | 0-0 |
| FC Sochaux-Montbéliard | 1-0 | 1-2 | 1-0 | 4-0 | 1-0 | 1-1 | 1-2 | 0-2 | 0-2 | 2-0 | 2-1 | 1-1 | 1-0 | 0-0 | 1-2 | 3-0 | 2-1 | ■ | 1-2 | 2-0 |
| Racing Club de Strasbourg | 1-0 | 3-1 | 2-0 | 1-0 | 5-0 | 1-1 | 2-2 | 1-2 | 0-1 | 1-0 | 3-1 | 0-0 | 0-2 | 3-1 | 3-1 | 1-0 | 1-1 | 0-0 | ■ | 1-4 |
| Toulouse FC | 3-1 | 1-2 | 1-0 | 1-0 | 2-3 | 2-1 | 0-0 | 1-0 | 0-2 | 1-3 | 1-1 | 0-0 | 2-1 | 1-0 | 2-1 | 0-2 | 0-2 | 0-0 | 2-0 | ■ |

## Division 1

| | | Pd | Wn | Dw | Ls | GF | GA | Pts | |
|---|---|---|---|---|---|---|---|---|---|
| 1. | OLYMPIQUE LYONNAIS (LYON) | 38 | 22 | 13 | 3 | 56 | 22 | 79 | |
| 2. | Lille Olympique SC Metropole (Lille) | 38 | 18 | 13 | 7 | 52 | 29 | 67 | |
| 3. | AS de Monaco FC (Monaco) | 38 | 15 | 18 | 5 | 52 | 35 | 63 | |
| 4. | Stade Rennais FC (Rennes) | 38 | 15 | 18 | 5 | 49 | 42 | 55 | |
| 5. | Olympique de Marseille (Marseille) | 38 | 15 | 10 | 13 | 49 | 42 | 55 | |
| 6. | AS de Saint-Étienne (Saint-Étienne) | 38 | 12 | 17 | 9 | 47 | 34 | 53 | |
| 7. | Racing Club de Lens (Lens) | 38 | 13 | 13 | 12 | 45 | 39 | 52 | |
| 8. | Association de La Jeunesse Auxerroise (Auxerre) | 38 | 14 | 10 | 14 | 48 | 47 | 52 | |
| 9. | Paris Saint-Germain FC (Paris) | 38 | 12 | 15 | 11 | 40 | 47 | 51 | |
| 10. | FC Sochaux-Montbéliard (Montbéliard) | 38 | 13 | 11 | 14 | 42 | 41 | 50 | |
| 11. | Toulouse FC (Toulouse) | 38 | 12 | 10 | 16 | 36 | 43 | 46 | |
| 12. | Racing Club de Strasbourg Football (Strasbourg) | 38 | 12 | 12 | 14 | 42 | 43 | 48 | |
| 13. | Olympique GC de Nice-Côte d'Azur (Nice) | 38 | 10 | 16 | 12 | 38 | 45 | 46 | |
| 14. | AC Ajaccio (Ajaccio) | 38 | 10 | 15 | 13 | 36 | 40 | 45 | |
| 15. | FC de Metz (Metz) | 38 | 10 | 14 | 14 | 33 | 45 | 44 | |
| 16. | FC Girondins de Bordeaux (Bordeaux) | 38 | 8 | 20 | 10 | 37 | 41 | 44 | |
| 17. | FC Nantes-Atlantique (Nantes) | 38 | 10 | 13 | 15 | 33 | 38 | 43 | |
| 18. | Stade Malherbe Caen-CBN (Caen) | 38 | 10 | 12 | 16 | 36 | 60 | 42 | R |
| 19. | Sporting Club de Bastia (Bastia) | 38 | 11 | 8 | 19 | 32 | 48 | 41 | R |
| 20. | FC Istres-Ville Nouvelle (Istres) | 38 | 6 | 14 | 18 | 25 | 51 | 32 | R |
| | | 760 | 248 | 264 | 248 | 826 | 826 | 1008 | |

## Top goal-scorers

1) Alexander FREI                                          (Stade Rennais FC)                    20
2) Mickaël PAGIS                                           (Racing Club de Strasbourg)           15
3) Pascal FEINDOUNE                                        (AS de Saint-Étienne)                 13
   Araujo dall'IGNA ILAN                                   (FC Sochaux-Montbéliard)              13
   "PAULETA" (Pedro Miguel Carreiro Resendes)             (Paris Saint-Germain FC)              13
   Juninho PERNAMBUCO                                      (Olympique Lyonnais)                  13

| Division 2 | Pd | Wn | Dw | Ls | GF | GA | Pts | |
|---|---|---|---|---|---|---|---|---|
| 1. AS Nancy-Lorraine (Nancy) | 38 | 21 | 8 | 9 | 54 | 33 | 71 | P |
| 2. Mans Union 72 (Le Mans) | 38 | 20 | 8 | 10 | 51 | 30 | 68 | P |
| 3. ES Troyes Aube Champagne (Troyes) | 38 | 20 | 8 | 10 | 61 | 48 | 68 | P |
| 4. Dijon Football Côte-d'Or (Dijon) | 38 | 14 | 15 | 9 | 44 | 34 | 57 | |
| 5. FC La Berrichonne (Châteauroux) | 38 | 14 | 15 | 9 | 51 | 43 | 57 | |
| 6. CS Sedan-Ardennes (Sedan) | 38 | 16 | 9 | 13 | 38 | 38 | 57 | |
| 7. En Avant de Guingamp (Guingamp) | 38 | 15 | 11 | 12 | 53 | 43 | 56 | |
| 8. Montpellier-Hérault SC (Montpellier) | 38 | 15 | 10 | 13 | 44 | 39 | 55 | |
| 9. Stade Brestois 92 (Brest) | 38 | 13 | 16 | 9 | 38 | 34 | 55 | |
| 10. FC Lorient Bretagne-Sud (Lorient) | 38 | 14 | 8 | 16 | 47 | 51 | 50 | |
| 11. Grenoble Foot 38 (Grenoble) | 38 | 12 | 12 | 14 | 45 | 50 | 48 | |
| 12. FC de Gueugnon (Gueugnon) | 38 | 12 | 12 | 14 | 30 | 40 | 48 | |
| 13. Amiens SC Football (Amiens) | 38 | 11 | 14 | 13 | 41 | 41 | 47 | |
| 14. Stade Lavallois Mayenne (Laval) | 38 | 13 | 8 | 17 | 43 | 51 | 47 | |
| 15. US de Créteil Lusitanos (Créteil) | 38 | 11 | 13 | 14 | 42 | 38 | 46 | |
| 16. Stade de Reims (Reims) | 38 | 10 | 13 | 15 | 34 | 55 | 43 | |
| 17. Havre AC Football Association (Le Havre) | 38 | 11 | 9 | 18 | 28 | 42 | 42 | |
| 18. Clermont Football Auvergne (Clermont Ferrand) | 38 | 8 | 15 | 15 | 34 | 39 | 39 | R |
| 19. Angers SC de l'Ouest (Angers) | 38 | 8 | 14 | 16 | 32 | 44 | 38 | R |
| 20. Chamois Niortais FC (Niort) | 38 | 9 | 8 | 21 | 38 | 55 | 35 | R |
| | 760 | 267 | 226 | 267 | 848 | 848 | 1027 | |

**Promoted**: AS d'Origine Arménienne de Valence (Valence), FC Sète 74 (Sète), Valenciennes FC (Valenciennes)

## Coupe de France Final   (Stade de France, Saint Denis – 04/06/05 – 77,617)

**AJ AUXERROISE (AUXERRE)**              **2-1**                        CS Sedan-Ardennes (Sedan)

*Benjani 37', Kalou 90'*                                                                  *Noro 64'*

**Auxerre**: Cool, Radet (Sagna 60'), Jaures, Mignot, Kaboul, Violeau, Cheyrou, Lachuer (Kalou 71'), Benjani, Mathis, Akale.

**Sedan**: Regnault, Ducourtioux, Belhadj, Hénin, Charpenet, Njanka (Budiate 89'), Mokake (Sabin 58'), Neumann, Noro, Gagnier, Citony.

## Semi-finals

Association de la Jeunesse Auxerroise (Auxerre)          2-1              Nîmes Olympique (Nîmes)
AS de Monaco FC (Monaco)                                 0-1              CS Sedan-Ardennes (Sedan)

## Quarter-finals

US Boulogne Côte d'Opale (Boulogne-sur-Mer)   1-2  (aet)  Association de la Jeunesse Auxerroise (Auxerre)
AS de Monaco FC (Monaco)                       1-0  (aet)  Clermont Football Auvergne (Clermont Ferrand)
Nîmes Olympique (Nîmes)                        4-3  (aet)  FC Sochaux-Montbéliard (Montbéliard)
CS Sedan-Ardennes (Sedan)                      2-1  (aet)  Grenoble Foot 38 (Grenoble)

# 2005-06

| 2005-06 Division 1 | Ajaccio | Auxerre | Girond. Bordeaux | Lille Olympique | Mans UC 72 | FC de Metz | AS de Monaco | AS Nancy-Lor. | FC Nantes | Olymp. Lyonnais | Olymp. Marseille | OGC de Nice | Paris St-Germain | RC de Lens | RC Strasbourg | AS St-Étienne | FC Sochaux | Stade Rennais | Toulouse FC | ES Troyes Aube |
|---|---|---|---|---|---|---|---|---|---|---|---|---|---|---|---|---|---|---|---|---|
| AC Ajaccio | ■ | 1-0 | 0-2 | 3-3 | 0-0 | 0-1 | 1-0 | 1-0 | 0-2 | 1-3 | 3-1 | 0-3 | 1-1 | 0-0 | 0-0 | 3-1 | 0-1 | 0-1 | 1-0 | 0-1 |
| AJ Auxerroise | 2-0 | ■ | 1-0 | 3-2 | 0-0 | 1-1 | 2-1 | 0-1 | 4-0 | 0-2 | 1-2 | 2-0 | 2-0 | 1-0 | 4-0 | 0-0 | 3-0 | 2-0 | 2-0 | 3-0 |
| FC Girondins de Bordeaux | 1-0 | 1-0 | ■ | 1-0 | 2-2 | 3-3 | 1-0 | 1-0 | 0-0 | 1-1 | 1-1 | 1-0 | 0-2 | 1-0 | 2-1 | 0-0 | 1-1 | 2-0 | 2-0 | 2-0 |
| Lille Olympique SC | 2-0 | 1-1 | 3-2 | ■ | 4-0 | 3-1 | 0-1 | 1-0 | 2-0 | 4-0 | 0-0 | 4-0 | 0-0 | 0-0 | 2-0 | 2-0 | 3-0 | 1-0 | 0-0 | 1-2 |
| Mans UC 72 | 1-0 | 0-2 | 1-0 | 1-1 | ■ | 2-0 | 0-0 | 0-0 | 0-0 | 1-2 | 3-0 | 2-0 | 0-0 | 0-0 | 2-0 | 0-1 | 2-1 | 4-0 | 1-1 | 1-0 |
| FC de Metz | 2-0 | 1-2 | 0-1 | 0-2 | 0-0 | ■ | 2-1 | 0-0 | 1-4 | 0-4 | 1-0 | 1-0 | 1-0 | 0-1 | 0-0 | 0-1 | 0-1 | 0-1 | 2-2 | 2-4 |
| AS de Monaco FC | 3-0 | 0-2 | 0-1 | 0-1 | 2-0 | 3-0 | ■ | 2-2 | 1-1 | 2-1 | 1-0 | 0-0 | 1-1 | 0-0 | 1-1 | 1-0 | 4-1 | 0-2 | 1-1 | 1-1 |
| AS Nancy-Lorraine | 0-0 | 1-3 | 0-0 | 0-0 | 1-0 | 1-1 | 0-1 | ■ | 0-0 | 0-2 | 1-1 | 0-0 | 1-1 | 1-2 | 1-2 | 2-0 | 0-2 | 6-0 | 2-0 | 2-1 |
| FC Nantes Atlantique | 0-2 | 3-2 | 0-1 | 1-1 | 1-0 | 0-0 | 0-0 | 3-0 | ■ | 0-1 | 1-3 | 0-0 | 0-0 | 2-0 | 4-3 | 1-1 | 3-1 | 0-2 | 2-0 | 1-1 |
| Olympique Lyonnais | 3-2 | 1-1 | 0-0 | 1-3 | 8-1 | 4-0 | 2-1 | 1-0 | 3-1 | ■ | 2-1 | 2-1 | 2-0 | 1-1 | 1-0 | 4-0 | 1-0 | 1-4 | 1-1 | 2-1 |
| Olympique de Marseille | 1-1 | 1-0 | 0-2 | 1-1 | 1-1 | 3-1 | 2-1 | 6-0 | 2-1 | 1-1 | ■ | 1-0 | 1-0 | 1-1 | 2-2 | 2-0 | 0-0 | 1-0 | 0-0 | 2-1 |
| OGC de Nice | 1-0 | 1-0 | 0-1 | 2-0 | 1-0 | 2-1 | 2-0 | 1-0 | 1-1 | 1-1 | 0-1 | ■ | 1-0 | 0-0 | 3-1 | 0-1 | 1-2 | 2-1 | 2-1 | 1-1 |
| Paris Saint-Germain FC | 2-4 | 4-1 | 3-1 | 2-1 | 0-1 | 4-1 | 0-0 | 1-0 | 2-0 | 0-1 | 0-0 | 1-2 | ■ | 3-4 | 1-0 | 2-2 | 3-1 | 2-0 | 2-0 | 2-1 |
| Racing Club de Lens | 1-0 | 7-0 | 1-1 | 4-2 | 2-0 | 0-0 | 1-1 | 1-2 | 3-1 | 1-1 | 2-0 | 2-2 | 1-1 | ■ | 2-1 | 2-1 | 0-0 | 1-0 | | 1-0 |
| Racing Club de Strasbourg | 2-2 | 0-0 | 0-0 | 2-2 | 1-2 | 2-1 | 1-2 | 1-3 | 0-1 | 0-4 | 0-1 | 0-0 | 1-1 | 1-1 | ■ | 0-1 | 0-0 | 0-1 | 2-4 | 2-0 |
| AS de Saint-Étienne | 0-0 | 1-1 | 1-1 | 0-2 | 3-0 | 2-0 | 1-1 | 0-2 | 1-0 | 0-0 | 2-1 | 0-1 | 3-0 | 2-0 | 0-2 | ■ | 0-0 | 0-0 | 1-3 | 1-1 |
| FC Sochaux-Montbéliard | 3-1 | 1-0 | 0-3 | 0-0 | 0-0 | 1-1 | 2-1 | 0-2 | 1-0 | 0-4 | 0-1 | 1-1 | 0-1 | 1-1 | 1-1 | 4-0 | ■ | 1-0 | 0-1 | 1-1 |
| Stade Rennais FC | 3-0 | 3-1 | 2-2 | 2-2 | 1-0 | 2-1 | 1-3 | 0-2 | 0-3 | 1-3 | 3-2 | 1-0 | 1-1 | 4-1 | 2-1 | 0-1 | 2-1 | ■ | 4-1 | 2-0 |
| Toulouse FC | 3-0 | 2-0 | 1-1 | 0-0 | 0-2 | 2-0 | 3-3 | 1-1 | 1-0 | 1-0 | 1-0 | 0-2 | 1-0 | 1-1 | 1-2 | 1-1 | 1-2 | 0-1 | ■ | 2-1 |
| ES Troyes Aube | 3-0 | 1-1 | 1-1 | 1-0 | 1-3 | 0-0 | 0-0 | 1-2 | 1-0 | 0-1 | 0-1 | 1-2 | 1-1 | 1-1 | 1-1 | 0-0 | 2-1 | 2-1 | 3-1 | ■ |

## Division 1

| | | Pd | Wn | Dw | Ls | GF | GA | Pts | |
|---|---|---|---|---|---|---|---|---|---|
| 1. | OLYMPIQUE LYONNAIS (LYON) | 38 | 25 | 9 | 4 | 73 | 31 | 84 | |
| 2. | FC Girondins de Bordeaux (Bordeaux) | 38 | 18 | 15 | 5 | 43 | 25 | 69 | |
| 3. | Lille Olympique SC Metropole (Lille) | 38 | 16 | 14 | 8 | 56 | 31 | 62 | |
| 4. | Racing Club de Lens (Lens) | 38 | 14 | 18 | 6 | 48 | 34 | 60 | |
| 5. | Olympique de Marseille (Marseille) | 38 | 16 | 12 | 10 | 44 | 35 | 60 | |
| 6. | Association de La Jeunesse Auxerroise (Auxerre) | 38 | 17 | 8 | 13 | 50 | 39 | 59 | |
| 7. | Stade Rennais FC (Rennes) | 38 | 18 | 5 | 15 | 48 | 49 | 59 | |
| 8. | Olympique GC de Nice-Côte d'Azur (Nice) | 38 | 16 | 10 | 12 | 36 | 31 | 58 | |
| 9. | Paris Saint-Germain FC (Paris) | 38 | 13 | 13 | 12 | 44 | 38 | 52 | |
| 10. | AS de Monaco FC (Monaco) | 38 | 13 | 13 | 12 | 42 | 36 | 52 | |
| 11. | Mans Union Club 72 (Le Mans) | 38 | 13 | 13 | 12 | 33 | 36 | 52 | |
| 12. | AS Nancy-Lorraine (Nancy) | 38 | 12 | 12 | 14 | 35 | 37 | 48 | |
| 13. | AS de Saint-Étienne (Saint-Étienne) | 38 | 11 | 14 | 13 | 29 | 39 | 47 | |
| 14. | FC Nantes-Atlantique (Nantes) | 38 | 11 | 12 | 15 | 37 | 41 | 45 | |
| 15. | FC Sochaux-Montbéliard (Montbéliard) | 38 | 11 | 11 | 16 | 34 | 47 | 44 | |
| 16. | Toulouse FC (Toulouse) | 38 | 10 | 11 | 17 | 36 | 47 | 41 | |
| 17. | ES Troyes Aube Champagne (Troyes) | 38 | 9 | 12 | 17 | 37 | 47 | 39 | |
| 18. | AC Ajaccio (Ajaccio) | 38 | 8 | 9 | 21 | 27 | 53 | 33 | R |
| 19. | Racing Club de Strasbourg Football (Strasbourg) | 38 | 5 | 14 | 19 | 33 | 56 | 29 | R |
| 20. | FC de Metz (Metz) | 38 | 6 | 11 | 21 | 26 | 59 | 29 | R |
| | | 760 | 262 | 236 | 262 | 811 | 811 | 1022 | |

AS Saint-Étienne vs Toulouse FC played on 15th January 2006 was abandoned after 15 minutes due to frozen pitch when the scoreline stood at 0-0. The match was replayed on 1st February 2006 and finished 1-3.

## Top goal-scorers

| | | | |
|---|---|---|---|
| 1) | "PAULETA" (Pedro Miguel Carreiro Resendes) | (Paris Saint-Germain FC) | 21 |
| 2) | "FRED" Frederico Chaves Guedes | (Olympique Lyonnais) | 14 |
| | Peter ODEMWINGIE | (Lille Olympique SC) | 14 |
| 4) | Daniel COUSIN | (Racing Club de Lens) | 13 |
| 5) | Sylvain WILTORD | (Olympique Lyonnais) | 13 |

| Division 2 | Pd | Wn | Dw | Ls | GF | GA | Pts | |
|---|---|---|---|---|---|---|---|---|
| 1. Valenciennes FC (Valenciennes) | 38 | 21 | 11 | 6 | 51 | 28 | 74 | P |
| 2. CS Sedan-Ardennes (Sedan) | 38 | 19 | 14 | 5 | 50 | 32 | 71 | P |
| 3. FC Lorient Bretagne-Sud (Lorient) | 38 | 18 | 12 | 8 | 49 | 26 | 66 | P |
| 4. Stade Malherbe Caen-CBN (Caen) | 38 | 18 | 12 | 8 | 56 | 35 | 66 | |
| 5. Dijon Football Côte-d'Or (Dijon) | 38 | 16 | 12 | 10 | 47 | 32 | 60 | |
| 6. Sporting Club de Bastia (Bastia) | 38 | 16 | 10 | 12 | 47 | 40 | 58 | |
| 7. Havre AC Football Association (Le Havre) | 38 | 13 | 16 | 9 | 48 | 41 | 55 | |
| 8. US de Créteil Lusitanos (Créteil) | 38 | 13 | 15 | 10 | 46 | 33 | 54 | |
| 9. En Avant de Guingamp (Guingamp) | 38 | 12 | 14 | 12 | 36 | 32 | 50 | |
| 10. Grenoble Foot 38 (Grenoble) | 38 | 12 | 12 | 14 | 42 | 45 | 48 | |
| 11. FC de Gueugnon (Gueugnon) | 38 | 11 | 15 | 12 | 29 | 37 | 48 | |
| 12. Montpellier-Hérault SC (Montpellier) | 38 | 12 | 11 | 15 | 34 | 43 | 47 | |
| 13. FC Istres-Ville Nouvelle (Istres) | 38 | 12 | 11 | 15 | 33 | 45 | 47 | |
| 14. Stade de Reims (Reims) | 38 | 10 | 15 | 13 | 32 | 31 | 45 | |
| 15. FC La Berrichonne (Châteauroux) | 38 | 10 | 14 | 14 | 48 | 48 | 44 | |
| 16. Amiens SC Football (Amiens) | 38 | 9 | 16 | 13 | 32 | 44 | 43 | |
| 17. Stade Brestois 92 (Brest) | 38 | 9 | 15 | 14 | 34 | 48 | 42 | |
| 18. Clermont Football Auvergne (Clermont Ferrand) | 38 | 10 | 8 | 20 | 35 | 59 | 38 | R |
| 19. Stade Lavallois Mayenne (Laval) | 38 | 9 | 8 | 21 | 38 | 59 | 35 | R |
| 20. FC Sète 74 (Sète) | 38 | 4 | 11 | 23 | 31 | 60 | 23 | R |
| | 760 | 254 | 252 | 254 | 818 | 818 | 1014 | |

Promoted: Chamois Niortais FC (Niort), FC Libourne Saint-Seurin (Libourne) and Tours FC (Tours).

## Coupe de France Final  (Stade de France, Saint Denis – 29/04/2006 – 79,061)

**PARIS SAINT-GERMAIN FC (PARIS)**         **2-1**         Olympique de Marseille (Marseille)

*Kalou 6', Dhorasoo 49'*                                                              *Maoulida 67'*

**Paris Saint-Germain**: Letizi, Rothen (Paulo Cesar 87'), Mendy, Rozehnal, Yepes, Armand, M'Bami, Cissé, Dhorasoo, Kalou, Pauleta.

**Marseilles**: Barthez, Pagis (Oruma 38'), Beye (Nasri 80'), Déhu, Civelli, Taiwo, Cana, Lamouchi, Ribéry, Maoulida, Niang.

## Semi-finals

| | | |
|---|---|---|
| FC Nantes-Atlantique (Nantes) | 1-2 | Paris Saint-Germain FC (Paris) |
| Olympique de Marseille (Marseille) | 3-0 | Stade Rennais FC (Rennes) |

## Quarter-finals

| | | |
|---|---|---|
| Calais Racing Union FC (Calais) | 0-1 | FC Nantes-Atlantique (Nantes) |
| Olympique Lyonnais (Lyon) | 1-2 | Olympique de Marseille (Marseille) |
| Paris Saint-Germain FC (Paris) | 2-1 | Lille Olympique SC Metropole (Lille) |
| Stade Rennais FC (Rennes) | 5-3 | Montpellier-Hérault SC (Montpellier) |

# 2006-07

| 2006-07 Division 1 | AJ Auxerroise | Giron. Bordeaux | Lille Olympique | Lorient B-Sud | Mans UC 72 | AS de Monaco | AS Nancy-Lorr. | FC Nantes | Olymp. Lyonnais | Olymp. Marseille | OGC de Nice | Paris St-Germain | RC de Lens | AS St-Étienne | CS Sedan-Ard. | FC Sochaux | Stade Rennais | Toulouse FC | ES Troyes Aube | Valenciennes FC |
|---|---|---|---|---|---|---|---|---|---|---|---|---|---|---|---|---|---|---|---|---|
| AJ Auxerroise | ■ | 0-0 | 2-1 | 2-1 | 2-3 | 2-1 | 2-0 | 1-0 | 0-0 | 0-3 | 0-0 | 0-0 | 1-0 | 1-1 | 2-2 | 1-0 | 1-0 | 1-0 | 1-0 | 1-1 |
| FC Girondins de Bordeaux | 0-0 | ■ | 0-1 | 1-1 | 1-0 | 1-0 | 3-0 | 0-1 | 1-2 | 1-0 | 3-2 | 0-0 | 1-0 | 1-0 | 3-1 | 2-0 | 1-2 | 2-0 | 2-1 | 2-1 |
| Lille Olympique SC | 1-1 | 3-0 | ■ | 1-0 | 0-2 | 1-1 | 0-1 | 0-0 | 1-2 | 1-0 | 1-0 | 1-0 | 4-0 | 2-2 | 2-1 | 2-0 | 1-1 | 1-3 | 4-0 | 0-2 |
| FC Lorient Bretagne-Sud | 2-1 | 0-1 | 1-1 | ■ | 2-1 | 0-0 | 2-0 | 3-1 | 1-3 | 2-1 | 0-0 | 0-1 | 1-0 | 0-0 | 2-0 | 1-3 | 0-0 | 0-1 | 0-0 | 1-0 |
| Mans UC 72 | 2-2 | 1-1 | 1-1 | 1-1 | ■ | 0-2 | 0-0 | 1-1 | 0-1 | 2-0 | 1-0 | 1-1 | 1-1 | 2-1 | 3-2 | 2-2 | 0-0 | 2-0 | 2-0 | 3-2 |
| AS de Monaco FC | 2-1 | 0-0 | 3-1 | 2-2 | 2-1 | ■ | 2-0 | 2-1 | 1-0 | 1-2 | 0-0 | 1-2 | 0-0 | 1-2 | 2-1 | 3-0 | 0-2 | 1-3 | 0-0 | 3-0 |
| AS Nancy-Lorraine | 1-0 | 2-1 | 1-3 | 0-1 | 1-1 | 1-0 | ■ | 1-0 | 0-3 | 2-0 | 3-0 | 0-3 | 2-1 | 0-2 | 3-1 | 5-2 | 0-0 | 2-1 | 1-0 | 1-0 |
| FC Nantes Atlantique | 1-1 | 0-0 | 1-1 | 0-2 | 0-0 | 1-0 | 2-1 | ■ | 1-3 | 2-1 | 1-0 | 1-1 | 0-0 | 2-2 | 0-1 | 0-2 | 0-2 | -:+ | 1-1 | 2-5 |
| Olympique Lyonnais | 1-0 | 1-2 | 4-1 | 1-0 | 2-1 | 0-0 | 1-0 | 3-1 | ■ | 1-1 | 1-1 | 3-1 | 3-0 | 2-1 | 1-0 | 3-3 | 0-0 | 1-1 | 2-0 | 2-1 |
| Olympique de Marseille | 3-1 | 2-1 | 4-1 | 0-1 | 2-0 | 2-1 | 2-1 | 0-0 | 1-4 | ■ | 3-0 | 1-1 | 0-1 | 2-1 | 1-0 | 4-2 | 2-0 | 3-0 | 2-1 | 1-0 |
| OGC de Nice | 0-0 | 2-1 | 2-1 | 3-0 | 3-3 | 1-1 | 0-0 | 1-1 | 1-4 | 2-1 | ■ | 1-0 | 1-2 | 2-1 | 2-2 | 0-0 | 1-1 | 0-1 | 3-0 | 2-0 |
| Paris Saint-Germain FC | 0-1 | 0-2 | 1-0 | 2-3 | 2-0 | 4-2 | 0-0 | 4-0 | 1-1 | 1-3 | 0-0 | ■ | 1-3 | 0-2 | 4-2 | 0-0 | 1-0 | 0-0 | 2-1 | 1-2 |
| Racing Club de Lens | 1-0 | 3-0 | 1-1 | 1-1 | 2-1 | 1-0 | 2-2 | 2-0 | 0-4 | 1-1 | 0-0 | 1-2 | ■ | 3-3 | 1-1 | 3-1 | 0-0 | 2-0 | 1-0 | 3-0 |
| AS de Saint-Étienne | 2-3 | 0-2 | 2-1 | 2-0 | 2-0 | 0-1 | 1-0 | 2-1 | 1-3 | 1-2 | 2-1 | 1-0 | 3-2 | ■ | 1-2 | 1-2 | 1-3 | 3-0 | 3-1 | 3-0 |
| CS Sedan-Ardennes | 2-2 | 1-1 | 2-0 | 3-1 | 1-2 | 0-1 | 2-2 | 1-1 | 0-1 | 0-0 | 1-1 | 2-0 | 2-2 | 2-2 | ■ | 1-1 | 1-0 | 0-2 | 1-2 | 1-1 |
| FC Sochaux-Montbéliard | 1-1 | 2-1 | 0-0 | 1-1 | 2-0 | 2-1 | 2-1 | 1-2 | 0-1 | 1-0 | 1-1 | 3-2 | 0-3 | 1-0 | 1-1 | ■ | 0-0 | 4-2 | 1-0 | 1-0 |
| Stade Rennais FC | 3-1 | 0-0 | 1-2 | 4-1 | 1-1 | 1-1 | 1-1 | 2-0 | 1-0 | 0-2 | 1-0 | 1-0 | 1-0 | 0-0 | 0-2 | 2-1 | ■ | 3-2 | 1-1 | 1-0 |
| Toulouse FC | 2-0 | 3-1 | 1-0 | 0-0 | 0-1 | 1-1 | 2-2 | 0-4 | 2-0 | 3-0 | 1-0 | 1-3 | 0-1 | 1-0 | 3-1 | 1-2 | 1-0 | ■ | 1-1 | 3-0 |
| ES Troyes Aube | 3-3 | 1-0 | 1-1 | 3-0 | 2-2 | 0-4 | 0-0 | 1-0 | 1-0 | 1-1 | 2-0 | 1-1 | 3-0 | 3-1 | 3-2 | 0-1 | 2-2 | 1-2 | ■ | 1-3 |
| Valenciennes FC | 1-3 | 2-0 | 0-3 | 0-0 | 1-1 | 2-2 | 1-0 | 1-0 | 0-0 | 0-0 | 0-1 | 0-0 | 1-3 | 1-0 | 2-1 | 0-0 | 3-1 | 0-0 | 3-1 | ■ |

## Division 1

| | | Pd | Wn | Dw | Ls | GF | GA | Pts | |
|---|---|---|---|---|---|---|---|---|---|
| 1. | OLYMPIQUE LYONNAIS (LYON) | 38 | 24 | 9 | 5 | 64 | 27 | 81 | |
| 2. | Olympique de Marseille (Marseille) | 38 | 19 | 7 | 12 | 53 | 38 | 64 | |
| 3. | Toulouse FC (Toulouse) | 38 | 17 | 7 | 14 | 44 | 43 | 58 | |
| 4. | Stade Rennais FC (Rennes) | 38 | 14 | 15 | 9 | 38 | 30 | 57 | |
| 5. | Racing Club de Lens (Lens) | 38 | 15 | 12 | 11 | 47 | 41 | 57 | |
| 6. | FC Girondins de Bordeaux (Bordeaux) | 38 | 16 | 9 | 13 | 39 | 35 | 57 | |
| 7. | FC Sochaux-Montbéliard (Montbéliard) | 38 | 15 | 12 | 11 | 46 | 48 | 57 | |
| 8. | Association de la Jeunesse Auxerroise (Auxerre) | 38 | 13 | 15 | 10 | 41 | 41 | 54 | |
| 9. | AS de Monaco FC (Monaco) | 38 | 13 | 12 | 13 | 45 | 38 | 51 | |
| 10. | Lille Olympique SC Metropole (Lille) | 38 | 13 | 11 | 14 | 45 | 43 | 50 | |
| 11. | AS de Saint-Étienne (Saint-Étienne) | 38 | 14 | 7 | 17 | 52 | 50 | 49 | |
| 12. | Mans Union Club 72 (Le Mans) | 38 | 11 | 16 | 11 | 45 | 46 | 49 | |
| 13. | AS Nancy-Lorraine (Nancy) | 38 | 13 | 10 | 15 | 37 | 44 | 49 | |
| 14. | FC Lorient Bretagne-Sud (Lorient) | 38 | 12 | 13 | 13 | 33 | 40 | 49 | |
| 15. | Paris Saint-Germain FC (Paris) | 38 | 12 | 12 | 14 | 42 | 42 | 48 | |
| 16. | Olympique GC de Nice-Côte d'Azur (Nice) | 38 | 9 | 16 | 13 | 34 | 40 | 43 | |
| 17. | Valenciennes FC (Valenciennes) | 38 | 11 | 10 | 17 | 36 | 48 | 43 | |
| 18. | ES Troyes Aube Champagne (Troyes) | 38 | 9 | 12 | 17 | 39 | 54 | 39 | R |
| 19. | CS Sedan-Ardennes (Sedan) | 38 | 7 | 14 | 17 | 46 | 58 | 35 | R |
| 20. | FC Nantes-Atlantique (Nantes) | 38 | 7 | 13 | 18 | 29 | 49 | 34 | R |
| | | 760 | 264 | 232 | 264 | 855 | 855 | 1024 | |

FC Nantes vs Toulouse FC played on 19th May 2007 was abandoned after 87 minutes following a pitch invasion by the Nantes fans when the scoreline stood at 0-0. The match was subsequently awarded as a victory to Toulouse FC (-:+) with a 0-0 scoreline being recorded.

## Top goal-scorers

| | | | |
|---|---|---|---|
| 1) | Steve SAVIDAN | (Valenciennes FC) | 13 |
| 2) | Mamadou NIANG | (Olympique de Marseille) | 12 |
| | "PAULETA" (Pedro Miguel Carreiro Resendes) | (Paris Saint-Germain FC) | 12 |
| 4) | Ismaël BANGOURA | (Mans Union Club 72) | 11 |
| | Aruna DINDANE | (Racing Club de Lens) | 11 |
| | "FRED" Frederico Chaves Guedes | (Olympique Lyonnais) | 11 |
| | Seydou KEITA | (Racing Club de Lens) | 11 |

| Division 2 | Pd | Wn | Dw | Ls | GF | GA | Pts | |
|---|---|---|---|---|---|---|---|---|
| 1. FC de Metz (Metz) | 38 | 22 | 10 | 6 | 54 | 22 | 76 | P |
| 2. Stade Malherbe Caen-CBN (Caen) | 38 | 19 | 14 | 5 | 65 | 40 | 71 | P |
| 3. Racing Club de Strasbourg Football (Strasbourg) | 38 | 19 | 13 | 6 | 47 | 33 | 70 | P |
| 4. Amiens SC Football (Amiens) | 38 | 21 | 6 | 11 | 57 | 42 | 69 | |
| 5. Grenoble Foot 38 (Grenoble) | 38 | 15 | 14 | 9 | 51 | 39 | 59 | |
| 6. Havre AC Football Association (Le Havre) | 38 | 15 | 11 | 12 | 52 | 38 | 56 | |
| 7. FC La Berrichonne (Châteauroux) | 38 | 15 | 9 | 14 | 42 | 44 | 54 | |
| 8. Dijon Football Côte d'Or (Dijon) | 38 | 14 | 12 | 12 | 44 | 47 | 54 | |
| 9. Sporting Club de Bastia (Bastia) | 38 | 14 | 11 | 13 | 52 | 49 | 53 | |
| 10. FC de Gueugnon (Gueugnon) | 38 | 13 | 9 | 16 | 47 | 52 | 48 | |
| 11. Stade de Reims (Reims) | 38 | 12 | 11 | 15 | 43 | 46 | 47 | |
| 12. AC Ajaccio (Ajaccio) | 38 | 12 | 11 | 15 | 44 | 50 | 47 | |
| 13. En Avant de Guingamp (Guingamp) | 38 | 11 | 13 | 14 | 45 | 44 | 46 | |
| 14. Stade Brestois 92 (Brest) | 38 | 10 | 15 | 13 | 40 | 40 | 45 | |
| 15. Montpellier-Hérault SC (Montpellier) | 38 | 11 | 11 | 16 | 41 | 48 | 44 | |
| 16. Chamois Niortais FC (Niort) | 38 | 10 | 14 | 14 | 36 | 44 | 44 | |
| 17. FC Libourne Saint-Seurin (Libourne) | 38 | 12 | 8 | 18 | 43 | 52 | 44 | |
| 18. US de Créteil Lusitanos (Créteil) | 38 | 9 | 13 | 16 | 33 | 50 | 40 | R |
| 19. FC Istres-Ville Nouvelle (Istres) | 38 | 8 | 11 | 19 | 35 | 63 | 35 | R |
| 20. Tours FC (Tours) | 38 | 6 | 8 | 24 | 30 | 58 | 26 | R |
| | 760 | 268 | 224 | 268 | 901 | 901 | 1028 | |

Promoted: Angers SC de l'Ouest (Angers), US Boulogne-Côte d'Opal (Boulogne-sur-Mer) and Clermont Football Auvergne (Clermont Ferrand).

## Coupe de France Final   (Stade de France, Saint Denis – 12/05/2007 – 79,797)

**FC SOCHAUX-MONTBÉLIARD**          **2-2** (aet)          Olympique de Marseille (Marseille)

*Beli 67', Le Tallec 116'*          *(5-4 on penalties)*          *Cissé 04', 98'*

**FC Sochaux:** Richert, Pichot, Afolabi, Bréchet, Tosic, Ziani, N'Draw, Pitau (Brunel 106'), Leroy, Beli (Le Tallec 104'), Grax (Birsa 73').

**Marseille:** Carrasso, Beye, Zubar, Rodriguez, Taiwo, M'Bami (Maoulida 94'), Cana, Ribery, Nasri, Niang (Oruma 73'), Cissé.

## Semi-finals

| | | |
|---|---|---|
| FC Montceau Bourgogne (Montceau/M.) | 0-2 | FC Sochaux-Montbéliard (Montbéliard) |
| Olympique de Marseille (Marseille) | 3-0 | FC Nantes-Atlantique (Nantes) |

## Quarter-finals

| | | |
|---|---|---|
| FC Montceau Bourgogne (Montceau/M.) | 1-0 | Racing Club de Lens (Lens) |
| Olympique de Marseille (Marseille) | 5-0 | Vannes Olympique Club (Vannes) |
| CS Sedan-Ardennes (Sedan) | 1-1 (aet) | FC Nantes-Atlantique (Nantes) |
| | (FC Nantes-Atlantique won 5-4 on penalties) | |
| FC Sochaux-Montbéliard (Montbéliard) | 2-1 | Paris Saint-Germain FC (Paris) |

# 2007-08

| 2007-08 Division 1 | AJ Auxerroise | Giron. Bordeaux | Lille Olympique SC | FC Lorient B-Sud | Mans UC 72 | FC de Metz | AS de Monaco FC | AS Nancy-Lorraine | Olympique Lyonnais | Olympique de Marseille | OGC de Nice | Paris Saint-Germain FC | RacingClub de Lens | RC de Strasbourg | AS de Saint-Étienne | FC Sochaux-Mont. | Stade Malherbe Caen | Stade Rennais FC | Toulouse FC | Valenciennes FC |
|---|---|---|---|---|---|---|---|---|---|---|---|---|---|---|---|---|---|---|---|---|
| AJ Auxerroise | | 0-2 | 0-1 | 5-3 | 3-0 | 0-0 | 1-0 | 0-0 | 1-3 | 2-0 | 2-0 | 0-1 | 0-0 | 1-1 | 1-3 | 0-1 | 1-0 | 0-2 | 1-0 | 2-0 |
| FC Girondins de Bordeaux | 4-1 | | 0-0 | 2-2 | 1-2 | 3-0 | 2-1 | 2-1 | 1-3 | 2-2 | 0-0 | 3-0 | 1-0 | 3-0 | 1-0 | 2-0 | 2-1 | 3-0 | 4-3 | 2-1 |
| Lille Olympique SC | 0-2 | 1-1 | | 0-0 | 3-1 | 1-1 | 0-1 | 2-1 | 0-1 | 1-1 | 1-1 | 0-0 | 2-1 | 0-3 | 3-0 | 1-1 | 5-0 | 3-1 | 3-2 | 3-0 |
| FC Lorient Bretagne-Sud | 1-1 | 1-0 | 1-1 | | 0-0 | 2-0 | 2-1 | 0-0 | 2-1 | 1-2 | 0-0 | 1-0 | 1-0 | 1-0 | 1-1 | 2-1 | 0-0 | 0-1 | 1-0 | 1-3 |
| Mans UC 72 | 3-0 | 1-2 | 1-1 | 0-0 | | 1-0 | 1-0 | 2-1 | 1-0 | 0-0 | 2-0 | 0-2 | 3-2 | 0-1 | 3-2 | 0-2 | 1-1 | 1-1 | 1-1 | 2-0 |
| FC de Metz | 0-1 | 0-1 | 1-2 | 1-2 | 4-3 | | 1-4 | 0-0 | 1-5 | 1-2 | 1-2 | 0-0 | 1-2 | 1-2 | 0-1 | 1-2 | 2-1 | 1-1 | 0-2 | 2-1 |
| AS de Monaco FC | 3-0 | 0-6 | 0-0 | 1-0 | 3-1 | 2-0 | | 1-3 | 0-4 | 2-3 | 1-1 | 1-2 | 2-0 | 3-0 | 1-1 | 1-0 | 0-0 | 1-2 | 0-2 | 0-0 |
| AS Nancy-Lorraine | 4-1 | 1-0 | 2-0 | 2-0 | 1-1 | 2-1 | 2-0 | | 1-1 | 1-1 | 2-1 | 1-0 | 2-1 | 3-0 | 2-0 | 1-1 | 1-0 | 2-3 | 1-0 | 0-0 |
| Olympique Lyonnais | 2-0 | 4-2 | 1-1 | 2-0 | 3-2 | 2-0 | 3-1 | 1-0 | | 1-2 | 0-0 | 4-2 | 3-0 | 5-0 | 1-0 | 4-1 | 2-2 | 1-1 | 3-2 | 2-0 |
| Olympique de Marseille | 2-1 | 1-2 | 1-3 | 0-0 | 1-0 | 3-1 | 2-0 | 2-2 | 3-1 | | 0-2 | 2-1 | 1-0 | 4-3 | 2-0 | 0-1 | 6-1 | 0-0 | 1-2 | 3-1 |
| OGC de Nice | 1-2 | 1-1 | 0-0 | 1-2 | 0-0 | 3-1 | 0-2 | 1-0 | 0-0 | 0-2 | | 2-1 | 1-0 | 1-0 | 3-0 | 0-0 | 3-1 | 1-1 | 1-1 | 1-0 |
| Paris Saint-Germain FC | 3-1 | 0-2 | 1-1 | 1-3 | 0-0 | 3-0 | 1-1 | 0-0 | 2-3 | 1-1 | 2-3 | | 3-0 | 1-0 | 1-1 | 0-0 | 0-1 | 1-3 | 1-2 | 1-1 |
| Racing Club de Lens | 2-0 | 2-2 | 1-2 | 1-1 | 3-1 | 1-1 | 0-0 | 1-0 | 3-0 | 3-3 | 0-0 | 0-0 | | 2-2 | 3-2 | 3-2 | 1-1 | 1-2 | 1-1 | 0-0 |
| Racing Club de Strasbourg | 3-0 | 1-1 | 0-1 | 0-0 | 0-1 | 2-3 | 0-2 | 0-0 | 1-2 | 0-0 | 0-1 | 1-2 | 2-1 | | 3-0 | 0-2 | 1-4 | 3-0 | 2-0 | 0-0 |
| AS de Saint-Étienne | 0-0 | 0-0 | 0-0 | 1-0 | 4-1 | 2-0 | 4-0 | 4-0 | 1-1 | 0-0 | 0-0 | 0-1 | 2-0 | 2-0 | | 1-0 | 3-0 | 2-0 | 0-0 | 3-1 |
| FC Sochaux-Montbéliard | 1-1 | 0-1 | 1-1 | 1-1 | 1-3 | 0-0 | 0-3 | 1-1 | 1-2 | 2-1 | 1-0 | 1-2 | 0-2 | 0-0 | 1-1 | | 1-1 | 0-0 | 0-1 | 1-0 |
| Stade Malherbe Caen | 0-0 | 5-0 | 1-0 | 0-0 | 3-2 | 1-2 | 1-1 | 0-0 | 1-0 | 1-2 | 1-0 | 3-0 | 1-4 | 2-0 | 1-3 | 2-2 | | 2-2 | 2-1 | 1-0 |
| Stade Rennais FC | 1-2 | 0-2 | 2-2 | 2-0 | 3-0 | 2-0 | 0-1 | 0-2 | 0-2 | 3-1 | 1-1 | 2-0 | 3-1 | 3-0 | 1-0 | 0-2 | 1-2 | | 2-1 | 1-0 |
| Toulouse FC | 2-0 | 0-1 | 1-0 | 0-0 | 1-1 | 0-0 | 0-0 | 1-1 | 1-0 | 0-0 | 1-1 | 1-1 | 1-1 | 1-3 | 0-2 | 1-2 | 1-1 | 0-0 | | 2-1 |
| Valenciennes FC | 3-0 | 3-1 | 0-0 | 3-0 | 1-2 | 0-0 | 1-0 | 1-1 | 1-2 | 2-1 | 1-2 | 0-0 | 1-2 | 2-0 | 2-0 | 3-1 | 3-0 | 3-0 | 3-1 | |

## Division 1

| | | Pd | Wn | Dw | Ls | GF | GA | Pts | |
|---|---|---|---|---|---|---|---|---|---|
| 1. | OLYMPIQUE LYONNAIS (LYON) | 38 | 24 | 7 | 7 | 74 | 37 | 79 | |
| 2. | FC Girondins de Bordeaux (Bordeaux) | 38 | 22 | 9 | 7 | 65 | 38 | 75 | |
| 3. | Olympique de Marseille (Marseille) | 38 | 17 | 11 | 10 | 58 | 45 | 62 | |
| 4. | AS Nancy-Lorraine (Nancy) | 38 | 15 | 15 | 8 | 44 | 30 | 60 | |
| 5. | AS de Saint-Étienne (Saint-Étienne) | 38 | 16 | 10 | 12 | 47 | 34 | 58 | |
| 6. | Stade Rennais FC (Rennes) | 38 | 16 | 10 | 12 | 47 | 44 | 58 | |
| 7. | Lille Olympique SC Metropole (Lille) | 38 | 13 | 18 | 7 | 45 | 32 | 57 | |
| 8. | Olympique GC de Nice-Côte d'Azur (Nice) | 38 | 13 | 16 | 9 | 35 | 30 | 55 | |
| 9. | Mans Union Club 72 (Le Mans) | 38 | 14 | 11 | 13 | 46 | 49 | 53 | |
| 10. | FC Lorient Bretagne-Sud (Lorient) | 38 | 12 | 16 | 10 | 32 | 35 | 52 | |
| 11. | Stade Malherbe Caen-CBN (Caen) | 38 | 13 | 12 | 13 | 48 | 53 | 51 | |
| 12. | AS de Monaco FC (Monaco) | 38 | 13 | 8 | 17 | 40 | 48 | 47 | |
| 13. | Valenciennes FC (Valenciennes) | 38 | 12 | 9 | 17 | 42 | 40 | 45 | |
| 14. | FC Sochaux-Montbéliard (Montbéliard) | 38 | 10 | 14 | 14 | 34 | 43 | 44 | |
| 15. | Association de la Jeunesse Auxerroise (Auxerre) | 38 | 12 | 8 | 18 | 33 | 52 | 44 | |
| 16. | Paris Saint-Germain FC (Paris) | 38 | 10 | 13 | 15 | 37 | 45 | 43 | |
| 17. | Toulouse FC (Toulouse) | 38 | 9 | 15 | 14 | 36 | 42 | 42 | |
| 18. | Racing Club de Lens (Lens) | 38 | 9 | 13 | 16 | 43 | 52 | 40 | R |
| 19. | Racing Club de Strasbourg Football (Strasbourg) | 38 | 9 | 8 | 21 | 34 | 55 | 35 | R |
| 20. | FC de Metz (Metz) | 38 | 5 | 9 | 24 | 28 | 64 | 24 | R |
| | | 760 | 264 | 232 | 264 | 868 | 868 | 1024 | |

FC de Metz had 1 point deducted following racist chanting by their fans during the home match versus Valenciennes FC on 16th February 2008. However, this decision was reversed on appeal and the point was reinstated.

## Top goal-scorers

| | | | |
|---|---|---|---|
| 1) | Karim BENZEMA | (Olympique Lyonnais) | 20 |
| 2) | Mamadou NIANG | (Olympique de Marseille) | 18 |
| 3) | Djibril CISSÉ | (Olympique de Marseille) | 16 |
| | Bafétimbi GOMIS | (AS de Saint-Étienne) | 16 |
| 5) | Fernando CAVENAGHI | (FC Girondins de Bordeaux) | 15 |

## Division 2

| | | Pd | Wn | Dw | Ls | GF | GA | Pts | |
|---|---|---|---|---|---|---|---|---|---|
| 1. | Havre AC Football Association (Le Havre) | 38 | 22 | 12 | 4 | 66 | 30 | 78 | P |
| 2. | FC Nantes-Atlantique (Nantes) | 38 | 19 | 13 | 6 | 58 | 34 | 70 | P |
| 3. | Grenoble Foot 38 (Grenoble) | 38 | 17 | 12 | 9 | 44 | 30 | 63 | P |
| 4. | CS Sedan-Ardennes (Sedan) | 38 | 15 | 13 | 10 | 46 | 40 | 58 | |
| 5. | Clermont Football Auvergne (Clermont Ferrand) | 38 | 14 | 15 | 9 | 50 | 41 | 57 | |
| 6. | ES Troyes Aube Champagne (Troyes) | 38 | 15 | 12 | 11 | 46 | 44 | 57 | |
| 7. | Stade Brestois 92 (Brest) | 38 | 15 | 12 | 11 | 38 | 38 | 57 | |
| 8. | Montpellier-Hérault SC (Montpellier) | 38 | 14 | 12 | 12 | 43 | 32 | 54 | |
| 9. | AC Ajaccio (Ajaccio) | 38 | 14 | 12 | 12 | 37 | 41 | 54 | |
| 10. | Angers SC de l'Ouest (Angers) | 38 | 13 | 14 | 11 | 39 | 35 | 53 | |
| 11. | Sporting Club de Bastia (Bastia) | 38 | 14 | 9 | 15 | 45 | 46 | 49 | (-2) |
| 12. | En Avant de Guingamp (Guingamp) | 38 | 11 | 15 | 12 | 41 | 37 | 48 | |
| 13. | Stade de Reims (Reims) | 38 | 12 | 10 | 16 | 44 | 52 | 46 | |
| 14. | Amiens SC Football (Amiens) | 38 | 11 | 12 | 15 | 49 | 51 | 45 | |
| 15. | FC La Berrichonne (Châteauroux) | 38 | 11 | 12 | 15 | 34 | 42 | 45 | |
| 16. | US Boulogne-Côte d'Opal (Boulogne-sur-Mer) | 38 | 12 | 7 | 19 | 37 | 54 | 43 | |
| 17. | Dijon Football Côte d'Or (Dijon) | 38 | 9 | 15 | 14 | 32 | 51 | 42 | |
| 18. | Chamois Niortais FC (Niort) | 38 | 11 | 8 | 19 | 38 | 48 | 41 | R |
| 19. | FC Libourne Saint-Seurin (Libourne) | 38 | 7 | 11 | 20 | 41 | 62 | 32 | R |
| 20. | FC de Gueugnon (Gueugnon) | 38 | 5 | 12 | 21 | 39 | 59 | 27 | R |
| | | 760 | 261 | 238 | 261 | 867 | 867 | 1019 | (-2) |

Sporting Club de Bastia (Bastia) had 2 points deducted following racist chanting by their fans in the Round 7 match versus FC Libourne Saint-Seurin.

Promoted: Nîmes Olympique (Nîmes), Tours FC (Tours) and Vannes Olympique Club (Vannes).

## Coupe de France Final   (Stade de France, Saint Denis – 24/05/2008 – 79,204)

**OLYMPIQUE LYONNAIS (LYON)**          **1-0**                    Paris Saint-Germain FC (Paris)

*Govou 103'*                                *(aet)*

**Olympique Lyonnais**: Coupet, Réveilleire, Squillaci, Boumsong, Grosso, Govou, Toulalan, Juninho (Clerc 118'), Kallström (Bodmer 68'), Fred (Keita 73'), Benzema.

**Paris Saint-Germain**: Alonzo, Ceará, Camara, Yepes, Armand, Chantôme (Mendy 83'), Bourillon (Souza 104'), Clément, Rothen, Pauleta (Luyindula 79'), Diané.

## Semi-finals

| | | |
|---|---|---|
| Amiens SC Football (Amiens) | 0-1 | Paris Saint-Germain FC (Paris) |
| Olympique Lyonnais (Lyon) | 1-0 | CS Sedan-Ardennes (Sedan) |

## Quarter-finals

| | | |
|---|---|---|
| Amiens SC Football (Amiens) | 1-0 | Dijon Football Côte d'Or (Dijon) |
| FC Girondins de Bordeaux (Bordeaux) | 0-0  (aet) | CS Sedan-Ardennes (Sedan) |
| | (CS Sedan-Ardennes won 4-3 on penalties) | |
| US de la Jeanne d'Arc (Carquefou) | 0-1 | Paris Saint-Germain FC (Paris) |
| Olympique Lyonnais (Lyon) | 1-0 | FC de Metz (Metz) |

# 2008-09

| 2008-09 Division 1 | AJ Auxerroise | Giron. Bordeaux | Grenoble 38 | Havre AC | Lille Olympique | FC Lorient B-Sud | Mans UC 72 | AS de Monaco FC | AS Nancy-Lorr. | FC Nantes | Olymp. Lyonnais | Olymp. Marseille | OGC de Nice | Paris St-Germain | AS St-Étienne | FC Sochaux | Stade Caen | Stade Rennais | Toulouse FC | Valenciennes FC |
|---|---|---|---|---|---|---|---|---|---|---|---|---|---|---|---|---|---|---|---|---|
| AJ Auxerroise | ■ | 0-2 | 2-0 | 3-0 | 2-0 | 0-0 | 2-0 | 0-1 | 1-1 | 2-1 | 0-0 | 0-2 | 0-1 | 1-2 | 1-0 | 1-0 | 2-1 | 0-0 | 1-1 | 0-0 |
| FC Girondins de Bordeaux | 2-0 | ■ | 1-1 | 4-0 | 2-2 | 1-0 | 3-2 | 1-0 | 1-0 | 2-0 | 1-0 | 1-1 | 2-1 | 4-0 | 1-1 | 3-0 | 2-1 | 1-1 | 2-1 | 2-1 |
| Grenoble Foot 38 | 0-0 | 0-1 | ■ | 0-0 | 0-0 | 1-3 | 2-1 | 1-0 | 0-0 | 0-1 | 0-2 | 0-3 | 0-0 | 0-0 | 1-0 | 0-1 | 2-1 | 1-0 | 1-0 | 0-0 |
| Havre AC Football Assoc. | 1-2 | 0-3 | 0-1 | ■ | 0-1 | 1-3 | 1-2 | 2-3 | 2-3 | 0-2 | 0-1 | 0-1 | 1-0 | 1-3 | 2-4 | 2-1 | 1-2 | 1-0 | 0-1 | 2-1 |
| Lille Olympique SC | 3-2 | 2-1 | 2-1 | 3-1 | ■ | 1-1 | 1-3 | 2-1 | 3-2 | 2-0 | 2-0 | 1-2 | 1-1 | 0-0 | 3-0 | 3-2 | 2-2 | 1-0 | 1-1 | 1-0 |
| FC Lorient Bretagne-Sud | 0-2 | 1-2 | 1-1 | 1-1 | 3-1 | ■ | 1-1 | 1-1 | 1-0 | 3-0 | 0-0 | 1-2 | 0-1 | 0-1 | 3-1 | 1-2 | 1-1 | 1-2 | 1-0 | 1-1 |
| Mans UC 72 | 0-2 | 1-3 | 1-1 | 2-0 | 0-1 | 0-1 | ■ | 0-1 | 2-0 | 0-2 | 1-3 | 1-1 | 1-2 | 0-1 | 1-0 | 2-0 | 2-0 | 2-2 | 1-2 | 1-0 |
| AS de Monaco FC | 0-1 | 3-4 | 1-0 | 0-1 | 0-2 | 2-0 | 3-0 | ■ | 3-1 | 1-2 | 0-1 | 0-1 | 1-2 | 1-0 | 2-2 | 1-1 | 1-1 | 3-1 | 3-2 | 1-1 |
| AS Nancy-Lorraine | 0-2 | 1-0 | 2-0 | 2-1 | 0-0 | 2-2 | 2-2 | 0-1 | ■ | 2-0 | 0-2 | 1-2 | 1-2 | 1-1 | 1-2 | 1-1 | 1-1 | 0-0 | 0-0 | 2-0 |
| FC Nantes-Atlantique | 2-1 | 1-2 | 1-1 | 1-2 | 0-2 | 1-1 | 1-4 | 1-1 | 0-1 | ■ | 2-1 | 1-1 | 2-0 | 1-4 | 1-0 | 1-1 | 1-1 | 1-1 | 1-1 | 2-0 |
| Olympique Lyonnais | 0-2 | 2-1 | 2-0 | 3-1 | 2-2 | 1-1 | 2-0 | 2-2 | 2-1 | 3-0 | ■ | 0-0 | 3-2 | 0-0 | 1-1 | 2-0 | 3-1 | 1-1 | 3-0 | 0-0 |
| Olympique de Marseille | 4-0 | 1-0 | 4-1 | 2-0 | 2-2 | 2-3 | 0-0 | 0-0 | 0-3 | 2-0 | 1-3 | ■ | 2-1 | 2-4 | 3-1 | 2-1 | 2-1 | 4-0 | 2-2 | 0-0 |
| OGC de Nice | 2-0 | 2-2 | 0-0 | 0-0 | 0-1 | 2-0 | 2-2 | 0-0 | 2-1 | 2-1 | 1-3 | 0-2 | ■ | 1-0 | 3-1 | 1-1 | 2-2 | 0-1 | 0-2 | 2-0 |
| Paris Saint-Germain FC | 1-2 | 1-0 | 3-0 | 3-0 | 1-0 | 3-2 | 3-1 | 0-0 | 4-1 | 1-0 | 1-0 | 1-3 | 2-1 | ■ | 2-1 | 2-0 | 0-1 | 0-1 | 0-1 | 2-2 |
| AS de Saint-Étienne | 2-0 | 1-1 | 0-2 | 2-0 | 2-1 | 1-4 | 1-1 | 2-0 | 0-0 | 2-1 | 0-1 | 0-3 | 0-1 | 1-0 | ■ | 2-1 | 3-2 | 0-3 | 2-2 | 4-0 |
| FC Sochaux-Montbéliard | 0-1 | 0-0 | 1-2 | 1-1 | 1-1 | 1-1 | 2-1 | 3-0 | 2-1 | 2-1 | 0-2 | 1-0 | 1-0 | 1-1 | 1-0 | ■ | 2-2 | 3-0 | 1-2 | 1-1 |
| Stade Malherbe Caen | 1-0 | 0-1 | 2-2 | 0-1 | 0-1 | 1-1 | 3-1 | 2-2 | 1-2 | 3-0 | 0-1 | 0-1 | 1-1 | 0-1 | 2-0 | 2-0 | ■ | 1-1 | 0-0 | 3-1 |
| Stade Rennais FC | 2-0 | 2-3 | 1-0 | 1-1 | 2-1 | 3-1 | 2-2 | 2-1 | 1-1 | 0-0 | 3-0 | 4-4 | 1-0 | 1-0 | 1-0 | 1-0 | 1-0 | ■ | 0-0 | 0-0 |
| Toulouse FC | 1-0 | 3-0 | 2-0 | 2-1 | 0-0 | 1-1 | 2-0 | 0-0 | 3-0 | 1-0 | 0-0 | 0-0 | 2-2 | 4-1 | 3-1 | 2-1 | 0-1 | 0-0 | ■ | 0-0 |
| Valenciennes FC | 2-0 | 1-2 | 1-1 | 3-2 | 2-0 | 3-1 | 0-2 | 3-1 | 0-1 | 1-1 | 2-0 | 1-3 | 1-0 | 2-1 | 1-0 | 2-2 | 2-0 | 0-0 | 0-1 | ■ |

## Division 1

| | | Pd | Wn | Dw | Ls | GF | GA | Pts | |
|---|---|---|---|---|---|---|---|---|---|
| 1. | FC GIRONDINS DE BORDEAUX (BORDEAUX) | 38 | 24 | 8 | 6 | 64 | 34 | 80 | |
| 2. | Olympique de Marseille (Marseille) | 38 | 22 | 11 | 5 | 67 | 35 | 77 | |
| 3. | Olympique Lyonnais (Lyon) | 38 | 20 | 11 | 7 | 52 | 29 | 71 | |
| 4. | Toulouse FC (Toulouse) | 38 | 16 | 16 | 6 | 45 | 27 | 64 | |
| 5. | Lille Olympique SC Metropole (Lille) | 38 | 17 | 13 | 8 | 51 | 39 | 64 | |
| 6. | Paris Saint-Germain FC (Paris) | 38 | 19 | 7 | 12 | 49 | 38 | 64 | |
| 7. | Stade Rennais FC (Rennes) | 38 | 15 | 16 | 7 | 42 | 34 | 61 | |
| 8. | Association de la Jeunesse Auxerroise (Auxerre) | 38 | 16 | 7 | 15 | 35 | 35 | 55 | |
| 9. | Olympique GC de Nice-Côte d'Azur (Nice) | 38 | 13 | 11 | 14 | 40 | 41 | 50 | |
| 10. | FC Lorient Bretagne-Sud (Lorient) | 38 | 10 | 15 | 13 | 47 | 47 | 45 | |
| 11. | AS de Monaco FC (Monaco) | 38 | 11 | 12 | 15 | 41 | 45 | 45 | |
| 12. | Valenciennes FC (Valenciennes) | 38 | 10 | 14 | 14 | 35 | 42 | 44 | |
| 13. | Grenoble Foot 38 (Grenoble) | 38 | 10 | 14 | 14 | 24 | 37 | 44 | |
| 14. | FC Sochaux-Montbéliard (Montbéliard( | 38 | 10 | 12 | 16 | 40 | 48 | 42 | |
| 15. | AS Nancy-Lorraine (Nancy) | 38 | 10 | 12 | 16 | 38 | 47 | 42 | |
| 16. | Mans Union Club 72 (Le Mans) | 38 | 10 | 10 | 18 | 43 | 54 | 40 | |
| 17. | AS de Saint-Étienne (Saint-Étienne) | 38 | 11 | 7 | 20 | 40 | 56 | 40 | |
| 18. | Stade Malherbe Caen-CBN (Caen) | 38 | 8 | 13 | 17 | 42 | 49 | 37 | R |
| 19. | FC Nantes-Atlantique (Nantes) | 38 | 9 | 10 | 19 | 33 | 54 | 37 | R |
| 20. | Havre AC Football Association (Le Havre) | 38 | 7 | 5 | 26 | 30 | 67 | 26 | R |
| | | 760 | 268 | 224 | 268 | 858 | 858 | 1028 | |

## Top goal-scorers

| | | | |
|---|---|---|---|
| 1) | André-Pierre GIGNAC | (Toulouse FC) | 24 |
| 2) | Karim BENZEMA | (Olympique Lyonnais) | 17 |
| | Guillaume HOARAU | (Paris Saint-Germain FC) | 17 |
| 4) | Michel BASTOS | (Lille Olympique SC Metropole) | 14 |
| | Ireneusz JELEN | (Assoc. Jeunesse Auxerroise) | 14 |
| | Steve SAVIDAN | (Stade Malherbe Caen-CBN) | 14 |

| Division 2 | Pd | Wn | Dw | Ls | GF | GA | Pts | |
|---|---|---|---|---|---|---|---|---|
| 1. Racing Club de Lens (Lens) | 38 | 20 | 8 | 10 | 47 | 35 | 68 | P |
| 2. Montpellier-Hérault SC (Montpellier) | 38 | 19 | 9 | 10 | 61 | 36 | 66 | P |
| 3. US Boulogne-Côte d'Opal (Boulogne-sur-Mer) | 38 | 20 | 6 | 12 | 51 | 36 | 66 | P |
| 4. Racing Club de Strasbourg Football (Strasbourg) | 38 | 18 | 11 | 9 | 57 | 45 | 65 | |
| 5. FC de Metz (Metz) | 38 | 17 | 12 | 9 | 48 | 35 | 63 | |
| 6. Tours FC (Tours) | 38 | 17 | 10 | 11 | 50 | 41 | 61 | |
| 7. Angers SC de l'Ouest (Angers) | 38 | 13 | 14 | 11 | 46 | 42 | 53 | |
| 8. Dijon Football Côte d'Or (Dijon) | 38 | 14 | 10 | 14 | 43 | 46 | 52 | |
| 9. CS Sedan-Ardennes (Sedan) | 38 | 13 | 12 | 13 | 46 | 49 | 51 | |
| 10. Vannes Olympique Club (Vannes) | 38 | 14 | 9 | 15 | 34 | 45 | 51 | |
| 11. Sporting Club de Bastia (Bastia) | 38 | 13 | 9 | 16 | 38 | 47 | 48 | |
| 12. Clermont Football Auvergne (Clermont Ferrand) | 38 | 12 | 11 | 15 | 46 | 50 | 47 | |
| 13. En Avant de Guingamp (Guingamp) | 38 | 10 | 16 | 12 | 37 | 35 | 46 | |
| 14. Stade Brestois '92 (Brest) | 38 | 13 | 6 | 19 | 45 | 50 | 45 | |
| 15. FC La Berrichone (Châteauroux) | 38 | 11 | 11 | 16 | 40 | 46 | 44 | |
| 16. AC Ajaccio (Ajaccio) | 38 | 11 | 11 | 16 | 44 | 56 | 44 | |
| 17. Nîmes Olympique (Nîmes) | 38 | 11 | 11 | 16 | 32 | 46 | 44 | |
| 18. Amiens SC Football (Amiens) | 38 | 9 | 16 | 13 | 35 | 40 | 43 | R |
| 19. ES Troyes Aube Champagne (Troyes) | 38 | 9 | 11 | 18 | 39 | 48 | 38 | R |
| 20. Stade de Reims (Reims) | 38 | 7 | 15 | 16 | 40 | 51 | 36 | R |
| | 760 | 271 | 218 | 271 | 879 | 879 | 1031 | |

Promoted: AC Arlésien (Avignon), FC Istres Ouest Provence (Istres) and Stade Lavallois Mayenne (Laval).

Note: AC Arlésien (Avignon) changed their name to AC Arles-Avignon (Avignon) on 16th June 2009.

## Coupe de France Final  (Stade de France, Saint Denis – 09/05/2009 – 80,056)

**EN AVANT DE GUINGAMP (GUINGAMP)**     **2-1**     Stade Rennais FC (Rennes)

*Eduardo 72', 83'*                                                      *Bocanegra 69'*

**Guingamp:** Gauclin, Deroff, Bassila, Koné, Felipe, Mathis, Colleau (Sène 72'), Oruma, Gilson Silva (Ogunbiyi 70'), Soumah, Eduardo.

**Stade Rennais:** Douchez, Fanni, M'Bia, Hansson, Bocanegra, Lemoine, Cheyrou (Kembo-Ekoko88'), Leroy, Danzé (Pagis 79'), Sow (Gyan 86'), Thomert.

## Semi-finals

| | | |
|---|---|---|
| Grenoble Foot 38 (Grenoble) | 0-1 | Stade Rennais FC (Rennes) |
| Toulouse FC (Toulouse) | 1-2 | En Avant de Guingamp (Guingamp) |

## Quarter-finals

| | | |
|---|---|---|
| Grenoble Foot 38 (Grenoble) | 2-0 | AS de Monaco FC (Monaco) |
| CS Sedan-Ardennes (Sedan) | 1-3 | En Avant de Guingamp (Guingamp) |
| Stade Rennais FC (Rennes) | 2-0 | Rodez Aveyron Football (Rodez) |
| Toulouse FC (Toulouse) | 1-1  (aet) | Lille Olympique SC Metropole |

(Toulouse FC won 7-6 on penalties)

# 2009-10

| 2009-10 Division 1 | AJ Auxerroise | Giron. Bordeaux | US Boulogne | Grenoble 38 | Lille Olympique | FC Lorient B-Sud | Mans UC 72 | AS de Monaco FC | Montpellier-Hérault | AS Nancy-Lorraine | Olymp. Lyonnais | Olymp. Marseille | OGC de Nice | Paris St-Germain | RC de Lens | AS St-Étienne | FC Sochaux-Mont. | Stade Rennais FC | Toulouse FC | Valenciennes FC |
|---|---|---|---|---|---|---|---|---|---|---|---|---|---|---|---|---|---|---|---|---|
| AJ Auxerroise | ■ | 1-0 | 0-0 | 2-0 | 3-2 | 4-1 | 2-1 | 2-0 | 2-1 | 1-3 | 0-3 | 0-0 | 2-0 | 1-1 | 0-0 | 1-0 | 0-1 | 1-0 | 1-1 | 1-0 |
| FC Girondins de Bordeaux | 1-2 | ■ | 0-0 | 1-0 | 3-1 | 4-1 | 3-0 | 1-0 | 1-1 | 1-2 | 2-2 | 1-1 | 4-0 | 1-0 | 4-1 | 3-1 | 2-0 | 1-0 | 1-0 | 0-1 |
| US Boulogne Côte d'Opal | 0-0 | 0-2 | ■ | 2-1 | 2-3 | 2-0 | 1-3 | 1-3 | 0-2 | 1-2 | 0-0 | 1-2 | 3-3 | 2-5 | 2-1 | 0-1 | 0-0 | 1-0 | 1-1 | 0-2 |
| Grenoble Foot 38 | 5-0 | 1-3 | 2-0 | ■ | 0-2 | 1-2 | 1-1 | 0-0 | 2-3 | 1-2 | 1-1 | 0-2 | 1-1 | 4-0 | 1-2 | 1-2 | 2-2 | 0-4 | 1-0 | 0-1 |
| Lille Olympique SC | 1-2 | 2-0 | 3-1 | 1-0 | ■ | 1-2 | 3-0 | 4-0 | 4-1 | 3-1 | 4-3 | 3-2 | 1-1 | 3-1 | 1-0 | 4-0 | 1-0 | 0-0 | 1-1 | 4-0 |
| FC Lorient Bretagne-Sud | 0-0 | 1-0 | 5-0 | 2-2 | 2-1 | ■ | 1-0 | 2-2 | 2-2 | 3-1 | 1-3 | 1-2 | 4-1 | 1-1 | 1-0 | 4-0 | 1-0 | 1-1 | 1-1 | 3-2 |
| Mans UC 72 | 0-1 | 2-1 | 1-1 | 1-0 | 1-2 | 0-3 | ■ | 1-1 | 2-2 | 2-1 | 2-2 | 1-2 | 0-1 | 1-0 | 3-0 | 1-1 | 0-0 | 1-3 | 1-3 | 2-1 |
| AS de Monaco FC | 0-0 | 0-0 | 1-0 | 0-0 | 0-4 | 2-0 | 1-1 | ■ | 4-0 | 2-1 | 1-1 | 1-2 | 3-2 | 2-0 | 2-0 | 1-2 | 2-0 | 1-0 | 1-0 | 2-1 |
| Montpellier-Hérault SC | 1-1 | 0-1 | 1-0 | 1-0 | 2-0 | 2-1 | 2-1 | 0-0 | ■ | 0-2 | 0-1 | 2-0 | 1-0 | 1-1 | 1-0 | 2-1 | 2-0 | 3-1 | 1-1 | 2-1 |
| AS Nancy-Lorraine | 0-1 | 0-3 | 1-3 | 0-2 | 0-4 | 1-0 | 3-2 | 4-0 | 0-0 | ■ | 0-2 | 0-3 | 2-0 | 0-0 | 5-1 | 0-1 | 2-1 | 1-2 | 0-0 | 1-1 |
| Olympique Lyonnais | 2-1 | 0-1 | 2-0 | 2-0 | 1-1 | 1-0 | 2-0 | 3-0 | 1-2 | 3-1 | ■ | 5-5 | 2-0 | 2-1 | 1-0 | 1-1 | 0-2 | 1-1 | 2-1 | 1-0 |
| Olympique de Marseille | 0-2 | 0-0 | 2-0 | 2-0 | 1-0 | 1-1 | 2-1 | 1-2 | 4-2 | 3-1 | 2-1 | ■ |  | 4-1 | 1-0 | 1-0 | 3-0 | 3-1 | 1-1 | 5-1 |
| OGC de Nice | 0-1 | 1-1 | 2-2 | 2-1 | 1-1 | 1-0 | 1-0 | 1-3 | 0-2 | 2-3 | 4-1 | 1-3 | ■ | 1-0 | 0-0 | 1-0 | 0-0 | 1-1 | 1-0 | 3-2 |
| Paris Saint-Germain FC | 1-0 | 3-1 | 3-0 | 4-0 | 3-0 | 0-3 | 3-1 | 0-1 | 1-3 | 1-1 | 1-1 | 0-3 | 0-1 | ■ | 1-1 | 3-0 | 4-1 | 1-1 | 1-0 | 2-2 |
| Racing Club de Lens | 2-0 | 4-3 | 3-0 | 1-1 | 1-1 | 1-1 | 2-1 | 3-0 | 0-1 | 2-1 | 0-2 | 1-0 | 2-0 | 1-1 | ■ | 1-0 | 0-0 | 2-2 | 0-2 | 1-1 |
| AS de Saint-Étienne | 1-1 | 3-1 | 0-1 | 1-0 | 1-1 | 0-2 | 2-0 | 3-0 | 1-0 | 0-0 | 0-1 | 0-0 | 0-2 | 0-0 | 1-4 | ■ | 0-0 | 0-0 | 0-1 | 0-2 |
| FC Sochaux-Montbéliard | 1-2 | 2-3 | 0-3 | 1-0 | 2-1 | 1-0 | 1-0 | 1-0 | 1-1 | 0-4 | 0-1 | 1-0 | 1-4 | 1-2 | 0-2 |  | ■ | 2-0 | 1-0 | 2-5 |
| Stade Rennais FC | 0-1 | 4-2 | 3-0 | 4-0 | 1-2 | 1-0 | 2-1 | 1-0 | 3-0 | 0-0 | 1-2 | 1-1 | 2-2 | 1-0 | 1-1 | 1-0 | 1-2 | ■ | 4-1 | 0-3 |
| Toulouse FC | 0-3 | 1-2 | 1-0 | 4-0 | 0-2 | 0-1 | 2-0 | 0-0 | 0-0 | 0-0 | 0-0 | 1-1 | 0-2 | 1-0 | 3-1 | 2-0 | 3-2 | 0-1 | ■ | 0-1 |
| Valenciennes FC | 0-0 | 2-0 | 1-1 | 2-0 | 1-0 | 0-0 | 0-1 | 3-1 | 1-1 | 1-3 | 2-2 | 3-2 | 2-1 | 2-3 | 0-0 | 1-0 | 1-1 | 0-2 | 1-3 | ■ |

## Division 1

| | | Pd | Wn | Dw | Ls | GF | GA | Pts | |
|---|---|---|---|---|---|---|---|---|---|
| 1. | OLYMPIQUE DE MARSEILLE (MARSEILLE) | 38 | 23 | 9 | 6 | 69 | 36 | 78 | |
| 2. | Olympique Lyonnais (Lyon) | 38 | 20 | 12 | 6 | 64 | 38 | 72 | |
| 3. | Association de la Jeunesse Auxerroise (Auxerre) | 38 | 20 | 11 | 7 | 42 | 29 | 71 | |
| 4. | Lille Olympique SC Metropole (Lille) | 38 | 21 | 7 | 10 | 72 | 40 | 70 | |
| 5. | Montpellier-Hérault SC (Montpellier) | 38 | 20 | 9 | 9 | 50 | 40 | 69 | |
| 6. | FC Girondins de Bordeaux (Bordeaux) | 38 | 19 | 7 | 12 | 58 | 40 | 64 | |
| 7. | FC Lorient Bretagne-Sud (Lorient) | 38 | 16 | 10 | 12 | 54 | 42 | 58 | |
| 8. | AS de Monaco FC (Monaco) | 38 | 15 | 10 | 13 | 39 | 45 | 55 | |
| 9. | Stade Rennais FC (Rennes) | 38 | 14 | 11 | 13 | 52 | 41 | 53 | |
| 10. | Valenciennes FC ( Valenciennes) | 38 | 14 | 10 | 14 | 50 | 50 | 52 | |
| 11. | Racing Club de Lens (Lens) | 38 | 12 | 12 | 14 | 40 | 44 | 48 | |
| 12. | AS Nancy-Lorraine (Nancy) | 38 | 13 | 9 | 16 | 46 | 53 | 48 | |
| 13. | Paris Saint-Germain FC (Paris) | 38 | 12 | 11 | 15 | 50 | 46 | 47 | |
| 14. | Toulouse FC (Toulouse) | 38 | 12 | 11 | 15 | 36 | 36 | 47 | |
| 15. | Olympique GC de Nice-Côte d'Azur (Nice) | 38 | 11 | 11 | 16 | 41 | 57 | 44 | |
| 16. | FC Sochaux-Montbéliard (Montbéliard) | 38 | 11 | 8 | 19 | 28 | 52 | 41 | |
| 17. | AS de Saint-Étienne (Saint-Étienne) | 38 | 10 | 10 | 18 | 27 | 45 | 40 | |
| 18. | Mans Union Club 72 (Le Mans) | 38 | 8 | 8 | 22 | 36 | 59 | 32 | R |
| 19. | US Boulogne-Côte d'Opal (Boulogne-sur-Mer) | 38 | 7 | 10 | 21 | 31 | 62 | 31 | R |
| 20. | Grenoble Foot 38 (Grenoble) | 38 | 5 | 8 | 25 | 31 | 61 | 23 | R |
| | | 760 | 283 | 194 | 283 | 916 | 916 | 1043 | |

## Top goal-scorers

| | | | |
|---|---|---|---|
| 1) | MAMADOU NIANG | (Olympique de Marseille) | 18 |
| 2) | Kevin GAMIERO | (FC Lorient Bretagne-Sud) | 17 |
| 3) | LISANDRO LÓPEZ | (Olympique Lyonnais) | 15 |
| | MEVLÜT Erdinç | (Paris Saint-Germain FC) | 15 |

| Division 2 | Pd | Wn | Dw | Ls | GF | GA | Pts | |
|---|---|---|---|---|---|---|---|---|
| 1. Stade Malherbe Caen-CBN (Caen) | 38 | 18 | 15 | 5 | 52 | 30 | 69 | P |
| 2. Stade Brestois '92 (Brest) | 38 | 20 | 7 | 11 | 53 | 34 | 67 | P |
| 3. AC Arles-Avignon (Avignon) | 38 | 16 | 12 | 10 | 43 | 39 | 60 | P |
| 4. FC de Metz (Metz) | 38 | 14 | 14 | 10 | 43 | 39 | 56 | |
| 5. Angers SC de l'Ouest (Angers) | 38 | 15 | 10 | 13 | 46 | 43 | 55 | |
| 6. Clermont Football Auvergne (Clermont Ferrand) | 38 | 15 | 9 | 14 | 48 | 41 | 54 | |
| 7. Havre AC Football Association (Le Havre) | 38 | 14 | 10 | 14 | 45 | 50 | 52 | |
| 8. Stade Lavallois Mayenne (Laval) | 38 | 11 | 18 | 9 | 49 | 41 | 51 | |
| 9. Dijon Football Côte d'Or (Dijon) | 38 | 12 | 15 | 11 | 52 | 46 | 51 | |
| 10. Nîmes Olympique (Nîmes) | 38 | 13 | 12 | 13 | 37 | 43 | 51 | |
| 11. Tours FC (Tours) | 38 | 11 | 16 | 11 | 47 | 46 | 49 | |
| 12. CS Sedan-Ardennes (Sedan) | 38 | 11 | 16 | 11 | 46 | 46 | 49 | |
| 13. AC Ajaccio (Ajaccio) | 38 | 13 | 9 | 16 | 41 | 42 | 48 | |
| 14. Vannes Olympique Club (Vannes) | 38 | 11 | 13 | 14 | 40 | 49 | 46 | |
| 15. FC Nantes-Atlantique (Nantes) | 38 | 12 | 9 | 17 | 43 | 54 | 45 | |
| 16. FC La Berrichone (Châteauroux) | 38 | 10 | 14 | 14 | 50 | 54 | 44 | |
| 17. FC Istres Ouest Provence (Istres) | 38 | 11 | 11 | 16 | 34 | 52 | 44 | |
| 18. En Avant de Guingamp (Guingamp) | 38 | 9 | 16 | 13 | 35 | 40 | 43 | R |
| 19. Racing Club de Strasbourg Football (Strasbourg) | 38 | 9 | 15 | 14 | 42 | 49 | 42 | R |
| 20. Sporting Club de Bastia (Bastia) | 38 | 10 | 9 | 19 | 40 | 48 | 39 | R |
| | 760 | 255 | 250 | 255 | 886 | 886 | 1015 | |

Promoted: Évian Thonon Gaillard FC (Gaillard), Stade de Reims (Reims), ES Troyes Aube Champagne (Troyes).

Mans Union Club 72 (Le Mans) changed their name to Le Mans FC.

## Coupe de France Final    (Stade de France, Saint Denis  – 01/05/2010 – 75,000)

**PARIS SAINT-GERMAIN FC (PARIS)    1-0  (aet)**                AS de Monaco FC (Monaco)

*Hoarau 107'*

**Paris Saint-Germain:** Edel, Jallet (Traoré 117'), Camara, Sakho, Armand, Makelele, Clément, Giuly (Luyindula 77'), Sessegnon, Hoarau, Mevlüt (Ceará 105').

**AS Monaco:** Ruffier, Modesto, Mongongu, Puygrenier, Traoré, Eduardo Costa (Sagbo 110'), Mangani (Haruna 55'), Pino (Maazou 86'), Alonso, Nenê, Park.

## Semi-finals

| | | |
|---|---|---|
| AS de Monaco FC (Monaco) | 1-0 | Racing Club de Lens (Lens) |
| US Quevilly (Le Petit-Quevilly) | 0-1 | Paris Saint-Germain FC (Paris) |

## Quarter-finals

| | | |
|---|---|---|
| Assoc. Jeunesse Auxerroise (Auxerre) | 0-0  (aet) | Paris Saint-Germain FC (Paris) |
| | (Paris Saint-Germain FC won 6-5 on penalties) | |
| AS de Monaco FC (Monaco) | 4-3 | FC Sochaux-Montbéliard (Montbéliard) |
| US Quevilly (Le Petit-Quevilly) | 3-1 | US Boulogne-Côte d'Opal (Boulogne-sur-Mer) |
| Racing Club de Lens (Lens) | 3-1 | AS de Saint-Étienne (Saint-Étienne) |

# 2010-11

| 2010-11 Division 1 | AC Arles-Avignon | AJ Auxerroise | Giron. Bordeaux | Stade Brestois '92 | Stade Mal. Caen | RC de Lens | Lille Olympique | FC Lorient B-Sud | Olymp. Lyonnais | Olymp. Marseille | AS Monaco FC | Montpellier-Hér. | AS Nancy-Lorraine | OGC de Nice | Paris-St Germain | Stade Rennais | AS de St-Étienne | FC Sochaux-Mont. | Toulouse FC | Valenciennes FC |
|---|---|---|---|---|---|---|---|---|---|---|---|---|---|---|---|---|---|---|---|---|
| AC Arles-Avignon | | 0-4 | 2-4 | 1-1 | 3-2 | 0-1 | 0-1 | 3-3 | 1-1 | 0-3 | 0-2 | 0-0 | 1-1 | 0-0 | 1-2 | 0-1 | 0-1 | 1-3 | 1-0 | 0-1 |
| AJ Auxerroise | 1-1 | | 0-1 | 0-1 | 1-1 | 1-1 | 1-1 | 2-2 | 4-0 | 1-1 | 1-1 | 1-0 | 2-2 | 2-0 | 1-0 | 2-1 | 2-2 | 2-0 | 1-2 | 1-1 |
| FC Girondins de Bordeaux | 0-0 | 3-0 | | 0-2 | 1-2 | 2-2 | 1-1 | 1-0 | 2-0 | 1-1 | 0-1 | 2-0 | 2-1 | 2-0 | 1-0 | 0-0 | 2-0 | 0-4 | 1-2 | 1-1 |
| Stade Brestois '92 | 0-0 | 1-1 | 1-3 | | 1-3 | 4-1 | 1-2 | 0-0 | 1-1 | 0-0 | 2-0 | 0-0 | 2-1 | 0-0 | 2-2 | 2-0 | 2-0 | 1-1 | 0-2 | 1-0 |
| Stade Malherbe Caen | 2-0 | 2-0 | 0-0 | 0-2 | | 1-1 | 2-5 | 0-2 | 3-2 | 2-2 | 0-0 | 2-0 | 2-3 | 0-0 | 1-2 | 1-0 | 1-0 | 0-3 | 1-1 | 2-2 |
| Racing Club de Lens | 0-1 | 1-1 | 1-0 | 1-1 | 2-0 | | 1-4 | 2-3 | 1-3 | 0-1 | 2-2 | 2-0 | 1-2 | 1-0 | 0-0 | 2-1 | 2-3 | 0-1 | 1-1 | |
| Lille Olympique SC | 5-0 | 1-0 | 1-1 | 3-1 | 3-1 | 1-0 | | 6-3 | 1-1 | 1-3 | 2-1 | 3-1 | 3-0 | 1-1 | 0-0 | 3-2 | 1-1 | 1-0 | 2-0 | 1-1 |
| FC Lorient Bretagne-Sud | 2-0 | 1-2 | 5-1 | 2-0 | 0-1 | 3-0 | 1-1 | | 2-0 | 2-2 | 2-1 | 0-0 | 0-0 | 1-2 | 1-1 | 2-0 | 0-0 | 1-1 | 0-0 | 2-1 |
| Olympique Lyonnais | 5-0 | 1-1 | 0-0 | 1-0 | 0-0 | 3-0 | 3-1 | 3-0 | | 3-2 | 0-0 | 3-2 | 4-0 | 1-0 | 2-2 | 1-1 | 0-1 | 2-1 | 2-0 | 1-1 |
| Olympique de Marseille | 1-0 | 1-1 | 2-1 | 3-0 | 1-2 | 1-1 | 1-2 | 2-0 | 1-1 | | 2-2 | 4-0 | 1-0 | 4-2 | 2-1 | 1-0 | 2-1 | 2-1 | 2-2 | 2-2 |
| AS de Monaco FC | 0-0 | 2-0 | 2-2 | 0-1 | 2-2 | 1-1 | 1-0 | 3-1 | 0-2 | 0-0 | | 0-0 | 0-1 | 1-1 | 1-1 | 1-0 | 0-2 | 2-1 | 0-0 | 0-2 |
| Montpellier-Hérault SC | 3-1 | 1-1 | 1-0 | 0-0 | 0-0 | 1-4 | 1-0 | 3-1 | 1-2 | 1-2 | 0-1 | | 1-2 | 1-1 | 1-0 | 0-1 | 1-2 | 2-0 | 1-0 | 2-1 |
| AS Nancy-Lorraine | 0-0 | 3-1 | 0-0 | 0-2 | 2-0 | 4-0 | 0-1 | 1-0 | 2-3 | 1-2 | 0-4 | 1-2 | | 3-0 | 2-0 | 0-3 | 1-1 | 1-0 | 0-2 | 2-0 |
| OGC de Nice | 3-2 | 1-0 | 2-1 | 1-1 | 0-4 | 0-0 | 0-2 | 2-0 | 2-2 | 1-0 | 3-2 | 0-1 | 1-1 | | 0-3 | 1-2 | 2-1 | 1-0 | 2-0 | 0-0 |
| Paris Saint-Germain FC | 4-0 | 2-3 | 1-2 | 3-1 | 2-1 | 0-0 | 2-2 | 0-0 | 1-0 | 2-1 | 2-2 | 2-2 | 2-2 | 0-0 | | 0-0 | 3-1 | 2-1 | 2-1 | 3-1 |
| Stade Rennais | 4-0 | 0-0 | 0-0 | 2-1 | 1-1 | 2-0 | 1-1 | 1-2 | 1-1 | 0-2 | 1-0 | 0-1 | 0-2 | 2-0 | 1-0 | | 0-0 | 2-1 | 3-1 | 1-0 |
| AS de Saint-Étienne | 2-0 | 1-1 | 2-2 | 2-0 | 1-1 | 3-1 | 1-2 | 1-4 | 1-1 | 1-1 | 3-0 | 2-1 | 0-2 | 1-1 | 1-2 | | | 3-2 | 2-1 | 1-1 |
| FC Sochaux-Montbéliard | 2-1 | 1-1 | 1-1 | 2-1 | 3-2 | 3-0 | 0-0 | 2-0 | 0-2 | 1-2 | 3-0 | 0-0 | 1-0 | 4-0 | 3-1 | 5-1 | 2-1 | | 1-3 | 2-1 |
| Toulouse FC | 2-1 | 0-1 | 2-0 | 2-0 | 1-0 | 1-1 | 1-1 | 3-0 | 2-0 | 0-1 | 0-1 | 1-0 | 1-1 | 1-0 | 0-2 | 1-2 | 0-1 | 0-1 | | 0-0 |
| Valenciennes FC | 3-0 | 1-1 | 2-2 | 3-0 | 2-1 | 1-1 | 1-1 | 0-0 | 2-1 | 3-2 | 0-0 | 0-1 | 1-1 | 2-1 | 1-2 | 2-0 | 1-1 | 1-1 | 2-1 | |

## Division 1

| | | Pd | Wn | Dw | Ls | GF | GA | Pts | |
|---|---|---|---|---|---|---|---|---|---|
| 1. | LILLE OLYMPIQUE SC METROPOLE (LILLE) | 38 | 21 | 13 | 4 | 68 | 36 | 76 | |
| 2. | Olympique de Marseille (Marseille) | 38 | 18 | 14 | 6 | 62 | 39 | 68 | |
| 3. | Olympique Lyonnais (Lyon) | 38 | 17 | 13 | 8 | 61 | 40 | 64 | |
| 4. | Paris Saint-Germain FC (Paris) | 38 | 15 | 15 | 8 | 56 | 41 | 60 | |
| 5. | FC Sochaux-Montbéliard (Montbéliard) | 38 | 17 | 7 | 14 | 60 | 43 | 58 | |
| 6. | Stade Rennais FC (Rennes) | 38 | 15 | 11 | 12 | 38 | 35 | 56 | |
| 7. | FC Girondins de Bordeaux (Bordeaux) | 38 | 12 | 15 | 11 | 43 | 42 | 51 | |
| 8. | Toulouse FC (Toulouse) | 38 | 14 | 8 | 16 | 38 | 36 | 50 | |
| 9. | Association de la Jeunesse Auxerroise (Auxerre) | 38 | 10 | 19 | 9 | 45 | 41 | 49 | |
| 10. | AS de Saint-Étienne (Saint-Étienne) | 38 | 12 | 13 | 13 | 46 | 47 | 49 | |
| 11. | FC Lorient Bretagne-Sud (Lorient) | 38 | 12 | 13 | 13 | 46 | 48 | 49 | |
| 12. | Valenciennes FC ( Valenciennes) | 38 | 10 | 18 | 10 | 45 | 41 | 48 | |
| 13. | AS Nancy-Lorraine (Nancy) | 38 | 13 | 9 | 16 | 43 | 48 | 48 | |
| 14. | Montpellier-Hérault SC (Montpellier) | 38 | 12 | 11 | 15 | 32 | 43 | 47 | |
| 15. | Stade Malherbe Caen-CBN (Caen) | 38 | 11 | 13 | 14 | 46 | 51 | 46 | |
| 16. | Stade Brestois '92 (Brest) | 38 | 11 | 13 | 14 | 36 | 43 | 46 | |
| 17. | Olympique GC de Nice-Côte d'Azur (Nice) | 38 | 11 | 13 | 14 | 33 | 48 | 46 | |
| 18. | AS de Monaco FC (Monaco) | 38 | 9 | 17 | 12 | 36 | 40 | 44 | R |
| 19. | Racing Club de Lens (Lens) | 38 | 7 | 14 | 17 | 35 | 58 | 35 | R |
| 20. | AC Arles-Avignon (Avignon) | 38 | 3 | 11 | 24 | 21 | 70 | 20 | R |
| | | 760 | 250 | 260 | 250 | 890 | 890 | 1010 | |

## Top goal-scorers

1) Moussa SOW          (Lille Olympique SC Metropole)    25
2) Kévin GAMEIRO       (FC Lorient Bretagne-Sud)         22
3) Grégory PUJOL       (Valenciennes FC)                 17
   Youssef EL-ARABI    (Stade Malherbe Caen-CBN)         17
   Lisandro LÓPEZ      (Olympique Lyonnais)              17

| Division 2 | Pd | Wn | Dw | Ls | GF | GA | Pts | |
|---|---|---|---|---|---|---|---|---|
| 1. Évian Thonon Gaillard FC (Gaillard) | 38 | 18 | 13 | 7 | 63 | 41 | 67 | P |
| 2. AC Ajaccio (Ajaccio) | 38 | 17 | 13 | 8 | 45 | 37 | 64 | P |
| 3. Dijon Football Côte d'Or (Dijon) | 38 | 17 | 11 | 10 | 55 | 40 | 62 | P |
| 4. Le Mans FC (Le Mans) | 38 | 17 | 11 | 10 | 48 | 37 | 62 | |
| 5. CS Sedan-Ardennes (Sedan) | 38 | 15 | 14 | 9 | 57 | 37 | 59 | |
| 6. Angers SC de l'Ouest (Angers) | 38 | 14 | 15 | 9 | 41 | 32 | 57 | |
| 7. Clermont Football Auvergne (Clermont Ferrand) | 38 | 12 | 16 | 10 | 51 | 49 | 52 | |
| 8. US Boulogne-Côte d'Opal (Boulogne-sur-Mer) | 38 | 13 | 13 | 12 | 35 | 41 | 52 | |
| 9. Havre AC Football Association (Le Havre) | 38 | 12 | 13 | 13 | 43 | 38 | 49 | |
| 10. Stade de Reims (Reims) | 38 | 12 | 13 | 13 | 53 | 51 | 49 | |
| 11. FC Istres Ouest Provence (Istres) | 38 | 12 | 13 | 13 | 45 | 47 | 49 | |
| 12. Tours FC (Tours) | 38 | 13 | 10 | 15 | 52 | 59 | 49 | |
| 13. FC Nantes-Atlantique (Nantes) | 38 | 11 | 14 | 13 | 38 | 40 | 47 | |
| 14. FC La Berrichone (Châteauroux) | 38 | 12 | 11 | 15 | 41 | 47 | 47 | |
| 15. Stade Lavallois Mayenne FC (Laval) | 38 | 11 | 14 | 13 | 36 | 43 | 47 | |
| 16. ES Troyes Aube Champagne (Troyes) | 38 | 13 | 7 | 18 | 35 | 45 | 46 | |
| 17. FC de Metz (Metz) | 38 | 10 | 15 | 13 | 43 | 40 | 45 | |
| 18. Vannes Olympique Club (Vannes) | 38 | 12 | 8 | 18 | 39 | 61 | 44 | R |
| 19. Nîmes Olympique (Nîmes) | 38 | 9 | 10 | 19 | 35 | 46 | 37 | R |
| 20. Grenoble Foot 38 (Grenoble) | 38 | 7 | 12 | 19 | 36 | 60 | 33 | R |
| | 760 | 257 | 246 | 257 | 891 | 891 | 1017 | |

Promoted: Amiens SC (Amiens), En Avant de Guingamp (Guingamp) and Sporting Club de Bastia (Bastia).

## Coupe de France Final   (Stade de France, Saint Denis – 14/05/2011 – 79,000)

Paris Saint-Germain FC (Paris)          **0-1**          LILLE OLYMPIQUE SC METROPOLE

*Obraniak 87'*

**Paris Saint-Germain:** Coupet, Ceará, Camara, Sakho, Tiéné, Chantôme, Makélélé (Clément 48'), Bodmer (Erdinç 69'), Giuly (Touré 90'), Nenê, Hoarau.

**Lille Olympique:** Landreau, Debuchy, Rami, Chedjou, Béria, Mavuba, Gueye (de Melo 63'), Cabaye, Gervinho, Hazard (Dumont 89'), Sow (Obraniak 79').

## Semi-finals

| | | |
|---|---|---|
| Olympique GC de Nice (Nice) | 0-2 | Lille Olympique SC Metropole (Lille) |
| Angers SC de l'Ouest (Angers) | 1-3 | Paris Saint-Germain FC (Paris) |

## Quarter-finals

| | | |
|---|---|---|
| Stade de Reims (Reims) | 2-3 (aet) | Olympique GC de Nice (Nice) |
| Stade Olympique de Chambéry Football | 0-3 | Angers SC de l'Ouest (Angers) |
| Paris Saint-Germain FC (Paris) | 2-0 (aet) | Le Mans FC (Le Mans) |
| Lille Olympique SC Métropole (Lille) | 0-0 (aet) | FC Lorient Bretagne-Sud (Lorient) |

(Lille Olympique SC won 5-3 on penalties)

| 2011-12 Division 1 | AC Ajaccio | AJ Auxerroise | Giron. Bordeaux | Stade Brestois '92 | Stade Malh. Caen | Dijon Football | Évian Gaillard | Lille Olympique | FC Lorient B-Sud | Olymp. Lyonnais | Olymp. Marseille | Montpellier-Hér. | AS Nancy-Lorraine | OGC de Nice | Paris St-Germain | Stade Rennais FC | AS St-Étienne | FC Sochaux-Mont. | Toulouse FC | Valenciennes FC |
|---|---|---|---|---|---|---|---|---|---|---|---|---|---|---|---|---|---|---|---|---|
| AC Ajaccio | ■ | 2-1 | 0-2 | 0-0 | 2-2 | 2-1 | 1-1 | 2-3 | 1-1 | 1-1 | 1-0 | 1-3 | 0-0 | 1-1 | 1-3 | 1-0 | 1-1 | 2-1 | 0-2 | 3-1 |
| AJ Auxerroise | 4-1 | ■ | 2-4 | 4-0 | 1-1 | 2-2 | 0-2 | 1-3 | 1-1 | 0-3 | 2-2 | 1-2 | 1-3 | 2-1 | 1-1 | 0-1 | 0-0 | 4-1 | 2-0 | 2-0 |
| FC Girondins de Bordeaux | 1-1 | 1-1 | ■ | 1-1 | 2-0 | 1-1 | 0-0 | 1-1 | 1-0 | 1-0 | 2-1 | 2-2 | 2-0 | 1-2 | 1-1 | 2-0 | 1-2 | 1-0 | 2-0 | 2-1 |
| Stade Brestois '92 | 1-1 | 1-0 | 0-2 | ■ | 1-1 | 1-1 | 2-2 | 3-1 | 3-1 | 1-1 | 1-0 | 2-2 | 0-1 | 1-0 | 0-1 | 0-1 | 2-2 | 2-0 | 0-0 | 1-0 |
| Stade Malherbe Caen | 0-0 | 2-1 | 1-0 | 0-0 | ■ | 3-0 | 2-2 | 1-2 | 1-0 | 1-0 | 1-2 | 1-3 | 1-2 | 1-1 | 2-2 | 0-2 | 1-4 | 1-3 | 0-1 | 1-0 |
| Dijon Football Côte d'Or | 1-1 | 0-2 | 2-0 | 1-0 | 2-0 | ■ | 3-1 | 0-2 | 2-0 | 1-2 | 2-3 | 1-1 | 0-2 | 3-0 | 1-2 | 1-5 | 1-2 | 0-0 | 1-1 | 1-2 |
| Évian Thonon Gaillard FC | 2-1 | 3-1 | 0-0 | 0-1 | 2-4 | 0-1 | ■ | 0-3 | 2-1 | 1-3 | 2-0 | 4-2 | 2-0 | 1-0 | 2-2 | 1-3 | 1-2 | 2-3 | 2-1 | 2-1 |
| Lille Olympique SC | 4-1 | 2-2 | 4-5 | 2-0 | 3-0 | 2-0 | 1-1 | ■ | 1-1 | 3-1 | 3-2 | 0-1 | 4-1 | 4-4 | 2-1 | 2-0 | 3-0 | 2-2 | 2-1 | 4-0 |
| FC Lorient Bretagne-Sud | 2-0 | 1-1 | 1-1 | 2-1 | 0-0 | 0-0 | 0-1 | 0-1 | ■ | 0-1 | 2-1 | 2-1 | 2-1 | 1-0 | 1-2 | 0-2 | 3-0 | 1-1 | 0-0 | 2-0 |
| Olympique Lyonnais | 1-1 | 2-1 | 3-1 | 1-1 | 1-2 | 3-1 | 2-1 | 2-1 | 3-2 | ■ | 2-0 | 2-1 | 3-1 | 3-4 | 4-4 | 1-2 | 2-1 | 2-1 | 3-2 | 4-1 |
| Olympique de Marseille | 2-0 | 3-0 | 0-0 | 1-1 | 1-1 | 1-2 | 2-0 | 2-0 | 2-1 | 2-2 | ■ | 1-3 | 1-0 | 2-0 | 3-0 | 0-1 | 0-0 | 2-2 | 0-1 | 1-1 |
| Montpellier-Hérault SC | 3-0 | 3-1 | 1-0 | 1-0 | 3-0 | 5-3 | 2-2 | 1-0 | 4-0 | 1-0 | 1-0 | ■ | 2-0 | 1-0 | 0-3 | 4-0 | 1-0 | 2-1 | 1-1 | 1-0 |
| AS Nancy-Lorraine | 2-2 | 0-0 | 2-2 | 2-1 | 1-1 | 1-2 | 1-1 | 1-1 | 2-2 | 2-0 | 1-3 | 1-0 | ■ | 1-0 | 2-1 | 0-0 | 3-2 | 1-2 | 0-3 | 1-1 |
| OGC de Nice | 3-0 | 1-0 | 3-0 | 0-0 | 1-0 | 1-1 | 1-1 | 0-1 | 2-0 | 1-3 | 1-1 | 0-1 | 1-1 | ■ | 0-0 | 2-0 | 0-2 | 1-1 | 1-1 | 2-0 |
| Paris Saint-Germain FC | 4-1 | 3-2 | 1-1 | 1-0 | 4-2 | 2-0 | 3-1 | 0-0 | 0-1 | 2-0 | 2-1 | 2-2 | 0-1 | 2-1 | ■ | 3-0 | 2-0 | 6-1 | 3-1 | 2-1 |
| Stade Rennais FC | 3-1 | 1-1 | 1-0 | 1-1 | 3-2 | 5-0 | 3-2 | 1-1 | 2-0 | 1-1 | 1-2 | 0-2 | 1-1 | 3-1 | 1-1 | ■ | 1-1 | 1-0 | 0-1 | 1-1 |
| AS de Saint-Étienne | 3-1 | 1-1 | 2-3 | 2-1 | 2-0 | 1-0 | 0-2 | 1-3 | 4-2 | 0-1 | 0-0 | 1-1 | 1-0 | 2-3 | 0-1 | 4-0 | ■ | 1-0 | 1-1 | 1-0 |
| FC Sochaux-Montbéliard | 0-2 | 0-0 | 0-3 | 2-1 | 1-2 | 1-0 | 1-1 | 0-1 | 1-1 | 2-1 | 1-0 | 1-3 | 1-0 | 2-0 | 0-1 | 2-6 | 2-1 | ■ | 3-0 | 1-1 |
| Toulouse FC | 0-2 | 1-0 | 3-2 | 0-0 | 1-0 | 2-0 | 2-1 | 0-0 | 1-1 | 3-0 | 1-0 | 1-1 | 1-0 | 0-0 | 1-3 | 1-0 | 0-1 | 2-0 | ■ | 2-0 |
| Valenciennes FC | 1-2 | 2-1 | 1-2 | 0-0 | 3-1 | 4-0 | 0-3 | 0-0 | 2-0 | 1-0 | 1-1 | 1-0 | 1-0 | 2-0 | 3-4 | 1-0 | 1-2 | 3-0 | 2-0 | ■ |

## Division 1

| | | Pd | Wn | Dw | Ls | GF | GA | Pts | |
|---|---|---|---|---|---|---|---|---|---|
| 1. | MONTPELLIER-HÉRAULT SC (MONTPELLIER) | 38 | 25 | 7 | 6 | 68 | 34 | 82 | |
| 2. | Paris Saint-Germain FC (Paris) | 38 | 23 | 10 | 5 | 75 | 41 | 79 | |
| 3. | Lille Olympique SC Metropole (Lille) | 38 | 21 | 11 | 6 | 72 | 39 | 74 | |
| 4. | Olympique Lyonnais (Lyon) | 38 | 19 | 7 | 12 | 64 | 51 | 64 | |
| 5. | FC Girondins de Bordeaux (Bordeaux) | 38 | 16 | 13 | 9 | 53 | 41 | 61 | |
| 6. | Stade Rennais FC (Rennes) | 38 | 17 | 9 | 12 | 53 | 44 | 60 | |
| 7. | AS de Saint-Étienne (Saint-Étienne) | 38 | 16 | 9 | 13 | 49 | 45 | 57 | |
| 8. | Toulouse FC (Toulouse) | 38 | 15 | 11 | 12 | 37 | 34 | 56 | |
| 9. | Évian Thonon Gaillard FC (Gaillard) | 38 | 13 | 11 | 14 | 54 | 55 | 50 | |
| 10. | Olympique de Marseille (Marseille) | 38 | 12 | 12 | 14 | 45 | 41 | 48 | |
| 11. | AS Nancy-Lorraine (Nancy) | 38 | 11 | 12 | 15 | 38 | 48 | 45 | |
| 12. | Valenciennes FC ( Valenciennes) | 38 | 12 | 7 | 19 | 40 | 50 | 43 | |
| 13. | Olympique GC de Nice-Côte d'Azur (Nice) | 38 | 10 | 12 | 16 | 39 | 46 | 42 | |
| 14. | FC Sochaux-Montbéliard (Montbéliard) | 38 | 11 | 9 | 18 | 40 | 60 | 42 | |
| 15. | Stade Brestois '92 (Brest) | 38 | 8 | 17 | 13 | 31 | 38 | 41 | |
| 16. | AC Ajaccio (Ajaccio) | 38 | 9 | 14 | 15 | 40 | 61 | 41 | |
| 17. | FC Lorient Bretagne-Sud (Lorient) | 38 | 9 | 12 | 17 | 35 | 49 | 39 | |
| 18. | Stade Malherbe Caen-CBN (Caen) | 38 | 9 | 11 | 18 | 39 | 59 | 38 | R |
| 19. | Dijon Football Côte d'Or (Dijon) | 38 | 9 | 9 | 20 | 38 | 63 | 36 | R |
| 20. | Association de la Jeunesse Auxerroise (Auxerre) | 38 | 7 | 13 | 18 | 46 | 57 | 34 | R |
| | | 760 | 272 | 216 | 272 | 956 | 956 | 1032 | |

## Top goal-scorers

1) Olivier GIROUD (Montpellier-Hérault SC) 21
   "NENE" Anderson Luis de Carvalho (Paris Saint-Germain FC) 21
3) Eden HAZARD (Lille Olympique SC) 20
4) Pierre-Emerick AUBAMEYANG (AS de Saint-Étienne) 16
   Lisandro LÓPEZ (Olympique Lyonnais) 16

| Division 2 | Pd | Wn | Dw | Ls | GF | GA | Pts | |
|---|---|---|---|---|---|---|---|---|
| 1. Sporting Club de Bastia (Bastia) | 38 | 21 | 8 | 9 | 61 | 36 | 71 | P |
| 2. Stade de Reims (Reims) | 38 | 18 | 11 | 9 | 54 | 37 | 65 | P |
| 3. ES Troyes Aube Champagne (Troyes) | 38 | 17 | 13 | 8 | 45 | 35 | 64 | P |
| 4. CS Sedan-Ardennes (Sedan) | 38 | 15 | 14 | 9 | 56 | 45 | 59 | |
| 5. Clermont Football Auvergne (Clermont Ferrand) | 38 | 15 | 13 | 10 | 48 | 39 | 58 | |
| 6. Tours FC (Tours) | 38 | 15 | 11 | 12 | 44 | 43 | 56 | |
| 7. En Avant de Guingamp (Guingamp) | 38 | 15 | 10 | 13 | 46 | 43 | 55 | |
| 8. AS de Monaco FC (Monaco) | 38 | 13 | 13 | 12 | 41 | 48 | 52 | |
| 9. FC Nantes-Atlantique (Nantes) | 38 | 14 | 9 | 15 | 51 | 42 | 51 | |
| 10. FC Istres Ouest Provence (Istres) | 38 | 13 | 12 | 13 | 46 | 44 | 51 | |
| 11. Angers SC de l'Ouest (Angers) | 38 | 13 | 12 | 13 | 44 | 45 | 51 | |
| 12. Racing Club de Lens (Lens) | 38 | 12 | 12 | 14 | 42 | 48 | 48 | |
| 13. AC Arles-Avignon (Avignon) | 38 | 10 | 18 | 10 | 34 | 41 | 48 | |
| 14. FC La Berrichone (Châteauroux) | 38 | 14 | 6 | 18 | 38 | 54 | 48 | |
| 15. Havre AC Football Association (Le Havre) | 38 | 11 | 14 | 13 | 38 | 34 | 47 | |
| 16. Stade Lavallois Mayenne FC (Laval) | 38 | 12 | 11 | 15 | 46 | 50 | 47 | |
| 17. Le Mans FC (Le Mans) | 38 | 11 | 12 | 15 | 39 | 40 | 45 | |
| 18. FC de Metz (Metz) | 38 | 10 | 12 | 16 | 30 | 44 | 42 | R |
| 19. US Boulogne-Côte d'Opal (Boulogne-sur-Mer) | 38 | 7 | 15 | 16 | 40 | 47 | 36 | R |
| 20. Amiens SC (Amiens) | 38 | 4 | 14 | 20 | 29 | 57 | 26 | R |
| | 760 | 260 | 240 | 260 | 872 | 872 | 1020 | |

Promoted: Nîmes Olympique (Nîmes), Chamois Niortais FC (Niort) and Gazélec FC Ajaccio (Ajaccio).

## Coupe de France Final    (Stade de France, Saint Denis – 28/04/2012 – 76,293)

**OLYMPIQUE LYONNAIS (LYON)**     **1-0**     US Quevilly (Le Petit-Quevilly)

*López 28'*

**Lyon:** Lloris, Réveillère, Cris, Lovren (Koné 18'), Cissokho, Källström, Gourcuff (Grenier 67'), Gonalons, López, Lacazette, Gomis (Briand 81').

**Quevilly:** El Kharroubi, Vardin, Weis, Beaugrard, Vanoukia, Diarra (Ouahbi 77'), Jouan, Laup (Ayina 81'), Capelle, Valéro (Herouat 57'), Colinet.

## Semi-finals

| Gazélec FC Ajaccio (Ajaccio) | 0-4 | Olympic Lyonnais (Lyon) |
|---|---|---|
| US Quevilly (Le Petit-Quevilly) | 2-1 | Stade Rennais FC (Rennes) |

## Quarter-finals

| US Quevilly (Le Petit-Quevilly) | 3-2 (aet) | Olympique de Marseille (Marseille) |
|---|---|---|
| Gazélec FC Ajaccio (Ajaccio) | 1-0 | Montpellier-Hérault SC (Montpellier) |
| Valenciennes FC (Valenciennes) | 1-3 | Stade Rennais FC (Rennes) |
| Paris Saint-Germain FC (Paris) | 1-3 | Olympic Lyonnais (Lyon) |

# 2012-2013

| 2012-13 Division 1 | AJ Ajaccio | SC de Bastia | Giron. Bordeaux | Stade Brestois '92 | Évian Gaillard | Lille Olympique | FC Lorient B-Sud | Olymp. Lyonnais | Olymp. Marseille | Montpellier-Hér. | AS Nancy-Lorraine | OGC de Nice | Paris St-Germain | Stade de Reims | Stade Rennais FC | AS St-Étienne | FC Sochaux-Mont. | Toulouse FC | ES Troyes Aube | Valenciennes FC |
|---|---|---|---|---|---|---|---|---|---|---|---|---|---|---|---|---|---|---|---|---|
| AJ Ajaccio | ■ | 0-0 | 1-0 | 1-0 | 2-0 | 1-3 | 1-0 | 3-1 | 0-2 | 2-1 | 1-1 | 0-2 | 0-0 | 2-0 | 2-4 | 0-0 | 0-1 | 2-3 | 0-1 | 1-1 |
| SC de Bastia | 1-0 | ■ | 3-1 | 4-0 | 0-0 | 1-2 | 2-1 | 4-1 | 1-2 | 3-1 | 4-2 | 0-1 | 0-4 | 2-1 | 0-2 | 0-3 | 0-0 | 0-0 | 3-2 | 2-3 |
| Girondins de Bordeaux | 2-2 | 1-0 | ■ | 0-2 | 2-1 | 1-1 | 1-1 | 0-4 | 1-0 | 4-2 | 3-2 | 1-1 | 0-1 | 0-0 | 1-0 | 0-0 | 2-2 | 1-0 | 0-0 | 2-0 |
| Stade Brestois '92 | 1-1 | 3-0 | 1-1 | ■ | 1-0 | 1-2 | 2-0 | 1-1 | 1-2 | 1-2 | 1-2 | 0-2 | 0-3 | 0-2 | 0-2 | 0-1 | 0-2 | 0-1 | 2-1 | 2-1 |
| Évian Thonon Gaillard FC | 1-1 | 3-0 | 2-3 | 0-2 | ■ | 0-2 | 1-1 | 1-1 | 1-1 | 0-1 | 1-1 | 4-0 | 0-1 | 2-2 | 4-2 | 2-2 | 5-1 | 0-4 | 2-0 | 2-0 |
| Lille Olympique SC | 2-0 | 0-0 | 2-1 | 1-0 | 1-2 | ■ | 5-0 | 1-1 | 0-0 | 4-1 | 1-1 | 0-2 | 1-2 | 3-0 | 2-0 | 1-1 | 3-3 | 2-0 | 1-1 | 2-1 |
| FC Lorient Bretagne-Sud | 4-4 | 4-1 | 0-4 | 4-0 | 2-1 | 2-0 | ■ | 1-1 | 0-1 | 2-1 | 3-0 | 1-1 | 1-3 | 2-2 | 2-2 | 3-1 | 2-0 | 1-0 | 3-2 | 1-1 |
| Olympique Lyonnais | 2-0 | 5-2 | 0-2 | 1-0 | 0-0 | 1-3 | 3-1 | ■ | 0-0 | 1-0 | 1-1 | 3-0 | 0-1 | 3-0 | 2-0 | 1-1 | 1-2 | 3-1 | 4-1 | 3-2 |
| Olympique de Marseille | 0-0 | 2-1 | 1-0 | 1-0 | 1-0 | 1-0 | 0-3 | 1-4 | ■ | 3-2 | 0-1 | 2-2 | 2-2 | 0-0 | 3-1 | 1-0 | 2-0 | 2-1 | 2-1 | 1-0 |
| Montpellier-Hérault SC | 3-0 | 4-0 | 1-0 | 2-1 | 2-3 | 0-0 | 2-0 | 1-2 | 0-1 | ■ | 1-0 | 3-1 | 1-1 | 3-1 | 2-0 | 1-1 | 2-0 | 1-1 | 1-1 | 3-1 |
| AS Nancy-Lorraine | 1-1 | 1-2 | 1-1 | 1-0 | 3-1 | 2-2 | 2-1 | 0-3 | 0-1 | 0-2 | ■ | 1-0 | 0-1 | 1-2 | 1-3 | 0-3 | 1-1 | 0-1 | 1-0 | 1-1 |
| OGC de Nice | 0-1 | 2-2 | 0-1 | 4-2 | 3-2 | 2-2 | 1-1 | 1-1 | 0-1 | 2-0 | 2-1 | ■ | 2-1 | 2-0 | 1-0 | 1-0 | 3-0 | 1-0 | 3-1 | 5-0 |
| Paris Saint-Germain FC | 0-0 | 3-1 | 0-0 | 3-1 | 4-0 | 1-0 | 2-2 | 1-0 | 2-0 | 1-0 | 3-0 | 2-1 | ■ | 1-0 | 1-2 | 1-2 | 2-0 | 2-0 | 4-0 | 1-1 |
| Stade de Reims | 1-1 | 1-2 | 0-0 | 0-0 | 1-2 | 1-1 | 1-0 | 1-0 | 0-1 | 3-1 | 2-0 | 3-1 | 1-0 | ■ | 1-0 | 1-0 | 1-1 | 1-1 | 1-1 | 0-1 |
| Stade Rennais FC | 1-1 | 3-2 | 0-2 | 2-2 | 0-1 | 2-0 | 1-2 | 0-1 | 2-2 | 2-1 | 0-2 | 0-3 | 0-2 | 1-0 | ■ | 2-2 | 2-2 | 2-0 | 1-2 | 2-0 |
| AS de Saint-Étienne | 4-2 | 3-0 | 0-2 | 4-0 | 1-0 | 1-2 | 0-2 | 1-0 | 2-0 | 4-1 | 4-0 | 4-0 | 2-2 | 0-0 | 2-0 | ■ | 0-1 | 2-2 | 2-0 | 1-0 |
| FC Sochaux-Montbéliard | 0-0 | 2-3 | 2-2 | 1-2 | 2-1 | 1-1 | 1-0 | 1-1 | 1-3 | 1-3 | 0-1 | 3-2 | 1-0 | 0-1 | 1-2 | 0-1 | ■ | 1-2 | 3-1 | 1-1 |
| Toulouse FC | 2-4 | 0-0 | 0-0 | 3-1 | 0-0 | 4-2 | 0-1 | 3-0 | 0-1 | 2-0 | 2-1 | 3-4 | 0-4 | 1-1 | 2-2 | 2-1 | 2-0 | ■ | 2-2 | 2-2 |
| ES Troyes Aube Champagne | 3-2 | 0-0 | 1-0 | 2-1 | 1-0 | 1-1 | 2-2 | 1-2 | 1-0 | 1-1 | 3-3 | 1-1 | 0-1 | 4-2 | 2-3 | 2-2 | 0-0 | 0-2 | ■ | 0-1 |
| Valenciennes FC | 3-0 | 3-4 | 0-0 | 2-1 | 2-1 | 1-3 | 6-1 | 0-2 | 4-1 | 1-1 | 0-0 | 0-2 | 0-4 | 1-0 | 4-1 | 0-0 | 3-1 | 0-0 | 2-1 | ■ |

## Division 1

| | | Pd | Wn | Dw | Ls | GF | GA | Pts | |
|---|---|---|---|---|---|---|---|---|---|
| 1. | PARIS SAINT-GERMAIN FC (PARIS) | 38 | 25 | 8 | 5 | 69 | 23 | 83 | |
| 2. | Olympique de Marseille (Marseille) | 38 | 21 | 8 | 9 | 42 | 36 | 71 | |
| 3. | Olympique Lyonnais (Lyon) | 38 | 19 | 10 | 9 | 61 | 38 | 67 | |
| 4. | Olympique GC de Nice-Côte d'Azur (Nice) | 38 | 18 | 10 | 10 | 57 | 46 | 64 | |
| 5. | AS de Saint-Étienne (Saint-Étienne) | 38 | 16 | 15 | 7 | 60 | 32 | 63 | |
| 6. | Lille Olympique SC Metropole (Lille) | 38 | 16 | 14 | 8 | 59 | 40 | 62 | |
| 7. | FC Girondins de Bordeaux (Bordeaux) | 38 | 13 | 16 | 9 | 40 | 34 | 55 | |
| 8. | FC Lorient Bretagne-Sud (Lorient) | 38 | 14 | 11 | 13 | 57 | 58 | 53 | |
| 9. | Montpellier-Hérault SC (Montpellier) | 38 | 15 | 7 | 16 | 54 | 51 | 52 | |
| 10. | Toulouse FC (Toulouse) | 38 | 13 | 12 | 13 | 49 | 47 | 51 | |
| 11. | Valenciennes FC ( Valenciennes) | 38 | 12 | 12 | 14 | 49 | 53 | 48 | |
| 12. | Sporting Club de Bastia (Bastia) | 38 | 13 | 8 | 17 | 50 | 66 | 47 | |
| 13. | Stade Rennais FC (Rennes) | 38 | 13 | 7 | 18 | 48 | 59 | 46 | |
| 14. | Stade de Reims (Reims) | 38 | 10 | 13 | 15 | 33 | 42 | 43 | |
| 15. | FC Sochaux-Montbéliard (Montbéliard) | 38 | 10 | 11 | 17 | 41 | 57 | 41 | |
| 16. | Évian Thonon Gaillard FC (Gaillard) | 38 | 10 | 10 | 18 | 46 | 53 | 40 | |
| 17. | AC Ajaccio (Ajaccio) | 38 | 9 | 15 | 14 | 39 | 51 | 40 | -2 |
| 18. | AS Nancy-Lorraine (Nancy) | 38 | 9 | 11 | 18 | 38 | 58 | 38 | R |
| 19. | ES Troyes Aube Champagne (Troyes) | 38 | 8 | 13 | 17 | 43 | 61 | 37 | R |
| 20. | Stade Brestois '92 (Brest) | 38 | 8 | 5 | 25 | 32 | 62 | 29 | R |
| | | 760 | 272 | 216 | 272 | 967 | 967 | 1030 | (-2) |

AC Ajaccio had 2 points deducted, with a further point deduction suspended, following incidents during a 2011-12 league match against Olympique Lyonnais.

## Top goal-scorers

| | | | |
|---|---|---|---|
| 1) | Zlatan Ibrahimovic | (Paris Saint-Germain FC) | 30 |
| 2) | Pierre-Emerick Aubameyang | (AS Saint-Étienne) | 19 |
| | Darío Cvitanich | (OGC Nice) | 19 |
| 4) | Bafétimbi Gomis | (Olympique Lyonnais) | 16 |

## Division 2

| | | Pd | Wn | Dw | Ls | GF | GA | Pts | |
|---|---|---|---|---|---|---|---|---|---|
| 1. | AS de Monaco FC (Monaco) | 38 | 21 | 13 | 4 | 64 | 33 | 76 | P |
| 2. | En Avant de Guingamp (Guingamp) | 38 | 20 | 10 | 8 | 63 | 38 | 70 | P |
| 3. | FC Nantes-Atlantique (Nantes) | 38 | 19 | 12 | 7 | 54 | 29 | 69 | P |
| 4. | Stade Malherbe Caen-CBN (Caen) | 38 | 17 | 12 | 9 | 48 | 28 | 63 | |
| 5. | Angers SC de l'Ouest (Angers) | 38 | 17 | 10 | 11 | 52 | 39 | 61 | |
| 6. | Havre AC Football Association (Le Havre) | 38 | 16 | 11 | 11 | 52 | 47 | 59 | |
| 7. | Dijon Football Côte d'Or (Dijon) | 38 | 15 | 14 | 9 | 52 | 49 | 59 | |
| 8. | Nîmes Olympique (Nîmes) | 38 | 17 | 7 | 14 | 52 | 42 | 58 | |
| 9. | Association de la Jeunesse Auxerroise (Auxerre) | 38 | 13 | 10 | 15 | 51 | 53 | 49 | |
| 10. | Tours FC (Tours) | 38 | 12 | 13 | 13 | 40 | 49 | 49 | |
| 11. | AC Arles-Avignon (Avignon) | 38 | 10 | 16 | 12 | 36 | 48 | 46 | |
| 12. | Racing Club de Lens (Lens) | 38 | 9 | 18 | 11 | 39 | 53 | 45 | |
| 13. | FC Istres Ouest Provence (Istres) | 38 | 11 | 10 | 17 | 38 | 45 | 43 | |
| 14. | Clermont Football Auvergne (Clermont Ferrand) | 38 | 9 | 16 | 13 | 33 | 47 | 43 | |
| 15. | Chamois Niortais FC (Niort) | 38 | 8 | 18 | 12 | 39 | 42 | 42 | |
| 16. | FC La Berrichone (Châteauroux) | 38 | 8 | 18 | 12 | 43 | 47 | 42 | |
| 17. | Stade Lavallois Mayenne FC (Laval) | 38 | 10 | 12 | 16 | 47 | 54 | 42 | |
| 18. | Le Mans FC (Le Mans) | 38 | 11 | 7 | 20 | 39 | 62 | 40 | R |
| 19. | CS Sedan-Ardennes (Sedan) | 38 | 6 | 13 | 19 | 41 | 58 | 28 | -3 |
| 20. | Gazélec FC Ajaccio (Ajaccio) | 38 | 6 | 10 | 22 | 34 | 54 | 25 | -3 |
| | | 760 | 255 | 250 | 255 | 917 | 917 | 1009 | (-6) |

CS Sedan-Ardennes and Gazélec FC Ajaccio each had 3 points deducted.

## Coupe de France Final   (Stade de France, Saint-Denis – 31/05/2013 – 77,000)

**FC GIRONDINS DE BORDEAUX (BORDEAUX)**   **3-2**   Évian Thonon Gaillard FC (Gaillard)

*Diabaté 39', 89', Saivet 53'*                     *Sagbo 51', Dja Djédjé 70'*

**Bordeaux:** Carrasso, Mariano, Sané, Henrique, Trémoulinas, Sertic, Plašil (Poko 67'), Obraniak, Saivet, Maurice-Belay, Diabaté.

**Évian:** Laquait, Djédjé, Betão, Cambon, Wass, Rabiu (Tié Bi 83'), Sorlin, Ninkovic (Barbosa 60'), Bérigaud, Khlifa, Sagbo (Angoula 90+1').

## Semi-finals

| | | |
|---|---|---|
| Évian Thonon Gaillard FC (Gaillard) | 4-0 | FC Lorient Bretagne-Sud (Lorient) |
| ES Troyes Aube Champagne (Troyes) | 1-2 | FC Girondins de Bordeaux (Bordeaux) |

## Quarter-finals

| | | |
|---|---|---|
| ES Troyes Aube Champagne (Troyes) | 3-0 | AS Nancy-Lorraine (Nancy) |
| AS de Saint-Étienne (Saint-Étienne) | 1-2 | FC Lorient Bretagne-Sud (Lorient) |
| Évian Thonon Gaillard FC (Gaillard) | 1-1  (aet) | Paris Saint-Germain FC (Paris) |
| | (Évian Thonon Gaillard FC won 4-1 on penalties) | |
| Racing Club de Lens (Lens) | 2-3 | FC Girondins de Bordeaux (Bordeaux) |

# 2013/2014

| 2013/14 Division 1 | AC Ajaccio | SC de Bastia | Giron. Bordeaux | Évian Thonon | Guingamp | Lille Olympique | FC Lorient B-Sud | Olymp. Lyonnais | Olymp. Marseille | AS de Monaco | Montpellier-Hér. | FC Nantes | OGC de Nice | Paris St.-Germain | Stade de Reims | Stade Rennais FC | AS Saint-Étienne | FC Sochaux-Mont. | Toulouse FC | Valenciennes FC |
|---|---|---|---|---|---|---|---|---|---|---|---|---|---|---|---|---|---|---|---|---|
| AC Ajaccio | | 1-1 | 1-1 | 2-3 | 1-2 | 2-3 | 1-2 | 2-1 | 1-3 | 1-4 | 1-1 | 0-1 | 0-0 | 1-2 | 2-1 | 3-1 | 0-1 | 1-1 | 2-2 | 1-3 |
| SC de Bastia | 2-1 | | 1-0 | 2-0 | 3-2 | 1-1 | 4-1 | 1-3 | 0-0 | 0-2 | 0-0 | 0-0 | 1-0 | 0-3 | 2-0 | 1-0 | 0-2 | 2-2 | 2-1 | 2-0 |
| FC Girondins de Bordeaux | 4-0 | 1-0 | | 2-1 | 5-1 | 1-0 | 3-2 | 1-2 | 1-1 | 0-2 | 2-0 | 0-3 | 1-1 | 0-2 | 0-0 | 2-2 | 2-0 | 4-1 | 0-1 | 2-1 |
| Évian Thonon Gaillard FC | 1-1 | 2-1 | 1-1 | | 1-2 | 2-2 | 0-4 | 2-1 | 1-2 | 1-0 | 2-2 | 2-0 | 2-0 | 2-0 | 1-1 | 1-2 | 1-2 | 1-1 | 2-1 | 0-1 |
| En Avant de Guingamp | 2-1 | 1-1 | 0-1 | 0-1 | | 0-0 | 2-0 | 0-1 | 1-3 | 0-2 | 1-2 | 1-0 | 1-0 | 1-1 | 1-2 | 2-0 | 0-0 | 5-1 | 2-0 | 1-0 |
| Lille Olympique SC | 3-0 | 2-1 | 2-1 | 3-0 | 1-0 | | 1-0 | 0-0 | 1-0 | 2-0 | 2-0 | 0-0 | 0-2 | 1-3 | 1-2 | 1-1 | 1-0 | 2-0 | 1-0 | 1-0 |
| FC Lorient Bretagne-Sud | 1-0 | 1-1 | 3-3 | 1-1 | 2-0 | 1-4 | | 2-2 | 0-2 | 2-2 | 4-4 | 2-1 | 3-0 | 0-1 | 0-0 | 2-0 | 1-0 | 2-1 | 1-3 | 2-1 |
| Olympique Lyonnais | 3-1 | 4-1 | 1-1 | 3-0 | 2-0 | 0-0 | 0-1 | | 2-2 | 2-3 | 0-0 | 3-1 | 4-0 | 1-0 | 0-1 | 0-0 | 1-2 | 2-0 | 1-1 | 1-1 |
| Olympique de Marseille | 3-1 | 3-0 | 2-2 | 2-0 | 1-0 | 0-0 | 1-0 | 4-2 | | 1-2 | 2-0 | 0-1 | 0-1 | 1-2 | 2-3 | 0-1 | 2-1 | 2-1 | 2-2 | 2-1 |
| AS de Monaco FC | 1-0 | 3-0 | 1-1 | 1-1 | 1-1 | 1-1 | 1-0 | 2-1 | 2-0 | | 4-1 | 3-1 | 1-0 | 1-1 | 3-2 | 2-0 | 2-1 | 2-1 | 0-0 | 1-2 |
| Montpellier-Hérault SC | 2-0 | 0-2 | 1-1 | 1-1 | 1-1 | 0-1 | 0-2 | 5-1 | 2-3 | 1-1 | | 1-1 | 3-1 | 1-1 | 3-0 | 0-0 | 0-1 | 2-1 | 2-1 | 0-0 |
| FC Nantes-Atlantique | 2-2 | 2-0 | 0-0 | 3-0 | 1-0 | 0-1 | 1-0 | 1-2 | 1-1 | 0-1 | 2-1 | | 2-0 | 1-2 | 0-0 | 0-3 | 1-3 | 1-0 | 1-2 | 2-1 |
| OGC de Nice | 2-0 | 2-0 | 1-2 | 3-1 | 1-0 | 1-0 | 1-2 | 0-1 | 1-0 | 0-3 | 2-2 | 0-0 | | 0-1 | 1-0 | 2-1 | 0-1 | 1-0 | 0-2 | 4-0 |
| Paris Saint-Germain | 1-1 | 4-0 | 2-0 | 1-0 | 2-0 | 2-2 | 4-0 | 4-0 | 2-0 | 1-1 | 4-0 | 5-0 | 3-1 | | 3-0 | 1-2 | 2-0 | 5-0 | 3-0 | 3-0 |
| Stade de Reims | 4-1 | 4-2 | 1-0 | 1-0 | 1-1 | 2-1 | 1-1 | 0-2 | 1-1 | 1-1 | 2-4 | 0-0 | 1-0 | 0-3 | | 1-3 | 2-2 | 0-1 | 1-2 | 3-1 |
| Stade Rennais FC | 2-0 | 3-0 | 1-1 | 0-0 | 0-2 | 0-0 | 1-1 | 2-0 | 1-1 | 2-0 | 2-2 | 1-3 | 0-0 | 1-3 | 2-1 | | 3-1 | 1-2 | 2-3 | 2-2 |
| AS de Saint-Étienne | 3-1 | 2-2 | 2-1 | 1-0 | 1-0 | 2-0 | 3-2 | 1-2 | 1-1 | 2-0 | 2-0 | 2-0 | 1-1 | 2-2 | 4-0 | 0-0 | | 3-1 | 1-2 | 3-0 |
| FC Sochaux-Mont. | 0-0 | 1-1 | 2-0 | 0-3 | 1-0 | 0-2 | 2-0 | 1-3 | 1-1 | 2-2 | 0-2 | 1-0 | 2-0 | 1-1 | 0-2 | 2-1 | 0-0 | | 2-0 | 2-0 |
| Toulouse FC | 1-1 | 1-3 | 1-1 | 1-1 | 0-0 | 1-2 | 1-0 | 0-0 | 1-1 | 0-2 | 1-1 | 1-1 | 1-0 | 2-4 | 3-2 | 0-5 | 0-0 | 5-1 | | 3-1 |
| Valenciennes FC | 2-3 | 3-2 | 0-1 | 0-1 | 1-1 | 0-1 | 1-1 | 1-2 | 0-1 | 1-2 | 1-1 | 2-6 | 2-1 | 0-1 | 1-1 | 2-1 | 1-3 | 2-2 | 3-0 | |

## Division 1

| | | Pd | Wn | Dw | Ls | GF | GA | Pts | |
|---|---|---|---|---|---|---|---|---|---|
| 1. | PARIS SAINT-GERMAIN FC (PARIS) | 38 | 27 | 8 | 3 | 84 | 23 | 89 | |
| 2. | AS de Monaco FC (Monaco) | 38 | 23 | 11 | 4 | 63 | 31 | 80 | |
| 3. | Lille Olympique SC Metropole (Lille) | 38 | 20 | 11 | 7 | 46 | 26 | 71 | |
| 4. | AS de Saint-Étienne (Saint-Étienne) | 38 | 20 | 9 | 9 | 56 | 34 | 69 | |
| 5. | Olympique Lyonnais (Lyon) | 38 | 17 | 10 | 11 | 56 | 44 | 61 | |
| 6. | Olympique de Marseille (Marseille) | 38 | 16 | 12 | 10 | 53 | 40 | 60 | |
| 7. | FC Girondins de Bordeaux (Bordeaux) | 38 | 13 | 14 | 11 | 49 | 43 | 53 | |
| 8. | FC Lorient Bretagne-Sud (Lorient) | 38 | 13 | 10 | 15 | 48 | 53 | 49 | |
| 9. | Toulouse FC (Toulouse) | 38 | 12 | 13 | 13 | 46 | 53 | 49 | |
| 10. | Sporting Club de Bastia (Bastia) | 38 | 13 | 10 | 15 | 42 | 56 | 49 | |
| 11. | Stade de Reims (Reims) | 38 | 12 | 12 | 14 | 44 | 52 | 48 | |
| 12. | Stade Rennais FC (Rennes) | 38 | 11 | 13 | 14 | 47 | 45 | 46 | |
| 13. | FC Nantes-Atlantique (Nantes) | 38 | 12 | 10 | 16 | 38 | 43 | 46 | |
| 14. | Évian Thonon Gaillard FC (Gaillard) | 38 | 11 | 11 | 16 | 39 | 51 | 44 | |
| 15. | Montpellier-Hérault SC (Montpellier) | 38 | 8 | 18 | 12 | 45 | 53 | 42 | |
| 16. | En Avant de Guingamp (Guingamp) | 38 | 11 | 9 | 18 | 34 | 42 | 42 | |
| 17. | Olympique GC de Nice-Côte d'Azur (Nice) | 38 | 12 | 6 | 20 | 30 | 44 | 42 | |
| 18. | FC Sochaux-Montbéliard (Montbéliard) | 38 | 10 | 10 | 18 | 37 | 61 | 40 | R |
| 19. | Valenciennes FC ( Valenciennes) | 38 | 7 | 8 | 23 | 37 | 65 | 29 | R |
| 20. | AC Ajaccio (Ajaccio) | 38 | 4 | 11 | 23 | 37 | 72 | 23 | R |
| | | 760 | 272 | 216 | 272 | 931 | 931 | 1032 | |

AS de Monaco FC initially had 2 points deducted following crowd trouble in a game during the 2012/2013 season, but this deduction was subsequently overturned.

## Top goal-scorers

| | | | |
|---|---|---|---|
| 1) | Zlatan Ibrahimovic | (Paris Saint-Germain FC) | 26 |
| 2) | Vincent Aboubakar | (FC Lorient Bretagne-Sud) | 16 |
| | Wissam Ben Yedder | (Toulouse FC) | 16 |
| | Edinson Cavani | (Paris Saint-Germain FC) | 16 |
| | André-Pierre Gignac | (Olympique Marseille) | 16 |
| | Salomon Kalou | (Lille Olympique SC) | 16 |

| Division 2 | | Pd | Wn | Dw | Ls | GF | GA | Pts | |
|---|---|---|---|---|---|---|---|---|---|
| 1. | FC de Metz (Metz) | 38 | 22 | 10 | 6 | 55 | 28 | 76 | P |
| 2. | Racing Club de Lens (Lens) | 38 | 17 | 14 | 7 | 58 | 40 | 65 | P |
| 3. | Stade Malherbe Caen-CBN (Caen) | 38 | 18 | 10 | 10 | 65 | 44 | 64 | P |
| 4. | AS Nancy-Lorraine (Nancy) | 38 | 16 | 13 | 9 | 47 | 37 | 61 | |
| 5. | Chamois Niortais FC (Niort) | 38 | 15 | 13 | 10 | 51 | 47 | 58 | |
| 6. | Dijon Football Côte d'Or (Dijon) | 38 | 14 | 15 | 9 | 53 | 42 | 57 | |
| 7. | Stade Brestois '92 (Brest) | 38 | 15 | 11 | 12 | 38 | 32 | 56 | |
| 8. | Tours FC (Tours) | 38 | 15 | 10 | 13 | 63 | 56 | 55 | |
| 9. | Angers SC de l'Ouest (Angers) | 38 | 14 | 13 | 11 | 46 | 45 | 55 | |
| 10. | ES Troyes Aube Champagne (Troyes) | 38 | 15 | 7 | 16 | 56 | 44 | 52 | |
| 11. | US de Créteil Lusitanos (Créteil) | 38 | 12 | 14 | 12 | 57 | 58 | 50 | |
| 12. | Havre AC Football Association (Le Havre) | 38 | 11 | 15 | 12 | 43 | 43 | 48 | |
| 13. | AC Arles-Avignon (Avignon) | 38 | 10 | 16 | 12 | 36 | 38 | 46 | |
| 14. | Clermont Football Auvergne (Clermont Ferrand) | 38 | 10 | 15 | 13 | 31 | 38 | 45 | |
| 15. | Nîmes Olympique (Nîmes) | 38 | 10 | 14 | 14 | 49 | 54 | 44 | |
| 16. | Association de la Jeunesse Auxerroise (Auxerre) | 38 | 10 | 13 | 15 | 35 | 45 | 43 | |
| 17. | Stade Lavallois Mayenne FC (Laval) | 38 | 10 | 12 | 16 | 44 | 52 | 42 | |
| 18. | FC La Berrichone (Châteauroux) | 38 | 10 | 10 | 18 | 43 | 59 | 40 | |
| 19. | FC Istres Ouest Provence (Istres) | 38 | 9 | 9 | 20 | 48 | 74 | 36 | R |
| 20. | Cercle Athlétiais Bastiais (Bastia) | 38 | 4 | 12 | 22 | 21 | 63 | 24 | R |
| | | 760 | 257 | 246 | 257 | 939 | 939 | 1017 | |

Due to financial irregularities, the DNCG, French football's financial watchdog, declared that Racing Club de Lens would not be allowed promotion into Ligue 1 for the 2014/2015 season. However, when the season commenced, Lens were allowed to play in Ligue 1 as the appeals process was still underway.

## Coupe de France Final   (Stade de France, Saint-Denis – 03/05/2014 – 80,000)

| Stade Rennais FC (Rennes) | **0-2** | **EN AVANT DE GUINGAMP (GUINGAMP)** |
|---|---|---|

*Pereira 37', Yatabaré 46'*

**Rennes**: Costil, Danzé, Kana-Biyik, Armand, Moreira, Konradsen (Oliveira 62'), Doucouré, Makoun (Pajot 68'), Grosicki (Ntep 52'), Alessandrini, Toivonen.

**Guingamp**: Samassa, Pereira, Kerbrat, Sorbon, Lévêque, Sankharé, Mathis, Beauvue (Atik 84'), Langil (Giresse 79'), Mandanne (Diallo 69'), Yatabaré.

## Semi-finals

| Stade Rennais FC (Rennes) | 3-2 | Angers SC de l'Ouest (Angers) |
|---|---|---|
| En Avant de Guingamp (Guingamp) | 3-1 (aet) | AS de Monaco FC (Monaco) |

## Quarter-finals

| AS Moulins (Moulins) | 0-0 (aet) – 2-4 on penalties | Angers SC de l'Ouest (Angers) |
|---|---|---|
| AS de Cannes Football (Cannes) | 0-2 | En Avant de Guingamp (Guingamp) |
| AS de Monaco FC (Monaco) | 6-0 | Racing Club de Lens (Lens) |
| Stade Rennais FC (Rennes) | 2-0 | Lille Olympique SC Metropole (Lille) |

# 2014/2015

| 2014/15 Division 1 | SC de Bastia | Giron. Bordeaux | Stade Mal. Caen | Évian Thonon | EA Guingamp | RC de Lens | Lille Olympique | FC Lorient B-Sud | Olymp. Lyonnais | Olymp. Marseille | FC de Metz | AS de Monaco | Montpellier-Hér. | FC Nantes | OGC de Nice | Paris St-Germain | Stade de Reims | Stade Rennais FC | AS Saint-Étienne | Toulouse FC |
|---|---|---|---|---|---|---|---|---|---|---|---|---|---|---|---|---|---|---|---|---|
| SC de Bastia | ■ | 0-0 | 1-1 | 1-2 | 0-0 | 1-1 | 2-1 | 0-2 | 0-0 | 3-3 | 2-0 | 1-3 | 2-0 | 0-0 | 2-1 | 4-2 | 1-2 | 2-0 | 1-0 | 1-0 |
| FC Girondins de Bordeaux | 1-1 | ■ | 1-1 | 2-1 | 1-1 | 2-1 | 1-0 | 3-2 | 0-5 | 1-0 | 1-1 | 4-1 | 2-1 | 2-1 | 1-2 | 3-2 | 1-1 | 2-1 | 1-0 | 2-1 |
| Stade Malherbe Caen | 1-1 | 1-2 | ■ | 3-2 | 0-2 | 4-1 | 0-1 | 2-1 | 3-0 | 1-2 | 0-0 | 0-3 | 1-1 | 1-2 | 2-3 | 0-2 | 4-1 | 0-1 | 1-0 | 2-0 |
| Évian Thonon Gaillard FC | 1-2 | 0-1 | 0-3 | ■ | 2-0 | 2-1 | 0-1 | 1-0 | 2-3 | 1-3 | 3-0 | 1-3 | 1-0 | 0-2 | 1-0 | 0-0 | 2-3 | 1-1 | 1-2 | 1-0 |
| En Avant de Guingamp | 1-0 | 2-1 | 5-1 | 1-1 | ■ | 2-0 | 0-1 | 3-2 | 1-3 | 0-1 | 0-1 | 1-0 | 0-2 | 0-1 | 2-7 | 1-0 | 2-0 | 0-1 | 0-2 | 2-1 |
| Racing Club de Lens | 1-1 | 1-2 | 0-0 | 0-2 | 0-1 | ■ | 1-1 | 0-0 | 0-2 | 0-4 | 2-0 | 0-3 | 0-1 | 1-0 | 2-0 | 1-3 | 4-2 | 0-1 | 0-1 | 1-0 |
| Lille Olympique SC | 1-0 | 2-0 | 1-0 | 1-0 | 1-2 | 3-1 | ■ | 2-0 | 2-1 | 0-4 | 0-0 | 0-1 | 0-0 | 2-0 | 0-0 | 1-1 | 3-1 | 3-0 | 1-1 | 3-0 |
| FC Lorient Bretagne-Sud | 2-0 | 0-0 | 2-1 | 0-2 | 4-0 | 1-0 | 1-0 | ■ | 1-1 | 1-1 | 3-1 | 0-1 | 0-0 | 1-2 | 0-0 | 1-2 | 0-1 | 0-3 | 0-1 | 0-1 |
| Olympique Lyonnais | 2-0 | 1-1 | 3-0 | 2-0 | 3-1 | 0-1 | 3-0 | 4-0 | ■ | 1-0 | 2-0 | 2-1 | 5-1 | 1-0 | 1-2 | 1-1 | 2-1 | 2-0 | 2-2 | 3-0 |
| Olympique de Marseille | 3-0 | 3-1 | 2-3 | 1-0 | 2-1 | 2-1 | 2-1 | 3-5 | 0-0 | ■ | 3-1 | 2-1 | 0-2 | 2-0 | 4-0 | 2-3 | 2-2 | 3-0 | 2-1 | 2-0 |
| FC de Metz | 3-1 | 0-0 | 3-2 | 1-2 | 0-2 | 3-1 | 1-4 | 0-4 | 2-1 | 0-2 | ■ | 0-1 | 2-3 | 1-1 | 0-0 | 2-3 | 3-0 | 0-0 | 2-3 | 3-2 |
| AS de Monaco FC | 3-0 | 0-0 | 2-2 | 2-0 | 1-0 | 2-0 | 1-1 | 1-2 | 0-0 | 1-0 | 2-0 | ■ | 0-0 | 1-0 | 0-1 | 0-0 | 1-1 | 1-1 | 1-1 | 4-1 |
| Montpellier-Hérault SC | 3-1 | 0-1 | 1-0 | 2-0 | 2-1 | 3-3 | 1-2 | 1-0 | 1-5 | 2-1 | 2-0 | 0-1 | ■ | 4-0 | 2-1 | 1-2 | 3-1 | 0-0 | 0-2 | 2-0 |
| FC Nantes-Atlantique | 0-2 | 2-1 | 1-2 | 2-1 | 1-0 | 1-0 | 1-1 | 1-1 | 1-1 | 1-0 | 0-0 | 0-1 | 1-0 | ■ | 2-1 | 0-2 | 1-1 | 1-1 | 0-0 | 1-2 |
| OGC de Nice | 0-1 | 1-3 | 1-1 | 2-2 | 1-2 | 2-1 | 3-1 | 1-3 | 2-1 | 1-0 | 0-1 | 1-1 | 0-0 | | ■ | 1-3 | 0-0 | 1-2 | 0-0 | 3-2 |
| Paris Saint-Germain FC | 2-0 | 3-0 | 2-2 | 4-2 | 6-0 | 4-1 | 6-1 | 3-1 | 1-1 | 2-0 | 3-1 | 1-1 | 0-0 | 2-1 | 1-0 | ■ | 3-2 | 1-0 | 5-0 | 3-1 |
| Stade de Reims | 2-1 | 1-0 | 0-2 | 3-2 | 2-3 | 0-0 | 2-0 | 1-3 | 2-4 | 0-5 | 0-0 | 1-3 | 1-0 | 3-1 | 0-1 | 2-2 | ■ | 1-0 | 1-2 | 2-0 |
| Stade Rennais FC | 0-1 | 1-1 | 1-4 | 6-2 | 1-0 | 2-0 | 2-0 | 1-0 | 0-1 | 1-1 | 1-1 | 2-0 | 0-4 | 0-0 | 2-1 | 1-1 | 1-3 | ■ | 0-0 | 0-3 |
| AS de Saint-Étienne | 1-0 | 1-1 | 1-0 | 3-0 | 2-1 | 3-3 | 2-0 | 2-0 | 3-0 | 2-2 | 1-0 | 1-1 | 1-0 | 1-0 | 5-0 | 0-1 | 3-1 | 0-0 | ■ | 0-1 |
| Toulouse FC | 1-1 | 2-1 | 3-3 | 1-0 | 1-1 | 0-2 | 3-2 | 2-3 | 2-1 | 1-6 | 3-0 | 0-2 | 1-0 | 1-1 | 2-3 | 1-1 | 1-0 | 2-1 | 1-1 | ■ |

## Division 1

| | | Pd | Wn | Dw | Ls | GF | GA | Pts | |
|---|---|---|---|---|---|---|---|---|---|
| 1. | PARIS SAINT-GERMAIN FC (PARIS) | 38 | 24 | 11 | 3 | 83 | 36 | 83 | |
| 2. | Olympique Lyonnais (Lyon) | 38 | 22 | 9 | 7 | 72 | 33 | 75 | |
| 3. | AS de Monaco FC (Monaco) | 38 | 20 | 11 | 7 | 51 | 26 | 71 | |
| 4. | Olympique de Marseille (Marseille) | 38 | 21 | 6 | 11 | 76 | 42 | 69 | |
| 5. | AS de Saint-Étienne (Saint-Étienne) | 38 | 19 | 12 | 7 | 51 | 30 | 69 | |
| 6. | FC Girondins de Bordeaux (Bordeaux) | 38 | 17 | 12 | 9 | 47 | 44 | 63 | |
| 7 | Montpellier-Hérault SC (Montpellier) | 38 | 16 | 8 | 14 | 46 | 39 | 56 | |
| 8. | Lille Olympique SC Metropole (Lille) | 38 | 16 | 8 | 14 | 43 | 42 | 56 | |
| 9. | Stade Rennais FC (Rennes) | 38 | 13 | 11 | 14 | 35 | 42 | 50 | |
| 10. | En Avant de Guingamp (Guingamp) | 38 | 15 | 4 | 19 | 41 | 55 | 49 | |
| 11. | Olympique GC de Nice-Côte d'Azur (Nice) | 38 | 13 | 9 | 16 | 44 | 53 | 48 | |
| 12. | Sporting Club de Bastia (Bastia) | 38 | 12 | 11 | 15 | 37 | 46 | 47 | |
| 13. | Stade Malherbe Caen-CBN (Caen) | 38 | 12 | 10 | 16 | 54 | 55 | 46 | |
| 14. | FC Nantes-Atlantique (Nantes) | 38 | 11 | 12 | 15 | 29 | 40 | 45 | |
| 15. | Stade de Reims (Reims) | 38 | 12 | 8 | 18 | 47 | 66 | 44 | |
| 16. | FC Lorient Bretagne-Sud (Lorient) | 38 | 12 | 7 | 19 | 44 | 50 | 43 | |
| 17. | Toulouse FC (Toulouse) | 38 | 12 | 6 | 20 | 43 | 64 | 42 | |
| 18. | Évian Thonon Gaillard FC (Gaillard) | 38 | 11 | 4 | 23 | 41 | 62 | 37 | R |
| 19. | FC de Metz (Metz) | 38 | 7 | 9 | 22 | 31 | 61 | 30 | R |
| 20. | Racing Club de Lens (Lens) | 38 | 7 | 8 | 23 | 32 | 61 | 29 | R |
| | | 760 | 292 | 176 | 292 | 947 | 947 | 1052 | |

Following Racing Club de Lens' disputed promotion the previous season, the club were allowed to play in Ligue 1. However, on 29th January 2015, the club's appeal was lost and it was announced that they would automatically relegated to Ligue 2 for the 2015-16 season, regardless of where the team finished in the league table.

## Top goal-scorers

| | | | |
|---|---|---|---|
| 1) | Alexandre Lacazette | (Olympique Lyonnais) | 27 |
| 2) | André-Pierre Gignac | (Olympique de Marseille) | 21 |
| 3) | Zlatan Ibrahimovic | (Paris Saint-Germain FC) | 19 |
| 4) | Edinson Cavani | (Paris Saint Germain FC) | 18 |

| **Division 2** | | **Pd** | **Wn** | **Dw** | **Ls** | **GF** | **GA** | **Pts** | |
|---|---|---|---|---|---|---|---|---|---|
| 1. | ES Troyes Aube Champagne (Troyes) | 38 | 24 | 6 | 8 | 61 | 24 | 78 | P |
| 2. | Gazélec FC Ajaccio (Ajaccio) | 38 | 18 | 11 | 9 | 49 | 37 | 65 | P |
| 3. | Angers SC de l'Ouest (Angers) | 38 | 18 | 10 | 10 | 47 | 30 | 64 | P |
| 4. | Dijon Football Côte d'Or (Dijon) | 38 | 17 | 10 | 11 | 44 | 34 | 61 | |
| 5. | AS Nancy-Lorraine (Nancy) | 38 | 15 | 13 | 10 | 53 | 39 | 58 | |
| 6. | Stade Brestois '92 (Brest) | 38 | 14 | 15 | 9 | 41 | 27 | 57 | |
| 7. | Havre AC Football Association (Le Havre) | 38 | 14 | 13 | 11 | 47 | 37 | 55 | |
| 8. | Stade Lavallois Mayenne FC (Laval) | 38 | 11 | 21 | 6 | 41 | 34 | 54 | |
| 9. | Association de la Jeunesse Auxerroise (Auxerre) | 38 | 12 | 16 | 10 | 48 | 42 | 52 | |
| 10. | FC Sochaux-Montbéliard (Montbéliard) | 38 | 13 | 13 | 12 | 39 | 37 | 52 | |
| 11. | Chamois Niortais FC (Niort) | 38 | 11 | 17 | 10 | 41 | 42 | 50 | |
| 12. | Clermont Football Auvergne (Clermont Ferrand) | 38 | 12 | 13 | 13 | 43 | 47 | 49 | |
| 13. | Nîmes Olympique (Nîmes) | 38 | 12 | 10 | 16 | 44 | 57 | 46 | |
| 14. | US de Créteil Lusitanos (Créteil) | 38 | 10 | 15 | 13 | 44 | 52 | 45 | |
| 15. | Tours FC (Tours) | 38 | 12 | 8 | 18 | 49 | 54 | 44 | |
| 16. | Valenciennes FC ( Valenciennes) | 38 | 10 | 12 | 16 | 34 | 51 | 42 | |
| 17. | AC Ajaccio (Ajaccio) | 38 | 9 | 14 | 15 | 32 | 42 | 41 | |
| 18. | Union Sportive Orléans Loiret Football (Orléans) | 38 | 9 | 13 | 16 | 36 | 47 | 40 | R |
| 19. | FC La Berrichone (Châteauroux) | 38 | 7 | 11 | 20 | 31 | 63 | 32 | R |
| 20. | AC Arles-Avignon (Avignon) | 38 | 7 | 9 | 22 | 31 | 59 | 30 | R |
| | | 760 | 255 | 250 | 255 | 855 | 855 | 1015 | |

It was initially announced that Nîmes Olympique would be relegated at the end of the season as a sanction for match fixing the previous season. However, this ruling was subsequently overturned.
AC Arles-Avignon were relegated two levels into the Championnat de France Amateur for financial reasons.

## Coupe de France Final    (Stade de France, Saint-Denis – 30/05/2015 – 80,000)

Association de la Jeunesse Auxerroise (Auxerre) **0-1**        **PARIS SAINT-GERMAIN FC (PARIS)**

*Cavani 64'*

**Auxerre**: Léon, Aguilar, Puygrenier, Fontaine, Djellabi, Mulumba (Vincent 86'), Ben Idir, Berthier (Nabab 80'), Sammaritano, Baby (Viale 82'), Diarra.

**Paris Saint-Germain**: Douchez, van der Wiel, Silva, Luiz, Maxwell, Motta, Verratti, Matuidi, Lucas (Lavezzi 73'), Cavani, Ibrahimovic.

## Semi-finals

| | | |
|---|---|---|
| Association de la Jeunesse Auxerroise (Auxerre) | 1-0 | En Avant de Guingamp (Guingamp) |
| Paris Saint-Germain FC (Paris) | 4-1 | AS de Saint-Étienne (Saint-Étienne) |

## Quarter-finals

| | | |
|---|---|---|
| US Boulogne | 1-1  (aet) – 3-4 on penalties | AS de Saint-Étienne (Saint-Étienne) |
| Paris Saint-Germain FC (Paris) | 2-0 | AS de Monaco FC (Monaco) |
| Stade Brestois '92 (Brest) | 0-0  (aet) – 2-4 on penalties | AJA Auxerroise (Auxerre) |
| US Concarnoise (Concarneau) | 1-2 | En Avant de Guingamp (Guingamp) |

# 2015/2016

| 2015/16 Division 1 | Angers SCO | SC de Bastia | Giron. Bordeaux | Stade Mal. Caen | Gazélec Ajaccio | EA Guingamp | Lille Olympique | FC Lorient B-Sud | Olymp. Lyonnais | Olymp. Marseille | AS de Monaco | Montpellier-Hér. | FC Nantes | OGC de Nice | Paris St-Germain | Stade de Reims | Stade Rennais FC | AS Saint-Étienne | Toulouse FC | ES Troyes Aube |
|---|---|---|---|---|---|---|---|---|---|---|---|---|---|---|---|---|---|---|---|---|
| Angers SC de l'Ouest | ■ | 1-0 | 1-1 | 2-0 | 0-0 | 0-0 | 2-0 | 5-1 | 0-3 | 0-1 | 3-0 | 2-3 | 0-0 | 1-1 | 0-0 | 0-0 | 0-2 | 0-0 | 2-3 | 1-0 |
| SC de Bastia | 1-0 | ■ | 1-0 | 1-0 | 1-2 | 3-0 | 1-2 | 0-0 | 1-0 | 2-1 | 1-2 | 1-0 | 0-0 | 1-3 | 0-2 | 2-0 | 2-1 | 0-1 | 3-0 | 2-0 |
| FC Girondins de Bordeaux | 1-3 | 1-1 | ■ | 1-4 | 1-1 | 1-0 | 1-0 | 3-0 | 3-1 | 1-1 | 3-1 | 0-0 | 2-0 | 0-0 | 1-1 | 1-2 | 4-0 | 1-4 | 1-1 | 1-0 |
| Stade Malherbe Caen | 0-0 | 0-0 | 1-0 | ■ | 2-0 | 2-1 | 1-2 | 1-2 | 0-4 | 1-3 | 2-2 | 2-1 | 0-2 | 2-0 | 0-3 | 0-2 | 1-0 | 1-0 | 1-0 | 2-1 |
| Gazélec Ajaccio | 0-2 | 3-2 | 2-0 | 1-0 | ■ | 0-0 | 2-4 | 1-1 | 2-1 | 1-1 | 0-1 | 0-4 | 1-1 | 3-1 | 0-4 | 2-2 | 1-1 | 0-2 | 2-2 | 2-3 |
| En Avant de Guingamp | 2-2 | 1-0 | 2-4 | 1-1 | 2-1 | ■ | 1-1 | 2-2 | 0-1 | 2-0 | 3-3 | 2-2 | 2-2 | 2-3 | 0-2 | 1-2 | 0-2 | 2-0 | 2-0 | 4-0 |
| Lille Olympique SC | 0-0 | 1-1 | 0-0 | 1-0 | 1-0 | 0-0 | ■ | 3-0 | 1-0 | 1-2 | 4-1 | 2-0 | 0-1 | 1-1 | 0-1 | 1-1 | 1-0 | 1-0 | 1-0 | 1-3 |
| FC Lorient Bretagne-Sud | 3-1 | 1-1 | 3-2 | 2-0 | 1-0 | 4-3 | 0-1 | ■ | 1-3 | 1-1 | 0-2 | 1-1 | 0-0 | 0-0 | 1-2 | 2-0 | 1-1 | 0-1 | 1-1 | 4-1 |
| Olympique Lyonnais | 0-2 | 2-0 | 3-0 | 4-1 | 2-1 | 5-1 | 0-0 | 0-0 | ■ | 1-1 | 6-1 | 2-4 | 2-0 | 1-1 | 2-1 | 1-0 | 1-2 | 3-0 | 3-0 | 4-1 |
| Olympique de Marseille | 1-2 | 4-1 | 0-0 | 0-1 | 1-1 | 0-0 | 1-1 | 1-1 | 1-1 | ■ | 3-3 | 2-2 | 1-1 | 0-1 | 1-2 | 1-0 | 2-5 | 1-1 | 1-1 | 6-0 |
| AS de Monaco FC | 1-0 | 2-0 | 1-2 | 1-1 | 2-2 | 3-2 | 0-0 | 2-3 | 1-1 | 2-1 | ■ | 2-0 | 1-0 | 0-3 | 2-2 | 1-1 | 1-0 | 4-0 | 3-1 |  |
| Montpellier-Hérault SC | 0-2 | 2-0 | 0-1 | 1-2 | 0-2 | 2-1 | 3-0 | 2-1 | 0-2 | 0-1 | 2-3 | ■ | 2-1 | 0-2 | 0-1 | 3-1 | 2-0 | 1-2 | 2-0 | 4-1 |
| FC Nantes-Atlantique | 2-0 | 0-0 | 2-2 | 1-2 | 3-1 | 1-0 | 0-3 | 2-1 | 0-0 | 0-1 | 0-0 | 0-2 | ■ | 1-0 | 1-4 | 1-0 | 0-2 | 2-1 | 1-1 | 3-0 |
| OGC de Nice | 2-1 | 0-2 | 6-1 | 2-1 | 3-0 | 0-1 | 0-0 | 2-1 | 3-0 | 1-1 | 1-2 | 1-0 | 1-2 | ■ | 0-3 | 2-0 | 3-0 | 2-0 | 1-0 | 2-1 |
| Paris Saint-Germain FC | 5-1 | 2-0 | 2-2 | 6-0 | 2-0 | 3-0 | 0-0 | 3-1 | 5-1 | 2-1 | 0-2 | 0-0 | 4-0 | 4-1 | ■ | 4-1 | 4-0 | 4-1 | 5-0 | 4-1 |
| Stade de Reims | 2-1 | 0-1 | 4-1 | 0-1 | 1-2 | 0-1 | 1-0 | 4-1 | 4-1 | 1-0 | 0-1 | 2-3 | 2-1 | 1-1 | 1-1 | ■ | 2-2 | 1-1 | 1-3 | 1-1 |
| Stade Rennais FC | 1-0 | 1-2 | 2-2 | 1-1 | 1-0 | 0-3 | 1-1 | 2-2 | 2-2 | 0-1 | 1-1 | 1-0 | 4-1 | 1-4 | 0-1 | 3-1 | ■ | 0-1 | 3-1 | 1-1 |
| AS de Saint-Étienne | 1-0 | 2-1 | 1-1 | 1-2 | 2-0 | 3-0 | 0-1 | 2-0 | 0-2 | 1-1 | 3-0 | 2-0 | 1-4 | 0-2 | 3-0 | 1-1 |  | ■ | 0-0 | 1-0 |
| Toulouse FC | 1-2 | 4-0 | 4-0 | 2-0 | 1-1 | 1-2 | 1-1 | 2-3 | 2-3 | 1-1 | 1-1 | 1-1 | 0-0 | 2-0 | 0-1 | 2-2 | 1-2 | 2-1 | ■ | 1-0 |
| ES Troyes Aube Champagne | 0-1 | 1-1 | 2-4 | 1-3 | 0-0 | 0-1 | 1-1 | 0-1 | 0-1 | 1-1 | 0-0 | 0-0 | 0-1 | 3-3 | 0-9 | 2-1 | 2-4 | 0-1 | 0-3 | ■ |

## Division 1

| | | Pd | Wn | Dw | Ls | GF | GA | Pts | |
|---|---|---|---|---|---|---|---|---|---|
| 1. | PARIS SAINT-GERMAIN FC (PARIS) | 38 | 30 | 6 | 2 | 102 | 19 | 96 | |
| 2. | Olympique Lyonnais (Lyon) | 38 | 19 | 8 | 11 | 67 | 43 | 65 | |
| 3. | AS de Monaco FC (Monaco) | 38 | 17 | 14 | 7 | 57 | 50 | 65 | |
| 4. | Olympique GC de Nice-Côte d'Azur (Nice) | 38 | 18 | 9 | 11 | 58 | 41 | 63 | |
| 5. | Lille Olympique SC Metropole (Lille) | 38 | 15 | 15 | 8 | 39 | 27 | 60 | |
| 6. | AS de Saint-Étienne (Saint-Étienne) | 38 | 17 | 7 | 14 | 42 | 37 | 58 | |
| 7. | Stade Malherbe Caen-CBN (Caen) | 38 | 16 | 6 | 16 | 39 | 52 | 54 | |
| 8. | Stade Rennais FC (Rennes) | 38 | 13 | 13 | 12 | 52 | 54 | 52 | |
| 9. | Angers SC de l'Ouest (Angers) | 38 | 13 | 11 | 14 | 40 | 38 | 50 | |
| 10. | Sporting Club de Bastia (Bastia) | 38 | 14 | 8 | 16 | 36 | 42 | 50 | |
| 11. | FC Girondins de Bordeaux (Bordeaux) | 38 | 12 | 14 | 12 | 50 | 57 | 50 | |
| 12. | Montpellier-Hérault SC (Montpellier) | 38 | 14 | 7 | 17 | 49 | 47 | 49 | |
| 13. | Olympique de Marseille (Marseille) | 38 | 10 | 18 | 10 | 48 | 42 | 48 | |
| 14. | FC Nantes-Atlantique (Nantes) | 38 | 12 | 12 | 14 | 33 | 44 | 48 | |
| 15. | FC Lorient Bretagne-Sud (Lorient) | 38 | 11 | 13 | 14 | 47 | 58 | 46 | |
| 16. | En Avant de Guingamp (Guingamp) | 38 | 11 | 11 | 16 | 47 | 56 | 44 | |
| 17. | Toulouse FC (Toulouse) | 38 | 9 | 13 | 16 | 45 | 55 | 40 | |
| 18. | Stade de Reims (Reims) | 38 | 10 | 9 | 19 | 44 | 57 | 39 | R |
| 19. | Gazélec FC Ajaccio (Ajaccio) | 38 | 8 | 13 | 17 | 37 | 58 | 37 | R |
| 20. | ES Troyes Aube Champagne (Troyes) | 38 | 3 | 9 | 26 | 28 | 83 | 18 | R |
| | | 760 | 272 | 216 | 272 | 960 | 960 | 1032 | |

Starting with this season, it was initially decided that there would be a reduction in the number of relegation places from Ligue 1 from three to two. However, this decision was appealed and overturned so at the end of the season, three teams were relegated.

## Top goal-scorers

| | | | |
|---|---|---|---|
| 1) | Zlatan Ibrahimovic | (Paris Saint-Germain FC) | 38 |
| 2) | Alexandre Lacazette | (Olympique Lyonnaise) | 21 |
| 3) | Edinson Cavani | (Paris Saint-Germain FC) | 19 |
| 4) | Michy Batshuayi | (Olympique de Marseille) | 17 |
| | Hatem Ben Arfa | (OGC de Nice) | 17 |
| | Wissam Ben Yedder | (Toulouse FC) | 17 |

## Division 2

| | | Pd | Wn | Dw | Ls | GF | GA | Pts | |
|---|---|---|---|---|---|---|---|---|---|
| 1. | AS Nancy-Lorraine (Nancy) | 38 | 21 | 11 | 6 | 60 | 32 | 74 | P |
| 2. | Dijon Football Côte d'Or (Dijon) | 38 | 20 | 10 | 8 | 62 | 36 | 70 | P |
| 3. | FC de Metz (Metz) | 38 | 19 | 8 | 11 | 54 | 39 | 65 | P |
| 4. | Havre AC Football Association (Le Havre) | 38 | 19 | 8 | 11 | 52 | 37 | 65 | |
| 5. | Red Star FC (Saint-Ouen) | 38 | 18 | 10 | 10 | 43 | 38 | 64 | |
| 6. | Racing Club de Lens (Lens) | 38 | 15 | 13 | 10 | 39 | 35 | 58 | |
| 7. | Clermont Football Auvergne (Clermont Ferrand) | 38 | 16 | 10 | 12 | 56 | 53 | 58 | |
| 8. | Association de la Jeunesse Auxerroise (Auxerre) | 38 | 15 | 10 | 13 | 47 | 46 | 55 | |
| 9. | Tours FC (Tours) | 38 | 11 | 14 | 13 | 36 | 41 | 47 | |
| 10. | Stade Brestois '92 (Brest) | 38 | 12 | 11 | 15 | 34 | 41 | 47 | |
| 11. | Football Bourg-en-Bresse Péronnas 01 (Bourg-en-Bresse) | 38 | 13 | 8 | 17 | 47 | 59 | 47 | |
| 12. | Valenciennes FC ( Valenciennes) | 38 | 10 | 14 | 14 | 39 | 43 | 44 | |
| 13. | Stade Lavallois Mayenne FC (Laval) | 38 | 9 | 17 | 12 | 35 | 42 | 44 | |
| 14. | Nîmes Olympique (Nîmes) | 38 | 13 | 12 | 13 | 50 | 52 | 43 | -8 |
| 15. | FC Sochaux-Montbéliard (Montbéliard) | 38 | 9 | 15 | 14 | 34 | 36 | 42 | |
| 16. | Chamois Niortais FC (Niort) | 38 | 8 | 18 | 12 | 38 | 45 | 42 | |
| 17. | AC Ajaccio (Ajaccio) | 38 | 9 | 15 | 14 | 34 | 42 | 42 | |
| 18. | Évian Thonon Gaillard FC (Gaillard) | 38 | 9 | 12 | 17 | 41 | 41 | 39 | R |
| 19. | US de Créteil Lusitanos (Créteil) | 38 | 8 | 10 | 20 | 42 | 66 | 34 | R |
| 20. | Paris FC (Paris) | 38 | 4 | 18 | 16 | 32 | 51 | 30 | R |
| | | 760 | 258 | 244 | 258 | 875 | 875 | 1010 | (-8) |

Nîmes Olympique had 8 points deducted following match fixing during the 2013-14 season.
Évian Thonon Gaillard FC were demoted two levels due to financial difficulties.

## Coupe de France Final    (Stade de France, Saint-Denis – 21/05/2016 – 80,000)

Olympique de Marseille (Marseille)    **2-4**    **PARIS SAINT-GERMAIN FC (PARIS)**
*Thauvin 12', Batshuayi 87'*    *Matuidi 2', Ibrahimovic 47' pen, 82', Cavani 57'*

**Marseille:** Mandanda, Manquillo, Nkoulou, Rekik, Mendy, Thauvin (Nkoudou 81'), Isla, Diarra, Barrada (Dja Djédjé 70'), Batshuayi, Fletcher (Cabella 60').

**Paris Saint-Germain:** Sirigu, Aurier, Marquinhos, Silva, Maxwell, Matuidi, Stambouli (Luiz 75'), Rabiot, Di María, Cavani (Lucas 75'), Ibrahimovic (Kurzawa 90').

## Semi-finals

| | | |
|---|---|---|
| FC Lorient Bretagne-Sud (Lorient) | 0-1 | Paris Saint-Germain FC (Paris) |
| FC Sochaux-Montbéliard (Montbéliard) | 0-1 | Olympique de Marseille (Marseille) |

## Quarter-finals

| | | |
|---|---|---|
| FC Lorient Bretagne-Sud (Lorient) | 3-0 | Gazélec FC Ajaccio (Ajaccio) |
| FC Sochaux-Montbéliard (Montbéliard) | 3-2 (aet) | FC Nantes-Atlantique (Nantes) |
| AS de Saint-Étienne (Saint-Étienne) | 1-3 | Paris Saint-Germain FC (Paris) |
| US Granville (Granville) | 0-1 | Olympique de Marseille (Marseille) |

# 2016/2017

| 2016/17 Division 1 | Angers SC | SC de Bastia | Giron. Bordeaux | Stade Mal. Caen | Dijon FCO | EA Guingamp | Lille Olympique | FC Lorient B-Sud | Olymp. Lyonnais | Olymp. Marseille | FC de Metz | AS de Monaco | Montpellier-Hér. | AS Nancy | FC Nantes | OGC de Nice | Paris St-Germain | Stade Rennais FC | AS Saint-Étienne | Toulouse FC |
|---|---|---|---|---|---|---|---|---|---|---|---|---|---|---|---|---|---|---|---|---|
| Angers SC de l'Ouest | ■ | 3-0 | 1-1 | 2-1 | 3-1 | 3-0 | 1-0 | 2-2 | 1-2 | 1-1 | 2-1 | 0-1 | 2-0 | 1-0 | 0-2 | 0-1 | 0-2 | 0-0 | 1-3 | 0-0 |
| SC de Bastia | 1-2 | ■ | 1-1 | 1-1 | 0-0 | 1-0 | 0-1 | 2-0 | 0-3 | 1-2 | 2-0 | 1-1 | 1-1 | 0-0 | 2-2 | 1-1 | 0-1 | 1-0 | 0-0 | 2-1 |
| FC Girondins de Bordeaux | 0-1 | 2-0 | ■ | 0-0 | 3-2 | 3-0 | 0-1 | 2-1 | 1-1 | 1-1 | 3-0 | 0-4 | 5-1 | 1-1 | 1-0 | 0-0 | 0-3 | 1-1 | 3-2 | 1-0 |
| Stade Malherbe Caen | 2-3 | 2-0 | 0-4 | ■ | 3-3 | 1-1 | 0-1 | 3-2 | 3-2 | 1-5 | 3-0 | 0-3 | 0-2 | 1-0 | 0-2 | 1-0 | 0-6 | 0-1 | 0-2 | 1-0 |
| Dijon Football Côte d'Or | 3-2 | 1-2 | 0-0 | 2-0 | ■ | 3-3 | 0-0 | 1-0 | 4-2 | 1-2 | 0-0 | 1-1 | 3-3 | 2-0 | 0-1 | 0-1 | 1-3 | 3-0 | 0-1 | 2-0 |
| En Avant de Guingamp | 1-0 | 5-0 | 1-1 | 0-1 | 4-0 | ■ | 1-0 | 1-0 | 2-1 | 2-1 | 1-0 | 1-2 | 1-1 | 1-0 | 2-0 | 0-1 | 2-1 | 1-1 | 0-2 | 2-1 |
| Lille Olympique SC | 1-2 | 2-1 | 2-3 | 4-2 | 1-0 | 3-0 | ■ | 0-1 | 0-1 | 0-0 | 0-2 | 1-4 | 2-1 | 1-0 | 3-0 | 1-2 | 0-1 | 1-1 | 1-1 | 1-2 |
| FC Lorient Bretagne-Sud | 1-1 | 0-3 | 1-1 | 1-0 | 2-3 | 3-1 | 1-0 | ■ | 1-0 | 1-4 | 5-1 | 0-3 | 2-2 | 0-2 | 1-2 | 0-1 | 1-2 | 2-1 | 2-1 | 1-1 |
| Olympique Lyonnais | 2-0 | 2-1 | 1-3 | 2-0 | 4-2 | 1-3 | 1-2 | 1-4 | ■ | 3-1 | 5-0 | 1-2 | 5-1 | 4-0 | 3-2 | 3-3 | 1-2 | 1-0 | 2-0 | 4-0 |
| Olympique de Marseille | 3-0 | 1-0 | 0-0 | 1-1 | 1-2 | 2-0 | 2-0 | 2-0 | 0-0 | ■ | 1-0 | 1-4 | 5-1 | 3-0 | 2-1 | 2-1 | 1-5 | 2-0 | 4-0 | 0-0 |
| FC de Metz | 2-0 | 1-0 | 0-3 | 2-2 | 2-1 | 2-2 | 3-2 | 3-3 | 0-3 | 1-0 | ■ | 0-7 | 2-0 | 2-1 | 1-1 | 2-4 | 2-3 | 1-1 | 0-0 | 1-1 |
| AS de Monaco FC | 2-1 | 5-0 | 2-1 | 2-1 | 2-1 | 2-2 | 4-0 | 4-0 | 1-3 | 4-0 | 5-0 | ■ | 6-2 | 6-0 | 4-0 | 3-0 | 3-1 | 3-0 | 2-0 | 3-1 |
| Montpellier-Hérault SC | 1-0 | 2-1 | 4-0 | 3-2 | 1-1 | 1-1 | 0-3 | 2-0 | 1-3 | 3-1 | 0-1 | 1-2 | ■ | 0-0 | 2-3 | 1-1 | 3-0 | 1-1 | 2-0 | 0-1 |
| AS Nancy-Lorraine | 2-0 | 1-0 | 0-2 | 2-0 | 1-0 | 0-2 | 1-2 | 2-3 | 0-0 | 4-0 | 0-3 | 0-3 |  | ■ | 1-1 | 1-0 | 1-2 | 3-0 | 3-1 | 0-0 |
| FC Nantes-Atlantique | 2-1 | 1-0 | 0-1 | 1-0 | 3-1 | 4-1 | 0-0 | 1-0 | 0-6 | 3-2 | 0-3 | 0-1 | 1-0 | 0-2 | ■ | 1-1 | 0-2 | 1-2 | 0-0 | 1-1 |
| OGC de Nice | 0-2 | 1-1 | 2-1 | 2-2 | 2-1 | 3-1 | 1-1 | 2-1 | 2-0 | 3-2 | 0-0 | 4-0 | 2-1 | 3-1 | 4-1 | ■ | 3-1 | 1-0 | 1-0 | 3-0 |
| Paris Saint-Germain FC | 2-0 | 5-0 | 2-0 | 1-1 | 3-0 | 4-0 | 2-1 | 5-0 | 2-1 | 2-0 | 3-0 | 1-1 | 2-0 | 1-0 | 2-0 | 2-2 | ■ | 4-0 | 1-1 | 0-0 |
| Stade Rennais FC | 1-1 | 1-2 | 1-1 | 2-0 | 1-1 | 1-0 | 2-0 | 1-0 | 1-1 | 3-2 | 1-1 | 2-3 | 1-0 | 2-0 | 1-1 | 2-2 | 0-1 | ■ | 2-0 | 1-1 |
| AS de Saint-Étienne | 2-1 | 1-0 | 2-2 | 0-1 | 1-1 | 1-0 | 3-1 | 4-0 | 2-0 | 0-0 | 2-2 | 1-1 | 3-1 | 0-0 | 1-1 | 0-1 | 0-5 | 1-1 | ■ | 0-0 |
| Toulouse FC | 4-0 | 4-1 | 4-1 | 0-1 | 0-0 | 2-1 | 1-1 | 3-2 | 1-2 | 0-0 | 1-2 | 3-1 | 1-0 | 1-1 | 0-1 | 1-1 | 2-0 | 0-0 | 0-3 | ■ |

## Division 1

| | | Pd | Wn | Dw | Ls | GF | GA | Pts | |
|---|---|---|---|---|---|---|---|---|---|
| 1. | AS DE MONACO FC (MONACO) | 38 | 30 | 5 | 3 | 107 | 31 | 95 | |
| 2. | Paris Saint-Germain FC (Paris) | 38 | 27 | 6 | 5 | 83 | 27 | 87 | |
| 3. | Olympique GC de Nice-Côte d'Azur (Nice) | 38 | 22 | 12 | 4 | 63 | 36 | 78 | |
| 4. | Olympique Lyonnais (Lyon) | 38 | 21 | 4 | 13 | 77 | 48 | 67 | |
| 5. | Olympique de Marseille (Marseille) | 38 | 17 | 11 | 10 | 57 | 41 | 62 | |
| 6. | FC Girondins de Bordeaux (Bordeaux) | 38 | 15 | 14 | 9 | 53 | 43 | 59 | |
| 7 | FC Nantes-Atlantique (Nantes) | 38 | 14 | 9 | 15 | 40 | 54 | 51 | |
| 8. | AS de Saint-Étienne (Saint-Étienne) | 38 | 12 | 14 | 12 | 41 | 42 | 50 | |
| 9. | Stade Rennais FC (Rennes) | 38 | 12 | 14 | 12 | 36 | 42 | 50 | |
| 10. | En Avant de Guingamp (Guingamp) | 38 | 14 | 8 | 16 | 46 | 53 | 50 | |
| 11. | Lille Olympique SC Metropole (Lille) | 38 | 13 | 7 | 18 | 40 | 47 | 46 | |
| 12. | Angers SC de l'Ouest (Angers) | 38 | 13 | 7 | 18 | 40 | 49 | 46 | |
| 13. | Toulouse FC (Toulouse) | 38 | 10 | 14 | 14 | 37 | 41 | 44 | |
| 14. | FC de Metz (Metz) | 38 | 11 | 10 | 17 | 39 | 72 | 43 | |
| 15. | Montpellier-Hérault SC (Montpellier) | 38 | 10 | 9 | 19 | 48 | 66 | 39 | |
| 16. | Dijon Football Côte d'Or (Dijon) | 38 | 8 | 13 | 17 | 46 | 58 | 37 | |
| 17. | Stade Malherbe Caen-CBN (Caen) | 38 | 10 | 7 | 21 | 36 | 65 | 37 | |
| 18. | FC Lorient Bretagne-Sud (Lorient) | 38 | 10 | 6 | 22 | 44 | 70 | 36 | POR |
| 19. | AS Nancy-Lorraine (Nancy) | 38 | 9 | 8 | 21 | 29 | 52 | 35 | R |
| 20. | Sporting Club de Bastia (Bastia) | 38 | 8 | 10 | 20 | 29 | 54 | 34 | R |
| | | 760 | 286 | 188 | 286 | 991 | 991 | 1046 | |

The game between Sporting Club de Bastia and Olympique Lyonnais was abandoned at half-time (when the scoreline was 0-0) after Bastia fans invaded the pitch and attacked the Lyon players. The match was duly awarded 3-0 to Lyon.

After being relegated to Ligue 2, Sporting Club de Bastia were relegated another division to the Championnat National due to financial difficulties. However, the French Football Federation subsequently announced that Bastia were denied entry to this division and the club took the place of its reserve team in the Championnat National 3 (the 5th tier).

## Top goal-scorers

| | | | |
|---|---|---|---|
| 1) | Edinson Cavani | (Paris Saint-Germain FC) | 35 |
| 2) | Alexandre Lacazette | (Olympique Lyonnais) | 28 |
| 3) | Radamel Falcao | (AS de Monaco FC) | 21 |
| 4) | Bafétimbi Gomis | (Olympique de Marseille) | 20 |
| 5) | Mario Balotelli | (OGC de Nice) | 15 |
| | Kylian Mbappé | (AS de Monaco FC) | 15 |
| | Ivan Santini | (Stade Malherbe Caen) | 15 |
| | Florian Thauvin | (Olympique de Marseille) | 15 |

## Promotion/Relegation play-off

The 18th placed Ligue 1 team, FC Lorient Bretagne-Sud (Lorient), played the 3rd placed Ligue 2 team, ES Troyes Aube Champagne, to decide promotion or relegation:

| | | |
|---|---|---|
| ES Troyes Aube Champagne (Troyes) | 2-1 | FC Lorient Bretagne-Sud (Lorient) |
| FC Lorient Bretagne-Sud (Lorient) | 0-0 | ES Troyes Aube Champagne (Troyes) |

ES Troyes Aube Champagne won 2-1 on aggregate to win promotion to Ligue 1.
FC Lorient Bretagne-Sud were relegated to Ligue 2.

## Division 2

| | | Pd | Wn | Dw | Ls | GF | GA | Pts | |
|---|---|---|---|---|---|---|---|---|---|
| 1. | Racing Club de Strasbourg Football (Strasbourg) | 38 | 19 | 10 | 9 | 63 | 47 | 67 | P |
| 2. | Amiens SC Football (Amiens) | 38 | 19 | 9 | 10 | 56 | 38 | 66 | P |
| 3. | ES Troyes Aube Champagne (Troyes) | 38 | 19 | 9 | 10 | 59 | 43 | 66 | POP |
| 4. | Racing Club de Lens (Lens) | 38 | 18 | 11 | 9 | 59 | 40 | 65 | |
| 5. | Stade Brestois '92 (Brest) | 38 | 19 | 8 | 11 | 58 | 44 | 65 | |
| 6. | Nîmes Olympique (Nîmes) | 38 | 17 | 13 | 8 | 58 | 40 | 64 | |
| 7. | Stade de Reims (Reims) | 38 | 14 | 13 | 11 | 42 | 39 | 55 | |
| 8. | Havre AC Football Association (Le Havre) | 38 | 14 | 12 | 12 | 39 | 31 | 54 | |
| 9. | Gazélec FC Ajaccio (Ajaccio) | 38 | 13 | 12 | 13 | 47 | 51 | 51 | |
| 10. | Chamois Niortais FC (Niort) | 38 | 12 | 13 | 13 | 45 | 57 | 49 | |
| 11. | AC Ajaccio (Ajaccio) | 38 | 13 | 9 | 16 | 47 | 58 | 48 | |
| 12. | Clermont Football Auvergne (Clermont Ferrand) Foot | 38 | 11 | 13 | 14 | 46 | 48 | 46 | |
| 13. | FC Sochaux-Montbéliard (Montbéliard) | 38 | 11 | 13 | 14 | 38 | 43 | 46 | |
| 14. | Valenciennes FC ( Valenciennes) | 38 | 10 | 15 | 13 | 44 | 44 | 45 | |
| 15. | Football Bourg-en-Bresse Péronnas 01 (Bourg-en-Bresse) | 38 | 11 | 11 | 16 | 49 | 58 | 44 | |
| 16. | Tours FC (Tours) | 38 | 10 | 13 | 15 | 55 | 60 | 43 | |
| 17. | Association de la Jeunesse Auxerroise (Auxerre) | 38 | 11 | 10 | 17 | 28 | 40 | 43 | |
| 18. | Union Sportive Orléans Loiret Football (Orléans) | 38 | 11 | 9 | 18 | 41 | 54 | 38 | -4 |
| 19. | Red Star FC (Saint-Ouen) | 38 | 8 | 12 | 18 | 36 | 56 | 36 | R |
| 20. | Stade Lavallois Mayenne FC (Laval) | 38 | 5 | 15 | 18 | 33 | 52 | 30 | R |
| | | 760 | 265 | 230 | 265 | 943 | 943 | 1021 | (-4) |

Union Sportive Orléans Loiret Football had 4 points deducted after failing to comply with financial reporting obligations.

## Promotion/Relegation play-off

The 18th placed Ligue 2 team, Union Sportive Orléans Loiret Football, played the 3rd placed Championnat National team, Paris FC, to decide the final promotion/relegation spot:

| | | |
|---|---|---|
| Paris FC (Paris) | 0-1 | Union Sportive Orléans Loiret Football (Orléans) |
| Union Sportive Orléans Loiret Football (Orléans) | 1-0 | Paris FC (Paris) |

Union Sportive Orléans Loiret Football won 2-0 on aggregate to retain their place in Ligue 2.
However, Paris FC were also subsequently promoted to take the vacant place caused following the relegation of Sporting Club de Bastia from Ligue 1.


## Coupe de France Final   (Stade de France, Saint-Denis – 27/05/2017 – 78,000)

| | | |
|---|---|---|
| Angers SC de l'Ouest (Angers) | **0-1** | **PARIS SAINT-GERMAIN FC (PARIS)** |

*Cissokho 90+1' (o.g.)*

**Angers**:  Letellier, Cissokho, Traoré, Thomas, Manceau, N'Doye, Santamaria (Bérigaud 90+2'), Mangani, Pépé (Tait 84'), Diedhiou (Bamba 63'), Ekambi.

**Paris Saint-Germain**:  Areola, Aurier, Marquinhos, Silva, Maxwell, Verratti, Motta, Matuidi, Di María, Cavani, Draxler (Pastore 72').

## Semi-finals

| | | |
|---|---|---|
| Angers SC de l'Ouest (Angers) | 2-0 | En Avant de Guingamp (Guingamp) |
| Paris Saint-Germain FC (Paris) | 5-0 | AS de Monaco FC (Monaco) |

## Quarter-finals

| | | |
|---|---|---|
| Angers SC de l'Ouest (Angers) | 2-1 | FC Girondins de Bordeaux (Bordeaux) |
| US Avranches Mont Saint Michel (Avranches) | 0-4 | Paris Saint-Germain FC (Paris) |
| AS de Monaco FC (Monaco) | 2-1 | Lille Olympique SC Metropole (Lille) |
| Étoile Football Club Fréjus Saint-Raphaël (Fréjus) | 0-1 | En Avant de Guingamp (Guingamp) |

# 2017/2018

| 2017/18 Division 1 | Amiens SC | Angers SCO | Giron. Bordeaux | Stade Mal. Caen | Dijon FCO | EA Guingamp | Lille Olympique | Olymp. Lyonnais | Olymp. Marseille | FC de Metz | AS de Monaco | Montpellier-Hér. | FC Nantes | OGC de Nice | Paris St-Germain | Stade Rennais FC | AS Saint-Étienne | RC Strasbourg | Toulouse FC | ES Troyes Aube |
|---|---|---|---|---|---|---|---|---|---|---|---|---|---|---|---|---|---|---|---|---|
| Amiens SC Football | ■ | 0-2 | 1-0 | 3-0 | 2-1 | 3-1 | 3-0 | 1-2 | 0-2 | 2-0 | 1-1 | 1-1 | 0-1 | 3-0 | 2-2 | 0-2 | 0-2 | 3-1 | 0-0 | 1-1 |
| Angers SC de L'Ouest | 1-0 | ■ | 2-2 | 3-0 | 2-1 | 3-0 | 1-1 | 3-3 | 1-1 | 0-1 | 0-4 | 1-1 | 0-2 | 1-1 | 0-5 | 1-2 | 0-1 | 1-1 | 0-1 | 3-1 |
| FC Girondins de Bordeaux | 3-2 | 0-0 | ■ | 0-2 | 3-1 | 3-1 | 2-1 | 3-1 | 1-1 | 2-0 | 0-2 | 0-2 | 1-1 | 0-0 | 0-1 | 0-2 | 3-0 | 0-3 | 4-2 | 2-1 |
| Stade Malherbe Caen | 1-0 | 0-2 | 1-0 | ■ | 2-1 | 0-0 | 0-1 | 1-2 | 0-2 | 1-0 | 1-2 | 1-3 | 3-2 | 1-1 | 0-0 | 2-2 | 0-1 | 2-0 | 0-0 | 1-0 |
| Dijon Football Côte d'Or | 1-1 | 2-1 | 3-2 | 2-0 | ■ | 3-1 | 3-0 | 2-5 | 1-3 | 1-1 | 1-4 | 2-1 | 1-0 | 3-2 | 1-2 | 2-1 | 0-1 | 1-1 | 3-1 | 3-1 |
| En Avant de Guingamp | 1-1 | 1-1 | 2-1 | 0-0 | 4-0 | ■ | 1-0 | 0-2 | 3-3 | 2-2 | 3-1 | 0-0 | 0-3 | 2-5 | 0-3 | 2-0 | 2-1 | 2-0 | 1-1 | 4-0 |
| Lille Olympique SC | 0-1 | 1-2 | 0-0 | 0-2 | 2-1 | 2-2 | ■ | 2-2 | 0-1 | 3-1 | 0-4 | 1-1 | 3-0 | 1-1 | 0-3 | 1-2 | 3-1 | 2-1 | 1-0 | 2-2 |
| Olympique Lyonnais | 3-0 | 1-1 | 3-3 | 1-0 | 3-3 | 2-1 | 1-2 | ■ | 2-0 | 2-0 | 3-2 | 0-0 | 2-0 | 3-2 | 2-1 | 0-2 | 1-1 | 4-0 | 2-0 | 3-0 |
| Olympique de Marseille | 2-1 | 1-1 | 1-0 | 5-0 | 3-0 | 1-0 | 5-1 | 2-3 | ■ | 6-3 | 2-2 | 0-0 | 1-1 | 2-1 | 2-2 | 1-3 | 3-0 | 2-0 | 2-0 | 3-1 |
| FC de Metz | 0-2 | 1-2 | 0-4 | 1-1 | 1-2 | 1-3 | 0-3 | 0-5 | 0-3 | ■ | 0-1 | 0-1 | 1-1 | 2-1 | 1-5 | 1-1 | 3-0 | 3-0 | 1-1 | 0-1 |
| AS de Monaco FC | 0-0 | 1-0 | 2-1 | 2-0 | 4-0 | 6-0 | 2-1 | 3-2 | 6-1 | 3-1 | ■ | 1-1 | 2-1 | 2-2 | 1-2 | 2-1 | 1-0 | 3-0 | 3-2 | 3-2 |
| Montpellier-Hérault SC | 1-1 | 2-1 | 1-3 | 1-0 | 2-2 | 1-1 | 3-0 | 1-1 | 1-1 | 1-3 | 0-0 | ■ | 0-1 | 2-0 | 0-0 | 0-1 | 0-1 | 1-1 | 2-1 | 1-1 |
| FC Nantes-Atlantique | 0-1 | 1-0 | 0-1 | 1-0 | 1-1 | 2-1 | 2-2 | 0-0 | 0-1 | 1-0 | 1-0 | 0-2 | ■ | 1-2 | 0-1 | 1-1 | 0-3 | 1-0 | 2-1 | 1-0 |
| OGC de Nice | 1-0 | 2-2 | 1-0 | 4-1 | 1-0 | 2-0 | 2-1 | 0-5 | 2-4 | 3-1 | 4-0 | 1-0 | 1-1 | ■ | 1-2 | 1-1 | 1-0 | 1-2 | 0-1 | 1-2 |
| Paris Saint-Germain FC | 2-0 | 2-1 | 6-2 | 3-1 | 8-0 | 2-2 | 2-1 | 2-0 | 3-0 | 5-0 | 7-1 | 4-0 | 4-1 | 3-0 | ■ | 0-2 | 3-0 | 5-2 | 6-2 | 2-0 |
| Stade Rennais FC | 2-0 | 1-0 | 1-0 | 0-1 | 2-2 | 0-1 | 1-0 | 1-2 | 0-3 | 1-2 | 1-1 | 1-1 | 2-1 | 0-1 | 1-4 | ■ | 1-1 | 2-1 | 2-1 | 2-0 |
| AS de Saint-Étienne | 3-0 | 1-1 | 1-3 | 2-1 | 2-2 | 2-0 | 5-0 | 0-5 | 2-2 | 3-1 | 0-4 | 0-1 | 1-1 | 1-0 | 1-1 | 2-2 | ■ | 2-2 | 2-0 | 2-1 |
| Racing Club de Strasbourg | 0-1 | 2-2 | 0-2 | 0-0 | 3-2 | 0-2 | 3-0 | 3-2 | 3-3 | 2-2 | 1-3 | 0-0 | 1-2 | 1-1 | 2-1 | 2-1 | 0-1 | ■ | 2-1 | 2-1 |
| Toulouse FC | 1-0 | 2-0 | 0-1 | 2-0 | 0-1 | 2-1 | 2-3 | 1-2 | 1-2 | 0-0 | 3-3 | 1-0 | 1-1 | 1-2 | 0-1 | 3-2 | 0-0 | 2-2 | ■ | 1-0 |
| ES Troyes Aube Champagne | 1-0 | 3-0 | 0-1 | 3-1 | 0-0 | 0-1 | 1-0 | 0-5 | 2-3 | 1-0 | 0-3 | 0-1 | 0-1 | 0-2 | 0-2 | 1-1 | 2-1 | 3-0 | 0-0 | ■ |

## Division 1

| | | Pd | Wn | Dw | Ls | GF | GA | Pts | |
|---|---|---|---|---|---|---|---|---|---|
| 1. | PARIS SAINT-GERMAIN FC (PARIS) | 38 | 29 | 6 | 3 | 108 | 29 | 93 | |
| 2. | AS de Monaco FC (Monaco) | 38 | 24 | 8 | 6 | 85 | 45 | 80 | |
| 3. | Olympique Lyonnais (Lyon) | 38 | 23 | 9 | 6 | 87 | 43 | 78 | |
| 4. | Olympique de Marseille (Marseille) | 38 | 22 | 11 | 5 | 80 | 47 | 77 | |
| 5. | Stade Rennais FC (Rennes) | 38 | 16 | 10 | 12 | 50 | 44 | 58 | |
| 6. | FC Girondins de Bordeaux (Bordeaux) | 38 | 16 | 7 | 15 | 53 | 48 | 55 | |
| 7. | AS de Saint-Étienne (Saint-Étienne) | 38 | 15 | 10 | 13 | 47 | 50 | 55 | |
| 8. | Olympique GC de Nice-Côte d'Azur (Nice) | 38 | 15 | 9 | 14 | 53 | 52 | 54 | |
| 9. | FC Nantes-Atlantique (Nantes) | 38 | 14 | 10 | 14 | 36 | 41 | 52 | |
| 10. | Montpellier-Hérault SC (Montpellier) | 38 | 11 | 18 | 9 | 36 | 33 | 51 | |
| 11. | Dijon Football Côte d'Or (Dijon) | 38 | 13 | 9 | 16 | 55 | 73 | 48 | |
| 12. | En Avant de Guingamp (Guingamp) | 38 | 12 | 11 | 15 | 48 | 59 | 47 | |
| 13. | Amiens SC Football (Amiens) | 38 | 12 | 9 | 17 | 37 | 42 | 45 | |
| 14. | Angers SC de l'Ouest (Angers) | 38 | 9 | 14 | 15 | 42 | 52 | 41 | |
| 15. | Racing Club de Strasbourg Football (Strasbourg) | 38 | 9 | 11 | 18 | 44 | 67 | 38 | |
| 16. | Stade Malherbe Caen-CBN (Caen) | 38 | 10 | 8 | 20 | 27 | 52 | 38 | |
| 17. | Lille Olympique SC Metropole (Lille) | 38 | 10 | 8 | 20 | 41 | 67 | 38 | |
| 18. | Toulouse FC (Toulouse) | 38 | 9 | 10 | 19 | 38 | 54 | 37 | PO |
| 19. | ES Troyes Aube Champagne (Troyes) | 38 | 9 | 6 | 23 | 32 | 59 | 33 | R |
| 20. | FC de Metz (Metz) | 38 | 6 | 8 | 24 | 34 | 76 | 26 | R |
| | | 760 | 284 | 192 | 284 | 1033 | 1033 | 1044 | |

## Top goal-scorers

| | | | |
|---|---|---|---|
| 1) | Edinson Cavani | (Paris Saint-Germain FC) | 28 |
| 2) | Florian Thauvin | (Olympique de Marseille) | 22 |
| 3) | Memphis Depay | (Olympique Lyonnais) | 19 |
| | Neymar | (Paris Saint-Germain FC) | 19 |
| 5) | Mario Balotelli | (OGC de Nice) | 18 |
| | Radamel Falcao | (AS de Monaco FC) | 18 |
| | Nabil Fekir | (Olympique Lyonnais) | 18 |
| | Mariano Díaz | (Olympique Lyonnais) | 18 |

## Promotion/Relegation play-offs

A play-off competition to decide promotion or relegation was held at the end of the season. This involved the 3rd, 4th and 5th-placed teams in Ligue 2, and the 18th-placed team in Ligue 1.

## Final

| | | |
|---|---|---|
| AC Ajaccio (Ajaccio) | 0-3 | Toulouse FC (Toulouse) |
| Toulouse FC (Toulouse) | 1-0 | AC Ajaccio (Ajaccio) |

Toulouse FC won 4-0 on aggregate to retain their place in Ligue 1.

## Semi-final

| | | |
|---|---|---|
| AC Ajaccio (Ajaccio) | 2-2 (aet) | Havre AC Football Association (Le Havre) |

(AC Ajaccio won 5-3 on penalties)

## Quarter-final

| | | |
|---|---|---|
| Havre AC Football Association (Le Havre) | 2-0 | Stade Brestois '92 (Brest) |

| __Division 2__ | __Pd__ | __Wn__ | __Dw__ | __Ls__ | __GF__ | __GA__ | __Pts__ | |
|---|---|---|---|---|---|---|---|---|
| 1. Stade de Reims (Reims) | 38 | 28 | 4 | 6 | 74 | 24 | 88 | P |
| 2. Nîmes Olympique (Nîmes) | 38 | 22 | 7 | 9 | 75 | 37 | 73 | P |
| 3. AC Ajaccio (Ajaccio) | 38 | 20 | 8 | 10 | 62 | 43 | 68 | PO |
| 4. Havre AC Football Association (Le Havre) | 38 | 19 | 9 | 10 | 53 | 34 | 66 | PO |
| 5. Stade Brestois '92 (Brest) | 38 | 18 | 11 | 9 | 58 | 43 | 65 | PO |
| 6. Clermont Football Auvergne (Clermont Ferrand) | 38 | 17 | 12 | 9 | 54 | 36 | 63 | |
| 7. FC Lorient Bretagne-Sud (Lorient) | 38 | 18 | 8 | 12 | 61 | 46 | 62 | |
| 8. Paris FC (Paris) | 38 | 16 | 13 | 9 | 46 | 36 | 61 | |
| 9. FC La Berrichone (Châteauroux) | 38 | 17 | 9 | 12 | 50 | 50 | 60 | |
| 10. FC Sochaux-Montbéliard (Montbéliard) | 38 | 15 | 8 | 15 | 51 | 62 | 53 | |
| 11. Association de la Jeunesse Auxerroise (Auxerre) | 38 | 13 | 8 | 17 | 51 | 55 | 47 | |
| 12. Union Sportive Orléans Loiret Football (Orléans) | 38 | 12 | 10 | 16 | 52 | 61 | 46 | |
| 13. Valenciennes FC ( Valenciennes) | 38 | 12 | 9 | 17 | 50 | 64 | 45 | |
| 14. Racing Club de Lens (Lens) | 38 | 11 | 10 | 17 | 48 | 49 | 43 | |
| 15. Chamois Niortais FC (Niort) | 38 | 11 | 9 | 18 | 47 | 60 | 42 | |
| 16. Gazélec FC Ajaccio (Ajaccio) | 38 | 11 | 8 | 19 | 35 | 60 | 41 | |
| 17. AS Nancy-Lorraine (Nancy) | 38 | 9 | 11 | 18 | 39 | 54 | 38 | |
| 18. Football Bourg-en-Bresse Péronnas 01 (Bourg-en-Bresse) | 38 | 10 | 6 | 22 | 50 | 87 | 36 | POR |
| 19. US Quevilly-Rouen Métropole (Le Petit-Quevilly) | 38 | 9 | 6 | 23 | 45 | 66 | 33 | R |
| 20. Tours FC (Tours) | 38 | 5 | 8 | 25 | 34 | 68 | 23 | R |
| | 760 | 293 | 174 | 293 | 1035 | 1035 | 1053 | |

## Promotion/Relegation play-off

The 18th placed Ligue 2 team played the 3rd placed Championnat National team to decide the final promotion/relegation spot:

| | | |
|---|---|---|
| Grenoble Foot 38 (Grenoble) | 2-1 | Football Bourg-en-Bresse Péronnas 01 |
| Football Bourg-en-Bresse Péronnas 01 | 0-0 | Grenoble Foot 38 (Grenoble) |

Grenoble Foot 38 won 2-1 on aggregate and were promoted to Ligue 2.
Football Bourg-en-Bresse Péronnas 01 were relegated to the Championnat National.

## Coupe de France Final   (Stade de France, Saint-Denis – 08/05/2018 – 73,772)

| | | |
|---|---|---|
| Vendée Les Herbiers Football (Les Herbiers) | **0-2** | **PARIS SAINT-GERMAIN FC (PARIS)** |

*Lo Celso 26', Cavani 74' pen*

**Les Herbiers**: Pichot, Marie, Fofana, Dequaire, Pagerie, Vanbaleghem (Dabasse 62'), Bongongui, Flochon, Germann (Gboho 63'), Eickmayer (Couturier 88').
**Paris Saint-Germain**: Trapp, Dani Alves (Meunier 86'), Silva, Marquinhos, Berchiche, Lo Celso, Motta (Draxler 68'), Rabiot, Mbappé (Pastore 86'), Cavani, Di María.

## Semi-finals

| | | |
|---|---|---|
| Vendée Les Herbiers Football (Les Herbiers) | 2-0 | FC Chambly Oise (Chambly) |
| Stade Malherbe Caen-CBN (Caen) | 1-3 | Paris Saint-Germain FC (Paris) |

## Quarter-finals

| | | |
|---|---|---|
| FC Chambly Oise (Chambly) | 1-0 | Racing Club de Strasbourg Football (Strasbourg) |
| Paris Saint-Germain FC (Paris) | 3-0 | Olympique de Marseille (Marseille) |
| Vendée Les Herbiers Football (Les Herbiers) | 0-0  (aet) | Racing Club de Lens (Lens) |
| | (Les Herbiers Football won 4-2 on penalties) | |
| Stade Malherbe Caen-CBN (Caen) | 1-0 | Olympique Lyonnais (Lyon) |

# 2018/2019

| 2018/19 Division 1 | Amiens SC | Angers SCO | Giron. Bordeaux | Stade Mal. Caen | Dijon FCO | EA Guingamp | Lille Olympique | Olymp. Lyonnais | Olymp. Marseille | AS de Monaco | Montpellier-Hér | FC Nantes | OGC de Nice | Nîmes Olymp. | Paris St-Germain | Stade de Reims | Stade Rennais FC | AS Saint-Étienne | RC Strasbourg | Toulouse FC |
|---|---|---|---|---|---|---|---|---|---|---|---|---|---|---|---|---|---|---|---|---|
| Amiens SC Football | ■ | 0-0 | 0-0 | 1-0 | 1-0 | 2-1 | 2-3 | 0-1 | 1-3 | 0-2 | 1-2 | 1-2 | 1-0 | 2-1 | 0-3 | 4-1 | 2-1 | 2-2 | 0-0 | 0-0 |
| Angers SC de l'Ouest | 0-0 | ■ | 1-2 | 1-1 | 1-0 | 0-1 | 1-0 | 1-2 | 1-1 | 2-2 | 1-0 | 1-0 | 3-0 | 3-4 | 1-2 | 1-1 | 3-3 | 1-1 | 2-2 | 0-0 |
| FC Girondins de Bordeaux | 1-1 | 0-1 | ■ | 0-0 | 1-0 | 0-0 | 1-0 | 2-3 | 2-0 | 2-1 | 1-2 | 3-0 | 0-1 | 3-3 | 2-2 | 0-1 | 1-1 | 3-2 | 0-2 | 2-1 |
| Stade Malherbe Caen | 1-0 | 0-1 | 0-1 | ■ | 1-0 | 0-0 | 1-3 | 2-2 | 0-1 | 0-1 | 2-2 | 0-1 | 1-1 | 1-2 | 1-2 | 3-2 | 1-2 | 0-5 | 0-0 | 2-1 |
| Dijon Football Côte d'Or | 0-0 | 1-3 | 0-0 | 0-2 | ■ | 2-1 | 1-2 | 0-3 | 1-2 | 2-0 | 1-1 | 2-0 | 0-1 | 0-4 | 0-4 | 1-1 | 3-2 | 0-1 | 2-1 | 2-1 |
| En Avant de Guingamp | 1-2 | 1-0 | 1-3 | 0-0 | 1-0 | ■ | 0-2 | 2-4 | 1-3 | 1-1 | 1-1 | 0-0 | 0-0 | 2-2 | 1-3 | 0-1 | 2-1 | 0-1 | 1-1 | 1-2 |
| Lille Olympique SC | 2-1 | 5-0 | 1-0 | 1-0 | 1-0 | 3-0 | ■ | 2-2 | 3-0 | 0-1 | 0-0 | 2-1 | 4-0 | 5-0 | 5-1 | 1-1 | 3-1 | 3-1 | 0-0 | 1-2 |
| Olympique Lyonnais | 2-0 | 2-1 | 1-1 | 4-0 | 1-3 | 2-1 | 2-2 | ■ | 4-2 | 3-0 | 3-2 | 1-1 | 0-1 | 2-0 | 2-1 | 1-1 | 0-2 | 1-0 | 2-0 | 5-1 |
| Olympique de Marseille | 2-0 | 2-2 | 1-0 | 2-0 | 2-0 | 4-0 | 1-2 | 0-3 | ■ | 1-1 | 1-0 | 1-2 | 1-0 | 2-1 | 0-2 | 0-0 | 2-2 | 2-0 | 3-2 | 4-0 |
| AS de Monaco FC | 2-0 | 0-1 | 1-1 | 0-1 | 2-2 | 0-2 | 0-0 | 2-0 | 2-3 | ■ | 1-2 | 1-0 | 1-1 | 1-1 | 0-4 | 0-0 | 1-2 | 2-3 | 1-5 | 2-1 |
| Montpellier-Hérault SC | 1-1 | 2-2 | 2-0 | 2-0 | 1-2 | 2-0 | 0-1 | 1-1 | 3-0 | 2-2 | ■ | 1-1 | 1-0 | 3-0 | 3-2 | 2-4 | 2-2 | 0-0 | 1-1 | 2-1 |
| FC Nantes-Atlantique | 3-2 | 1-1 | 1-0 | 1-1 | 3-0 | 5-0 | 2-3 | 2-1 | 3-2 | 1-3 | 2-0 | ■ | 1-2 | 2-4 | 3-2 | 0-0 | 0-1 | 1-1 | 0-1 | 4-0 |
| OGC de Nice | 1-0 | 0-0 | 1-0 | 0-1 | 0-4 | 3-0 | 2-0 | 1-0 | 0-1 | 2-0 | 1-0 | 1-1 | ■ | 2-0 | 0-3 | 0-1 | 2-1 | 1-1 | 1-0 | 1-1 |
| Nîmes Olympique | 3-0 | 3-1 | 2-1 | 2-0 | 2-0 | 0-0 | 2-3 | 2-3 | 3-1 | 1-0 | 1-1 | 1-0 | 0-1 | ■ | 2-4 | 0-0 | 3-1 | 1-1 | 2-2 | 0-1 |
| Paris Saint-Germain FC | 5-0 | 3-1 | 1-0 | 3-0 | 4-0 | 9-0 | 5-0 | 3-1 | 3-1 | 5-1 | 1-0 | 1-1 | 3-0 | | ■ | 4-1 | 4-1 | 4-0 | 2-2 | 1-0 |
| Stade de Reims | 2-2 | 1-1 | 0-0 | 2-2 | 0-0 | 2-1 | 1-1 | 1-0 | 2-1 | 1-0 | 0-1 | 1-0 | 1-1 | 0-3 | 3-1 | ■ | 2-0 | 0-2 | 2-1 | 0-1 |
| Stade Rennais FC | 1-0 | 1-0 | 2-0 | 3-1 | 2-0 | 1-1 | 3-1 | 0-1 | 1-1 | 2-2 | 0-0 | 1-1 | 0-0 | 4-0 | 1-3 | 0-2 | ■ | 3-0 | 1-4 | 1-1 |
| AS de Saint-Étienne | 0-0 | 4-3 | 3-0 | 2-1 | 3-0 | 2-1 | 0-1 | 1-2 | 2-1 | 0-1 | 3-0 | 2-1 | 0-1 | 2-0 | 1-1 | | | ■ | 2-1 | 2-0 |
| Racing Club de Strasbourg | 3-1 | 1-2 | 1-0 | 2-2 | 3-0 | 3-3 | 1-1 | 2-2 | 1-1 | 2-1 | 1-3 | 2-3 | 2-0 | 0-1 | 1-1 | 4-0 | 0-2 | 1-1 | ■ | 1-1 |
| Toulouse FC | 0-1 | 0-0 | 2-1 | 1-1 | 2-2 | 1-0 | 0-0 | 2-2 | 2-5 | 1-1 | 0-3 | 1-0 | 1-1 | 1-0 | 0-1 | 1-1 | 2-2 | 2-3 | 1-2 | ■ |

## Division 1

| | | Pd | Wn | Dw | Ls | GF | GA | Pts | |
|---|---|---|---|---|---|---|---|---|---|
| 1. | PARIS SAINT-GERMAIN (PARIS) | 38 | 29 | 4 | 5 | 105 | 35 | 91 | |
| 2. | Lille Olympique SC Metropole (Lille) | 38 | 22 | 9 | 7 | 68 | 33 | 75 | |
| 3. | Olympique Lyonnais (Lyon) | 38 | 21 | 9 | 8 | 70 | 47 | 72 | |
| 4. | AS de Saint-Étienne (Saint-Étienne) | 38 | 19 | 9 | 10 | 59 | 41 | 66 | |
| 5. | Olympique de Marseille (Marseille) | 38 | 18 | 7 | 13 | 60 | 52 | 61 | |
| 6. | Montpellier-Hérault SC (Montpellier) | 38 | 15 | 14 | 9 | 53 | 42 | 59 | |
| 7. | Olympique GC de Nice-Côte d'Azur (Nice) | 38 | 15 | 11 | 12 | 30 | 35 | 56 | |
| 8. | Stade de Reims (Reims) | 38 | 13 | 16 | 9 | 39 | 42 | 55 | |
| 9. | Nîmes Olympique (Nîmes) | 38 | 15 | 8 | 15 | 57 | 58 | 53 | |
| 10. | Stade Rennais FC (Rennes) | 38 | 13 | 13 | 12 | 55 | 52 | 52 | |
| 11. | Racing Club de Strasbourg Football (Strasbourg) | 38 | 11 | 16 | 11 | 58 | 48 | 49 | |
| 12. | FC Nantes-Atlantique (Nantes) | 38 | 13 | 9 | 16 | 48 | 48 | 48 | |
| 13. | Angers SC de l'Ouest (Angers) | 38 | 10 | 16 | 12 | 44 | 49 | 46 | |
| 14. | FC Girondins de Bordeaux (Bordeaux) | 38 | 10 | 11 | 17 | 34 | 42 | 41 | |
| 15. | Amiens SC Football (Amiens) | 38 | 9 | 11 | 18 | 31 | 52 | 38 | |
| 16. | Toulouse FC (Toulouse) | 38 | 8 | 14 | 16 | 35 | 57 | 38 | |
| 17. | AS de Monaco FC (Monaco) | 38 | 8 | 12 | 18 | 38 | 57 | 36 | |
| 18. | Dijon Football Côte d'Or (Dijon) | 38 | 9 | 7 | 22 | 31 | 60 | 34 | PO |
| 19. | Stade Malherbe Caen-CBN (Caen) | 38 | 7 | 12 | 19 | 29 | 54 | 33 | R |
| 20. | En Avant de Guingamp (Guingamp) | 38 | 5 | 12 | 21 | 28 | 68 | 27 | R |
| | | 760 | 270 | 220 | 270 | 972 | 972 | 1030 | |

## Top goal-scorers

| | | | |
|---|---|---|---|
| 1) | Kylian Mbappé | (Paris Saint-Germain FC) | 33 |
| 2) | Nicolas Pépé | (Lille Olympique SC) | 22 |
| 3) | Edinson Cavani | (Paris Saint-Germain FC) | 18 |
| 4) | Florian Thauvin | (Olympique de Marseille) | 16 |
| 5) | Moussa Dembélé | (Olympique Lyonnais) | 15 |
| | Radamel Falcao | (AS de Monaco FC) | 15 |
| | Neymar | (Paris Saint-Germain FC) | 15 |

## Promotion/Relegation play-offs

A play-off competition to decide promotion or relegation was held at the end of the season. This involved the 3rd, 4th and 5th-placed teams in Ligue 2, and the 18th-placed team in Ligue 1.

### Final

| | | |
|---|---|---|
| Racing Club de Lens (Lens) | 1-1 | Dijon Football Côte d'Or (Dijon) |
| Dijon Football Côte d'Or (Dijon) | 3-1 | Racing Club de Lens (Lens) |

Dijon Football Côte d'Or won 4-2 on aggregate to retain their place in Ligue 1.

### Semi-final

| | | |
|---|---|---|
| ES Troyes Aube Champagne (Troyes) | 1-2 (aet) | Racing Club de Lens (Lens) |

### Quarter-final

| | | |
|---|---|---|
| Paris FC (Paris) | 1-1  (aet) | Racing Club de Lens (Lens) |
| | (Racing Club de Lens won 5-4 on penalties) | |

| | Division 2 | Pd | Wn | Dw | Ls | GF | GA | Pts | |
|---|---|---|---|---|---|---|---|---|---|
| 1. | FC de Metz (Metz) | 38 | 24 | 9 | 5 | 60 | 23 | 81 | P |
| 2. | Stade Brestois '92 (Brest) | 38 | 21 | 11 | 6 | 64 | 35 | 74 | P |
| 3. | ES Troyes Aube Champagne (Troyes) | 38 | 21 | 8 | 9 | 51 | 28 | 71 | PO |
| 4. | Paris FC (Paris) | 38 | 17 | 14 | 7 | 36 | 22 | 65 | PO |
| 5. | Racing Club de Lens (Lens) | 38 | 18 | 9 | 11 | 49 | 28 | 63 | PO |
| 6. | FC Lorient Bretagne-Sud (Lorient) | 38 | 17 | 12 | 9 | 51 | 41 | 63 | |
| 7. | Havre AC Football Association (Le Havre) | 38 | 13 | 15 | 10 | 45 | 40 | 54 | |
| 8. | Union Sportive Orléans Loiret Football (Orléans) | 38 | 15 | 7 | 16 | 51 | 53 | 52 | |
| 9. | Grenoble Foot 38 (Grenoble) | 38 | 13 | 11 | 14 | 43 | 47 | 50 | |
| 10. | Clermont Football Auvergne (Clermont Ferrand) | 38 | 11 | 15 | 12 | 44 | 37 | 48 | |
| 11. | FC La Berrichone (Châteauroux) | 38 | 11 | 15 | 12 | 37 | 42 | 48 | |
| 12. | Chamois Niortais FC (Niort) | 38 | 11 | 14 | 13 | 34 | 41 | 47 | |
| 13. | Valenciennes FC ( Valenciennes) | 38 | 11 | 10 | 17 | 52 | 61 | 43 | |
| 14. | AS Nancy-Lorraine (Nancy) | 38 | 12 | 6 | 20 | 36 | 50 | 42 | |
| 15. | Association de la Jeunesse Auxerroise (Auxerre) | 38 | 10 | 11 | 17 | 34 | 36 | 41 | |
| 16. | FC Sochaux-Montbéliard (Montbéliard) | 38 | 11 | 8 | 19 | 27 | 43 | 41 | |
| 17. | AC Ajaccio (Ajaccio) | 38 | 9 | 13 | 16 | 29 | 45 | 40 | |
| 18. | Gazélec FC Ajaccio (Ajaccio) | 38 | 9 | 12 | 17 | 30 | 54 | 39 | POR |
| 19. | AS Béziers (Béziers) | 38 | 9 | 11 | 18 | 33 | 50 | 38 | R |
| 20. | Red Star FC (Saint-Ouen) | 38 | 7 | 9 | 22 | 28 | 58 | 30 | R |
| | | 760 | 270 | 220 | 270 | 834 | 834 | 1030 | |

## Promotion/Relegation play-off

The 18th placed Ligue 2 team played the 3rd placed Championnat National team to decide the final promotion/relegation spot:

| | | |
|---|---|---|
| Le Mans FC (Le Mans) | 1-2 | Gazélec FC Ajaccio (Ajaccio) |
| Gazélec FC Ajaccio (Ajaccio) | 0-2 | Le Mans FC (Le Mans) |

Le Mans FC won 3-2 on aggregate and were promoted to Ligue 2, while Gazélec FC Ajaccio were relegated to the Championnat National.

## Coupe de France Final   (Stade de France, Saint-Denis – 27/04/2019 – 75,000)

| | | |
|---|---|---|
| **STADE RENNAIS FC (RENNES)** | **2-2  (AET)** | Paris Saint-Germain FC (Paris) |
| *Kimpembe 40' (o.g.),  Mexer Goal 66'* | (6-5 on penalties) | *Dani Alves 13',  Neymar 21'* |

**Rennes**:  Koubek, Traoré, Da Silva, Mexer, Bensebaini, André, Grenier, Sarr, Ben Arfa, Bourigeaud (Siliki 106'), Niang.

**Paris Saint-Germain**:  Areola, Dagba (Diaby 106' (Nkunu 120+1')), Marquinhos, Kimpembe, Bernat, Verratti, Dani Alves, Draxler (Cavani 91'), Di María (Paredes 75'), Mbappé, Neymar.

## Semi-finals

| | | |
|---|---|---|
| Olympique Lyonnais (Lyon) | 2-3 | Stade Rennais FC (Rennes) |
| Paris Saint-Germain FC (Paris) | 3-0 | FC Nantes-Atlantique (Nantes) |

## Quarter-finals

| | | |
|---|---|---|
| Amicale Sportive de Vitré (Vitré) | 0-2 | FC Nantes-Atlantique (Nantes) |
| Paris Saint-Germain FC (Paris) | 3-0 | Dijon Football Côte d'Or (Dijon) |
| Stade Rennais FC (Rennes) | 2-0 | Union Sportive Orléans Loiret Football (Orléans) |
| Olympique Lyonnais (Lyon) | 3-1 | Stade Malherbe Caen-CBN (Caen) |

# 2019/2020

| 2019/20 Division 1 | Amiens SC | Angiers FCO | Giron. Bordeaux | Stade Brestois | Dijon FCO | Lille Olympique | Olymp. Lyonnais | Olymp. Marseille | FC de Metz | AS de Monaco | Montpellier-Hér. | FC Nantes | OGC de Nice | Nîmes Olymp. | Paris St-Germain | Stade de Reims | Stade Rennais FC | AS Saint-Étienne | RC Strasbourg | Toulouse FC |
|---|---|---|---|---|---|---|---|---|---|---|---|---|---|---|---|---|---|---|---|---|
| Amiens SC Football | ■ | | 1-3 | 1-0 | 1-1 | 1-0 | 2-2 | 3-1 | 0-1 | 1-2 | 1-2 | 1-2 | | | 4-4 | 1-1 | | | 0-4 | 0-0 |
| Angers FC de l'Ouest | 1-1 | ■ | 3-1 | 0-1 | 2-0 | 0-2 | | 0-2 | 3-0 | 0-0 | 1-0 | 2-0 | 1-1 | 1-0 | | 1-4 | | 4-1 | 1-0 | |
| FC Girondins de Bordeaux | | | ■ | 2-2 | 2-2 | | 1-2 | 0-0 | 2-0 | 2-1 | 1-1 | 2-0 | 1-1 | 6-0 | 0-1 | | | 0-1 | | 0-1 |
| Stade Brestois '92 | 2-1 | 0-1 | 1-1 | ■ | 2-0 | | 2-2 | | 2-0 | | 1-1 | 0-0 | | 1-2 | 1-0 | 0-0 | 3-2 | 5-0 | | 1-1 |
| Dijon Football Côte d'Or | | | 0-2 | 3-0 | ■ | 1-0 | | 0-0 | 2-2 | 1-1 | 2-2 | 3-3 | | 0-0 | 2-1 | | 2-1 | 1-2 | 1-0 | 2-1 |
| Lille Olympique SC | | 2-1 | 3-0 | 1-0 | 1-0 | ■ | 1-0 | 1-2 | 0-0 | | 2-1 | 2-1 | | 2-2 | 0-2 | | 1-0 | 3-0 | 2-0 | 3-0 |
| Olympique Lyonnais | 0-0 | 6-0 | 1-1 | | 0-0 | 0-1 | ■ | 2-0 | | | 0-1 | 2-1 | | 0-1 | | 0-1 | 2-0 | 1-1 | | 3-0 |
| Olympique de Marseille | 2-2 | 0-0 | 3-1 | 2-1 | | 2-1 | 2-1 | ■ | | 1-1 | 1-3 | | 3-1 | | 0-2 | 1-1 | 1-0 | 2-0 | 1-0 | |
| FC de Metz | 1-2 | | 1-2 | | | 0-2 | 1-1 | | ■ | 3-0 | 2-2 | 1-0 | | 2-1 | 0-2 | 1-1 | 0-1 | 3-1 | 1-0 | 2-2 |
| AS de Monaco FC | 3-0 | 1-0 | | 4-1 | 1-0 | 5-1 | 0-3 | 3-4 | | ■ | 1-0 | | 3-1 | 2-2 | 1-4 | 1-1 | 3-2 | | | 1-3 |
| Montpellier-Hérault SC | 4-2 | 0-0 | 4-0 | 2-1 | | 1-0 | | 1-1 | 3-1 | | ■ | 2-1 | 1-0 | 1-3 | | 0-1 | 1-0 | | | 3-0 |
| FC Nantes-Atlantique | | 1-2 | 0-1 | | 1-0 | 0-1 | | 0-0 | 0-0 | 0-1 | 1-0 | ■ | 1-0 | | 1-2 | 1-0 | 1-0 | 2-3 | | 2-1 |
| OGC de Nice | 2-1 | 3-1 | 1-1 | 2-2 | 2-1 | 1-1 | 2-1 | 1-2 | 4-1 | 2-1 | | | ■ | 1-3 | 1-4 | 2-0 | 1-1 | | | 3-0 |
| Nîmes Olympique | 1-1 | 1-0 | | 3-0 | 2-0 | | 0-4 | 2-3 | 1-1 | 3-1 | | 0-1 | 1-2 | ■ | 2-0 | 0-1 | 0-1 | | | 1-0 |
| Paris Saint-Germain FC | 4-1 | 4-0 | 4-3 | | 4-0 | 2-0 | 4-2 | 4-0 | | 3-3 | 5-0 | 2-0 | | 3-0 | ■ | 0-2 | | 2-0 | | 4-0 |
| Stade de Reims | | 0-0 | 1-1 | 1-0 | 1-2 | 2-0 | 1-1 | | 0-1 | 0-0 | 1-0 | | 1-1 | 0-0 | | ■ | 1-0 | 3-1 | 0-0 | |
| Stade Rennais FC | 3-1 | 2-1 | 1-0 | 0-0 | | 1-1 | | 0-1 | | 5-0 | 3-2 | 1-2 | 2-1 | 2-1 | 0-1 | | ■ | 2-1 | | 3-2 |
| AS de Saint-Étienne | 2-2 | | 1-1 | 1-1 | | 1-0 | | 0-1 | 1-0 | 0-0 | 0-2 | 4-1 | 1-1 | | | 0-4 | 1-1 | ■ | | 2-2 |
| Racing Club de Strasbourg | 0-0 | | | | 1-2 | 1-2 | | 1-1 | 2-2 | 1-0 | 2-1 | 1-0 | 4-1 | | | 3-0 | 0-2 | 2-1 | ■ | 4-2 |
| Toulouse FC | 2-0 | 0-2 | 1-3 | 2-5 | 1-0 | 2-1 | 2-3 | 0-2 | | 1-2 | | | | 0-2 | | | 0-1 | 0-2 | 0-1 | ■ |

| | Division 1 | Pd | Wn | Dw | Ls | GF | GA | Pts | PPG | |
|---|---|---|---|---|---|---|---|---|---|---|
| 1. | PARIS SAINT-GERMAIN FC (PARIS) | 27 | 22 | 2 | 3 | 75 | 24 | 68 | 2.52 | |
| 2. | Olympique de Marseille (Marseille) | 28 | 16 | 8 | 4 | 41 | 29 | 56 | 2.00 | |
| 3. | Stade Rennais FC (Rennes) | 28 | 15 | 5 | 8 | 38 | 24 | 50 | 1.79 | |
| 4. | Lille Olympique SC Metropole (Lille) | 28 | 15 | 4 | 9 | 35 | 27 | 49 | 1.75 | |
| 5. | Olympique GC de Nice-Côte d'Azur (Nice) | 28 | 11 | 8 | 9 | 41 | 38 | 41 | 1.46 | |
| 6. | Stade de Reims (Reims) | 28 | 10 | 11 | 7 | 26 | 21 | 41 | 1.46 | |
| 7. | Olympique Lyonnais (Lyon) | 28 | 11 | 7 | 10 | 42 | 27 | 40 | 1.43 | |
| 8. | Montpellier-Hérault SC (Montpellier) | 28 | 11 | 7 | 10 | 35 | 34 | 40 | 1.43 | |
| 9. | AS de Monaco FC (Monaco) | 28 | 11 | 7 | 10 | 44 | 44 | 40 | 1.43 | |
| 10. | Racing Club de Strasbourg Football (Strasbourg) | 27 | 11 | 5 | 11 | 32 | 32 | 38 | 1.41 | |
| 11. | Angers SC de l'Ouest (Angers) | 28 | 11 | 6 | 11 | 28 | 33 | 39 | 1.39 | |
| 12. | FC Girondins de Bordeaux (Bordeaux) | 28 | 9 | 10 | 9 | 40 | 34 | 37 | 1.32 | |
| 13. | FC Nantes-Atlantique (Nantes) | 28 | 11 | 4 | 13 | 28 | 31 | 37 | 1.32 | |
| 14. | Stade Brestois '92 (Brest) | 28 | 8 | 10 | 10 | 34 | 37 | 34 | 1.21 | |
| 15. | FC de Metz (Metz) | 28 | 8 | 10 | 10 | 27 | 35 | 34 | 1.21 | |
| 16. | Dijon Football Côte d'Or (Dijon) | 28 | 7 | 9 | 12 | 27 | 37 | 30 | 1.07 | |
| 17. | AS de Saint-Étienne (Saint-Étienne) | 28 | 8 | 6 | 14 | 29 | 45 | 30 | 1.07 | |
| 18. | Nîmes Olympique (Nîmes) | 28 | 7 | 6 | 15 | 29 | 44 | 27 | 0.96 | |
| 19. | Amiens SC Football (Amiens) | 28 | 4 | 11 | 13 | 31 | 50 | 23 | 0.82 | R |
| 20. | Toulouse FC (Toulouse) | 28 | 3 | 4 | 21 | 22 | 58 | 13 | 0.46 | R |
| | | 558 | 209 | 140 | 209 | 704 | 704 | 767 | | |

Play was suspended indefinitely on 13th March 2020 due to the effects of the COVID-19 pandemic in the country. On 28th April 2020, it was announced that neither Ligue 1 or Ligue 2 would resume again this season as the French government had banned all sporting events until September 2020. It was decided that final league positions would be calculated based on a points per game basis with head to head results deciding the ranking of teams with an identical points per game record. Paris Saint-Germain FC were duly announced as Champions and Amiens SC Football and Toulouse FC were relegated to Ligue 2.

Olympique GC de Nice-Côte d'Azur finished ahead of Stade de Reims due to a better head-to-head record.

FC Girondins de Bordeaux finished ahead of FC Nantes-Atlantique due to a better head-to-head record.

The 18th-placed Ligue 1 team would normally compete in the Promotion-Relegation play-offs at the end of the season with a team from Ligue 2 to decide whether they would remain in Ligue 1 for the 2020-21 season, but the play-offs were cancelled so Nîmes Olympique remained in Ligue 1.


## Top goal-scorers

| | | | |
|---|---|---|---|
| 1) | Wissam Ben Yedder | (AS de Monaco FC) | 18 |
| | Kylian Mbappé | (Paris Saint-Germain FC) | 18 |
| 3) | Moussa Dembélé | (Olympique Lyonnais) | 16 |
| 4) | Neymar | (Paris Saint-Germain FC) | 13 |
| | Victor Osimhen | (Lille Olympique SC) | 13 |
| 6) | Habib Diallo | (FC Metz) | 12 |
| | Mauro Icardi | (Paris Saint-Germain FC) | 12 |

In Ligue 2, after the season was ended early on 28th April 2020, it was decided that the final league positions at the time of abandonment would stand. FC Lorient were therefore declared champions and won promotion to Ligue 1 alongside RC Lens. Following the cancellation of the play-offs, AC Ajaccio remained in Ligue 2 and Le Mans FC and Union Sportive Orléans Loiret Football were relegated to Le Championnat.

| | Division 2 | Pd | Wn | Dw | Ls | GF | GA | Pts | |
|---|---|---|---|---|---|---|---|---|---|
| 1. | FC Loient Bretagne-Sud (Lorient) | 28 | 17 | 3 | 8 | 45 | 25 | 54 | P |
| 2. | Racing Club de Lens (Lens) | 28 | 15 | 8 | 5 | 39 | 24 | 53 | P |
| 3. | AC Ajaccio (Ajaccio) | 28 | 15 | 7 | 6 | 38 | 22 | 52 | |
| 4. | ES Troyes Aube Champagne (Troyes) | 28 | 16 | 3 | 9 | 34 | 25 | 51 | |
| 5. | Clermont Football Auvergne (Clermont Ferrand) | 28 | 14 | 8 | 6 | 35 | 25 | 50 | |
| 6. | Havre AC Football Association (Le Havre) | 28 | 11 | 11 | 6 | 38 | 25 | 44 | |
| 7. | Valenciennes FC ( Valenciennes) | 28 | 11 | 9 | 8 | 24 | 20 | 42 | |
| 8. | En Avant de Guingamp (Guingamp) | 28 | 10 | 9 | 9 | 40 | 33 | 39 | |
| 9. | Grenoble Foot 38 (Grenoble) | 28 | 7 | 14 | 7 | 27 | 29 | 35 | |
| 10. | FC Chambly Oise (Chambly) | 28 | 9 | 8 | 11 | 26 | 32 | 35 | |
| 11. | Association de la Jeunesse Auxerroise (Auxerre) | 28 | 8 | 10 | 10 | 31 | 30 | 34 | |
| 12. | AS Nancy-Lorraine (Nancy) | 28 | 6 | 16 | 6 | 27 | 26 | 34 | |
| 13. | Stade Malherbe Caen-CBN (Caen) | 28 | 8 | 10 | 10 | 33 | 34 | 34 | |
| 14. | FC Sochaux-Montbéliard (Montbéliard) | 28 | 8 | 10 | 10 | 28 | 30 | 34 | |
| 15. | FC La Berrichone (Châteauroux) | 28 | 9 | 7 | 12 | 22 | 38 | 34 | |
| 16. | Rodez Aveyron Football (Rodez) | 28 | 8 | 8 | 12 | 31 | 34 | 32 | |
| 17. | Paris FC (Paris) | 28 | 7 | 7 | 14 | 22 | 40 | 28 | |
| 18. | Chamois Niortais FC (Niort) | 28 | 6 | 8 | 14 | 30 | 41 | 26 | |
| 19. | Le Mans FC (Le Mans) | 28 | 7 | 5 | 16 | 30 | 45 | 26 | R |
| 20. | Union Sportive Orléans Loiret Football (Orléans) | 28 | 4 | 7 | 17 | 21 | 43 | 19 | R |
| | | 560 | 196 | 168 | 196 | 621 | 621 | 756 | |

**Coupe de France Final**   (Stade de France, Saint-Denis – 24/07/2020 – 2,805)

**PARIS SAINT-GERMAIN FC (PARIS)**         **1-0**         AS de Saint-Étienne (Saint-Étienne)

*Neymar 14'*

**Paris Saint-Germain**: Navas, Kehrer (Dagba 20'), Silva, Marquinhos, Bakker, Di María, Paredes (Verratti 75'), Gueye, Neymar, Icardi, Mbappé (Sarabia 33').

**Saint-Étienne**: Moulin, Debuchy (Krasso 83'), Fofana, Perrin, Kolodziejczak, Camara (Neyou 46'), M'Vila, Maçon (Moukoudi 34'), Boudebouz (Nordin 75'), Bouanga, Hamouma (Khazri 46').

## Semi-finals

| | | |
|---|---|---|
| Olympique Lyonnais (Lyon) | 1-5 | Paris Saint-Germain FC (Paris) |
| AS de Saint-Étienne (Saint-Étienne) | 2-1 | Stade Rennais FC (Rennes) |

## Quarter-finals

| | | |
|---|---|---|
| ASM Belfort Football (Belfort) | 0-3 | Stade Rennais FC (Rennes) |
| Dijon Football Côte d'Or (Dijon) | 1-6 | Paris Saint-Germain FC (Paris) |
| Olympique Lyonnais (Lyon) | 1-0 | Olympique de Marseille (Marseille) |
| SAS Épinal (Épinal) | 1-2 | AS de Saint-Étienne (Saint-Étienne) |